New Frontiers in Microsimulation Modelling

Public Policy and Social Welfare
A Series Edited by the European Centre

 European Centre Vienna

Volume 36

Asghar Zaidi / Ann Harding / Paul Williamson (Eds.)

New Frontiers in Microsimulation Modelling

Routledge
Taylor & Francis Group

LONDON AND NEW YORK

First published 2009 by Ashgate Publishing

Published 2019 by Routledge
2 Park Square, Milton Park, Abingdon, Oxon OX14 4RN
52 Vanderbilt Avenue, New York, NY 10017

Routledge is an imprint of the Taylor & Francis Group, an informa business

Copy-editing and DTP: Willem Stamatiou
European Centre for Social Welfare Policy and Research
Berggasse 17, 1090 Vienna, Austria

British Library Cataloguing-in-Publication Data. A catalogue record for this book is available from the British Library.

ISBN 13: 978-0-7546-7647-8 (pbk)

Contents

8

List of Figures and Tables

Figures

Tables

Preface – Orcutt's Vision 50 Years On

Michael Wolfson

The inaugural meeting of the International Microsimulation Association took place in August 2007 in Vienna. This volume presents a selection of the papers presented at that meeting. The meeting also marked the 50th anniversary of Guy Orcutt's seminal paper setting out his vision for socio-economic microsimulation modeling (Orcutt, 1957). It is fitting, therefore, as the preface to this book to reflect briefly on Orcutt's original vision for microsimulation modeling of socio-economic phenomena.[1]

Guy Orcutt began his academic career in the 1940s in the centre of one of the most exciting developments in economics – the construction of the System of National Accounts (SNA). The SNA represented a success both in conceptual terms – a coherent and policy-oriented framework for describing the major sectors and financial relationships in an economy, and in empirical terms – with the estimation and articulation of the relevant aggregate data tables (Watts, 1991).

One of the first applications of the SNA was the construction of macro-econometric simulation models, and Orcutt became involved in the issues of time series estimation. Indeed he built his own regression analyser – arguably one of the first PCs in the world – and brought it with him to England in the late 1940s when he was invited to join Richard Stone at the newly formed Department of Applied Economics in Cambridge. But the time series data then available amounted at most to a few dozen time periods – not nearly enough data for serious hypothesis testing. Moreover, as a result of

---

1   This preface draws substantially on my opening address to the 1st General Conference of the International Microsimulation Association in Vienna, 2007. I wish to thank Alice Nakamura, Guy Orcutt's daughter, and Steve Gribble, Geoff Rowe, Chantal Hicks and Martin Spielauer from the microsimulation unit at Statistics Canada, for valuable discussions. I alone remain responsible for these remarks.

aggregation, all the real behavioural detail, which was obviously occurring at the level of individuals and firms, was being lost.

Guy Orcutt's words in this regard are clear enough in his 1957 paper. After outlining a number of fundamental concerns with the programme of macroeconomic theory and empirical work, Orcutt stated, "Existing models of our socio-economic system have proved to be of rather limited predictive usefulness. ...current models... only predict aggregates and fail to predict distributions...insufficient evidence remains in highly aggregative economic time series for effective testing of economic hypotheses. ... if nonlinear relationships are present, then stable relationships at the micro level are quite consistent with the absence of stable relationships at the aggregate level."

This last statement reflects an economics literature beginning to recognize just how restrictive the conditions for aggregation really are (e.g. Gorman, 1959), as well as the famous Cambridge controversies in capital theory (Cohen and Harcourt, 2003). But beyond these fundamental criticisms of the macroeconomic work of the time, he had a concrete proposal ..." This paper presents a first step in meeting the need for a new type of model of a socio-economic system designed to capitalize on our growing knowledge about (micro or elemental) decision-making units. ... aggregates will be obtained from the simulated models in a fashion analogous to the way a census or survey obtains aggregates relating to real socio-economic systems."

Recall that Orcutt was already familiar with various sorts of computing, having built from scratch his own regression analyser. So it was natural that he would be well aware of the growing power of computers, one of the critical enabling technologies for microsimulation. For Orcutt's vision, then, "... the model would be simulated on a large electronic machine such as the IBM 704 or the UNIVAC II or some improved successor to these powerful giants."

Interestingly, one of the main computing issues he worried about in 1957 was the generation of random numbers, "The only operation that might be elaborated on usefully in this paper is that of random sampling. ... the procedure either would be to produce and store adequate quantities of (random) numbers on magnetic tapes or to introduce a subroutine...." Progress in computing has been such that we barely give a thought to the question of random number generation today. The photo shows one of these "powerful giants" to which Orcutt was referring, an IBM 704. This computer could perform 40,000 instructions per second. Today's PCs are at least five orders of magnitude faster.

Orcutt's 1957 paper concluded with three notable points. First, "These models could be used either for unconditional forecasting or for predictions of what would happen given specified external conditions and governmental actions." In other words, the models would have practical applications.

But it was also his intention that these kinds of models be relevant for research. "Such models also would improve (research) by keeping the interrelated nature of the system in the consciousness of the investigator...". He certainly appreciated the concerns, for example, that underlay the Walrasian view of an economy, with many simultaneously interacting agents. But he strongly rejected any approach that was not firmly grounded in real data. He was definitely not a fan of the axiomatic, data-starved but increasingly fashionable mathematization of economics.

Finally, he clearly recognized that the "...final success of the ideas sketched in this paper will require a long-term effort by many individuals of widely assorted abilities." This idea, that scientific progress could only be achieved by the organization of a multi-skilled team, with long-term funding and appropriate infrastructure, is taken for granted in fields as diverse as astronomy, genetics, and climate change, but even 50 years later, this is generally not the case in the social sciences.

Following his seminal 1957 paper, Guy Orcutt dedicated decades of his career precisely to forming and securing the funds for such team efforts. He had some considerable successes. The 1961 and 1976 books he co-authored report on the results of two such modeling efforts (Orcutt et al. 1961 and Orcutt et al. 1976).

He also continued to push for models that were comprehensive, that encompassed the whole of the economy. While he strongly rejected general equilibrium models, he certainly embraced what might better be called "general interaction models". He also fully appreciated the need for appropriate data, and therefore supported, for example, the efforts of Richard and Nancy Ruggles with regard to the development of explicit microdata foundations for the System of National Accounts (Ruggles and Ruggles, 1975).

He still carried his formative experiences in macroeconomics, so that in his major dynamic microsimulation model, DYNASIM, "Operating in conjunction with this micro model is a sub model of the macroeconomy. This model provides an environment within which the micro model operates so that activities at the micro level can be influenced by macroeconomic conditions."

It was also his vision that market interactions be explicitly modeled. "While the intent of interaction of many different types of decision units through markets remains as part of the original conception of microanalytic modeling, the implementation presented in this book still falls short of the dream…" Unfortunately, Guy Orcutt eventually became frustrated and disillusioned by his inability to muster the resources for the teamwork needed for successful microsimulation efforts, and by the continued resistance of the mainstream economics profession to the ideas of microanalytic simulation.

There were, of course, a few glimmers of recognition in mainstream economics of the profound issues which had motivated Guy Orcutt to conceive and champion an empirically grounded microanalytic approach. One of the most biting was Axel Leijonhufvud's wonderful tongue in cheek anthropological study, "Life Among the Econ" (Leijonhufvud, 1973). "The young Econ, or 'grad', is not admitted to adulthood until he has made a 'modl' exhibiting a degree of workmanship acceptable to the elders of the 'dept' in which he serves his apprenticeship. … …The Math-Econ are in many ways the most fascinating, and certainly the most colorful, of Econ castes. … show(ing) many cultural patterns that we are wont to associate with religious orders or sects … (They) make exquisite modls finely carved from bones of walras. If some of these are 'useful' … it is clear that this is purely coincidental in the motivation for their manufacture." Leijonhufvud was attempting, along the same lines as Guy Orcutt, to warn the economics profession that their lone ranger research approach, imbued with physics envy and ascribing the highest status to mathematical elegance rather than realism and usefulness, was going down the wrong path.

In the same year, Frank Hahn delivered an inaugural lecture on becoming a University Professor at Cambridge (Hahn, 1973). Hahn was one of the high priests in the inner sanctum of the "math econ" caste, in Leijonhufvud's ethnology. He took the opportunity in this lecture, with his usual immodesty, to explicate the main challenges to general equilibrium (or GE) theory – criticisms which he was at least willing to recognize and discuss, unlike so many other math econ high priests of the day. "I turn now to the most difficult of the remaining questions of how to characterize the equilibrium of the economy as a whole. … The definition which I want to adopt is the following: an economy is in equilibrium when it generates messages which do not cause agents to change the theories which they hold or the policies (behaviours) they pursue."

This was a fascinating attempt to rescue GE theory – essentially by appealing to a vision that sounds very much like microanalytic, or what some now call multi-agent, simulation. But the tremendous irony was that this was the death knell for GE theory, for the simple reasons that while Hahn was certainly correct in his diagnosis of the challenge to GE theory, his new concept of an equilibrium could never obtain. However, orthodox economic theory has proven remarkably resistant to the challenges of realism and practical utility. Hence Guy Orcutt's frustration.

In contrast, Sandia Corporation, which since WWII has been primarily associated with nuclear weapons research, and is presumably focused on practicalities, obtained a patent that appears essentially identical to Orcutt et al.'s DYNASIM (USPO). The "summary of the invention" opens with the words, "The present invention provides a method for predicting changes in an economy, using a microsimulation model. The economy to be microsimulated comprises a plurality of decision makers. Decision makers include, for example, households, government, industry, and banks." (The granting of this patent suggests that the U.S. patent office is not very familiar with microsimulation and its novelty, and that some of the chapters in this volume may be "infringing" the Sandia patent.)

Half a century after Guy Orcutt's seminal vision, to what extent has it been realized? There is no question that in terms of computing power, progress has been spectacular. But perhaps the greatest challenge remaining is with regard to data, particularly for dynamic models. Essentially what is needed is "multi-multi-mi-lo" data sets – richly multivariate, multi-level, microdata which are longitudinal. Even in a relatively well-endowed and sophisticated national statistical office like Statistics Canada, dynamic microsimulation work is continually constrained by data availability. These constraints are most acute for estimating changes over time in co-evolving characteristics – even those which have been at the centre of Orcutt's modeling efforts since the early 1960s like nuptiality and labour force activity. In the health area, there are still major gaps in data on the joint dynamics of basic risk factors like smoking, obesity, hypertension and cholesterol.

Further, judging by the chapters in this volume, microsimulation models are still lacking the full range of agents in the economy as envisaged by Orcutt, particularly firms. And aside perhaps from marriage in dynamic models, individuals do not interact with each other; there is nothing like the standard economic notion of markets. The explicit macroeconomic feedbacks in Orcutt's original vision and in DYNASIM are generally absent in microsimulation models, with the notable exception of some chapters in Part IV of this volume.

The spectacular growth in computing power and the still considerable growth in rich micro data sets has been accompanied by a flowering of statistical estimation methods. Especially from a dynamic microsimulation model point of view, some are blind alleys – such as the recently fashionable trajectory analysis. On the other hand, there is a richness of numerically intensive methods which could be better exploited. For example, Rowe and Binder (2008) have developed a novel and powerful approach to cross-validation in order to assess alternative non-nested functional forms for behavioural dynamics of various sorts. The core idea is to validate estimated equations by using them to predict out-of-sample values, which has become feasible in survey data from complex sample designs where bootstrap weights have been produced to enable users to do their own variance estimation.

Explicit modeling of agent behaviour, particularly in static models, has been quite limited. But the chapters in Part II of this volume illustrate recent developments. There is of course some behaviour in dynamic models as described in a number of chapters in Part III – Orcutt's "operating characteristics" for agents are obviously essential. But agents still are generally not endowed with any explicit decision-making, let alone the kind of theory formation in Frank Hahn's attempt to reformulate GE theory. On the other hand, over the past 20 years there has been a remarkable growth in agent-based models of a more theoretical sort, many of which are described in the on-line Journal of Artificial Societies and Social Simulation (JASSS). These "toy" or abstract models, in contrast to the "industrial strength" applied policy models presented in this volume, do include a growing richness of interactions among co-evolving agents, thereby realizing a central portion of Orcutt's vision.

Still, it has been 50 years since Orcutt's seminal paper, and there are some ways in which his original vision should be adapted.

One of the most striking discoveries in modern cosmology has been dark matter and dark energy. Current theory holds that only about 4% of the "stuff" in the known universe is familiar kinds of matter. Analogously, time and again in contemporary microanalytic multivariate statistical estimations, it is rare that more than 10% of the observed variation or heterogeneity in real populations is "explained" by the independent variables. The bad news, then, is that the large majority of what is to be to understood and predicted is unknown. But the good news, with dynamic microsimulation models, is that this unexplained heterogeneity can still be incorporated explicitly into the modeling by characterizing its distribution. Even though this is computationally more intensive, it is readily done with modern computing.

Another adaptation of Orcutt's original vision is the tradeoff between a single omnibus all-encompassing model like his original DYNASIM, and more targeted and purpose-built models. Microsimulation at Statistics Canada, for example, has evolved toward a powerful modeling environment, the ModGen language used for writing microsimulation models (Statistics Canada – ModGen), as well as tools for harnessing parallel processing on multiple PCs, and then a family of similar models, but with each tailored to specific questions. Many of the modules are common across several versions of Statistics Canada's LifePaths and POHEM models, but others may be scaled back or greatly elaborated, depending on the question under study.

A renewed vision for socio-economic microsimulation should also include building bridges between the industrial strength applied models which are the essential focus of this volume, and the vibrant community of "toy" or agent-based modelers (e.g. JASSS, various issues) that has been growing over the past several decades. Initially, the most important bridges are simply awareness of each other's work. The notion of any empirical grounding for many of the agent-based models is still a ways off. On the other hand, Statistics Canada's ModGen simulation environment has enabled an agent-based model on the theory of price indices (Wolfson, 1999), and is being used in the creation of "industrial strength" infectious disease models. Developing linkages between some of the ideas and issues being addressed by the more theoretical agent-based models and applied dynamic microsimulation models should prove fruitful.

Finally, it is apt to close this preface with a few reflections on the coming decade for microsimulation. First, applied microsimulation modeling has already moved into other fields, most notably health. For example, a recent paper in Nature has modeled pandemic flu in the US using a database constructed essentially from the full population census of several hundred million interacting agents, with a 12-hour time step (Eubank et al., 2004). A similar effort in Canada also starts with a database constructed from the population census (Pourbohloul et al., 2005). One of the key questions here is the nature of the contact networks for the spread of infection, and the dynamics of these contact patterns.

The Clinton health reform debate in the US, well over a decade ago, has already entailed the development of several microsimulation models of health care (e.g. Lewin Group). But the frontier goes well beyond health care, which is typically treated in static models like another tax or transfer programme, to population health itself. For health in this appropriately broader sense, quantitative characterizations of the natural histories of diseases, their impacts not only on mortality but also on functional status, proximal risk factors like obesity, as well as distal social determinants, are essential. Dynamic microsimulation modeling is uniquely suited to addressing core realities which are generally ignored in the reigning spreadsheet or differential equation approaches. In particular, microsimulation models can easily incorporate the realities of population heterogeneity, co-morbidity, complex networks of causal factors for disease and risk factor etiology, and competing risks, as is well illustrated in the Will et al. (2001) study of the cancer drug Tamoxifen using Statistics Canada's POHEM (POpulation HEalth Model).

Another promising area is social indicators. The same Richard Stone who invited Guy Orcutt to Cambridge in the late 1940s to work on the SNA, decades later became concerned with the narrowness of the perspective on society offered by the then highly successful SNA. As a result, he developed a new approach called the System of Social and Demographic Statistics (SSDS; UN, 1975). Stone's SSDS builds on the familiar notion of life expectancy, one of the most widely used indicators in the world. But few realize that it is the result of a simulation. Dynamic microsimulation modeling offers a wonderful opportunity to build a family of social indicators that generalize life expectancy and other multi-state life table measures, particularly in a way that can realize Sir Richard Stone's vision of the SSDS (Wolfson, 1997).

Yet another promising area for further development is illustrated by Euromod (see Chapter 8), a wonderful example of the extension of microsimulation models to a multi-country context.

Another strategic direction for microsimulation modeling is for it to become firmly implanted in national statistical agencies. In Statistics Canada, for example, microsimulation is now the basis for specialized demographic projections for subpopulations such as those characterized by "visible minority" status. The underlying microsimulation model, DemoSim, is expected to evolve into the primary methodology for all demographic projections. DemoSim (formerly known as PopSim) runs directly on the population census microdata (Belanger et al., 2005; Caron Malenfant, 2009). This is strategic, in the spirit of Guy Orcutt's vision, because it will broaden the base of support for microsimulation infrastructure within a statistical agency, and hopefully diffuse as a best practice to other statistical offices.

Finally, microsimulation modeling still has not achieved the kind of scientific status it deserves. One reason is that many potential users are concerned about the "black box" nature of microsimulation models. An important step, therefore, is for microsimulation modeling to become a "glass box" activity, including for example public availability of the model and open source code. The papers in this volume, and the formation of the International Microsimulation Association which the volume reflects, have clearly been significant steps in this direction.

References

Bélanger, A./Caron Malenfant, É./Martel, L./Carrière, Y./Hicks, C./Rowe, G. (2005) 'Population Projections of Visible Minority Groups, Canada, Provinces and Regions', Statistics Canada, Catalogue no. 91-541.

Caron Malenfant, É. (2009) 'An Overview of DemoSim, Statistics Canada's Microsimulation Model for Demographic Projections', General Conference of the International Microsimulation Association, Biennial Meeting, Ottawa, June 8-10, 2009.

Cohen/Harcourt, G. (2003) 'Retrospectives: Whatever Happened to the Cambridge Capital Theory Controversies?', *The Journal of Economic Perspectives*, 17 (1): 199-214.

Eubank, S./Guclu, H/Anil Kumar, V. S./Marathe, M. V./Srinivasan, A./Toroczkai, Z./Wang, N. (2004) 'Modelling Disease Outbreaks in Realistic Urban Social Networks', *Nature* 429: 180-184.

Hahn, F.H. (1973) "On the Notion of Equilibrium in Economics, An Inaugural Lecture". Cambridge University Press.

JASSS – http://jasss.soc.surrey.ac.uk/JASSS.html

Leijonhufvud, A. (1973) 'Life Among the Econ', *Western Economic Journal*, XI (3), September.

Lewin Group – http://www.lewin.com/Expertise/HealthReform/

Orcutt, G.H. (1957) 'A new type of socio-economic system', *Review of Economics and Statistics* 58 (2): 773-797 (reprinted with permission in *International Journal of Microsimulation* 1 (1): 3-9, Autumn, at http://www.microsimulation.org/IJM/V1_1/IJM_1_1_2.pdf).

Orcutt, Guy H./Greenberger, M./Korbel, J./Rivlin, A.M. (1961) *Microanalysis of Socioeconomic Systems: A Simulation Study*. New York: Harper.

Orcutt, Guy H./Caldwell, S./Wertheimer, I.I. (1976) *Policy Exploration Through Microanalytic Simulation*. Washington D.C: The Urban Institute.

Pourbohloul, B./Meyers, L.A./Skowronski, D.M./Krajden, M./Patrick, D.M./Brunham, R.C. (2005) 'Modeling Control Strategies of Respiratory Pathogens', *Emerging Infectious Diseases*, 11 (8): 1249-1256.

Rowe, G./Binder, D. (2008) "Can Bootstrap Replicates be used for Cross-validation?", 2008 Proceedings of the Survey Research Methods Section. American Statistical Association Annual Meeting.

Ruggles, R./Ruggles, N.D. (1975) 'The Role of Microdata in National Economic and Social Accounts', *Review of Income and Wealth*, 21 (2): 203-216.

Statistics Canada – ModGen http://www.statcan.gc.ca/microsimulation/modgen/modgen-eng.htm

United Nations (1975) *Towards a System of Social and Demographic Statistics (SSDS)*. Studies in Methods, Series F, No. 18, ST/ESA/STAT/SER F/18. New York.

USPO, Patent number 791724 filed 1997-01-29, granted January 10, 2006.

Watts, H.W. (1991) 'Distinguished Fellow. An Appreciation of Guy Orcutt', *Journal of Economic Perspectives*, 5 (I): 171-1.

Will, B.P./Nobrega, K.M./Berthelot, J.M./Flanagan, W./Wolfson, M.C./Logan, D.M./Evans, W.K. (2001) 'First Do No Harm: Extending the Debate on the Provision of Preventive Tamoxifen', *British Journal of Cancer*, 85 (9): 1280-1288.

Wolfson, M. (1997) 'Sketching LifePaths: A New Framework for Socio-Economic Accounts', in: Conte, R./Hegselmann, R./Terna, P. (eds.), *Simulating Social Phenomena*, Lecture Notes in Economics and Mathematical Systems 456, Springer.

Wolfson, M. (1999) 'New Goods and the Measurement of Real Economic Growth: Results Using the XEcon Experimental Economy', *Canadian Journal of Economics*, April.

Chapter 1

New Frontiers in Microsimulation Modelling: Introduction

Paul Williamson / Asghar Zaidi / Ann Harding

1   Introduction

As Michael Wolfson notes in his preface, this volume draws together some of the key contributions made to the first General Conference of the International Microsimulation Association. The conference, held in Vienna in 2007, took as its theme "Celebrating 50 years of Microsimulation", and marked the 50th Anniversary of the paper in which Guy Orcutt first outlined his vision for a new type of socio-economic modelling (Orcutt, 1957).

Orcutt's original vision for microsimulation entailed an empirically-based, multi-agent, micro-macro modelling approach. Initial fulfilment of this vision was hampered by a range of computational and data constraints. The gradual overcoming of these barriers has shaped the subsequent history of microsimulation, resulting in ever-increasing model sophistication and diversity. The outcome, at the risk of over-simplification, is the emergence of three basic types of microsimulation model. The first is the "static" cross-sectional tax-benefit calculator, which allows assessment of the distributional impacts of changes in state fiscal and welfare policies at a given point in time. The focus of such models is moving towards increasingly comprehensive coverage of the tax-benefit system, inter-country comparison and improved modelling of behavioural responses to changes in tax and benefit rates.

The second is the "dynamic" model, in which population characteristics are projected forwards through a process of regular updating of the characteristics of the individuals within the model (typically using an annual time-step). These models have become increasingly ambitious in terms of the range of population attributes and behaviours updated, and the sample size modelled.[1]

Third is the "micro-macro" model, which uses outputs from micro-simulation models as inputs to macro-economic models and vice versa, in order to better capture the interplay between individual behaviours and the macro-economic environment within which they operate. Again these types of models have seen increasing sophistication, including more comprehensive micro- or macro-elements and greater micro-macro integration. A consistent thread running through all three types of model, distinctive to microsimulation, is a commitment to empiricism and policy relevance, and a concern for the distributional impacts of policy decisions.

For those interested in tracking the historical developments in microsimulation, the single best repository of knowledge is the irregular "series" of edited volumes documenting the proceedings from past microsimulation conferences (Orcutt et al., 1986; Harding, 1996; Mitton et al., 2000; Gupta and Kapur, 2000; Gupta and Harding, 2007; Harding and Gupta, 2007). As the latest in the series, this present volume documents the most recent developments. These include advances in spatial modelling (section 2), discrete-choice behavioural modelling (section 3), improvements in the modelling of demographic events, labour supply, life-time earnings and pensions (section 4) and endeavours to more firmly integrate microsimulation models in a broader micro-macro modelling framework (section 5). The advances in each of these areas are summarized in more detail below. We conclude by outlining some likely future trends in microsimulation modelling, and considering the role that the International Microsimulation Association might have to play in helping to shape this future.

2 Spatial modelling

Spatial microsimulation is a fast-growing modelling technique used to develop synthetic datasets describing household characteristics at a local (sub-regional) level (Birkin and Clarke, 1988; Williamson et al., 1998; Voas and Williamson, 2000; Ballas et al., 2005; Chin et al., 2005, 2007; Lymer et al., 2008). Such data construction is often achieved by combining aggregate

---

1 See Zaidi and Rake (2001) for a review of major dynamic microsimulation models; the paper also discusses pros and cons of alternative empirical choices to be made in building a dynamic microsimulation model. Harding (2007) offers a summary of challenges and opportunities of dynamic microsimulation models.

census data with a detailed sample survey dataset. The method produces detailed portrayals of the household composition and mix of neighbourhoods, which can be used to inform analysis of spatial variations in the impact of policy initiatives in areas such as taxation and benefits, education, and health. Part I of this volume comprises a series of chapters that outline the latest advances in spatial microsimulation modelling. These include refinements in the creation of a plausible spatially-detailed starting population, dealing with within-city moves, modelling shopping flows and their interaction retail development location, and, finally, the forecasting of sub-regional expenditure patterns.

In Chapter 2, *Birkin, Wu and Rees* make the case for producing a spatially-detailed dynamic microsimulation model, specified at a sub-city scale, in order to fill the gaps left by official projections, which are generally either for larger spatial units and/or lacking any more than a rudimentary age/sex breakdown. They then outline the basic structure of Moses, an ambitious attempt to produce such a model. In order to make the problem tractable, Moses limits its ambitions to the modelling of demographic transitions, migration and housing. Even so, a number of methodological challenges are faced, including the integration of migration and household formation, the modelling of housing stock dynamics and the handling of student migration. The chapter highlights these challenges, but concentrates on one: the use of a spatial interaction model to inform the microsimulation of within-city moves or "relocations". Simulation results confirm that the patterns of microsimulated relocations correspond closely to those of the underlying spatial interaction model, which in turn shows broad agreement with observed flows. The chapter finishes, however, on a note of caution. Whilst the potential utility of spatial microsimulation is high, the challenges, not least concerning adequate validation of the results, remain many and significant.

One of the most substantial challenges usually facing spatial microsimulators is the lack of a spatially detailed starting population. In Chapter 3, *Tanton, McNamara, Harding and Morrison* revisit this challenge, describing the creation of a synthetic population through the reweighting of survey data to local area census benchmarks. The reweighting is undertaken using a generalized regression algorithm, GREGWT, created by the Australian Bureau of Statistics. Whereas Australian census data capture gross household income, the reweighted survey data capture current disposable income (post-tax and transfers). Importantly, disposable, rather than gross,

33

income is required to identify households living in poverty. The reweighted survey data, therefore, allow the authors to derive headcount estimates of the number of persons living in poor households for small geographical units (Statistical Local Areas) across the South East of Australia. The results confirm previous findings of widespread rural poverty, but also highlight the existence of pockets of poverty within major urban areas, sometimes cheek-by-jowl with pockets of extreme affluence.

In Chapter 4, *Van Leeuwen, Clarke and Rietveld* demonstrate the clear potential of spatial microsimulation for aiding local planning decisions through the development of a model of local retail choice, SIMtown. In particular they emphasize how spatial microsimulation can allow planners to consider a range of possible spatial developments. Their contribution falls into three parts. First, they generate the by now familiar pre-requisite of a spatially-detailed micro-population. In doing so, they demonstrate that the accuracy of the reconstructed population improves with both the size of the survey being reweighted and with the number of local constraints that the reweighting process is required to satisfy. For this reason, restricting the reweighting process to the use of local survey respondents only is shown to be counter-productive. Second, the authors undertake multinomial logistic regression analysis of shopping survey data to derive probabilistic models, for a variety of retail types, of destination choice. In doing so they find that, in contrast to population reconstruction, behavioural models derived using local responses match the reality better than models based upon analysis of all responses. Third, the authors combine their behavioural models and spatially-detailed micro-populations to explore the predicted impacts of contrasting retail developments (including the opening of a supermarket and a retail centre). The model results are shown to allow the sub-regional winners and losers from such a development to be identified, whether in terms of specific urban centres or socio-demographic subgroups.

In Chapter 5, *Anderson, de Agostini, Laidoudi, Weston and Zong* draw together a number of innovative strands to produce spatially-detailed estimates and forecasts of the share of household expenditures allocated to a range of communications and media-related products, measured in terms of both money and time. First, they use survey data to estimate non-linear demand functions for household expenditures upon a range of telephony and media items. Second, they estimate future values for the explanatory variables underpinning these demand functions, using first-order autoregressive functions fitted to time-series data. Third, they substitute these values into

34

the demand functions to yield forecast expenditure shares. The resulting overall changes in forecast expenditure shares are shown to be theoretically plausible and in line with observed trends. Fourth, the authors identify, for each item of household expenditure, the most closely associated (predictive) set of census-based variables, the values of which are themselves projected forwards, separately, using a constrained linear regression approach, for each small geographic area within the region of study. Fifth, iterative proportional fitting is used to reweight the original expenditure survey data to these projected small-area values. The authors then demonstrate good geographic model fit by comparing survey-based small-area estimates with observations derived independently from the census and from corporate billing information. They conclude by highlighting the utility of information on local market share and revenue for service providers whose costs, infrastructure and revenues are themselves spatially variable.

3 Work incentives and labour supply

A policy issue that has received much greater modelling attention during the past decade is work incentives, with which Part II of this volume engages. Structural population ageing, resulting from lower fertility rates and increased longevity, is expected to have adverse fiscal consequences for modern welfare states. This is partly due to the expected higher outlays in pensions and health and aged care programmes that the growing number of elderly will generate. But it is also due to the slower forecasted growth in taxation revenue and GDP associated with population ageing, with labour supply growth expected to be slower than in recent decades.

In this environment, it is not surprising that the governments have become much more concerned about whether welfare and tax programmes are adversely affecting incentives to work. In many countries, the labour force participation rates of sole parents and partnered mothers have been the subject of extensive scrutiny. Questions have been raised about whether income-tested cash transfers for children have imposed high effective marginal tax rates upon mothers and about the availability and price of child care (Harding et al., 2006). The impact of tax and social security programmes on labour supply and effective tax rates for the working age population has also been placed under the spotlight (Immervol, 2004). Nearer the end of the working life, a particular issue has been whether pension schemes have provided undue incentives to retire early (Cotis, 2003).

One of the key weaknesses of the traditional static microsimulation models is that they only deal with the first-round effects of policy change, before behaviour has adjusted (Bourguignon and Spadaro, 2005). In recent years, the "arithmetic" static microsimulation models have been complemented by discrete choice models simulating behavioural responses in labour supply. Early work in this field includes research by Blundell et al. (2000) on the likely effect of the introduction of the Working Families Tax Credit in the UK and analysis by Aaberge et al. (2000) of the impact of replacing current income taxes with a flat tax in three European countries. Another notable contribution was that of Creedy et al. (2002), who employed discrete choice models to reflect the interaction between tax rates and labour supply. In Part II of this volume more recent developments are charted. This includes extending model coverage to the economically inactive, the introduction of labour market wage-rates dependent upon supply and demand, cross-country analyses and improved modelling of female labour supply decisions.

36

In Chapter 6, *Labeaga, Oliver and Spadaro* extend their earlier work on analysing the impact on income distribution of possible and implemented reforms to the Spanish tax system (Oliver and Spadaro, 2007) to also consider labour supply responses. Much existing work on labour supply behavioural responses excludes those sections of the population who are economically inactive, such as pensioners, students and the disabled. This is because of the difficulty of estimating likely labour supply responses for such groups. The authors argue that this contradicts the basic thrust of microsimulation, which attempts to retain the heterogeneity apparent within the population. Accordingly, Labeaga, Oliver and Spadaro combine behavioural results for those sections of the Spanish population for whom labour supply can be estimated with arithmetic results for the remaining part of the population within their sample. They assess the major structural reforms made to the Spanish income tax system in 1999, as well as the impact of two other possible reform options – first, a reform which replaces the 1999 income tax system with a "vital minimum", consisting of a tax allowance per equivalent adult and a proportional tax on taxable income and, second, a "basic income" reform, which consists of a universal lump-sum transfer allocated to each household plus a flat tax on taxable income. They find that the scenarios simulated have only a limited impact on the efficiency of the economy (as measured by labour supply effects) but that the "basic income" reforms would lead to considerable improvements in the welfare of the poorest households.

In Chapter 7, *Barlet, Blanchet and Le Barbanchon* also seek to push outwards the earlier boundaries of microsimulation. As described above, one of the growth areas for microsimulation in the past decade has been the development of models incorporating changes in labour supply in response to changes in the tax-transfer environment. These models have concentrated upon individuals' decisions to enter the labour market – and/or to supply a larger or smaller number of hours of labour – in the face of the current or possible alternative tax or social transfer programmes. Such models have provided a useful impact to policy debates in an environment when the purpose of policy reform has often been to improve work incentives and raise labour force participation rates. However, one weakness of the labour supply behavioural microsimulation models has been that they typically assume that those who want new jobs or want to increase their working hours will be able to do so – in other words, that the number of jobs will increase so as to match any growth in labour supply.

Barlet, Blanchet and Le Barbanchon take a novel approach in Chapter 7, sketching out a new microsimulation model for simulating labour market demand and supply. The importance of such a new direction has been emphasized by public policy developments in France during the past 15 years, which have been specifically aimed at affecting the demand side of the labour market. The most important of these has been the reduction of employer's social security contributions for those employees on low wages, designed to boost labour demand through the lowering of labour costs. The authors develop a model where the unit on the supply side is an individual and on the demand side is a job. The model is updated every year for such events as aged workers retiring, new workers entering the labour market, the outcomes of "wage negotiations" and a host of other factors. The authors run three experimental simulations to illustrate the capacities of the new model – a 25% increase in the number of new labour market entrants each year (broadly similar to the past impact of the baby boom cohort in the French labour market); an increase in minimum wage; and the elimination of the lower social security employer contribution rates for low wage workers (thus restoring the uniform contribution rates that prevailed at the beginning of the 1990s).

In Chapter 8 the focus upon labour market issues continues, but here the emphasis is upon the role of in-work benefits and their effects upon income redistribution and work incentives. Figari's analysis utilizes EUROMOD, a unique multi-country microsimulation modelling infrastructure developed during the past decade to carry out European comparative social science research (Sutherland, 2007). The EUROMOD static microsimulation model allows Figari to examine the impact of "policy swapping", introducing two types of in-work benefits into four Southern European counties – Greece, Italy, Portugal and Spain. "In-work" benefits provide cash transfers or tax credits to individuals with low earnings and belong to the "make work pay" group of policies that are conditional on the employment status of the recipient and have been introduced in recent years in the US, the UK and New Zealand. In Italy, Greece and Spain, fewer than 49% of women with low education are in paid employment, raising the possibility that an in-work benefit could raise participation significantly. Figari simulates two policy options – first, a family based in-work benefit, similar in structure to the UK Working Tax Credit and, second, an individually based in-work benefit operating like a low wage subsidy. He finds that there is a trade-off between the redistribution and incentive effects of in-work benefits. The family-based in-work benefits are better targeted at the poorest families – but this comes at the price of the deterioration in work incentives for women in couples. On the other hand, individually-based in-work benefits improve incentives for such women to work – but are less redistributive towards those at the bottom of the income spectrum.

This concern about female labour supply is also continued in the following chapter, Chapter 9, by *Kalb and Thoresen*. The authors develop broadly comparable behavioural microsimulation models for Australia and Norway and use them to examine the impacts upon parents' labour supply and the costs to government of a substantial reduction in child care centre fees. While the two models are both based on discrete choice labour supply models, they have been adapted to reflect the different institutional arrangements in each country – in particular, the rationing of child care due to supply shortages in Norway. The authors find that mothers' participation in the labour market is strikingly different, with 60% of mothers with a 1-4 year-old child participating in the labour force in Australia compared with 80% in Norway. The authors simulate a 50% reduction in child care fees and find that the change increases the labour supply of both mothers and fathers in both countries, albeit with a greater effect in Norway due to a more elastic labour supply. However, the results also suggest that encouraging labour supply by reducing child care fees for everyone is relatively costly and could have adverse affects on the income distribution, with only modest gains in terms of increased working hours. Thus, once again, there appears to be a trade-off between redistributive goals and improving work incentives.

4   Demographic issues, social security and retirement incomes

Most OECD countries are facing the prospect of rapid demographic change in the decades ahead. Three factors are responsible for this change. The first factor is the ageing of the baby boom generation: this generation was born in 1945 and in the following one to two decades after that, and a large number of these people have been retiring from the early 2000s onwards. The main predicament has been that this phenomenon of the high baby boom did not continue and, instead, it was followed – at least in Europe – by a much lower fertility rate. From one perspective, this can be regarded as a success of societal development, as societies offered much more choice to women – and women had much better control over whether and when to have children and how many children to have in the family. Among the consequences, however, have been either a lower number of births per woman or the postponement of births to a later age. The other key phenomenon associated with demographic change is the rise in life expectancy, particularly at older ages. Today, those who make it to the age of 60 to 65 years have much higher chances of surviving until much later in life. The demographic change observed can be seen as a sign of progress for our societies – but it also raises concerns, in particular, for social security and pension policy. Part III of the book includes chapters that address issues linked with demographic change, social security, earnings and retirement incomes. Also considered are a range of issues relating to the validation and evaluation of model-based estimates of earnings and pensions.

Baroni, Eklöf, Hallberg, Lindh and Žamac, in Chapter 10, illustrate how the agent-based microsimulation model, IFSIM, could be used as an approach to evaluate policy changes that affect fertility decisions. The policy in question is a change to the Swedish parental leave benefit system, in which the minimum level of benefit that is received when no prior earnings are available is increased. The motivation is to see how such a policy change might affect fertility timing and fertility rates. The authors argue that although microsimulation models have come a long way forward in modelling individual heterogeneity, they are not well suited for the study of fertility behaviour. This is principally because the social interactions that are viewed as an important factor in fertility decisions are better captured by the agent-based approach. The main advantage of such a simulation model is that the whole effect of many different social insurance systems can be accounted for, including the macro feedback on the individual level of other agents' choices. They find that the policy of raising the minimum benefit has a negligible impact on completed fertility – and that this is also true regarding the overall cost to the transfer systems. Thus, Sweden has little to gain or lose by implementing the policy in question. The authors argue that many other issues can be investigated with this agent-based approach, but observe that it is important that such models are validated by appropriate rules of thumb.

In Chapter 11, *Blanchet and Le Minez* describe the main features of the dynamic microsimulation model for France, DESTINIE, which has been progressively developed over the last 15 years at the French National Statistical Institute (INSEE). The authors discuss how the development of DESTINIE has followed the evolution of pension policy issues in France. The authors provide details on pension entitlement rules for a "full rate" pension, that made the use of the microsimulation modelling approach particularly attractive in France. They present results based on this model of retirement behaviour, concerning age at retirement before and after the 1993 and 2003 pension reforms, for both private and public sector workers. They also discuss the relevance and limits of these results, with clear indications on how the model can be further developed.

In Chapter 12, *Morrison* estimates internal rates of return from the Canada Pension Plan (CPP) to subgroups, on the basis of attributes other than the birth year or gender. He makes use of the DYNACAN longitudinal dynamic microsimulation model for Canada. The subgroups of interest are: those with low lifetime earnings, ever-married, immigrants, early retirees, and the disabled. The approach adopted highlights the usefulness of the measure of internal rates of return in evaluating the effectiveness of CPP's existing or possible alternative provisions, to these subgroups. Arguments are presented in favour of using the internal rates of return analyses as a standard part of policy evaluation processes. In a second extension of the author's earlier work, this chapter also presents results for real after-tax internal rates of return for the Canada Pension Plan. The analysis provides a first look at internal rates of return, calculated based on participants' net gains and losses. The findings are that the real after-tax rates of return are lower than the before-tax rates, but are still positive for all cohorts for both men and women, and for all of the examined subgroups by gender. The chapter provides practical, policy-oriented, and policy-relevant results.

Chapter 13, by *Rowe and Moore*, provides an overview of the steps being taken to validate simulations of lifetime employment careers in the

Statistics Canada dynamic microsimulation model, LifePaths. This evaluation serves two purposes: i) to outline the credibility of the simulation of career-long employment and earnings patterns, and to determine how these deficiencies might possibly be remedied; and ii) to document, as far as possible, the degree of realism that might be expected of simulations of the future by examining simulations of the past. One key finding of this validation exercise is that LifePaths is currently generating far too many job transitions. Despite these issues, preliminary validation results show that LifePaths can provide highly credible simulations of career wages. The authors conclude that LifePaths can credibly be used to simulate and evaluate issues relating to the Canadian retirement income system. Life-Paths' success is to be attributed to the efforts that went into assembling pertinent data in estimating employment and earnings equations, and to the sophistication of its analytical techniques. In that sense, LifePaths' current success is seen to be a testimony to the value of data integration inherent in all microsimulation modelling work.

Chapter 14 is contributed by the research team of the UK's ESRC SAGE Research Group. The authors, *Zaidi, Evandrou, Falkingham, Johnson and Scott*, report on the work undertaken in constructing the labour market module in the SAGE dynamic microsimulation model for Great Britain. They emphasize three steps in simulating life course trajectories of employment and earnings: estimation of credible predictors of employment transitions and earnings dynamics from existing datasets; implementation of estimated employment and earnings equations on the base data; and the validation for logic and consistency of simulated results. The chapter provides a meticulous description of work undertaken for these three steps within the SAGE model and points to generic lessons drawn. Authors conclude that the logic testing and statistical evaluation of simulated results showed that the SAGE model produces a realistic distribution of employment and earnings, which was related to individual circumstances in a way that no static or macro model could achieve. Nonetheless, they identify that a further validation of the long-term trajectories of employment and earnings will be necessary. They mention that the absence of period and cohort effects will inevitably entail some degree of doubt about their simulated results. They also caution for the Monte Carlo and other sources of variation, such as sampling and imputation variation in the base data and variation in parameter estimates, and these variations must be accounted for when exploring the effects of different economic and social policy scenarios of the future.

41

In Chapter 15, *O'Donoghue, Leach and Hynes* analyse how the results from econometric models of earnings are applied to dynamic microsimulation models, using data for Ireland and the UK. The authors provide an in-depth assessment of the effects of different accounting periods and payment mechanisms for recorded earnings. Such differences may lead to inaccuracies in model estimation through the different variance in earnings across groups – and this could subsequently have a significant impact on the simulation of earnings. The authors find that a number of choices that are not usually incorporated into dynamic microsimulation models have very important impacts upon the performance of earnings equations: i) estimating earnings models on a subset of the population that did not enter the labour market in the previous year; ii) splitting the sample into a low-earnings variability and another group to avoid problems associated with heteroscedasticity; and iii) using a narrower definition of income excluding lump-sum payments and using a shorter accounting period such as weekly earnings.

In Chapter 16, *Willekens* emphasizes the fact that the ultimate aim of microsimulation is to produce a virtual population that is representative of a real population – and then to use the virtual population to study character-istics of the real population and to perform experiments that are not possible in real populations. However, one of the major weaknesses of microsimulation is the credibility of the model for the real population and processes. If the model is a weak representation, then the results of microsimulation will lack credibility. The author argues that continuous-time microsimula-tion modelling has clear advantages over microsimulation in discrete time units. The key advantage is that the dates of events and the sequences of events can be determined accurately using the theory of competing risks and continuous-time multistate transition models. Willekens points out that the *R* programming environment makes it easier to implement continuous-time microsimulation. These developments substantially reduce the program-ming costs and the computing time is also not substantially larger than in discrete-time microsimulation. These developments are expected to enhance the use of continuous-time microsimulation in the study of life histories.

Capéau, Decoster, De Swerdt and Orsini, in Chapter 17, analyse the dis-tributional impact of lowering social security contributions and compensat-ing for the revenue loss by an increase in indirect taxes. For this empirical application, a link is made between two existing Belgian microsimulation models – MODÉTÉ for the tax-benefit system, and ASTER for the indirect tax part. The behavioural models were estimated to predict changes in expenditure behaviour and in labour supply (a discrete choice model). The authors simulate the impact of the reform with and without taking into account the labour supply reaction. The authors find that with fixed labour supply there are considerable distributional effects, with the current generation of pensioners being most liable to pay the bill as they do not profit from the reduced tax on labour income, but do pay higher consumption prices. However, this assessment of gain or loss is sensitive to the decision to neglect or integrate leisure in the welfare concept used to assess the effect of the reform. Moving to the second simulation, incorporating labour supply changes, flexible labour supply is assumed for couples only. The results confirm the findings from many other papers: the labour supply effect is mainly found at the extensive margin of labour market participation. For the welfare analysis, the picture of gainers and losers evidently is affected by the weight attached to the lost leisure for individuals who enter the labour market or increase their labour supply.

Blander and Nicaise, in Chapter 18, estimate a joint (Markovian) model of employment and poverty states, taking into account that educational attainment is endogenous. Using this model, the authors evaluate the impact of different policies on poverty alleviation (by ex-post microsimulation). The three policies evaluated are: increasing the coverage of the minimum income; activation of the unemployed poor; and raising the educational level of vulnerable groups. Using the duration of poverty spells or the poverty probability as the evaluation criterion, the authors find that (a) increased coverage of the guaranteed minimum income has adverse effects, (b) activation has large short-term and small long-term positive effects, and (c) raising the educational level of vulnerable groups has lasting positive effects. The dynamic approach adopted in this chapter can be seen to be much more realistic in predicting the impact of such poverty-reducing policies. Given the high degree of mobility into and out of poverty, the net effects of anti-poverty measures appear to be much smaller than a static model would predict. Moreover, depending on the type of policy adopted, long-term effects may be much greater or smaller than short-term effects.

5   Macro-micro linkages and environmental policies

Another prominent trend in microsimulation in the past decade has been an attempt to link microsimulation models to macro-economic models. The supreme advantage of microsimulation models is that they allow detailed analysis of the winners and losers from a policy reform – but the potential downside is that they ignore the possible economy-wide effects of that reform, such as an increase in interest rates or unemployment. In contrast, the various types of general equilibrium models capture these economy-wide impacts, but at the price of providing no detailed distribution of outcomes, with the household sector typically being represented by a single representative household. Not surprisingly, numerous attempts are now being made to link macro- and micro-models, with the goal of harnessing the power of both types of models. Part IV of the book reports on some of the latest attempts to better integrate the two approaches.

In Chapter 19, *Foertsch and Rector* report on an attempt to capture the second-round effects caused by a series of proposed changes to the US tax system. Their solution involves the use of outputs from a microsimulation of the federal individual income tax system to calibrate a macroeconomic model of the US economy (the "Global Insight" model), and vice versa. The microsimulation model captures changes in the tax system, such as falling marginal tax rates, which lead to changes in macroeconomic behaviours and outcomes (higher levels of investment, jobs growth etc.), which in turn lead to changes in individual behaviour (higher rates of labour market participation, higher post-tax incomes) and so on. Although this iterative calibration process sounds like a potentially computationally very expensive solution, in the example presented only three iterations are required to reduce the gap between microsimulation and macroeconomic model outputs, at the end of a 10-year projection period, to $0.6 billion. The results from the combined models confirm the importance of taking dynamic revenue feedbacks (second-round effects) into account. At face-value, the proposed tax changes are forecast to lead to a loss in tax revenue of $992 billion dollars over the period 2007-16. Allowing for dynamic revenue feedbacks the projected loss in revenues decreases by nearly a third to $696 billion dollars.

Brown, Harris, Picton, Thurecht, Yap, Harding, Dixon and Richardson, in Chapter 20, move the focus on to the micro-level links between health and employment outcomes and wider macro-economic implications that ensue. Specifically, they describe an approach to evaluating a proposed health intervention programme targeted at preventing or ameliorating Type 2

Diabetes – a health challenge of increasing concern not only in Australia but across the developed world. In their work Brown et al. use survey data to first of all produce a cell-based projection of future cases of Type 2 Diabetes. These results are fed into a microsimulation model of future household labour supply, with health status being used as one of the key predictors of labour supply. The outcomes from this model are fed, finally, into a computable general equilibrium model of the macro-economy. Collectively, these linked models allow not only the types of analysis conventionally associated with microsimulation models (such as the estimation of the costs associated with the proposed programme of intervention and of the number of cases of diabetes avoided), but also of the total costs to the economy. The results presented show that this latter contribution is vital. Taken from the viewpoint of health care alone, the costs of intervention are greater than the projected savings in future treatment costs. However, the additional labour supply freed-up by a healthier workforce leads to an estimated AUD $6.4 billion net increase in GDP by the end of the projection period.

In Chapter 21, *Clauss and Schubert* sketch out the structure of the combined CGE/microsimulation model being developed in the Centre for European Economic Research (ZEW) in Germany. ZEW have developed the STSM tax and benefit microsimulation model, for analysis of the impact of taxes, social security contributions and transfers on the private incomes and labour supply of private households in Germany. They have also constructed the PACE-L static general equilibrium model. To link the two models, the authors first run the microsimulation model to derive those parameters which will be subsequently required to run the CGE model, such as the gross wage and disposable income for different types of households. These microsimulation outcomes are fed into the labour supply component of the CGE model, with wages and unemployment rates initially being held constant. In the second round, the labour supply changes arising from policy reform are allowed to affect wages and unemployment. In turn, these then feed back into the labour supply module, with interaction occurring between the two modules until convergence occurs. The authors conclude with some examples of where the availability of both macro- and micro-results has contributed greatly to public policy development.

In Chapter 22, *Stølen, Texmon and Nielsen* outline an integrated micro-macro approach to assessing the future fiscal impact of current and future immigration flows. Using a cohort-component demographic projection model, a series of macro-projections of plausible population futures are first generated, with scenarios ranging from balanced (zero) to constantly high net immigration. These aggregate projections are used as constraints on the demographic trajectories of the dynamic microsimulation model MOSART. Through MOSART, Stølen et al. are able to disaggregate the tax and benefit histories (and futures) of Norway's immigrant and non-immigrant populations. For immigrants, labour market participation rates are modelled, differentiated by age, sex and point of origin. Alternative labour participation scenarios are also assessed. Through these simulations Stølen et al. are able to demonstrate that future fiscal (pension) and service (education, health) pressures will be attributable almost entirely to demographic ageing. In this context immigration is shown to have the potential to play a small but helpful role in ameliorating these pressures, at least up until the model time-horizon of 2050. Beyond this, as Stølen et al. observe, immigrants from previous decades will themselves start to enter retirement, potentially adding significantly to the existing demographic pressures. Stølen et al conclude by briefly outlining the planned next stage in their analysis, which is to feed their macro-demographic projections and their microsimulation-based estimates of labour supply, pension expenditures and public service demands, as exogenous inputs to Statistics Norway's dynamic computable general equilibrium model, reflecting an overall project arc of linkage from macro to micro and then back to macro.

In Chapter 23, *Bardazzi, Oropallo and Pazienza* demonstrate how a firm-based microsimulation model (DIECOFIS) can be used to assess the potential for energy taxes – specifically carbon taxes – to encourage a reduction in industrial carbon emissions. Their chapter falls into two parts. First, an ex ante analysis confirms the overall fiscal neutrality of a carbon tax reform introduced in Italy in 1998 – although it also confirms that, as a result, some energy-intensive industrial sectors are likely to experience non-trivial reductions in gross operating surplus. The second part of the chapter reviews what changes in firm behaviour actually arose following the introduction of a watered-down version of the originally proposed carbon tax. This ex post analysis uncovers significant between-firm variations in response. In part this is attributed to sector-specific energy requirements; in part to differing elasticity of demand between large and small firms. The latter finding is thought to reflect the economies of scale and longer time horizons enjoyed by large firms when placing bulk contracts for purchasing energy supplies. The remaining challenge is to close the loop and feed the observed ex post behavioural responses into an ex ante analysis of a next round of possible energy tax reforms.

6   Conclusion

Orcutt's original vision for a fully integrated and comprehensive micro-macro model of the socio-economic system remains unfulfilled. However, as we have shown above, the microsimulation community is making significant strides towards fulfilling this goal. Areas of innovation captured in this volume include improvements in discrete-choice modelling, spatial resolution and micro-macro integration.

Looking towards the future, the pace of development is such that forecasting the advances to be made over the next 50 years would be foolhardy. With more modest ambition, we can at least project forwards current trends. Continued advances in behavioural modelling can be expected, fuelled by the increased provision of longitudinal data, ongoing refinement of existing analytical techniques and growing engagement with the agent-based modelling community. Similar advances are anticipated in the fields of spatial modelling and micro-macro linkage. The "realm" of microsimulation will also continue to expand, having moved well beyond its original tax-transfer focus to embrace arenas such as child support, pharmaceutical benefits and environmental issues (Brown et al. 2004; Harding and Percival, 2007). New application areas are emerging, most notably in the health arena, covering the modelling of both disease (demand) and its treatment (supply). At the same time, microsimulation continues to be embraced by practitioners from an ever-widening range of countries – the most recent notable additions being China and Japan. Finally, we anticipate that microsimulation models of all types will continue to become ever more firmly embedded as key tools in national policy-making, a trend most recently reflected by the planned adoption of dynamic microsimulation to produce official demographic projections for Statistics Canada.

As editors, we trust that this current volume, drawing upon the proceedings of the first General Conference of the International Microsimulation Association (IMA), will go some way towards making this future, and Orcutt's vision, a reality. As the elected serving officers of the association, we also hope that this volume helps fulfil in part the IMA's goal of serving the wider microsimulation community through the dissemination of knowledge. A second General Conference has already been organized, to be held in Ottawa in June 2009, and the publication of this volume is timed to coincide with it. Other dissemination pathways include the association's website, email discussion lists and associated academic journal. For more details of these and other initiatives, please visit the association's website: www.microsimulation.org

References

Aaberge, R./Colombino, U./Strom, S. (2000) 'Welfare Effects of Proportional Taxation: Empirical Evidence from Italy, Norway and Sweden', *Journal of Population Economics*, 13 (4): 595-621.

Ballas, D./Clarke, G.P./Wiemers, E. (2005) 'Building a Dynamic Spatial Microsimulation Model for Ireland', *Population Place and Space*, 11: 157-172.

Birkin, M./Clarke, M. (1988) 'SYNTHESIS – A Synthetic Spatial Information System for Urban and Regional Analysis: Methods and Examples', *Environment and Planning* A, 20: 1645-1671.

Blundell, R./Duncan, A./McCrae, J./Meghir, C. (2000) 'The Labour Market Impact of the Working Families Tax Credit', *Fiscal Studies*, 21: 75-106.

Bourguignon, F./Spadaro, A. (2005) 'Microsimulation as a Tool for Evaluating Redistribution Policies', *Journal of Economic Inequality*, 4 (1): 77-106.

Brown, L./Abello, A./Phillips, B./Harding, A. (2004) 'Moving Towards an Improved Micro-Simulation Model of the Australian Pharmaceutical Benefits Scheme', *Australian Economic Review*, 37 (1): 41-61.

Chin, S.F./Harding, A. (2007) 'spatialMSM – NATSEM's Small Area Household Model for Australia', in Gupta, A and Harding, A (eds), *Modelling Our Future: Population Ageing, Health and Aged Care*, Model 22, International Symposia in Economic Theory and Econometrics, Volume 16, Elsevier B. V., Amsterdam, pp. 563-566.

Chin, S.F./Harding, A./Lloyd, R./McNamara, J./Phillips, B./Vu, Q. (2005) 'Spatial Microsimulation Using Synthetic Small Area Estimates of Income, Tax and Social Security Benefits', *Australasian Journal of Regional Studies*, 11 (3): 303-336.

Cotis, J. (2003) 'Population Ageing: Facing the Challenge', *OECD Observer*, September.

Creedy, J./Duncan, A.S./Harris, M./Scutella, R. (2002) *Microsimulation Modelling of Taxation and the Labour Market: The Melbourne Institute Tax and Transfer Simulation.* Cheltenham: Edward Elgar Publishing.

Gupta, A./Kapur, V. (2000) *Microsimulation in Government Policy and Forecasting.* Amsterdam: North-Holland, Elsevier.

Gupta, A./Harding, A. (Eds.) (2007) *Modelling Our Future: Population Ageing, Health and Aged Care*, International Symposia in Economic Theory and Econometrics, Volume 16. Amsterdam: Elsevier B.V.

Harding, A. (2007) Challenges and Opportunities of Dynamic Microsimulation Modelling, Plenary paper presented to the 1st General Conference of the International Microsimulation Association, Vienna, 21 August 2007.

Harding, A. (Ed.) (1996) *Microsimulation and Public Policy*, Contributions to Economic Analysis Series. Amsterdam: North Holland.

Harding, A./Gupta, A. (Eds.) (2007) *Modelling Our Future: Population Ageing, Social Security and Taxation*, International Symposia in Economic Theory and Econometrics, Volume 15. Amsterdam: Elsevier B.V.

Harding, A./Percival, R. (2007) 'The Australian Child Support Reforms: A Case Study of the Use of Microsimulation Modelling in the Policy Development Process', *Australian Journal of Public Administration*, 66 (4): 422-437.

Harding, A./Payne, A./Vu, Q.N./Percival, P. (2006) 'Trends in Effective Marginal Tax Rates, 1996-97 to 2006-07', *AMP NATSEM Income and Wealth Report* Issue 14, September (available from www.amp.com.au/ampnatsemreports).

Immervoll, H. (2004) *Average and Marginal Effective Tax Rates Facing Workers in the EU: A Micro-Level Analysis of Levels, Distributions and Driving Factors.* OECD Social, Employment and Migration Working Paper No 19. Paris: OECD.

Lymer, S./Brown, L./Yap, M./Harding, A. (2008) 'Regional Disability Estimates for New South Wales in 2001 Using Spatial Microsimulation', *Applied Spatial Analysis and Policy,* 1 (2): 99-116

Mitton, L./Sutherland, H./Weeks, M. (2000) *Microsimulation Modelling for Policy Analysis: Challenges and Innovations.* Cambridge: Cambridge University Press.

Oliver, X./Spadaro, A. (2007) 'Basic Income or Vital Minimum? A Note on the Distributive Effects of Possible Reforms of the Spanish Income Tax', pp. 361-387 in: Harding, A./Gupta, A. (Eds.), *Modelling Our Future: Population Ageing, Social Security and Taxation,* International Symposia in Economic Theory and Econometrics, Vol. 15. Amsterdam: Elsevier B. V.

Orcutt, G.H. (1957) 'A New Type of Socio-economic System', *Review of Economics and Statistics* 58 (2): 773-797 (reprinted with permission in *International Journal of Microsimulation* 1 (1): 3-9, Autumn, at http://www.microsimulation.org/IJM/V1_1/IJM_1_1_2.pdf).

Orcutt, G./Merz, J./Quinke, H. (1986) *Microanalytic Simulation Models to Support Social and Financial Policy.* Amsterdam: North-Holland, Elsevier.

Sutherland, H. (2007) 'EUROMOD', pp. 563-566 in Gupta, A./Harding, A. (Eds.), *Modelling Our Future: Population Ageing, Health and Aged Care,* Model 22, International Symposia in Economic Theory and Econometrics, Volume 16. Amsterdam: Elsevier B. V.

Voas, D./Williamson, P. (2000) 'An Evaluation of the Combinatorial Optimisation Approach to the Creation of Synthetic Microdata', *International Journal of Population Geography,* 6: 349-366.

Williamson, P./Birkin, M./Rees, P.H. (1998) 'The Estimation of Population Microdata by Using Data from Small Area Statistics and Samples of Anonymised Records', *Environment and Planning* A, 30 (5): 785-816.

Zaidi, A./Rake, K. (2001) *Dynamic Microsimulation Models: A Review and Some Lessons for SAGE,* ESRC-SAGE discussion Paper no. 2. London: London School of Economics.

Part I:
Spatial Modelling

Chapter 2

Moses: Dynamic Spatial Microsimulation with Demographic Interactions

Mark Birkin / Belinda Wu / Phil Rees

1   Introduction

Microsimulation models have been used extensively to address distributional questions in a population. The work on dynamics is perhaps less voluminous, but still substantial (a comprehensive review is provided by O'Donoghue, 2001; for a more recent statement of challenges and issues, see Harding, 2007). The challenges in dynamic modelling of a population are considerable, yet multiplied further when there are several sub-populations, as within a spatial microsimulation. In order to moderate this problem, the most popular approach has been "static dynamic" (e.g. Ballas et al., 2004), in which a base population is regenerated synthetically to match independent forecasts of the overall population structure. In addition to the question of dimensionality – the existence of multiple sub-populations by definition includes parallel modelling of a number of demographic groups – the most important challenge is to capture interactions between these sub-populations, and in a geographical context in particular to assess patterns of migration within and between local neighbourhoods. While the well-known Sverige

This research has been sponsored by the ESRC Award Number RES-149-25-0034. Moses is a node of the National Centre for e-Social Science. More information about Moses, including code and documentation for the dynamic model as well as papers and presentations, is available at www.ncess.ac.uk/research/moses. More information about the National Centre for e-Social Science is available at www.ncess.ac.uk. Census output is Crown copyright and is reproduced with the permission of the Controller of HMSO and the Queen's Printer for Scotland. 2001 Census, Output Area Boundaries. Crown copyright 2003.

model is one notable earlier attempt to capture spatial dynamics within a microsimulation framework (Rephann and Holm, 2004) this model adopts quite large spatial units and treats regions as closed systems without attempting to model local interactions. On the other hand, the SMILE model (Ballas et al., 2005) includes migration between Irish counties. The work of Duley (1989) incorporates small area migration data only in the context of inter-censal population updating. This report therefore documents a distinctive attempt to meet the challenge of modelling spatial dynamics with local demographic interactions.

It will be seen that the difficulties to be surmounted in constructing a spatial microsimulation model with explicit dynamics remain formidable. Nevertheless the benefits from successful prosecution of such a campaign would be extensive. The advantages in representing demographic processes through microsimulation, in contrast to traditional cohort-based approaches, have been eloquently stated by van Imhoff and Post (1998: 105-107), turning on the detailed simultaneous representation of multiple demographic characteristics, and the representation of interactions between processes and between individuals. Such a model could also provide unique and valuable benefits to urban planners and policy-makers, with responsibility for far-reaching policy decisions regarding questions from sustainable development, environmental quality, housing and transport to equity and efficiency in the provision of health, education, social care, and the regulation of an extensive range of public and private services from retailing to crime prevention (Clarke and Birkin, 2008). Typically such decisions are made in the context of a very limited understanding of demographic trends and processes, whether independently or in response to specific policy influences (for example, if I approve this new housing programme, to what extent will it meet future housing needs: and how will it affect housing market behaviours in such a way that those needs are themselves changed?).

The remainder of the chapter is structured as follows. In Section 2, the Moses model is introduced and the major demographic components are described. A substantial section is then devoted to the means for modelling migration between local neighbourhoods. The fourth section of the chapter presents some indicative results and model benchmarks, before the chapter concludes with a discussion and review of next steps.

2   Structure of the Moses model

2.1   *Overview*

The overall structure of the Moses model is illustrated in Figure 1. The model is currently expressed as ten distinct *functions* which are in turn combined into three *module* groups – demographic transitions, migration and housing. Before commenting on these three module groups, a number of preliminary observations concerning the model are necessary.

Figure 1:   The structure of the Moses dynamic model

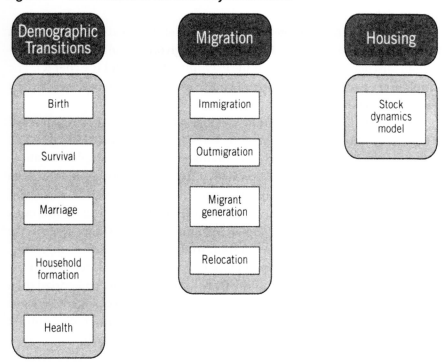

The Moses dynamic model builds on a baseline simulation or *Population Reconstruction Model* (PRM) which recreates the entire UK population as an array of households and their constituent members (Birkin et al., 2006). Both private households and communal establishments are represented. The PRM uses synthetic records from the 2001 Census Sample of Anonymised Records (SAR) which provides quite an extensive array of social and demographic characteristics for each household. The base population is constructed using a genetic algorithm which reweights the SAR to local neighbourhood profiles from the Census Small Area Statistics. The algorithm has been shown to perform well. For the purpose of the dynamic model prototype which is reported here, a subset of important household and individual characteristics are extracted from the PRM. The household characteristics are location, housing type and household size. The individual characteristics are age, sex, marital status, social class, ethnicity and health. Each of these individual and household attributes is projected throughout the course of the simulation.

The spatial units adopted within the model are census wards, of which there are more than 11,000 in England, although only 33 in the Leeds Metropolitan District, which is used as the exemplar throughout the chapter. The simulation operates in discrete time intervals of one year, and runs from a base year of 2001 until 2031.

The order in which the various demographic modules are implemented is also worthy of further discussion. Van Imhoff and Post (1998: 116-117) note four alternative procedures involving simultaneous implementation, versus sequential implementation with a fixed order of events, a random order of events, or one in which the most likely event is itself simulated for each individual. In this application, a fixed order of events has been implemented in the sequence shown in Figure 1. There is some logic to the ordering – for example, the demographic transitions come before migration, because if there is a spatial dependence (e.g.mortality rates depend on the place of residence) then this is more likely to be historically embedded than newly acquired. Nevertheless it is recognized that the sequence is to some degree arbitrary, and that some further investigation of alternatives might be justified at some point in the future course of this research.

2.2 *Transition probabilities*

Each of the demographic processes within this functional group may be expressed in the form of a simulation equation of the following nature:

$$P\left[x_1(t), x_2(t+1)\right] = R(x)\, f\left[S(x)\right] \tag{1}$$

in which P $[x_1(t),x_2(t+1)]$ is a transition probability from state x_1 at time t to state x_2 at time t+1; S(x) is a set of individual and household attributes which are predictive of these transition probabilities, and R(x) are attributes which are expected to be independent and uncorrelated. In simple terms, for the purpose of any transition the model divides demographics into two groups – those which affect the process and those which do not. Table 1 shows, for each of the transition processes, the characteristics affecting each process (marked "Yes") and the independent characteristics (marked "No"). The data sources are also noted in Table 1. The 2001 Census provides base populations for local neighbourhoods, including wards. ONS Vital Statistics are counts of births and deaths for small areas. The British Household Panel Survey (BHPS) is a longitudinal survey of the UK population since 1991 covering many social and demographic trends as well as attitudes, lifestyles and behavioural data.

Table 1:   Data inputs and dependencies for demographic transitions

	Birth	Survival	Marriage	Household formation	Health
Housing variables					
Location	Yes	Yes	No	No	Yes
Household type	No	No	No	No	No
Housing size	No	No	Yes	Yes	No
Individual variables					
Age	Yes	Yes	Yes	Yes	Yes
Sex	Yes	Yes	Yes	Yes	Yes
Marital status	Yes	No	Yes	Yes	No
Ethnicity	No	No	No	No	No
Social group	No	No	No	No	No
Health	No	No	No	No	Yes
Data					
BHPS	No	No	Yes	Yes	Yes
ONS Vital Statistics	Yes	Yes	No	No	No
2001 Census	Yes	Yes	No	No	Yes

In its structure, the model is rather more straightforward than many existing dynamic simulation models, such as CORSIM (Caldwell,1996) and its many offspring. For example, O'Donoghue (2001) notes the existence of 900 equations in 28 equation-based processes in CORSIM, with processes including labour force participation and income dynamics in addition to basic demographic transitions. However the spatial component renders Moses distinctive with respect to demographics. Consider the survival module as an example. The Moses survival function applies mortality rates based on the sex and exact age (from 0 to 100 years) of individuals by location. Therefore for a model of the city of Leeds disaggregated fairly coarsely into 33 census wards the simulation requires 33 x 2 x 101 = 6,666 survival parameters. If one then allows that these parameters might evolve through each of 30 model iterations, then in the order of 200,000 parameters are required for the survival model alone!

In practice this level of detail is kept manageable through secondary modelling of the parameter estimates, which turns the task from a multiplicative to an additive process. National survival rates are estimated for each age and sex combination (202 calculations). These are then adjusted to known small area death rates by five-year age-sex cohorts (20 x 2 x 33 = 1,320 calculations). Then we apply a simple evolutionary rule, such as a 1% improvement in all survival rates in year 12 of the simulation (30 parameters).

Nevertheless parameter estimation remains a formidable challenge, particularly when one considers that current assumptions are very much towards the straightforward end of what might in principle be accommodated. Thus there are no interactions between say health status and survival rates. To take a second example, fertility rates in the model are differentiated by age of mother, by marital status and by location. However no allowances are made for variations in age-specific birth rates by either ethnic or social group, both of which are well-known to influence reproduction (Forste and Tienda,1996; de la Croix and Doepke, 2003).

2.3 Migration

The functions in this group provide the means to simulate the movement of individuals and households within the urban area, including the introduction of new individuals from outside the city region ('immigration"), as well as outmigration to other locations ('emigration"). The movement of individuals within the city region is referred to as "relocation" in order to distinguish this important phase from the other migration processes. The conjunction of two previously distinct individuals, or groups of individuals, within a single housing unit is referred to as "household formation".

In Table 2, the variable relationships and data sources for the migration processes are described. The immigration and emigration functions both comprise two sub-models, accounting for sub-national and international migration flows. Migrant profiles for sub-national flows can be obtained at a ward level from the 2001 Census Special Migration Statistics, while the profiles for international flows are derived from the International Passenger Survey (IPS). In the case of outmigration, the movement is modelled in a two-stage process, in which migrants are at first "generated" using profiles derived from the British Household Panel Survey. This procedure is described in more detail in Section 3. The migrants are split into local and sub-national migrants. Local migrants can then be passed across to the relocation function for assignment within the Leeds area. Sub-national migrants require no further action. Although logically one region's sub-national emigrants are another region's sub-national immigrants this connection is not effected within the current model structure, as it imposes too great a burden on the data processing and file sharing within the model architecture. It is much more straightforward to implement the model as a series of self-contained regional models with external interactions than to try and construct an all-encompassing national model. This strategy also has the advantage that each region can be calibrated and validated independently. Attempting to validate a single national model would be a daunting challenge indeed.

Once the characteristics of potential migrants have been determined, then emigrants can be identified within the synthetic population by Monte Carlo sampling in the usual way.[1] Immigrants present greater problems since they are entering the population from an external and unknown source. Inmigrants are created in the model by "cloning" members of the baseline population, i.e. existing households or residents with the right characteristics are duplicated from existing members of the database (cf. Chenard, 2000).

The purpose of the household formation routine is to produce new household units through the aggregation of pairs of existing households. Panel data are used to establish the rate of household formation by age and sex, and the affinity between partners by age, gender and social class. The household formation rates are used to create a pool of movers within each geographical area. Pairs of individuals within the mover pool are then united in accordance with the affinity distributions. Although the household formation routine belongs logically within the migration module, there is a sense in which it is misplaced within the current specification since we

59

---

1   In other words, the probability of emigration according to the characteristics of the individual. A number is drawn at random between 0 and 1. If the emigration probability exceeds the random number, then the status of "emigrant" is applied to this individual.

make the simplifying assumption that both partners in this procedure are already located within the same small geographical area. This decision is justified in view of the lack of easily accessible data on the spatial dimension of household formation. It could potentially be enhanced through further analysis for example of local parish records, but such work lies beyond the scope of the current project and is likely to remain so.

Table 2:   Data inputs and dependencies in the migration functions

	Immigration	Emigration	HH formation	Relocation
Housing variables				
Location	Yes	Yes	No	Yes
Household type	No	No	No	Yes
Housing size	No	Yes	Yes	Yes
Individual variables				
Age	Yes	Yes	Yes	Yes
Sex	Yes	Yes	Yes	Yes
Marital status	No	Yes	Yes	Yes
Ethnicity	Yes	No	No	No
Social group	No	No	No	Yes
Health	No	No	No	No
Data				
2001 Census	No	No	No	Yes
SMS	Yes	Yes	No	Yes
IPS	Yes	Yes	No	No
BHPS	No	Yes	Yes	Yes
Moses	Yes	No	No	No

Such local flows are captured quite richly within the 2001 Census Special Migration Statistics (SMS), allowing disaggregation by age and sex, and by mover groups (complete or partial households). However the problem with SMS is that this provides a single snapshot view of movement at a period in time, and the same rates cannot be expected to persevere indefinitely, for example in the face of evolving transport, housing and economic patterns. The relocation function therefore requires further secondary modelling of neighbourhood interaction patterns within the city. Because this feature of the Moses model is both important and distinctive, the next section of this chapter is devoted to a more detailed discussion of modelling local migration.

In common with the discussion from the previous section, it must be noted again that in many respects the migration module incorporates assumptions which present a rather simplified view of reality. For example, the failure to establish a link between ethnicity and emigration means that the important processes of return migration[2] are not currently encapsulated within the model. Another example might be the absence of a link between health and migration. In particular, towards the end of the lifecycle deterioration into poor health might be envisaged as an important driver of household change and movement into institutional accommodation. Of course these features may be justified on the grounds that any model must perforce represent an abstracted and simplified view. The general point perhaps is that the model can represent *transitions* but not *events*. This point is picked up again in the concluding section of the chapter.

2.4 Housing module

In many microsimulation models, housing stock may be unimportant or of secondary interest. For example, in static models it may be appropriate to assume a simple assignment relationship between population and housing (specifically, that every household has a house!). However in truly dynamic models which attempt to trace the evolution of a population for small geographical areas housing stock dynamics play an important role, because housing markets will not be in equilibrium with respect to demographic shifts. In other words, the composition and movement of urban populations will depend on the underlying distribution of housing stock. Such dynamics in the housing market have been recognized for a long time with respect to dynamic microsimulation. For example the idea of vacancy chains is widespread in the literature (Hooimeijer and Oskamp, 1996). Vacancy chains are implicit in the Moses model. Thus whenever a new migrant is identified, or a new household is formed through the coalescence of two existing households, then a vacancy is created so the stock of housing available to new movers is increased. However the model is also inspired by analogy with demographic accounts, such that housing stock can also be adjusted through "natural change" and "migration". In this case, birth or fertility rates reflect

61

---

2   The short-term influx of economic migrants coming into the UK to find work, but in the long term returning to their country of origin. The importance of this group has been the subject of much debate in the literature on international migration – see for example Dustmann et al. (1996).

new house builds in an area, while mortality rates equate to the demolition of current stock. In a housing market context, migration is not physical but relates to change in use, for example the conversion of old warehouse units into residential accommodation, or perhaps the use of residential property for retail businesses. Finally, we can also recognize that there will always be an element of the housing stock which lies vacant at a point in time.

The Moses housing module therefore recognizes changes in the housing market through a set of independent transitions. At a point in time, the housing stock comprises a set of occupied households and a set of vacant households. During an iteration of the simulation, the stock is increased by new house building, by changes of use and by complete households moving from a property and into the mover pool. The available housing stock is reduced by the demolition of housing and by any change of use from residential to non-residential activity. Vacant housing is then repopulated by migrants from the mover pool.

In practice, the migration experiments reported in Section 3 have been undertaken with a rather simple view of urban housing markets, in which the initial stock of occupied housing is known (from the 2001 Census), and to which vacant housing is added at a uniform rate across all locations. From here, housing market growth is essentially demand-driven, so that new housing construction takes place where it is most needed. Other simulations (not reported here) have been undertaken in which housing stock evolves in accordance with published local plans, and others in which brownfield expansion is conducted more aggressively.

A much more accurate view of current housing conditions is possible of course. Recent research at the Centre for Applied Spatial Analysis, University College London, has looked at the integration of Ordnance Survey Mastermap, the electoral roll, aerial photography and other sources to provide a detailed picture for parts of London (Crooks and Hudson-Smith, 2008). The application of such a methodology to Leeds and other areas is currently under consideration. However housing market dynamics can only ever be partially informed by current building and development plans. An important contribution of dynamic simulation must be to understand, through the exploration of various scenarios, how things might look under alternative views of the future. For example, where might we be if the housing market is able to respond freely to the choices and needs of residents, and does this contrast with the view under current strategic plans and proposals?

3   Spatial Interaction Models (SIM) for migration

The operation of the relocation sub-module is considered in some detail in the following sections. First the problem of identifying potential migrants is considered, and then a method for the assignment of migrants within the local area is introduced. Finally, the means by which meso-scale assignment models can be combined with micro-level simulation modelling are discussed and evaluated.

3.1   Identification of movers

Data from five waves (2000-2004) of the British Household Panel Survey (BHPS) have been used to assess the key determinants of migration. BHPS is a longitudinal study of approximately 9,000 households and 16,000 individuals, and captures a very wide range of social and attitudinal information (University of Essex, 2005). The BHPS includes "individual mover status" which captures "whether sample members have moved since (the) previous wave" (Taylor et al., 2005). The BHPS also includes a household reference code and an individual reference code. The household reference code is unique to each wave of collection, but the individual codes are consistent between waves. Therefore the mover status of each individual can be attributed by applying a cross-sectional match between successive waves of the survey using individual person identifiers. A test is then applied to establish whether an individual has the same household companions, and changes in membership are traced according to the demographics of household members (age, sex and marital status).

   Once the mover status of each individual in a household has been established, three mover groups can be identified. The first group is households which move in their entirety, the second group is individuals leaving a household, and the third group is partial household moves in which more than one individual leaves the household and more than one person stays behind. We want to establish the factors which drive variations in the migration probabilities for each of these groups. However analysis of the data led quickly to the conclusion that partial moves and individual moves could be combined with little loss of accuracy. For example, in the 2003 wave, we have 855 household moves and 693 individual moves, but only 229 partial moves. Therefore only two categories remain: "type 1 moves" involving an entire household, and "type 2 moves" involving the separation of a single individual from a household.

The generation of movement probabilities from a single wave is not possible. Consider the situation in which a household has four members, and each is a mover since the last wave. Any of the following could be true:

1) The four household members have moved as a unit.
2) One household with two members has "merged" with another household of two members.
3) A household with three members has moved as a unit. It has been joined by an individual splitting from another household.
4) Four individuals have come from larger households, and combined to form a new household.

With the terminology introduced above then case 1 is a type 1 move; case 2 is two type 1 moves; case 3 is a type 1 move and a type 2 move; case 4 is four type 2 moves. Other possibilities can also be envisaged. In order to disentangle household moves from individual moves, we therefore need to link together data from successive waves of the BHPS, and alongside the mover flag to indicate whether each individual is part of the same household.[3]

64

Table 3:   Analysis of movers in the British Household Panel Survey

			Number of Moves			
Wave	Year	Panel Size	Individuals	Households	Individuals	Households
8	1999	10906	9716	5178	236	472
9	2000	15623	13579	7287	328	596
10	2001	15603	10232	5608	448	334
11	2002	18867	12511	6757	602	397
12	2003	16597	14358	7708	292	584
Total		77596	60396	32538	1906	2383

From this procedure, 1906 individual moves and 2383 household moves were identified across six linked waves of the BHPS, as shown in Table 3. We then analysed individual moves for each of the following person characteristics: Age (in 7 categories), Sex (2), Household size (4), Marital status (6), Headship (2), Ethnicity (3), Health status (6), Occupation (10), Home ownership (3), Tenure (4). For households, the same characteristics were analysed for the household reference person, except for headship which is clearly redundant.

---

3   Because there is no common link between households between waves, this process is not trivial. Therefore we had to write code to find an individual mover at time t, find the same individual at time t-1, then compare the other individuals in the same household at t and t-1.

A chi-squared test was employed to test the importance of each potential predictor variable. Figure 2a shows that single-person households tend to favour flats at all stages of the lifecycle, although this trend is strongest for the younger age groups. Figure 2b shows that larger households tend to have a stronger preference for housing, and this preference is most pronounced amongst families in the intermediate age ranges.

Figure 2:   Housing preference by household size

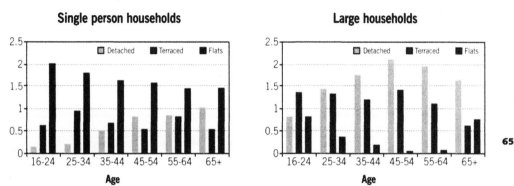

Figure 3:   The Leeds Metropolitan Area

A procedure for the distribution of migrants using a doubly constrained spatial interaction model has been fully described elsewhere (Wu et al., 2008: Appendix 1). The fit of this model can be assessed most easily through a regression of observed against zonal interactions which generates a reasonable, although not a spectacular, relationship, explaining about 65% of the variance in local migration patterns. Further diagnostic information is shown in Table 4, which can in turn be interpreted with reference to the local geography which is illustrated in Figure 3. Here the model fitness is assessed by small area: in the table, these are ranked from worst to best. There is a general pattern for the poorest fits to be in the more central areas. For example, Seacroft has a very high level of intra-ward moves, but because this is quite a small zone in proximity to several others, the model tends to predict quite a lot of cross-boundary movement. The model is most robust in the free-standing peripheral towns, i.e. Wetherby, Pudsey, Otley, Morley and Guiseley (Aireborough).

Table 4: Ward level diagnostics for the Doubly Constrained Spatial Interaction Model (for explanation, see text)

Zone	Name	Model fit	Observed	Predicted	Ratio
28	Seacroft	0.13	3.18	3.50	0.91
30	Weetwood	0.28	3.71	3.12	1.18
32	Whinmoor	0.54	3.76	4.00	0.94
2	Armley	0.56	2.78	3.35	0.83
27	Roundhay	0.56	5.09	4.24	1.20
15	Hunslet	0.58	2.49	3.96	0.63
33	Wortley	0.59	2.91	3.81	0.76
18	Moortown	0.61	4.04	3.90	1.04
7	Chapel Allerton	0.62	3.31	3.54	0.94
26	Rothwell	0.63	3.39	4.3	0.79
16	Kirkstall	0.65	4.04	3.22	1.25
11	Halton	0.66	4.00	4.35	0.92
25	Richmond Hill	0.68	2.89	3.90	0.74
5	Bramley	0.69	3.25	3.68	0.88
3	Barwick & Kippax	0.70	4.76	3.94	1.21
6	Burmantofts	0.71	2.77	3.65	0.76
29	University	0.72	3.11	3.08	1.01
12	Harehills	0.72	3.03	3.64	0.83
13	Headingley	0.75	3.03	3.14	0.96
17	Middleton	0.75	3.20	3.96	0.81
9	Cookridge	0.76	4.96	4.46	1.11
4	Beeston	0.77	2.83	3.76	0.75
10	Garforth	0.79	3.21	3.88	0.83
21	North	0.79	4.45	4.59	0.97
14	Horsforth	0.80	4.34	4.13	1.05
23	Pudsey North	0.87	3.99	4.16	0.96
24	Pudsey South	0.90	3.19	4.01	0.80
19	Morley North	0.91	3.37	4.21	0.80
8	City & Holbeck	0.93	2.94	3.65	0.81
20	Morley South	0.94	2.85	3.76	0.76
22	Otley	0.95	4.33	3.52	1.23
1	Aireborough	0.97	4.20	3.51	1.20
31	Wetherby	0.99	4.75	3.50	1.36

The table also shows the relationship between observed and predicted distance moved by ward, but this shows no clear pattern and is uncorrelated with goodness of fit.

Zones are as shown in Figure 3. "Model fit" is the correlation (R-squared) between observed and predicted migration flows to each other zone; "Obs" is the average migration distance observed within the Special Migration Statistics (SMS); "Pred" is the average migration distance predicted by the doubly-constrained spatial interaction model (DCSIM); "Ratio" is the ratio between the observed and predicted migration distances.

3.2   Integration of the models

Once a set of aggregate flow patterns has been obtained from the spatial interaction model (SIM), these may be used to determine individual flow patterns in an obvious way. Thus individual behaviours can simply be sampled from the SIM using the normal Monte Carlo procedures, in which location preferences would be given by:

$$p(j,m \mid i,k) = T_{ij}^{km} \bigg/ \sum_{jm} T_{ij}^{km} \qquad (2)$$

where T_{ij}^{km} is the number of households of type k with housing type m who migrate from zone i to zone j; and $p(j,m \mid i,k)$ is the probability that households of type k living in i will move to housing type m in zone j.

This methodology has been adopted recently by Nakaya et al. (2007) and originally suggested by Birkin and Clarke (1987). The necessary steps in the microsimulation model can be described verbally in the following process:

1. Identify a set of migrant households. Create a list of available housing by destination and housing type.
2. Create a list of mover households by zone of origin and demographic group.
3. For each migrant (selected at random), assign a choice probability for each available housing unit, and apply a Monte Carlo sampling procedure to select a specific destination.
4. Once a housing unit is assigned, remove it from the choice set and move to the next migrant.

Compared with the spatial interaction model, then the origin and destination terms are embedded within the migrant selection process (i.e. the list of available destinations sums to housing stock and the number of migrants sums to the number of movers in each zone). Furthermore the role of the balancing factors is automatically regulated by the adoption of a one-to-one assignment of migrants to housing units. In other words, we assert that the Monte Carlo procedure and the SIM will produce equivalent results when each individual preference is described by the utility function:

$$U_{ij}^{km} = e^{-\beta d_{ij} + \lambda^{km}} \tag{3}$$

where d_{ij} is the distance from zone i to zone j, and the probabilities are simply:

$$p(j, m \mid i, k) = U_{ij}^{km} \bigg/ \sum_{jm} U_{ij}^{km} \tag{4}$$

There are some similarities between this assertion and the well-known equivalence between meso-level spatial interaction models and individual level random utility models (Domencich and McFadden, 1975), although a formal description of this equivalence is at best difficult, and perhaps impossible because of the Monte Carlo sampling involved within the present choice model. Therefore the only way to demonstrate this equivalence is through simulation once again. Parameters from the SIM calibration were used to generate the utility function (3), then the preference function (4) was deployed within the simulation framework described above. The results from the two models (T_{ij}) were correlated. The resulting correlation yielded an r^2 of 0.95. Furthermore, the correlation between the microsimulation (MSM) results and the observed flows are very similar to the equivalent comparison for the SIM at $r^2 = 0.65$. Of course a perfect correspondence within this process cannot be expected for two reasons. In the first place, the sampling procedure within the microsimulation is randomized. Secondly, and more important, the microsimulation incorporates an integerized version of the SIM, i.e. all the flows in the MSM are whole numbers, while the SIM has fractional flows. Without being able to state that the assertion has been fully proven, at the very least, it seems that the implementation of a microsimulation model, where the choice function (4), represents a close approximation to the SIM.

Of course there are numerous ways in which the representation of migration processes might be improved within this modelling framework. For example, the distance deterrence parameters of the SIM might be made spatially disaggregate, or the resolution of the population might be refined by social class, ethnicity or other characteristics. One hypothesis worth exploring is that housing stock is not a subtle enough discriminator of neighbourhood attractiveness, and other metrics are required including measures of environmental quality, the performance of local services (health, education, crime prevention) or social preferences between different demographic groups. A more ambitious development might be the explicit regulation of demand through a house price mechanism. Some broader requirements and priorities are considered in the discussion in Section 5. Next, however, some indicative model results will be evaluated.

4   Evaluation of model results

In this section, indicative results from the simulation will be assessed. The model was run in single-year intervals for 30 time periods starting in 2001. Appropriate assumptions were adopted in relation to key demographic trends:

- Total period fertility rates in 2001 were close to an all-time low. A steady increase in the Total Period Fertility Rate was assumed from approximately 1.65 in 2001 to 1.8 in 2011, then staying constant until 2031.
- Mortality rates were reduced by 1% per annum throughout all 30 years of the simulation for both genders at ages 60 and over. For ages under 60, there was no change in the baseline mortality rates.
- Steady profiles of inmigration and outmigration were maintained from 2001 onwards. However the overall migration rates were adjusted to balance the official sub-national population projections (ONS, 2007).
- Housing stock was allowed to grow in accordance with the demand for accommodation. An arbitrary vacancy rate of 2% was applied to all areas and housing types in 2001. This vacancy rate was maintained throughout the simulation, so that new house building matches the needs of new migrants and home-starters. The rate of new building is assumed to be identical for all areas and housing types.

- Rates of marriage, household formation, and change in health status are assumed constant in relation to the various drivers from the baseline calibration.

For the Leeds area, comparative demographic profiles between Moses and ONS estimates are provided in Figures 4 and 5. While the trends amongst both schoolchildren (Figure 4) and the more elderly age ranges (Figure 5) are similar between Moses and ONS, the evolutionary patterns are not completely identical and may again point to some minor alignment issues between the underlying projection methods and assumptions.

Figure 4: Demographic profiles for Leeds: Schoolchildren

4a. Model estimates (source: Moses)   **4b. Government estimates (source: ONS, 2007)**

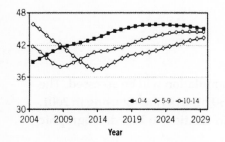
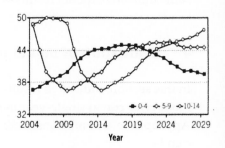

Figure 5: Demographic profiles for Leeds: Elderly

5a. Model estimates (source: Moses)   **5b. Government estimates (source: ONS, 2007)**

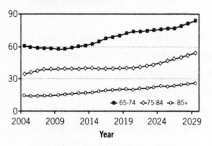
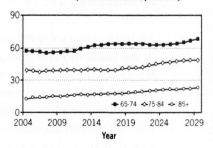

A different set of outputs is shown in Figures 6 and 7. First, in Figure 6, changes in the ethnic composition of the population can be seen. Whilst the white population grows fairly sluggishly, minority populations – in particular those EU migrants from new accession countries who are subsumed within the "other" category – grow much more rapidly. Equivalent analyses are not available from official sources, although these conclusions are rather similar to other work undertaken by geographers on behalf of Yorkshire's Regional Development Agency (Stillwell et al., 2006). In Figure 7 growth in the elderly populations (the increase in the number of people aged 85 and over) is shown in various parts of the city. It is moderately striking that not only is there significant growth in all areas, but also that change is especially acute in certain areas – often, and perhaps not surprisingly, those that start with the heaviest concentrations to begin with.[4] Again this analysis cannot be reproduced from official sources which are incapable of disaggregation below the metropolitan area scale (i.e. the entire region covered by Figure 7).

Figure 6:   Population dynamics by ethnicity (metropolitan scale)

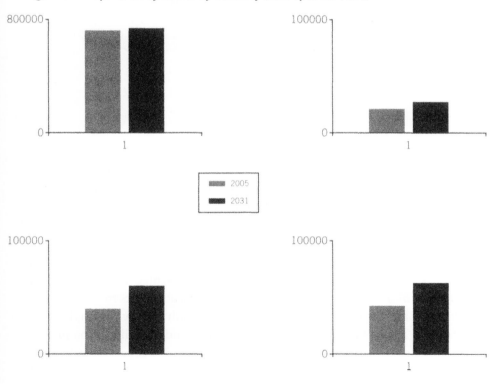

---

4   The highest concentrations in the elderly population of Leeds are generally in the Aire and Wharfe valleys to the north of the city: especially the wards of Aireborough, Cookridge, North, Otley and Wetherby – see Figure 3.

**Figure 7:   Increase in the elderly (85+) population, 2005-2030
(neighbourhood scale)**

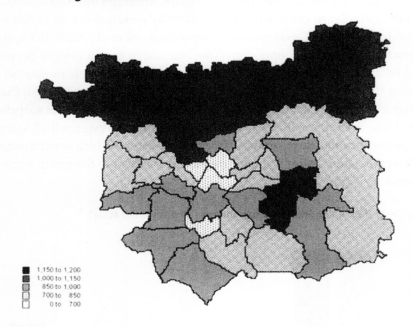

1,150 to 1,200
1,000 to 1,150
850 to 1,000
700 to 850
0 to 700

72

Finally, in Figure 8 we can see changes in the ancillary health variable over time. The ability to project future distributions of social, economic and demographic phenomena could be of great interest to policy users with an interest in the planning of future patterns of service delivery and resource allocation (Edward, 2008) and represents one of the major motivations for the Moses project (Birkin et al., 2005). Of course the validation of such estimates represents a major conceptual and practical challenge. Whilst this illustration shows overall quality of health, as represented in both the census data and BHPS, there is no reason why other characteristics from either the census, BHPS or other sources such as the Health Survey for England or National Travel Survey, might not be estimated and modelled dynamically in a similar way. The authors are currently engaged in separate projects on behalf of third parties with an interest in health care, the provision of social services, education, transport, housing and the accumulation of personal and inherited wealth, which are all exploring the extent to which such activities might be helpful in different applied contexts.

Figure 8: Increase in the proportion of the population with poor health, 2005-2030 (neighbourhood scale)

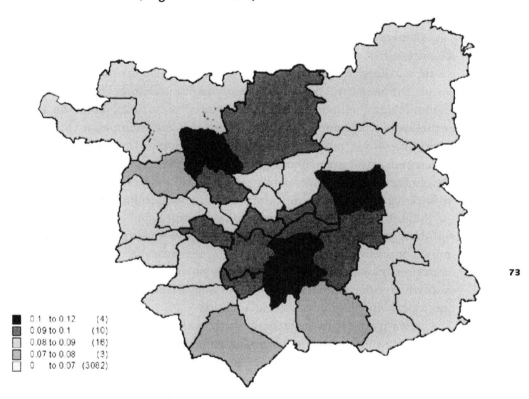

■	0.1 to 0.12	(4)
▨	0.09 to 0.1	(10)
□	0.08 to 0.09	(16)
▨	0.07 to 0.08	(3)
□	0 to 0.07	(3082)

5 Discussion and next steps

This chapter has described progress to date in the development of Moses, a dynamic spatial microsimulation model of the UK population. It has been seen that such a model presents many challenges, some of which have been addressed effectively, others at best partially resolved. It is appropriate to begin this discussion with a restatement of the case for needing such a model. It may be argued that three particular benefits are spatial disaggregation, the provision of compositional detail and methodological refinement.

In relation to spatial disaggregation, it was remarked that official sub-national projections extend only to the metropolitan area level, and this is insufficient to support decisions regarding the planning and delivery of local services from retailing to health care, from housing to the prevention of crime. With respect to compositional detail, it has been shown that characteristics like health care and ethnicity can be added which provide much needed richness to the standard demographics of age and gender.

It has been asserted, although not yet fully demonstrated, that further characteristics, whether demographic, economic or social, perhaps even in relation to lifestyles and attitudes, might be modelled in a similar way and would further extend the value of the dynamic modelling. The capacity for methodological refinement might be regarded as a critical part of the intellectual case for dynamic microsimulation. Limited examples are included within the Moses model as described in this chapter: for example, the interdependence between marriage and fertility rates, and the deployment of disaggregate survival rates across geographical areas represent an increase in sophistication relative to cohort-based demographic models. There is no doubt that further decomposition might add value – for example, is it sufficient to assume constant fertility rates between ethnic groups? Could more complex forecasts explore interdependencies between social class, education, housing and wealth? Whether such disaggregation adds value, and which aspects demand the closest and earliest attention, remains a question for further reflection and analysis.

A complementary perspective on the question of methodology is provided by the authors in another recent paper (Wu et al., 2008), in which the problem of student migration is treated with special care. In this paper, the authors argue that many serious weaknesses in standard demographic models are induced through the particular difficulty of dealing with student migrants, who move between and around cities in unusual ways. It is proposed that the microsimulation approach provides a natural means for the isolation of the student sub-population, and it is also suggested that individual-based methods including agent-based simulation may be an effective means to introduce specific rule-based behaviours for student "agents". This connection is particularly relevant in the current context if we regard student migration as an example of a demographic event – in effect the decision to move into and through university education. The idea of events, in contrast to transitions, was introduced in Section 2. It is possible that much greater power might be added to dynamic simulation models through the adoption of an events-driven perspective, with each of these events attracting multiple transitions. Thus the decision to get married might associate directly with a desire to move house and have children, perhaps even a change of job. The progression towards ill health might be accompanied by the dissolution of a household and an associated migration into the care of a family member or other provider. In short, many possibilities for methodological refinement might be explored on the foundations of a dynamic modelling framework which have been laid down here.

In fairness, it should be recognized that whether dynamic spatial microsimulation models can really generate sufficiently robust population estimates to support resource allocation and planning decisions within our cities, and if so over what kinds of time horizon, remains an open question. Although benchmarks against official estimates may provide reassurance to a degree, the validation of model projections against a future yet to be revealed must by definition be hugely uncertain. There are a number of potential routes towards validation of these model estimates which all need further evaluation. Possible strategies include running the model backwards to a known prior state; interim evaluation of model updates (e.g. comparing 2001-based "projections" against 2008/09 data); and ongoing monitoring of model projections into the future. Given that policy-makers must nevertheless make important decisions about the future in the light of some kind of evidence or assessment, and given that at the very least surely it is possible to add quantitative evidence on the basis of specified assumptions and scenarios, the authors remain optimistic that there is value to be extracted from this exercise. Furthermore this chapter has set out to articulate dynamic spatial microsimulation as a worthwhile intellectual challenge in its own right.

References

Ballas, D./Clarke, G./Dorling, D./Eyre, H./Thomas, B./Rossiter, D. (2004) 'SimBritain: A Spatial Microsimulation Approach to Population Dynamics', *Population, Space and Place*, 11: 13-34.

Ballas, D./Clarke G./Wiemers, E. (2005) Building a dynamic spatial microsimulation model for Ireland, *Population, Space and Place*, 11: 157-172.

Birkin, M./Clarke, M. (1987) 'Comprehensive models and efficient accounting frameworks for urban and regional systems', pp. 169-195 in: Griffith, D./Haining, R. (eds.), *Transformations through space and time*. The Hague: Martinus Nijhoff.

Birkin, M./Clarke, M./Chen, H./Dew, P./Keen, J./Rees, P./Xu, J. (2005) MoSeS: Modelling and Simulation for e-Social Science, *Proceedings of the First International Conference on e-Social Science*, National Centre for e-Social Science, Manchester; available online: http://www.ncess.ac.uk/events/conference/2005/papers/papers/ncess2005_paper_Birkin1.pdf,accessed October 2008.

Birkin, M. / Turner, A. / Wu, B. (2006) 'A Synthetic Demographic Model of the UK Population: Methods, Progress and Problems', *Proceedings of the Second International Conference on e-Social Science*, NCeSS, Manchester; available online: http://www.ncess.ac.uk/events/conference/2006/papers/papers/BirkinSyntheticDemographicModelOfUKPopulation.pdf; accessed October 2008.

Caldwell, S.B. (1996) 'Health, Wealth, Pensions and Life Paths: The CORSIM Dynamic Microsimulation Model', in: Harding, A. (ed.), *Microsimulation and Public Policy*. Amsterdam: Elsevier.

Chenard, D. (2000) 'Individual alignment and group processing: an application to migration processes in DYNACAN', in: Mitton, L. / Sutherland, H. / Weeks, M. (eds.), *Microsimulation Modelling for Policy Analysis: Challenges and Innovations*. Cambridge University Press.

Clarke, M. / Birkin, M. (2008) MoSeS: SimCity for Real, Digital Geography in a Web 2.0 World, Barbican, London.

de la Croix, D. / Doepke, M. (2003) 'Inequality and Growth: Why Differential Fertility Matters', *American Economic Review*, 93 (4): 1091-1113.

Crooks, A. / Hudson-Smith, A. (2008) The Fine Scale Spatial Dynamics of the Greater London Housing Market, GISRUK, Manchester. Available online at http://www.casa.ucl.ac.uk/andrew/repastmodels/gisruk/crooks_smith_Theseira_GISRUK2008.pdf, accessed July 2008.

Domencich, T. / McFadden, D. (1975) *Urban Travel Demand: A Behavioural Analysis*. Amsterdam: North Holland.

Duley, C. (1989) A model for updating Census-based household and individual information for inter-censal years. Unpublished PhD thesis, School of Geography, University of Leeds.

Dustmann, C. / Bentolila, S. / Faini, R. (1996) 'Return Migration: The European Experience', *Economic Policy*, 11: 213-250.

Edward, O. (2008) 'Real-life SimCities: How digital geographers are using predictive computer models to improve the way we plan and run our cities', *Geographical Magazine*, August.

Forste, R. / Tienda, M. (1996) 'What's behind racial and ethnic fertility differentials', *Population and Development Review, Vol 22*, Supplement: Fertility in the United States: New Patterns New Theories, 109-133.

Fotheringham, A.S. / Rees, P. / Champion, T. / Kalogirou, S. / Tremayne, A.R. (2004) 'The development of a migration model for England & Wales: overview & modelling outmigration', *Environment & Planning A*, 36 (9): 1633-1672

Harding, A. (2007) Challenges and Opportunities of Dynamic Microsimulation Modelling, Plenary paper presented to the 1st General Conference of the International Microsimulation Association, Vienna, 21 August 2007.

Hooimeijer, P. / Oskamp, A. (1996) 'A Simulation Model of Residential Mobility and Housing Choice', *Journal of Housing and the Built Environment*, 11: 313-336.

van Imhoff, E. / Post, W. (1998) 'Microsimulation methods for population projection.', *Population: An English Selection*, 10: 97-138.

Nakaya, T. / Fotheringham, A.S. / Clarke, G. / Ballas, D. (2007) 'Retail Modelling Combining Meso & Micro Approaches', *Journal of Geographical Systems*.

O'Donoghue, C. (2001) 'Dynamic microsimulation: a survey', *Brazilian Electronic Journal of Economics* 4 (2): 45-61.

Office for National Statistics (2007) *Sub-national population projections, 2004-2029*. London: HMSO.

Ott, J./Rao, D. (1985) 'A chi-square test to distinguish allelic association from other causes of phenotypic association between two loci', *Genetic Epidemiology*, 2 (1): 79-84.

Rephann, T. J./Holm, E. (2004) 'Economic-Demographic Effects of Immigration', *International Regional Science Review*, 27: 379-410.

Stillwell, J./Rees, P./Boden, P. (2006) *Yorkshire and the Humber Population Projections: Age and Ethnicity*. School of Geography, University of Leeds.

Taylor, M. (ed.) with Brice, J./Buck, N./Prentice-Lane, E. (2005) *British Household Panel Survey User Manual, Volume B*. Colchester: University of Essex.

University of Essex (2005) Institute for Social and Economic Research, British Household Panel Survey; Waves 1-13, 1991-2004 [computer file]. Colchester, Essex: UK Data Archive. SN: 5151.

Wu, B./Birkin, M./Rees, P. (2008) 'A spatial microsimulation model with student agents', *Computers Environment and Urban Systems* 32: 440-453.

Chapter 3

Small Area Poverty Estimates for Australia's Eastern Seaboard in 2006

**Robert Tanton / Justine McNamara /
Ann Harding / Thomas Morrison**

1 Background

There is increasing interest within Australia about the extent to which the benefits of the economic boom over the past decade may not have been evenly distributed among all Australians. One focus of this interest has been the examination of geographic differences in advantage and disadvantage, with a growing body of work examining aspects of disadvantage at a small area level. This includes work by Baum and colleagues focusing on multiple measures of socio-economic disadvantage (Baum et al., 2005), and Vinson's (2001; 2004; 2007) work on small area estimates of disadvantage, social cohesion and resilience. A series of studies by Gregory and Hunter (Gregory and Hunter, 1996; Hunter, 2003) use census data to map regional disparities in advantage and disadvantage within Australia's cities. Regional differences in housing affordability and the impact of housing assistance have also been studied (Melhuish et al., 2004; Taylor et al., 2004), along with spatial trends in income inequality (Harding et al., 2004). Part of the value of these small area estimates of disadvantage are that they allow

This study was funded under ARC project DP664429: *Opportunity and Disadvantage: Differences in Wellbeing Among Australia's Adults and Children at a Small Area Level*. The authors would also like to acknowledge the efforts of the many past and present NATSEM staff who have contributed to the development of the spatial microsimulation techniques critical to this study. They include: Anthea Bill, Marcus Blake, Susan Day, Anthony King, Stephen Leicester, Rachel Lloyd, Tony Melhuish, Binod Nepal, Ben Phillips, Shih-Foong Chin, Thomas Morrison and Elizabeth Taylor.

decision-makers to assess where policies are best targeted. For example, a policy which can be introduced at a regional level to counter poverty and disadvantage will have the greatest impact if it is introduced into an area with high poverty rates.

Internationally there is also interest in the spatial distribution of poverty and disadvantage. The UK has indicators of deprivation for small areas (see Office of the Deputy Prime Minister Neighbourhood Renewal Unit, 2004), as do Scotland (Noble et al., 2003), New Zealand (Salmond and Crampton, 2002) and many other countries. The US Census Bureau publishes small area poverty data (see U.S. Census Bureau, 2008), and the World Bank provides information and software for poverty mapping (see Bedi et al., 2007). The World Bank website on poverty mapping makes it clear that poverty mapping is designed to assist policy-makers.

This study focuses on regional differences in income poverty, and builds on earlier work by NATSEM examining this issue (see Lloyd et al., 2001; Chin et al., 2006; and Harding et al., 2006). Poverty has been difficult to study at a small area level in Australia due to a lack of suitable data. The Australian Census of Population and Housing (which forms the primary basis for many small area studies) collects income information, but not in a way that is suitable for the measurement of income poverty. The usual method of measuring income poverty, within Australia and internationally, is to calculate disposable income (that is, income inclusive of cash transfers and net of income tax), apply an equivalence scale to that income so as to take account of differences in household size and composition, and then set a poverty line at some level of equivalent disposable income (in Australia usually 50% of the median equivalized income, but internationally more often 60% of this amount). The Australian census provides only gross income, with no information about income tax, and provides this income measure only in ranges, not actual dollar figures.

In this study, we overcome these data deficiencies by using spatial microsimulation techniques to produce synthetic estimates of income poverty at a small area level. We have used these techniques (described below) to produce earlier estimates of poverty (see Lloyd et al., 2001; Chin et al., 2006), but in this chapter we use updated methodology and more recent data to produce synthetic small area poverty rates for 2006. In this chapter, we present results only for the four states and territories along Australia's eastern seaboard, which together make up approximately 79% of Australia's total population

The remainder of this chapter is arranged as follows. Section 2 provides details of the methodology used to produce our poverty estimates, and Section 3 presents results from the modelling. Section 4 summarizes the material presented in this chapter, and discusses work still to be done.

2   Methodology

2.1   *Measurement of poverty*

The definition and measurement of poverty is highly contested in Australia and internationally. There is no firm consensus among researchers or policy-makers about the best way to define and measure poverty (see Harding et al., 2001; McNamara et al., 2007; and Saunders, 2005 for a discussion of debates around these issues). In general, there has been a move in recent years towards multidimensional measures of poverty and disadvantage, based on a number of theoretical frameworks including Amartya Sen's concept of capabilities and the concept of social exclusion (see, for example, Headey, 2005; Saunders, 2005). However, it is widely acknowledged that headcount measures of income poverty, despite their deficiencies, continue to be an important part of assembling evidence about disadvantage, and a number of recent Australian studies use income poverty as a primary poverty measure (see, for example, Marks, 2007; Saunders and Bradbury, 2006).

A headcount poverty measure provides a straightforward, easily understood and widely accepted measure of disadvantage. As our focus in this study is on comparisons between regions, our priority is to use a consistent and well-understood measure of disadvantage.

Additional debates about the measurement of income poverty (relating, for example, to the quality of income data, and the correct place to draw the poverty line) are also ongoing, but as Marks (2007) notes, agreement has been reached about some issues. He notes that disposable income (that is, income after taxes and cash transfers) is viewed as the best measure of income to use for the calculation of poverty, and that this should be adjusted in some way for household size (Marks 2007: 2).

In this study, current disposable household income is used as the basis for measuring poverty. The use of household rather than individual income assumes income-sharing within households. The modified OECD equivalence scale (widely recognized internationally) is used to adjust these household incomes for household size and composition.[1] Persons are then ranked by their household incomes, and the poverty line is set at 50% of the median equivalized household income, so that all persons with household income falling below this figure are deemed to be in poverty. Further details about the technical issues involved in the choice of income measure, equivalence scale and poverty line can be found in Greenwell et al. (2001) and Saunders (2005).

In interpreting the results in this chapter, it is important to be aware that income poverty is only one measure of disadvantage, and that headcount measures of poverty are very sensitive to definitional changes. It could be that using different measures of disadvantage, or using an alternative definition of poverty, could produce somewhat different spatial patterns to those shown here.

2.2 *Spatial unit and geographic coverage*

This study focuses only on the three states and one territory that make up the eastern section of Australia: New South Wales, Victoria, Queensland and the Australian Capital Territory (ACT). As noted earlier, these four regions make up about 79% of the total Australian population, and the capital cities of the states are Australia's largest three cities. Work is continuing on developing up-to-date regional poverty estimates for Australia's remaining states and territories.

The primary spatial unit used in this study is the Statistical Local Area (SLA). There are 1,353 SLAs in Australia in the 2001 Australian Standard Geographical Classification (ASGC) (ABS 2001). SLAs vary substantially in population size, and in this study, focusing on the eastern seaboard states, SLAs in Brisbane and Canberra are generally smaller in population and more homogenous than those elsewhere. To partly overcome this problem, we present most of our results in population-weighted quintiles and deciles of poverty.

---

1   In this study, this scale has been used to give a value of 1 to the first adult in the household, 0.5 to any second and subsequent adults, and 0.3 to dependent children (defined here as children aged 0 to 15, which differs from some earlier poverty research, in which full-time students living at home up to age 24 were sometimes also allocated the dependent child weight).

2.3 Spatial microsimulation

The results presented in this chapter are produced using a spatial microsimulation model developed by NATSEM. Spatial microsimulation techniques provide small area data that may not be available from other sources, and also incorporate the ability to model the impact of policy changes at a small area level (Melhuish et al., 2002; Chin et al., 2005). A number of techniques exist to conduct spatial microsimulation.

Internationally, methods for spatial microsimulation include combinatorial optimization, which is a reweighting technique that uses a probabilistic method (see Voas and Williamson, 2000; and Williamson, 2007) and deterministic methods implemented in the UK and Ireland using an iterative proportional fitting method (see Ballas et al., 2005a, 2005b; Anderson, 2007). Other spatial microsimulation models that use a dynamic approach and geocoded small area administrative data exist in Europe (SVERIGE – see Rephann, 2001).

Our work uses a reweighting technique, which involves creating a set of weights representing synthetic households for each small area being modelled. These weights are then applied to a poverty flag variable generated using the equivalized disposable household income in STINMOD, NATSEM's national microsimulation model of Australia's tax and social security system (Lloyd, 2007). If the equivalized disposable household income is less than half the Australian median income, then the poverty flag is set to one; otherwise it is zero. This process produces estimates of the number and proportion of persons in income poverty for each small area included in the modelling.

Details of the development of the spatial microsimulation methodology at NATSEM have been reported at length elsewhere (see, for example, Chin and Harding 2006, 2007; Melhuish et al., 2002; Melhuish et al., 2004). Here, we will describe the major steps that are involved in the production of the synthetic poverty estimates produced for this chapter, and will note the changes introduced to the modelling for these estimates compared with earlier NATSEM regional poverty estimates (reported in Lloyd et al., 2001 and Chin et al., 2006).

2.3.1 Producing regional weights

The first step in producing regional poverty estimates involves combining information from two sources – the Australian Census of Population and

Housing 2001, and data from the most recent income surveys conducted by the Australian Bureau of Statistics. The census, as noted earlier, has insufficient information to produce poverty rates, but includes variables that broadly relate to poverty at a very detailed regional level. The Survey of Income and Housing Costs, on the other hand, provides the detailed information about income needed to calculate income poverty, but at a very low level of spatial disaggregation. To produce a set of household weights for each small area included in the modelling, we benchmark the Survey of Income and Housing Costs to the census, using variables that are available in both data sources. The census benchmark variables used to produce the regional estimates for this study are shown in Table 1.

Table 1: Benchmarks used in the reweighting algorithm

Census XCP [1] table	
X46b	Income by Tenure by Household Type
X13	Labour Force Status by Sex and Age
X44	Landlord Type by Weekly Rent
X46	Income by Tenure by Household Type
X45	Type of non-private dwelling
X41	Monthly Housing Loan Repayment by Weekly Household Income
X47	Dwelling Structure by Household Type by Family Type
X48	Number of persons usually resident
X40	Weekly Rent by Weekly Household Income

Note: (1) XCP refers to the Census 2001 Expanded Community Profile Tables.

For this study, we combine data from two separate years of the Survey of Income and Housing Costs – 2002/03 and 2003/04. This is done to maximize our sample size, and thus improve our estimates of regional poverty. In order to combine these two separate survey years with 2001 Census data, we first merged the two income surveys, then converted all dollar amounts in each of these surveys to 2001 values. We then re-coded the benchmarking variables where necessary to ensure that data were categorized identically across the income surveys and the census. Finally, we used the GREGWT reweighting algorithm to reweight the combined income surveys using the census benchmark variables. The GREGWT algorithm is a generalized regression routine written in the SAS programming language, and developed by the ABS (Bell, 2000). It conducts iterative calculations to derive an optimal set of household weights for each SLA, using a regression approach to minimize the difference for each benchmark class between the census count and the estimated count. When the difference between the two counts – known as the residual – is at or close to zero, the iterations stop (Chin and Harding, 2006) – a process known as convergence. The output from the GREGWT run is a set of household weights for each SLA in Australia, with these weighted survey households closely matching the characteristics of households in each SLA as recorded in the census data.

GREGWT residuals (that is, the difference between the census count and the estimated count for each of the benchmark variables) for the vast majority of small areas in Australia are very small, and the household weights produced for these areas can then be used to calculate small area poverty rates and other regional characteristics associated with the benchmark variables. However, for some small areas, especially those with unusual characteristics or very small populations, the residuals are very large, and the algorithm does not converge. These small areas are then dropped from any further analysis. Table 2 shows each of the states and territories for which estimates are produced in this chapter, and the number of non-convergent SLAs within each. While the ACT has a reasonably large percentage of non-convergent SLAs, almost all these have either extremely low populations, or very unusual characteristics (for example, they may consist entirely or almost entirely of military bases or universities). As shown in the final right hand column of Table 2, only a very small minority of households live in the SLAs for which we are not able to produce accurate results.

85

Table 2:   **Non-convergent SLAs**

State/territory	Total number of SLAs	Number of non-convergent SLAs	Percent of non-convergent SLAs	Percent of all households in that State/Territory living in non-convergent SLAs
New South Wales	199	4	2.0%	2.1%
Victoria	200	6	3.0%	0.3%
Queensland	454	13	2.9%	0.4%
Australian Capital Territory	107	19	17.8%	0.9%

Source: ABS Census of Population and Housing 2001; Survey of Income and Housing Costs 2002/03; Survey of Income and Housing Costs 2003/04; authors' calculations.

2.3.2 Applying the weights to the variable(s) of interest

The final steps in spatial microsimulation involve applying the set of household weights for each convergent SLA that has been produced by the GREGWT process to the variable or variables of interest – in this case, income poverty.

The most recent ABS survey data available to use as the basis for measuring income poverty is the 2003/04 Survey of Income and Housing Costs. In order to produce more recent estimates of income poverty, we used NATSEM's static microsimulation model of Australia's tax and social security system – STINMOD – to uprate incomes, cash transfer, and tax arrangements to reflect the 2006/07 financial year world. NATSEM's static microsimulation model – STINMOD – simulates the impact of major federal government cash transfers, income tax and the Medicare levy on individuals and families in Australia. STINMOD is used by the Australian Treasury, the Department of Families Community Services and Indigenous Affairs, and other government agencies in policy formulation. (For additional information about STINMOD, see the STINMOD technical papers 1 to 7, available on the NATSEM website.) The version of STINMOD used in this study (a modified version of STINMOD/06B) is a set of simulated unit records based on the same income surveys we used to produce our regional weights – the ABS Surveys of Income and Housing for 2002/03 and 2003/04.

As we wanted to model the regional distribution of income poverty as of 2006, we also needed to inflate our weights by projected population changes, as the set of weights produced through the reweighting process reflects small area populations in 2001. To do this, we applied a population uprating factor to each household weight within each SLA, using small area household projections produced by the ABS (ABS, 2004).

Our final adjustment to the set of regional weights was to multiply each weight for each household for each SLA by the number of persons within that household (including children), so as to produce estimates of individuals in poverty, rather than households in poverty.

Using the STINMOD synthetic unit record dataset, we created a binary poverty flag variable for each household within this dataset (using a poverty definition and methodology described in the following section). Note that the STINMOD dataset covers the whole of Australia, not just the states and territory which we modelled at a regional level, so that the poverty flag variable was based on the distribution of incomes across the whole of Australia. We then applied our regional weights to this poverty flag variable, providing a final dataset which contained the estimated number and estimated proportion of people in poverty in each converging SLA in 2006. Our results (see Section 3) are presented as population-weighted deciles, with SLAs in the bottom quintile having the lowest proportions of people in poverty, and SLAs in the top quintile having the highest proportions of people in poverty. Because the quintiles are population-weighted, the SLAs in each quintile represent approximately one-fifth of persons living in SLAs within that quintile, rather than one-fifth of SLAs. Note that this is not exact, because if a break-point for a quintile happens in a large SLA, the whole population of that SLA has to be assigned to the quintile, which means there may be slightly more than 20% of people in a quintile. Some of our results are also presented as population-weighted deciles, created using the same methodology as the quintiles.

It should be noted that some regions which, for example, show a low proportion of people in poverty, may nevertheless contain subgroups of individuals who are experiencing a high level of poverty. These within-area differences are not able to be examined in the sort of geographical analysis undertaken here. However, the strength of spatial analysis is that it allows us to locate areas where there is a heavy concentration of income poverty.

3 Results

Figure 1 shows the estimated distribution of poverty across Australia's eastern seaboard, using population-weighted quintiles of income poverty. The darkest colour on the map represents those areas where the proportion of people in poverty is in the top quintile. This map makes it clear that areas outside Australia's capital cities are more likely to have higher proportions of people in poverty than within capital cities. Large areas of rural NSW, western Victoria and south-eastern coastal regions fall into the top quintile of income poverty. Clusters of non-capital city areas showing lower rates of income poverty include areas in north Queensland to the west and south of Mackay (regions which include some mining towns), a large cluster of SLAs in south-eastern New South Wales and north-eastern Victoria, as well as the areas surrounding Sydney, Melbourne and Canberra.

While the capital cities generally have fewer top quintile SLAs, there are clusters of income-poor suburbs within these cities. For example, in Sydney the suburbs to the south-west of the city generally show higher rates of poverty than those to the north of the city. In Melbourne and Brisbane, there are several clusters of SLAs with relatively high rates of poverty. Canberra shows somewhat less variation than the other capital cities, and those areas that do show up on the Canberra map as being in the top poverty quintile are in fact areas of very low population.

In order to examine regional variations in poverty further, and to examine geographical differences between areas of very low poverty and very high poverty, we calculated population-weighted deciles (rather than quintiles) of poverty. SLAs falling into the bottom two deciles (lowest proportions of persons in poverty) and those falling into the top two deciles (highest proportion of persons in poverty) are shown in Figure 2.

This map shows again the tendency for rural areas to have higher proportions of people living in poverty than major urban areas – and very few rural SLAs fall into the top two (least poor) deciles of income poverty. In the cities, more of a mix between relatively high and relatively low poverty areas is evident. For example, in Melbourne there are a number of adjoining SLAs in which some small areas fall into the highest or second-highest decile of income poverty, while others fall into the lowest or second-lowest decile.

While the maps clearly demonstrate geographical differences in poverty, it is also important to understand the magnitude of the differences in advantage and disadvantage between areas. Table 3 provides this information, showing where the poverty rate within each decile falls as a proportion of the overall poverty rate for the SLAs included in the modelling. Recall that our deciles are population-weighted, and therefore are deciles of people, not deciles of SLAs. Thus some deciles contain much more than 10% of the total number of SLAs, and some much less. While the number of persons in each decile is roughly 10% of the total, this is not always the case as we cannot split SLAs across deciles, so that if a large SLA falls at the boundary of a decile, its total population will go into that grouping.

As shown in the table, the differences between poverty rates across deciles are substantial, with people living in SLAs in the least poor decile having a poverty rate of only around half of the overall average rate across New South Wales, Victoria, Queensland, and the ACT, compared to people living in SLAs in the poorest decile, where the poverty rate is over one and a half times the average rate. When we examine ranges of poverty rates within deciles, these differences are even more marked, with the least poor SLA within the bottom decile having a poverty rate of only .14 of the mean rate, while the most poor SLA within the top decile have a poverty rate of over two and a half times the mean.

Figure 1:   Population-weighted quintiles of poverty by SLA, 2006

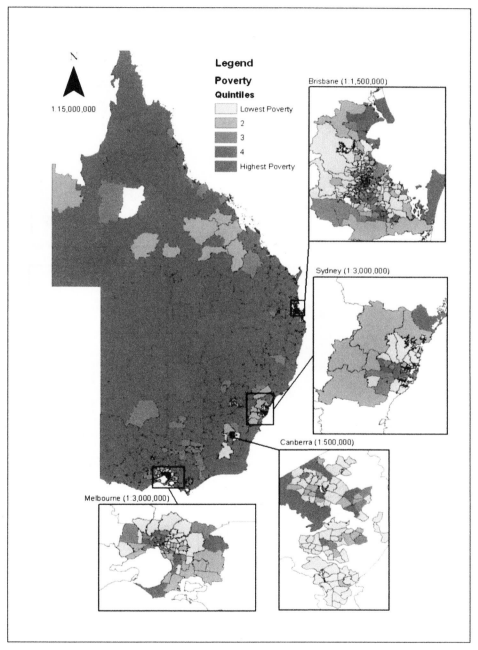

Data source: Authors' calculations.

Figure 2: Population-weighted deciles of poverty by SLA, 2006

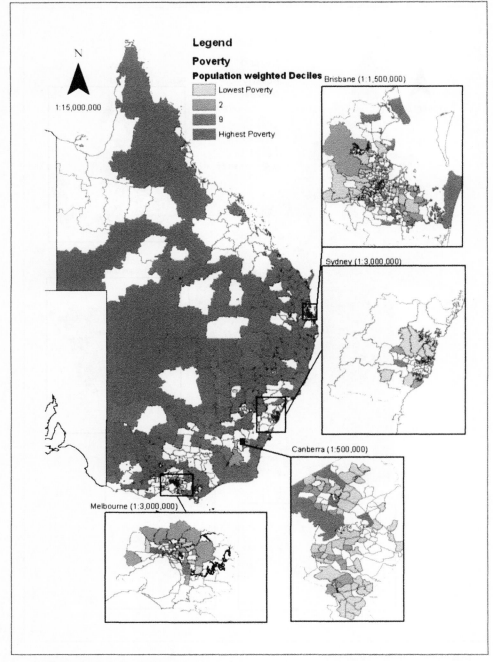

Data source: Authors' calculations.

Table 3:   Decile poverty rates as a proportion of the mean poverty rate across
            all SLAs modelled, 2006

Decile of poverty	Number of SLAs	Number of persons	Decile poverty rate as proportion of mean poverty rate	Range of proportions of mean poverty rate within decile
1 – Least poor	105	1425991	0.52	0.14-0.61
2	82	1423352	0.68	0.61-0.73
3	77	1432888	0.78	0.73-0.83
4	80	1408532	0.87	0.83-0.92
5	56	1271331	0.96	0.92-0.98
6	80	1605060	1.03	1.00-1.06
7	70	1422310	1.10	1.06-1.15
8	79	1426587	1.20	1.15-1.24
9	91	1434324	1.31	1.24-1.36
10 – Most poor	198	1430940	1.53	1.36-2.73
Total	918	14281315	na	na

4   Conclusion and next steps

These initial results from regional modelling suggest that, at least in relation to income poverty, rural areas in Australia continue to experience greater concentrations of hardship than capital cities – and, in particular, that areas of very low poverty are much more likely to be urban than rural. This tendency accords with earlier estimates of the regional distribution of income poverty, including studies that have looked at the differences between capital cities and balance of state at a broad level (Chin et al., 2006; Ciurej et al., 2006; Lloyd et al., 2001), which generally show higher levels of poverty in rural than capital city locations. Other research using wider measures of disadvantage, for example Vinson's work on small area disadvantage (2001; 2004; 2007) has also tended to find greater rural than urban disadvantage.

There are also substantial overlaps between the areas our spatial microsimulation techniques indicate to have high concentrations of income poverty, and areas which other research using alternative disadvantage indicators and non-simulated data find to be highly advantaged or disadvantaged. For example, Vinson finds the Queensland areas west of Mackay moderately advantaged (Vinson, 2007), and our study finds these same areas falling into the second quintile of income poverty (that is, having the second-lowest proportion of people in poverty).

However, it is important to note that one of the strengths of small area analysis is its ability to show exceptions to general geographic trends, and, as noted above, there are numerous areas within capital cities which have high or moderately high estimated levels of income poverty. While concentrations of very low levels of income poverty are rare outside the capital cities, there are also nevertheless many rural areas which do not fall into the bottom (poorest) quintile of income poverty. These sorts of differentiations within broad regions shown in our results accord well with analyses such as Vinson's work discussed above, and the work on regional disparities published by Baum and colleagues (Baum et al., 2005).

It should also be noted that the conclusions about lower poverty rates within the cities might be affected if we took greater account of differentials in the cost of living between the cities and the bush. While it is difficult to fully account for such differentials, one obvious possibility is to subtract housing costs from income and then calculate after-housing poverty rates. There is evidence to suggest that taking housing costs into account in the calculation of regional differences in advantage and disadvantage reduces, but does not eliminate, some of the differences in income poverty between capital city and non-capital city areas (see McNamara et al., 2007).

The magnitude of the differences we found in the poverty rates for different spatial areas underlines the importance of estimating and analysing data at a high level of spatial disaggregation. Existing studies of trends in poverty at a national level may in fact disguise differences between areas, and possible above-average increases or decreases in poverty within small areas. Future work may be able to track small area trends in poverty over time, in order to provide further insights into the ways national poverty trends may possibly play out differently within and across small areas.

The spatial microsimulation work undertaken for this study demonstrates the ability of this sort of estimation to produce data about disadvantage useful for policy-makers and service providers. However, considerable further work is continuing to add value to the results presented here.

While these results have been validated against earlier estimates produced by NATSEM (Chin et al., 2006), and found to match well with those figures, further validation against more recent data is still being undertaken. In addition, as noted earlier, estimates for Australia's remaining states and territories are still being calculated. In the near future, detailed data from Australia's 2006 census will be released (only basic data have so far been released), and this will also be incorporated into our modelling. Although we have addressed the issue of differing population sizes between SLAs to some extent by presenting our results in population-weighted quantiles, we will in the future look at aggregating results for some areas with very small SLAs (for example, in Canberra and Brisbane) to bring them into closer alignment with average SLA population sizes.

Perhaps the most important developments in this work relate to the ability of spatial microsimulation to be used for evidence-based policy-making. Additional regional work at NATSEM is using projection methodologies to produce estimates of population characteristics into the future, so that policy-makers can use these estimates as needs-based planning indicators. Also, because our regional weights are applied to the output file from STINMOD, our regional models have the capability not just to estimate the regional distribution of poverty, as demonstrated in this chapter, but, more importantly, to model possible policy responses to the alleviation of disadvantage.

References

Australian Bureau of Statistics (ABS) (2001) *Statistical Geography Volume 1. Australian Standard Geographical Classification (ASGC) 2001*. Australian Bureau of Statistics, Canberra, Cat. No. 1216.0.

ABS (2004) *Household and Family Projections 2001-2026, Australia*, Cat. No.3236.0, ABS, Canberra.

Anderson, B. (2007) *Creating small-area Income Estimates: spatial microsimulation modelling*. London: Department for Communities and Local Government.

Ballas, D./Clarke, G./Dorling, F./Eyre, H./Thomas, B./Rossiter, D. (2005a) 'SimBritain: a spatial microsimulation approach to population dynamics', *Population, Space and Place* 11 (1): 13-34.

Ballas, D./Clarke, G./Wiemers, E (2005b) 'Building a dynamic spatial microsimulation model for Ireland', *Population, Space and Place* 11 (3): 157-172.

Baum, S./O'Connor, K./Stimson, R. (2005) *Fault Lines Exposed: Advantage and Disadvantage across Australia's Settlement System*. Clayton, Victoria: Monash University ePress.

Bedi, T./Coudouel, A./Simler, K. (2007) *More than a pretty picture: Using poverty maps to design better policies and interventions*. Washington: World Bank.

Bell, P. (2000) GREGWT and TABLE macros – Users guide, Unpublished. Australian Bureau of Statistics.

Chin, S.F./Harding, A. (2006) 'Regional Dimensions: Creating synthetic small-area microdata and spatial microsimulation models', Technical Paper 33, Canberra, NATSEM.

Chin, S.F./Harding, A. (2007) 'SpatialMSM – NATSEM's Small Area Household Model for Australia', pp. 563-566 in: Gupta, A./Harding, A (eds), *Modelling Our Future: Population Ageing, Health and Aged Care*, International Symposia in Economic Theory and Econometrics, Volume 16. Amsterdam: Elsevier B. V.

Chin, S.F./Harding, A./Lloyd, R./McNamara, J./Phillips, B./Vu, Q. (2005) 'Spatial microsimulation using synthetic small-area estimates of income, tax and social security benefits', *Australasian Journal of Regional Studies* 11 (3): 303-336.

Chin, S.F./Harding, A./Tanton, R. (2006) 'A spatial portrait of disadvantage: income poverty by Statistical Local Area in 2001'. Paper presented at the ANZRSAI Conference, Beechworth Victoria, 26-29 September 2006.

Ciurej, M./Tanton, R./Sutcliffe, A. (2006) *Analysis of the regional distribution of relatively disadvantaged areas using 2001 SEIFA*. Canberra: ABS, Pub. # 1351.0.55.013.

Greenwell, H./Lloyd, R./Harding, A. (2001) 'An introduction to poverty measurement issues'. NATSEM Discussion Paper No. 55. National Centre for Social and Economic Modelling, University of Canberra.

Gregory, B./Hunter, B. (1996) 'An exploration of the relationship between changing inequality of individual, household and regional income in Australian cities', *Urban Policy and Research* 14 (3): 171-182.

Harding, A./Lloyd, R./Bill, A./King, A. (2006) 'Assessing Poverty and Inequality at a Detailed Regional Level: New Advances in Spatial Microsimulation', pp 239-261 in: McGillivray, M./Clarke, M. (eds), *Understanding Human Well-being*. Helsinki: United Nations University Press.

Harding, A./Lloyd, R./Greenwell, H. (2001) *Financial Disadvantage in Australia 1900 to 2000: The persistence of poverty in a decade of growth*. The Smith Family, Camperdown, NSW, November 2001 (available from www.natsem.canberra.edu.au)

Harding, A./Yap, M./Lloyd, R. (2004) 'Trends in Spatial Income Inequality, 1996 to 2001', AMP. NATSEM Income and Wealth Report, Issue No 8, September 2004 (available from www.amp.com.au/ampnatsemreports)

Headey, B. (2005) 'A framework for assessing poverty, disadvantage and low capabilities in Australia'. Paper presented at the HILDA Survey Research Conference, Melbourne, September 29-30 2005.

Hunter, B. (2003) 'Trends in neighbourhood inequality of Australian, Canadian and US cities since the 1970s', *The Australian Economic History Review* 32 (1): 22-44.

Lloyd, R. (2007) 'STINMOD: use of a static microsimulation model in the policy process in Australia', in: Harding, A./Gupta, A. (eds), *Modelling our Future: Population Ageing, Social Security and Taxation,* International Symposia in Economic Theory and Econometrics, Volume 15. Amsterdam: Elsevier B. V.

Lloyd, R./Harding, A./Greenwell, H. (2001) 'Worlds Apart: Postcodes with the Highest and Lowest Poverty Rates in Today's Australia', paper presented at the National Social Policy Conference, Sydney, July 2001.

McNamara, J./Tanton, R./Phillips, B. (2006) 'The regional impact of housing costs and assistance on financial disadvantage: positioning paper'. Australian Housing and Urban Research Institute, Melbourne.

McNamara, J./Tanton, R./Phillips, B. (2007) 'The regional impact of housing costs and assistance on financial disadvantage: final report'. Australian Housing and Urban Research Institute, Melbourne.

Marks, G.N. (2007) 'Income poverty, subjective poverty and financial stress'. Social Policy Research Paper No 29, FaCSIA, Canberra.

Melhuish, T./Blake, M./Day, S. (2002) 'An evaluation of synthetic household populations for Census collection districts created using Spatial Microsimulation techniques', 26th Australian and New Zealand Regional Science Association International (ANZRSAI) Annual Conference, Gold Coast, Queensland, Australia, 29 September - 2 October 2002, National Centre for Social and Economic Modelling, University of Canberra.

Melhuish, T./King, A./Taylor, E. (2004) *The regional impact of Commonwealth rent assistance.* Australian Housing and Urban Research Institute.

Noble, M./Wright, G./Dibben, M./Smith, C./Ratcliffe, G./McLennan, D. (2003) *Scottish Index of Deprivation 2003.* Edinburgh: Scottish Executive.

Office of the Deputy Prime Minister Neighbourhood Renewal Unit (2004) *The English Indices of Deprivation 2004 (Revised).* London: Office of the Deputy Prime Minister.

Rephann, T. (2001) 'Economic-demographic effects of immigration: Results from a dynamic, spatial microsimulation model', paper presented at the 2001 Annual meeting of the Mid-Atlantic Division of the Association of American Geographers, Maryland.

Salmond, C./Crampton, P. (2002) *NZDep2001 Index of Deprivation.* Wellington: Department of Public Health, Wellington School of Medicine and Health Sciences.

Saunders, P. (2005) *The Poverty Wars: Reconnecting Research with Reality.* Sydney, NSW.: UNSW Press.

Saunders, P./Bradbury, B. (2006) 'Monitoring trends in poverty and income distribution: data, methodology and measurement', *The Economic Record* 82 (258): 341-364.

Taylor, E./Harding, A./Lloyd, R./Blake, M. (2004) 'Housing unaffordability at the Statistical Local Area level: New estimates using spatial microsimulation', paper presented at the ANZRSAI, Wollongong, September 2004.

U.S. Census Bureau (2008) Small area income and poverty estimates (http://www.census.gov/hhes/www/saipe) [accessed 15 October 2008].

Vinson, T. (2001) *Unequal in Life, The Distribution of Social Disadvantage in Victoria and NSW.* Melbourne: Jesuit Social Services, Ignatius Centre for Social Policy and Research.

Vinson, T. (2004) *Community adversity and resilience: the distribution of social disadvantage in Victoria and New South Wales and the mediating role of social cohesion.* Richmond, Victoria: Jesuit Social Services.

Vinson, T. (2007) *Dropping off the edge: the distribution of disadvantage in Australia.* A report of Jesuit Social Services and Catholic Social Services Australia.

Voas, D./Williamson, P. (2000) 'An evaluation of the combinatorial optimisation approach to the creation of synthetic microdata', *International Journal of Population Geography* 6: 349-366.

Williamson, P. (2007) 'Combinatorial Optimisation instruction manual', Working Paper 2007/1, Population Microdata Unit, Department of Geography, University of Liverpool.

Chapter 4

Microsimulation as a Tool in Spatial Decision Making: Simulation of Retail Developments in a Dutch Town

Eveline S. van Leeuwen / Graham P. Clarke / Piet Rietveld

1 Introduction

A major challenge in a (spatial) planning process is "how to handle spatial complexity". Therefore, many different tools are used to understand spatial patterns. Many of them are respectively used to promote, present and discuss spatial complexities. For example, concepts, cartographic representations and scenarios are useful examples of communicative tools in the field of planning (Van Duinen, 2004; Healey, 2004; Jensen and Richardson, 2004). However, although they are based on situations of actual space, they often lack a basis of accurate geographical information (Van Leeuwen et al., 2007).

Microsimulation models (MSM) are models that can include *communicative* qualities along with more *analytical* qualities. In these models, agents represent members of a population for the purpose of studying how individual (i.e. micro) behaviours generate aggregate (i.e. macro) regularities from the bottom up (e.g. Epstein, 1999). This brings about a very natural instrument to anticipate trends in the environment through monitoring and early warning as well as to predict and value the short-term and long-term consequences of implementing certain policy measures (Saarloos, 2006).

Whereas many planning approaches focus either on predictions based on actual situations or on pathways to reach a desired situation, MSM tends to focus on a kind of space that is "in between", namely on *possible* situations. This approach fits in the planning field that needs accurate information about possible developments, while recognizing the limitations of such knowledge in practice, such as the existence of high spatial "system uncertainties" together with high "decision stakes" (Funtowicz and Ravetz, 1993). In addition, these uncertainties require the exploration of a *bandwidth* of possible spatial developments, as can be achieved with MSM. Simulations can be helpful in showing spatial dynamics, especially if linked to geographical information systems (Ballas and Clarke, 2000). These dynamic insights are useful in planning activities, such as problem-setting and discussions about consequences of future (spatial) decisions.

An important subject of discussion, in many European countries, is the future development of retail activities. These developments are illustrative examples of complex decisions affecting both physical and social aspects of space. As such, MSM can be used to break through scales, for example by showing "regional" impacts of "local" actions. This is crucial for planners and designers who are often involved in multi-faceted problems (Van Leeuwen et al., 2007).

In this chapter, we show how MSM can be used to explore the effects of a range of possible retail developments in a medium-sized town. To achieve this the creation of a micro-population is required that includes household characteristics known to determine shopping behaviour (see Figure 1). Prior to the modelling reported in this chapter, therefore, a literature review on

Figure 1:   The creation of a micro-population by simulation

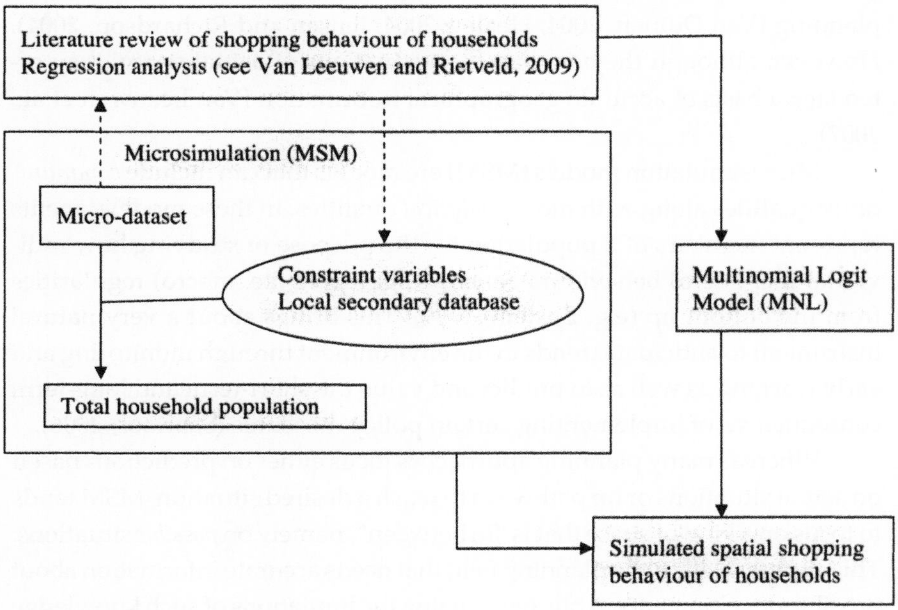

the determinants of spatial shopping behaviour and a regression analysis of questionnaire results have already been performed. From these, we know which variables provide possible relevant constraints for the creation of a spatially-detailed micro-population, and which variables are relevant to the construction of behavioural models of retail activity.

In this chapter, we describe the development of an MSM model, called SIMtown, through which a database of the total household population with relevant shopping characteristics in and around a Dutch town is simulated. Furthermore, we describe how we developed the multinomial logistic (MNL) model that relates a set of household and spatial characteristics to the revealed location choice for shopping. The MNL model derives the probability that a household makes a certain choice, in this case to shop in the town itself, in the direct hinterland (7 km zone), in the extended hinterland (16 km zone) or in the "rest of the world". Therefore we developed four utility functions. The simulated micro-population will be used to analyse the effect of a retail development at different locations on the behaviour of individual households.

To promote MSM as a useful tool in spatial planning, we will begin with a thorough description of the simulation of the micro-population (including the choice of constraints and micro-dataset). Then we will link the micro-population to the behavioural model, in this case a MNL model. In the last part of the chapter, we will simulate different, possible, retail developments in and around Nunspeet, a Dutch medium-sized town.

2   MSM framework design

2.1   The micro-dataset

For the simulation we have chosen two different towns: Oudewater and Nunspeet. The small town Oudewater (10,000 inhabitants), is situated in a relatively urbanized area with many other small towns, 7 km from Woerden (50,000 inhabitants) and 25 km from Utrecht (250,000 inhabitants). The medium-sized town Nunspeet (20,000 inhabitants), on the other hand, is situated in a more rural region, with a large nature area nearby, 7 km from Elburg (11,000 inhabitants) and 10 km from Harderwijk (40,000 inhabitants). The population of these towns will be simulated at the zip-code level (small areas with in general a population of between 100-4,000 persons). The area of

Oudewater and the direct hinterland consist of 18 different zip-code areas, the locality of Nunspeet has 9.

There are numerous ways of building a spatial microsimulation model. When no survey or micro data exist on the spatial behaviour of activities being modelled, the variables have to be built up sequentially using conditional probability rules. Techniques such as iterative proportional fitting and Monte Carlo sampling have typically been used in these cases (Birkin and Clarke, 1988: 1989). However, if a survey of individual or household behaviour is available then most researchers advocate reweighting that survey so that it fits small-area geographies known from the Census. Thus, households or individuals are effectively cloned if they match the characteristics of households in the study areas. The micro-dataset we use for the reweighting is taken from a transnational project, the European Union research project "Marketowns".[1] The dataset consists of information about characteristics of the household (such as number and age of persons, car ownership, income level, length of residence) and the employment situation in the household (such as single or double income, place of job, hours worked). This information was collected in 2002 using self-completion survey techniques sent to households living in 6 Dutch towns (of which Oudewater and Nunspeet are 2) and a 7 km zone (direct hinterland) around these towns. In total, the dataset consists of 1,500 completed surveys, around 250 per town.

When simulating a micro-population, one often has to choose between different possible micro-datasets, such as (larger) national micro-datasets with general data or smaller, local, more specific ones. To see whether it is essential to use local information instead of general information, we will compare the outcomes of a simulation using the total dataset for one simulation and only the households living in either Oudewater or Nunspeet for another. In addition, we will also compare the outcomes from simulations with different numbers of constraint variables.

It is also important to note that there are a number of reweighting methodologies. Ballas et al. (2005) provide a useful review of the alternatives. Although many techniques would produce good fits between the two

1   Information contained in this chapter is drawn from the MARKETOWNS project which is funded by the European Commission under the Fifth Framework Programme for Research and Technology Development, Contract QLRT -2000-01923. The project involves the collaboration of The University of Reading (UK), the University of Plymouth (UK), Joint Research Unit INRA-ENESAD (France), Agricultural Economics Research Institute LEI (The Netherlands), Polish Academy of Sciences (Poland) and The University of

data sources, previous studies (Williamson et al., 1998; Ballas, 2001) have shown that, for situations such as that described above, the combinatorial optimization using simulated annealing technique works most effectively in terms of finding the combination of records which best fits known small-area statistical constraints.

2.2 Constraint variables

Constraint variables are used to fit the survey micro-data to the known census data in each of the zip-code areas. The choice of which variables to use is an important one as it affects the outcomes. In some models, the order of constraints in the model, as well as the number of distinguished classes also has an effect on the results. Unfortunately, there are few publications suggesting "rules" to follow or guidelines for good practice (although see the discussion in Chin and Harding 2006 and Smith et al., 2007). Furthermore, the best variables to be used as constraints are not always available for the smallest areas.

As shown in Figure 1, a literature review and a regression analysis were conducted in an earlier stage of this research, in order to make a pre-selection of constraint variables related to shopping behaviour. This has been described in Van Leeuwen and Rietveld (2009). Unfortunately, in our case, some of the information was only available at the municipality level instead of zip-code level. In these cases we tried to match it, as well as possible, to the smaller areas, as is described in the next section. We used 7 constraint variables in total (all of which are found in both the census and survey data).

2.2.1 Type of household

The constraint variable "type of household" refers to the composition of the household. We made a distinction between single households, households with young children (under 18 years) and other households. This information is available at the zip-code level, although the Dutch Bureau of Statistics (CBS) uses "households with children" instead of "households with young children". We adapted this by using information about the age of the children (available at the municipality level).

2.2.2 Income level

The level of income of the households is measured by means of deciles. We used national decile-groups.[2] Unfortunately, this information is not available for zip-codes but only for municipalities. To be able to make a distinction between the different zip-codes in the municipality we used the level of urbanization: we combined information about total number of households per income level in each municipality with the level of urbanization of the zip-codes. Because data were available about (relative) income levels of more or less urbanized zip-codes, it was possible to redistribute the number of households in each decile at the municipality level to the lower level.

2.2.3 Car ownership

We used car ownership as a constraint variable because it appeared to be significant in the regression analysis and most of the information is available. Four classes are distinguished: households owning no car, owning 1 car, owning 2 cars and owning more than 2 cars. For each zip-code we know the total number of cars. Again, we used the level of urbanization to redistribute the number of cars per municipality over the zip-codes.

2.2.4 Job in zone A, B or C

The place of job is a relevant variable, as it plays a significant role in the logit model. Therefore it is important to include it as a constraint. It was possible to include 3 constraints; having a job in zone A (the town itself), zone B (7 km hinterland) and/or zone C (7-16 km hinterland). We started with a file from 2001, describing (for each municipality) where most of the persons have a job. For up to 30 towns, the number of persons working there and living in the municipality concerned is given. As the municipality borders do not correspond with our zones (A, B and C) we used the number of households and the number of jobs available at zip-code level to disaggregate the totals. We checked the outcomes with available information about the total number of working persons per zip-code and it appeared accurate.

---

2   All the Dutch households are sorted according to their level of income. Then 10 equal groups, according to the number of households in each group, are distinguished. The highest income level of each group is used as class boundaries (so-called deciles).

102

2.2.5 Agricultural or non-agricultural households

Finally we used the constraint of number of households living on a farm and number of households who do not. Although this variable was not included in the regression analysis, it could make sense to use this variable as location characteristics for farm households can be different from those of non-farm households, for example, in terms of accessibility or remoteness. The information on number of farms is available at zip-code level, although only for the year 2004. We used this information, bearing in mind that the actual number might have been slightly higher in 2002.

In addition to the constraint variables, two control variables are used. These variables are not part of the reweighting procedure, but are used to check if the results are reliable (hence are an important part of the calibration process). The control variables are number of persons (instead of households) and the number of single- and double-income households.

2.3 *Validation and variable selection*

To evaluate the outcomes of the different simulation models, we used the standardized absolute error measure (SAE) as described by Voas and Williamson (2001). The measure sums the discrepancies divided by the number of expected households (Equation 1):

$$TAE = \sum_k \left| T_k - E_k \right|$$

$$SAE = TAE / N \qquad (1)$$

in which T_k is the observed count of cell k (e.g. zip-code 3448), E_k the expected count for cell k and N the total expected count for the whole table (e.g. Oudewater as a whole). Of course, it is also necessary to have an error-threshold. Clarke and Madden (2001) suggest an error threshold of at least 80% of the areas with less than 20% error (SAE<0.20) for spatial models generally. Smith et al. (2007) work with a model that simulates persons with diabetes, which is a relatively rare disease, and therefore works towards an error threshold of less than 10% error (SAE<0.10) in 90% of the output areas. However, as noted above, there are no hard and fast rules in the literature regarding what is an acceptable level of accuracy which must in part depend upon the quality and comparability of the datasets being matched.

To analyse the effect of the constraint variables on the outcomes, we simulated 7 different models (see Table 1) with 3 different datasets (respectively all, Nunspeet and Oudewater households). The models differ in the selection and number of constraint variables; and in the dataset they are being used to reweight (the total micro-dataset or only the part related to the specific town). It is interesting to look at the differences between these models, to learn whether it is better to have more constraint variables, and how use of a larger or smaller and more site-specific micro-dataset affects the outcomes.

The different outcomes are evaluated with the help of standardized absolute errors (SAE) for income, jobs, kind of household and the total model: The lower the SAE, the better. In total, we ran 28 models as shown in Table 2.

Table 1: Constraint variables included in the six different models

Model	Constraints
3C	JobA, JobB, Household
3CC	Income, JobA, JobB
4C	Household, JobA, JobB, Income
5Ccars	Household, Income, JobA, JobB, Cars
5Cfarm	Household, Income, JobA, JobB, Farm
6C	Household, Income, JobA, JobB, JobC, Cars
7C	Household, Income, JobA, JobB, JobC, Cars, Farm

When we, first of all, compare the differences between the four datasets, it appears that Nunspeet has in general lower SAEs compared to Oudewater. This can be explained by the larger number of more heterogeneous zip-codes in the Oudewater region. Furthermore, we can see that in almost all cases the use of the total dataset results in a better fit compared to the town-specific datasets. A reason for this can be the "richness" of the database: the town-specific micro-datasets consist or around 250 households, the total database of 1,450 households from 6 different towns.

Considering the choice of number and specific constraints, Table 2 shows that, in general, the best results are achieved by the model with a larger number of constraint variables. The average SAE values are lowest for the 6C model, highest for the 3C and 3CC model. However, when we look at the scores for the separate constraints, it appears that the 3C model works very well for the "type of household" variable and the 3CC model very well

Table 2: **Standardized Absolute Error (SAE) of the constraint variables income, jobs and household for simulation models with different constraints and different datasets**

Database Model	Oudewater		Nunspeet	
	Total	Selection	Total	Selection
	SAE		SAE	
Income				
3C	0.50	0.53	0.38	0.42
3CC	0.06	0.14	0.06	0.13
4C	0.10	0.16	0.07	0.13
5Ccars	0.19	0.23	0.16	0.19
5Cfarm	0.10	0.26	0.07	0.14
6C	0.18	0.25	0.16	0.18
7C	0.19	0.34	0.15	0.16
Jobs (A,B,C)				
3C	0.15	0.16	0.05	0.11
3CC	0.15	0.17	0.07	0.11
4C	0.15	0.16	0.06	0.11
5Ccars	0.16	0.16	0.06	0.14
5Cfarm	0.20	0.17	0.11	0.14
6C	0.05	0.04	0.04	0.08
7C	0.12	0.08	0.10	0.12
Household				
3C	0.11	0.14	0.06	0.10
3CC	0.31	0.33	0.26	0.24
4C	0.18	0.24	0.13	0.14
5Ccars	0.14	0.17	0.11	0.12
5Cfarm	0.15	0.20	0.09	0.13
6C	0.18	0.22	0.10	0.13
7C	0.15	0.20	0.08	0.11
Average*				
3C	0.20	0.22	0.15	0.15
3CC	0.18	0.21	0.19	0.14
4C	0.16	0.19	0.09	0.12
5Ccars	0.15	0.16	0.09	0.14
5Cfarm	0.17	0.20	0.10	0.13
6C	0.10	0.12	0.08	0.11
7C	0.13	0.14	0.11	0.12

Note: *Average SAE values of the variables: income, job A, job B, job C, household, and car ownership.

for the income variable. This indicates that, in general, more constraints lead to a better model. However, when only a small number of variables are very important, it is better to use a limited number of constraints.

Finally, it appears that not all variables are good constraint variables. In our example, it seems that the variable farm-household disturbs the results of the job variables; both the 5C farm and the 7C model show high errors for these variables and therefore the 6C model has a better fit than the 7C model. However, this "disturbance" occurs most strongly in the Oudewater model. In this town, the agricultural sector is more important compared to Nunspeet. Thus, it seems that different constraint variables could be relevant in different towns (see Smith et al. 2008 for more details on building microsimulation models within cities by taking variations in geodemographics into account).

To summarize, we can conclude from this simulation exercise that in general a larger number of (relevant) constraint variables, as well as a larger dataset result in the best fit of the simulation model. However when only a small number of variables are important, it is better to use a limited number of constraints.

2.4   SIMtown, the final framework

The model chosen for the final simulation is the 6C model in which constraints related to household type, income, job in zone A, job in zone B, job in zone C and car ownership are included. We used these six constraint variables to reweight the total dataset (consisting of 1,500 Dutch households).

Unfortunately, the calculated weights are not 100% correct. This is due to the fact that we only want to work with "complete" households (not with 0.7 household), so that the calculated weights (in decimals) need to be rounded to integers, which can cause small number problems. However, after some final improvements, the SAE values indicate that we simulated two usable micro-population datasets (see Table 3).

For further validation, we can also look at the results for the control variables, the values of which were not directly constrained as part of the reweighting process. Table 4 shows the SAE values for the two control variables, number of persons and number of single- and double-income households. It still appears that the simulation is (relatively) robust. For Nunspeet, the number of persons is very well simulated. Considering that the number of single and double income households is a more difficult variable to simulate (related to jobs and only households with two or more adults are considered), these results are satisfying as well.

Table 3: SAE values for the constraint variables

	SAE average		% of areas with SAE < 0.10	
	Oudewater	Nunspeet	Oudewater	Nunspeet
Income (1-10)	0.07	0.08	95	90
Cars (= 0)	0.11	0.04	60	100
Job A	0.01	0.01	100	100
Job B	0.04	0.02	100	100
Job C	0.02	0.01	100	100
Household (1-3)	0.11	0.04	65	90
Total	0.06	0.03	100	100

Table 4: SAE values for the control variables "number of persons" and "number of single- and double-income households"

		SAE average	% zip-codes SAE < 0.10	% zip-codes SAE < 0.20
Oudewater	persons	0.11	80	90
	single/double income	0.16	40	100
Nunspeet	persons	0.04	90	100
	single/double income	0.19	0	80

In our opinion, and based on the constraint and control variables of the simulation of households, the new micro-population of both Oudewater and Nunspeet is a good representation of the actual population. For the second part of this chapter we choose to focus on Nunspeet. An important reason for this is the regional spatial structure. In Oudewater, the spatial structure of cities, towns, roads and railways is relatively complicated. In addition, the larger city of Woerden is partly situated in zone B and partly in zone C. This makes it complicated to develop an accurate behavioural model. In Nunspeet, the spatial situation is easier to understand and to analyse.

3   SIMtown and the shopping destination

In Section 2, we simulated a micro-population for the area of Nunspeet and its hinterland in two ways: using all the households and only the Nunspeet households respectively. During the validation of the results of the simulations, it appeared that the micro-population simulated with all households resulted in the most accurate outcomes.

In similar fashion it is possible to develop two MNL models to predict the spatial shopping behaviour of households: a general model based on the same 1,500 households and a local model, based on the questionnaire responses from a selected town (in the case of Nunspeet around 200 households). In this second part, we will make the choice for a local or a general MNL model.

3.1 The Multinomial Logit Model (MNL)

To study existing linkages between Nunspeet and its hinterland, four zones are distinguished. The town of Nunspeet is classified as zone A, then circles are drawn of 7 km and 16 km around Nunspeet, respectively labelled as zones B and C. The area outside the 16 km circle is labelled as zone D, rest of the world.[3]

The MNL model aims at deriving the probability that a household (i) makes a certain choice, in this case to shop in zone A (town), B (hinterland), C (16 km zone) or in D (the rest of the world). Therefore we developed four utility functions (Equations 2-5).

$$U_i(A) = a\,\text{lndist}_{iA} + \beta\,\text{lnfloor}_{iA} + \gamma\,\text{job}_{iA} + \delta(\text{lndist}_{iA} \times \text{car}_i) + \theta(\text{age}_i \times \text{lndist}_{iA}) + \iota\,\text{lnyear}_i + \varepsilon_{iA} \tag{2}$$

$$U_i(B) = a\,\text{lndist}_{iB} + \beta\,\text{lnfloor}_{iB} + \gamma\,\text{job}_{iB} + \delta(\text{lndis}_{iB} \times \text{car}_i) + \theta(\text{age}_i \times \text{lndist}_{iB}) + \iota\,\text{lnyear}_i + \varepsilon_{iB} \tag{3}$$

$$U_i(C) = a\,\text{lndist}_{iC} + \beta\,\text{lnfloor}_{iC} + \gamma\,\text{job}_{iC} + \delta(\text{lndist}_{iC} \times \text{car}_i) + \theta(\text{age}_i \times \text{lndist}_{iC}) + \iota\,(0) + \varepsilon_{iC} \tag{4}$$

$$U_i(D) = \gamma\,\text{job}_{iD} + \zeta\,\text{income}_i + \eta\,\text{kids}_i + \kappa\,\text{Oudewater}_i + \lambda\,\text{Gemert}_i + \nu\,\text{Nunspeet}_i + \xi\,\text{Schagen}_i + o\,\text{Bolsward}_i + \varepsilon_{iD} \tag{5}$$

Important variables in the utility functions dealing with zones A, B and C are: distance to the shop (*Indist*)[4]; floor space in the zone (*Infloor*)[5]; job in the zone (*job*); the interaction of having a car (*car*) with distance; the interaction of age of household head (*age*) with distance; and the length of residence

---

3   These zones are chosen in the Marketowns project. 7 km is thought to be the maximum distance at which households do their daily or weekly shopping. In the Netherlands, 7 km is a distance which usually takes around 30 minutes by bike.

4   Distance to the nearest place with a substantial shop in the concerning zone.

5   Floor space of shops in the nearest place (zip-code) with a substantial shop in the concerning zone.

within zones A and B (*Inyear*). In the utility function of the rest of the world (zone D), having a job there is included, as well as the level of income of the households, having children or not and a dummy variable for each town. Because the utility of a household to shop in the distinguished zones depends on the kind of shopping, we run this model three times; for groceries, fun-shopping[6] and goal-shopping[7]. Table 5 shows the model specifications and the parameter values.

Although the general and specific MNL models are almost the same, the explained variance differs; the R^2adj. (measure of explained variance) of the local logit model of Nunspeet is significantly higher than the R^2adj. of the general logit model for all three product groups. This suggests better outcomes using the local model. In the next step, we use the simulated micro-population as input for the two logit models.

3.2 Micro-population as (new) input for the MNL models

Table 5 compares the results of the Marketowns questionnaire against the local- and the general MNL model predictions (for three product groups and four zones) and at the right-hand side the differences between the outcomes of the models and the questionnaires.

The logit model of the spatial behaviour of households for buying groceries explains most of the variance (R^2adj. of 0.60 for the general model, 0.73 for the Nunspeet model) when compared to fun- or goal-shopping. This also results in good outcomes: the average share of grocery shopping in zone A predicted by the Nunspeet model is almost as high as the average value from the questionnaires, 57% compared to 59%. For zone B, the share of purchases is underestimated (with around 3%) and for zone C overestimated, which results in an accurate prediction of the share in zone D.

Also for fun-shopping, the models predict the share of purchases in zone A relatively accurately, but the share in zone B is underestimated. Furthermore, fun-shopping in zone D is overestimated. When looking at goal-shopping, it appears zone A is slightly overestimated in the Nunspeet model. The share in zone B is again underestimated in both models.

Overall, both models tend to estimate the share of purchases in zone A very well. However, they underestimate the share of purchases in zone B. Furthermore, the local, Nunspeet model results in the most similar outcomes compared with the characteristics of the questionnaire. Therefore we will use this model for the retail development simulations.

---

6   Shopping for cloths, shoes, and different kind of luxuries.
7   Shopping for furniture, gardening products, do-it-yourself products.

Table 5: Multinomial Logit Model specifications and parameter values for three product groups and two models; the first one using the characteristics of all households (n=1,500) and the second one using only the characteristics of households living in Nunspeet (n=200)

Determinants of shopping destination	Groceries		Fun		Goal	
	All HH[1]	Nun[2] HH	All HH	Nun HH	All HH	Nun HH
InDIST	-1.34***	-1.35**	-0.65***	-0.48	-1.15***	-1.79**
InFLOOR	0.59***	0.98***	0.37***	0.40	0.28***	0.44**
JOB	0.50***	0.39	0.18**	0.04	0.40***	0.47*
CAR*Indist	0.08	-0.31	0.08	-0.10	0.47**	0.55
AGE*Indist	0.002	0.002	-0.001	-0.001	-0.001	0.006
InYEAR	0.26***	0.31*	0.02	0.16	0.07*	0.10
INCOME	0.08	0.01	0.14***	0.15**	0.10**	0.07
KIDS	-0.13	-0.27	-0.44***	-0.41	0.33*	0.46
Oudewater	0.24		1.73***		-0.43	
Gemert	0.51		1.87***		-0.34	
Nunspeet	0.09	3.67	2.03***	2.45	-0.38	1.06
Schagen	-0.31		0.82		-0.51	
Bolsward	-0.21		1.83***		-0.12	
R²adj	0.60	0.73	0.13	0.22	0.30	0.47

Notes: [1] HH = households, [2] Nun = Nunspeet
*** Significant at the 0.01% level; ** significant at the 0.05% level; * significant at the 0.1% level

Table 6: Spatial shopping behaviour of households (share of purchases in four zones) according to the questionnaires, the Nunspeet logit model and the general logit model

Kind of Shopping	Zone	Average (%)			Difference between results questionnaires and logit models (%)	
		Question-naires	Nunspeet logit model	General logit model	Nunspeet logit model	General logit model
Groceries	A	59	57	54	-1.5	-4.8
	B	36	33	33	-2.7	-2.4
	C	5	8	11	3.7	6.2
	D	0	1	1	0.5	0.4
Fun	A	32	33	31	1.1	-0.6
	B	29	21	20	-7.9	-8.9
	C	9	11	12	1.9	2.7
	D	31	35	37	4.9	6.7
Goal	A	46	49	46	3.2	0.8
	B	37	33	31	-4.1	-5.2
	C	12	12	15	-0.3	2.8
	D	6	7	7	1.2	1.6

4   Simulated impacts of new retail developments

Until recently, the development of out-of-town retail centres was not permitted in the Netherlands. Nowadays, the national government has handed planning responsibility over to local governments, so they can decide whether out-of-town retail centres are permitted in their area. Obviously, this decision is not easily made. For local policy-makers it is difficult to assess all possible spatial and socio-economic developments and to finally make a decision. This is where microsimulation can prove useful (cf. Van Leeuwen et al., 2007). MSM can offer useful insights into the current situation and new developments at the small geographical level as it can effectively turn the sample data from the questionnaire into a full dataset for every household in the Nunspeet region. This means that under-over-biases of household types in the questionnaire are removed (see also Tomoki et al., 2007). Furthermore, the database contains many combinations of household features, thus improving the quality of model predictions.

4.1   Current situation

A first useful outcome of SIMtown is a picture of the current situation. The complex reweighting procedure leads to robust estimation of current flows of purchases relative to questionnaire-based estimates, which suffer from bias due to the under- and over-representation of certain household types. Table 7 shows, for each town located in the Nunspeet region (see Figure 2), the total share of products bought in the four distinguished zones.

Not surprisingly, households living in Nunspeet buy most products (71%) in the centre of Nunspeet. However, households from Vierhouten and Hulshorst, two small settlements, also tend to shop in zone A (Nunspeet).

Table 7:   Share of total purchases bought in the four zones per settlement (%)

Town	Zone			
	A	B	C	D
Nunspeet	71	6	5	18
Hierden	19	15	38	29
Vierhouten	44	10	12	35
Hulshorst	55	6	13	26
Elburg	11	59	9	20
't Harde	17	41	14	28
Doornspijk	30	36	9	25

Figure 2:   Schematic map of Nunspeet and its hinterland

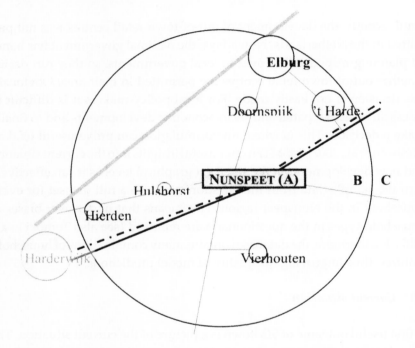

4.1.1 Spatial distribution of households with a low income

The outcomes of SIMtown also include information about other, related subjects. It enables us, for example, to get insights into specific household groups which may have difficulties in accessing certain stores or centres, information which is often difficult to get at a high level of spatial resolution. Figure 3 (a,b) shows the spatial distribution of older households (with a head 65 years and older) and young households (with a head 35 years and younger) with a relatively low income (income deciles 1-3). The dot-patterns show the share of these poorer households without a car.

Figure 3(a) shows that, in Nunspeet and Vierhouten especially, a relatively large share of the population consists of elderly persons with a low income: between 10 and 15%. In the western part of Nunspeet, as much as 60 to 75% of these households do not own a car. For these households, local facilities are extremely important. By contrast, in Hierden, only 6% of the households consist of elderly with low income and around half of them own a car.

The share of the total population of young households with low income is much lower, between 2 and 5%. The majority of households with a head younger than 35 have a medium-high income. In addition, most of the young households with low income own a car.

Figure 3 (a,b): Share in total population of (a) older households (per zip-code) with low income and that portion of them without a car; (b) same for younger households

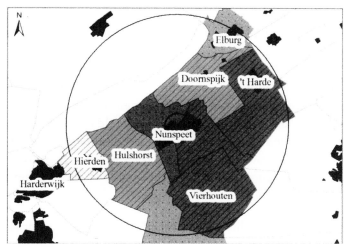

Share of older households (head >= 65) with low income:
☐ 1-5 % ☐ 5-10% ■ 10-15% Out of area
No car: ⊡ 45-60% ▨ 60-75%

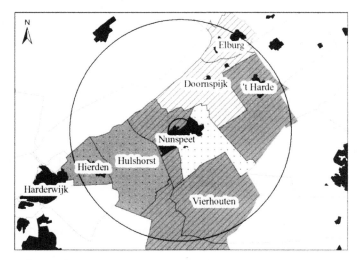

Share of young households (head <= 35) with low income:
☐ 2-3% ■ 4-5% Out of area
No car: ⊡ 20-25% ▨ 25-30%

4.4.2 Spatial distribution of recently arrived households

Another interesting topic, which is often difficult to extract from spatial databases, is the distribution and characteristics of new households in an area. The Nunspeet micro-population includes information about how long a household resides in the area, enabling us to select households living 5 years or shorter in Nunspeet and its hinterland. Generally, around 10% of the total population recently (less than 5 years ago) moved to the Nunspeet area (see Table 8).

Figure 4 shows the spatial distribution of older and younger households who have recently arrived in Nunspeet. Most of them, between 30-50% are young households, whilst only a small number, between 1 and 15%, are elderly. Interestingly, most older households choose Nunspeet, Doornspijk and 't Harde for their new residence, while younger households are particularly interested in Hierden and Hulshorst. In addition, SIMtown also offers information about several characteristics of the newcomers, such as their income level.

114

Table 8:   Share of households living 5 years or shorter in the Nunspeet region

Town	Zip-code	Living 5 years or shorter in Nunspeet						
			of which old (head>=65)			of which young (head<=35)		
		Total (%)	total	High* income (%)	Low** income (%)	total	High* income (%)	Low** income (%)
Hierden	3849	11.3	0.5	0	100	4.7	45	11
Nunspeet	8071	8.0	0.9	11	89	2.9	45	7
Nunspeet	8072	7.4	0.8	13	75	2.5	48	12
Vierhouten	8076	9,0	0.6	0	100	3.2	31	19
Hulshorst	8077	7.3	0.0	-	-	2.9	41	7
Elburg	8081	8.6	0.7	14	71	3.1	48	13
't Harde	8084	8.3	1.0	20	70	2.9	55	10
Doornspijk	8085	8.5	0.9	22	67	2.8	39	11

Notes: * 3 highest income deciles.

    ** 3 lowest income deciles.

Table 8 shows the share of the older and younger households in the recently moved households with relatively high and low incomes. As expected, most older households which recently moved to the Nunspeet region, have low incomes. However, there is a considerable degree of differentiation: in 't Harde and Doornspijk around one fifth of the new elderly have a high income. Again as expected, many recently moved young households often receive a high income. Many of them have dual incomes with at least one of the jobs in the region.

Figure 4 (a,b):   Share in total recently moved (<5 years) households of (a) older households; (b) same for younger households

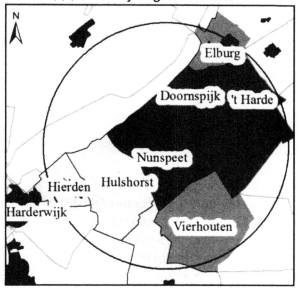

Share of older households (head >= 65) just moved to the area:

☐ 1-5%   ☐ 5-10%   ■ 10-15%   ☐ Out of area

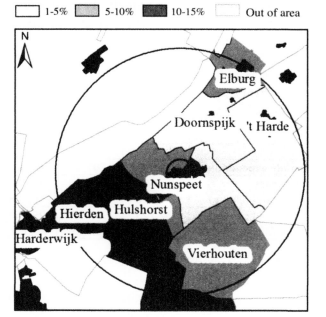

Share of young households (head <=35) just moved to the area:

☐ 30-35%   ☐ 35-40%   ■ 40-45%   ☐ Out of area

4.2 Simulations of future developments

Apart from giving insight into the current situation, MSM is especially useful for exploring the likely effects of future developments, using the MNL-derived utility functions to model household responses to proposed changes in retail environment. These changes can be summarized into monthly expenditures per household and per zone. They can also be used to obtain insight into the effect of developments on specific sub-sets of households. In what follows we use SIMtown to explore the consequences of two types of retail development – the building of a new supermarket and the building of a new retail centre.

4.2.1 Building a new supermarket

In Nunspeet, the municipality is considering allowing a large supermarket chain to build a new store in the centre of the town. The total new shopping area would be 1,240 m², a considerable amount compared to the existing 7,000 m². With the help of the MNL model and the micro-population dataset we can simulate the effect of this new supermarket. In addition, we can also simulate three alternatives: 1) what if the supermarket would be built elsewhere in a large town in the hinterland (Elburg); 2) in a small town in the hinterland ('t Harde); or 3) in a small city in zone C (Harderwijk at 10 km distance). We measure the effect in "changing expenditures per zone per month". Table 9 shows the results.

Table 9: The effects of a new supermarket on the total grocery expenditures in the four zones (in monthly expenditures per zone)

	Monthly expenditures per zone (€)				Regional effect (€)
Zone	A	B	C	D	A+B
Initial monthly expenditures*	3,131,331	1,881,465	467,806	57,515	
Store in Nunspeet	94,941	-66,276	-25,038	-3,627	28,665
Store in hinterland (Elburg)	-70,216	93,144	-19,458	-3,470	22,928
Store in hinterland ('t Harde)	-57,723	92,997	-29,767	-5,507	35,274
Store in zone C (Harderwijk)	-21,152	-6,585	28,559	-822	-27,737

Note: * of all households in town and hinterland.

It appears that, when the new supermarket is built in Nunspeet, the monthly revenues on groceries will increase there by €95,000 (3%) at the cost of revenues in the other zones. When building the store in a slightly smaller town in the hinterland (Elburg), the revenues there will increase by €93,000 (5%), leading to a significant loss in Nunspeet. Obviously, for Nunspeet the best option is to build the store in Nunspeet itself. However, for the region Nunspeet-Elburg, it would be best to build the supermarket in 't Harde.

4.2.2 Building a new Retail Centre

The Netherlands Institute of Spatial Planning (RPB) described in its study "Winkelen in Megaland" [shopping in Megaland] (Evers et al., 2005) six scenarios of future retail developments. First of all, following expert opinions, total floor space will increase by 12% by 2010.[8] The distribution of floor space over different kinds of shops (grocery, fun or goal) depends on the kind of development. For now, we will focus on two scenarios: first the development of a retail centre *in* the centre of Nunspeet, Elburg (medium town in hinterland) or 't Harde (small town in hinterland). Such a centre will consist of 80% fun- and 20% goal-shopping. The second scenario is the development of a retail centre just *outside* Nunspeet. Such a centre would consist of 10% grocery, 60% fun- and 30% goal-shopping.

Contrary to the development of a new supermarket in Nunspeet (zone A), the development of a whole retail centre results in a larger regional effect compared to building it in the centre of Elburg (see Table 10). The extra local monthly revenues are 15% higher in Nunspeet compared to Elburg, mostly as a result of lower revenues in zones C and D. This can be explained by the fact that Nunspeet already has a larger supply of fun-shopping and thus a stronger regional function. Adding more shops makes such a centre more important for this kind of shopping.

Interestingly, building a retail centre in 't Harde instead of Elburg results in a higher regional effect because of less revenues in zones C and D. 't Harde has a population of around 6,000 households not including tourists and soldiers encamped there. When the retail centre is built in 't Harde, these people, as well as people from surrounding areas, will be less attracted to shop in zones C or D. For the Nunspeet-Elburg region, it would be best to have a new retail centre both in Nunspeet and in Elburg.

---

8   This leads to an increasing floor space of 4,600 m² in zone A and 3,300 m² in zone B.

Table 10: Changing flow of total expenditures (grocery, fun- and goal-shopping) for scenario 1 for different possible locations

Scenario 1	Monthly expenditures per zone (€)				Regional effect (€)
Zone	A	B	C	D	A+B
Initial monthly expenditures*	6,369,958	4,048,063	1,335,940	1,917,850	10,418,021
Centre in Nunspeet	100,224	-29,338	-18,433	-52,453	70,885
Centre in Elburg	-31,752	83,298	-13,382	-38,164	51,546
Centre in 't Harde	-19,849	76,800	-15,632	-41,319	56,951
Centre in Nunspeet and Elburg	67,723	52,499	-31,253	-88,969	120,222

Note: * of all households in town and hinterland.

Scenario 2, building a retail centre just *outside* a town (see Table 11), can only be simulated for Nunspeet because of the structure of the data. In this scenario, a retail centre will be developed just *outside* Nunspeet and also the kind of shops differs slightly from scenario 1.

Table 11 shows the effects, which appear to be rather large; more than 10% growth of total revenues in zone B. This is mainly a result of households living in Nunspeet spending less money on (fun) shopping in town or zone D and much more in the new centre located in zone B. Now that the distance to a shopping centre with a substantial floor space in zone B has decreased significantly (from Elburg to nearby Nunspeet) many Nunspeet households are more likely to go shopping there. Also the households living just around Nunspeet (in the hinterland) are likely to choose this new retail centre. However, in addition to buying less in Nunspeet, they also tend to buy less in zones C and D when this new retail centre is developed. The predicted total regional effect is a growth of 2% of total revenues.

Table 11: Changing flow of total expenditures (grocery, fun- and goal-shopping) for scenario 2

Scenario 2	Monthly expenditures per zone (€)				Regional effect (€)
Zone	A	B	C	D	A+B
Initial monthly expenditures*	7,790,159	4,707,255	1,814,834	4,117,902	
Centre just outside Nunspeet	-317,059	535,515	-31,643	-186,812	218,456

Note: * of all households in town and hinterland.

4.2.3 Micro-results

SIMtown allows us to take a closer look at the results and to see which kind of households are most likely to change their shopping behaviour; to buy less in zone A and more in the new retail centre just outside Nunspeet.

In the model, the Nunspeet households are divided between two zip-codes: 8072 located most closely to the new out-of-town retail centre, and 8071, a little bit further away. In the first zip-code, older households with low income and a car in particular tend to go to the new retail centre. They spend 10% less in zone A and 15% more of their total expenditures in the new centre. From the other part of Nunspeet (zip-code 8071), middle-aged households with medium income, households with children and often a job in zone B more often go to the new shopping mall. However, they only buy 6% less in zone A and 7% more in the new centre.

Of course, households living in the smaller towns in the hinterland of Nunspeet would also buy products in the shopping centre: older households with low income and no car living in Vierhouten or Doornspijk, as well as younger households with low-medium income, households with no children and households with a job nearby are predicted to spend 10% more of their total expenditures in the new place, and 5% less in zone A. As expected, especially (older) households with low incomes and no car, as well as (young) rich households with a car and job outside the region, are least likely to change their shopping behaviour by spending (more) money in the new retail centre at the cost of Nunspeet.

From this analysis, it would appear that building extra shops in existing shopping areas, such as the centre of Nunspeet or Elburg, would result in some (minor) changes in the shopping behaviour of households. However, developing an entire new retail centre in a smaller shopping area, such as 't Harde (Scenario 1) or outside a medium-sized town such as Nunspeet (Scenario 2), would result in a much more significant change. The reason for this is that these latter developments create (totally) new opportunities for the households, changing the distance, and therefore the travel costs (in time or money), to convenient shopping areas.

5   Conclusions

The aim of this chapter was to show the usefulness of spatial MSM in spatial decision-making. Therefore, as described in the first part of the chapter, we developed a MSM named SIMtown. During the development process, a number of choices had to be made, for example concerning the micro-dataset and the constraint variables. Unfortunately, literature dealing with these kinds of choices, which are very important for the development of a MSM model, is rare. From our experiments it appears that the best micro-dataset was generated by reweighting the large general dataset, instead of the small, local one. Although the households in the general dataset are not specifically related to the town population which was to be simulated, it resulted in the lowest statistical errors. Furthermore, we decided to use a (relatively) large number of constraint variables, namely six. However, not all available constraint variables were included: the variable "being an agricultural household or not" did not add anything to the model. The last choice to be made was which MNL-based behavioural model to use: the one derived using local (town-specific) or general (all) questionnaire responses. We found that the locally derived model explained most of the variance and gave the best results. Thus, from our analysis we can conclude that the best results come from a MSM framework using a large micro-dataset, a (relatively) large number of relevant constraint variables and a local behavioural model.

In the second part of the chapter the Dutch town Nunspeet was used as case-study area. From the simulations of retail developments in Nunspeet using SIMtown, it has been shown that MSM can be a useful tool in spatial planning. First of all, it provides a picture of the current situation, which is not available from existing statistics. It was shown that the facilities in Nunspeet are mostly used by households living in Nunspeet itself, but also by households living in villages nearby, such as Vierhouten and Hulshorst. Also more complex and detailed spatial information, such as the share of older households with a low income and no car, becomes available through the MSM. Secondly, SIMtown was used to simulate potential future retail developments. Building a new store, close to existing shops, was shown not to result in major changes. The model also allows different kinds of shopping to be taken into account: when focusing on fun shopping, it appears that Nunspeet, which already has a more important regional function, profits more from new developments than for example the smaller town Elburg.

However, the most important changes occur when a new retail centre is developed at a new location, such as in a small shopping area in a smaller town as 't Harde or outside a medium-sized town as Nunspeet. The reason for this is that these developments create (totally) new opportunities for households, changing the distance and therefore the travel costs (in time or money) to convenient shopping areas. Nevertheless, the development of a new retail centre just outside Nunspeet only leads to 4% less purchases in the centre itself. The micro-results show that in particular older households with low income and a car tend to go to the new retail centre. They spend 10% less in the centre of Nunspeet and 15% more of their total expenditures in the new centre.

For local decision-makers, these insights (as well as the range of possible outcomes) are very useful, enabling them to put the effects of proposed retail developments into perspective, both for themselves and for the possibly affected stakeholders.

References

Ballas, D. (2001) 'A spatial microsimulation approach to local labour market policy analysis', unpublished PhD thesis, School of Geography, University of Leeds.

Ballas, D./Clarke, G.P. (2000) 'GIS and microsimulation for local labour market analysis'. *Computers, Environment and Urban Systems*, 24: 305-330.

Ballas, D./Rossiter, D./Thomas, B./Clarke, G.P./Dorling, D. (2005) 'Geography matters: simulating the local impacts of national social policies', Joseph Rowntree Foundation, York.

Birkin, M./Clarke, M. (1988) 'SYNTHESIS – A Synthetic spatial information system for urban and regional analysis: methods and examples', *Environment and Planning* A, 20: 1645-1671.

Birkin, M./Clarke, M. (1989) 'The generation of individual and household incomes at the small area level', *Regional Studies*, 23: 535-548

Chin, S-F./Harding, A. (2006) 'Regional Dimensions: Creating synthetic small-area microdata and spatial microsimulation models', Technical Paper 33, NATSEM, Canberra.

Clarke, G.P./Madden, M. (eds.) (2001) *Regional Science in Business*. Berlin: Springer.

Epstein, J.M. (1999) 'Agent-based computational models and generative social science', *Complexity*, 4 (5): 41-60.

Evers, D./van Hoorn, A./van Oort, F. (2005) *Winkelen in Megaland [Shopping in Megaland]*.Den Haag: Ruimtelijk Planbureau.

Funtowicz, S.O./Ravetz, J.R. (1993) 'Science For The Post-Normal Age', *Futures*, 25: 739-755.

Healey, P. (2004) 'The treatment of space and place in the new strategic spatial planning in Europe', *International Journal of Urban and Regional Research*, 28: 45-67.

Jensen, O.B./Richardson, T. (2004) *Making European space: mobility, power and territorial identity*. London: Routledge.

Nakaya, T./Fotheringham, A.S./Hanaoka, K./Clarke, G.P./Ballas, D./Yano, K. (2007) 'Combining microsimulation and spatial interaction models for retail location analysis', *Journal of Geographical Systems*, 9: 345-369.

Saarloos, D.J.M. (2006) 'A Framework for a Multi-Agent Planning Support System', PhD thesis. Eindhoven: Eindhoven University Press Facilities.

Smith, D.M./Harland, K./Clarke, G.P. (2007) 'SimHelath:estimating small area populations using deterministic spatial microsimulation in Leeds and Bradford', Working Paper 07/06, Univeristy of Leeds, Leeds.

Smith, D./Clarke, G.P./Harland, K. (2008) 'Improving the synthetic data generation process in spatial microsimulation models', *Environment and Planning A*.

Van Duinen, L.B.J. (2004) 'Planning Imagery - The emergence and development of new planning concepts in Dutch national spatial policy, PhD thesis. University of Amsterdam

Van Leeuwen, E.S./Hagens, J.E./Nijkamp, P. (2007) 'Multi-Agents Systems: A Tool in Spatial Planning. An example of micro-simulation use in retail development', *disP*, 170 (3): 19-32.

Van Leeuwen, E.S./Rietveld, P. (2009) 'Spatial Consumer Behaviour in Small and Medium-sized Towns'. Amsterdam: Department of Spatial Economics, VU University.

Voas, D./Williamson, P. (2001) 'Evaluating Goodness-of-Fit Measures for Synthetic Microdata', *Geographical & Environmental Modeling*, 5 (2): 177-200

Williamson, P./Birkin, M./Rees, P.H. (1998) 'The estimation of population microdata using data from small area statistics and samples of anonymised records', *Environment and Planning A*, 30: 785-816.

Chapter 5

Time and Money in Space: Estimating Household Expenditure and Time Use at the Small Area Level in Great Britain

Ben Anderson / Paola de Agostini / Selma Laidoudi / Antonia Weston / Ping Zong

There is an increasing need to develop small-area estimates of a range of socio-economic indicators both for public policy and commercial applications. In the case of the former indicators of exclusion and deprivation as well as ill-health and other social burdens are obvious examples whilst in the case of the latter it is more usually wealth, consumption and lifestyle that is of interest.

Estimating such variables at small-area levels has pre-occupied social and economic geographers as well as a number of commercial data providers for some time. In this chapter we present a spatial microsimulation approach to the estimation of two distinct forms of "consumption" –

The research reported in this chapter was supported by the ESRC (RES-341-25-0004), BT and the Department of Communities and Local Government.

The ONS Time Use survey was collected by Ipsos-RSL and sponsored by the Office for National Statistics, the Department for Culture, Media and Sport; Department for Education and Skills; Department of Health; Department for Transport, Local Government and the Regions and the Economic and Social Research Council. It is distributed by the UK Data Archive, University of Essex, Colchester. The data is copyright and is reproduced with the permission of the Controller of HMSO and the Queen's Printer for Scotland.

The Expenditure and Food Survey was collected by the Office for National Statistics and sponsored by the Office for National Statistics and the Department for Environment, Food and Rural Affairs. It is distributed by the UK Data Archive, University of Essex, Colchester. The data is copyright and is reproduced with the permission of the Controller of HMSO and the Queen's Printer for Scotland.

Census data were originally created and funded by the Office for National Statistics and are distributed by the Census Dissemination Unit, MIMAS (University of Manchester). Output is Crown copyright and is reproduced with the permission of the Controller of HMSO and the Queen's Printer for Scotland.

This chapter uses data provided through EDINA UKBORDERS with the support of the ESRC and JISC and uses boundary material which is copyright of the Crown.

household expenditure on telecommunications (ICT) related services and household time-use. Both are interesting examples of data which are (mostly) not available at the small-area level from any public UK data source and yet are important to the analysis of current social behaviour, public policy or commercial strategies.

Whilst the spatial estimation of income has long been a key research activity (Williamson, 2005) there appear to have been relatively few attempts to estimate small-area distributions of household consumption and expenditure (Hanaoka and Clarke, 2006) and similarly few attempts to project these distributions forwards in time (Ballas et al., 2005). Understanding the spatial nature of time-use adds a key dimension to this analysis both in terms of the spatial distribution of the effects of public policy interventions and the spatial distribution of activities which indicate certain kinds of markets or lifestyles. Whilst such analysis is relatively common in transport research (Buliung and Kanaroglou, 2007) it is almost unknown in other areas of sociological interest such as media-use and leisure.

This chapter reports preliminary results from a research programme intended to do both – to produce estimates of expenditure and time-use at small-area levels in the UK, to project them forwards in time and to conduct scenario analyses through static spatial microsimulation. The programme draws on econometric approaches to the analysis of expenditure (demand) as well as traditional approaches to microsimulation and forecasting and combines them with a spatial microsimulation method to produce spatial estimates. In this chapter we focus on just four aspects of the model – the use of a system approach to modelling time-use and expenditure, the forecasting of co-variates using an autoregression method, the use of geographical re-zoning and constrained regression techniques to produce projected census distributions and finally the use of the model for the microsimulation of future scenarios.

1   Spatially simulating time and money

There has been considerable recent interest in the estimation of non-census variables at the small-area level using a range of approaches that go under the term "spatial microsimulation". These have been driven by an agenda that assumes that

> "Governments need to predict the outcomes of their actions
> and produce forecasts at the local level." (Openshaw, 1995)

This agenda requires the creation of datasets which measure the attributes of individuals, households and which generate a synthetic census made up of these units to produce robust estimates of these attributes at the small-area level (Ballas et al., 1999; Birkin and Clarke, 1989; Clarke, 1996; Williamson et al., 1998; Chin et al., 2005).

Common to these efforts is the use of a number of variables from the UK decennial population census tables which describe the socio-demographics of small areas, known as *constraints*, together with the same variables from a representative sample survey to generate a synthetic population of households and/or individuals complete with all attributes measured by the sample survey. There are a wide range of possible methods to combine these data and they have recently been extensively tested and reviewed in the context of studies of population, income and health distributions (Ballas and Clarke, 2001; Ballas et al., 2005b; Ballas et al., 1999; Ballas et al., 2005a).

The key value of the approach is that the product is a population dataset constructed by giving each sample survey unit a series of weights, one for each small area, so that the sum of weights for each small area is equal to the number of units required for that small area (e.g. 1,000 households) and cross-tabulations of weighted units for each small area match those recorded by the census. Thus the sum of weights for each small area is equal to the number of units recorded in that area by the census. By attaching weights to surveyed units it is possible to, in effect, create a synthetic census containing all the variables from the sample survey and to use this to estimate the small-area distributions of each of them.

As an example, the ONS Time Use Survey (ONS-TU-2000) has a household sample size of 6,414. If each small area requires 1,000 households than a naïve weighting would fit the ONS-TU-20000 households into each small area by allocating each household a weight of 1,000/6,4141. Of course, this would create an unrealistic set of identical areas. Instead, we adjust the household weights so that they sum to reflect the actual number and socio-economic constitution of households in each small area, as recorded in the 2001 Census. A similar approach allows us to use the UK Expenditure and Food Survey (EFS) to estimate small-area distributions of household expenditure.

However this approach provides us with just one snapshot in time, and a historical one at that. To generate more recent estimates we could use more recent time-use datasets (e.g. 2005) but we would have to assume no change in the Census socio-demographic distributions at the small-area levels. More realistically, and indeed to generate forecasts, we need to be able to project both the Census and the survey dataset forwards in time and we discuss our approach to this below.

Having constructed the synthetic census micro-data (i.e. households or individuals) it is then possible to use standard microsimulation techniques (Mitton et al., 2000) to develop models linking a range of socio-demographic and other independent variables to the social outcomes under study. By varying the future distributions of the values of the independent variables under specific scenarios it then becomes possible to estimate the spatial distributions of such outcomes. It is this ability to conduct microlevel scenario analyses which marks the approach in this chapter from those which simply seek to produce spatial indicators or estimates of "current levels". Whilst our work has included all regions of the UK, for the sake of clarity we restrict the results presented here to the Eastern region of England.

2   Overview of methods

Figure 1 gives an overview of the modelling method. In this case it shows the pooled Expenditure and Food Surveys (EFS) for 1995-2004 being used as the basis for two sets of analyses. The first is the estimation of a series of demand system ("causal") models that link expenditure to socio-economic characteristics. These models are crucial to the microsimulation of alternative future scenarios. The second is the calculation of autoregressive model (AR) coefficients for the system model variables over time which are then used to project the EFS data forwards – in this case to 2006. The system models are then re-estimated using the new (forecast) values of their variables to produce the projected expenditure for the projected EFS households for the given year. Finally this projected household dataset is used as input to the spatial microsimulation process which, in this example, uses a projected (i.e. synthetic) 2006 small-area micro-population.

In this chapter we use 2001 Census data in conjunction with the UK Expenditure and Food Survey (EFS) to estimate the small-area distributions of household expenditure; and in conjunction with the 2000 ONS Time Use Survey (ONS-TU-2000) to estimate spatial variability in time-use.

In the remainder of this chapter we discuss the elements of this process in more detail.

Figure 1:   Forecasting approach – 2006 as an example

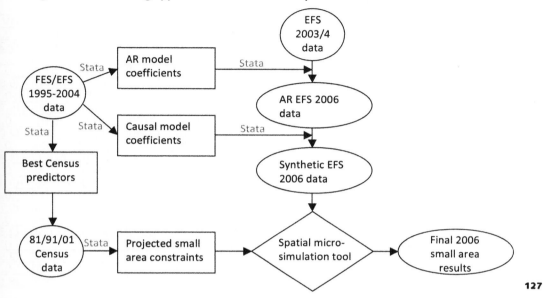

127

3   Demand system approaches to the analysis of time and money

The analysis of the share of expenditure devoted to different items has a long tradition in microeconomics and a commonly used econometric model of goods demand is the Almost Ideal Demand System (AIDS) proposed by Deaton and Muellbauer (1980a, 1980b) which proposes the utility function to be a linear model. This model relates share of household expenditure on specific items with income (or total expenditures) and prices whilst controlling also for the demographic characteristics of the household. Banks et al. (1997) proposed an extension of this linear model, QUAIDS (Quadratic Almost Ideal Demand System), which introduces a quadratic term in log real income (expenditure). They found that the QUAIDS model was useful in capturing the complexity of income effects in cases in which the Engel curves (relationship between income and expenditure) were of primary interest and estimation was conducted using household level data. We have used this non-linear system approach to model expenditures on some key telecommunications-related expenditure items grouped into eight categories (phone landline, mobile, satellite, cable, TV, internet, CDs and DVDs) with the aim of exploring changes in household spending patterns on these items from 1994 to 2004.

Table 1:   Demand system model estimation results (*t* values in parenthesis)

	Landline	Mobile	Satellite	Cable	TV	Internet	CDs	DV
Constant	-0.29	0.22	0.16	0.08	0.38	0.01	0.24	0
	-(22.12)	(18.78)	(25.09)	(17.24)	(36.73)	(1.40)	(30.59)	(27.
beta								
ICT exp	-0.32	0.02	0.03	0.02	0.16	0.00	0.06	0.
	-(68.10)	(4.97)	(13.90)	(11.44)	(44.19)	(2.10)	(19.91)	(9.8
Price of Landline	0.23	0.00	-0.03	-0.01	-0.09	-0.01	-0.05	-0
	(38.21)	(0.66)	-(16.03)	-(8.33)	-(27.74)	-(9.76)	-(18.93)	-(16.
Price of Mobile	0.00	-0.01	0.00	0.00	0.00	0.00	0.01	0.
	(0.66)	-(6.44)	(4.09)	(1.50)	(0.96)	-(0.29)	(5.65)	-(2.0
Price of Satellite	-0.03	0.00	0.01	0.00	0.01	0.00	0.00	0.
	-(16.03)	(4.09)	(11.40)	(6.30)	(8.19)	(3.54)	(3.08)	(1.
Price of Cable	-0.01	0.00	0.00	0.00	0.01	0.00	0.00	0.
	-(8.33)	(1.50)	(6.30)	(5.48)	(9.83)	(3.57)	-(1.96)	-(4.
Price of TV	-0.09	0.00	0.01	0.01	0.04	0.01	0.02	0.
	-(27.74)	(0.96)	(8.19)	(9.83)	(13.45)	(6.95)	(17.76)	(9.
Price of Internet	-0.01	0.00	0.00	0.00	0.01	0.00	0.00	0.
	-(9.76)	-(0.29)	(3.54)	(3.57)	(6.95)	-(3.50)	(7.06)	(2.8
Price of CDs	-0.05	0.01	0.00	0.00	0.02	0.00	0.01	0.
	-(18.93)	(5.65)	(3.08)	-(1.96)	(17.76)	(7.06)	(2.61)	(2.
Price of DVDs	-0.04	0.00	0.00	0.00	0.01	0.00	0.01	0.
	-(16.71)	-(2.09)	(1.40)	-(4.10)	(9.72)	(2.82)	(2.99)	(9.
lambda								
ICT exp^2	-0.03	0.00	0.00	0.00	0.03	0.00	0.00	0.
	-(51.78)	-(8.37)	-(1.78)	(1.34)	(65.28)	-(3.69)	(8.57)	(2.
Year	-0.05	0.05	0.01	0.01	0.00	0.02	-0.01	-0
	-(21.17)	(22.98)	(7.23)	(8.92)	(0.33)	(20.21)	-(9.42)	-(15.
Year^2	0.00	0.00	0.00	0.00	0.00	0.00	0.00	0.
	(7.64)	-(6.80)	-(8.80)	-(8.77)	(0.25)	-(7.33)	(4.16)	(11.
Education of HOH	0.01	0.02	0.00	0.00	-0.03	0.01	0.00	0.
	(4.68)	(6.93)	-(2.30)	-(3.85)	-(10.35)	(8.51)	-(2.42)	-(2.8
N. workers	0.01	0.00	0.00	0.00	-0.01	0.01	0.00	0.
	(3.45)	-(0.13)	-(3.26)	-(6.83)	-(9.31)	(13.38)	(6.00)	(1.
Age of HOH	0.00	0.00	0.00	0.00	0.00	0.00	0.00	0
	(15.38)	-(26.31)	-(2.08)	-(3.56)	(21.44)	-(6.81)	-(3.36)	-(7.
Household size	-0.38	-0.48	-0.31	0.29	-0.12	-0.14	-0.43	1.
	-(1.88)	-(1.99)	-(3.15)	(2.82)	-(0.91)	-(1.09)	-(2.61)	(2.
N. persons 0-4	0.39	0.47	0.32	-0.29	0.13	0.14	0.41	-1.
	(1.93)	(1.95)	(3.21)	-(2.83)	(0.99)	(1.08)	(2.52)	-(2.
N. persons 5-17	0.39	0.47	0.31	-0.29	0.12	0.14	0.43	-1
	(1.92)	(1.96)	(3.17)	-(2.82)	(0.89)	(1.10)	(2.61)	-(2.
N. persons 18-44	0.37	0.48	0.31	-0.29	0.12	0.14	0.44	-1.
	(1.86)	(1.96)	(3.17)	-(2.84)	(0.90)	(1.07)	(2.65)	-(2.
N. persons 45-64	0.38	0.49	0.31	-0.29	0.10	0.14	0.43	-1.
	(1.90)	(2.03)	(3.19)	-(2.82)	(0.74)	(1.11)	(2.61)	-(2.
N. persons 65+	0.38	0.50	0.31	-0.29	0.10	0.14	0.43	-1.
	(1.89)	(2.05)	(3.17)	-(2.83)	(0.73)	(1.09)	(2.61)	-(2.
RMSE*100	4.32	3.41	1.03	0.48	3.11	0.49	1.27	0.

Notes: RMSE: Root mean squared error measures the average deviation of the predicted values from the observed values and is an accepted measure of fit (Cranfield et al., 2003). Thus RMSE for Landline is 4.32/100 representing an average deviation of 0.04% of share of expenditure.

A positive beta coefficient shows that the share of ICT expenditure on that item increases as the price increases (c.f. Landline).

A positive lambda coefficient indicates that the greatest increase is at the lowest end of the overall ICT expenditure scale (cf. TV) whilst a negative lambda coefficient indicates that a decrease in share occurs at the highest level of overall ICT expenditure (cf. Landline).

A t-value > 1.96 indicates a statistically significant coefficent at the 95% level.

HOH: Head of Household.

Table 2:   System goodness-of-fit measures

	Log-Likelihood Value	SRMSE * 100	IIA	LRT [χ^2]
QUAIDS	278680.84	3.214	0.009	6073.55 (p < 0.0001)

Notes: SRMSE & IIA both provide an indicator of whole system fit and are very low (Cranfield et al., 2003) indicating a strongly performing model. LRT: Lagrange ratio test indicates lambda are significantly different from zero thus confirming non-linearity.

For each expenditure share modelled, the predictors used include overall ICT expenditure (and its square) as a proxy for income, a price index for each item of expenditure and basic household demographics such as the education level of the head of household, the number of workers in the household, the age of the head of household, the number of persons and the number of persons in certain age groups. A time-term (the survey year) was also included. This model took three days to estimate on a PC cluster and the results are shown in Table 1 with further goodness of fit statistics report in Table 2. The co-efficients labelled beta indicate the (linear) effect of prices on expenditure on the relevant item whilst those labelled lambda indicate the non-linear effects of demographics and year. These models provide a good fit to the data (RMSE values are low) and Figure 2 shows the observed and estimated shares of overall ICT expenditure on landlines, mobiles and internet subscriptions for the observed survey period and confirm that the model produces plausible estimates.

We have also applied this approach to modelling the demand for time. In this case there are two main differences between our approach and that of Banks et al. Firstly, where standard demand models use proportion of expenditure ("share") in order to control for total expenditure, we use actual time spent since we can assume that all persons only have 24 hours in their day. Secondly we currently do not consider the price of time. Whilst it would be possible to include hourly wage rates for each individual and also, potentially, the opportunity costs of outsourcing activities such as child care, we leave this for future work.

Figure 2: Estimated and observed shares of expenditures (1994-2003)

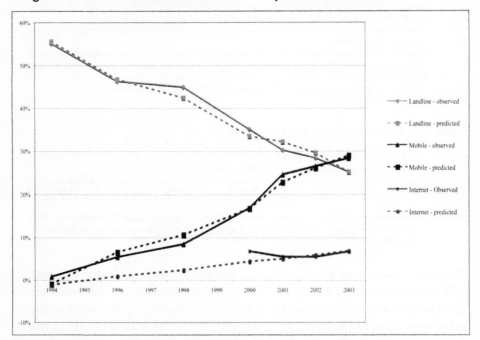

The results (not shown) suggest that all the activities considered are negatively related (i.e. substitutable) to each other. Older people, and those who are married or separated spend more time on health and family care. People with a post-secondary school level education spend more time on social life and entertainment. Married people also spend more time at work. The level of total personal income is significant and positively related to the amount of time spent working and in social activities compared to the lower income class. Middle-high income classes appear to spend more time using the internet even when socio-economic status is controlled. Individuals in households with children spend more time at work, in health and family care and in social and sport activities. On the other hand those living in a household with more adults spend less time on all those activities. Individuals living in the North and South-West and East of England allocate more time to social life and entertainment compared to London and the other regions whilst people without a car have less opportunity of providing health and family care than those having more than two cars.

4 Forecasting expenditure co-variates

Having established the explanatory variables in our demand system models, we next need to project or forecast them forwards in time. Unlike other forecasting models, such as Palombini and Sapio's (1999) consumer Weighted Impact Structural Evaluation case-study, or Cracknell and Mason's (1999) direct forecasting, we use time-series methods to forecast the explanatory variables for the future years in which we have no observed data. The use of time series models for forecasting may be attractive if there is a sufficiently long enough time-series so that an effective time-series model can be built and in the case of the Expenditure surveys we have yearly data starting in the early 1990s.

Here we use a simple autoregressive process of an AR(I) or first order one regressive process time series which represents one year lagged dependence as follows.

Equation 1: $\quad X_t = \alpha + \beta_1 X_{t-1} + \varepsilon_t \ t=1, 2, \ldots .T$ (1)

In this first order autoregressive model, α is an intercept parameter, β is an unknown parameter and ε is an uncorrelated random error with mean zero and constant variance σ^2. This is an autoregressive time-series model of the first order, since X_t depends only on its value in the previous period, X_{t-1}, plus a random disturbance. In this case X is the value of the causal variables identified in the previous section.

We therefore took the means, variances and covariances from the data and estimated the future values of the time-series data by applying the derived parameters and error terms to each household in our baseline household survey data. We develop this forecast recursively, first obtaining the n=1, i.e. t+1 period ahead forecast, then the n=2, i.e. t+2 period ahead forecast and so on. This process is continued until the n-step-ahead forecast is obtained separately for each explanatory variable.

While some causal variables can be forecasted with a reasonable level of accuracy (e.g. as explanatory variables for example, telephone, mobile phone, internet, cable, satellite, income, number of persons in employment), others are more difficult to forecast such as changes in demographics and changes in age groups. The latter need more precise population statistical analysis than could be attempted in this work. In addition where we need to increase the ages of the sample we would need to implement a model of attrition (death) and replacement of younger age cohorts. This kind of dynamic model exists but was outside the scope of the work reported here. We therefore do not age the sample data assuming instead that households with a given age distribution will be similar in all relevant respects in 2003 to households with the same age distribution in 2006, 2011 and 2016 with the exception of the explanatory (demand system) variables listed above. This is of course a brave assumption and building a more realistic dynamic model is the subject of ongoing research.

Figure 3:   Observed (1994-2003) and forecast (2004-2016) mean weekly household expenditure

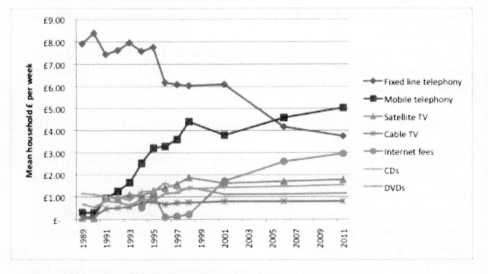

Note: Observed data from ONS Expenditure and Food Surveys.

Once the explanatory variables have been forecast using the AR(I) process, the new expenditure variables can then be calculated for each case (household) for each year by substitution into the demand system model. This is an unconditional forecasting approach taking the effects of changes in all influenced factors into account simultaneously rather than assuming a time-specific causal chain.

This approach yields plausible results as Figure 3 indicates. We have a forecast decline in estimated fixed line telephony expenditure and increase in mobile expenditure. Interestingly this method does not forecast a complete substitution between the two as mobile spending rises less fast than fixed line spending declines. Spending on Internet fees shows a steady increase as more households go online (bearing in mind generally decreasing prices) although the rate of increase is perhaps rather lower than would be anticipated as narrowband access products are phased out in favour of (initially) more expensive broadband access.

5   Identifying census constraint variables

Having forecast the survey data we now need to take it through the spatial microsimulation process. As discussed below we use the iterative proportional fitting procedure (Deming and Stephan, 1940; Wong, 1992) to calculate weights for each household for each of the n census areas using a number of constraint variables which are available from both the census (as household counts) and the survey data (as microdata). Whilst there appear to be many different household level variables in the Census output they are essentially different combinations of the following:

- Household response person (HRP) characteristics: Age, gender, marital status, NS-SEC, ethnicity, religion, employment status.
- Household characteristics: accommodation type, tenure, number cars/ vans, number rooms, composition, presence of long-term limiting illness, presence of children, number of persons, number of children.

The first key test of the potential utility of these variables is the extent to which they predict the outcome variable of interest. This is relatively easy to assess using standard regression techniques and using the r square value as an indicator of the value of the constraint variables (Chin and Harding, 2006). Whilst Chin and Harding report the use of repeated bi-variate regressions to test each variable independently, we used a stepwise multivariate method (Anderson, 2007a, 2007b). This approach means that correlations between constraint variables are taken into account and thus the "pure" effects of each constraint can be revealed whilst the use of the stepwise technique automatically includes only those variables which have a statistically significant effect on the model and orders the resulting "best constraints" in decreasing order of their effects. This is critical to the performance of the simulation since it is the constraint with the greatest effect which must be fitted last. The overall model R-squared score is then an indicator of how well the included constraints predict the outcome variables at the household level and thus a confidence indicator for the robustness of the eventual results.

As an example Table 3 shows the results of stepwise regression models for the four best performing time-use variables on weekdays. The r^2 values suggest that the simulation for dml1_1 (Work time) and dml1_8 (Mass media) are likely to be the most robust followed by dml1_3 (Household and family care) and dml1_5 (Social life and entertainment). Whilst there is currently no accepted view of what a "good" result might be, the values are towards the upper end of the range of bi-variate results reported by Chin and Harding (2006).

Table 3:   Preliminary constraint variables in decreasing order of statistical power for the selected top-level time-use categories

dml1_1 (Work)	dml1_3 (Household and family care)	dml1_5 (Social life and entertainment)	dml1_8 (Mass media)
Employment status	Number of earners	Employment status	Age of HRP
Number of children	Composition	Tenure	Employment status
Age of HRP	Number of children		HRP non-white
Number of earners	Gender of HRP		
R sq = 52.8%	R sq = 18.2%	R sq = 10.7%	R sq = 30.3%

134

It should be clear that different constraints will be identified as optimal indicators for different outcome variables. Thus each outcome that we wish to spatially microsimulate could potentially require *different* census constraint data in contrast to a generic solution using a single set of constraints (in a fixed order) such as Ballas et al.'s SimBritain approach (2005a).

6   Projecting small-area census data

The final piece in the jigsaw is to produce synthetic small-area tables for the selected constraint variables for future Census and inter-censual years by defining a set of geographical zones that can be held constant over time, despite the continual changes to UK zonal geography. Census 2001 wards were selected primarily because the errors involved during the geographical re-zoning are potentially smaller at ward level than at the smaller census output area/enumeration district levels. The method creates consistent geographical zones where the most contemporary zone is taken as the reference zone to which all earlier data are updated (Gregory and Ell, 2005; Norman et al., 2003). This was implemented using an intersection/union operation between the historic (1981, 1991) and contemporary (2001) zone boundaries to create fragmented zones each with unique identifiers for both the historic and contemporary zones and then aerial interpolation was used to produce the re-allocated Census data. Postcodes were used as a proxy for population distribution and weights were calculated from the proportion or share of postcodes that the historic zone has within the total of the contemporary zone. These were used to re-weight the historical census data and allocate the weighted values to each fragment before the fragments were re-aggregated to Census 2001 wards.

Our analysis suggests that the method does not lose significant numbers of households and that postcode losses during re-zoning are very low at the level of the individual countries (England, Scotland and Wales) and still minimal at the individual ward level. The conversion weights developed by this methodology when tested using the degree of fitness measure discussed in Simpson (2002) are good – 84% and 87% for the 1981 and 1991 data respectively.

Having produced a historical dataset containing re-zoned small-area Census data for 1981-2001 it was then necessary to project these data forwards in time. In contrast to Ballas et al.'s exponential linear smoothing approach (Ballas et al., 2005), linear regression was chosen as the least-worse alternative since with only three data points we have no basis for using a more complex model form and because constrained linear regression is the least complex to implement and interpret.

In addition three conditions (1-3) were applied:

1.   The total number of households for all census constraints of a particular census variable should not exceed the total number of households in each ward.

2.   The total number of households in each ward should not be negative, nor should the number of households for any of the 18 census constraints.

3.   The total number of projected households in each government region should be equal or closely approximate that of the total number of households forecast by the UK Government's household projection models.

Constraints were projected in terms of proportions of households to avoid having to control each year for changing household numbers and were projected for 2006, 2011 and 2016 by constrained linear regression on condition that the sum of all fractions of census constraints belonging to a census variable is "1".

In order to forecast the number of households for each ward for years 2006, 2011 and 2016, we used linear regression on condition that the number of households is not negative. As above a linear approach was chosen as being the simplest to implement given our limitation to three data points. Whilst a more complex curve fit could have been used, the lack of additional data points means that we have no basis for assuming any particular kind of curve. In addition the UK Government's official household projections give, in general, a linear trend so we feel that this approach is defensible.

The result is that of the 10,072 wards projected, 4 had zero households in 2006, 8 had zeros in 2011 and 15 in 2016. The projection of zero households is a result of a decreasing linear trend in household numbers for these areas from 1981 and so could result from mis-alignments of 1981, 1991 and 2001 boundaries during the interpolation process and/or real decline. In order to progress we used the most recent non-zero household numbers. Given that very few wards show this behaviour we do not believe that it fundamentally altered the results.

The projected numbers of households were then re-normalized for each government region to fit official projections (*England*: ONS, 2005; *Wales*: ONS, 2005; *Scotland*: ONS, 2005; SES, 2005). This step removed the divergence between the estimated total number of households in each government region and the official estimates. Finally the projected number of households was multiplied by the projected constraint variable fractions to produce the projected small-area constraint counts.

A selection of the forecast constraints is shown in Table 4 and reflects forecasts of patterns that have been revealed by analysis of the 1991 and 2001 censuses such as that by Dorling and Thomas (2004). The only trends which may be significantly debatable are the rate at which the rise in households with two or more cars begins to flatten, and the relative distributions of retired and inactive persons which may well be driven by definitional problems in the historical Census datasets.

Table 4: UK household and demographic trends (excl. Northern Ireland), 1981-2016

Constraint	1981	Census 1991	2001	2006	Forecast 2011	2016	% change 01-06	% change 06-11	% change 11-16
Households (renorm)	19,500,592	21,929,611	23,853,464	25,233,696	26,119,671	27,003,050	5.79	3.51	3.38
Cars									
No Car	7,696,634	7,310,974	6,552,696	6,181,603	5,653,248	5,113,032	-5.66	-8.55	-9.56
1 Car	8,788,671	9,544,042	10,436,644	10,840,189	11,098,067	11,353,893	3.87	2.38	2.31
2+ Cars	3,015,346	5,074,590	6,864,142	8,211,904	9,368,356	10,536,125	19.63	14.08	12.47
Tenure									
Owned	10,851,975	14,484,152	16,288,627	18,332,609	19,684,810	20,962,346	12.55	7.38	6.49
Socially Rented	6,468,169	5,379,152	4,752,840	4,071,772	3,478,379	2,953,930	-14.33	-14.57	-15.08
Other	2,180,452	2,066,333	2,811,618	2,829,315	2,956,482	3,086,774	0.63	4.49	4.41
Dependent Children									
No children	12,934,584	15,346,016	16,860,374	18,238,150	19,161,692	20,099,147	8.17	5.06	4.89
1 Child	2,730,391	2,760,965	2,999,450	3,022,950	3,036,740	3,045,047	0.78	0.46	0.27
2+ Children	3,835,667	3,822,652	3,993,640	3,972,596	3,921,239	3,858,856	-0.53	-1.29	-1.59
Martial Status									
Couple	12,707,599	11,404,410	10,650,569	9,913,694	8,943,154	7,887,085	-6.92	-9.79	-11.81
Single Parent	414,432	915,602	2,293,560	2,679,987	3,244,657	3,838,175	16.85	21.07	18.29
Single	4,243,449	5,873,758	7,223,587	8,079,646	8,901,083	9,757,042	11.85	10.17	9.62
Other	2,134,943	3,735,826	3,684,150	4,560,369	5,030,777	5,520,748	23.78	10.32	9.74
Socio-Economic Status									
High	3,902,958	4,751,818	6,541,051	7,216,911	7,836,356	8,363,557	10.33	8.58	6.73
Medium	2,378,910	2,811,976	3,276,253	3,541,524	3,732,679	3,906,983	8.10	5.40	4.67
Low	6,488,415	5,285,923	5,761,203	5,162,606	4,878,577	4,701,250	-10.39	-5.50	-3.63
Retired	2,697,218	5,567,522	6,186,136	7,692,497	8,485,815	9,107,180	24.35	10.31	7.32
Inactive	4,033,210	3,512,336	2,088,821	1,620,158	1,186,244	924,080	-22.44	-26.78	-22.10

7   Spatially microsimulating time and money in space

With this preparatory work in place we then used an iterative proportional fitting technique adapted from Ballas et al.'s SimBritain approach (Ballas et al., 2005a) to produce a list of weighted households in each zone for a given year. This method was chosen over others such as combinatorial optimization (Voas and Williamson, 2000) or simulated annealing (Ballas et al., 1999) as it was efficient to compute at the ward level for the whole of the UK and being deterministic, produces identical results with identical inputs.

Following Ballas et al. we implemented a regional weighting scheme so that only households belonging to the same region as the particular LSOA are allocated to it. Ballas et al. also report using a process of integerization to select the "best fit" n weighted households for a given area where n is the number of households required for the ward. Ballas et al. report that this integerization produced some extremely poor results when tested against the census distributions and described a swapping algorithm to swap households between their 1991 wards in order to reduce errors and produce a better fit.

Since it is inevitable that the integerization process will reduce within-zone variation and for our purposes it was not necessary that each small area was allocated a whole number of households, we did not implement the integeristion process. Instead our simplified method allowed the final household weights for each small area to remain fractional so that all possible survey households are retained. Our experience is that this simplified method produces distributions that perform at least as well as Ballas et al.'s more complex combination of integerization and household swapping.

The spatial microsimulation process was implemented as a java-based tool which produces an output file summarising the input variables of interest for each zone and in addition a large weights file (Table 5).

Table 5:   Example time-use simulation output file (partial)

Zone	region	HH_id	WEIGHT	dml1_1
E01015589	6	2	0.56	480
E01015589	6	3	0.56	485
E01015589	6	4	5.07	193.33
E01015589	6	5	0.7	280
E01015589	6	6	2.59	350

For each area this file records the weight attributed to survey households allocated to it. Notice that this weight could be zero. In this example the simulated survey variable (dml1_1) is the household's work time in minutes per day. In addition any number of other variables can be included provided that we can be confident that they are predicted by the chosen constraint variables.

Calculating the time-use indicator for each zone is thus a straightforward matter of summing the weighted survey variable (i.e. the sum of weight * dml1_1 in this case) for each area and dividing by the number of households in that area. Similarly any other statistic can be calculated – such as the median or the variance for each area.

Time in space

In this example we report the spatial distribution of two time-use variables – work and mass media time. We report work because banded personal work hours are available from the 2001 census and so can be used as a validation source at the small-area level. A rank order (Spearman) test at the ward level between the estimated mean household work time and the Census 2001 derived mean work hours[1] for all persons aged 16-74 shows that the simulation results are an excellent fit to the analogous Census results (Spearman rho = 0.8404, p < 0.001). This is confirmed by Figure 4, which shows the close relationship between the two albeit with some outliers.

Mass media usage on the other hand might be expected to be the inverse of work time and indeed Figure 5 shows a clear South West to North East gradient such that those areas closest to London and other cities show the highest levels of average household work time and this declines markedly towards the south east Essex, east Suffolk and north Norfolk coasts where mass media usage is highest. In the context of identifying the spatial distribution of latent demand for broadband-delivered media content the peripheral areas of the East of England may be of interest

---

1   Census work hours data are published in ranges. We have calculated the mean value for each range using the ONS 2000 time-use survey and then taken this value as the "midpoint" for each range in order to derive the census mean work time. This is particularly useful as it provides a specific value for the top-most census range which was "49 hours or more per week".

Figure 4:   Observed (Census 2001) vs. estimated (model) work hours

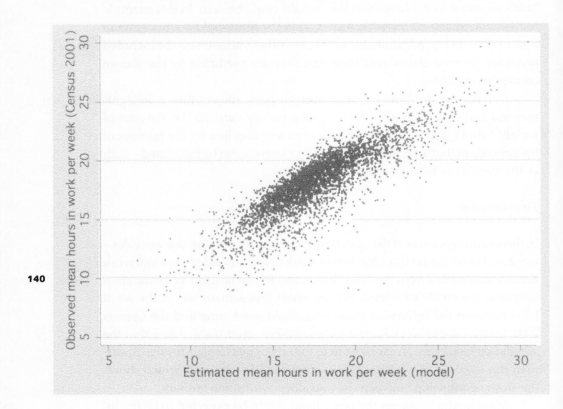

140

Figure 5: Estimated mean work time in 2001 (Eastern region, minutes per day, weekdays)

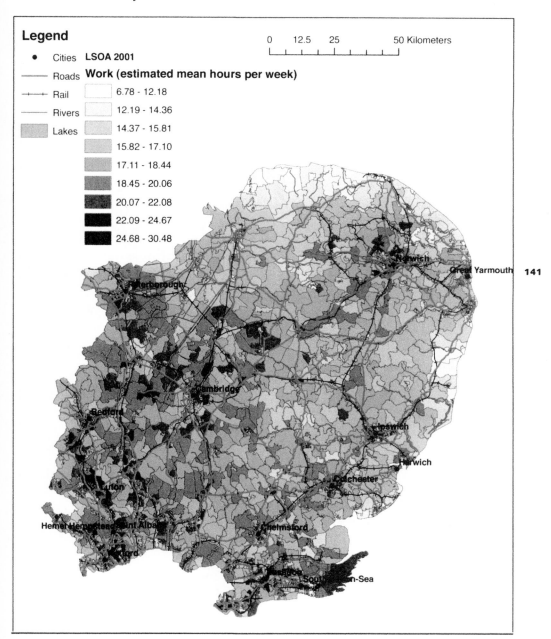

Figure 6: Estimated mean mass media time in 2001 (Eastern region, minutes per day, weekdays)

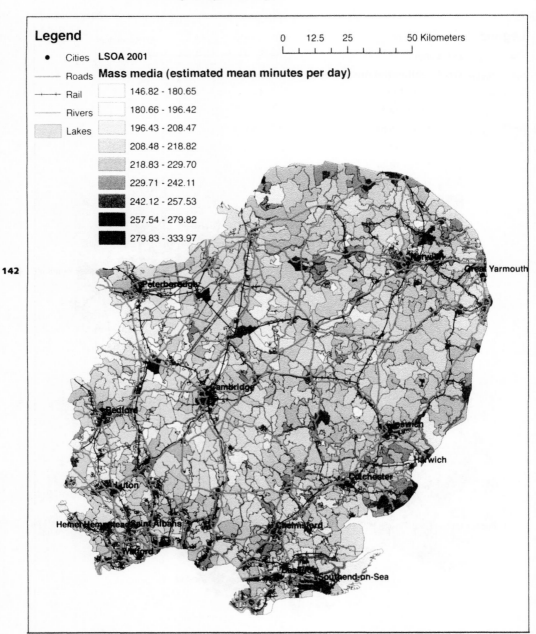

Money in space over time

Our final examples show results from the spatial microsimulation of household expenditure using exactly the same method as that described for time-use. The first set of results (Figure 7) show the validation of the ward level household telephony expenditure estimates using an extract from BT's residential household billing data for 2003 for part of the East of England. Whilst there were a number of wards where no BT expenditure is recorded either because they were accidentally excluded from the data extraction or because they were areas with few BT customers, there was a significant rank order correlation between the two at ward level (Spearman rho = 0.7796, p < 0.001). We therefore have some degree of confidence in these and other estimates produced by this method.

Figure 7: **Estimated total household weekly telephone expenditure (Census 2001, EFS 2001-2) vs. total weekly BT residential household expenditure in Q1 2003 (Eastern region subsample, Census wards)**

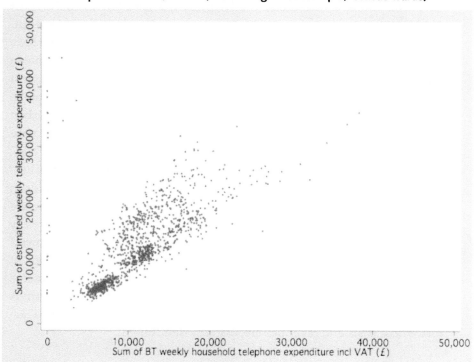

The second set of results show baseline-projected change in household expenditure on fixed line and mobile telephony and on internet subscriptions. As we can see (Figures 8 to Figure 10) mean household expenditure on fixed line telephony is projected to fall across the whole of the East of England whilst mobile telephony expenditure is projected to rise in those areas which in 2001 were estimated to have lowest mobile phone uptake. The distributions also reflect the incomplete substitution of mobile for fixed line expenditure as noted earlier. Thus those places with higher mobile expenditure growth are not necessarily those with the greatest reduction in expenditure on fixed line telephony.

In the case of expenditure on internet service subscriptions the greatest increases are to be found in the rural and north-eastern peripheries of the region as well as those urban areas where internet uptake was estimated to be lowest in 2001.

In our second example we use an econometric microsimulation to model new expenditure patterns in the underlying household expenditure data before the spatial microsimulation process begins. We tested the effect of 100% internet access from 2006 on a range of other household expenditures by extending our expenditure (demand) system models to include this variable. Figure 11 shows the spatial distribution of change for mean weekly telephony spend in the East of England and shows that the greatest impact is seen in those areas which would have had lowest internet uptake (the coastal areas with the highest average age and some deprived urban areas). Of course these areas may prove the most expensive to target with whatever intervention could raise internet uptake to 100%.

This problem is highlighted by Figure 12 which shows the total increased weekly spend, thus taking account of the number of households in each ward. We can see immediately that those areas which would generate the greatest increase (e.g. Mancroft in Norwich) in revenue are not *necessarily* (or even mostly) those with the greatest increase in mean household spend but are, rather obviously generally those with the largest populations of latent demand. In the context of decisions about infrastructure investments this difference is crucial and it should be immediately clear why these kinds of spatial microsimulation methods are proving of value to commercial actors whose costs and revenues are spatially distributed.

Figure 8: **Estimated change in mean weekly household spend on fixed line telephony 2001-2016 (Eastern region)**

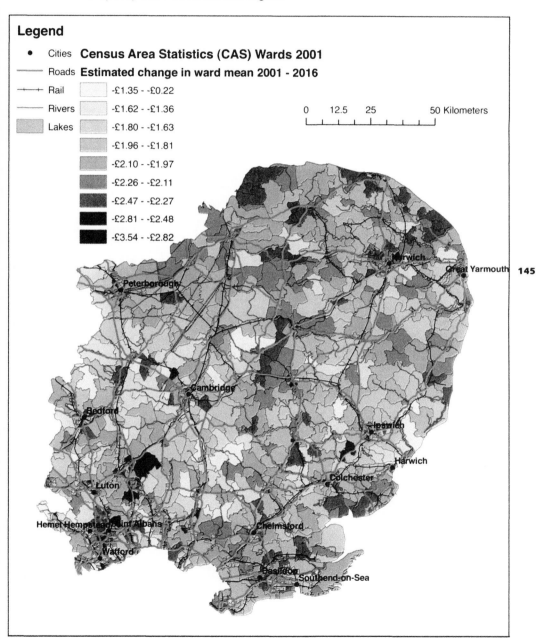

**Figure 9:   Estimated change in mean weekly household spend on mobile
telephony 2001-2016 (Eastern region)**

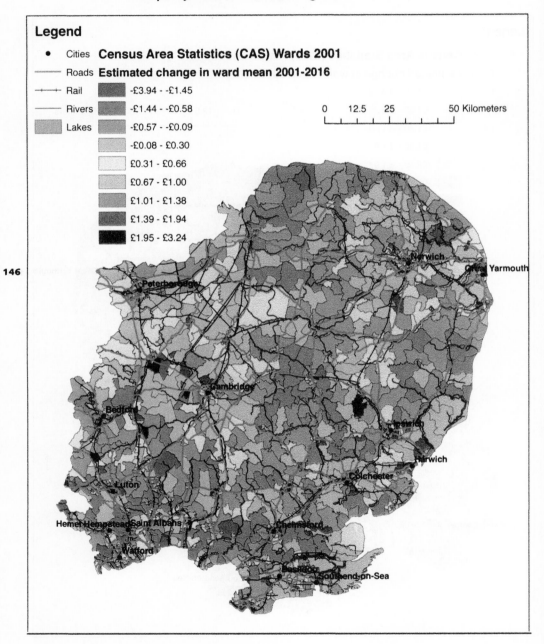

Figure 10: Estimated change in mean weekly household spend on internet subscriptions 2001-2016 (Eastern region)

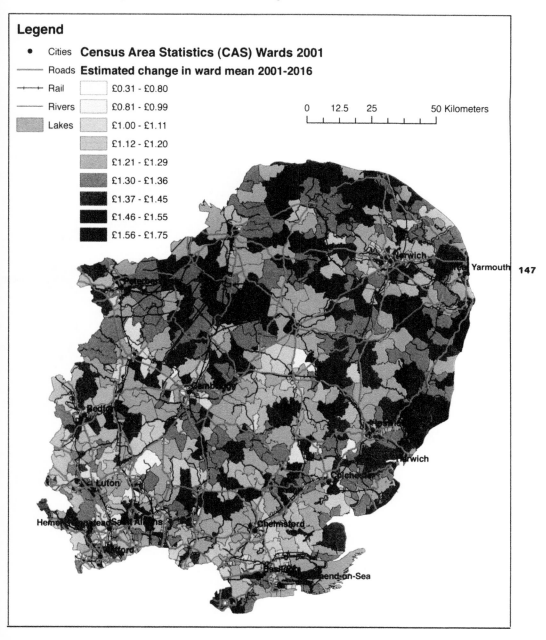

Figure 11: Estimated change in mean household weekly expenditure on fixed line telephony with 100% internet access in 2006

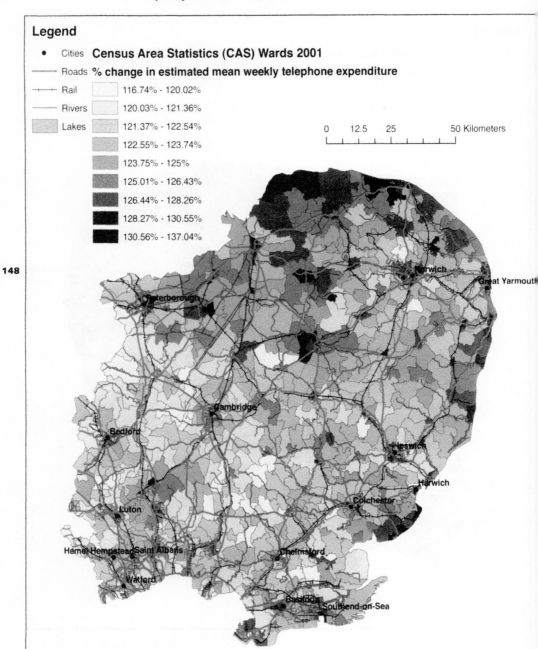

Figure 12: Estimated change in total household weekly expenditure per ward on fixed line telephony, assuming 100% internet access in 2006

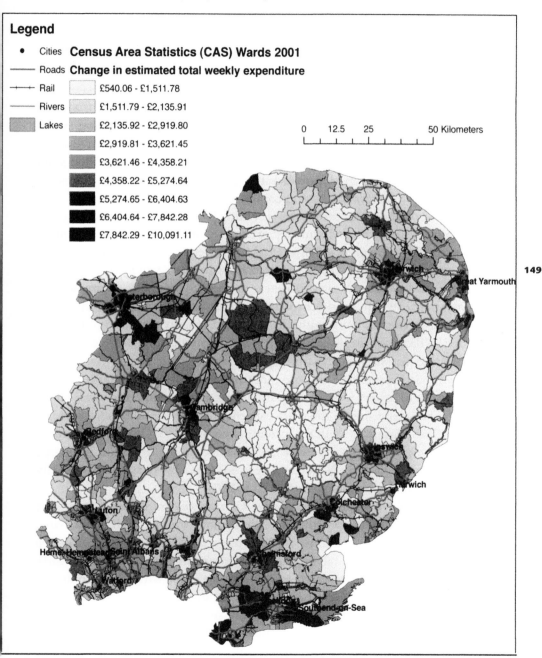

149

8   Conclusions

In summary this chapter has described a number of stages in the spatial microsimulation of time and money in space. We have shown how the need to develop small-area estimates of time-use and household expenditure for policy and commercial purposes can be met and results validated. We have also shown how a combination of relatively simple forecasting and microsimulation methods in combination with the projection of small-area census tables provides one way to estimate future small-area distributions of variables of interest. Whilst we have applied this to household time-use and expenditure the method is generic and could be applied to other household or individual outcomes provided that the census constraint variables are adequate predictors of these outcomes at the microdata level.

One of the major problems with using both expenditure and time-use data in this way is the frequency of zero reported time/money spent on apparently infrequent activities/goods. Differentiating between the non-recording due to error and the non-recording due to no activity/consumption is difficult where no other variables can be used to triangulate or impute data. One possibility is to use a form of regression-based imputation which enables the replacement of zeros with the modelled values based on a multivariate model (Bardazzi and Barnabani, 1998). This would require the assumption that, for example, those with internet access did actually use it in the way modelled and it is possible that this would produce significant over-estimates of behaviour. An alternative in the case of time-use – and indeed a valuable extension to the work reported here – would be to replace the 2000 time-use survey with the recently available 2005 ONS Omnibus time-use survey which should show increased recording of internet-mediated behaviour. If nothing else it could be used to analyse changes in (spatially microsimulated) time-use from 2001 to 2005.

Overall we believe that the use of demand system models to analyse time-use is a unique contribution, as is our attempt to produce small-area estimates of time-use. There have been few attempts to produce small-area estimates of household expenditure and thus this work provides an early contribution to this research area. Our experiences with the re-zoning of small-area statistics has suggested several new approaches including the aggregation of smaller area data from historical censuses as well as the exploration of other census projection methods and this is part of our on-going research programme. In addition we acknowledge that our household projection model is extremely simplistic. In our ongoing work we are investigating the development of a dynamic agent-based household expenditure model.

References

Anderson, B. (2007a) *Creating small area income estimates for England: spatial microsimulation modelling*. Ipswich: Chimera, University of Essex.

Anderson, B. (2007b) *Estimating time spent on-line at small area levels: a spatial microsimulation approach* (No. CWP-2007-01). Ipswich: Chimera, University of Essex.

Ballas, D./Clarke, G. (2001) 'Modelling the local impacts of national social policies: a spatial microsimulation approach', *Environment and Planning C: Government and Policy* 19: 587-606.

Ballas, D./Clarke, G./Dorling, D./Eyre, H./Thomas, B./Rossiter, D. (2005a) 'SimBritain: A Spatial Microsimulation Approach to Population Dynamics', *Population, Space and Place* 11: 13-34.

Ballas, D./Clarke, G./Dorling, D./Rigby, J./Wheeler, B. (2005b) *Using Geographical Information Systems and spatial microsimulation for the analysis of health inequalities*. Paper presented at the 10th International Symposium on Health Information Management Research – iSHIMR 2005.

Ballas, D./Clarke, G./Turton, I. (1999, 25-28 July, 1999) *Exploring Microsimulation Methodologies for the Estimation of Household Attributes*. Paper presented at the 4th International Conference on GeoComputation, Mary Washington College, Virginia, USA.

Ballas, D./Rossiter, D./Thomas, B./Clarke, G./Dorling, D. (2005) *Geography Matters*. York: Joseph Rowntree Foundation.

Banks, J./Blundell, R./Lewbel, A. (1997) 'Quadratic engel curves and consumer demand', *The Review of Economics and Statistics* 79 (4): 527-539.

Bardazzi, R./Barnabani, M. (1998) 'Modelling Zero Expenditures on Italian Household Consumption', *Economic Notes* 1: 55-96.

Birkin, M./Clarke, G. (1989) 'The generation of individual and household incomes at the small area level', *Regional Studies* 23 (6): 535-548.

Buliung, R./Kanaroglou, P. (2007) 'Activity-Travel Behaviour Research: Conceptual Issues, State of the Art, and Emerging Perspectives on Behavioural Analysis and Simulation Modelling', *Transport Reviews* 27 (2): 151-187.

Chin, S.-F./Harding, A. (2006) *Regional Dimensions: Creating Synthetic Small-area Microdata and Spatial Microsimulation Models*. Canberra: National Centre for Social and Economic Modelling, University of Canberra.

Chin, S.-F./Harding, A./Lloyd, R./McNamara, J./Phillips, B./Vu, Q. (2005) 'Spatial Microsimulation Using Synthetic Small Area Estimates of Income, Tax and Social Security Benefits', *Australasian Journal of Regional Studies* 11 (3): 303-336.

Clarke, G. (ed.) (1996) *Microsimulation for Urban and Regional Policy Analysis*. London: Pion.

Cracknell, D./Mason, C. (1999) 'Forecasting telephony Demand Against a Background of major Structure Change', pp. 203-215 in: Loomis, D./Taylor, L. (eds.), *The Future of the Telecommunications Industry – Forecasting and Demand Analysis*. Dordrecht: Kluwer Academic Publishers.

Cranfield, J.A.L. / Eales, J.S. / Hertel, T.W. / Preckel, P.V. (2003) 'Model selection when estimating and predicting consumer demands using international, cross section data', *Empirical Economics* 28 (2): 353-364.

Deaton, A.S. / Muellbaeur, J. (1980a) 'An Almost Ideal Demand System', *American Economic Review* 70: 312-336.

Deaton, A.S. / Muellbaeur, J. (1980b) *Economics and Consumer Behaviour.* Cambridge: Cambridge University Press.

Deming, W.E. / Stephan, F.F. (1940) 'On a least square adjustment of sampled frequency tables when the expected marginal totals are known', *Annals of Mathematical Statsictics* 6: 427-444.

Dorling, D. / Thomas, B. (2004) *People and places: a 2001 census atlas of the UK.* Bristol: Policy Press.

Gregory, I.N. / Ell, P. S. (2005) 'Breaking the boundaries: geographical approaches to integrating 200 years of the census', *Journal – Royal Statistical Society Series A* 168 (2): 419-437.

Hanaoka, K. / Clarke, G. (2006) 'Spatial microsimulation modelling for retail market analysis at the small-area level', *Computers, Environment and Urban Systems* 31 (2): 162-187.

Mitton, L. / Sutherland, H. / Weeks, M.J. (2000) *Microsimulation modelling for policy analysis: challenges and innovations.* Cambridge: Cambridge University Press.

Norman, P. / Rees, P. / Boyle, P. (2003) 'Achieving Data Compatibility Over Space and Time: Creating Consistent Geographical Zones', *International Journal of Population Geography* 9: 365-386.

ONS (2005) *Household numbers and projections: Regional Trends 38.* London: Office for National Statistics.

Openshaw, S. (ed.) (1995) *Census Users' Handbook.* London: GeoInformation International.

Palombini, I.M. / Sapio, B. (1999) 'Analysis of Customer Expectations for the Introduction of New Telecommunications Services', in: Loomis, D. / Taylor, L. (eds.), *The Future of the Telecommunications Industry — Forecasting and Demand Analysis.* Dordrecht: Kluwer.

SES (2005) *Household Projections for Scotland: 2002-Based.* Edinburgh: Scottish Executive Statistics.

Simpson, L. (2002) 'Geography conversion tables: a framework for conversion of data between geographical units', *International Journal of Population Geography* 8 (1): 69-82.

Voas, D. / Williamson, P. (2000) 'An evaluation of the combinatorial optimisation approach to the creation of synthetic microdata', *International Journal of Population Geography* 6 (5): 349-366.

Williamson, P. (2005) *Income Imputation for Small Areas.* Liverpool: University of Liverpool.

Williamson, P. / Birkin, M. / Rees, P. (1998) 'The estimation of population microdata by using data from small area statistics and samples of anonymised records', *Environment and Planning A* 30: 785-816.

Wong, D. (1992) 'The Reliability of Using the Iterative Proportional Fitting Procedure', *Professional Geographer* 44 (3): 340-348.

Part II:
Work Incentives and Labour Supply

Chapter 6

Work Incentives, Redistribution Policies and the Equity-Efficiency Trade Off: Evidence from Spain

José M. Labeaga / Xisco Oliver / Amedeo Spadaro

1   Introduction

Over the past 20 years, there have been wide-scale changes in the Spanish redistribution system.[1] Since 1979, the year of the creation of income tax, two main reforms have been implemented. In 1989, a large-scale reform provided married wage-earners with the possibility of making separate tax declarations. The Personal Income Tax (PIT) system was again reformed in 1999, and the subsequent equity and efficiency effects have been the subject of both political and academic debate.

The evaluation of the reform has been carried out mainly via arithmetical simulation techniques. Castañer et al. (2000) use the Taxpayers Panel of the Spanish Tax Agency (*Panel de Declarantes por IRPF*) to examine the implications of the reform in terms of redistribution and welfare. They show that the 1999 scheme reduces total redistribution, mainly through the reduction of tax receipts. Using the European Community Household Panel and the microsimulation model GLADHISPANIA, Oliver and Spadaro (2003, 2007) find similar results. Levy and Mercader-Prats (2002) focus on the analysis of the withholding mechanism and the efficiency effects of the new income tax system. They show that the 1999 reform failed to reduce the compliance costs of taxpayers. Sanchís and Sanchís (2001) simulate the new PIT system, taking into account the effects on household consumption of a VAT increase introduced to compensate for the fall in income tax revenue.

---

1   An historical description can be found in Cantó et al. (2002).

The authors acknowledge financial support from the Spanish Government (ECO2008-06395-C05-02; SEJ2005-08783-C04-03). The usual disclaimers apply.

The main pitfall of arithmetical analysis is the absence of behavioural reactions. With respect to the labour market, for example, some of the changes introduced by the reform are particularly designed to provide incentives for the participation of certain groups. Even if this was not the case, we may expect some effects on household consumption/labour supply patterns, at least in the medium to long run. The main concern of this chapter is to shed some light on these issues by measuring the impact of the reforms on labour supply behaviour and evaluating their effects on individual and social welfare.

There have been very few attempts to evaluate the Spanish PIT reforms including labour supply behavioural reactions (Labeaga and Sanz, 2001; García and Suarez, 2002; Prieto and Alvarez, 2002; and Castañer et al., 2004). In all of these papers, the labour supply model is based on the traditional continuous approach (see Hausman, 1981 and 1985a) that has been recognized as suffering from several problems. One is the lack of identification of the responses of hours to marginal changes in taxes (see, for instance, Van Soest, 1995); another is the under-identification of wage effects due to misspecification of dynamic components (see McCurdy, 1992 or Arellano *et al.*, 1999). The principal inconvenience of using this methodology is that the behavioural restrictions it imposes are too strong, requiring that the labour supply function globally satisfies the Slustky conditions. As a result, the estimation results suffer from a lack of robustness, which reduces their usefulness for policy evaluation (see MaCurdy et al., 1990, and MaCurdy, 1992).

Such weaknesses have pushed researchers towards the estimation of total income elasticities (Feldstein, 1995; Auten and Carroll, 1999; Gruber and Saez, 2002) or the estimation of direct utility functions by a discretization of the labour supply alternatives (Van Soest, 1995; Aaberge et al., 1995; Hoynes, 1996; Bingley and Walker, 1997; Keane and Moffit, 1998 and Blundell et al., 2000). This second approach has been heavily employed in the recent analysis of tax reforms. Since behavioural changes probably occur at the corner or kink points of the labour supply function, this method has the advantage of capturing them, providing the analyst with an estimation of the elasticity at the extensive margin. Moreover, this methodology allows us to avoid the computational and analytical difficulties associated with utility maximization under non-linear and non-convex budget constraints. This is because the budget constraint is now directly modelled in the utility function. It also enables us to consider fixed costs, simultaneous participation and the intensity of work choices, as well as spouses' joint labour supply decisions.

An excellent application of behavioural microsimulation based on discrete choice models, which illustrates very well the potential of this approach, is that of Blundell et al. (2000), which evaluates the likely effect of the introduction of the Working Families Tax Credit (WFTC) in the UK. They estimate, separately, a discrete labour supply model for married couples and single parents on a sample of UK households in the Family Resources Survey for 1995 and 1996. The particularity of the model lies in its ability to include child care costs, which vary with hours of work. They then use their results to simulate labour supply responses under the new budget constraint using the TAXBEN microsimulation model developed at the Institute for Fiscal Studies. The results show that the introduction of behavioural responses reduces the estimated cost of the WFTC programme by 14% from its level in the purely arithmetical scenario. This is mostly due to an increase in labour force participation by single mothers. Similar analysis has been carried out to evaluate recent reforms in the US (Hoynes, 1996 and Keane and Moffit, 1998), Italy, Norway and Sweden (Aaberge et al., 2000), the Netherlands (Das and Van Soest, 2001), Germany (Bonin et al., 2002) and France (Bargain, 2005).

A striking feature of the papers cited above is that policy evaluation is carried out using only the sub-sample for which it is possible to estimate labour supply responses. The inactive population (i.e. pensioners, students, handicapped, etc.) is excluded from the global analysis of the reforms. This feature is somewhat in contradiction with the standard microsimulation practice that, on the contrary, makes substantial efforts to retain all of the population heterogeneity in the evaluation exercise (see Bourguignon and Spadaro, 2006). Moreover, structural reform, such as that in 1999 in Spain, covers the whole population and produces global welfare effects that should be incorporated in any evaluation exercise.

In our opinion, one potential solution to these problems is to carry out a microsimulation exercise combining arithmetic and behavioural instruments in order to adjust the after-tax figures and produce results for the population as a whole. In this chapter, first, we use the estimation results from Labeaga et al. (2008) to compute the *ex post* patterns of labour supply (and utility) of these agents. Second, we perform an arithmetical simulation on the remaining part of the population in the sample. This procedure allows us to obtain a global evaluation of both the efficiency and welfare impacts of the reforms considered.

Given the policy implications of the evaluation results, in addition to the 1999 reform, we also consider other hypothetical scenarios inspired by the basic income – flat tax (BIFT) and vital minimum – flat tax (VMFT) philosophies (see Atkinson, 1995). The objective of these exercises is to shed light on the potential of BIFT and VMFT to reduce inequality and to increase social welfare in Spain (see Oliver and Spadaro, 2003, 2007).

The structure of the chapter is as follows. Section 2 describes the dataset, the microsimulation model and the main features of the systems simulated (1998 PIT, 1999 PIT and the simulated BIFT and VMFT). The evaluation of the different policy scenarios is carried out in Section 3. Section 4 concludes.

2   Data, microsimulation model and main features of redistribution systems

We use the Spanish data from the European Community Household Panel (ECHP). The last Spanish wave when we constructed the microsimulation model was that of 1995. Given that we are interested in comparing the 1998 and 1999 scenarios, and that the monetary variables in the 1995 wave are from 1994, we update them using the nominal growth rate (inflation plus real growth). To update incomes from 1994 to 1998 we use the factor 1.281; from 1994 to 1999 the updating factor is 1.335. In Table A1 (see Annex) we compare household net income in the 1998 and 1999 ECHP waves (actually available but not yet implemented in the microsimulation model) with that in our updated dataset. After updating net income, we convert to gross income using the microsimulation model GLADHISPANIA, in which we can compute, from net incomes, social contributions, total income tax and also the monthly amounts that are withheld from income in anticipation of the yearly income tax bill. This is carried out via a fixed-point algorithm which iterates until it reaches the withholdings, income tax and social insurance contribution patterns which best fit the net incomes observed in the data.[2] The results of the model's calibration are shown in Table A2, where they are compared to the corresponding aggregate figures reported in official statistics. The number of households in the database is 6,522. After dropping 102 observations due to missing information about the household head (which we need to compute income tax accurately), we have 6,420 households, representative of the total number of households in the Spanish population (12,068,375 in 1995, source INE). The descriptive statistics of the variables

---

2   A full description of the microsimulation model (GLADHISPANIA), of the dataset and of the net to gross algorithm is contained in Oliver and Spadaro (2004a).

used in the econometric section are given in Table A3. The scenarios which we simulate using GLADHISPANIA are described below.

The 1998 and 1999 Spanish direct redistribution systems

The model replicates social contributions levied on wages (for employers and employees) and on self-employed workers and income taxes. Table A4 sets out the social contribution rates of firms and employees and the maximum and minimum contribution base-rates for 1998 and 1999.

With respect to the 1998 system, the 1999 reform moved from a PIT structure in which individuals' specific conditions were taken into account mainly by means of tax deductions to one in which they are reflected in tax allowances. Some of the 1998 tax deductions were included in the subsistence-level minimum income (i.e. personal and family tax deductions); others became tax deductions on different kinds of expenditure (i.e. tax deductions on employee wages) and some were eliminated altogether (i.e. house rentals). Nevertheless, the main feature of the reform (for our purposes) is the reduction in both tax brackets (from 9 to 6) and tax rates (as can be seen in Table A5). In particular maximum and minimum marginal taxes fell asymmetrically: the former was reduced from 56% to 48%, whilst the latter fell from 20% to 18%.

The Basic Income-Flat Tax (BIFT) and the Vital Minimum-Flat Tax (VMFT)

As mentioned above, the debate over the suitability of the reforms to the Spanish redistribution system is still open. Recently, alternative schemes based on a flat tax mechanism have been proposed (Oliver and Spadaro, 2003). The underlying idea is to simplify the tax structure and, at the same time, to introduce a sort of "citizens' income". In order to explore the ensuing implications on welfare and redistribution, we carry out simulations of the basic income-flat tax reform (BIFT) and the vital minimum-flat tax (VMFT) reforms. Both replace the 1999 PIT leaving the social security contributions scheme unchanged.

The VMFT reform replaces the 1999 PIT with a vital minimum, which consists of a tax allowance per equivalent adult[3] and a proportional tax on taxable income. The BIFT reform consists of a universal lump-sum transfer, called the "basic income" (i.e. an amount of money that the government allocates to each household, independent of income and status) plus a flat tax on taxable income. As for VMFT, we take into account the number of household members, yielding a basic income per equivalent adult.

---

3   The equivalence scale used is the square root of the number of household members.

The advantages or disadvantages of a VMFT or BIFT scheme are well known in the literature (see Atkinson, 1995) and summarised in Table A6. The main problem is the labour supply disincentives that a high flat tax may engender. The econometric model used in the next section takes these disincentives into account and quantifies their impact.

We run four simulations for different flat rates. To facilitate the redistribution analysis, the basic income or vital minimum has been chosen to respect the government's budget constraint (with respect to our year of reference, 1999) in an arithmetical framework. In Table A7, we show the four simulated scenarios. We start from the maximum marginal tax rate of the 1999 system (46%), which allows 4,632 euros of annual basic income per equivalent adult (and 13,997 euros as the vital minimum), and we reduce the flat tax rate to 38%, 30% and 25%.

3 Evaluation of the Spanish reforms: efficiency and welfare effects

The details of the econometric methodology as well as the results obtained are given in Labeaga et al. (2008).

The simulation of the effects of the reforms is carried out at both the individual and the social level. First, we quantify the efficiency costs by looking at changes in household labour supply. Given the discrete nature of the labour supply alternatives, the results are reported in terms of transition matrices (Section 3.1). The second step is the identification of winners and losers. This is done by comparing individual utility before and after the reform (Section 3.2).

The third and fourth evaluation exercises concern the social welfare effects of each reform. In Section 3.3 we compare the scenarios we have simulated, ordering them by a social welfare function which sums individuals' weighted indirect utility. The weights capture the social planner's inequality aversion. Several specifications are tested in order to carry out sensitivity analysis with respect to the social welfare function used.

In Section 3.4, an alternative social evaluation method is explored: this is based on a social welfare function which assigns weights to individual utilities measured in terms of equivalent incomes (King, 1983). With respect to the previous method, this approach has the advantage of not depending on the cardinalization of the individual utility function.

3.1 Efficiency effects

One of our main goals is to quantify the efficiency costs (measured in terms of hours of work) of the reforms. The reference scenario is the one in force in 1999. Tables A8 and A9 show the transition matrices for each reform. Rows (i) contain the observed distribution of working hours in 1999, whereas columns (j) show the predicted distribution under each simulated scenario. Each cell a_{ij} of the matrix (for $i \neq j$) shows the number of individuals (households) changing from the observed alternative i to the predicted alternative j. The diagonal elements refer to the number of individuals (households) that do not change their labour supply following the reform.

In Table A8 we present the results for the sub-sample of singles. The values to the right of the diagonal reflect individuals who increase their labour supply after the reform and vice versa. The first point to note is that almost all individuals remain on the diagonal, which means that the reforms have very little impact on labour supply. Comparing the 1999 scenario to that in 1998, we observe that two individuals who do not work in 1999 worked 40 hours in 1998, and three individuals working 40 hours or more reduce their labour supply (one of whom stops working). Along the same lines, the BIFT-25% scenario does not affect labour supply much either. This is due to the reduced flat tax and basic income. Three individuals increase their labour supply and three decrease it. The second point is that, as expected, the higher the marginal tax rate, the greater the labour supply effects. Under the BIFT-38% scenario, average hours of work fall by 3%. Under the BIFT-46% scenario, 6.2% of individuals reduce their labour supply (5% of individuals decide to stop working). The VMFT scheme produces only small labour market disincentives: total working hours remain almost constant.

Table A9 presents the transition matrices for couples. As there are nine possible alternatives, combining hours of work of the household head and his/her spouse, the table is somewhat more complicated. In this case, not all of the elements to the right (left) of the diagonal represent an increase (fall) in total hours of work. We may observe substitution between spouses' working hours. For example, under the scenario BIFT-38% we observe that 0.5% of the households (5 out of 1,015) move from 0_40 to 40_0. This means that under the 1999 system the household head does not work and the spouse works 40 hours; after the reform the head of the household works 40 hours and the spouse stops working (there is substitution between partners' hours of work). As in the previous case, two facts should be stressed.

First, the majority of households are on the diagonal, which implies that, on aggregate, they do not change their labour supply. Second, the higher is the marginal tax rate, the greater are the labour supply effects.

When comparing the 1998 system to that in 1999 we observe very few changes. We obtain more or less the same results under the scenario VMFT. With a flat tax of 25% or 30% there are no households entering or exiting the labour market. With a flat tax of 38% or 46% only one household stops working while another starts working. The picture is different under BIFT. In terms of total hours of work, the BIFT-38% reform reduces labour supply by 3%, while the BIFT-46% reform reduces hours of work by 4.3%. Again, the extreme case is BIFT-46%, in which 0.6% of households stop working and 4.7% clearly reduce their labour supply.

The main conclusion of this analysis is that, on average, the efficiency effects are negligible for all of the scenarios examined and for each household type. The only exceptions are for the BIFT scenarios with high flat tax rates (38% and 46%). Here, the average change in labour supply is around 5-6% (which cannot be considered as "negligible" in terms of the political feasibility of the reform).

3.2 Winners and losers

A first approximation of the welfare effects may be obtained by looking at the households whose utility increases after the reform (winners) and those for whom it falls (losers). In each reform there are winners and losers, but their distribution over the income deciles is not uniform. We find out which part of the population benefits or loses by analysing the distribution over income deciles. Unfortunately, this does not allow us to rank the reforms unequivocally in terms of social welfare.

The utility function is computed using the parameters estimated in Labeaga et al. (2008). For households that are not potential workers we calculate utility as follows. First, fiscal units are identified, following the criteria established by the Tax Agency (parents and children under 18 or disabled children). If the fiscal unit is a couple, the estimated coefficients for couples are used. On the other hand, if the fiscal unit is composed of one parent, without a spouse, the coefficients for singles are used. The other household members (grandparents, uncles, children over 18…) are treated as singles. Figure 1 presents the results for the whole sample; winners and losers from each reform are shown by income deciles.

Figure 1:   Winners and losers from reform options compared with 1999 system (whole sample)

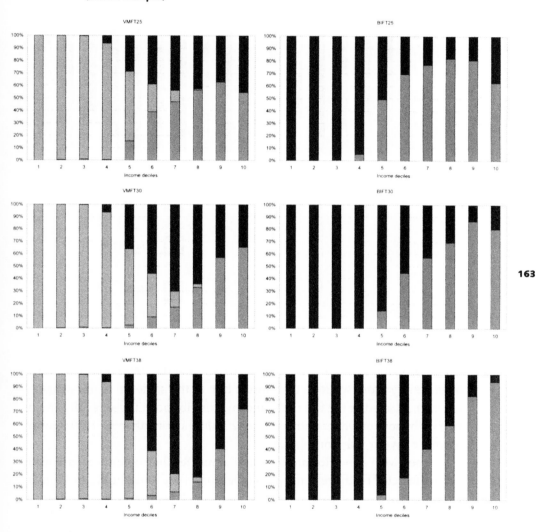

163

Figure 1: Winners and losers (whole sample) (continued)

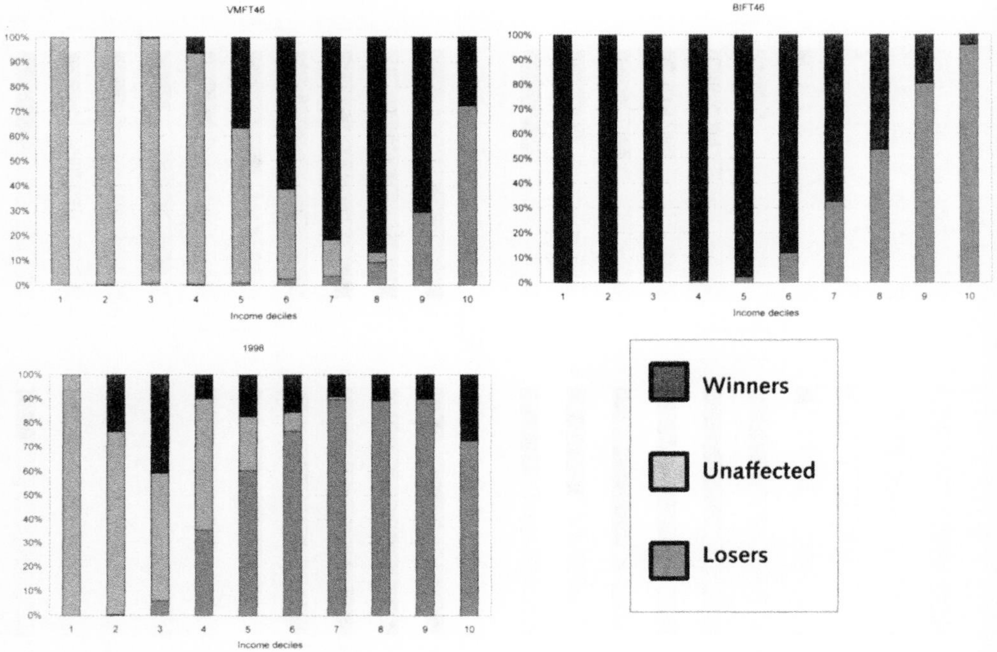

Comparing the 1998 and 1999 systems we see that the 1999 scenario is characterised by more winners than losers but, at the same time, the winners are concentrated at the top of the income distribution. These results are in line with those of Oliver and Spadaro (2004*b*) showing that the 1999 reform seems to favour rich households.

The VMFT scenarios produce similar results: the poorer deciles (1 to 4) are not affected by the reforms. This is because these households are largely exempt from income tax and are thus unaffected by the reform. In the other deciles we find more losers than winners: this is because the marginal tax rate increases. In particular, from the fourth to the seventh or eighth decile the number of winners increases progressively, and then decreases (except for the VMFT-25% reform, in which the winners represent between 35 and 45%, starting from the sixth decile). The losers appear in the fifth decile and their number increases progressively (except under VMFT-25%, where they are fewer in the last decile due to the low marginal tax rate). Except for the VMFT-25% reform, the number of winners always exceeds the number of losers.

The BIFT reforms affect everyone. Due to the presence of a basic income, the first deciles are composed of winners; the losers are concentrated in the higher deciles. Starting from the fourth and fifth deciles, the number of losers increases progressively. The higher is the basic income given to each household, the higher is the number of winners. From the comparison between the BIFT and the VMFT scenarios we see that, despite similar effects at higher incomes, the treatment of poor households in the BIFT increases the number of winners. This result can thus be considered as an argument in favour of BIFT.

3.3 *Social welfare evaluation: an optimal taxation approach*

One possible way to analyse the social desirability of the reforms consists in computing, under each of the systems evaluated, a social welfare function assigning a certain weight to each individual depending on the utility they obtain in each of the situations. This approach is typical in the optimal taxation framework (Mirrlees, 1971; Stern, 1976). This procedure has the advantage of summarizing in one number the welfare associated with each reform. However, it does require the specification of a social welfare function, which depends on the particular cardinalization of the utility function. The social welfare function used here is the following:[4]

$$W = \frac{1}{\lambda} \sum U_s(y,L,X)^\lambda + \frac{1}{\lambda} \sum \left[\pi * U_c(y,L,X) \right]^\lambda \tag{1}$$

where U_s and U_c represent singles' and couples' utility respectively, π is a parameter weighting couples' utility in the social welfare function, and λ is a parameter in $(-\infty, 1]$, capturing the social planner's aversion to inequality. For $\lambda = 1$, the planner puts the same marginal weight on every household (this is the utilitarian specification), while for $\lambda \rightarrow -\infty$ the government is only interested in the welfare of the poorest household (the Rawlsian specification).

The results are shown in Figure 2, in which we set $\pi = 2$.[5] On the x-axis, λ takes values from -2 (a social welfare function with greater inequality

---

4   To decrease the computational burden, the utility for couples and singles has been normalized to their respective means. The results of this section must be interpreted bearing in mind that they are not independent of the particular social welfare function used for the evaluation.

5   Other plausible values of the π parameter yield the same conclusions. These results are available upon request.

aversion) to 1 (utilitarian). On the y-axis, we show the percentage increase or decrease in social welfare with respect to the reference scenario (1999).

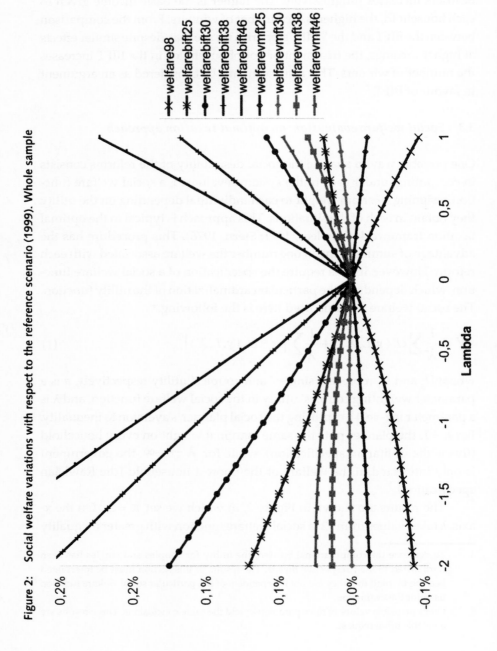

Figure 2: Social welfare variations with respect to the reference scenario (1999). Whole sample

The reform that seems to be optimal[6] (among the alternatives evaluated), for any social planner's inequality aversion specification, is BIFT-46%. The effects, in terms of welfare, of a higher basic income dominate the efficiency losses (in terms of labour supply) of a higher tax rate. This is certainly due to the small implicit extensive elasticities estimated in Labeaga et al. (2008). Other BIFT reforms with lower marginal tax rates are still more desirable than the VMFT or 1999 systems. The only exception occurs between the BIFT-25% and the VMFT-46% and VMFT-38% for utilitarian specifications of the social welfare function: in these cases the two VMFT schemes yield higher social welfare. The reason is that the lower level of basic income that can be assigned with a marginal tax of 25% is not sufficient to compensate, in terms of welfare, for the efficiency loss resulting from the higher (25%) marginal tax rate for poor households[7].

3.4 Social welfare evaluation: computing equivalent incomes

We complete the policy evaluation by computing equivalent incomes.[8] These allow us to construct a social welfare function in terms of money metric utility that does not depend on the cardinalization of the utility functions used.[9] A prior step to computing equivalent incomes is to calculate the equivalent variation for each household. This is defined by the amount of money that we must give to (or take away from) household i before the reform so that the household is unaffected by the reform. A positive (negative) equivalent variation indicates households which increase (decrease) their utility after the reform.

Equivalent incomes, Ye, may be computed using the equivalent variation VE for each household. The equivalent income is defined in terms of indirect utility, $V(\cdot)$, as:

$$V(t_a, Ye) = V(t, m) \tag{2}$$

where t_a is the reference price. Using the cost function:

---

6   In the sense that it yields the maximum value of social welfare.

7   Similar results are obtained from a separate analysis of couples and singles.

8   See Labeaga et al. (2008), King (1983) and Creedy and Duncan (2002).

9   Other money metric utility measures exist, such as the compensating variation or consumer surplus. The advantage of equivalent variation over the other measures is that the reference prices are those pre-reform. This property renders the comparison between the reforms easier.

$$Ye = E(t_a, V(t_b, m_b))$$ (3)

where $E(\cdot)$ is the cost function, t_a are prices before the reform and $V(t_b, m_b)$ is the utility level achieved after the reform. Using the 1999 system as the reference, equivalent income is:

$$Ye = y^0 + VE$$ (4)

This equivalent income is a measure of the welfare of each agent that does not depend on the cardinalization of the utility function used. It is then possible to build a social welfare function in the following way:

$$BS = \frac{1}{N\lambda} \sum (Ye)^\lambda$$ (5)

where, as in Section 3.3, λ is a parameter in $(-\infty, 1]$ which captures inequality aversion; N is the number of households.

Table 1:   Equivalent variations for each reform option (in euros)

Decile	1998 Disposable income (1)	46% BIFT (4,632) (2)	46% VMFT (13,997) (3)	38% BIFT (3,526) (4)	38% VMFT (12,002) (5)	30% BIFT (2,421) (6)	30% VMFT (9,589) (7)	25% BIFT (1,730) (8)	25% VMFT (7,737) (9)
1	0	4,729	0	3,600	0	2,472	0	1,767	0
2	1	4,441	0	3,353	3	2,264	1	1,590	0
3	6	3,099	0	2,227	0	1,351	2	811	0
4	-31	2,452	0	1,689	8	925	17	435	3
5	-150	2,134	115	1,396	104	641	92	213	7
6	-257	1,369	355	801	349	219	166	-117	-52
7	-301	717	688	324	482	-86	208	-291	-90
8	-337	-170	979	-273	597	-384	173	-449	-155
9	-407	-1,471	823	-1,143	259	-779	-132	-629	-312
10	-561	-4,011	-1,638	-2,436	-933	-809	-173	161	496
Mean	-204	1,328	132	953	87	581	35	349	-10

The distribution by income deciles of the equivalent variation for each reform is presented in Table 1. Again, the pre-reform scenario is the 1999 system. Table 1 shows that, on average, there is a loss of 200 euros per household under the 1998 system; this figure is larger for the top income deciles. On the contrary, the BIFT schemes produce significant improvements in terms of average welfare: the large positive equivalent variations for the bottom deciles compensate for the losses suffered by the top deciles. The BIFT schemes produce average equivalent variation figures of 1328€ (for a tax rate of 46%), 953€ (38%), 581€ (30%) and 349€ (25%). Under VMFT schemes, there is a small increase in average welfare resulting from the positive amounts computed for the deciles from 5 to 8-9.

Figures 3 and 4 show the results of the computation of the welfare function (5) for values of λ from -2 to 1. They represent the changes in social welfare *(BS)* using the system in force in 1999 as the reference scenario. In Figure 3 we compare the 1999, 1998 and VMFT scenarios. In Figure 4 we compare the reference system (1999) and the BIFT scenarios.[10] The first, and most important, result is that BIFT-46%, BIFT-38%, BIFT-30% and BIFT-25% yield (in that order) the highest values of social welfare independent of λ. Comparing Figures 3 and 4 we see that the rise in social welfare associated with BIFT is 50-60 times higher than that from VMFT. The basic income-flat tax scenarios seem to represent the best trade-off between equity and efficiency. They are much more effective in raising social welfare than a vital minimum-flat tax mechanism, independent of the social planner's aversion to inequality.

The other interesting result is that, with this social welfare evaluation methodology, VMFT schemes, and the 1998 and the 1999 systems produce very similar effects (see Figure 3). This is particularly true for social planners who are inequality-averse. The explanation is intuitive: the more Rawlsian the planner the less weight is given to changes at the middle or the top of the distribution. Since VMFT, 1999 and 1998 schemes have similar impacts on poorer households, their evaluation is practically the same.

The fact that this social evaluation technique suggests that basic income flat tax schemes are the most socially desirable redistribution mechanisms reinforces the results obtained in Section 3.3: the small labour supply effects and the large increase in the welfare of poor households support the BIFT mechanism as a powerful instrument for income redistribution.

---

10   We present the simulation results in two separate Figures in order to make them clearer, given the large difference in scale between the BIFT changes and those from the other scenarios.

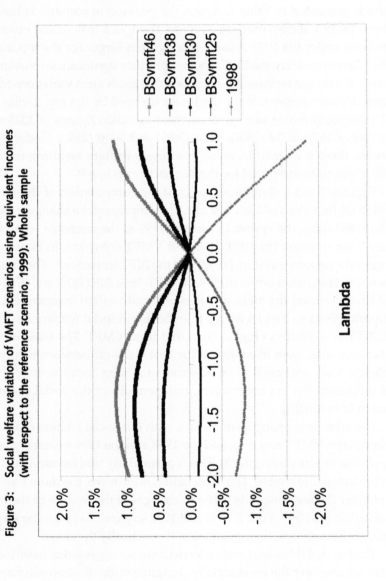

Figure 3: Social welfare variation of VMFT scenarios using equivalent incomes (with respect to the reference scenario, 1999). Whole sample

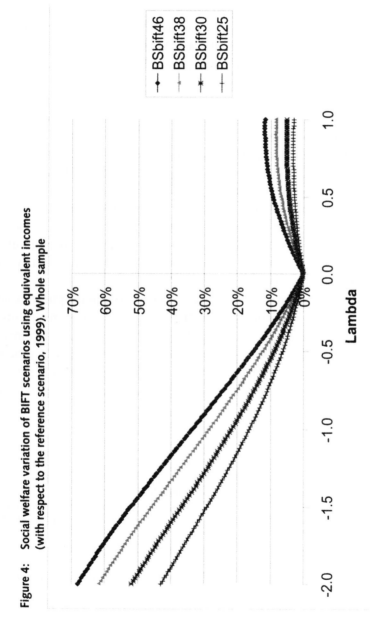

Figure 4: Social welfare variation of BIFT scenarios using equivalent incomes (with respect to the reference scenario, 1999). Whole sample

4   Conclusions

In this chapter we have evaluated the efficiency and welfare effects (both at the individual and social levels) of recent reforms of the Spanish Income Tax system, compared to some BIFT and VMFT alternatives. The analysis is carried out using a microsimulation model in which labour supply reactions are explicitly taken into account.

We have shown that the scenarios simulated have only a limited impact on the efficiency of the economy (as measured by labour supply effects). The welfare effects of the VMFT reforms are limited. On the other hand, the BIFT schemes lead to considerable improvements in the welfare of the poorest households (and thus social welfare). These results are robust to different social welfare evaluation techniques.

In our opinion, the contributions of this chapter are both methodological and policy-oriented. From a methodological point of view we have pointed out the limits and the short cuts of behavioural microsimulation analysis but, at the same time we have shown that it is a powerful tool for the *ex ante* evaluation of public policies.

With respect to policy, the main contribution of this chapter consists in highlighting the potential of a basic income–flat tax scheme as an institutional redistribution mechanism which can both reduce inequality and increase social welfare in Spain. Its feasibility depends on the associated efficiency costs (in terms of reductions in labour supply) that may result: given the results of our econometric estimations, it seems that these costs are small.

References

Aaberge, R. / Colombino, U. / Strom, S. (1995) 'Labor Supply Responses and Welfare Effects of Tax Reforms', *Scandinavian Journal of Economics* 97: 635-659.

Aaberge, R. / Colombino, U. / Strom, S. (2000) 'Welfare effects of proportional taxation: empirical evidence from Italy, Norway and Sweden', *Journal of Population Economics* 13 (4): 595-621.

Aaberge, R. / Colombino, U. / Vennemo, T. (2005) *"Evaluating Alternative Representations of the Choice Sets in Models of Labour Supply"*, mimeo.

Agencia Tributaria (2001) 'Informe anual de recaudación tributaria', *Servicio de auditoría interna*.

Anuario de Estadísticas Laborales y de Asuntos Sociales (2002) del Ministerio de Trabajo y Asuntos Sociales.

Arellano, M. / Bover, O. / Labeaga, J. M. (1999) 'Autoregressive Models with Sample Selectivity for Panel Data', chapter 2 in Hsiao, C. / Lahiri, K. / Lee, L.F. / Pesaran, M.H. (eds), *Analysis of Panels and Limited Dependent Variable Models.* Cambridge University Press.

Atkinson, A.B. (1995) *Public Economics in Action: A Basic Income-Flat Tax Proposal.* Oxford: Clarendon Press.

Auten, G. / Carroll, R. (1999) 'The Effect of Income Taxes on Household Income', *Review of Economics and Statistics* 81: 681-693.

Bargain (2005) 'On Modelling Household Labour Supply with Taxation', IZA DP No. 1455

Bingley, P. / Walker I. (1997) 'The Labour Supply, Unemployment and Participation of Lone Mothers in In-Work Transfer Programmes', *The Economic Journal*, 107: 1375-90.

Blundell, R. / Duncan, A. / McCrae, J. / Meghir, C. (2000) 'The Labour Market Impact of the Working Families-Tax Credit', *Fiscal Studies* 21: 75-104.

Bonin, H. / Kempe, W. / Schneider, H. (2002) "Household labour supply effects of low-wage subsidies in Germany", IZA DP, No. 637.

Bourguignon, F. / Spadaro, A. (2006) 'Microsimulation as a Tool for Evaluating Redistribution Policies', *Journal of Economic Inequality* 4 (1): 77-106.

Cantó, O. / Gago, A. / Gradín, C. / Del Río, C., (2002) 'La política fiscal en España durante el periodo 1982-1996', *Hacienda Pública Española, special issue:* 253-288.

Castañer, J.M. / Onrubia, J. / Paredes, R. (2000) 'Efectos de la reforma del IRPF sobre la renta disponible, su distribución y sobre el bienestar social', *Economistas* 84: 183-199.

Castañer, J.M. / Romero, D. / Sanz, J.F. (2004) *"Simulación sobre los hogares españoles de la reforma de IRPF de 2003. Efectos sobre oferta laboral, recaudación, distribución y bienestar"*, XI Encuentro de Economía Pública, Barcelona, February 5th and 6th, 2004.

Creedy, J. / Duncan, A.S. (2002) 'Behavioural Microsimulation with Labour Supply Responses', *Journal of Economic Surveys* 16: 1-39.

Das, M. / Van Soest, A. (2001) 'Family Labour Supply and Proposed Tax Reforms in the Netherlands', *De Economist*.

Feldstein, M. (1995), "The Effect of Marginal Tax Rates on Taxable Income: A Panel Study of the 1986 Tax Reform Act", *Journal of Political Economy* 103: 551-572.

García, J. / Suárez, M. J. (2002) 'La reforma del IRPF y la oferta laboral de las mujeres casadas', *Revista de Economía Aplicada* 10: 53-77.

Gruber, J. / Saez, E. (2002) 'The elasticity of taxable income: evidence and implications', *Journal of Public Economics* 84: 1-32.

Hausman J. (1981) 'Labour Supply', in: Aaron and Pechman (eds.), *How Taxes Affect Economic Behaviour.* Washington DC: The Brookings Institution.

Hausman J. (1985a) 'The Econometrics of Nonlinear Budget Sets', *Econometrica* 53: 1255-1282.

Hausman, J., (1985b) 'Taxes and Labour Supply', in: Auerbach, A. / Feldstein, M. (eds.), *Handbook of Public Economics*, Vol. 1. Amsterdam: North Holland.

Hoynes, H. (1996) 'Welfare Transfers in Two Parent Families: Labour Supply and Welfare Participation Under AFDC-UP', *Econometrica* 64: 295- 332.

Keane, M. / Moffit, R. (1998) 'A Structural Model of Multiple Welfare Program Participation and Labour Supply', *International Economic Review* 39: 553-589.

King, M. (1983) 'Welfare Analysis of Tax Reforms Using Household Data', *Journal of Public Economics* 21: 183-214.

Labeaga, J.M. / Oliver, X. / Spadaro, A. (2008) 'Discrete Choice Models of Labour Supply, Behavioural Microsimulation and the Spanish Tax Reforms', *Journal of Economic Inequality* 6 (3): 247-263.

Labeaga, J.M./Sanz, J.F. (2001) 'Oferta de trabajo y fiscalidad en España. Hechos recientes y tendencias tras el nuevo Impuesto sobre la Renta de las Personas Físicas', *Papeles de Economía Española* 87: 230-243.

Levy, H./Mercader-Prats, M. (2002) 'Simplifying the personal income tax system: lessons from the 1998 Spanish Reform', *Fiscal Studies* 23: 419-443.

MaCurdy, T.E. (1992) 'Work disincentive effects of taxes: a re-examination of some evidence', *American Economic Review* 24: 265-289.

MaCurdy, T./Green, D./Paarsch, H. (1990) 'Assessing Empirical Approaches for Analyzing Taxes and Labour Supply', *Journal of Human Resources* 25: 415-490.

Memoria de la Administración Tributaria (2001) *Ministerio de Economía y Hacienda.* Secretaría de Estado de Hacienda.

Mirrlees, J.A. (1971) 'An Exploration of the Theory of Optimal Income Taxation', *Review of Economic Studies* 39: 175-208.

Oliver, X./Spadaro, A. (2003) "Renta mínima o mínimo vital? Un análisis sobre los efectos redistributivos de posibles reformas del sistema impositivo español". *DEA Working Paper Series nº1.* Universitat de les Illes Balears. <http://www.uib.es/depart/deaweb/deawp/>

Oliver, X./Spadaro, A. (2004a) "A Technical Description of GLADHISPANIA: A Spanish Micro-Simulation Tax-Benefit Model". *DEA Working Paper Series nº7.* Universitat de les Illes Balears. <http://www.uib.es/depart/deaweb/deawp/>

Oliver, X./Spadaro, A. (2004b) 'Are Spanish Governments Really Averse to Inequality? A Normative Analysis using the 1999 Spanish Tax Reform', *Investigaciones Económicas* 28: 551-566.

Oliver, X./Spadaro, A. (2007) 'Basic Income or Vital Minimum? A Note on the Distributive Effects of Possible Reforms of the Spanish Income Tax', pp. 361-383 in: Harding, A./Gupta, A. (eds.), *Modeling our Future: Population Ageing, Social Security and Taxation.* International Symposium in Economic Theory and Econometrics, Vol. 15. Amsterdam: Elsevier.

Prieto, J./Álvarez, S. (2002) "Análisis de las ganancias de bienestar asociadas a los efectos de la reforma del IRPF sobre la oferta laboral de la familia española", *Instituto de Estudios Fiscales, DT 7.*

Sanchís, J.A./Sanchís, A.S. (2001) 'Análisis de simulación de los efectos distributivos de la reforma del IRPF de 1999', in: Labeaga, J.M./Mercader-Prats, M. (eds.), *Desigualdad, redistribución y bienestar: una aproximación a partir de la microsimulación de reformas fiscales.* Madrid: Instituto de Estudios Fiscales.

Stern, N. (1976) 'On the specification of models of optimum income taxation', *Journal of Public Economics* 6: 123-162.

Stern, N. (1986) 'On the Specification of Labour Supply Functions', in: Blundell, R./Walker, I. (eds.), *Unemployment, Search and Labour Supply.* Cambridge University Press.

Van Soest, A. (1995) 'Structural Models of Family Labour Supply. A Discrete Choice Approach', *Journal of Human Resources,* 30: 63-88.

Annex A

Table A1: **Comparison of updated 1995 ECHP with 1998 and 1999 ECHP (in Euro)**

Household mean disposable income	PHOGUE	PHOGUE 1995 (updated)	Difference
1998	18,334	18,130.6	-1.11%
1999	18,375	19,311	5.09%

Table A2: **Calibration of GLADHISPANIA (in billions of Euro)**

	1998			1999		
	Official Statistics	Gladhis-pania	Differ-ence	Official Statistics	Gladhis-pania	Differ-ence
	(1)	(2)	(3) = (2-1)/1	(4)	(5)	(6) = (5-4)/4
Personal Income Tax collection[a]	39.2	39.1	-0.25%	39.54	37.83	-4.33%
Average income Tax rate[c] = (net tax/ taxable income)	15.13%	15.59%	3.03%	23.15%	23.87%	3.12%
Employee Social Security contributions[b]	13.7	13.37	-2.40%	2,424	14.26	-2.13%

(a)   Source: Informe Anual de Recaudación Tributaria de 2001.

(b)   Source: Anuario de Estadísticas Laborales y de Asuntos Sociales 2002.

(c)   Source: Memoria de la Administración Tributaria 2001.

Table A3: Descriptive statistics of the variables used in the econometric section

SINGLES			COUPLES		
Variable	Mean	Standard Deviation	Variable	Mean	Standard deviation
Yearly Disposable Income	14,692	9,559	Yearly Disposable Income	24,030	15,756
Weekly Hours of Leisure	135.22	17			
			Children (in %):		
Age	41.8	11.3	no children	24.3	
Education (in %):			one child	30.4	
university graduate	37.1		two children	38.3	
secondary school	21.2		three children or more	7.0	
less than secondary school	41.7				
			Head of the household:		
Children (in %):			Weekly Hours of Leisure	127.7	11.6
no children	83.4		Age	38.9	8.3
one child	10.4		Education (in %):		
two children	5.02		university graduate	30.8	
three children	1.16		secondary school	19.9	
			less than secondary school	49.3	
			Spouse:		
			Weekly Hours of Leisure	153.1	18.5
			Age	36.6	8.1
			Education (in %):		
			university graduate	25.6	
			secondary school	20.7	
			less than secondary school	53.7	
Number of observations	259		**Number of observations**	1,015	

Table A4: Social Security contribution and Monthly Minimum and Maximum Base (in Euro)

	1998		1999			
Minimum base	477 (= minimum wage/12)		485.7 (= minimum wage/12)			
Maximum base	2,360		2,402.7			
	Firm		**Worker**		**Total**	
Contribution Items	**1998**	**1999**	**1998**	**1999**	**1998**	**1999**
General contingencies	23.6%	23.6%	4.7%	4.7%	28.3%	28.3%
Mean no. of industrial accidents and professional illnesses	4%	4%	0%	0%	4%	4%
Unemployment						
Full-time worker (permanent worker)	6.2%	6.2%	1.6%	1.6%	7.8%	7.8%
Full-time worker (temporary worker)	6.2%	6.7%	1.6%	1.6%	7.8%	8.3%
Part-time worker	6.2%	7.7%	1.6%	1.6%	7.8%	9.3%
Social welfare fund	0.4%	0.4%	0%	0%	0.4%	0.4%
Professional training	0.6%	0.6%	0.1%	0.1%	0.7%	0.7%

Table A5: Tax rates schedule (in Euro)

1998				1999	
Single Person's income tax return		**Family income tax return**		**Single person's and family income tax return**	
Bracket	Tax rate	Bracket	Tax rate	Bracket	Tax rate
0-2,806.73	0	0-5,415.12	0	0-3,606.07	0.18
2,806.73-6,977.75	0.2	5,415.12-13,492.72	0.2	3,606.07-12,621.25	0.24
6,977.75-13,793.23	0.23	13,492.72-19,028.04	0.246	12,621.25-24,641.50	0.283
13,793.23-21,005.37	0.28	19,028.04-26,390.44	0.29	24,641.50-39,666.08	0.372
21,005.37-30,621.57	0.32	26,390.44-35,255.37	0.33	39,666.08-66,111.33	0.45
30,621.57-40,838.77	0.39	35,255.37-47,485.97	0.39	> 66,111.33	0.48
40,838.77-51,837.29	0.45	47,485.97-59,716.56	0.45		
51,837.29-63,106.27	0.52	59,716.56-72,938.83	0.53		
> 63,106.27	0.56	> 72,938.83	0.56		

Table A6: Advantages and disadvantages of the reforms based on a flat tax

Advantages	Disadvantages
✓ Eliminating all the current allowances and deductions would broaden the tax base. Then, all sources of income are treated equally (horizontal equity).	✓ These schemes can affect labour supply of the more productive people if the flat tax is too high.
✓ Simplicity for taxpayers, and consequently, more transparency, since all income is taxed at the same rate)	✓ High rates can cause capital flows toward other countries with better capital fiscal treatment.
✓ Simplicity for the Treasury Department, and thus, minor collection costs and less tax evasion.	✓ Lower flat taxes can generate redistribution towards the rich.

Table A7: BIFT and VMFT: simulated scenarios (in Euro)

	BIFT	VMFT
Flat tax	Basic Income	Vital Minimum
46%	4,632	13,997
38%	3,526	12,002
30%	2,421	9,589
25%	1,730	7,737

Table A8: Singles transition matrixes (the reference system is the one of 1999)

		1998				
		0	30	40	50	Total
1999	0	48		2		50
	30		34			34
	40	1		127		128
	50		1	1	45	47
	Total	49	35	130	45	259
		BIFT25				
		0	30	40	50	Total
1999	0	48		2		50
	30		34			34
	40	1		126	1	128
	50			1	46	47
	Total	49	34	129	47	259
		BIFT30				
		0	30	40	50	Total
1999	0	50				50
	30		34			34
	40	3		124	1	128
	50		1	1	45	47
	Total	53	35	125	46	259
		BIFT38				
		0	30	40	50	Total
1999	0	50				50
	30	2	31	1		34
	40	3	1	120	4	128
	50	2	1		44	47
	Total	57	33	121	48	259
		BIFT46				
		0	30	40	50	Total
1999	0	50				50
	30	2	31	1		34
	40	8	1	115	4	128
	50	3	1	1	42	47
	Total	63	33	117	46	259

Table A8 (continued)

		VMFT25				
		0	30	40	50	Total
1999	0	49		1		50
	30		34			34
	40			127	1	128
	50			1	46	47
	Total	49	34	129	47	259
		VMFT30				
		0	30	40	50	Total
1999	0	49		1		50
	30		34			34
	40			127	1	128
	50			2	45	47
	Total	49	34	130	46	259
		VMFT38				
		0	30	40	50	Total
1999	0	49		1		50
	30		33	1		34
	40		1	126	1	128
	50			3	44	47
	Total	49	34	131	45	259
		VMFT46				
		0	30	40	50	Total
1999	0	48	1	1		50
	30		33	1		34
	40	1	1	124	2	128
	50	1		3	43	47
	Total	50	35	129	45	259

Table A9: Couples transition matrixes (the reference system is the one of 1999)

	hm_hf	0_0	0_25	0_40	40_0	40_25	40_40	50_0	50_25	50_40	Total
					1998						
	0_0	4						1			5
	0_25		5								5
	0_40			58							58
	40_0				395		1	1			397
1999	40_25				1	59					60
	40_40						194				194
	50_0							203	1		204
	50_25								24		24
	50_40				1					67	68
	Total	4	5	58	397	59	195	205	25	67	1015

	hm_hf	0_0	0_25	0_40	40_0	40_25	40_40	50_0	50_25	50_40	Total
					BIFT25						
	0_0	5									5
	0_25		5								5
	0_40	1		54	3						58
	40_0	1			393			2		1	397
1999	40_25				4	56					60
	40_40			1			188	5			194
	50_0	2			1			201			204
	50_25								24		24
	50_40				1		1	1		65	68
	Total	9	5	55	402	56	189	209	24	66	1015

	hm_hf	0_0	0_25	0_40	40_0	40_25	40_40	50_0	50_25	50_40	Total
					BIFT30						
	0_0	5									5
	0_25		5								5
	0_40	1		54	3						58
	40_0	1			395			1			397
1999	40_25			1	5	54					60
	40_40	1		1	4		182	6			194
	50_0	2			1			201			204
	50_25			1					23		24
	50_40				2		1	1		64	68
	Total	10	5	57	410	54	183	209	23	64	1015

	hm_hf	0_0	0_25	0_40	40_0	40_25	40_40	50_0	50_25	50_40	Total
					BIFT38						
	0_0	5									5
	0_25		5								5
	0_40	1		52	5						58
	40_0	1			396						397
1999	40_25			1	6	52		1			60
	40_40	1		1	14	1	169	8			194
	50_0	3			2			199			204
	50_25			1					23		24
	50_40			2	2			1		63	68
	Total	11	5	57	425	53	169	209	23	63	1015

Table A9 (continued)

	hm_hf	0_0	0_25	0_40	40_0	40_25	40_40	50_0	50_25	50_40	Total
					BIFT46						
	0_0	5									5
	0_25		5								5
	0_40	1		52	5						58
	40_0	1			396						397
1999	40_25			1	8	49	1	1			60
	40_40	1		1	20	1	158	13			194
	50_0	3			7			194			204
	50_25			1					23		24
	50_40			3	7			1		57	68
	Total	11	5	58	443	50	159	209	23	57	1015

	hm_hf	0_0	0_25	0_40	40_0	40_25	40_40	50_0	50_25	50_40	Total
					VMFT25						
	0_0	5									5
	0_25		5								5
	0_40			58							58
	40_0				393			3		1	397
1999	40_25				2	58					60
	40_40			1			188	5			194
	50_0							204			204
	50_25								24		24
	50_40						1	1		66	68
	Total	5	5	59	395	58	189	213	24	67	1015

	hm_hf	0_0	0_25	0_40	40_0	40_25	40_40	50_0	50_25	50_40	Total
					VMFT30						
	0_0	5									5
	0_25		5								5
	0_40			56	1	1					58
	40_0				393			3	1		397
1999	40_25			1	3	56					60
	40_40			1	4	1	182	6			194
	50_0							204			204
	50_25								24		24
	50_40						1	1		66	68
	Total	5	5	58	401	58	183	214	25	66	1015

	hm_hf	0_0	0_25	0_40	40_0	40_25	40_40	50_0	50_25	50_40	Total
					VMFT38						
	0_0	4		1							5
	0_25		5								5
	0_40			56	1	1					58
	40_0				389	1		5	1	1	397
1999	40_25			1	3	55		1			60
	40_40	1		1	10	1	173	8			194
	50_0							203	1		204
	50_25								24		24
	50_40			1		1				66	68
	Total	5	5	60	403	59	173	217	26	67	1015

Table A9 (continued)

	Hm_hf	0_0	0_25	0_40	40_0	40_25	40_40	50_0	50_25	50_40	Total
					VMFT46						
1999	0_0	4		1							5
	0_25		5								5
	0_40			56	1	1					58
	40_0				388	1	1	5	1	1	397
	40_25			1	4	54	1				60
	40_40	1			13	1	170	9			194
	50_0				2			201	1		204
	50_25								24		24
	50_40			2	1		1			64	68
	Total	5	5	60	409	57	173	215	26	65	1015

Note: hm = hours of male; hf = hours of female

Chapter 7

Microsimulating Supply/Demand Interactions on a Labour Market: a Prototype

Muriel Barlet / Didier Blanchet / Thomas Le Barbanchon

1 Introduction

There is a long tradition of microsimulation models being applied to labour
market issues but most of them concentrate on supply-side aspects – i.e. the
incidence of taxes or social transfers on households' decisions to enter the
labour market and/or their decisions to supply a larger or smaller number
of hours. The evaluation of *demand-side* policies generally relies on other
instruments. In France, the most important of these demand-side policies
over the last 15 years has been the reduction of employer's contributions on
low wages, the idea being to boost labour demand through the reduction of
labour costs. Many efforts have been devoted to assessing the impact of this
policy (L'Horty, 2006), the dominant tools being macro-econometric or CGE
models for *ex ante* evaluations and micro-econometric techniques for *ex post*
evaluations, whose general principle is to perform controlled comparisons
of elementary units (firms or individuals) who benefit or do not benefit from
the policy under review (Crépon and Desplatz, 2001).

Such instruments have proved useful and should remain so in the
future, but all of them have their limits. Macro-econometric or CGE models
remain too aggregate to simulate adequately the detailed impact of policies that are strongly modulated according to workers' characteristics. And

An earlier version of this paper was presented at the seminar of the *"Département des Etudes
Economiques d'Ensemble"*, INSEE. We thank participants to this seminar and more specifically
its discussant, François Legendre, for his very helpful comments, as well as participants to the
first IMA conference. Any errors or shortcomings of this new version remain ours.

micro-econometric evaluation techniques are always suspected of insufficient control for various sources of bias, such as unobserved heterogeneity among elementary units or general equilibrium effects.

Given these limits, it is interesting to explore whether microsimulation models could be enriched to deal simultaneously with these two dimensions of labour supply and labour demand. The obvious advantage of microsimulation is to allow the description of targeted policies at a very detailed level. The reason why it has not been more extensively used for analysing demand-side policies, at this stage, probably stems from doubts about the ability to deal in a simple way with interactions between supply and demand or other general equilibrium effects. Some models are starting however to emerge that address this question, and which are at the confluent between traditional microsimulation and the more recent current of agent-based computational economics (ACE, see Colander et al., 2008, or LeBaron and Tesfatsion, 2008). Examples of such models are Fagiolo (2004) and Neugart (2008). The present model is a prototype belonging to this family.

Just to give a flavour of what this model tries to do, one can describe it as providing an integrated simulation of entries into and exits from the labour force and of the process of job creation/destruction. Jobs can destruct due to general or idiosyncratic shocks on productivity, on wages, on prices or on demand. Existing jobs become vacant due to retirement or spontaneous exits by employees. New jobs are created according to expected profitability and global demand for goods and services. A matching process takes place between vacant jobs and unemployed people, segmented by skill level. Wage negotiations also take place each year for insiders. The model can deliver predictions on many variables: unemployment and employment rates, gross and net flows on the labour market, wages, tenure, and duration of unemployment spells, with the possibility of differentiating all the data according to age and skill level.

At this stage, all this is done on a dynamic sample of individuals and jobs that is not directly derived from empirical data, but constructed in order to reflect basic characteristics of the French labour market. In that sense, this version of the model differs from "standard" microsimulation models that are generally based on survey data or on individual data drawn from administrative sources. Basing the model on actual micro-data has been left for future research at this stage. Yet the model is clearly a model of microsimulation in the sense that it fully simulates interactions between economic agents at the micro-level, taking into account the heterogeneity that exists between all these agents, and taking into account factors that randomly affect that heterogeneity.

Our chapter is organized as follows. The next section will present the main choices retained for the general structure of the model. The following one will present the calibration and the results of a central simulation. The last section will examine how the model reacts to various shocks or policy changes: demographic shocks, modification of the minimum wage and changes in the level of employers' contributions. Although still a prototype, the model is already able to provide orders of magnitudes for the impact of such shocks or changes that make sense. On the other hand, these results should be still considered as preliminary. The calibration of the model remains very imperfect, and more systematic explorations of its properties are required before moving to operational applications.

2   The general structure of the model

2.1   *Choosing the basic unit on the demand side: firms or jobs?*

The general architecture of the model derives from a compromise between objectives and achievability. The objective is to simultaneously simulate labour-supply by individuals and labour demand by firms in a dynamic framework. The first strategic choice to make is to characterize the elementary units that the model will simulate. On the supply-side, the choice is natural: the elementary unit is the individual (eventually taking into account the structure of his household in later versions). On the demand-side, the choice is more open: are we going to simulate firms, or local units, or even groups of firms? Such a problem was already raised in Orcutt's seminal paper (1957) and the difficulty in choosing the appropriate level of analysis is certainly an additional reason for the under-development of demand-oriented models.

The main problem with the "firm", "local unit" or "group" approaches is the very strong heterogeneity of these units. The population of firms is made up of a few big entities and very large numbers of smaller entities. Keeping firms of both types in a unique microsimulated sample would be extremely tricky. Usually, in business surveys, this problem is solved by using weights that differ according to firms' sizes. The same approach might be used in a microsimulation context if we were only interested in simulating the behaviour of these firms, i.e. the demand-side of the labour market. However, applying the same strategy in a model that matches firms and workers would imply these workers' weights to depend upon the size of their firms. The weights would then have to vary when workers moved from one firm to another and/or when the sizes of their firms fluctuated. And what about the weight to be applied when the worker falls into unemployment? It seems difficult to find an elegant way to deal with this first problem.

In addition, the heterogeneity according to size is associated with a high amount of *qualitative* heterogeneity. In the model, we would have to simulate firms' decisions to open vacancies, to close jobs, to define the qualification required for each job… Can we simulate such decisions in the same way for micro-firms or large ones? Do we even have a reasonable micro-model of how such decisions are actually taken in large production units?

Finally, in a dynamic context, another issue would be the difficulty of accounting for the *demography* of firms. Differential growth of firms, closures, creations, and reorganization constitute a permanent process that continuously reshapes the population of firms and a lot of energy would be required to model that process in a satisfactory way.

As a consequence, even if microsimulating hiring or firing decisions at the firm level would be full of insights and remains a long-term objective, we have decided to choose a simpler approach that models labour demand directly at the level of jobs. Jobs will be created or destroyed without regard for the kind of unit they belong to. This simpler solution is also the one chosen in theoretical matching models. Such a solution limits somewhat the range of effects that the model will be able to analyse. For instance, the model will not be able to simulate policies that are aimed at firms with some specific sizes. But the advantages of this approach largely outweigh its drawbacks, at least at this stage.

2.2 *What sources for inter-individual heterogeneity?*

A second central choice for the architecture of the model consists in choosing the criteria according to which individuals or jobs are going to differentiate from each other. We want a model that describes wage heterogeneity and the different individual probabilities of being unemployed. Obviously, this could be done in a single good/type of job framework. All individuals would produce the same good in equivalent jobs but with different efficiencies. High-qualified and non-qualified workers would be perfectly substitutable and would compete to produce this unique good. But this would obviously under-exploit the possibilities offered by microsimulation. At the other extreme, one could imagine fully differentiated goods, in the spirit of models of monopolistic competition. In that case, we would have to define demand and price functions for each job, a solution that is clearly excessively demanding.

The solution that has been retained is intermediate. We define a limited number of products/types of jobs, which will be equal to four in the following application. These four types of products/jobs correspond to four qualification levels, i.e. product number 1 will be the typical product or service produced by unskilled (US) workers, up to product 4 that will be the typical good/service produced by high-skilled (HS) workers. For each type of good, a unit price and an overall demand will be introduced in the model. For instance, Price(HS) will be the market price of the good produced by high-skilled workers. The kind of good/service produced will be a characteristic of the job, but the ability for a given worker to occupy a given job will depend on his qualification. High skill workers will be – in principle – able to work on all existing kinds of jobs, while unskilled workers can only work on US-type of jobs for the production of "US-type" goods/ services. This possibility for skilled workers to work on less skilled jobs has been introduced with the idea of simulating downgrading effects, although this possibility will not be used in this chapter.

2.3 An overview of what the model describes at a given point in time

Given all these clarifications, we are now able to give a complete list of variables simulated by the model at a given point in time. At the beginning of a given period, there is a certain number of jobs indexed by j, each of them belonging to one of the four types ($k=NQ$ to HQ) and a certain number of individuals indexed by i. Variables associated with individual i are:

- age,
- qualification equal to US, LS, MS and HS,
- the efficiencies of this worker in the four types of jobs,
- his/her current employment status of the individual,
- the identifier j(i) of his/her current job, if employed,
- his/her gross wage,
- the length of the current unemployment spell (or of the last one if the individual is currently working).

We have a parallel set of variables defined for jobs:

- the job level (i.e. the kind of good/service produced by that job which is equivalent to the minimum qualification level required to hold that job),
- the identification number i(j) of the individual who holds the job (hence i[j]=j[i]),
- the real production (volume) on that job if occupied: it will be equal to the efficiency level of the jobholder.
- this production valued at current prices,
- the labour cost, equal to the wage augmented with social contributions.
- the mark-up by the employer, i.e. the relative gap between production and the labour cost.
- the number of periods already spent by the current holder on this job,
- the duration of the contract if it is a short-term one.

190   From these individual variables, the model derives two kinds of aggregate variables: those which are of interest as output variables (whose list can be enlarged depending on user's needs) and those that are also requested as inputs for some of the steps of the simulation. For instance, average unemployment levels will play a role in individual wage negotiations; or the average mark-up for employers will play a role in the evolutions of labour demand. The model also uses a small set of macro variables that are not derived from micro-level information: prices for the four types of goods belong to this category since the model treats them as exogenous, the implicit assumption being that we are in a small open economy where prices are determined by the international environment.

2.4 Simulation of a typical time period: the first steps

We now move on to the description of events that are simulated over a given time period. Currently, the time step of the model is one year but it could be modified with relatively few changes (albeit at higher calibration costs). The simulation is sequential. Broadly speaking, during a time period, we first simulate demographic evolutions, then different forms of separations occur, followed by some wage-negotiations by workers who remain in their jobs. The last step is the simulation of new hirings, except in the case of very adverse economic conditions, where no new hirings at all would be demanded by employers. Let's examine these different steps in more detail.

At the beginning of the period, age and durations in employment or unemployment are first increased by one year. Then aged workers retire and new individuals enter the labour market. In the baseline scenario, the rotation rate of the population is equal to the inverse of the working-age length (40 years) and is the same for all qualifications. The young people who enter the labour market are first considered as unemployed.

In the second step, three different kinds of separations take place. The first two ones are modelled in a very simple way.

- We first simulate the end of short-term contracts with some conversions of the most profitable ones into permanent contracts.
- We then simulate exogenous separations: at each period such separations occur for a fraction δ of jobs. This rate of exogenous separations encompasses all aspects of labour supply behaviour that are not modelled elsewhere. Namely, the exogenous separation represents quit decisions and job-to-job mobility.

The third type of separation is economic lay-offs, whose probability increases when mark-up rates decrease and that become systematic for jobs on which the mark-up rate is less than a minimum threshold.

This mark-up rate is computed for each job but it has both global and individual determinants. Global determinants include technological shocks or shocks on prices. We are not going to present any results of this kind, but such macro-shocks can be simulated with the model. Another group of global determinants of the mark-up rate are social security contributions or the minimum wage: we shall discuss simulations where these two policy parameters change. At the individual level, the most critical individual determinant of the mark-up rate is individual efficiency. Individual efficiencies already differ across individuals when they enter the labour force. Then, at each time period, workers face idiosyncratic productivity shocks simulated as random walks, with a positive drift that accounts for learning by doing effects (especially true for the most qualified). To sum up, an individual can be laid-off either because of macro- or micro-shocks on the value of what he/she produces, or because of adverse changes in his labour cost due, for instance, to social contributions or minimum wage policies.

Once all these different categories of separations have been simulated, we simulate wage bargaining for insiders, i.e. for individuals that have remained in their job. It is done at the individual level, but here again under the influence of the macro-economic context. We make the assumption that each insider knows the maximal wage above which he/she would be fired for sure (it corresponds to the one paid by an employer gaining the minimum mark-up on the job). The insider determines a target wage between his/her current wage and this maximal wage. The cursor between these two wage levels is modulated according to the current unemployment rate for his or her level of qualification. It must be noticed that such a wage bargaining process precludes downward wage flexibility, an hypothesis that we considered as realistic, but that remains disputable. Symmetrically, partial upward inertia is generated by supposing that only one part of the gap between the current wage and the target is filled each time. It is noteworthy that, with all these assumptions, tenure will be an indirect determinant of the mark-up rate. The longer an individual has been in a job, the higher his wage and the lower the mark-up for the employer.

2.5 Completing the simulation for a given year: job creations and matching

At the end of this first series of events, the amount of employment is necessarily lower than the one that prevailed at the end of the previous period. The last step of the simulation will consist either in increasing the number of matches between jobs and individuals to fit the production targets of this new period, or eventually simulating some additional separations in the case of very adverse economic conditions.

How do we compute production targets for each type of jobs/goods? In the current version of the model, this target production is nothing else than the production of the previous period, corrected by one or two factors, among the three following ones: a "classical" factor and one of two "Keynesian" factors that have been introduced to account for cyclical macroeconomic movements.

The "classical" factor is linked to the difference between the current mean mark-up rate and a reference mark-up rate. If the mean mark-up rate for a given qualification is below this reference (resp. above), the desired production capacity will be lower (resp. greater) than the previous target production.

The two "Keynesian" factors are never simultaneously effective. The first one puts an exogenous upper limit to the demand for goods (Keynesian depression). The second parameter is an exogenous factor of Keynesian stimulation that has the effect of boosting the growth of labour demand beyond what would naturally result from changes in the mark-up rate. In the baseline scenario, these parameters are ineffective: by default the model evolves in a "classical" environment.

Target employment is then computed by dividing target production by the average efficiency observed among employed workers. Two situations may occur:

- Either the employment target is less than the level of employment that has resulted from separations simulated during the first stage. Such a case is not very likely but, in such an event, the model simulates the requested number of additional separations (by decreasing order of individual mark-up rates).

- Or the employment target is higher than the number of jobs still occupied after separations or lay-offs. In that case, there is a simulation of hires. For each qualification, workers unemployed for more than 1 year (we exclude the workers fired in the current period) are listed. A fraction of them is randomly selected to become employed. This selection can be viewed as a simple way to represent the friction in the hiring process and will certainly have to be improved in future versions of the model. If the number of the unemployed selected is greater than the target employment, we randomly exclude the surplus. Then we match the selected unemployed with vacancies. It is worth noting that, at the end of this process, target employment may still not be reached. Such a case will correspond to a case of demand rationing: employers are not able to fill all the vacancies that they have posted.

How is the wage determined for each new individual match? We suppose that the employer cannot observe his/her employee's efficiency when he/she is hired. It is only one year after the match that this productivity is fully known to the employer, eventually leading to a lay-off if it appears excessively low. This will lead to a strong concentration of "economic" separations among individuals with low experience. Because employers lack the relevant information, hiring wages are set according to the following norm: if individuals are employed for their first time, their wage is the minimum wage (for the non-qualified workers) or a multiple (increasing by the qualification) of the minimum wage; for individuals that have already worked, hiring wages are a fixed markdown on their last wage.

The type of contract, short-term or permanent contract, is randomly attributed among the new hired workers.

This hiring process is the last step of the simulation for year t. At the end of this step, the employed population can be divided between two groups. The first one corresponds to workers with at least one year of tenure in their current job, who have renegotiated their wages during this particular year. This wage bargaining may have brought them closer to the risky zone (i.e. prone to economic lay-off). The second group is made up of newly hired workers that are still not attached to their jobs, in the sense that their employers do not know yet if their efficiency is high enough to make the match profitable. This makes them strongly exposed to the risk of being laid-off at the next period.

3 Model calibration and data initialization

The calibration and simulations presented hereafter are conducted on a population representing around $1/2000^{th}$ of wage-earners in the French private sector (8,250 individuals). This relatively small sample is the one that is used for the development of the model. Its small size naturally affects the stability of results, which is another reason for cautiousness in their interpretation.

The objective of the calibration is to make the characteristics of the simulated population as close as possible to a set of observable statistics of the French labour market. First, we want to reproduce average "static" features of the labour market by qualification. We devote special attention to unemployment rates, average wages and the number of people working under short-term contracts. We also want average mark-up rates to lie in a reasonable range around observed values. We complete these static controls by checks of some dynamic properties. We try to reproduce the labour market turnover by qualification. In other words, we try to simultaneously adjust unemployment rates and average employment duration. Growth rates of wages are also taken into account.

Regarding individual heterogeneity, we seek to reproduce the proportions of workers whose wages lie in specific intervals above the minimum wage. We could have been more demanding by taking care of other distributional characteristics of wages or employment durations. Matching the variance or the median of such distributions is left for future work.

First we describe the empirical data that are going to be used for calibration. Then we explain how, for a given set of parameters, we generate the full distribution of characteristics for the populations of persons and jobs simulated by the model. We then explain how parameters have been calibrated in order to make the characteristics of these simulated populations as close as possible to data. This is done by combining exogenous information, guesstimates and indirect inference for the few parameters on which we had very little information *a priori*.

3.1 Data

The calibration of the model is based on two different datasets: the *"enquête emploi"* (labour force survey) and the *"Déclarations annuelles de données sociales"* (DADS). The *enquête emploi* is a quarterly survey. Since 2002, it has provided a longitudinal dataset where individuals appear six consecutive quarters. It contains information about employment status, earnings, hours worked and relatively detailed individual characteristics. The DADS is a longitudinal dataset available from 1976-2004, which provides information on every job held in the private, state-owned, local government and non-profit sectors by every worker in France.

We exploit the LFS sample to compute target moments relative to unemployment (rate of unemployment by qualification, duration of unemployment...) and the DADS sample to compute target moments for wages (means, standard deviation and growth rate). We calculate the distribution of workers among the four different job levels and the numbers in short-term contracts thanks to the LFS dataset.

The qualification of employees depends on his/her socio-occupational category. For unemployed people, we use the socio-occupational category of their previous job; for unemployed people who have never worked, we use their level of education.

It is important to note that rates of unemployment used for the calibration and that are going to be simulated are bigger than the usual measures – because the reference population is not the whole labour force but the labour force minus civil servants, self-employed and company managers.

3.2 Initialization of individual characteristics

The model includes many parameters, and what we must build with these parameters is a full sample of the population and of jobs that will adequately reproduce the main features of the French labour market. We shall first explain how the sample is built for given values of parameters and we shall then explain in the next section, how parameters are themselves optimized to generate a sample with desirable characteristics.

How is the individual base built? Two steps are needed. The first step consists in approximating the distributions of individual characteristics by sampling individuals and jobs from a priori distributions. These distributions are intuited both from data (for example wage distributions by qualification) and from the structure of the model. This first step includes four substeps.

- We first build the population of individuals. Qualifications are attributed according to existing data. We randomly assign ages.
- Individual efficiencies for these individuals are drawn from age-dependent distributions. The median values for productivities are constrained to unity. This is nothing else than an accounting convention consisting in using median productivities as measurement units for volumes of the four kinds of goods. Growth rates of productivity with age are chosen to parallel qualification-specific wage profiles. The heterogeneity within age groups is controlled through the first quartile of the distribution. It is chosen to get shares of low wage-earners as close as possible to observed ones.
- We then match individuals and jobs. Applying the reference mark-up to the productivity of each individual, we obtain real labour costs for each employee. We then choose prices for each type of good such that the mean nominal labour cost by qualification is reproduced. We thus obtain production in value by jobs and, taking into account social contributions, individual nominal wages.
- Finally, contract types and employment duration are randomly assigned within the specific population.

Once this first step has been completed, distributions that are obtained do not necessarily correspond to a steady-state situation. Dynamic simulations based on such a sample would be therefore affected by non-informative transitory changes. The final use we want to make of the model is rather to produce pure analytical variants showing how labour market equilibrium is displaced by some exogenous shock or policy change. Producing such variants requires starting from a steady or stationary state. Of course, what "stationary" will mean here does not correspond to a situation where all individuals are themselves in stationary states, quite the contrary. The concept is one of "dynamic" stationarity, where all individual situations go on evolving over time, but in a way that keeps constant all macro-characteristics of the sample. To reach such a dynamic steady state, we just need to simulate the model with fixed parameters until stabilization of all macro-economics characteristics. Convergence is generally obtained after approximately 20 iterations.

3.3 Calibration

By calibration, we mean the choice of parameters such that the resulting steady-state sample is as close as possible to median characteristics of the French labour market, such as described by data presented in Section 3.1.

The full description of the calibration of the model is beyond the scope of this chapter. As mentioned above, parameters have been divided into three distinct sets. A first group of parameters is directly observed or can be directly computed from real data. This is for instance the case for social contribution rates. In France, the rate of social contributions depends on the level of the gross wage. For employees paid at the minimum wage, the rate of contribution is 14%. For employees paid more than 1.6 times the minimum wage, the rate of contributions is 40%, with a progressive formula between these two thresholds.

A second set of parameters has been guesstimated. This is the case for parameters describing the process of wage negotiation. These parameters are the minimum and reference mark-up, the intensity of wage negotiation, the critical unemployment rate and the wage loss after an unemployment spell. If the mark-up is below the minimum mark-up the employee is automatically fired. If the mark-up lies between the minimum and the reference mark-up the employee is fired with a probability decreasing with the mark-up. The minimum and reference mark-ups have been set at 20% and 30% after several attempts. The value of the unemployment rate for which insiders fully stop negotiating their wages has been fixed at a very high value (40%). Otherwise 10% (wage negotiation intensity) of the gap between current and target wage is filled at each period. The hiring wages of the second or further employment spell are set 10% below the previous salary. For some other unobservable parameters, initial guesses were obtained by analytically solving a simplified version of the model without any individual heterogeneity. These parameters are the matching rates, the separation rates, and the inflows of short-term contracts.

Parameters from the last group have been estimated through indirect inference (see Gourieroux et al., 1993). The objective was to find values of these parameters that minimize the distance between a given set of moments of the real data and their model-predicted counterparts.

In our empirical implementation, the moments that we tried to match are: unemployment rates, mean wages, stocks of people working under short-term contracts and mean unemployment and employment durations for each level of qualification. Parameters that are estimated in this way are matching rates, the first quartiles of initial productivity distributions, the variances of productivity shocks, the separation rates, the prices of each variety and the inflows of short-term contracts. We use the inverse of the observed moments as the weighting matrix of the distance so that our objective function is

$$\sum_{i=1}^{I} (\,\beta_i(\Omega_s) - \beta_i^0\,)/\beta_i^0\,)^2$$

where I is the number of moments to match, β_i^0 is the observed value of the ith moment and $\beta_i(\Omega_s)$ is the simulated value of the ith moment when the structural parameters are equal to Ω_s. In order to find the value of Ω_s that minimizes the objective function, we simulate our model with a large set of different parameters. For each simulation, the random events affecting each individual have the same outcome. Consequently, the differences between each simulation are only due to parameters and not to random effects.

This calibration procedure leads to features of the simulated labour market (Table 1) that are relatively close to the observed features (especially concerning unemployment rates and mean wages). The employment duration is slightly too high for upper qualification (MQ and HQ). There is a trade-off between average wages, the shares of low-wage workers (below 1.3 and 1.6 times the minimum wage) and the unemployment rates of NQ and LQ workers. At this stage, it has not been possible to get a simultaneous adjustment of these three variables and the priority has been given to average wages and unemployment rates. Table 2 shows that this leads to a slight overestimation of the share of low-wage workers.

It is worth noting that, to some extent, the results produced with a $1/2000^{th}$ sized sample (first part of Table 1) are different from those obtained with a $1/500^{th}$ sized. As the sample size matters we may presume that with a $1/2000^{th}$ sized sample the model outcomes still strongly depend on the drawing of random effects. Because of this problem, it would have been better to carry out the calibration with a larger sample, but this would have resulted in exorbitant computation times. There is obviously a trade-off between the number of parameter values we are able to scan and the accuracy of the model outcomes. As we manage to use the same random draws in all our simulations (for calibration and variant) we think that this precision issue isn't excessively harmful for the conclusions of the following section.

Table 1: **Calibration results**

	Unem-ployment rates (%)	Wages (euros)	Wages growth (%)	Share of short-term contracts (%)	Mean unemploy-ment dura-tion (years)	Mean em-ployment duration (years)	Mark-up (%)
	1/2000th sized sample						
NQ	23.4	1 554	2.2	11.9	1.19	7.72	46.5
LQ	14.2	1 836	2.3	5.7	1.25	10.60	35.3
MQ	10.8	2 555	2.6	6.7	1.18	13.80	32.8
HQ	8.5	4 348	3.6	4.1	1.43	16.72	34.1
	1/500th sized sample						
NQ	22.9	1 581	2.3	11.7	1.17	8.14	45.3
LQ	13.9	1 834	2.3	5.5	1.25	10.64	35.0
MQ	10.6	2 543	2.6	6.6	1.23	13.76	32.7
HQ	7.4	4 507	3.6	3.9	1.41	17.22	33.6
	Observed						
NQ	23.8	1 496	1.1	12.6	1.11	7.71	Non-ob-served
LQ	16.2	1 760	1.6	6.5	1.08	10.84	Non-ob-served
MQ	10.5	2 324	1.6	6.4	1.03	10.97	Non-ob-served
HQ	8.3	4 116	3.1	4.3	1.04	11.13	Non-ob-served

Table 2: **Calibration results for wage distribution**

	<1.3 × minimum wage (%)	<1.6 × minimum wage (%)
1/2000th sized sample	26.5	46.8
1/500th sized sample	25.5	46.6
Observed	21.6	47.0

4   Some experimental simulations

Even if the calibration may still be improved, it is already interesting to look at how the model reacts to different shocks. We simulate three shocks: a demographic shock and two economic policy shocks.

The demographic shock consists of a permanent increase in the number of entrants to the labour market. Each year, the inflow is 25% greater than in the reference scenario. This scenario is not necessarily realistic, although it more or less reproduces what could have been, all else equal, the past impact of the baby boom on the French labour market. The purpose of this first simulation is essentially to check stability properties of our model.

The two economic policy scenarios directly impact labour costs. The first economic policy consists of an increase of the minimum wage from 1,200 euros up to 1,300 euros (scenario "Min W"). The increase is linear and progressive over 10 years. The second scenario consists of restoring uniform contribution rates for all workers (scenario called "Unif"), i.e. dismantling the system of tax exemptions that has been progressively set up in France for low-wage workers since 1993. We, however, assume that such a dismantling takes place progressively over 10 years.

4.1 A demographic shock

The demographic shock results in an increase in the working-age population. Because it takes time to absorb the extra unemployed, the unemployment rate increases in the short run. The short-term effect on the overall unemployment rate is around 0.5 percentage points (Table 3). This is similar to what Ouvrard and Rathelot (2006) obtained in a theoretical matching model. As efficiency increases with age, the mean efficiency over the whole population is lower than in the baseline scenario. Consequently, above frictional unemployment, extra classical unemployment is generated. In the medium run, the unemployment rate is expected to decrease gradually through three potential channels. The first channel is the mechanical increase in hirings due to the fact that the matching function depends primarily on the size of the unemployed population. Second, at the micro-economic level, the short-term increase in the unemployment rate leads to a decrease in wage claims. As a result, mark-up rates increase and separations due to adverse idiosyncratic efficiency shocks are less numerous. Third, the increase in mark-up rates may also have a macro-effect. In the classical setting that we retain here, this higher mark-up increases the level of production that is desired by firms. However, since the target employment is never a binding constraint in the "classical" environment, this third channel is ineffective.

In the long run, the first cohorts of this demographic shock are well absorbed into employment, and frictional unemployment is no longer an issue. Moreover, mean efficiency increases up to its baseline level, as these cohorts gain experience. This happens roughly 40 years after the beginning of the shock. After 50 years (result not shown), there is no effect on the unemployment rate. Regarding the stability properties, there is no overshooting phenomenon. In this simulation, mean wages adjust quickly enough to movements of the unemployment rate.

Table 3: **Effects of the demographic shock (results are shown in absolute deviation from baseline scenario averaged over 5 years)**

	After 5 years	After 15 years	After 40 years
Employment (in thousands)	171	1055	3307
Unemployment rate (in points)	0.5	0.4	0.0
Mean monthly wage (in euros)	-13	-55	-10

Reading guide: five years after the shock, the mean unemployment rate (averaged over 5 years around the fifth year after the shock) is 0.5 points greater than the mean unemployment rate averaged over the corresponding years in the baseline scenario.

4.2 *Economic policy shocks affecting labour costs*

The two economic policies are both simulated in two different environments: a "classical" situation in which the supply of goods is not constrained and a "Keynesian" situation in which it is the case. To simulate the "Keynesian" environment, the target production is progressively reduced by up to 3% below its "classical" potential over the 10 years preceding the shock. Then, during and after the shock, the target production is fully prevented from growing. Assuming a permanent situation of Keynesian depression is naturally an extreme assumption, which is just introduced to check the properties of this ultra-Keynesian regime. Before the shock, the unemployment rate is of course already higher in this "Keynesian" regime than for its "classical" counterpart.

The two environments share the same micro-economic channel through which differences between efficiency and real labour cost affect employment. Even in the "Keynesian" case, reductions in the margin between efficiency and real labour costs, i.e. decreases in the mark-up, lead to higher rates of "economic" separations. Because of hiring frictions, increases in these "economic" separations mechanically result in higher unemployment rates, whatever the overall employment target is. However, as a consequence of the higher unemployment rate in the "Keynesian" situation, people at work are more efficient, so there is a selection effect. As a result, the microeconomic channel is weaker in this "Keynesian" case. On the other hand, in this Keynesian setting, employment is also affected by the macro-constraint on global demand for all types of goods/qualifications.

Results are reported in Table 4 and commented from now on.

Table 4: Effects of economic policy shocks (to read the table see caption of Table 3)

	In "classical" environment			In "Keynesian" environment		
	After 5 years	After 10 years	LR (30 years)	After 5 years	After 10 years	LR (30 years)
Effects on employment (in thousands)						
Min W	-21.8	-54.4	-92.8	-2.2	-12.8	-26
Unif.	-193.2	-367	-299.8	-33.2	-81.4	-84.8
Effects on overall unemployment rate (in points)						
Min W	0.12	0.34	0.6	0.02	0.06	0.18
Unif.	1.18	2.22	1.82	0.18	0.48	0.52
Effects on the unemployment rate of non-qualified workers (in points)						
Min W	0.5	1.14	1.82	0.04	0.24	0.5
Unif.	2.28	4.12	3.48	0.44	1.06	1.08
Effects on mean monthly wage (in euros)						
Min W	3.8	9.2	10.2	3	8.2	14
Unif.	6.4	1.4	-24.4	-0.6	-3.8	-15
Effects on the mean monthly wage of the non-qualified workers (in euros)						
Min W	11.4	22.8	19	12.8	31	46.2
Unif.	-8.8	-43.6	-100.8	-4.4	-15	-48.2

4.2.1 Increasing the minimum wage

Increasing the minimum wage in a "classical" setting has a negative effect on employment that gradually deepens to attain around 100,000 workers less. As expected, the effect in the "Keynesian" situation is considerably weaker (almost four times) but remains unfavourable to employment. In both cases, the effects concentrate on NQ and LQ workers. Actually, 70% of employment losses concern non-qualified workers. The magnitude of our effects falls within the bracket that had been for instance proposed in a review of existing estimates by the CSERC (1999) that gave an impact of a 1% increase of the minimum wage that ran from -4000 or -20000 depending on models and assumptions.

Figure 1: **Evolution of the unemployment rate (left axis) and of the mean wage (right axis) for non-qualified workers in the Minimum wage increase scenario ("classical" environment)**

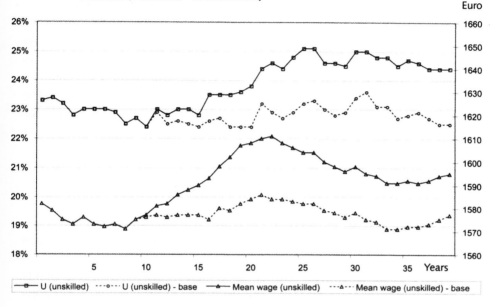

Figure 2: **Evolution of the share of workers whose wage is just above the minimum wage in the Minimum wage increase scenario ("classical" environment)**

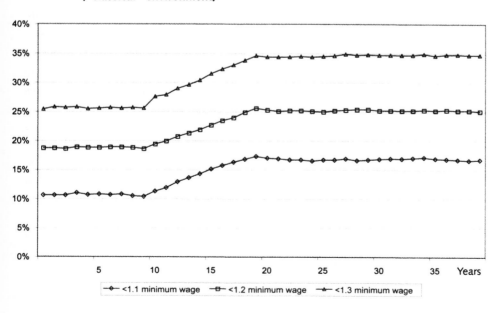

In the long run, workers gain on average 10 euros more in the "classical" environment. Wage increases are greater for non-qualified workers for whom it amounts to almost 20 euros (see Figure 1). This is only 20% of the initial increase in the minimum wage. This gap is due to the negative impact of unemployment on wage negotiations and to the lack of automatic diffusion of increases of the minimum wages. The absence of automatic diffusion is also responsible for the deformation on the left side of the wage distribution (see Figure 2). In the "Keynesian" environment, as the increase in the unemployment rate is lower, the wage rise is more intense especially for non-qualified workers. Here again, the magnitude of this final effect on wages is in line with figures gathered by the CSERC (1999).

4.2.2 Restoring flat contribution rates for low-wage workers

Restoring "normal" contribution rates for workers paid between the minimum wage and 1.6 times this minimum wage causes the loss of 300,000 jobs in the "classical" environment and 100,000 jobs in the "Keynesian" environment. The figures for the classical case are slightly below results in previous studies that have evaluated the impact of *introducing* such tax exemptions since the mid-1990s. This is partly due to the fact that the dismantling of these exemptions is progressive. Simulations of a sudden suppression of these exemptions (results not shown) lead to a much larger negative impact, at least in the short run (around 600,000 job losses).

Wages are influenced through two channels, which have opposite effects. On the one hand, higher unemployment moderates wage claims. On the other hand, as labour costs grow, the average efficiency of insiders increases. In the short run, the overall mean wage goes up because the share of non-qualified workers declines. In the long run, the first effect dominates (see Figure 3).

In both environments the number of unemployed people increases compared to what happens with unchanged social security contributions. The model needs some time to adjust to the new steady state. Higher labour costs should lead to decreasing wages. But the downward rigidity of insiders' wages precludes such a downward adjustment. The only way to get declining wages is through an increasing frequency of unemployment spells. This phenomenon is probably responsible for the unemployment rate overshooting observed in the medium run (see Figure 4).

Figure 3: **Evolution of the mean wage for NQ workers in the "Unif" scenario (re-harmonization of social security contribution rates)**

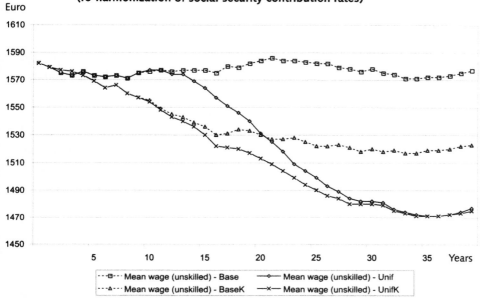

Figure 4: **Evolution of the overall unemployment rate in the "Unif" scenario (re-harmonization of social security contribution rates)**

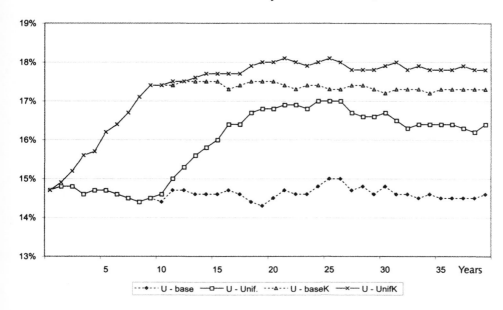

5 Conclusion

In this chapter, we have presented the first version of a microsimulation model that tries to describe the dynamic matching process between labour demand and supply with heterogeneous agents. Despite many simplifications and a calibration that remains preliminary, we checked that simulations of demographic shocks and typical French economic policies yield reasonable results that lie within the range of the consensus emerging from other *ex ante* or *ex post* evaluations. The model therefore illustrates the potential of microsimulation techniques for exploring the detailed consequences of policies oriented toward the demand side of the labour market, that have played an important role in France since the mid-1990s.

The version presented in this chapter remains, however, highly experimental. Beyond the technical questions of revising various aspects of specifications and of improving the calibration methodology, two major issues for further research are, respectively, to try to fully base the model on individual survey data or administrative data, and to develop the modelling of labour supply behaviour, in order to be able to fully retrace the interactions between exemptions of contributions on low-wage workers, minimum wage policies, and the impact of other social benefits on decisions to join the labour market.

206

References

Conseil d'Orientation pour l'Emploi (2006) *Rapport au Premier ministre relatif aux aides publiques.*

Colander, D./Howitt, P./Kirman, A./Leijonhufvud, A./Mehrling, P. (2008) 'Beyond DSGE models: toward an empirically based macroeconomics', *American Economic Review*, Papers and Proceedings, 98 (2): 236-240.

Conseil Supérieur de l'Emploi, des Revenus et des Coûts (1999) *Le SMIC : salaire minimum de Croissance*, La Documentation française.

Crépon, B./Desplatz, R. (2001) 'Une nouvelle évaluation des effets des allégements de charges sociales sur les bas salaires', *Economie et Statistique* 348.

Fagiolo, G./Dosi, G./Gabriele, R. (2004) 'Matching, bargaining and wage-setting in an evolutionary model of labor market and output dynamics', *Advances in Complex Systems* 14: 237-273.

Gourieroux, C./Monfort, A./Renault, E. (1993) 'Indirect Inference', *Journal of Applied Econometrics* 8 (S): 85-118.

LeBaron, B./Tesfatsion, L. (2008) 'Modelling macroeconomics as open-ended dynamic systems of interacting agents', *American Economic Review*, Papers and Proceedings, 98 (2): 246-250.

Neugart, M. (2008) 'Labour market policy evaluation with ACE', *Journal of Economic Behaviour and Organization* 67: 418-430.

L'Horty, Y. (2006) 'Dix ans d'évaluation des exonérations sur les bas salaires', *Connaissance de l'Emploi* 24.

Orcutt, G.H. (1957) 'A new type of socio-economic system', *Review of Economics and Statistics* 58 (2): 773-797 (reprinted with permission in *International Journal of Microsimulation* 1 (1): 3-9, Autumn, at http://www.microsimulation.org/IJM/V1_1/IJM_1_1_2.pdf).

Ouvrard, J.F./Rathelot, R. (2006) 'Demographic change and unemployment: what do macro-econometric models predict?', INSEE/DESE Working Paper, n° 2006/04.

Sterdyniak, H. (2007) 'Low-skilled Jobs: the French Strategy', OFCE Working Paper, n° 2007/15.

Chapter 8

Policy Swapping across Countries Using EUROMOD: The Case of In-Work Benefits in Southern Europe

Francesco Figari

1 Policy swapping analyses in the European Union

The aim of this chapter is to analyse the potential role of policy swapping analyses in the context of the Open Method of Coordination developed at the European Union level. Although the choice of policies to achieve specific targets is a responsibility of the Member States, the Open Method of Coordination developed at the European Union level in 2000, encourages mutual learning processes across countries. One approach to reach or to evaluate the feasibility of explicit targets measured by common indicators (Atkinson et al., 2002) is to exchange good practices between Member States in order to facilitate policy learning through a peer review approach (Atkinson, 2005). Although it is not easy to adopt policies and institutional

I am grateful to Stephen Jenkins for his supervision. Chiara Pronzato and participants at the first General Conference of the International Microsimulation Association (Vienna, August 2007) and at a workshop at the Instituto de Estudio Fiscales (Madrid, November 2007) made helpful comments.
This chapter uses EUROMOD version D5. EUROMOD is continually being improved and updated. Any remaining errors, results produced, interpretations or views presented are the author's responsibility. I am indebted to Holly Sutherland and all past and current members of the EUROMOD consortium for the construction and development of EUROMOD. This chapter uses data from the Household Budget Survey (HBS 2004) made available by National Statistical Service of Greece; the Survey of Household Income and Wealth (SHIW95) made available by the Bank of Italy; the European Community Household Panel (ECHP) User Data Base made available by Eurostat; and the Family Expenditure Survey (FES 2003) made available by the UK Office for National Statistics (ONS) through the Data Archive. Material from the FES is Crown Copyright and is used by permission. Neither the ONS nor the Data Archive bears any responsibility for the analysis or interpretation of the data reported here. An equivalent disclaimer applies for all other data sources and their respective providers cited in this acknowledgement.

processes employed in other Member States, countries can learn from each other and the Open Method of Coordination represents the context of such mutual exchange (Atkinson et al., 2005).

The process behind the Open Method of Coordination, made up of common recommendations, national action plans and joint evaluation reports, leaves the responsibility of each action to the national actors. No sanctions are established at European level for those countries which do not follow the recommendations. Nevertheless this process might contribute to initiate a virtuous circle of actions and policy reforms which the Member States are more interested to follow if the same strategies are under discussion in other countries and they form part of the social inclusion process established at the EU level (Ferrera et al., 2002).

Indeed one of the main instruments to achieve the objectives of the Lisbon Strategy for Employment and Growth (European Commission, 2004) was identified in the Open Method of Coordination as a way to encourage best practices and to achieve higher convergences towards common European targets, explicitly defined in terms of goals, encouraging and supporting the Member States to develop their own policies to achieve such targets. However, Member States face revenue constraints and political disputes that often reduce their capacity or willingness to implement national reforms necessary to reach the objectives agreed at the European level: a policy learning process might help such countries to develop their policies in line with what is implemented in other Member States. Policy learning across countries is particularly relevant when the need of policy alternatives is urgent. In most of the European countries, this is relevant for the policies aimed at reducing the risk of poverty of specific groups of the population on which no progress has been made in the last decade (Atkinson, 2009).

Policy swapping analyses are a specific way of policy learning across countries, performed with microsimulation models. They consist of borrowing policies that seem to be effective in one country and implementing them in other countries, in order to understand the effect of such tax-benefit instruments on different populations. On the one hand, policy swapping analyses overcome the limitations of aggregate analyses that can be misleading in the evaluation of the most effective way to achieve a given objective, in particular in a cross-country comparison. On the other hand, they require a comparable or even unified approach not only in terms of input micro-data but also in the way in which the interaction with the existing tax-benefit instruments is taken into account. A microsimulation approach allows the policy-makers to move from the established targets to the policy reforms that would lead to the achievement of such targets (Atkinson, 2009).

When the number of countries involved in the analysis is large and the tax-benefit instrument complex, a multi-country model such as EUROMOD, built with comparability and flexibility in mind, can be of great advantage. Such analyses enable the analyst to create a strict link between policies and outcomes and to understand this relationship, assessing the impact of any policy changes on the baseline scenario.

Previous studies show the extent to which national policies can improve their effectiveness by looking beyond national borders. This chapter presents a case-study that evaluates the trade-off between the redistributive and the incentive effects of the potential implementation of in-work benefits in the Southern European countries (Figari, 2009). These are policies that are aimed at contributing to make work pay and provide secure income which is one of the objectives of the European strategy to modernize social protection as part of the European social model (European Commission, 2004).

The rest of the chapter is organized as follows. Section 2 provides a brief description of EUROMOD and its high potential for policy swapping analyses. Section 3 illustrates the rationale for the potential implementation of different kinds of in-work benefits in the Southern European countries. The distributional effects in terms of poverty rates, distribution of gainers and income variation, as well as the incentive effects in terms of effective marginal tax rates and replacement rates, are presented in Section 4. Section 5 concludes.

2   EUROMOD: a tool for policy swapping analyses

EUROMOD is a unique multi-country infrastructure developed in the last decade in order to carry out European comparative social science research. EUROMOD covers the 15 pre-2004 European Union Member States plus Estonia, Hungary, Poland and Slovenia. Currently it is being extended to cover all the 27 Member States and using mainly the new European level micro-data source, namely EU-SILC (European Union Survey on Income and Living Conditions).

EUROMOD is a static microsimulation model which covers only monetary incomes. It combines information on relevant policy rules with detailed and representative data on individual and household circumstances drawn from national household income surveys. EUROMOD simulates most direct taxes, social contributions and cash benefits except those based on contributory history (as this information is not available from input datasets). Instruments which are not simulated are taken directly from the data.

For a limited number of countries (i.e. Belgium, Germany, Greece, Ireland, Italy, the Netherlands and the UK) it also includes estimates of private non-cash incomes (imputed rent for owner-occupied accommodation, consumption of own production and fringe benefits provided by the employers), and indirect taxes (Belgium, Greece, Ireland and the UK).

As with most tax-benefit models, EUROMOD enables us to assess the effect of consolidated tax-benefit systems on the main monetary social indicators and to evaluate the impact of actual or hypothetical policy changes with specification of revenue constraints. Moreover, EUROMOD enables us to analyse the impact of national policies within a European perspective and policies at the European Union level. Thus EUROMOD is of value in understanding how different policies in different countries may contribute to common objectives through (i) cross-country comparison of specific tax-benefit instruments, (ii) policy and whole system swapping, and (iii) analysis of the impact of common changes across countries (Lietz and Mantovani, 2007).

Alongside distributional effects, it gives the possibility of analysing the work incentives associated with a given policy reform and to derive the budget sets that an individual faces under different labour market choices (Immervoll, 2004).

The disposable income simulated by EUROMOD corresponds to market income and public pensions after taxes and social insurance contributions are deducted and cash benefits added. EUROMOD baseline results do not take into account non take-up of benefits or tax evasion. Therefore, the legal rules are assumed to be universally respected and the costs of compliance and claiming are assumed to be zero. This can result in the over-estimation of taxes and benefits and gives rise to differences between EUROMOD estimates of disposable income and income values recorded in the underlying datasets (Mantovani and Sutherland, 2003; Lietz and Sutherland, 2005). As a consequence, EUROMOD baseline outputs capture the intended effect of taxes and benefits rather than the actual performance. However, additional features of the model allow the user to take into account the effects of tax evasion (particularly relevant in Italy, Greece and Hungary) and benefit non-take up (Germany, Sweden and the UK).

One of the main aims of EUROMOD is to maximize comparability while maintaining transparency about real differences across countries (Sutherland, 2007). This goal is achieved by a user-friendly interface and a very flexible modular system design, without any part of the national tax-benefit system being hard-wired in the code. Any policy change can be implemented without reprogramming the code. Policy swapping exercises are particularly facilitated by the flexible definition of the units of assessment and income concepts in the model. The former are the group of people on which the tax-benefit rules are to be performed. The latter are the aggregations of monetary variables used as both input to tax-benefit algorithms (e.g. means for the calculation of social benefits, base of personal tax) and as output of the model (e.g. disposable income). Moreover, a standardized approach of defining and naming both input and output variables enables us to have the same variable names corresponding to a common income source across countries (Sutherland et al., 2008).

Baseline systems in EUROMOD have been validated and tested at micro (i.e. case-by-case validation) and macro level, comparing the aggregate indicators and distributive statistics with external sources and national microsimulation models. The results of the validation exercises are reported in the Country Reports (available on the EUROMOD web pages) and in Mantovani and Sutherland (2003) and Lietz and Sutherland (2005).

EUROMOD is free for academic use subject to the permission to use the original micro-data, on which EUROMOD relies. For further information see Sutherland (2007) and visit http://www.iser.essex.ac.uk/research/euromod.

One of the main motivations for building a multi-country model at the European level came from the attempts to investigate the different characteristics of the tax-benefit systems, in order to evaluate the potential impact of "borrowing" policies in place in other countries. Such kinds of social experiments are nowadays known as "policy swapping" exercises and they are particularly useful to understand the likely impact of any policies on a given population of interest, to capture the interaction between tax-benefit systems and the characteristics of such a population and to assess the effectiveness of national policies (Callan and Sutherland, 1997).

The pioneering work by Atkinson et al. (1988) looked at the implications of applying the British tax system based on personal deductions to the French population and replacing the existing *quotient familial*. Callan and Sutherland (1997) explored the impact of basic income schemes in the

UK and Ireland but they could not include more European countries in a consistent way due to limitations of the national models available at that time. The natural option seemed to be the development of EUROMOD, a consistent Europe-wide model especially designed to carry out cross country comparisons.

More recently a number of policy swapping exercises have been conducted, focused on child benefits and making use of EUROMOD.[1] Among others, Immervoll et al. (2001), Levy (2003), Levy et al. (2005 and 2008) studied the impact of implementing child support policies experienced abroad in Spain, Austria, the Netherlands and the UK (swapping policies among countries) and Poland (borrowing policies from Austria, France and the UK). These studies highlight the relevance of policy swapping exercises in distinguishing between the effects of level of spending, policy structure and impacts due to the characteristics of national populations.

Another area in which EUROMOD has been used to analyse the effect of policies borrowed from other countries is related to the in-work benefits that usually represent a strict link between the tax and the benefit system. The analysis of such benefits is a good example of where a microsimulation model can be exploited to analyse the work incentives related to the policy changes and the second-round effects allowing for behavioural adjustments. Bargain and Orsini (2006) use a structural labour supply model to assess the second-round effects of the British Working Families' Tax Credit and of an individualized tax credit in Finland, France and Germany. They find that only the individualized benefit might increase the employment rates, but with very high efficiency costs due to the structural characteristics of the economy and the population. Figari (2009) shows the effects of the implementation of in-work benefits in the Southern European countries, characterized by very different background conditions and tax-benefit systems.

3 The rationale for in-work benefits in the Southern European countries

In-Work Benefits (IWBs) provide cash transfers through the tax system to individuals with low earnings. They belong to the family of "make work pay" (OECD, 2003) policies since they are conditional on employment status of the recipient.

---

1   For an overview of EUROMOD uses see Lietz and Mantovani (2007) and EUROMOD Working Papers at http://www.iser.essex.ac.uk/research/euromod/working-papers

IWBs can be family-based or individually-based. Family-based IWBs are well-established in Anglo-Saxon countries. The Family Income Supplement was introduced in the UK in 1971 and it has been modified several times since then, with the introduction of the Working Family Tax Credit (1999) and most recently the Working Tax Credit (Brewer, 2003). The US, Ireland and New Zealand have also introduced family-based in-work benefit schemes (Eissa and Hoynes, 2004). Other countries, such as Australia, Canada, Belgium and France, have implemented individually-based IWBs, targeting individual family members rather than the family as a whole (OECD, 2003).[2]

The two different types of IWBs share common objectives in terms of enhancing labour market participation and financial resources of low income groups. However, individually-based IWBs tend to shift the aim from redistribution towards work-incentive aspects. From a purely employment-based point of view, the OECD recommends the implementation of individually-based IWBs (OECD, 2003). Family-based policies may discourage the labour market participation of the second earner mainly due to income effect: in a couple the additional employment income would lead the family to lose the eligibility of receiving the benefit with only marginal financial advantage. This scenario has been confirmed by ex ante and ex post analyses of the labour market implications of the British in-work benefits (Blundell et al., 2000; Brewer et al., 2006; Francesconi and Van der Klaauw, 2007) and may be crucial in those countries where non-employment is concentrated among wives. On the other hand, individually-based policies may be less well targeted to poor households, because individuals with low earnings would receive the benefit irrespective of partner's income and other non-labour income. This type of support to relatively poor individuals belonging to well-off families might be particularly common in countries characterized by the presence of multigenerational families.

Comparing the Southern European Countries with countries in which IWBs are well-established, the SECs show a number of common features that can make IWBs particularly well tailored as part of a reformed welfare system. Poverty and inequality rates are among the highest in the EU-15 (Eurostat, 2006): in 2003, the share of people at risk of poverty was around 19-21% against an EU-15 average of 17%. Inequality of income distribution was even more spread, with Gini indices ranging from 0.31 (Spain) to 0.38 (Portugal) against an EU-15 average of 0.30.

---

2   Other instruments as tax allowances are not considered IWBs in their strict sense because they are not refundable and the level of support increases with income.

The low level of general social protection nets is reflected by the share of GDP spent on social protection: it ranged from 19.7% in Spain to 26.4% in Italy compared with an EU-15 average of 28.3%. Generalized low earnings and the absence of generous income support schemes mean that more than half of the people at risk of poverty have a job. In other words, the working poor are at the very bottom of the income distribution. See Table 1 for detailed figures, in which also the UK is included given the relevance of the comparison with this country throughout the chapter.

Table 1: Social indicators, 2003

	At risk of poverty[a] %	Inequality of income distribution[a] Gini index	Social protection expenditures[b] % GDP
Greece	20	0.33	26.3
Italy	19	0.33	26.4
Portugal	21	0.38	24.3
Spain	20	0.31	19.7
UK	18	0.34	26.7
EU-15	17	0.30	28.3

Source: a) EUROSTAT (2006), b) EUROSTAT (2007). At risk of poverty defined as proportion of individuals with equivalent income below the 60% of median equivalent income.

Budget constraint charts summarize the institutional background and the public support available to families of different types. Figure 1 shows how net income (on the vertical axis) varies with gross earnings (on the horizontal axis) for a one-earner couple with two children (9 and 7 years old) and no other income sources at household level.[3] The 45° degree line represents the situation without taxes and benefits: a net income above such a line means net support from the state in addition to gross earnings. Greece, Italy and Spain are characterized by the absence of any generalized income support and individuals must rely exclusively on their own earnings that are not taxed up to the threshold corresponding to the personal allowance.

3 The baseline scenario refers to 2003 for Greece, Portugal and Spain; 2001 for Italy. From these years, no substantial reform has been implemented in the tax-benefit systems in particular with reference to minimum income schemes, in-work benefits and child benefits. In Italy the personal tax credits have been replaced by a more general personal tax allowance in 2003 with slightly regressive effects on the people at the bottom of the income distribution.

In Portugal, a guaranteed minimum income scheme applies to all citizens available for employment; it is means-tested at family level and its amount depends on the size of the household and it is indexed to the amount of the social age pension.

Figure 1:   Budget constraint charts – baseline scenario. One-earner couple with two children (9 and 7 years old)

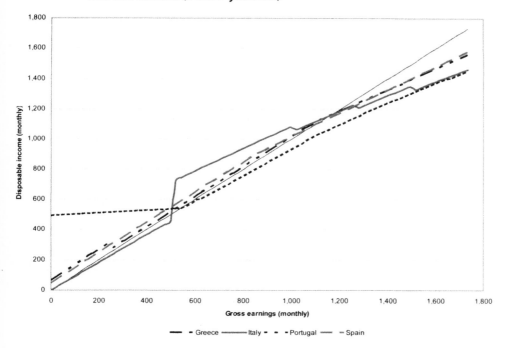

217

Note: The assumed hourly wage is €5, i.e. around the 30th percentile gross hourly wage in Greece, Italy and Spain, and around the 50th percentile in Portugal.

Source: Author's elaborations from EUROMOD.

In Greece (dotted-dashed line), Portugal (dotted line) and Spain (long dashed line), those with low earnings receive a relatively small refundable tax credit for children in education (in Greece) and an income-tested child benefit (in Portugal and Spain). In Italy (solid line) an individual receives a Family Allowance when she works as employee. The amount of this transfer is means-tested at family level and is related to family composition and to the number of days worked in a month.

In 2003 the SECs were far from the European average in terms of female education attainment and far from the Lisbon targets (European Commission, 2004) in terms of female labour market participation (i.e. 57% by 2005). The percentage of low-educated women ranged from 46% in Greece to 75% in Portugal, against an average level in the EU-15 and in the UK of fewer than 40%. Moreover, with the exception of Portugal, the employment rate of women was much lower than elsewhere: in Greece, Italy and Spain fewer than 40% of women with lower than secondary education level were in paid employment (Table 2).

Such employment rates refer to both women in couples and lone mothers. However, in the SECs, lone mothers, whose number has increased over the last decade, are more likely to work than women in couples due to the absence of relevant social protection schemes (Bradshaw et al., 1996).

Table 2: **Female education attainment and labour market participation, 2003**

	Low education, %	Employment rate, %
Greece	45.7	38.8
Italy	57.3	31.5
Portugal	75.4	63
Spain	54.2	36.4
UK	36.4	61.2
EU-15	38.7	44.3

Source: Author's calculations from Labour Force Surveys (2003). Low education: % of the female population aged 25-64 years having completed at most lower secondary education.

4 An example of policy swapping analysis[4]

The potential role of IWBs in order to promote social inclusion and to support the income of those at the bottom of the income distribution in the Southern European Countries can be particularly relevant when the focus is on the women, due to their low labour market participation and their role in family caring responsibilities.

The simulation of the family-based IWB (henceforth "IWB fam") uses the UK Working Tax Credit (WTC) as an exemplar (Brewer, 2003), replicating its structure with the parameters (i.e. thresholds of eligibility and the maxi-

---

4   This section draws on Figari (2009).

mum amount of the benefit) calibrated to obtain the same cost in terms of GDP in each country. This amount does not necessarily correspond to what it would be necessary to spend in order to achieve specific national goals in terms of redistribution of income and incentive effects, but it represents a common benchmark that makes possible cross-country comparisons.

The main eligibility condition for the Working Tax Credit is that at least one person in the family works 16 or more hours a week (30 or more if there are no children). The amount of the tax credit depends on family gross income (all main sources of income with the exception of children's earnings and a disregarded amount for pensions, capital and property income) and it varies according to the composition of the family. Above the given thresholds, the tax credit is tapered out at the rate of 37%.

Given the underlying income distributions, the demographic characteristics and the constraints in terms of total cost, the maximum amount of the simulated benefit for a lone parent or a couple working 30 or more hours a week is €4,405 per year in Italy, €3,475 in Greece, €2,600 in Spain and €2,369 in Portugal. The benefit is exhausted when the annual gross income of the family is respectively around €18,021 in Italy, €14,216 in Greece, €10,636 in Spain and €9,692 in Portugal.

The individually-based IWB (henceforth "IWB ind") is simulated as a wage subsidy (Phelps, 1994) for all individuals working 16 or more hours a week. The work requirement implies that the recipients are individuals characterized by low hourly wages (and not simply low earnings). This aspect should provide an incentive for working poor people to work at least part-time. Eligible individuals with gross earnings below the fifteenth percentile (α) of the earnings distribution are entitled to the full amount of the benefit, which is equal to an additional percentage of their earnings, calibrated to imply the same cost as each country's family-based IWB. The individually-based subsidy corresponds to an additional 21.1% of individual earnings in Italy, 20.9% in Spain, 14.6% in Greece and 13% in Portugal. Earnings above α reduce the entitlement at the rate of 37%.

Two assumptions underlie the simulations. First, the new IWBs simulated for the SECs do not respect revenue neutrality, given that their cost is not covered by additional resources. Second, the employee receives the full amount of the IWBs without any reduction in gross wage.

4.1 Is there a trade-off between the redistributive and the incentive effects?

The higher level of income at which the individually-based IWB is exhausted and the less stringent working hours' requirements compared with the family-based IWB, lead to a much larger number of household beneficiaries of the individually-based IWB than those recipients of the family-based IWB: 19% versus 11% in Greece and Italy, with percentages even higher in Spain (23% versus 14%) and Portugal (33% versus 17%). In some cases, more than one recipient of the individually-based IWB belongs to the same household and this increases the number of the individuals potentially entitled to receive the individually-based IWB. However, looking at the value of the IWBs, it emerges that the family-based IWBs are double the individually-based IWBs both in terms of average and maximum value. Average (and maximum) family-based IWBs range from €71 (€197) per month in Portugal to €152 (€367) in Italy. Average individually-based IWBs range from €31 (€57) in Portugal to €80 (€ 158) in Italy. Portugal and Italy are also the two countries that report, respectively, the highest and the lowest percentage of beneficiaries, which partly justifies the differences in the amount.

This is the first lesson derived from a cross-country perspective: given the same structure of the IWBs, the labour market characteristics and the underlying income distributions of a country drive the final results in a massive way. In Portugal, where a larger share of households than in other countries meet both the working hours' requirements (individuals working more than 16 hours per week) and the income threshold conditions (low wages and low family incomes), more resources would be necessary in order to give a substantial amount of benefits to those who are entitled to receive them. This confirms the risk that these policies might have too many beneficiaries when the wages are not dispersed enough (Boeri et al., 2000).

4.2 Redistributive effects

Looking at the reduction in poverty (see Table 3) after the implementation of IWBs, it emerges that the effect is much more evident when the poverty line is set as 40% of median equivalent income rather than as 60%, in particular after the family-based IWB. This is particularly true in the case of Italy (-25 %) and Portugal (-20 %). It contrasts with the situation experienced in other countries where individuals at the bottom of the income distribution rely on social assistance and income support schemes more than on their earnings (Bargain and Orsini, 2006). This implies that in the Southern European countries a policy oriented at the working poor, such as the IWBs, is also a means to support the poorest individuals.

With the exception of Spain, the contribution of family-based IWBs to reducing the share of people at risk of poverty is larger than that of individually-based IWBs. This is due to the larger generosity of family-based IWBs – and because they are means-tested at family level and, hence, they are better targeted towards the poorest families. Recipients of individually-based IWBs might belong to non-poor families, reducing the overall redistributive effects of the benefit.

Table 3:   Redistributive effects: impact on poverty

		Poverty line: 40%		Poverty line: 60%	
		Proportion poor	Δ	Proportion poor	Δ
Greece	Baseline	0.0819	- - -	0.1929	- - -
	IWB fam	0.0756	−7.68	0.1793	−7.02
	IWB ind	0.0785	−4.16	0.1867	−3.22
Italy	Baseline	0.0719	- - -	0.2018	- - -
	IWB fam	0.0541	−24.78	0.1816	−10.00
	IWB ind	0.0664	−7.68	0.1948	−3.47
Portugal	Baseline	0.0490	- - -	0.2089	- - -
	IWB fam	0.0394	−19.64	0.1971	−5.66
	IWB ind	0.0453	−7.55	0.2017	−3.46
Spain	Baseline	0.0592	- - -	0.1917	- - -
	IWB fam	0.0564	−4.73	0.1889	−1.45
	IWB ind	0.0559	−5.59	0.1828	−4.64

Note: Poverty line is kept constant as in the baseline scenario in order to take into account possible changes in median income. Δ: percentage difference against the baseline. The baseline scenario refers to 2003 for Greece, Portugal and Spain, 2001 for Italy.

Source: Figari (2009) based on EUROMOD.

However, in countries characterized by a large share of multigenerational households (10% of the total in Spain, 9% in Portugal, 6% in Greece and 4% in Italy), the redistributive effects of means-tested policies are not clear a priori. On the one hand, the presence of multi-family households does not allow family-based IWBs to be targeted at the very poorest households. On the other hand, it is likely that a larger number of individuals belonging to the same household receive the individually-based IWB, enhancing its redistributive effect. As a consequence, we observe households at the top of the income distribution receiving the IWBs and individually-based IWBs being more redistributive than family-based IWBs, such as happens in Spain.

Additional evidence of the clear distributional impact of the IWBs is given by the distribution of the average percentage variation in equivalent household disposable income after their introduction (see Table 4). The redistributive effect after family-based IWBs is more evident in all countries but Spain: the largest increase in income takes place among the poorest fifth, in particular in Italy (8%) and Portugal (5%), and it is decreasing along the income distribution. After individually-based IWBs, the increase in income is spread among the households in the first three quintile groups. This is particularly true in Spain, where the individually-based IWB leads to an increase in income larger than that after the family-based IWB.

Table 4:   Percentage variation in equivalent disposable income by quintile

		Income quintile				
		1	2	3	4	5
Greece	IWB fam	3.15	2.03	1.21	0.61	0.12
	IWB ind	1.17	1.39	1.33	1.00	0.25
Italy	IWB fam	8.32	2.36	0.51	0.20	0.09
	IWB ind	3.17	1.54	1.36	0.68	0.28
Portugal	IWB fam	4.98	2.36	1.92	0.40	0.17
	IWB ind	1.75	2.28	1.74	1.01	0.25
Spain	IWB fam	2.06	0.94	0.86	0.99	0.77
	IWB ind	1.75	1.81	1.19	1.01	0.29

Source: Figari (2009) based on EUROMOD.

Looking at the households whose income increases by at least 5%, gainers are concentrated among the poorest fifth (Italy and partly Portugal) and the second (Greece and Spain) quintile groups. With the exception of Spain, family-based IWBs lead to a larger share of gainers at the bottom of the income distribution than individually-based IWBs. However, in Greece and Italy, individually-based IWBs have a bigger impact on the households in the middle of the income distribution.

4.3 Work incentives

At the intensive margin, where the choice is whether or not to work a little bit more, Effective Marginal Tax Rates (EMTRs) give an estimate of the way in which the new fiscal regime modifies the pay-off of working longer hours or of obtaining a better-paid job.

Individuals in the phase-in region of the benefits are expected to face lower EMTRs. At the opposite extreme, individuals in the phase-out region are expected to face higher EMTRs and lower incentives to work a little more.

Figure 2 shows the distribution of average EMTRs considering only the recipients of the two IWBs. As expected, a general increase in the EMTRs is observed. Only in Italy and Spain do recipients of individually-based IWBs in the poorest quintile group face a reduction in the EMTRs, meaning that some of them are in the phase-in region of the benefit. Comparing the effect of the two benefits, individually-based IWBs lead to lower EMTRs than family-based IWBs, with substantial differences in particular at the bottom of the income distribution.

In all countries the beneficiaries of family-based IWBs face a large increase in average EMTRs across the entire income distribution, highlighting a potential financial disincentive for individuals to work a little more if this causes a reduction in benefits assessed at family level.

In general the level of the EMTRs after the benefits does not exceed 50% (with even lower values in Spain). Such levels cannot be accounted for as a potential reason of the poverty trap, a situation in which an individual has little incentive to work more and in which he cannot escape poverty by increasing his income. The absence of a strong disincentive to work, in particular for the individuals in the first quintiles, is due to the absence of generous social assistance schemes that in other countries may lead to EMTRs close to 100%.

In order to evaluate the work incentives at the extensive margin, where the choice is about working rather than being out of the labour market, a widely used measure is the replacement rate, being the ratio between household disposable income when the woman is out of work and household income when she works.

Table 5 shows the average replacement rates separately for lone mothers and women in couples, after their choice of working full-time and part-time. Being assessed at household level, such measures take into account any variation in the income of other household members.

224

Figure 2: **Distribution of average EMTRs – only IWB recipients**

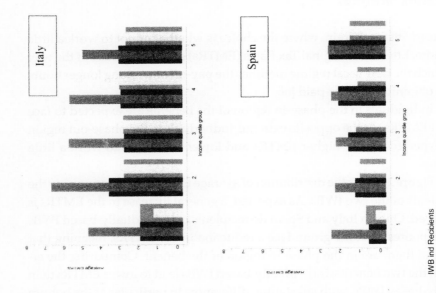

Source: Author's calculations based on EUROMOD.

Table 5:   Average Replacement rates

	Greece			Italy			Portugal			Spain		
	Base-line %	IWB fam Δ	IWB ind Δ	Base-line %	IWB fam Δ	IWB ind Δ	Base-line %	IWB fam Δ	IWB ind Δ	Base-line %	IWB fam Δ	IWB ind Δ
Lone mothers working full-time												
Mean	48.5	-2.5	-1.8	55.0	-1.2	-2.1	54.2	-1.9	-0.7	44.9	-0.2	-0.5
% whose rate rises		11.2	5.9		5.4	5.0		13.2	11.5		12.2	10.3
% whose rate falls		83.8	89.1		47.8	70.7		50.6	56.2		30.9	49.4
Lone mothers working part-time												
Mean	68.2	-4.2	-4.1	78.3	-2.9	-7.9	78.2	-6.8	-3.9	62.0	-1.4	-4.8
% whose rate rises		25.7	0.8		4.3	0.4		10.3	0.3		6.3	1.9
% whose rate falls		69.3	94.1		29.5	96.9		47.9	97.4		43.8	96.9
Women in couples working full-time												
Mean	61.6	0.2	-1.5	65.4	0.8	-1.5	62.4	1.3	-0.5	61.7	0.2	-0.6
% whose rate rises		46.5	15.4		14.3	5.3		31.9	12.1		12.6	9.2
% whose rate falls		52.6	83.7		9.8	64.1		10.6	43.2		8.1	43.3
Women in couples working part-time												
Mean	75.9	0.3	-2.5	79.0	0.7	-3.8	77.7	1.1	-2.6	75.0	0.3	-3.5
% whose rate rises		56.1	0.6		14.3	0.4		31.6	0.9		13.1	0.6
% whose rate falls		42.9	98.5		4.1	96.9		7.1	92.3		2.1	98.2

Source: Figari (2009) based on EUROMOD. Women aged 18-65 years old. Δ: change in replacement rate in percentage points.

For lone mothers both types of IWBs lead to lower replacement rates and hence a higher incentive to work compared to the baseline scenario, especially in Greece and Italy when they work full-time and in all countries when they work part-time. The reduction in replacement rates affects lone mothers both after individually-based IWBs and after family-based IWBs because lone mothers are likely to be entitled to both of them.

For women in couples the results are different because family-based IWBs in all countries lead to a potential disincentive effect to work (replacement rates slightly higher than in the baseline scenario), both if women work part-time or full-time. After the introduction of family-based IWBs, the proportion of women in couples whose replacement rates rise is higher than the proportion of women whose replacement rates fall. This is because women's participation in the labour market implies a reduction in the benefit received by their working partners. However replacement rates after individually-based IWBs are always lower than in the baseline scenario, showing a potential positive incentive effect to work. Between 43% (in Portugal and Spain) and 84% (in Greece) of the women working full-time face reduced replacement rates as do almost all women working part-time. These results confirm also for the Southern European countries what has been assessed in the UK about the employment effects of family-based in-work benefit policies (Blundell et al., 2000). Moreover, such disincentives for secondary earners in a couple are considered as one of the main obstacles in importing the British model of in-work benefit to other countries characterized by a relatively high female labour market participation (such as in Germany) (Haan and Myck, 2007).

5 Conclusions

In this chapter, the role of policy swapping analyses in the European Union has been analysed through a case-study related to the implementation of in-work benefits in the Southern European countries.

Policy swapping analyses are a specific way of policy learning across countries, performed with microsimulation models. They consist of borrowing policies that seem to be effective in one country and implementing them in other countries, in order to understand the effect of such tax-benefit instruments on different populations. A microsimulation approach allows the policy-makers to move from the established targets to the policy reforms that would lead to the achievement of such targets.

The analyses show the potential role of EUROMOD, the European-wide multi-country model, as a tool for cross-country comparative research. When the number of countries involved in the analysis is large and the tax-benefit instrument complex, a multi-country model such as EUROMOD, built with comparability and flexibility in mind, can be of great advantage.

Taking into account the institutional framework conditions in a cross-country comparative view, the implementation of two forms of in-work benefits in the Southern European countries has been considered. The increasing role played by in-work benefits in the Anglo-Saxon welfare systems, with positive evidence of redistributive effects and social inclusion of low-skilled workers, should indeed encourage other countries to evaluate the feasibility of implementing such policies.

Although the redistributive effects are modest and the IWBs cannot be considered as a primary tool in poverty reduction, they are a means to support the poorest. In general, family-based in-work benefits seem to be better targeted at the poorest families but the presence of multi-family households does not allow such policies to be targeted at the poorest households. Individually-based policies lead to better incentives to work both at the intensive and the extensive margin than family-based in-work benefits. In particular, women in couples, whose labour market participation is far below the European average, face higher incentives to work part-time or full-time after the introduction of individually-based policies while they face a lower incentive to work after the introduction of family-based in-work benefits.

The analyses confirm that in-work benefits might be one of the pillars of a redefined welfare system in the Southern European countries in order to enhance the economic position of the working poor and to increase female employment. In particular, despite the influence of the Anglo-Saxon models on policy-makers, individually-based IWBs seem to be more efficient if the enhancement of the labour market participation of women in couples is of fundamental concern. However, cash transfers must be complemented by an extension of child care provisions in order to allow women to find jobs that are not only more financially attractive but also reconcilable with other caring responsibilities.

As a general remark, the case-study presented in this chapter shows the extent to which a policy swapping analysis can be informative about the interaction between the structure of the tax-benefit instrument and the socio-economic characteristics of the population. Although it is not easy to adopt policies employed in other countries, mutual policy learning should be one of the key elements to improve the effectiveness of a tax-benefit system.

References

Atkinson, A.B. (2005) 'EUROMOD and the Development of EU Social Policy', EUROMOD Working Papers EM1/05.

Atkinson, A.B. (2009) 'An Enlarged Role for Tax Benefit Models', in: Lelkes, O./Sutherland, H. (eds.), *Tax and Benefit Policies in the Enlarged Europe. Assessing the Impact with Microsimulation Models*. Aldershot: Ashgate.

Atkinson, A.B./Bourguignon, F./Chiappori, A. (1988) 'What do we learn about tax reform from international comparisons? France and Britain', *European Economic Review* 32: 343-352.

Atkinson, A.B./Cantillon, B./Marlier, E./Nolan, B. (2002) *Social Indicators: the EU and Social Inclusion*. Oxford University Press.

Atkinson, A.B./Cantillon, B./Marlier, E./Nolan, B. (2005) *Taking Forward the EU Social Inclusion Process*. Luxembourg Presidency of the Council of the European Union.

Baldini, M./Bosi, P./Toso, S. (2002) 'Targeting Welfare in Italy: Old Problems and Perspectives on Reform', *Fiscal Studies* 23 (1): 51-75.

Bargain, O./Orsini, K. (2006) 'In-Work Policies in Europe: Killing Two Birds with One Stone', *Labour Economics* 13: 667-697.

Bertola, G. (2000) 'Policy Choices and Interactions with Existing Instruments', *OECD Economic Studies* 31: 185-196.

Blundell, R./Duncan, A./McCrae, J./Meghir, C. (2000) 'The Labour Market Impact of the Working Families Tax Credit', *Fiscal Studies* 21 (1): 75-104.

Boeri, T./Layard, R./Nickell, S. (2000) *Welfare-to-Work and the fight against long-term unemployment*.

Boeri, T./Perotti, R. (2001) *Less Pensions, More Welfare*. Bologna: Il Mulino.

Bradshaw, J./Kennedy, S./Kilkey, M./Hutton, S./Corden, A./Eardley, T./Holmes, H./Neale, J. (1996) *Policy and the Employment of Lone Parents: A Comparison of Policy in 20 Countries*. London: SPRC.

Brewer, M. (2001) 'Comparing In-Work Benefits and the Reward to Work for Families with Children in the US and the UK', *Fiscal Studies* 22 (1): 41-77.

Brewer, M. (2003) 'The New Tax Credits', *IFS Briefing Note* No. 35.

Brewer, M. (2006) 'Tax credits: fixed or beyond repair?', in: Chote, R. et al. (Eds.), *The IFS Green Budget: January 2006*. London: IFS.

Brewer, M./Duncan, A./Shephard, A./Suarez, M. J. (2006) 'Did Working Family Tax Credit work? The impact of in-work support on labour supply in Great Britain', *Labour Economics* 13: 699-720.

Callan, T./Sutherland, H. (1997) 'The impact of comparable policies in European countries: microsimulation approaches', *European Economic Review* 41: 627-633.

Eissa, N./Hoynes, H. (2004) 'Taxes and the Labour Market Participation of Married Couples: The Earned Income Tax Credit', *Journal of Public Economics* 88 (9-10): 1931-1958.

Esping-Andersen, G. (1990) *The Three Worlds of Welfare Capitalism*. Oxford: Polity Press.

European Commission (2004) *Facing the Challenge. The Lisbon Strategy for Growth and Employment*. Luxembourg: Office for Official Publications of the European Communities.

EUROSTAT (2006) *The Social Situation in the European Union 2005-2006*. European Commission.

EUROSTAT (2007) *Europe in Figures. Eurostat Yearbook 2006-07*. Eurostat Statistical books.

Ferrera, M. (1996) 'The "Southern" Model of Welfare in Social Europe', *Journal of European Social Policy* 6 (1): 17-37.

Ferrera, M./Matsaganis, M./Sacchi, S. (2002) 'Open Coordination against Poverty: The New EU 'Social Inclusion Process' ", *Journal of European Social Policy* 12 (3): 227-239.

Figari, F. (2009) "Can In-work Benefits Improve Social Inclusion in the Southern European Countries?", EUROMOD Working Papers EM4/09.

Francesconi, M./Van der Klaauw, W. (2007) 'The Socioeconomic Consequences of 'In-Work' Benefit Reform for British Lone Mothers', *Journal of Human Resources* 42 (1): 1-31.

Haan, P./Mick, M. (2007) 'Apply with Caution: Introducing UK-Style In-Work Support in Germany', *Fiscal Studies* 28 (1): 43-72.

Immervoll, H. (2004) 'Average and marginal effective tax rates facing workers in the EU. A micro-level analysis of levels, distributions and driving factors', *OECD Social, Employment and Migration Working Papers* No. 19. Paris: OECD.

Immervoll, H./Sutherland, H./de Vos, K. (2001) 'Reducing Child Poverty in the European Union: the Role of Child Benefits', in: Vleminckx, K./Smeeding, T. M. (eds.), *Child Well-Being, Child Povery and Child Poverty in Modern Nations*. Bristol: Policy Press.

Levy, H. (2003) "Child-targeted tax-benefit reform in Spain in a European context: a microsimulation analysis using EUROMOD", EUROMOD Working Paper, EM2/03.

Levy, H./Lietz, C./Sutherland, H. (2007) 'Swapping Policies: Alternative Tax-Benefit Strategies to Support Children in Austria, Spain and the UK', *Journal of Social Policies* 36 (4): 625-647.

Levy, H./Morawski, L./Myck, M. (2008) "Alternative tax-benefit strategies to support children in Poland", EUROMOD Working Paper, EM4/08.

Lietz, C./Mantovani, D. (2007) 'A Short Introduction to EUROMOD: An Integrated European Tax-Benefit Model', pp. 1-26 in: Bargain, O. (ed.), *Micro-simulation in action: Policy analysis in Europe using EUROMOD*, Research in Labor Economics, 25, Elsevier Ltd.

Lietz, C./Sutherland, H. (2005) "Social Indicators and other Income Statistics using EUROMOD: an assessment of the 2001 baseline and changes 1998-2001", EUROMOD Working Paper, EM7/04.

Mantovani, D./Sutherland, H. (2003) "Social Indicators and other Income Statistics using EUROMOD baseline: a Comparison with Eurostat and National Statistics", EUROMOD Working Paper, EM1/03.

OECD (2003) *Employment Outlook*. Paris: OECD.

OECD (2006) *Employment Outlook*. Paris: OECD.

Owens, J. (2006) 'Fundamental Tax Reform: An International Perspective', *National Tax Journal* LIX 1: 131-164.

Phelps, E. (1994) 'Raising the Employment and Pay of the Working Poor: Low Wage Employment Subsidies vs the Welfare State', *AER Papers and Proceedings*, May: 54-88.

Phelps, E. (2000) 'The importance of inclusion and the power of job subsidies to increase it', *OECD Economic Studies*, 31. Paris: OECD.

Sutherland, H. (2007) 'EUROMOD: the tax-benefit microsimulation model for the European Union', pp. 483-488: in Gupta, A./Harding, A. (eds.), *Modelling Our Future: population ageing, health and aged care*. International Symposia in Economic Theory and Econometrics Vol 16, Elsevier.

Sutherland, H./Figari, F./Lelkes, O./Levy, H./Lietz, C./Mantovani, D./Paulus, A. (2008) Improving the capacity and usability of EUROMOD – Final Report, EUROMOD Working Paper EM4/08.

Chapter 9

Behavioural Microsimulation: Labour Supply and Child Care Use Responses in Australia and Norway

Guyonne Kalb / Thor O. Thoresen

1   Introduction

The main purpose of this chapter is to discuss labour supply and child care modelling in a microsimulation context, and to report the results from this type of behavioural microsimulation with regard to female labour supply effects, distributional effects, and the costs to the government. Our interest is in changing transfer schemes to improve parents' labour supply. We show the effects of a move towards lower fees for care in child care centres in Norway and Australia.

We present two behavioural microsimulation models, developed in Australia and Norway respectively, to analyse such policy changes. The Norwegian model is based on a structural joint labour supply and child care choice model (Kornstad and Thoresen, 2007), whereas the Australian model is based on a two-step labour supply and child care choice model, in which a reduced-form bivariate tobit model for formal and informal care is used to impute care costs into a structural labour supply model (Doiron

This chapter was written when the second author visited the Department of Economics and the Melbourne Institute of Applied Economic and Social Research at the University of Melbourne. Both institutions are gratefully acknowledged for their hospitality. A previous version of this chapter was presented at the Australian Labour Market Research Workshop, 8-9 February 2007, and at the International Microsimulation Conference, 20-22 August 2007. We thank Prem Thapa and John Creedy for their comments on earlier versions of this chapter. The first author also acknowledges the financial support of the Australian Research Council, which funded this research through a Discovery Project Grant (# DP0770567).

and Kalb, 2005). These models are compared to other models developed in the literature.

The institutional features of the economies the models are set to operate in are important for two reasons. First, they provide guidelines on how to construct the model and, secondly, results from simulations of policy changes must be evaluated in the context of the objectives of the transfer schemes. Improved labour supply incentives arising from reduced fees must be balanced against increased government expenditure and adverse effects on the distribution of income.

Section 2 briefly reviews the literature on labour supply and child care modelling. After a quick comparison of Norway and Australia in terms of family transfer schemes, labour supply and income distributions, Section 3 presents the two behavioural microsimulation models to be used in the analysis. The labour supply effects and distributional effects from the microsimulations of the proposed policy changes are presented and discussed in Section 4. Section 5 concludes the chapter.

2   Joint labour supply and child care modelling

Before presenting our own empirical strategies when estimating joint labour supply and child care choice models in Section 3, we discuss some of the main issues and challenges in modelling labour supply behaviour of parents of preschoolers. We focus on models of parents' labour supply and child care choices.[1]

2.1   Simplification of the modelling: focus on mothers' labour supply

The simultaneous choice of child care and labour supply is a multidimensional issue, which creates a number of empirical challenges. Compromise along some dimension is often required in order to be able to address this issue. Analyses based on data from the U.S. and Canada appear to focus on quality issues, such as choice of mode of care, whereas there appears to be more attention towards availability issues in Europe (Wrohlich, 2006). This brief review does not endeavour to address all the methodological questions involved, but highlights quality and availability issues.

---

1   Heckman (1974) and Blau and Robins (1988) are two early contributions.

An additional simplification is that a predominant part of the literature focuses on the labour supply behaviour of single parents or mothers in two-parent households. In fact, the model presented in Section 3 for Australia (Doiron and Kalb, 2005) is one of the few couple-based models within this literature; Brink et al. (2007) is another example. In a few approaches, care by fathers is included among the care alternatives – see for instance Casper and O'Connell (1998), and Kimmel and Powell (2006).

We focus on the labour supply of married/cohabiting mothers in our analysis.

2.2 The utility functions of families of preschoolers

The standard framework of the joint labour supply and child care choice literature is to assume that families derive utility from leisure (L), consumption (C) and child care quality (Q):

$$U = v(L, C, Q),$$ (1)

where the inclusion of the child care quality component separates this approach from labour supply models without child care considerations. However, there is a large variety in how child care quality is incorporated in the different analyses. This reflects the fact that child care quality is an ambiguous concept; for instance it may refer to various forms of child development or to the well-being of children when in care.

It is usually assumed that care has a quality and quantity component, that there are different modes of care, that every child receives some amount of care from its parents, and that preschool children need non-parental arrangements for the time that both parents participate in the labour market. We discuss the link between hours of work and hours of care in Section 2.4. Care can be purchased from different types of care providers and informal types of care, such as care by grandparents, may be available. As an example, in analyses based on data from North America, as in Blau and Hagy (1998), two types of purchased care are often distinguished: centre-based care and care by a sitter in the sitter's or child's home.

As an example of how quality is addressed in the literature, Blau and Hagy (1998) present the following quality production function:

$$Q = Q(T, F, \mathbf{A}, I; \mathbf{X}, \eta_2)$$ (2)

where T is maternal child care time; F is non-parental child care time; A is a vector of attributes representing the quality of non-parental care; I is a categorical variable representing different combinations of employment and child care, which may also influence quality; X is a vector of observed exogenous variables; and η_2 represents unobserved household characteristics. The quality attributes of child care (A) include variables such as group size, staff/child ratio, and provider training. The model is estimated by employing a discrete-continuous approach, estimating a 14-state discrete choice model jointly with equations for a number of continuously distributed variables. Related approaches are followed by Michalopoulos and Robins (2000), Powell (2002), Lokshin (2004) and Wrohlich (2006).

The reduced-form approach of Blau and Hagy can be contrasted to frameworks that are more structural, in that they are more closely tied to an economic model of household behaviour. Examples are Michalopoulos et al. (1992), Ribar (1995) and Averett et al. (1997). For instance, Ribar estimates a model based on maximising a utility function, which is quadratic in income, labour supply and paid care utilization. The representation of quality in such models is challenging, since there are reasons to assume that two types of care are available to parents: purchased care and unpaid non-maternal care (such as care by a grandmother). The standard assumption is that both types of care are available to all. Under such circumstances, all parents would consume free care, unless additional identifying assumptions are introduced. Michalopoulos et al. (1992) assume that care costs are proportional to quality; Ribar (1995) introduces a dichotomous variable in the utility function, implicitly capturing negative utility of unpaid care utilization; and Averett et al. (1997) assume that informal care has an unobserved shadow price, reflecting psychic costs or quid-pro-quo agreements.

Different estimation methods are used for the structural models. For instance, Ribar (1995) employs a multinomial discrete choice approach, which is also the dominant empirical strategy within the part of the literature that focuses on mode choices. In contrast to most mode choice analyses, which rely on the conditional logit model with state-specific extreme value distributed error terms,[2] Ribar's model involves a more complex likelihood function (for instance, allowing some parameters to be stochastic).

The models for Norway (Kornstad and Thoresen, 2007) and Australia (Doiron and Kalb, 2005), used in this chapter, both belong to the structural part of the literature.

---

2   See the basic model in Van Soest (1995) and a survey of the literature in Creedy and
     Kalb (2005).

2.3   Measures of costs

Measuring real child care costs is a challenge and serious measurement problems can arise in deriving measures of statutory fee prices. The standard approach to derive measures of fees is to use information from the same data source which reports labour supply and child care choices. However, in such data, the child care fees are obviously endogenously chosen by the parents – and therefore they are contaminated by the preferences of the parents. Moreover, many studies based on U.S. data report that the price of child care is only observed for employed mothers (for example, Connelly and Kimmel, 2003), creating an additional measurement problem.

Studies that focus on detailed choice sets of care often employ multinomial logit frameworks, which require extensive imputation of counterfactuals. A popular approach to impute prices for each alternative is to estimate fee equations, often with controls for selectivity. An alternative approach is to match information from household surveys to information from care providers on fees and other attributes of care (for example, Blau and Hagy, 1998). Dependent on the modelling framework, other studies employ a hedonic approach to obtain prices that reflect quality (for example, Duncan et al., 2001).

2.4   The link between hours of care and hours of work

Another important issue is the assumption regarding the relationship between hours in care and hours in work. Do mothers need non-maternal care for as many hours as they work and do they spend all their non-work time with the child(ren)? Regarding the first question, a link between hours in care and hours in work is not always explicitly stated and taken into account in the empirical framework. According to Duncan et al. (2001), child care price effects tend to be overestimated when studies fail to respect the constraint that child care hours must at least equal work hours. This assumes that fathers play no role, which is the implicit assumption in many studies, since the role of fathers is often neglected.

The other question, to what extent mothers are allowed to enjoy "real leisure", in addition to their time in market work and time in care activities, has received some attention. Some studies, such as Blau and Hagy (1998), allow "non-working" mothers to utilize non-maternal care alternatives. Allowing such choices can be problematic due to a lack of information, as Powell (2002) reports that child care prices are not observed for "non-working" mothers.

2.5 Availability constraints

Several studies emphasize that rationing and availability of care are important when modelling the labour market behaviour of mothers with preschool children: many parents have no access to care. This question is not easily separated from the quality issue, since restrictions may be observed for some types of care, with certain quality attributes, whereas other modes of care, with other (lesser) quality characteristics, are available. For instance, many parents are constrained with regard to care from grandparents or other relatives simply because they live too far away. Davis and Connelly (2005) incorporate availability constraints in a model belonging to the reduced-form mode choice approach. They use information on geographical variations in the number of slots per children in different age groups in centres and family day care, and they use self-reported information on the availability of other care alternatives.

Due to the different institutional settings in Europe and the North-American countries, studies based on data from European countries pay more attention to rationing and availability. In many Northern European countries, the public sector is strongly involved in the supply of care; child care is often centre-based and centres are highly regulated and subsidized. However, often the number of slots in these centres has not been sufficient to meet the demand. This happened in the Nordic countries. In Southern European countries, the availability restrictions appear even more severe. According to Del Boca (2005), Italy has long queues for publicly provided care, a less developed market for private care, and substantial rigidities with respect to opening hours in centres.

Rationing is accounted for in different ways in the literature. Gustafsson and Stafford (1992) incorporate a variable representing the degree of rationing of centre-based care at the municipality level by comparing the number of mothers of pre-school children either working or in education with the number of centre-based care spaces. From a reduced-form logit analysis, they find that the elasticity of work (more than 30 hours) with respect to the price of child care is substantially influenced by rationing: the average elasticity is -0.06 for all and -1.9 for those not subject to rationing. Following Gustafsson and Stafford, Del Boca and Vuri (2007) use area-specific information to address the availability constraint. They also find that public policies to reduce child care costs will have different effects depending on families' access to care. Lokshin (2004) and Wrohlich (2006) use an alternative approach. In Lokshin, those in the sample without access to formal child care have reduced choice sets,[3] whereas Wrohlich argues that restrictions with respect to subsidized formal (subsidized) care can be translated into a price increase, raising the price of child care for families who have no access to formal care to the same level as for "private market" child care.

3   The Norwegian and Australian models

Before presenting the two microsimulation models for labour supply and child care responses for Norway and Australia in Sections 3.2 and 3.3, we briefly describe some main institutional features of Norway and Australia, highlighting the differences between the two countries.[4] These characteristics have consequences for the modelling approaches and form the background for interpreting the empirical results in Section 4.

The Norwegian and Australian models are similar in many ways. The behavioural responses are both based on discrete choice labour supply models, which have been adapted to suit the institutional arrangements in each country and the data available. For example, the Norwegian model allows for rationing of child care but the Australian model does not (since no information is available on this). This has the potential for understating the Australian response to child care price changes. However, this effect is expected to be limited since, from the data, there is no evidence that households lack access to formal child care or use less formal child care than they would like. One advantage of the Australian approach is that fathers' labour supply responses are taken into account.

3.1   *Main institutional features of Norway and Australia*

There are many similarities between Australia and Norway – both countries being rich in natural resources, possessing relatively ambitious welfare states, and belonging to high-growth economies over the last decades (Mehlum et al., 2006). The two countries are often found among the highest-ranked

---

3   This is similar to the approach followed by Kornstad and Thoresen (2007), see Section 3.2.
4   A detailed comparison can be found in Kalb and Thoresen (2007).

countries according to various indices, such as the Human Development Index from the United Nations. However, the two countries differ substantially with regard to the design and generosity of family support schemes, families' labour supply and income distributions. These three aspects are briefly compared in this subsection.

3.1.1 Family support transfers

Norway and Australia represent the polar opposites of family support schemes: the Nordic model of subsidized non-parental care and universal family income support versus a support scheme based on means-tested or income-tested transfers.[5]

Nevertheless, fertility rates in Australia and Norway are rather similar. In 2006, it was 1.81 for Australia (ABS, 2007) and 1.90 for Norway (Statistics Norway, 2007). Parental leave schemes are again rather different in the two countries. In Norway, families with both parents in paid employment prior to birth can choose between full compensation over a period of 44 weeks or 80% compensation over 54 weeks. Mothers without work experience prior to birth receive a cash transfer of NOK33,584 (2007 value).[6] The total cost of the parental leave scheme was about NOK11 billion in 2007.

In Australia, entitlements at the federal level are much lower. In principle, there is no paid maternity leave, although several individual employers are now offering women (and sometimes men) different amounts of paid leave (but this is often linked to tenure and/or returning to work within a certain period). Parental leave provisions include up to 52 weeks of *unpaid* parental leave for parents to take on a shared basis to care for their newborn child or newly adopted child under the age of five years. After the leave, parents have the right to be returned to the position held immediately before the start of parental leave or an equivalent position. In addition, there is a one-off payment of AU$4,133 per child paid at birth, costing the Government about 0.2 billion dollars in 2003/2004 (ABS, 2006).

In almost all industrialized countries, some sort of cash support conditional on the presence of children in families exists. The main difference between Norway and Australia is that the Australian Family Tax Benefit is income-tested partly on household income and partly on the primary

---

5 A third type is the in-work benefit schedules present in the U.K. and in the U.S.
6 For an approximate exchange rate between the Australian and Norwegian currencies, use 1AU$≈5NOK. In addition, with reference to exchange rates in June 2007: 1US$≈6NOK and 1AU$≈0.85US$.

carer's income. The Child Benefit schedule in Norway is paid to all mothers of children between 0 and 18 years of age. The total costs of the Child Benefit scheme exceeded NOK14.3 billion in 2007.

The first type of family payment in Australia, Family Tax Benefit part A, pays the maximum rate per child to all families with children on an annual income under $40,000. Some payment can still be received by families on relatively high incomes, with the minimum rate still being fully paid to families on an income of at least AU$88,620 per year. A second payment, Family Tax Benefit part B, is available to all single-earner families in Australia and only income-tested on the income of the secondary earner. The total cost of the Family Tax Benefit payments was AU$12.9 billion in 2003/2004.

In Norway, three types of care for preschool children can be distinguished: parents' own care and two types of non-parental care, consisting of centre-based care and child-minders. The centres are financed through national-level governmental subsidies; support from local governments; and parental fees.

The waiting lists for access to subsidized centre-based care were a main argument for the introduction of the Home Care Allowance. This scheme gives all parents of preschool children aged 1 or 2 a tax-free transfer in cash, depending only on utilization of public or private day care centres. The reform was introduced in order to make government transfers across different modes of care more equal. The allowance cost approximately NOK2 billion in 2007.

Introducing Home Care Allowance was controversial, because the transfer provides incentives to withdraw from the labour market and care for children at home (Kornstad and Thoresen, 2007). In response, the so-called "child care compromise" was introduced in 2004. It implies increased efforts to abolish queues for centre-based care and a substantial reduction in parental fees through introduction of maximum prices, applicable to all centre-based care. Finally, there is an income deduction scheme for child care expenses through the tax system.[7]

For 2007, the Norwegian government transferred approximately NOK13.7 billion to child care centres. The costs of the various financial programmes to increase the supply of centre-based care are not included in that measure.

---

7   Deductions for child care expenses are limited by an upper threshold; in 2007, this was set at NOK25,000 for the first child, to which NOK5,000 is added for each additional child.

In Australia, Child Care Benefit is available to parents who have non-parental care expenditures. There are different child care subsidy rates, depending on the number and age of children, the parents' incomes and labour market status, the type of child care that is used and the number of hours of child care that is used. A (small) minimum amount of AU$0.497 per hour (in 2006/2007) is payable to all child care users, independent of household income. In 2005/2006 the Australian government spent about AU$1.5 billion on the Child Care Benefit, slightly up from AU$1.4 billion in 2003/2004; see ABS (2006).

A second source of assistance to parents who pay for child care is the Child Care Tax Rebate. If a work/study test is passed and the family has received Child Care Benefit, any costs remaining after deducting the Child Care Benefit from child care costs from approved care can be rebated at 30% up to a maximum amount of AU$4,211 per child. There is no income test for this rebate.[8]

Comparing the costs of transfers in relation to aggregate economic measures such as tax revenues and GDP, different results are found for Australia and Norway. Summing the total costs of the various transfer programmes for families with dependent children, we find that the costs in Norway were approximately NOK43 billion. This was about 7.4% of the estimated tax revenue for mainland Norway in 2007, or about 2.7% of mainland GDP. The average expenditure per child under 18 years of age in the population is estimated at NOK39,716. Summing the costs of the Australian transfer programmes for 2003/2004 results in a total cost of AU$14.5 billion (excluding the Child Care Tax Rebate which was not yet introduced at that stage). This was about 6.9% of Commonwealth tax revenue.[9] Approximately 1.6% of GDP was used for family support, whereas approximately AU$2,853 was spent per child under 18 years of age, much less than in Norway.

3.1.2 Parents' attachment to the labour market

Mothers' participation in the labour market is strikingly different between the two countries, even though differences have decreased over recent years. For instance, Jaumotte (2003) compared female labour force participation in 1981 with that in 2001: Australia's participation rate of women aged between 25 and 54 increased from just over 50% to just over 70%, whereas

---

8   In 2008, the rebate percentage will increase to 50% and the rebatable amount will increase to AU$7,500.

9   The 2003/2004 tax revenue was AU$209 billion (ABS, 2005).

this rate increased from just over 70% to just over 80% in Norway. OECD (2006) reports a rate of 70.7 and 79.9% for Australia and Norway respectively in 2005.

The effect of children is much more pronounced in Australia. Figure 1 provides information on measures for partnered mothers' labour supply in Australia and Norway by age of the youngest child, and compares them to females without children in the same age group (20-45). It confirms that Norwegian mothers of pre-school children[10] have higher participation rates, work less often part-time and work on average more hours, compared to Australian mothers. As soon as the youngest child starts school (represented by age group 5-9), participation increases substantially in Australia but also in Norway, so there remains a substantial difference between mothers in the two countries. In fact, Norwegian mothers with a youngest child between 5 and 9 years of age have very similar connections to market work as females without children, except for lower part-time ratios in the latter group.

Women without children, selected to be of a comparable age as the women with children in this figure, participate equally in the labour market in Australia and Norway. Australian and Norwegian fathers in the same 20-45 age group also follow similar patterns with respect to labour force participation and are hardly affected by the presence of young children.

Figure 1: Labour market connections for married/cohabiting men and women, aged 20 to 45, by age of the youngest child

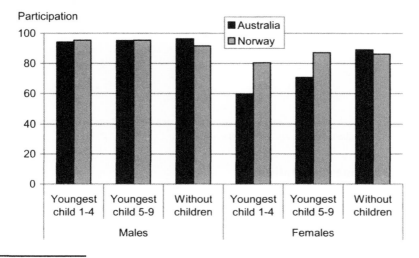

---

10   We restrict the comparison to families with children aged between 1 and 4, because Australian children usually enter preparatory school at the age of 5 and many Norwegian mothers of infants are on parental leave.

Figure 1 (continued)

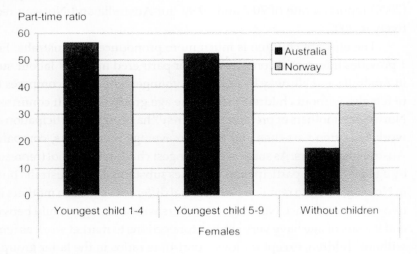

Source: Authors' calculations using the Survey of Income and Housing Costs 2003/2004 for Australia and the Labour Force Survey 2005 for Norway.

3.1.3 Income distributions

Redistributional objectives of family transfers, given the distribution of other income components, may contribute to the need for different transfer designs in Norway and Australia. Table 1 shows that, although overall Australia is more unequal, in accordance with previous findings for Norway and Australia (Gottschalk and Smeeding, 2000; Förster and Vleminckx,

2004), the subgroup of families with children has similar Gini coefficients in Norway and Australia. This similarity in income inequality seems mostly due to the targeted family payments in Australia.[11] When family payments are excluded from the post-tax income, the Gini coefficient increases substantially for Australia, indicating the importance of family payments for equality in Australia. Excluding the Child Benefit for Norway has a much smaller effect.

Table 1: **Estimates of income inequality and the distribution of family transfers across incomes in 2007**

	Australia		Norway	
	Gini coefficient	Concen-tration coefficient	Gini co-efficient	Concen-tration coefficient
Income inequality				
All	0.298		0.268	
all families with children 0-17	0.247		0.245	
same as above, excl. child benefit	0.319		0.262	
all families with preschoolers	0.245		0.245	
Distribution of child benefit, all families with children 0-17		-0.340		-0.079
Distribution of child care subsidies, all families with preschoolers[a]		-0.027		0.440

Note: a) For Norway this is done for households with children aged 1 or 2. Since fewer families in this group use centre-based care, it is expected that this estimate is larger than the estimate for the whole group of preschoolers.

The concentration indices are as expected for the family payments in the two countries (negative for Australia and close to zero for Norway), given that Australia targets these payments at poorer households and Norway provides universal child benefits. The targeting of child care subsidies in Australia is somewhat counterbalanced by the higher child care use by parents who are in the labour force (and therefore better off), resulting in a concentration index close to zero. Norway does not target child care subsidies and therefore only experiences the latter effect, causing the concentration coefficient to be positive and large.

---

11   Estimates presented in Table 1 are derived using the data sources of two microsimulation models of Norway and Australia; see descriptions of LOTTE (Norway) in Aasness et al. (2007) and of the Melbourne Institute Tax and Transfer Simulator (Australia) in Buddelmeyer et al. (2007). Standard methods in income distribution analysis are followed.

3.2   The Norwegian model for families with preschoolers

A decision model for Norwegian families with preschool children must at least include two important features of the Norwegian economy. Firstly, as described in Section 3.1.1, there are two types of non-parental care in Norway, which the model should take into account; care in centres and care by other paid caregivers, such as childminders. Secondly, as noted in Section 2.5, there is a focus on availability constraints in studies based on European data. A model for Norway should include the fact that some parents have more restricted choice sets than others. Therefore, parents who report that they are denied access to care, because of queues, have a more limited choice set in the model, similar to the approach of Lokshin (2004). Moreover, availability constraints are also taken into account by letting the number of opportunities vary across different discrete choices, arguing that in some of the discrete alternatives that households face, more opportunities are available.

The modelling framework is based on the notion that the parents choose one job for the mother and one child care alternative for each child. Thus, we have households maximising utility represented by $U(C_{kr}, H_k, k, r)$ – the utility of choosing job k and child care arrangement r, where C_{kr} is consumption/disposable income corresponding to job k and child care arrangement r and H_k is annual hours of work in job k for the mother. It is assumed that preferences can be specified as

$$U(C_{kr}, H_k, k, r) = v(C_{kr}, H_k) + \varepsilon^*(C_{kr}, H_k, k, r), \quad k \in B, \ r \in S, \tag{3}$$

where $v(C_{kr}, H_k)$ is the deterministic part of the utility function and $\varepsilon^*(C_{kr}, H_k, k, r)$ is a stochastic error term. This stochastic term captures the fact that the choice of the mother's job is not only influenced by working hours and wage rates, but also by the set of non-pecuniary attributes characterising job satisfaction. Similarly, child care options vary with regard to facilities, quality of staff, etc., as well as opening hours and fees. Many of these attributes are fixed for a given job or child care option. For instance, opening hours are fixed at child care centres, as frequently are hours of work and job satisfaction factors. A desire to alter such features would most likely require a job change or a change of care provider. Hence, we assume that labour supply and choice of child care are outcomes of discrete choices from finite sets of jobs and child care arrangements, where each job is assumed to have fixed working hours, a wage rate and a number of non-pecuniary characteristics, and each care alternative has fixed opening hours, a care fee and specific quality attributes.

We do not observe all variables and choice opportunities that are relevant to the decision-makers, such as the quality of non-parental child care or the variables determining job satisfaction, apart from hours of work and wage rates for participants in market work. To capture the effects of these non-pecuniary attributes on preferences, alternative specific stochastic error terms are introduced, which are assumed to be both independent of observed characteristics and of each other.

To simplify the choice process, we organize the job and child care alternatives into 11 categories (see Table 2). Regarding the link between hours of care and hours of work (discussed in Section 2.4), a fixed link (Ilmakunnas, 1997) is assumed to exist between hours of market work and hours of non-parental care for $j > 1$, so if $j > 1$ then $m = 1$ or $m = 2$ with the amount of non-parental care used equalling the hours of labour supply.[12] This means that the mother cannot work and take care of her child(ren) at the same time. However, mothers typically spend time with children when not working in the market. In that sense, "leisure" is assumed to contribute to the well-being of preschoolers. Reversely, we do not exclude the possibility of mothers out of the labour force using either of the two non-parental care alternatives. The combinations $j = 1$ and $m = 1$ or $j = 1$ and $m = 2$ suggest that non-parental care might be seen as a contributor to child care quality, not only as a substitute for parental care when this is unavailable.[13]

The mother is assumed to choose the job and child care arrangement that maximizes preferences subject to a standard budget constraint. A key feature of this model is that it follows from the model specification that the probability of choosing a job and child care arrangement from category (jm) depends on the number of jobs and care arrangements offered within this group, relative to the numbers in other groups. For instance, we know that there are more full-time than part-time opportunities both in the labour market and in the markets for child care. However, as no suitable information on these variations in opportunities is available, we treat the number

---

12   It is assumed that men provide no care during the working day. As seen in Figure 1 and evident from other data sources, males are predominantly full-time workers.

13   Approximately 3% of the parents use non-parental care even if the mother does not work. The hours of care used in these two categories are based on average amounts calculated from the data.

of alternatives as a latent variable to be estimated. In practice, we let the number of opportunities vary across states by allowing the number of options in combinations of long part-time work / child care centre ($j = 4$, $m = 1$), full-time work / child care centre ($j = 5, m = 1$) and not working / parental care ($j = 1, m = 3$) to differ relative to the other states. For the other states, the number of possibilities is normalized to one.

Table 2: Classification of jobs and child care arrangements

Mode of care (m)	Weekly working hours / weekly child care hours (j)				
	0	1-16	17-24	25-32	32+
Day care centre	$j=1, m=1$	$j=2, m=1$	$j=3, m=1$	$j=4, m=1$	$j=5, m=1$
Other paid care	$j=1, m=2$	$j=2, m=2$	$j=3, m=2$	$j=4, m=2$	$j=5, m=2$
Parental care	$j=1, m=3$	-	-	-	-

Regarding the rationing in the market for care in centres, mothers who report unsuccessful applications for centre-based care have more limited choice sets since they cannot choose care at centres ($m=1$). Then, based on a multinomial logit model, the probability P_{hjm} that household h chooses a job with the mother's hours of work in group j and a child care arrangement in mode m is:

$$P_{hjm} = \frac{\exp\left(v\left(\tilde{C}_{hjm}, \tilde{H}_{j'}, X_h\right) + \log\left(n_{jm}/n\right)\right)}{\exp\left(v\left(\tilde{C}_{h13}, \tilde{H}_1, X_h\right) + \log n_{13}\right) + \sum_{i=1}^{5}\sum_{l \in \Omega_h} \exp\left(v\left(\tilde{C}_{hil}, \tilde{H}_i, X_h\right) + \log n_{il}\right)}, (4)$$

where

$$\Omega_h = \begin{cases} (1,2) & \text{if household } h \text{ is constrained in the market for care at centers} \\ (1) & \text{otherwise} \end{cases},$$

n_{jm} is the number of opportunities in $B_j \times S_{jm}$, $\tilde{H}_j$ is the median working time in hours of work group j, and $\tilde{C}_{jm}$ is consumption, corresponding to working time, $\tilde{H}_j$, and the price of non-parental care, X_h is a taste modifying variable and n is the baseline value of number of jobs.

Note that there is no explicit assumption on quality differences between modes of care (only as captured by the state-specific error terms). However, it cannot be ruled out that estimates of n_{jm}/n include care quality effects or other state-specific effects.

Given that each household faces a number of job offers and care offers, a major challenge within this approach is to provide a reasonable representation of the wage and price distributions for each household across each category. This is extremely demanding with respect to information. We simplify by assuming that all parents face a fixed price across all non-parental care alternatives. Measures of the fees that the parents face in child care centres and in other paid care alternatives are derived from external sources (not the same data source as the information on choices are based on; see the discussion in Section 2.3): these are the Parental Pay Survey 1998 for centre-based care and a survey of childminders' child care production for other paid care. Thus, the care prices that families in the present analysis face vary with respect to modes of care (centres and other paid care). In addition, centre-based care price measures reflect families' geographical location and discount schemes with respect to siblings.

Wage measures are derived from a standard wage equation (log wage as dependent variable) controlling for selectivity. However, to take into account that wages vary across jobs, an individual-specific random effect is introduced by making 30 random draws from the normally distributed error term.

Data from the Home Care Allowance Survey 1998 are used in the estimation and in the simulation of the model, but in the simulations the data are projected to 2003. They were collected through postal interviews before the reform, with a response rate at 70%, and include detailed information on families' labour supply, use of child care and composition of income. Only married or cohabiting parents with at least one child between 1 and 5 years old are included in the analysis. Families that employ informal care by others, such as grandparents, are excluded from the analysis. According to our data, only a small number of families have access to this type of care. In addition, we exclude families where the mother is either a pensioner, student, on maternity leave, or on other types of paid leave. The final sample includes 768 observations. A number of checks have been carried out to assess the representativity of the sample. We find that there is close correspondence between the distribution of variables (such as mothers' education and age and the number of children) in this sample and a much larger sample of families with preschool children, collected from the 1998-wave of the Income Distribution Survey.

The budget constraint in each of the 11 states of Table 2 is defined by wage income (w_h times $\tilde{H}_j$), family income other than the mother's own earnings (I_h), the price of non-maternal child care (Q_m) and taxes (T):

$$\tilde{C}_{hjm} = w_h \tilde{H}_j + I_h - Q_m - T\left(w_h \tilde{H}_j, I_h, Q_m\right).$$

The tax-benefit model LOTTE (Aasness et al., 2007) is employed to derive family post-tax income (consumption) in each state. This model uses information from the Home Care Allowance Survey to establish (somewhat simplified) state-specific income tax returns for the households.[14]

In the estimation of the model, the deterministic component of the household's preferences is represented by a "Box-Cox" type utility function:

$$v\left(\tilde{H}_j,\tilde{C}_{hjm}\right)\equiv\gamma_0\frac{\tilde{C}_{hjm}^{\alpha_1}-1}{\alpha_1}+\frac{\left(1-\dfrac{\tilde{H}_j}{M}\right)^{\alpha_2}-1}{\alpha_2}X_h\beta \tag{5}$$

where $M = 8760$ is the total number of annual hours available to the mother, γ_0, α_1, α_2 and β are parameters, and X_h is the number of children below 19 years of age (see Kornstad and Thoresen (2007) for parameter estimates). For the utility function to be quasi-concave, we require $\alpha_1 < 1$ and $\alpha_2 < 1$. Note that if $\alpha_1 \to 0$ and $\alpha_2 \to 0$, the utility function converges to a log-linear function.

Figure 2: The distribution of observed and simulated choices, 11 states, families with children 1-5 years old

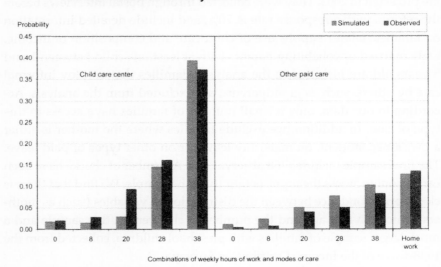

Corresponding to the classification of job and child care alternatives into 11 categories in Table 2, Figure 2 displays the actual frequencies of the dif-

---

14   Income tax return data are the standard database used in LOTTE.

ferent combinations and the relevant probability distributions, based on model simulations. The simulated probabilities are derived by calculating the average probability for each state, based on the individual probabilities from Equation (4). The category "Home work" includes alternatives where the mother is a caregiver at home, whereas non-parental care alternatives may also be used by mothers not participating in market work. Although the model provides a reasonably good fit, as measured by contrasting predicted and observed probability distributions, this is not conclusive evidence of acceptable model performance. A more rigorous test of the model is an examination of its capacity to predict effects of out-of-sample reforms, such as the ability to capture the effects of changes which were not part of the economic environment underlying the behaviour of economic agents used in the estimation of the model.

3.3 The Australian model for all couple families

Labour supply and child care demand are estimated in two separate steps. First, a reduced-form bivariate tobit model is estimated for formal care use and informal care cost (for details, see Doiron and Kalb, 2005). Explanatory variables include hours of work, number and age of children, presence of other adults in the household, and price of child care (from an external data source). The choice of the amount of care is continuous, depending on the amount of labour supply. There is no fixed link between hours of work and hours of formal care and cost of informal care. Instead, the link is estimated based on observed labour supply and child care use behaviour, allowing for unobserved heterogeneity.

The predicted demand for formal child care and cost of informal child care from this model is then used to impute child care costs for households in the Survey of Income and Housing Cost (SIHC) sample at the different levels of labour supply.[15] The SIHC is the main data set on which the policy simulations are based. Net child care costs are calculated from the predicted gross costs of child care and the predicted levels of child care benefits. These net costs are calculated using the characteristics of the household, predicted informal child care costs and predicted formal child care costs (computed from predicted formal child care demand multiplied by the average child

---

15   We have chosen 0, 5, 10, 15,…, 50 hours of labour supply for married women. Given the low number of married men working low part-time hours, they are assumed to choose from 0, 10, 20, 30, 40 or 50 hours.

care fees for that household). They are computed within the Melbourne Institute Tax and Transfer Simulator (MITTS), a microsimulation model for Australia. Any child care subsidies are deducted from formal costs, before adding the formal and informal costs together. No explicit account is taken of potential restrictions regarding child care availability, since no information is available on this. It is assumed there are no quality differences in care.

The labour supply model is described in detail in Kalb (2002). The approach follows most of the literature in adopting a neoclassical framework based on utility maximization (as described in Section 2.2) without an explicit consideration of child care quality. Only child care costs appear in the budget constraint. The rules of the relevant taxation and social security systems are used to obtain the net income of the household arising from its choices of labour supply.

The utility of couple families, $U(C, L_1, L_2)$, is maximized subject to a time constraint for each adult:

$$L_1 + H_1 = T \text{ and } L_2 + H_2 = T \tag{6}$$

and subject to a standard household budget constraint:

$$C = w_1 H_1 + w_2 H_2 + y_1 + y_2 + B(hc, w_1 H_1 + w_2 H_2 + y_1 + y_2) - \tau(B, w_1 H_1 + y_1, w_2 H_2 + y_2, hc) - cc(H_1, H_2, hc, w_1 H_1 + w_2 H_2 + y_1 + y_2) \tag{7}$$

where L_1 and L_2 indicate the leisure hours (including home production) of the husband and wife (married or de facto) respectively; H_1 and H_2 are the hours of work of husband and wife; T is the total time available for husband and wife; C indicates net income, which is assumed equal to household consumption; w_1 and w_2 are the gross wage rates of husband and wife; y_1 and y_2 are the non-labour incomes of husband and wife; hc is a set of household attributes; $B(.)$ is the amount of benefit a household is eligible for given its household characteristics hc and household income; τ is the tax function that indicates the amount of tax to be paid; and cc is the net child care cost to be paid.

The budget constraint for each household (including child care costs) can be constructed using MITTS. First, for each hours level allowed in the discrete choice labour supply model, a gross income level (together with all transfers and taxes) is computed within the MITTS model.[16] Then, for each household with children of 12 years or younger in the SIHC, a predicted net cost of child care is imputed, based on the characteristics of the household

---

16   Predicted wages are used for non-participants in the labour market. These are based on separate wage equations for married men and married women (see Kalb and Scutella, 2002).

(State, urban residency, number and age of children, and calculated gross income).

Rather than associating each household with one specific predicted child care cost amount *cc* in the labour supply model, recognising the uncertainty in predicted child care costs, we draw repeatedly from the joint distribution of formal and informal child care costs. A simulated maximum likelihood approach is used to estimate the model's parameters given these draws. The draws are generated by including a draw from the error term (individual-specific variation) when predicting child care costs and demand using the model. An advantage is that the calculation of the Child Care Benefits is more accurate in this approach compared to using expected child care costs, given that the subsidy payable for the average child care cost is not the same as the average Child Care Benefits based on potential outcomes for child care costs. The results presented in Section 4 are based on a model estimated using 10 draws.

Following Keane and Moffitt (1998), a quadratic specification is used for the utility function. This utility function is simple but quite flexible, in that it allows for the leisure of each person and income to be substitutes or complements. Parameters representing fixed costs of working are included in the utility function when positive labour choices are made. The fixed cost of the working parameter is subtracted from net income in the utility function to indicate the cost of working versus non-participation (following Callan and Van Soest, 1996). The fixed cost is zero when the relevant person is not working. In contrast to the Norwegian model, the utility of the preferred job/child care arrangement is independent of the number of opportunities in each category.

We include observed heterogeneity by allowing the linear preference and fixed cost parameters to depend on a range of exogenous personal and household characteristics such as the number and ages of children, and the age and education level of each parent. Unobserved heterogeneity is added to these parameters in the form of a normally distributed error term with zero mean and unknown variance.

Data from wave 2 of the Household, Income and Labour Dynamics in Australia (HILDA) Survey (conducted in 2002) are used to estimate the demand for child care. As expected, families with younger children (particularly of preschool age) and families with more adults in paid employment are more likely to use child care. Subsequently, data from the 2002/2003 Survey of Income and Housing Costs (SIHC) are augmented with parameters from the child care demand models, and used for labour supply modelling. Interviews for the 2002/2003 SIHC and the second wave of HILDA were conducted in the same financial year. It is therefore appropriate to combine information from the two data sets. The SIHC includes 3,404 couple families, 1,902 of which have dependent children. The SIHC is a representative survey of the Australian population conducted by the ABS.

Similar to the Norwegian measures of fees, an external source of data, the Child Care Census 2002 (Department of Family and Community Services, 2003), is used to obtain average hourly child care fees by age of the child and State of residency, which are then used in the modelling. In calculating average fees, the hourly fees of different types of child care are weighted by the number of children of a particular age using that type of child care. For these details and the estimated coefficients and properties of the model, see Kalb and Lee (2008).

4 Labour supply and distributional effects of changes in Australian and Norwegian child care subsidies

Although differences in family policies alone are unlikely to explain the disparities in mothers' labour supply in the two countries, the large differences in family support schemes are expected to contribute to the gap between the two countries. In subsection 4.1, we describe the effects of a substantial fee reduction following the so-called "child care compromise" in Norway (see Section 3.1.1), and in subsection 4.2 we simulate the effects of a similar reduction in child care fees in Australia. The results are summarized in Section 4.3. The focus is on the effects on married or cohabiting mothers' labour supply.

As labour incentives might come at a cost in terms of distributional effects, it is important to combine information about labour supply effects with descriptions of income distribution effects. We also provide measures of the total costs of changes, after taking behavioural adjustments into account.

4.1 Effects of reduced fees in centre-based care in Norway

As noted before, the design of Norwegian support schemes can be characterized as encouraging female labour supply. Recently, female labour supply incentives were further improved by the introduction of the so-called "child care compromise". In the following, we focus on the effects of fee reductions for centre-based care introduced by the "child care compromise".

The reform involves reducing fees for full-time care in day care centres down to NOK1,750 per month (in 2005 prices). In contrast, parents paid NOK2,800 per month on average for full-time care in centres run by local authorities in August 2003. As there is doubt that the policy-makers will reach the 1,750 level in the near future, we address effects of the fee reductions introduced so far, using the 2007 maximum fee of NOK2,330. Discounts for siblings and part-time care are taken into account.

The tax and transfer system for 2003 serves as a reference point or baseline when studying the effects. Thus, we project the data from the year of data collection, 1998, to 2003. The projection means that all income components, including female wage rates, are adjusted to 2003 levels by the wage growth in the period, that the prices of non-parental care are adjusted according to information on price changes in the period, and that the families are taxed according to the 2003 tax law. The maximum fee in 2007 is deflated to the 2003 level.

Results before and after the policy change are presented in terms of probabilities for various combinations of labour supply and child care. In accordance with features of Norwegian markets for non-parental care, we distinguish between centre-based care and other paid-care alternatives. The simulated probabilities are derived by calculating the average probability for each state, based on the individual choice probabilities. Similarly, measures of incomes are obtained by calculating average expected equivalized disposable income for each household member, before and after the policy reform.

The reduction in prices will increase demand for centre-based care, and it might therefore be unrealistic to allow mothers to choose freely under the prevailing conditions in the market for care at centres, even though the "child care compromise" aims at ending waiting lists for centre-based care. Under the assumption that the degree of rationing is at the same level as in the reference system, we expect that the depicted rate cuts will induce changes as described in Figure 3. The probability of "parental care/home work" is reduced, and the use of "full-time work/child care centre" increases substantially. In total, the mother's labour supply increases by about two hours per week on average, or about 6%. This corresponds to an increase of about 5,600 person-years.

Figure 3 also shows the probabilities for an alternative where the rate cut is combined with a no-rationing assumption, thus simulating the total effect of the "child care compromise". One may argue that this simulation provides a more realistic estimate of the effects, even though some families are still waiting for access. The behavioural effects are substantially stronger when removing the rationing constraint. Under this assumption, the overall effect on hours of work is an increase in labour supply by about 11%, or approximately 10,300 person-years.

Figure 3: Probabilities in baseline system compared to probabilities when maximum fees at child care centres are set at NOK2,330

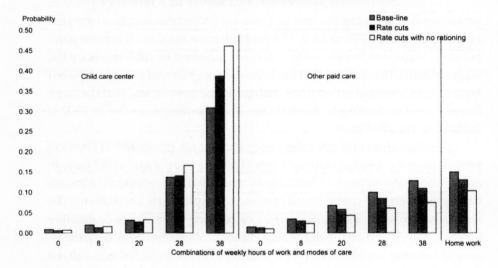

The effects of fee reductions on the distribution of incomes in the case of unchanged rationing are shown in Figure 4. The effects on incomes can be decomposed into two sources. Firstly, the reforms affect household incomes in a direct way, which refers to the effect on disposable income before behavioural adjustments. Secondly, alterations in the tax-benefit system make the mothers adjust behaviour – both with respect to labour supply and the choice of child care alternatives. These two effects are added together to obtain the total effect on incomes.

The income gains across quintiles, shown in Figure 4, reflect the fact that the indirect effects through working hours responses and changes in the use of child care centres are larger at the low end of the income distribution – while the direct effects are larger for high-income families, as there is a positive relationship between income and use of centre-based child care in the pre-reform situation. Combining the two effects, benefits are larger for high-income quintiles compared to the other quintiles, which confirms that reducing fees is not particularly beneficial for families at the low end of the income distribution.

It has been difficult to predict the costs of this reform, partly because of its two-fold character, which involves increasing availability and reducing prices at the same time.[17] For example, the fee reductions have increased demand, resulting in increased waiting lists for an unaltered supply of the services. Using information from budget proposals, we estimate the increase in operational costs of the reform in 2007 (when maximum fees are reduced to NOK2,370) to be NOK 6.4 billion, reflecting increased subsidies following from increased availability and from fee reductions. However, labour supply effects should be taken into account when calculating the budgetary costs. The tax revenue increase, induced by the larger tax base following from increased female labour supply, of approximately NOK1.3 billion[18] needs to be subtracted, resulting in an estimated total cost of NOK5.1 billion.

Figure 4: Effects on income distribution and on distribution of weekly working hours, Norway

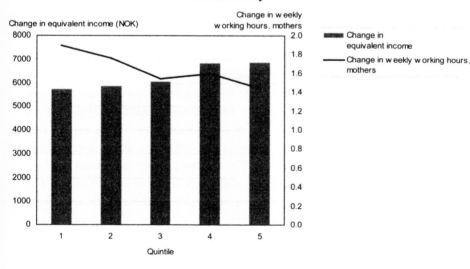

---

17 For instance, the official estimate of costs reported in Kornstad and Thoresen (2006) was too low.

18 Note that this estimate is derived from a simulation without availability restrictions and may somewhat overestimate the access to care in 2007, therefore representing a potentially upwardly biased estimate of the effect from an increased tax base.

This example clearly points out one of the dilemmas when designing family support schemes. The fee reduction encourages female labour supply, but it does not have advantageous distributional effects, at least with respect to the income distribution.

4.2 Effects of reduced fees of formal child care in Australia

To create a comparable policy change to the Norwegian fee reduction, we simulate a reduction in formal 2002/2003 child care fees by 50%, which is close (percentage wise) to the intended fee reduction of the Norwegian reform. The 2002/2003 tax and transfer system is similar to the current situation, except for the Child Care Tax Rebate, which was not introduced until 2004/2005.

The main component of the costs to the government is associated with halving child care fees. This cost is calculated by taking 50% of the original child care costs, and assuming that child care prices do not change as a result of this additional indirect subsidy. For all families together the cost is estimated at AU$0.9 billion per year and, for couple families only, the cost is estimated at AU$0.7 billion per year. Due to the lower child care fees, direct child care subsidies to families also decrease (assuming that families receive no more in subsidy than they pay for child care services).

Using behavioural microsimulation, we assess the effect of this policy on couples' labour supply.[19] The results show that women respond more than men to the increased net income resulting from lower child care fees. Women are usually more responsive to financial incentives and they are also more likely to be currently out of the labour force. Reducing the cost of child care will make it more attractive to enter the labour force. However, the effects are rather modest. The labour supply responses are low, reflecting the fact that many families with older children are not affected by the decrease in child care fees. On average, mothers increase their average working hours by 0.11 hours per week, indicating that the labour supply of Australian mothers is less elastic than the labour supply of Norwegian mothers. The effects are largest for mothers with children aged between 1 and 4, who are expected to increase their average working hours by 0.21 to 0.30 hours per week. Labour force participation increases the most (0.8 percentage points) for mothers of 1- to 2-year old children. A small positive effect of 0.01 hours per week on average is found for men.

---

19   The labour supply model only predicts the labour supply changes for wage and salary workers between 15 and 64 years of age. Those who are self-employed, full-time students or disabled remain at their observed labour supply in the simulation.

Additional tax revenue of AU$49 million and reduced expenditure of AU$48 million is expected due to increased labour supply. Overall, taking labour supply responses into account, the increase in government expenditure of AU$0.9 billion due to the policy change will be reduced by about AU$86 million.

Figure 5: **Effects on income distribution[a] and on weekly working hours from child care fee reductions, Australia**

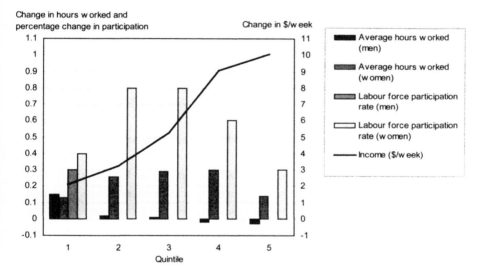

Note: a) Change in disposable income (net of child care cost) is calculated at fixed labour supply levels. At the moment, the change in income when allowing for labour supply responses cannot be calculated. However, given the small labour supply responses the results will be similar to those assuming fixed labour supply.

There is no distributional impact of this policy change on families with dependent children aged under 18 years of age, when labour supply is fixed (as is seen when computing Gini coefficients before and after the change). Comparing the average effect of the policy change by equivalized income quintiles, Figure 5 shows clear differences. Focusing on couple families only, Figure 5 shows that families in higher quintiles receive on average a larger increase in their equivalized disposable income than families in lower quintiles. However, the labour supply changes partly counteract this. The indirect effect (through labour supply changes) is higher for men in lower income quintiles and highest for women in the middle-income quintiles. Similarly, women in middle quintiles have higher labour supply responses than women in low- or high-income households. As in Norway, Figure 5 shows that the direct effects of the policy change are higher for the higher quintiles whereas the indirect effects are higher for the lower and middle quintiles, resulting in a combined effect which remains largest for the top quintile.

As expected, female labour supply is more affected than male labour supply in all quintiles. Figure 5 also reveals interesting differences between mothers and fathers in terms of the distributions of changes in working hours and labour force participation. Fathers belonging to the upper quintiles have very small (negative) responses to the policy change, whereas mothers' responses are larger (and positive). The reason for this difference is that households in the higher quintiles are much more likely to contain men who are already working substantial hours, thus offering less scope for increases in labour supply, whereas any of the quintiles are likely to contain families with women who are not working or working few hours.

4.3 The case for fee reductions in Australia and Norway

Summarising the results of child care fee reductions in Norway and Australia, we find that strengthening labour supply incentives in this way may have unfavourable distributional effects. Reduced child care fees in Norway encourage female labour supply, but the labour supply stimulating policy change also makes Norway's income distribution more unequal. That is, this simulation illustrates that there might be trade-offs between the aim of redistributing incomes and the objective to attract more women to market work.

The results for Australia support the same view as the results for Norway: encouraging labour supply by reducing child care fees for everyone is relatively costly, could have detrimental distributional effects and the gains in terms of working hours are limited. The main reason for effects not being stronger is that Australian married / de facto mothers are not found to be very responsive with respect to changes in child care costs. This indicates the importance in policy-making of having access to this type of information, provided by behavioural microsimulation models.

Despite the expected lack of success of reducing child care fees for all families, there remains a concern in Australia regarding relatively low labour force participation rates of mothers. High, and recently quickly increasing, prices for non-parental care in Australia may prevent low-income mothers from participating in the labour market. Alternative policies may be more effective than universal fee reductions.

5   Concluding remarks

In this chapter, we have discussed microsimulation modelling involving labour supply and child care responses, focusing on two such models for Norway and Australia. When applying the two models to predict the effects of fee reductions in the two countries we find very similar results: the differences appear mainly driven by somewhat more elastic labour supply in Norway compared to Australia.

Although results from such analyses provide valuable input for policymakers, we conclude by acknowledging that there are several unresolved issues, which need more attention. These involve shortcomings with respect to our own model specifications, as well as shortcomings in the literature more generally. For example, one major challenge is that fathers' involvement in care is likely to increase in the future, calling for models which endogenize fathers' labour supply.

References

Aasness, J./Dagsvik, J.K./Thoresen, T.O. (2007) 'LOTTE – The Norwegian Tax-Benefit Model System', pp. 513–518 in: Gupta, A./Harding, A. (eds.), *Modelling Our Future: Population Ageing, Health and Aged Care*, International Symposia in Economic Theory and Econometrics Volume 16. Amsterdam: Elsevier.

Australian Bureau of Statistics (ABS) (2005) *Taxation Revenue, Australia (reissue), 2003-04*, Catalogue no. 5506.0. Canberra.

ABS (2006) *Yearbook Australia, 2005*, Catalogue no. 1301.0. Canberra.

ABS (2007) *Births Australia, 2006*, Catalogue no. 3301.0. Canberra.

Averett, S.L./Peters, H.E./Waldman, D.M. (1997) 'Tax Credits, Labor Supply, and Child Care', *Review of Economics and Statistics* 79: 125-135.

Blau, D.M./Hagy, A.P. (1998) 'The Demand for Quality in Child Care', *Journal of Political Economy* 106: 104-146.

Blau, D.M./Robins, P.K. (1988) 'Child-Care Costs and Family Labor Supply', *Review of Economics and Statistics* 70: 374–381.

Brink, A./Nordblom, K./Wahlberg, R. (2007) 'Maximum Fee vs. Child Benefit: A Welfare Analysis of Swedish Child-Care Fee Reform', *International Tax and Public Finance* 14: 457-480.

Buddelmeyer, H./Creedy, J./Kalb, G. (2007) *Tax Policy Design and Behavioural Microsimulation Modelling*. Cheltenham: Edward Elgar.

Callan, T./Van Soest, A. (1996) 'Family Labour Supply and Taxes in Ireland', Working Paper No. 78, Economic and Social Research Institute, Dublin, Ireland.

Casper, L.M./O'Connell, M. (1998) 'Work, Income, the Economy, and Married Fathers as Child-Care Providers', *Demography* 45: 243-250.

Connelly, R./Kimmel, J. (2003) 'Marital Status and Full-Time/Part-Time Work Status in Child Care Choices', *Applied Economics* 35: 761-777.

Creedy, J./Kalb, G. (2005) 'Discrete Hours Labour Supply Modelling: Specification, Estimation and Simulation', *Journal of Economic Surveys* 19: 697-734.

Davis, E.E. / Connelly, R. (2005) 'The Influence of Local Price and Availability on Parent's Choice of Child Care', *Population Research and Policy Review* 24: 301-334.

Del Boca, D. (2005) 'Editorial Foreword', *Labour*, 19 (Special Issue): 1-4.

Del Boca, D. / Vuri, D. (2007) 'The Mismatch between Employment and Child Care in Italy: the Impact of Rationing', *Journal of Population Economics* 20: 805–832.

Department of Family and Community Services (2003) *2002 Census of Child Care Services*. Canberra: Commonwealth of Australia.

Doiron, D. / Kalb, G. (2005) 'Demands for Child Care and Household Labour Supply in Australia', *Economic Record* 81: 215–236.

Duncan, A. / Paull, G. / Taylor, J. (2001) 'Mothers' Employment and the Use of Child Care in the United Kingdom', IFS Working Papers WP01 / 23, Institute for Fiscal Studies, London.

Förster, M.F. / Vleminckx, K. (2004) 'International Comparisons of Income Inequality and Poverty: Findings from the Luxembourg Income Study', *Socio-Economic Review* 2: 191-212.

Gottschalk, P. / Smeeding, T.M. (2000) 'Empirical Evidence on Income Inequality in Industrialized Countries', pp. 261-307 in: Atkinson, A.B. / Bourguignon, F. (eds.), *Handbook of Income Distribution*, Volume 1. New York: Elsevier-North Holland.

Gustafsson, S. / Stafford, F. (1992) 'Child Care Subsidies and Labor Supply in Sweden', *Journal of Human Resources* 27: 204-230.

Heckman, J. (1974) 'Effects of Child Care Programs on Women's Work Effort', *Journal of Political Economy* 82: S136-163.

Ilmakunnas, S. (1997) 'Female Labour Supply and Work Incentives', Labour Institute for Economic Research, Finland.

Jaumotte, F. (2003) 'Labour Force Participation of Women: Empirical Evidence on the Role of Policy and Other Determinants in OECD Countries', *OECD Economic Studies*, No. 37, 2003 / 2.

Kalb, G. (2002) 'Estimation of Labour Supply Models for Four Separate Groups in the Australian Population', Working Paper No. 24 / 02, Melbourne Institute of Applied Economic and Social Research, University of Melbourne.

Kalb, G. / Lee, W.-S. (2008) 'Child care Use and Parents' Labour Supply in Australia', *Australian Economic Papers* 47: 272-295.

Kalb, G. / Scutella, R. (2002) 'Estimation of Wage Equations in Australia: Allowing for Censored Observations of Labour Supply', Melbourne Institute Working Paper No. 8 / 02, University of Melbourne.

Kalb, G. / Thoresen, T.O. (2007) 'The Case for Labour Supply Incentives: A Comparison of Family Policies in Australia and Norway', Working Paper No. 27 / 07, Melbourne Institute of Applied Economic and Social Research, University of Melbourne.

Keane, M. / Moffitt, R. (1998) 'A Structural Model of Multiple Welfare Program Participation and Labor Supply', *International Economic Review* 39: 553-589.

Kimmel, J. / Powell, L.M. (2006) 'Nonstandard Work and Child Care Choices of Married Mothers', *Eastern Economic Journal* 32: 397-419.

Kornstad, T. / Thoresen, T.O. (2006) 'Effects of Family Policy Reforms in Norway: Results from a Joint Labour Supply and Child care Choice Microsimulation Analysis', *Fiscal Studies* 27: 339-371.

Kornstad, T. / Thoresen, T.O. (2007) 'A Discrete Choice Model for Labor Supply and Child Care', *Journal of Population Economics* 20: 781-804.

Lokshin, M. (2004) 'Household Child care Choices and Women's Work Behavior in Russia', *The Journal of Human Resources* 39: 1094-1115.

Mehlum, H./Moene, K./Torvik, R. (2006) 'Institutions and the Resource Curse', *The Economic Journal* 116: 1-20.

Michalopoulos, C./Robins, P.K. (2000) 'Employment and Child Care Choices in Canada and the United States', *Canadian Journal of Economics* 33: 435-470.

Michalopoulos, C./Robins, P.K./Garfinkel, I. (1992) 'A Structural Model of Labor Supply and Child Care Demand', *Journal of Human Resources* 27: 166-203.

OECD (2006) *OECD Employment Outlook. Boosting Jobs and Incomes*, Paris.

Powell, L.M. (2002) 'Joint Labor Supply and Child care Choice Decisions of Married Mothers', *The Journal of Human Resources* 37: 106-128.

Ribar, D.C. (1995) 'A Structural Model of Child Care and the Labor supply of Married Women', *Journal of Labor Economics* 13: 558-597.

Statistics Norway (2007) Births, <http://www.ssb.no/english/subjects/02/02/10/fodte_en/>.

Van Soest, A. (1995) 'Structural Models of Family Labor Supply: A Discrete Choice Approach', *Journal of Human Resources* 30: 63-88.

Wrohlich, K. (2006) 'Labor Supply and Child care Choices in a Rationed Child Care Market', IZA DP No. 2053, The Institute for the Study of Labor.

Part III:
Demographic Issues, Social Security and Retirement Incomes

Chapter 10

Fertility Decisions – Simulation in an Agent-Based Model (IFSIM)

Elisa Baroni / Matias Eklöf / Daniel Hallberg /
Thomas Lindh / Jovan Žamac

1   Introduction

There are many different policy proposals to stimulate births, such as: direct lump sum payment at birth, increasing child benefits, child care provision, parental leave benefits, etc.

Many of the policy proposals that are discussed in countries with low fertility rates are already implemented in, for instance, Sweden. Most notably Sweden has a generous parental leave system and child care is heavily subsidized. Compared with low fertility rate countries that have TFR below 1.5 Sweden has a somewhat higher TFR about 1.8, and up to now Sweden has had relatively stable completed cohort fertility rates around 2. What has increased in Sweden, as well as in other countries, is the age at first birth. Today the average age of mothers at first birth is 29. There is thus a concern that if the trend in postponement of first child continues, it will be difficult for these generations to catch up and reach a completed cohort fertility of around 2. Besides this there are other known medical complications with postponing child birth, e.g. miscarriage and Down's syndrome. One explanation that has been put forward for this delay in first child birth

We are grateful for comments from participants at the 1st General Conference of the International Microsimulation Association in Vienna 2007. We are very grateful to Gustav Öberg who has programmed the simulation model IFSIM and with great patience implemented the experiments this chapter builds on. Funding from the Swedish Research Council is gratefully acknowledged.

is the university expansion. Students simply do not get as many children as non-students (SOU, 2003). It is an open question why this is the case but one hypothesis that we will elaborate on in this chapter is that the construction of many social insurance systems, including the parental leave system, to a large extent excludes students, at least in Sweden.

In Sweden, the basic levels of support (if not qualified) given in the unemployment insurance, sickness insurance, parental leave, and study allowance systems are very low. In order to qualify for reasonable levels in these systems, a history of employment is required. However, most students have not qualified because they have a limited work history. It is therefore financially difficult to support family formation before becoming established in the labour market. One hypothesis is that this explains the problems described above.

The purpose of this chapter is to investigate how an increase to the minimum parental leave benefit might affect fertility behaviour. One aspect that we are interested in is how it might affect fertility timing and fertility rates. Prolonged education per se must not be an obstacle for family formation. It could instead be that the existing parental leave system affects fertility timing by discouraging students from having children, through the qualification requirements. It is, however, not certain that timing in itself is enough to affect completed cohort fertility. Certainly, if the delay in first birth is so large that it occurs just before the ending of the reproductive period then long-run fertility rates must decrease. But if the delay is not as drastic, and there is still enough time to reach the amount of desired children then the long-run fertility rates could be unaffected by the delay in first birth.

If the policy change has the possibility of affecting either timing or the fertility rates then we are interested to see the economic consequences of this. For the state, an increase in minimum benefit constitutes a cost. This is however not the only effect. If it is a pure timing effect then the increased cost today has to be compared to the future decrease in parental leave payments. For those who already today receive the minimum parental leave benefit, it will constitute a pure cost to the state as the benefit increases. Even if the cost of the parental leave benefits in total increases it is not certain that the overall cost increases due to external effects.

There are external effects both from a timing change and from changes in the fertility rate. If the fertility rate changes we know that the age structure of the population will alter. That affects other intergenerational transfer systems, namely the educational and pension systems. If the economy is not a perfectly open one we also know that changes in the age structure will affect factor prices. The external effects from a pure timing change are somewhat harder to evaluate but there could be effects both for the human capital acquisition of the children as well as the human capital depreciation of the parents. That the age of the parents might affect the child's human capital accumulation is very likely, however it is very hard to evaluate the magnitude. When the parents take time off to raise children it will most likely constitute a depreciation of their human capital. This depreciation varies during the different stages of human capital accumulation (accumulation either through education or through work experience). It is however hard to determine the magnitudes of these effects.

To evaluate a policy change thus becomes cumbersome if accounting for the above-mentioned possibilities. For this reason we use an agent-based microsimulation model, the IFSIM model. The need to use simulations in complex systems is well known, however a note on the use of the agent-based approach is warranted. Although microsimulation models (e.g. SESIM, MOSAIC) have come a long way modeling individual heterogeneity, including accurate public transfer systems, and even incorporating dynamic behaviour, they are not well suited for the study of fertility behaviour. There are demographers that view social interactions as an important factor in the fertility decision, e.g. Lutz et al. (2006). To be able to capture this social dimension we apply the agent-based approach.[1] Naturally our contribution draws upon previous work using agent-based modeling (ABM) in demographic analysis, particularly for family formation, such as Todd and Billari (2003), Todd et al. (2005), and Billari et al. (2007). These ABM models, however, mostly focus on one narrow aspect (e.g. fertility, matching, etc.) and seldom incorporate an elaborate set of public transfer systems. Since we are interested in how a change to one particular transfer system might have external effects on other public transfer systems we try to model the transfer systems as done in microsimulation models but combine this with an agent-based approach to behaviour mechanisms. The main advantage of the simulation model is that the whole effect of many social insurance systems can be accounted for, including the macro feedback on the individual level of other agents' choices.

---

1   For a good introduction on ABM, including their application to economic research, there are good online resources. These include L. Tesfatsion's website, at http://www.econ. iastate.edu/tesfatsi/abmread.htm or http://en.wikipedia.org/wiki/Agent_based_ model.

The finding at this stage is that the policy of raising the minimum benefit has a negligible impact on completed fertility, but this is also true regarding the overall cost of the transfer systems. We see a marginal increase in the number of students that give birth but this mainly results in a tempo effect. The window of opportunity to have children is still large enough for individuals to educate themselves and still reach the desired number of children.

The rest of the chapter is organized as follows. Next we give some stylized facts concerning the development of fertility and education. Section 3 gives a model overview. In Section 4 we clarify the key mechanisms between our main variables of interest, in particular the parental leave benefits and the fertility decision. In Section 5 the results from our simulations are presented and Section 6 concludes the chapter.

2   Descriptive evidence on low fertility and education

Sweden, like many other European countries, has experienced a decline in period fertility since the 1970s. This decline in fertility can partly be explained by the tempo effect. As shown in Figure 1, the mother's average age at birth of first child has increased by roughly 2 years between 1993 and 2003, from 27 to 29.

Figure 1:   Age at birth of first child

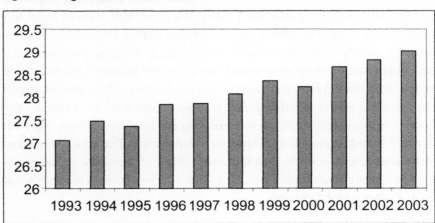

Source: LINDA.[2]

---

2   LINDA is a micro panel dataset covering administrative data for about 3% of the Swedish population. For a more detailed description of LINDA, see Edin and Fredriksson (2000).

The postponement of first child coincides with the expansion of the tertiary educational system during the 1990s. From 1993 to 2005 the numbers enrolled in universities increased from just over 200 thousand to just over 300 thousand, an increase of almost 50%. In Figure 2 we report the overall proportion of 20-34 years old in higher education between 1993 and 2005.

Figure 2:   Share of 20-34 years old in higher education

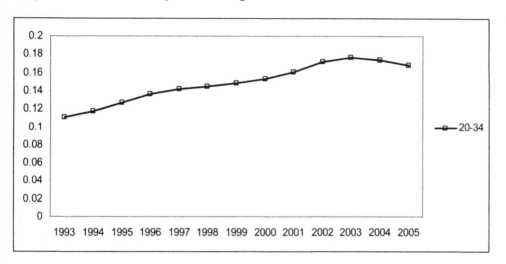

This trend of higher education participation and longer time spent in education might explain child-bearing postponement. From Skirbekk et al. (2006) we know that there is a large difference between high-educated and low-educated mothers with respect to their age at first birth. They find for Sweden that the average age of a woman at first birth varies between 24.1 (for someone with short secondary education) to 27.3 (for someone with completed tertiary education). The same trend is observed by Gustafsson et al. (2002). The probability to give birth (or adopt) differs substantially between students and non-students. Figure 3, which also depicts the fraction of students, shows that while a 30 year-old Swedish non-student female has a 14% probability of having a new child; the probability for the student counterpart is around 5-6%. The probability is also more stretched out over a wider age interval among students. Judging from the rather thick right tail, postponement of births is more pronounced among students than others.

Figure 3: **The probability to give birth (or adopt) by student status, and the fraction of students, by age, 2003**

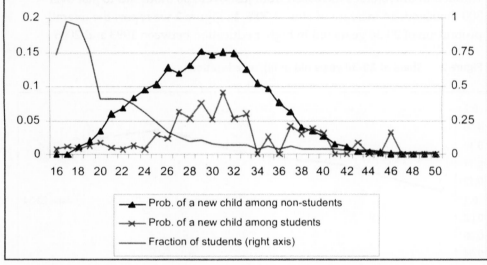

Source: LINDA.

These empirical findings motivates us to investigate if there are possible changes to the public transfer systems that might increase student fertility rates, and thus perhaps break the possible co-movement between education expansion and fertility delay.

3   Model overview

The IFSIM model consists of a small number of interacting modules. Due to space considerations we only give a brief overview of the model and focus on features that are important for this chapter.[3]

The model incorporates four key agents: individuals, households, networks and the State. Individuals are the main agent; they can be born, die, leave home, study, procreate, work or retire. Individuals are grouped into households which are separate agents. Networks are less tangible agents but still they exist as separate entities with a specific location and group composition. The final agent is the State which performs the tax and redis-

---

3   See Baroni et al. (2009) for a complete description of the IFSIM model.

tribution functions, including setting a local tax rate to keep the budget in balance, calculating and collecting income tax rates, paying teachers´ salaries, student allowances, parental leave, child care and pension benefits.

3.1 Demographic module

3.1.1 Initial population

The initial population comes directly from the Swedish micro dataset HUS from the year 1996. HUS is a representative sample with 2,931 individuals and 1,104 households.[4] We proportionally scale up this sample by factor 6 to 17,586 individuals (6,624 households) in the initial year of simulation. From this period onwards individuals are born inside the model and for these we have full life cycle records. For the initial individuals, from the HUS data, we do not have prior records, for instance earnings history. Rather than imputing their history with perhaps dubious methods we have chosen to disregard the first 100 periods of the simulation by which time all people in the initial dataset will be dead.

3.1.2 Ageing and mortality

The most basic life process simulated in the model is the process of ageing: at any period, the age of individuals is increased by one year. The maximum age an individual can reach is 110. Every year the individual has an exogenous probability of dying according to age-specific mortality rates for Sweden in 2006.

3.1.3 Social Networks

Every individual is, from birth, a member of a social network containing all those individuals to whom he or she is close. We follow Billari et al. (2007) in defining social closeness as a spatial area representing the individual's scope of interaction, by age group.

More specifically, agents are arranged along the surface of an imaginary cylinder, whose vertical length is broken into eight segments representing eight age groups. Each age group is therefore allocated to an imaginary sub-cylinder whose height is the age interval for that group, and whose

---

4   See Klevmarken and Olovsson (1993) and Flood et al. (1996).

circumference is in turn sliced into a different number of networks (each age group having different numbers of networks in them).

Each network is constructed as a segment on the circumference delimited by a corresponding angle. The model develops a procedure to then allocate each individual to a given network group within his or her own network space, by age group, and also to update his or her network in time, as the individual ages and moves between age groups and networks. A graphical representation of the network group organization is presented in Figure 4 below. For instance, one network could be the slice m in age group y and another one could be n, in age group $y+1$.

Figure 4:   Graphical representation of the network groups

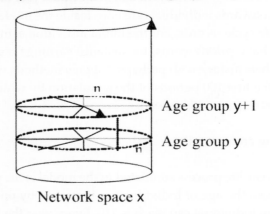

This means that the individuals will migrate between network groups as they age, and two individuals that belong to the same network group at one age, may belong to different groups at later ages. Furthermore, this implementation will allow for "spatial" migration as well as individuals could be allowed to change their "spatial" location, here measured as the angle on the circumference, over time.

Every newborn inherits a network angle which is the average of her parents' network angles plus a random term. A network angle is a technical construct which allows the individual to be placed, given his age, on a specific segment of the circumference throughout her life. At any point in time, his or her individual angle is compared against the angle determining where each network begins and ends (by age group), and placed within the network segment corresponding to his or her angle. In the same network the individual will therefore meet a subsample of other people in the same age group who happen to have a similar angle. In time, as the individual grows older and jumps between age groups, the composition of his or her network will change since different age groups are characterized by different network angles, hence individuals are shifted not only vertically but also "horizontally", so to say, depending on their own angle relative to the new age-group network configuration.

To sum it up, the individual's location within the cylinder space is determined by two coordinates: (i) their age group. This defines the location within the vertical y space, or in other words the sub-cylinder to which the individual belongs; (ii) the angle of the circumference within which the individual's network falls (corresponding to the interval on the circumference occupied by that network). This defines the horizontal x-coordinate.

3.1.4 Adolescents leaving home and partner matching

Starting from age 18, individuals living with their parents may leave the parental household and set up a household of their own. The decision to leave home is modeled as an exponential probability function increasing with age, and adjusted on the basis of a social pressure effect (i.e. how many people of similar age in the network who have left home). Those who leave home form a new single-headed household. Individuals thus match after leaving home (the matching procedure explained below).

In our baseline simulation, the majority of people, 84%, leave home by the age of 20. By age 24 everyone has left home.

Our matching procedure draws in particular from the work of Billari et al. (2007). Individuals still living with their parents are not allowed to match with, and matching is restricted to 18+. We regard this not to have a major effect in terms of delaying fertility since the majority have left the parental home by age 20.

The matching probability depends only on the linear age difference between the potential partners. The maximum age difference is set to three years. Although this matching procedure appears primitive, it does allow for assortative matching as university degree individuals match later in life and are thus more likely to match with another single university degree individual. Belonging to the same network increases the matching probability. Although matching is an ideal application for ABM we have here chosen to focus on the fertility behaviour and for this reason matching is treated simplistically.

3.1.5 Fertility

Matched females between ages 20 and 40 can give birth. Fertility is determined by biological, economic and social factors. We assume that, for some reason, a couple has a certain ideal number of children and that this preferred number of children is an average of the number of siblings that the woman and her partner have. This average is then adjusted by a small random number (with zero expectancy). The couples wish to reach this preferred number but if they succeed or not depends on biological, economic and social factors.

The biological factor captures the fact that all women are not capable of giving birth and that this ability varies with age. Biological ability is modelled according to the following function:

$$\Pr(Fertility_{BIO}) = \frac{\alpha - e^{\ln(\alpha)^{\frac{age-\eta}{40-\eta}}}}{\alpha - 1} . \tag{1}$$

Here α and η are set to 50 and 15 respectively. By doing so we obtain a biological fecundity that corresponds quite well to estimates in Menken et al. (1986) of infertility. For example, infertility at ages 20-24 would in this case amount to 7%, while it would be 22% for the age group 35-39. If a [0,1] uniform draw exceeds the probability given by (1) she will be classified as infertile and will not be able to have a child.

For those who instead are fertile, the actual probability of giving birth in a given year is determined by economic and social factors, which together will determine whether or not the woman gives birth.

The economic factor aims to capture both the decision of having or not having a child as well as the timing of having a child. One part evaluates the economic consequences of having a child while another part compares present income with the expected future income. The disposable income is affected by a new child due to (i) the fixed cost of a child (assumed to be a fixed amount for everyone), and (ii) varying costs of the temporary exit from the labour market. We base the expected difference in income due to a new child only on the mother's future income, not on the expected income of the household.

The functional form of the economic factor is

$$E = \left(0.5 + \left(\frac{e^{relativeNPV}}{1 + e^{relativeNPV}}\right)\right)\left(\frac{e^{Inc}}{1 + e^{IncFuture}}\right), \tag{2}$$

where *relativeNPV* captures the difference in net present value of the expected income stream with and without a child. It is a function of the expected relative difference in an individual's future discounted disposable income under the two states (having a child or not) and estimated over six years ahead. Different labour market situations (i.e. skilled or unskilled, or whether one is still in university) affect the expected projected income and the relative difference when considering having a child. Skilled expects a higher income growth than unskilled, although the initial level after education may be lower.

The other parameter in the economic factor, namely the expected change in income over the next five years, is represented by *Inc* and *IncFuture* in equation (2) which stands for the current income and the expected income five years later respectively. An individual with a higher growth obtains stronger incentives to postpone having a child compared to an individual having a low expected income growth.

Besides the economic factor there is also a social factor that affects fertility. The social pressure is meant to capture the effects that the social environment as well as the perceived biological "pressure" have on the individual's decision. The function for the social pressure is

$$S = \left(0.8 + 0.4\left(\frac{e^x}{1 + e^x}\right)\right)\frac{bio}{bioFuture}, \tag{3}$$

where x is the difference between the desired number of children and the currently actual number of children. The desired number of children is the average of the couple's siblings which emphasizes that social norms are set during youth. The ratio *bio/bioFuture* captures the awareness of the biological window of opportunity, where *bio* is the current biological fecundity rate and *bioFuture* is the fecundity rate five years ahead. After the age of 30 the biological fecundity rate decreases rapidly and this effect becomes important.

Having calculated the individual economic and social pressures, fertile women are then assigned their final probability of having a child in that given year according to the following Cobb Douglas function:

$$\Pr(Child) = \Pr(Fertility_{BIO})E^{\gamma_1}S^{\gamma_2}, \tag{4}$$

where γ_1 and γ_2, are scaling parameters used to control the relative weight that the social and economic pressures have on the final fertility rate. These are chosen to get as close fit as possible to the Swedish fertility rates. We compare the individual outcome against a random draw to assign an actual birth. We then calibrate this function to 2006 Swedish fertility data, by age (from Statistics Sweden).

Results of our calibration are shown in Figure 5. We obtain a plausible age-profile for giving birth. There is a slight overestimation for women between ages 23 to 26 and a higher peak. Considering that we have not put in any age-specific rates, except those coming from biological studies concerning female fecundity by age, the model fits the data quite well. The combination between economic and social pressure combined with the agents' rules of thumbs is able to fit the data surprisingly well.

Figure 5:   Simulated and actual (SCB in graph) fertility rates by age

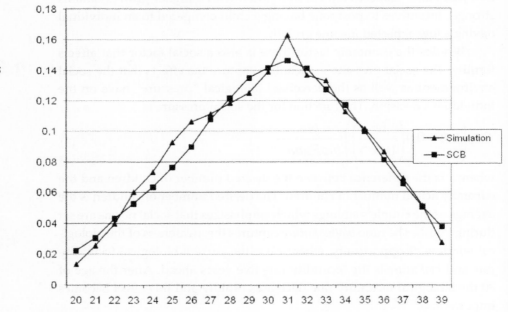

3.2   Educational module

When reaching age 7, all individuals are universally put into basic schooling up until the age of 16. If entering secondary school, the individual will stay in school another 3 years. The choice to apply to university is determined by three parts. First, there is a baseline probability assumed to capture the overall probability that any eligible individual enters the university. Second, we have a probability that captures the economic factors of university choice. This increases with the perceived economic pay-off of higher education. Third, there is a probability that embodies the social pressure and relates to the average participation rate at university within each network group.

The path into university entails one application step and one acceptance step. After the individuals decide whether to apply to university or not the applicants are ordered with respect to their accumulated human capital such that the ones with the highest human capital are accepted by the university. The number of individuals finally accepted is determined by a policy parameter, which we set to 30% of the 19-30 age group and thus roughly replicate the Swedish case.

Whether individuals apply to university or not depends on their expected life time incomes, and they form their expectations based on contemporary cross-section projections of disposable income by age. The mean projections are based on the full sample whereas a specific individual's position in the distribution of disposable incomes will depend on her position in the network group's distribution of human capital. This reflects the reasonable assumption that individuals with high accumulated human capital should expect to be positioned higher in the distribution of incomes. In other words, individuals eligible to apply will have higher propensity of applying to university if their expected costs of entering university (i.e. 5 years of foregone labour income net of tax and income while students) outweigh their future benefits in terms of higher future disposable incomes. Applicants are assumed to have the ability of comparing these net present values of expected future incomes from either going to work immediately or university studies.

If attending university, the student will be entitled to a student allowance for the duration of the course (5 years), amounting to a fixed proportion of average earnings (12%). Female students are not excluded from the event of having a new child. If so, the mother takes time off from the university studies to be on parental leave. In doing so she will receive parental leave benefit according to the rules described below in Section 3.4.1.

3.3 Modules for human capital formation, the labour market and consumption good production

We postulate a production technology that only depends on human capital (i.e. there are no savings into other types of productive assets). Human capital is the only asset and it is measured by the quality of labour embodied in each worker, for a given amount of schooling, training, work experience etc.

Human capital entails an externality embodied in the private accumulation of human capital. An increase in human capital, e.g. through an additional year of schooling or on-the-job training, has two distinct effects: (i) an increase in one's own marginal productivity or wages; (ii) an increase in the total human capital stock, which also enters the human capital production functions of current students. This spill-over effect is the key externality that generates endogenous growth in the model. The human capital stock aims to capture the quality of educational institutions and the ability of the system to transfer knowledge between individuals.

There are four main inputs into the production of human capital: (i) innate individual ability; (ii) ability acquired from parental influence and parental own human capital levels; (iii) ability acquired through formal education; (iv) skills and expertise acquired through on-the-job training.

The natal human capital is derived from the natal human capitals of both parents (cf. genetic and inheritable ability), and a random term. In the pre-school periods the human capital production function is a Cobb-Douglas type with the sum of parents' human capital and the child's own capital as input factors.

During schooling the human capital stock of the teachers, scaled by the number of students, enters the human capital production function along with the parents' human capital. Hence teaching capacity depends both on the number of teachers per student and their "competence". In the model teacher density is kept constant (at a fixed rate of 10 students per teacher) so that teaching quality only depends on the level of human capital.

After studies all individuals enter the labour market, and an individual's human capital then increases for every year of work until age 55, but proportionately less so as the individual ages. After reaching the age of 55 the human capital starts to depreciate at a growing rate. We assume that the rate of increase before age 55 is higher for university-educated than for those with less education, thus generating a steeper wage profile over life for the higher-educated.

We assume that workers work full-time. Retirement is deterministic. At age 65, individuals are automatically turned into pensioners entitled to retirement pension.

There are two sectors of production. The principal sector in the economy produces a single consumption good. The second sector is the educational sector described above. Those who are randomly designated to become a teacher in a given year do not participate in the production of the consumption good.[5]

The amount of consumption good produced depends entirely on the total human capital level of the labour force (excluding teachers). The production function follows a Cobb-Douglas shape with a time-dependent productivity factor. This is meant to capture the idea that returns to human capital investment are increasing, in line with endogenous growth theory, but after a certain level the situation might reverse since the externality from aggregate human capital follows a logistic curve. There are two input factors in the model; the total human capital of the primary or secondary level of education individuals, and the total human capital of the university (tertiary) individuals.

There are no monetary values in the model so earnings are represented by the share of total output produced going to each worker. The allocation of the produced good to workers is separated into two steps. First, the total produced goods are allocated to the two production factors (non-university and university degree individuals) such that the shares reflect each group's marginal product. Then, within each group, the consumption good units are allocated proportionally to the human capital of the individual. This implies for example that, as the supply of university degree individuals is reduced, their marginal product will increase and thereby increase their share of the produced goods. This will be observed by young individuals who will be more prone to choose university and thus increase the future supply of university degree individuals.

3.4 State, tax and benefit systems

The State calculates the total expenditure bill, by aggregating the costs of the education, teacher's salaries, student allowance, parental leave subsidies, child allowance and pensions.[6] Once total expenditures are calculated, the State will adapt the tax system so as to raise sufficient revenues to balance the budget (no debt is allowed). The tax system comprises a state and a lo-

---

5   After one year as a teacher, the individual returns to the pool of potential teachers, which consists of all non-students.

6   Teachers are paid a fixed rate of 40% of the average GDP per worker. The pension system is modelled according to the new Swedish system except for that we have a fixed retirement age at 65 and that we do not have any funded part. We only model the pay-as-you-go component which in reality comprises about 87% of the total public coverage.

cal tax. The state tax is a progressive tax paid by the top 20% of the income distribution. The local tax paid by everybody with positive earnings is a flat tax rate on earnings. It is residually derived to cover the part of total expenditure not covered by the state tax. The individual income tax will therefore be a combination of both the state tax (if eligible) and the local tax. The individual disposable income is therefore the sum of any earnings, pensions, student or parental allowances, minus the income tax.

3.4.1 The parental leave minimum benefit and the student allowance benefit

The parental leave minimum benefit is modeled according to the Swedish system in 2007, with some simplifications. In our model we assume that only the woman gets the benefit within the couple, hence the amount of the benefit is calculated on her eligible income.

The benefit comprises a minimum amount, for those who have no earnings history, and an insurance-related amount. The minimum amounts of the parental leave minimum benefit of the base and alternative scenarios are summarized in Table 1.

Table 1: The parental leave minimum benefit and the student allowance benefit

	Parental leave minimum amount		Student allowance
	Base	Alternative	Base / Alternative
Compensation per day (SEK)	180	800	95
Compensation per year (SEK)	65,700	292,000	34,560
As GDP per worker per year	22.8%	101.4%	12.0%
As BAs per year	164.3%	730.0%	86.4%

Note: 1 BA is 40,000 SEK (in 2007), and 10 SEK (Swedish Crown) is approx. 1 EURO. GDP per worker is the average earnings in the economy.

The minimum benefit part is for mothers with no previous earnings. In the base scenario it corresponds to 180 SEK per day (about 548 EURO per month), which is approx. equal to today's minimum benefit. This corresponds to about 23% of GDP per worker annually or 13.7% of the so-called Basic Amount equivalent (BA) per month.[7] Students that receive a child

---

7   In our model the BA is calculated to reproduce a level comparable with the Basic Amount for 2007, i.e. 40,000 SEK or roughly 4,000 Euro.

during their studying period would receive this amount unless they have prior earnings. In our alternative scenario we elaborate to see what happens when this minimum level is quadrupled to 800 SEK per day (about 2,433 EURO per month), which is about the level of average earnings in the model. In relation to the student allowance benefit, also described in Table 1, the minimum amount of the parental leave minimum benefit is about twice as high. As mentioned, a university student will be entitled to a student allowance for a 5-year period amounting to 12% of the average earnings per year (about 288 EURO per month).[8]

The income-related part is for individuals with previous earnings. They receive 80% of their earnings as parental leave benefit, but only up to the cap of 10 BAs.

The parental leave minimum benefit is paid for three years after the birth of the child, after which the individual returns to the previous labour market status.[9] Being on parental leave does not exclude per se the possibility to have another child, since the model allows women with a child older than one year of age to have another one.

One can note that parental leave minimum benefits are subject to income tax. The student allowance benefit is not.

4 Key interactions

In this final sub-section we clarify the mechanisms through which IFSIM produces interactions between our key variables of interest, in particular the parental leave benefit system and fertility.

As we recall, the economic pressure is calculated as the difference over the next six years in projected income with or without a child. Leaving aside the parental leave benefit, with a child projected income will always be lower than without (hence a negative economic incentive) since a child involves both direct (fixed) costs and indirect costs. The indirect costs will however vary depending on the initial individual conditions, i.e. the educational level, the human capital level, and the amount of work experience. Also the

---

8   In reality most students also have student loans. We assume that these loans are always paid back and the interest rate exactly equals indiviuals' discount rate and thus these loans do not affect individuals' decisions.

9   This length of the leave is longer than in reality. However, we do not include the right to benefits when taking care of a sick child nor do we include the effect of part-time work when raising children. We thus believe that adding a longer initial leave compensates for this.

expected wage commanded by the individual's skill group (high-skilled or low-skilled) will affect indirect costs as income projections are steeper for high-skilled. If someone highly educated has a child, she will face a higher opportunity cost to exit the labour market than someone of the same age with lower education, in terms of foregone income, although the direct cost of having a child will be the same. It follows that the parental leave benefit becomes the key variable in tipping more or less favourably economic incentives: for someone with a higher education to have a child now rather than later, the benefit must compensate sufficiently not only for the immediate loss of income, but also for the future loss stemming from human capital depreciation and lost years of (more highly paid) work experience.

For a student the opportunity cost of having a child consists of (i) the difference between the student allowance and the flat parental leave benefit and (ii) the loss in future income streams caused by the delay in finishing education. For a worker there is an opportunity cost of (i) the difference between a low-skill wage and an income-related parental leave benefit and (ii) the decrease in wage caused by depreciation of human capital and loss of on-the-job training.

When calibrated to the current Swedish system the opportunity cost for the student will be vastly greater than for the worker. The experiment we make lowers the direct loss by increasing the flat parental leave benefit but affects the future loss only indirectly by increasing future tax burdens. See below.

The parental leave benefit is currently set as an external parameter to roughly reflect the value of the Swedish benefit. When we increase it the model will also produce an indirect effect on fertility. This will be due to the fact that, in order to preserve revenue neutrality, an increase in the benefit will be matched by an increase in the local income tax, which will translate in lower disposable incomes for all. When projecting incomes, potential parents look at disposable incomes; hence such a tax increase will be included in their calculation and push down their own income forecasts. This implies that the opportunity cost of having a child is lower (due to taxation) hence there is an incentive for higher fertility. In essence there is a transfer from those with less children to those with many.

5   Results

The aim of this simulation is to investigate the overall effects of raising the minimum benefit in the parental leave system. The minimum parental leave is given only to females who have no previous work experience. Since we do not model unemployment this group is only students. In reality the unemployed could also receive the minimum benefit. Note that students may have earnings history since some enrol late in university education.

The base scenario represents the model of the current Swedish system (in which the minimum parental leave benefit amounts to the equivalent of ca. 180 SEK a day), while the alternative scenario is a simulation when the minimum level in the parental leave system is raised to the average wage (corresponding to 800 SEK a day).

We have chosen to look at the following variables: completed cohort fertility, age at first birth, share of students with children, share of people with their preferred number of children, share who receive the minimum parental leave benefit, government spending on parental leave and total government spending on intergenerational transfers.

Initial data were described above. All results that are presented are such that we let the model first run for 100 years to level off, then we look at the average for the following 50 years when we analyse the variables of interest. The calculated averages reported below are based on five runs for each of the scenarios. There are differences between the different runs, under the same scenario (due to monte-carlo variation), but they are negligible.

In Table 2 we see the results for the base scenario when the minimum benefit level is according to the Swedish current system, and for the alternative when the minimum benefit is based on the average wage. The alternative policy has more or less no impact on the aggregate results. We see that there are slightly more students that get children during their studying period under the alternative scenario. The completed cohort fertility (averaged over the 50 years) is smaller, among university educated than for the whole population, 1.6 compared to 1.8, but the difference is very small between the two scenarios.

Table 2: Summary for different variables under the base scenario and the alternative scenario, average of five simulations

	Base	Alt.
Completed cohort fertility, all women	1.78	1.80
Completed cohort fertility, university educated women	1.61	1.61
Share of female students that give birth (%)	8.7	9.3
Share of women with preferred number of kids (%)	70.0	71.1
Average age of mother at first birth	27.0	27.0
Share of women on parental leave, with the minimum amount:		
All (%)	7.1	7.3
Students (%)	26.6	31.0
Government spend on parental leave (% of GDP)	0.9	1.3
Total government cost (% of GDP)	57.6	57.8

There are some interesting conclusions which we can draw from our simulation experiment. First of all we see that increasing the minimum parental leave works as an incentive to higher fertility for students, as the share of students with children increases from 8.7 to 9.3%. We also see that the total share of parents on minimum parental leave increases marginally from 7.1 to 7.3%. As expected, the share is four times higher among students, and there is a greater increase among students also in relative terms. When it comes to the average age at first birth, we see no change but this might be explained by the fact that, although more university students are having children, only 4.1% of females in fertile ages are students, i.e. their weight in the average is very small (the share of students in the population is practically the same in both base and alternative scenarios). That is also possibly why, overall, we see that the improvement on the share of people who reach their desired number of children is very modest, as is the effect on the completed cohort fertility.

Increasing the minimum benefit is not effective in raising overall fertility since it targets a small population group (mainly students). In addition we simulate that the majority of students has prior earnings history. This might also suggest that, short of intervening on the earnings-related parental leave benefit, the economic pressure to have children after completing education remains low: more students might have children earlier than without the raise in minimum parental leave, but this anticipation is then "balanced out" by the negative economic pressure to have more children once they join the labour market. An interesting experiment for future analysis might therefore be to look at the effects of raising the earnings-related component of the parental leave benefit as well as the minimum.

How can it be that the government total costs do not increase when the minimum benefit is raised (and yet the total expenditure on parental leave benefits does increase)? Those additional individuals who get children during their study period instead of afterwards, receive a smaller benefit (since their benefit would be based on a higher income than the average income). This represents a saving in overall government expenditures which counterbalances the increase in the parental leave bill.

6 Concluding remarks

There are many policy proposals to raise the low fertility rates. To investigate if these different proposals will have any effect or not is not an easy task. We have in this chapter illustrated how agent-based modeling could be used as an approach for policy evaluation. To illustrate our approach we have considered a change to the Swedish parental leave benefit. The considered change has been to increase the minimum level of benefit that is received when no prior earnings are available. The result of the policy simulation is that there are no noticeable aggregate effects from the change. Sweden would have little to gain or loose by implementing such a policy. The negligible difference in numbers of births comes from the fact that, while students do get an incentive to have more children, they are a relatively small group in the population, and also they might simply anticipate the timing of birth but not increase the total number of children that they will have over their life cycle. Therefore raising the minimum parental leave benefit alone might not be sufficient to raise overall fertility unless it is accompanied by a raise in the income-related component of the benefit (affecting workers).

One of the major challenges in the agent-based approach is to find the rules of thumb and calibrating these. When it comes to the fertility rules we choose to calibrate these to the Swedish fertility rates by age in 2006. We deliberately did not choose the standard route to apply the empirical age-specific fertility rates to our individuals. Instead we tried to find rules of thumb that were not age-specific except for the pure biological impact. By doing so hopefully we avoid some of the standard critique that otherwise applies when it comes to policy changes of this sort. We actually manage to some extent to fit the empirical fertility rates by using economic and social aspects in the decision rules combined with the biological fertility ability.

Many other issues can be investigated with this agent-based approach. The key lies in the ability to validate the model by finding appropriate rules of thumb. In this chapter we have mainly focused on the fertility decision. The benefit of using an agent-based approach in this case is that the rules of thumb are more likely to be unaffected by the policy change than what most relationships in a standard microsimulation approach would be.

References

Baroni, E./Žamac, J./Öberg, G. (2009) 'IFSIM handbook', Working Paper 2009:7. Stockholm: Institute for Futures Studies.

Billari, F. C./Prskawetz, A./Fent, T./Diaz, B.A. (2007) 'The wedding ring: an agent-based marriage model based on social interactions', *Demographic Research* 17 (3), Vienna Institute of Demography.

Edin, P. A./Fredriksson, P. (2000) 'LINDA: Longitudinal individual data for Sweden', Uppsala University Economics Department Working Paper, 2000: 19.

Flood, L./Klevmarken, A./Olovsson, P. (1996) *Household market and non market activiteis (HUS), Volumes III-VI*. Department of Economics Uppsala University.

Gustafsson, S.S./Kenjoh, E./Wetzels, C.M. (2002) 'The role of education on postponement of maternity in Britain, Germany, the Netherlands and Sweden', pp. 55-79 in: Ruspini, E./ Dale, A. (eds.), *The Gender dimension of social change. The contribution of dynamic research to the study of women´s life courses*. Bristol, UK: The Policy Press.

Klevmarken, A./Olovsson, P. (1993) *Household Market and Non-market Activities, Procedures and Codes 1984–1991*. The Industrial Institute for Economic and Social Research.

Lutz, W./Skirbekk, V./Testa, M. R. (2006) 'The low fertility trap hypothesis: Forces that may lead to further postponement and fewer births in Europe', in *Vienna Yearbook of Population Research 2006*. Vienna: Austrian Academy of Sciences.

Menken, J./Trussell, J./Larsen, U. (1986) 'Age and Infertility', *Science* 233 (4771): 1389-1394.

SOU (2003) Studerande och trygghetssystemen, SOU 2003:130. Stockholm: Fritzes.

Skirbekk, V./Kohler, H. P./Prskawetz, A. (2006) 'The marginal effect of school leaving age on demographic events. A contribution to the discussion on causality', pp. 65-85 in: Gustafsson, S./Kalwij, A. (eds.), *Education and Postponement of Maternity*. Amsterdam: Kluwer Publications.

Todd, P.M./Billari, F.C./Simao, J. (2005) 'Aggregate age-at-marriage patterns from individual mate search heuristics', *Demography* 42 (3): 559-574.

Todd, P. M./Billari, F.C. (2003) 'Population-wide marriage patterns produced by individual mate search heuristics', pp. 117-137 in: Billari, F. C./Prskawetz, A. (eds.), *Agent-based Computational Demography*. Berlin: Springer-Verlag.

Chapter 11

Projecting Pensions and Age at Retirement in France: Some Lessons from the Destinie I Model

Didier Blanchet / Sylvie Le Minez

1 Introduction: the context

Public interest for the future of pensions in France has progressively gained importance at the end of the 1980s. During the 1970s and early 1980s, the policy orientation had been to increase the generosity of the system, through relatively generous indexation rules, and, in 1983, the generalization of retirement at age 60. This policy took place in a demographic context that remained relatively favourable. This period came to an end during the second half of the 1980s, and concern started to emerge about ways to ensure pension viability in a context of demographic ageing.

This concern stimulated demand for projections and simulations of pension reform scenarios. In a first step, these questions have been examined with aggregate models, e.g. the Margaret model that had been developed by the Forecasting Directorate at the Ministry of Finance (Vernière, 1990). Similar models continue to be used, but it was clear from the beginning that they could not answer all questions raised by pension reforms. Some of these questions require other tools, able to reasonably capture the complexity of the French pension system. This complexity has two dimensions. The first one stems from the fact that the system remains fragmented, with

The authors are indebted to the collective work of successive members of the Destinie team. Our comprehension of the model's properties has also greatly benefited from close examination by some of its final users, notably Marie Reynaud and Yves Guégano from the General Secretariat of the *Conseil d'Orientation des Retraites*. Any errors or shortcomings remain ours.

a multiplicity of coexisting schemes. The second one is due to the fact that, even for a given scheme, rules are quite complex and often display strong non-linearities whose impact is difficult to describe with a representative agent approach. Microsimulation imposed itself as one way to deal with this overall complexity, and it is for this reason that the Destinie microsimulation model has been progressively developed at the French National Statistical Institute (INSEE).

The aim of this chapter is to give an overview of the current characteristics of this model and to describe what are or have been its main applications. Developments of this model have more or less followed the evolution of questions that have been addressed to it. The first section of this chapter gives some details on one of the reasons that made microsimulation particularly attractive for the French case, which is the non-linearity of rules governing access to a "full rate" pension. Section 2 briefly describes the general structure retained by the first version of the model and its main developments over the last 10 years. Section 3 concentrates on how the model tries to simulate retirement behaviour, giving some results and discussing the relevance and limits of these results, with some indications on tracks that could be followed to overcome part of these limits.

2   The Destinie model: main features and developments

2.1   *Why microsimulation?*

Destinie was not created with the idea of replacing all other approaches to pension projections. It is clear that many questions related to pensions can be addressed with simpler or different models. In particular, macro-variants of pension projections used by the *Conseil d'Orientation des Retraites* (Pensions Advisory Committee) are produced by the French Ministry of Social Affairs using a very aggregate model. Such an instrument remains perfectly suited for quick evaluations of global variants concerning demographic or employment trends, or average pension/income ratios.

But microsimulation becomes necessary when we want to address the impact of detailed and complex changes in pension rules. One good illustration is the modelling of rules governing access to the so-called "full rate pension" (*retraite à taux plein*) in the largest scheme, the *Régime Général*, that provides the basic pension for wage-earners in the private sector.

This regime is often described as a regime where the normal retirement age (NRA) is 60, this being the result of the 1983 reform that lowered the minimum age required to get a "full rate" pension to 60. But presenting 60 as the normal retirement age was already an approximation of reality under these 1983 rules, and this approximation will be increasingly irrelevant from one cohort to the next after reforms that have been enacted in 1993 and 2003. The reason is that the condition for obtaining this full rate does not only involve age. It also involves the total number of years of contribution reached at that age. This second parameter has been little constraining until now, except for women with short careers, explaining that the median age at retirement still remains very close to 60 (and even lower due to various systems of early retirement), but it should play an increasing role in the future and accurate projections require an explicit treatment of this double condition.

To be more precise, let us introduce notations N and N_{tot} for the number of years of contributions to the *Régime Général* and to all kinds of regimes (hence $N_{tot} \geq N$). After the 1983 reform and until 1993, the general formula for computing benefits for an individual retiring at age A_r was:

$$P = \alpha\,(A_r, N_{tot}).\min(1, N/D).W \tag{1}$$

where W is a reference wage (at that time the average of the 10 best years of past wages truncated to the social security ceiling), where D was equal to 37.5 years and where $\alpha(A_r, N_{tot})$ was a proportionality coefficient whose exact formula was the following:
- A maximum value of 50% ("full rate") for either $A_r=65$ or $N_{tot} \geq D=37,5$.
- If none of these conditions were fulfilled, a reduction of α by 5 percentage points for each year missing to reach the closest of both, i.e. a 10% decline in the pension level.

The necessity to take into account the complexity of this formula has been increased by the 1993 pension reform. The two major aspects of this reform were:
- Less generous rules for computing W (a progressive change from the average of the 10 best years to the 25 best years, combined with a less generous rule for revalorizing these past wages before computing their average).
- A progressive increase of D from 37.5 years to 40 years.

The impact of such a reform is obviously highly dependent on distributional characteristics of the population. Knowing how the transition from the 10 to the 25 best years of one's career is going to affect the reference wage W depends on the distribution of individual careers between relatively flat ones for whom this aspect of the reform is rather neutral and upward sloping or irregular ones for which the impact of the reform is important. And computing the impact of shifting D from 37.5 to 40 years, either in terms of retirement behaviour or replacement levels, requires a projection of the distribution of N_{tot} within and around this 37.5-40 bracket.

It is with the idea of accurately simulating such distributive effects that the Destinie model started being developed in 1993.

2.2 The general structure of the model

Potentially, microsimulation is able to simulate very complex and disaggregated rules. But a balance must be found between refinement and tractability and Destinie did not escape this trade-off, especially given the fact that the model has been developed with a reduced team. In fact, the first version, that was essentially experimental, contained some relatively simplifying assumptions.

The main initial simplification has been to concentrate the model on the case of wage-earners from the private sector. This means that the initial version of the model did not try to describe and predict the case of other categories of workers. It also means that we did not address the case of heterogeneous careers mixing different regimes.

As seen below, the first limitation has been partially corrected since, with the introduction of a specific module dedicated to public sector employees, but the second limitation remains. The current version of the model assumes that careers are confined either to the private or the public sector. This limitation is problematic in a context where consequences of reforms for people with heterogeneous careers have become an important matter of concern and are often presented as a blind point in our knowledge of retirement conditions.

Another simplification has been imposed by the available data. At that time, there was no unified administrative data source covering both the population of pensioners and current contributors. As a result, we decided to base Destinie on individual data derived from a household survey, the 1991 Financial Assets Survey collected by INSEE. This survey provided basic demographic data as well as information about careers (individual educational attainment, years of service, earnings). It also provided data on assets. These are not used at this stage in the model, but there are still plans to use them to give better projections of global resources of pensioners' households.

With a few adjustments, this survey allowed the constitution of an initial base of some 15,000 households containing some 37,000 individuals. The main limit imposed by this data source is that information on past careers remained relatively poor: the main information is the total number of years spent in employment, used as a proxy for the number of years of contributions. This information is less precise than the one that we could have got from administrative data, and had to be complemented by several imputations. For instance, for all individuals in the sample, we have had to impute sequences of past wages, using the same kind of wage equations as the ones used for projections of future wages (see below), rescaled to be consistent both with current individual wages reported in the survey, and past evolutions of wages at the macro-level.

Another simplifying choice has been to describe relative social status with one single indicator, the school-leaving age: this variable codetermines labour market and demographic behaviour. It is of particular importance for computing pensions since it determines both career profiles and the maximum number of years of contributions that the individual can reach at age 60, hence the possibility to get the full rate at this age.

On the other hand, one element of relative complexity that we chose to introduce from the beginning is a relatively complete simulation of kinship ties, with the idea that simulating such an information could be useful for many questions related to ageing, e.g. projections of the level of informal support by relatives in case of old-age invalidity, or the intergenerational transmission of assets.

How does Destinie manage these kinship ties? The basic unit of observation is the individual, not the household, with all individuals identified by a unique identification number. But each individual record also includes a set of IDs for partner, parents and children, *living or not living* in the same household. In the initial database, those of these kinship ties that do not directly derive from the household structure of the Financial Assets Survey are artificially imputed: for instance, if one person aged 50 in the survey has declared to have his or her mother still alive, an artificial bidirectional link is created between this person and one widow drawn from the survey sample with adequate characteristics.

Once such links have been imputed, they are easy to update by simulating further unions *within* the sample, renewal of the sample being exclusively due to births from these unions and from net migration flows. The resulting database remains indexed by individual IDs and keeps a fully rectangular structure that is easier to manage than irregular structures where basic records describe households and are therefore of a variable length.

One way to characterize this approach is to view the microsimulation sample as a small endogamic subpopulation whose kinship structure tries to mimic the true structure that prevails in the French population, i.e. a kind of "compression" of the actual kinship structure within a limited sample. Of course, such an approach would be fully misleading if our purpose were to model the prevalence of a phenomenon such as consanguinity. But this is not what the model has been made for. As long as simpler ties are considered, we conjecture that this approach does not generate any excessive bias. For instance, this representation should not bias estimates of the probability to have surviving children for the oldest olds, or the probability to combine the burden of old parents and children still at home for people in the phase of transition between active life and retirement.

Apart from this specific treatment of kinship ties, the other characteristics of this initial version of Destinie were relatively standard. The model simulated both demographic and labour market trajectories from the initial year (1991 in the first version) up to 2040, using a mix of deterministic rules, behavioural hypotheses and random drawings. The demographic events are unions, breaking-ups, births of children, death and migrations. The parameters of equations for these events are adjusted so that the probabilities predicted by the model fit the long-term demographic projections made by the INSEE. Labour market events first include exit from school, assumed to coincide with entry on the labour market. This occurs at an age drawn in a way depending from school attainment of both parents. After that, people move between employment, unemployment and inactivity according to simple assumptions allowing consistency with "official" labour force forecasts made by INSEE.

Concerning earnings, the forecasting procedure involves two steps. First, each individual's theoretical earnings profile is derived from a wage equation where gender, school-leaving age and tenure are the main predictors. Fixed individual effects are then added to the theoretical profile in order to be consistent with wages observed in the survey. For projections, values predicted from these equations are augmented to take into account the impact of an exogenous rate of technical progress. All values are projected in real terms, i.e. the model does not simulate inflation (benefits indexed on inflation are therefore projected to be constant in the model).

The last event to be modeled is retirement. It is well known that defining retirement is not always straightforward, given the frequent non-coincidence between the last exit from employment and access to regular retirement. As will appear more clearly below, most modelling efforts in Destinie have been concentrated upon this second event, i.e. claiming of pension benefits. But Destinie does not ignore the fact that this does necessarily coincide with the exit from employment. The point is simply that such anticipated exits are simulated as exogenous realizations of a transition model, not as the outcome of a behavioural model. Now, in the very first version of the model, this behavioural model itself remained very simple: the individual was supposed to take up his or her pension at the age of eligibility to the "full rate". Pensions were then computed according to rules prevailing or expected for the *Régime Général* and for the two complementary schemes, ARRCO and AGIRC.

2.3   *Adaptations of the model to changing demands*

This first version of the model was essentially experimental and its main purpose was to demonstrate the feasibility and potential interest of such an instrument (Blanchet and Chanut, 1999). Although it had been developed with the idea of detailing the impact of the 1993 reform, this first version only gave very rough indications on the potential impact of this reform.

The following years have been devoted both to some general improvements or reestimations of parameters or data, and to the development of more specific modules that more or less directly responded to changes in policy interest.

The first kind of activity is part of a model's normal life and will not be discussed at length:

– Some efforts have been devoted to improving the demographic realism of the model (Robert-Bobée, 2001, 2002).
– A second adaptation has been to improve the modelling of labour market transitions, using estimated transition probabilities based on age, gender and education levels (Bonnet, 1997).
– The initial version of the model assumed perfectly parallel wage trajectories for individuals from the same cohort, gender and with the same

educational attainment, except for deviations caused by withdrawals from the labour force. To better represent the dispersion of wage trajectories, autoregressive random components have been added to wage equations (Colin, 1997).

– At the same time, updates of the initial database have been made using a new version of the Financial Assets Surveys (the 1997 edition). The initial sample of DESTINIE now contains about 20,000 households and 50 000 individuals.

Changes in the model that have been determined by the evolution of policy questions deserve more explanations. These major changes are described in Table 1.

Table 1: Partial list of policy questions and corresponding developments of the model

Year	Policy questions addressed by the model	Developments of new modules, when requested
1993-1996	Simulating consequences of the 1993 pension reform	First version of the model
1999	Testing the impact of reforms combining stronger conditions for retirement at the full rate with increased flexibility around this full rate	New module simulating the choice of age at retirement (Stock and Wise, 1990)
2003	Examining the extension of pension reform to the public sector	Development of a public sector module
2003	Computing the impact of measures giving access to retirement before 60 to people with long careers	
2005	Projecting the long-term costs of old-age invalidity	New module simulating transition to invalidity and the associated benefit (APA). Valorization of the fact that the model also projects kinship ties (simulation of the number of family members who are potential helpers for the dependant person)
2005-2006	Simulating the impact of alternative scenarios for survivors benefits	
2006	Simulating the impact of increased incentives to postponing retirement	

Policy questions that arose during the second half of the 1990s directly stemmed from the limits of the 1993 reform. Although this reform was not a marginal one, it was clear from the beginning that it was far from fully restoring viability for the French pension scheme. Among tools available to restore this balance, this 1993 reform had strongly relied on the reduction of replacement rates. According to evaluations by the COR, its long-term impact on pension levels could go as high as a 18% reduction in their average level compared to a no reform scenario. On the other hand, and this was also one of the conclusions of the first version of the Destinie model, the predictable impact of the reform on retirement ages appeared quite weak. Shifting the duration required for a full pension from 37.5 to 40 years was not expected to affect a large number of future retirees, at least until 2020, as this measure applied to cohorts whose age at entry on the labour market had remained significantly below 20 on the average.

One question was therefore to explore ways to go further in this direction. This was done in particular in the Charpin report (Charpin, 2000). This report explored the idea of increasing further this duration condition, but suggesting to counterbalance this change by increasing the margin of choice around this reference duration. Indeed, as noted above, both the pre- and post-1993 systems imposed a strong penalty on pensioners claiming for benefits before this normal retirement age, by more than 10% by year of anticipation, i.e. a much stronger adjustment than required by the so-called actuarial neutrality principle. Simultaneously, this system did not offer any incentive to postpone beyond this normal retirement age, since, as we have also seen above, years contributed beyond duration D were not taken into account into the computation of the pension level (except through a very minor impact on the reference wage W). The proposal was therefore to combine a strengthening of the condition on parameter D with a reduction of penalties ("*décote*") for retirement with $N_{tot}<D$ and the introduction of a bonus ("*surcote*") for departures with $N_{tot}>D$, bringing French rules closer to actuarial neutrality.

The problem with such a policy recommendation is to know how to predict its impact on actual retirement behaviour. As long as both anticipation and postponement were strongly discouraged, it was not very far from reality to assume that a very large majority of people retired exactly at the "full rate" or "normal" retirement age (NRA), as it was done in the first version of Destinie. But introducing more room for arbitrage around this NRA clearly called for a more sophisticated modelling of people's behaviour. Figure 1 stylizes the problem showing typical profiles of replacement rates. The first one corresponds to a pre-reform profile with a strong non-linearity around the NRA (point A). The second one corresponds to a post-reform scenario where entitlements are globally lower but with a lower degree of non-linearity around the new NRA (point B). The question with such a reform is to know how people will react to the shift between the two profiles. Will they move to the new NRA (point B)? Will they try to benefit from incentives to postpone beyond this new NRA (point B')? Or will they make use of the possibility to leave earlier with lower penalties than before (point B")?

Figure 1:   The ambiguous impact of pension reform on age at retirement

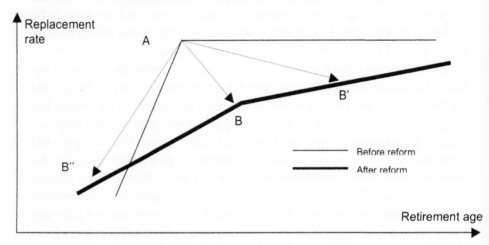

To try to answer these questions, a module has been added to the model that determines age at retirement according to an intertemporal income-leisure trade-off inspired by Stock and Wise (1990). The principle is to assume that each individual considering retirement compares the discounted flows of utility levels upon retiring now or at all other potential retirement ages. This model will be presented in more details in Section 3. It has been used both for simulating the impact of proposals that had been made *before* the 2003 reform, and for *ex post* simulations of consequences of this 2003 reform. For the private sector, this 2003 reform has combined a further increase of condition D up to 41.75 years by 2020 with a progressive reduction of the penalty for early withdrawal and the introduction of an incentive to post-ponement consisting in a (sub-actuarial) bonus of 3% on the pension level for each year worked beyond the NRA.

The other main challenge after the 1993 reform has been the extension of this reform to people working in the public sector, a sector that had been ignored in the first version of the model. A specific module has been developed to simulate pensions for this category. Here again, some simplifications had nevertheless to be made. This module considers an extensive definition of this public sector, including all categories of civil servants and employees working for public administrations, central or local, and also the employees of large public firms. This simplification is a strong one: actual rules are not fully homogeneous for all these categories of workers, and all of them did not get reformed simultaneously. While the 2003 reform actually changed rules for civil servants, it did not address the question of special schemes for large public firms. The other simplification is that, as mentioned above, the model still assumes purely homogeneous careers.

Nevertheless, this module has been a significant step forward towards a better representativity of the model. It takes into account the one-pillar structure of the pension system for civil servants, the fact that some of them had (and still have) possibilities to retire at 55, and the fact that this system does not cover the entirety of wages (it only applies to the base wage, not to premiums that represent a rather large part of total wages for highly skilled civil servants). For the pre-2003 reform conditions, it also takes into account the fact that civil servants leaving after 55 or 60 but without their 37.5 years of contribution only faced mild penalties. For the post-2003 conditions, it takes into account the main features of this reform, i.e. the convergence of D toward the level used in the private sector (40 years by 2008, 41.75 years by 2020), and the progressive alignment of penalties or bonuses for anticipated or delayed exits between the two sectors.

3   Projecting age at retirement: what did we learn?

We now concentrate on how the model has been used for answering the specific question of future retirement ages. We shall first re-expose the Stock and Wise model and the way it has been calibrated, then present some of the results derived from this module, and discuss both the positive and more problematic aspects of such exercises.

3.1   Applying the Stock and Wise model on French data

The problem is to model the decision of an individual facing a menu of retirement decisions of the kind that was displayed in Figure 1. Let's consider an individual who is not retired at the beginning of year t. If retirement takes place at time $r \geq t$, the individual expects to earn wages $(Y_t,...Y_{r-1})$ followed by a sequence of pension benefits $(B_r(r), B_{r+1}(r),...,B_s(r),...)$.[1] Utility derived from income when working or not working is respectively equal to U_w and U_r. The expected sum of discounted utilities with retirement at year r is equal to:

$$V_t(r) = \sum_{s=t}^{r-1} \beta^{s-t} S_t(s) U_w(Y_s) + \sum_{s=r}^{T} \beta^{s-t} S_t(s) U_r(B_s(r))$$

where β is a measure of time discounting and $S_t(s)$ is the survival probability at time s for an individual alive at t. The following specification is retained for utility functions:

$$U_w(Y_s) = \frac{Y_s^{1-\gamma}}{1-\gamma} \quad \text{and} \quad U_r(B_s) = \frac{[kB_s(r)]^{1-\gamma}}{1-\gamma}$$

where γ is a measure of risk aversion and k is an index of preference for leisure. The assumption is that the individual evaluates $V_t(r)$ for every age r between t and the maximum retirement age (65 years in the French case). He retires immediately if $V_t(t)$ is the highest of all these values. Otherwise he postpones, and the same decision process re-occurs in year t+1 incorporating any new information that appears between t and t+1. For individuals not retired but already inactive at time t, the rules are similar except that preretirement years are evaluated using the utility function U_r rather than U_w.

An econometric estimation of such a model on French data is difficult given the fact that, until 2003, the rigidity of French rules offered little space for the revelation of individual preferences. The parameters of the utility function were first estimated on administrative data collected by the Ministry of Social Affairs (Mahieu and Blanchet, 2004). However final values used in the model rather result from an *ad hoc* calibration because of the extreme concentration of observed retirement ages that makes structural estimations very unstable (Mahieu-Sédillot, 2000). The model retains uniform values for time preference ($\beta=0,97$) and risk aversion ($\gamma=0,5$). Some heterogeneity has been introduced concerning preference for leisure. The general rule is to assume a value of 2 on the average, with a standard deviation of 0.2. But this average value is raised to 2.5 for the so-called "active" categories in the public sector (policemen, primary school teachers...) to account for their strong propensity to use their right to retire as soon as at age 55.

---

[1]   As frequently done in the literature, incomes are before-tax incomes, assuming that this does not make an excessively large difference for the predictive performance of the model.

3.2 Main results

Tables 2 and 3 give some results based on this model of retirement behaviour concerning age at retirement before or after the 1993 and 2003 reforms, both for the private and the public sector. Table 2 is restricted to the private sector, since it presents results for the 1993 reform. Two causes of changes in age at retirement can be distinguished: even with the pre-1993 rule, increases in the age at entry into the labour force would have caused an increase of the average age at benefit claiming by 0.3 years, from 61.2 to 61.5. To this we must add the impact of the reform itself, including its interaction with this increasing age at entry on the labour market: this adds 0.6 years more, i.e. a nearly one-year increase between cohort 1935-1940 and cohort 1965-74.

Table 2:   Impact of the 1993 reform on average age at retirement

Cohort	Before the reform			After the reform			Average change due to reform		
	Total	Men	Women	Total	Men	Women	Total	Men	Women
1935-40	61.2	60.4	61.9	61.5	60.8	62.1	0.3	0.4	0.2
1940-44	61.3	60.4	62.2	61.6	60.6	62.5	0.2	0.2	0.3
1945-54	61.2	60.5	61.8	61.5	60.9	62.2	0.4	0.4	0.4
1955-64	61.1	60.7	61.4	61.5	61.1	61.9	0.5	0.4	0.5
1965-74	61.5	61.2	61.7	62.1	61.9	62.2	0.6	0.7	0.5

Source: Destinie model

Table 3:   Impact of the 2003 reform on average age at retirement, by education level

Cohort	Private sector					Public sector				
	Total	Educ level 1	Educ level 2	Educ level 3	Educ level 4	Total	Educ level 1	Educ level 2	Educ level 3	Educ level 4
Before the 2003 reform										
1945-54	61.5	61.3	61.1	61.7	62.9	58.6	57.4	58.1	58.8	60.7
1955-64	61.5	61.3	61.0	61.5	62.7	57.9	57.2	57.6	58.3	59.3
1965-74	62.1	61.5	61.7	62.2	63.4	58.6	57.3	58.5	59.2	60.0
After the 2003 reform										
1945-54	61.6	61.0	61.3	61.6	62.8	60.2	58.7	59.9	60.8	62.1
1955-64	61.9	61.4	61.7	62.2	62.8	60.1	59.6	60.0	60.3	60.9
1965-74	62.3	61.7	62.3	62.5	62.9	60.8	59.8	60.8	61.4	61.5
Average change due to reform										
1945-54	0.0	-0.4	0.1	0.4	0.2	1.6	1.3	1.8	1.9	1.4
1955-64	0.4	0.2	0.6	0.8	0.1	2.2	2.4	2.4	2.1	1.7
1965-74	0.2	0.3	0.6	0.4	-0.4	2.2	2.4	2.3	2.2	1.5

Source: Destinie model, Buffeteau and Godefroy (2005).

Table 3 shows the additional effect of the 2003 reform. To give an idea of the differential impact according to age at entry in the labour market, this second table splits the population of each cohort into four groups, defined by quartiles of the number of years of education (we have seen that this variable constitutes the proxy used by the model to describe relative social status for individuals). In the private sector, the additional impact of this new reform is weak compared to changes already generated by the 1993 reform. The impact is much more important in the public sector, with a final increase of 2.4 years for average age at retirement (but from a point of departure that is much lower).

Let us concentrate on the private sector first. In that case, Destinie results may appear as being much below what could have been expected from a reform that is relatively important. *A priori*, the Destinie model is a supply-side model where we would have expected people to react rather significantly to monetary incentives such as the introduction of the *surcote* in 2003. Why don't we find a stronger impact?

A closer analysis shows that this result can be explained if we take into account the full impact of the reform and the fact that Destinie is not exactly a pure supply-side model. As explained above in Section 2.2, the model incorporates the rationing of employment that strongly affects French workers before the normal retirement age, through the exogenous modelling of exits from employment *before* retirement. Returning to Figure 1, it is easy to see that we shall have a strong interaction effect between this rationing and reactions to the reform. Individuals who reach retirement age without being constrained on their labour supply can actually benefit from the monetary incentive to postpone beyond point B and will react positively to the reform. But individuals with exactly the same characteristics who arrive in the same zone after having lost their job will react in the opposite way. If they only have low non-labour incomes (e.g. low unemployment benefits), they will tend to claim for retirement benefits before the full rate and will be all the more induced to do so if the penalty for this anticipation is reduced, as it has been the case with the 2003 reform.

Table 4 confirms this analysis by showing that the weakness of the global impact results from the contradictory impact of new incentives on the groups of people still at work or no more at work before retirement. This table concerns the 1965-1974 cohort. It shows that the average impact of +0.2 years of postponement that appeared, for this cohort, in Table 4 is an average between a mean postponement of +0.8 for men and a mean anticipation of -0.4 years by women, with strong differentiation according to labour market status for each of the two genders. The contrast is already important for men, with an average postponement of 1.3 for those who are still at work versus only 0.3 for those who have already left employment. The contrast is much more important for women: women who remain at work until retirement have a postponement behaviour that is roughly equivalent to men's, while the relatively large number of those who are already out of employment have an opposite tendency to *anticipate* pension claiming, this high propensity being probably the result of lower resources than for men, the latter ones being more likely to benefit from generous unemployment or preretirement benefits until reaching a full-rate pension.

Table 4: **Impact of the 2003 reform on age at retirement depending on labour market situation before retirement (1965-1974 cohort, private sector only)**

Status before retirement	Men		Women	
	Relative weight	N. of years of postponement	Relative weight	N. of years of postponement
Working	52%	+1.3	34%	+1.4
Non-working	48%	+0.3	66%	-1.3
Total	100%	+0.8	100%	-0.4

Source: Destinie model and COR (2007).

The case of public sector employees is very different. For this category all changes in incentives go in the same direction: no exposition to unemployment risk before retirement, increasing rather than declining penalties for early retirement, higher education level associated to a higher age at entry into employment that makes the duration condition more constraining. The reform results in changes of the age at retirement ranging between +1.5 and +2.4 years.

On the whole, the global impact of the reform that is predicted by the model is an increase of the total labour force by about 640,000 people at the 2020 horizon. Another review of this result can be gained by looking at projected activity rates for the 60-64 age group. This is done in Figure 2. They give labour force participation rates for men and women in this age bracket under four scenarios, i.e. two counter-factual scenarios corresponding to what would have been projected with the pre-1993 or pre-2003 rules, a projection incorporating the impact of the 2003 reform and a variant of this projection where the impact of bonuses for people postponing retirement beyond the normal age is neutralized. One reason for proposing this scenario is that, in many cases, the timing of retirement remains constrained by the employers' ability to unilaterally terminate the labour contract at the NRA. Although removing this possibility was one of the aims of the 2003 reform, it has been reintroduced afterwards in several sectors under the pressure of employers themselves.

Figure 2: Projected labour force participation rates for the 60-64 age group, various scenarios

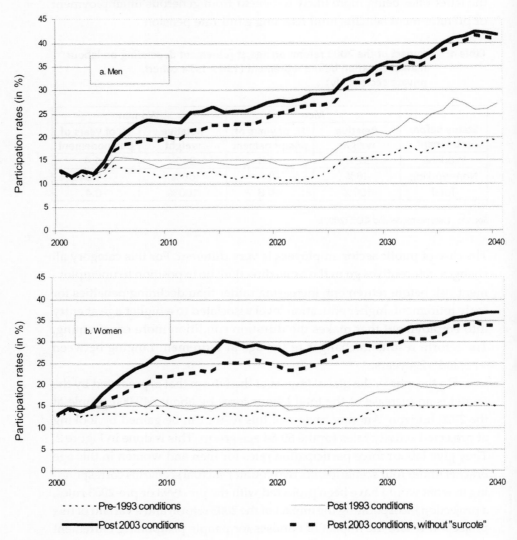

Globally, including the 1993 and the 2003 reform and the trend that would have occurred even without reform, LFP rates in 2020 are expected to be about 28% in the 60-64 age group both for men and women compared to respectively 12% for men and 15% for women in 2003. In the very long run, they would climb to a little more and little less than 40% for, respectively, men and women. A little more than 15 points of this increase would be due to the 2003 reform alone, among which 5 to 2 points are due to the impact of the *"surcote"*.

Is such a prediction realistic? On the whole, a 15-point increase in the total activity rate for this age bracket corresponds to less that one additional year on the labour market for the population as a whole. This is not that large. The model cannot be charged for excessive optimism concerning the incidence of financial incentives to postpone retirement.

However one can have some doubts on the timing of such a change. Figure 2 shows that this change is indeed very rapid, much more rapid than what seems to be shown by the first post-2003 observations. Actually, current employment trends for the 60-64 groups did not show any significant sign of increase since 2003. Part of this inertia can be due to one additional aspect of the 2003 reform that we have not commented so far, which is the possibility offered to people with very long careers (i.e. having started working at less than 16) to retire before 60, a measure intended to be transitory but that has had a strong success over the last years. But this point cannot be the sole explanation for the apparent inertia of behaviour, and this puts into question the relevance of the modelling approach that has been adopted by Destinie I, at least for the short run.

3.3   *About the limits of the Destinie I approach*

Poor performance in predicting short-term evolutions can be due to a variety of factors. Here, we shall try to give a brief list of these factors, discuss their importance – some of them are more relevant than others – and discuss options to solve these problems.

One first possibility is to incriminate the specification of the behavioural model itself. It is clear that the Stock and Wise model is only one option among others for simulating retirement behaviour and other options could have been chosen. The new version of the model currently under construction (Blanchet and Le Minez, 2007) will offer four other options: departure at the full rate, optimization based on instantaneous utility, optimization of

"Social Security wealth" (SSW), i.e. departure at the age that maximizes the expected flow of benefits during the whole retirement, or a decision based on the so-called "accrual", i.e. the rate of change of SSW when postponing retirement by one year. Relying on this list of options may at least have the pedagogical role of showing the amount of uncertainty that necessarily affects projections. It will also be possible to illustrate this uncertainty by varying the parameterization of the Stock and Wise approach. This will be much easier to do in the new model because such changes will not imply a complete re-running of the model.

Pursuing this line, one could wonder whether better predictions could be reached by including additional, "non monetary" determinants of retirement behaviour. An increasing stream of research actually emphasizes the importance of these non-monetary determinants, especially of health or working conditions (Afsa, 2006; Blanchet and Debrand, 2007). Its potential contribution to improving the realism of long-term predictions, however, needs relativization. If the question is to make a long-term projection on the incidence of financial reforms, the introduction of such covariates is of limited help: either we keep them constant in projections, and this is what our current approach with constant preference parameters implicitly does, or we wish to make the assumption that they are going to change over time, but the problem is to predict the path for this change. Under our current state of knowledge, predictions of these covariates would be essentially conventional.

A third possible criticism of the Destinie approach concerns the fact that the model remains excessively supply-oriented. We have already seen that, here again, the criticism has to be relativized. The current version of Destinie already includes demand-side constraints. One could even argue that it includes too many of them, by assuming relatively stable levels in non-employment before normal retirement age with the implied consequences that we have seen on postponement behaviour. In fact, the problem is not the absence of demand-side constraints in the model, but rather the fact that they are extrapolated in a relatively naïve fashion. Some room for improvement exists here, eventually with a better integration of supply- and demand-side effects, for instance if we follow the idea that the perspective of later retirement could change simultaneously the behaviour of both employees and employers much ahead of the new normal retirement age (Hairault et al., 2007).

However, efforts to improve the module that simulates retirement behaviour will remain vain if some other problems are not solved. The best of all possible models of retirement behaviour will still produce low-quality results if it is not based on good initial data or good projections of what determines pension entitlements. Biases in the estimation of past careers and poor prediction of future careers lead, for instance, to estimates of the number of years of contributions reached at age 60 that are biased either upwards or downwards, and we have seen how crucial this parameter is to explain behaviour in the French system. Improvements are also necessary at this level. They simultaneously concern the other segments of the model, essentially the labour market module, and the accurateness of the initial database or of the initial imputations that are used for projections. The new version of the model will also try to bring some significant improvements on these two aspects.

References

Afsa, C. (2006) 'L'estimation d'un coût implicite de la pénibilité du travail chez les travailleurs âgés', *Working Paper INSEE/DESE* n° G2006/10

Blanchet, D./Chanut, J.M. (1998) 'Projeter les retraites à long terme. Résultats d'un modèle de microsimulation', *Economie et Statistique*, 315: 95-106.

Blanchet, D./Pelé, L.P. (1999) 'Social security and retirement in France', pp. 101-133 in: Gruber, J./Wise, D.A. (Eds.), *Social Security and Retirement All Around the World*. NBER/ University of Chicago Press.

Blanchet, D./Debrand, T. (2007) 'Aspiration à la retraite, santé et satisfaction au travail : une comparaison européenne', *Working Paper INSEE/DESE* n° G2007/03

Blanchet, D./Le Minez, S. (2007) 'The Destinie II model : a progress report', 1st IMA conference, Vienna.

Bardaji, J./Sédillot, B./Walraet, E. (2002) 'Évaluation de trois réformes du Régime Général d'assurance vieillesse à l'aide du modèle de microsimulation DESTINIE', *Working Paper INSEE/DESE* n° G2002/07

Bardaji, J./Sédillot, B./Walraet, E. (2004) 'Les retraites du secteur public : projections à l'horizon 2040 à l'aide du modèle de microsimulation DESTINIE', *Working Paper INSEE/DESE* n° G2004/14

Bonnet, C./Mahieu, R. (1999) 'Microsimulation techniques applied to intergenerational transfers - Pensions in a dynamic framework: the case of France', *Working Paper INSEE/DESE* n° G99/06

Buffeteau, S./Godefroy, P. (2005) 'Conditions de départ en retraite selon l'âge de fin d'études : analyse prospective pour les générations 1945 à 1974', *Working Paper INSEE/DESE* n° G2005/01

Charpin, J.M. (1999) *L'avenir de nos retraites, rapport au premier ministre*. Paris: La Documentation Française.

Colin, C. (1999) 'Modélisation des carrières dans Destinie', *Working Paper INSEE/DESE* n° G99/02

Colin, C. (1999) 'Evolution de la dispersion des salaires : un essai de prospective par microsimulation', *Working Paper INSEE/DESE* n° G99/03

Colin, C./Legros, F./Mahieu, R. (1999) 'Bilans contributifs comparés des régimes de retraite du secteur privé et de la fonction publique', *Working Paper INSEE/DESE* n° G99/10

Conseil d'Orientation des Retraites (2006) *Retraites: perspectives 2020 et 2050, Troisième Rapport.* Paris: La Documentation Française.

Crenner, E. (2007) 'Projecting Living Standards and Poverty Rates for French Pensioners', 1st General Conference of the International Microsimulation Association, 20-22 August 2007, Vienna.

Division 'Redistribution et Politiques Sociales' (1999) 'Le modèle de microsimulation dynamique DESTINIE', *Working Paper INSEE/DESE* n° G99/13

Duée, M./Rebillard, C. (2004) 'La dépendance des personnes âgées : une projection à long terme', *Working Paper INSEE/DESE* n° G2004/02

Duée, M. (2005) 'La modélisation des comportements démographiques dans le modèle de microsimulation Destinie', *Working Paper INSEE/DESE* n° G2005/15

Hairault, J.O./Langot, F./Sopraseuth, T. (2006) 'Les effets à rebours de l'âge de la retraite sur le taux d'emploi des seniors', *Economie et Statistique* 397: 51-63

Mahieu, R./Blanchet, D. (2004) 'Estimating models of retirement behaviour on French data', pp. 235-284 in: Gruber, J./Wise, D.A. (Eds.), *Social Security Programs and Retirement around the world.* NBER/The University of Chicago Press.

Mahieu, R./Sédillot, B. (2000) 'Microsimulations of the retirement decision: a supply side approach', *Working Paper INSEE/DESE* n° G 2000/07

Mahieu, R./Sédillot, B. (2001) 'Départ à la retraite, irréversibilité et incertitude', *Working Paper INSEE/DESE* n° G2001/06

Robert-Bobée, I. (2001) 'Modelling demographic behaviours in the French microsimulation model Destinie: An analysis of future change in completed fertility', *Working Paper INSEE/DESE* n° G2001/14

Robert-Bobée, I. (2002) 'Les comportements démographiques dans le modèle de microsimulation Destinie - Une comparaison des estimations issues des enquêtes Jeunes et Carrières 1997 et Histoire Familiale 1999', *Working Paper INSEE/DESE* n° G2002/10

Stock, J./Wise, D. (1990) 'Pensions, the option value of work, and Retirement', *Econometrica,* 58 (5): 1151-1180.

Vernière, L. (1990) 'Les retraites pourront-elles être financées après l'an 2000 ?', *Economie et Statistique* 233: 19-27.

Walraet, E./Vincent, A. (2003) 'La redistribution intragénérationnelle dans le système de retraite des salariés du privé: une approche par microsimulation', *Economie et Statistique* 366: 31-56.

306

Chapter 12

Rates of Return in the Canada Pension Plan: Sub-populations of Special Policy Interest and Preliminary After-tax Results

Richard J. Morrison

1   Introduction

Calculations of internal rates of return are valuable for evaluating social security programmes. Canada's Office of the Chief Actuary regularly uses them in the statuary actuarial reports that assess the operation of the Canada Pension Plan (CPP). Those reports cite the Plan's positive rates of return as evidence that the CPP provides its participants with good value. The CPP's effectiveness in this respect is important because that programme's benefits provide a major source of Canadian seniors' incomes, ranking behind only (1) the collective returns to private investments (interest, dividends, and capital gains), and (2) private (employer) pensions.

Modern longitudinal microsimulation models and analyses are almost invariably team efforts. Thus, the results I present in this chapter owe a considerable debt to the other members of the DYNACAN team, past and present, and are possible only through their efforts. Inevitably, the results also owe a good deal to other colleagues and modelers, both in Canada and internationally. Beyond this general dependency and my appreciation for their various contributions, this particular analysis owes a special debt to Vesna Petrovic for her critical assistance in assembling a special purpose longitudinal database of the relevant persons, their characteristics, and their CPP transactions. I am further grateful to several members of the DYNACAN team for constructive comments that have improved both the chapter's substance, and its presentation. The responsibility for any remaining shortcomings is, of course, entirely my own. This chapter is a revised, updated, version of one presented at the first International Microsimulation Association conference, held in Vienna, August 20-22, 2007. I am grateful to the conference organizers for the opportunity to supplement the original chapter's results with preliminary findings on real after-tax internal rates of return for the Canada Pension Plan.

Disclaimer: The opinions expressed in this chapter are entirely those of the author. They are not necessarily shared by Human Resources and Social Development Canada, the government of Canada, nor Her Majesty in Right of Canada.

The DYNACAN longitudinal dynamic microsimulation model generates, for birth-year cohorts, series of CPP contributions and benefits that imply cohort-specific internal rates of return. Morrison (2004) shows that DYNACAN's projected rates lie close to those calculated using the Chief Actuary's ACTUCAN model, despite the very different approaches that the two models employ. Morrison (2000, 2007) provides a summary description of the DYNACAN model. Moreover, the flexibility associated with longitudinal microsimulation modeling and its micro-level data permit one to use DYNACAN to calculate rates of return differentiated by gender. Existing studies suggest that real (inflation-adjusted) internal rates of return for women are about 2% higher than the rates for men, but the real return rates are positive for both men and women (Morrison, 2004).

This chapter extends the calculation of internal rates of return to sub-populations divided by characteristics other than gender. The relevance is that, given the CPP's goals, cohort-specific rates of return for particular sub-populations should be, or can be expected to be, higher or lower than the corresponding value for the full population cohort. Thus, for example, we expect to find that rates are higher for ever-married persons, in part because they are the only ones who can receive survivor benefits. Given the social insurance component of the Canada Pension Plan, the rates should be, and are, higher for persons receiving disability benefits than for the general population. As well, to the extent that actuarial adjustments for early retirement are fair, one should expect that rates of return for those retiring early should be similar to, and not higher than, those for persons not taking up benefits until the CPP's normal retirement age of 65. This chapter displays comparisons of real internal rates of return for these sub-populations and others.

In a second extension of the earlier work, this chapter also presents preliminary results for real after-tax internal rates of return. It assesses the internal rates of return implicit in participants' losses in purchasing power when they contribute to the Plan and their gains in purchasing power when they receive benefits. The new measures reflect the impacts of tax relief in respect of contributions, and of the positive taxes and benefit reductions that apply upon benefit receipt. The resulting after-tax internal rates of return are smaller than the before-tax returns, but still are positive for both men and women, as well as for all of the several sub-populations examined.

The general organization of this chapter is straightforward:

- The initial sections provide greater context for the use of rates of return in assessing government social security programmes, specifically including the use of such rates in actuarial reports on the CPP. They outline the calculation of before-tax internal rates of return using data from the DYNACAN model.

- In addition, they confirm the consistency of the DYNACAN-generated rates of return with the before-tax rates reported by the Office of the Chief Actuary. As well, they update a previous DYNACAN analysis that derived gender-specific rates of return.
- Subsequent sections extend the calculations of sub-population-specific before-tax rates to selected groups of special policy interest, including those with low lifetime earnings, immigrants, early retirees, and the disabled. The discussion relates the calculated rate of return differentials to the design goals of the CPP, and to particular provisions within the CPP.
- The chapter also presents preliminary findings on the "effective" internal rates of return that result after one considers the tax relief accorded to CPP contributions, and the income taxes and benefit reductions associated with benefit receipt.
- A short concluding section addresses the utility of sub-population rates of return and after-tax internal rates of return as supplements to DYNACAN's extensive set of standard output tables and graphs, and as a useful tool for model validation.

Throughout, the chapter focuses on practical, policy-oriented, and policy-relevant results.

2 Internal rates of return

2.1 *Relevance of rate of return measures*

The legislation underlying the Canada Pension Plan requires the publication of periodic actuarial reports that assess the status and sustainability of the programme. The Office of the Chief Actuary, operating as an independent party within the Office of the Superintendent of Financial Institutions, prepares those reports with inputs from an actuarial valuation model, ACTUCAN. One recurring component of those CPP actuarial reports has been a table of before-tax internal rates of return, providing a measure of the value that members of a cohort receive from the CPP. The actuarial reports present the internal rates of return for several birth-year cohorts as a means of demonstrating how the evolution and maturation of the CPP affect cohorts differently, providing different cohorts with differing internal rates of return. As the most recently published statutory actuarial report, addressing the CPP as at 31 December 2006, notes –

> "The higher internal rates of return of the earlier cohorts mean that they are expected to receive better value from the CPP than those who follow. The differences provide an indication of the degree of intergenerational transfer present in the Plan. However, the fact that all of the rates in the table are greater than zero shows that each cohort is expected to realize a positive return from its investment in the CPP." (23rd Actuarial Report, 2007: 70)

It is relevant for DYNACAN's credibility that its before-tax internal rates of return, derived using DYNACAN's very different modeling approach, prove similar to ACTUCAN's. Moreover, a confirmation of the positive rates of return that appear in the actuarial reports provides collaborative evidence for the value of the Canada Pension Plan to its participants, and of the sustainability of that value for recent and future birth-year cohorts. As well, the power of longitudinal dynamic modeling permits the analysis of policy-relevant sub-populations that enable one to assess the extent to which the Canada Pension Plan is meeting its multiple design goals.

2.2 Definition of internal rate of return

Since one analysis in this chapter addresses the consistency of the DYNACAN rate of return results with those in the actuarial reports on the Canada Pension Plan, it is useful to begin with a characterization of an internal rate of return. As the Chief Actuary describes them in the most recent statutory actuarial report --

> "The internal rate of return is, with respect to a group of CPP participants born in a given year (i.e. a cohort), the unique interest rate resulting in the equality of:
> – the present value of past and future contributions paid or expected to be paid by and in respect of that cohort, and
> – the present value of past and future benefits earned or expected to be earned by that cohort." (23rd Actuarial Report, 2007: 70)

Informally, one may characterize a cohort's internal rate of return using the analogy of a bank account for which there is a fixed rate of interest for all positive or negative balances. Into this account, the members of a cohort, and their employers, pay all their prescribed CPP contributions. From it, they fund all of their benefits in the amounts prescribed by the CPP legislation and regulations. Upon the death of the last member of the cohort, one derives the internal rate of return as that level of interest rate such that the very last withdrawal exactly empties the bank account. That derived interest rate is the before-tax internal rate of return for the cohort.

There are several considerations relevant to using a policy model's internal rates of return to assess the operation of a social security programme. Major issues include the following:

- One must necessarily base the calculated rates of return on projections as well as historical data. Thus, as with all other outputs from longitudinal microsimulation models, the rates of return depend explicitly on one's assumptions about the life and earnings histories of cohorts, often including groups of persons not yet born.

- One can calculate the internal rates of return not only for cohorts, but also for significant sub-populations within those cohorts. The sub-population internal rates of return reflect the series of contributions and benefits for just those individuals belonging to the specified sub-population. These sub-populations may, depending on their defining characteristics, be subject to particular CPP provisions intended to implement particular policy objectives.

- Following the lead of the Office of the Chief Actuary, the DYNACAN team calculates before-tax internal rates of return on both nominal and real bases to reflect cohorts' differing experiences of inflation. However, for economy of presentation, this chapter uses the real rates of return for sub-populations of interest and for after-tax internal rates of return.

- The rates of return included in the first portion of this chapter are, as noted, real before-tax rates. That is, the rates depend on the gross contributions made by contributors, and the gross benefits received by beneficiaries. They do not reflect the impact on participants' purchasing power from the treatment of contributions and benefits by the positive tax system or various income-tested benefit programmes. A separate section later in the chapter provides preliminary results for real after-tax internal rates of return

2.3 *Calculating before-tax internal rates of return*

The mechanics of calculating internal rates of return are relatively straightforward. The DYNACAN model generates annual data for each synthetic individual. Besides demographic information on marital, disability, and

311

retirement status, the simulation generates work and earnings, and the resulting gross CPP contributions and benefits. The demographic life histories allow us to identify the individuals falling into various populations of special policy interest, e.g. the ever-disabled. Using DYNACAN's CPP contributions and benefits outputs, we compile, for any relevant cohort, or sub-population of the cohort, the appropriate time-subscripted contributions paid, and benefits received. The DYNACAN team has assembled these data from DYNACAN's standard outputs using a small number of programmes written in C and Perl. Collectively, the CPP contributions and benefits provide the time series of net benefits (benefits received less contributions made) that are the basis for the internal rate of return calculations. For the nominal rate of return calculations, one uses the unadjusted current dollar benefits and contributions. For the real rate of return calculations, one converts the net contributions to constant dollar values, using the consumer price index, as one assigns the various contributions and benefits to the appropriate elements of the series of net benefits.

The calculated rates of return inevitably depend on DYNACAN's success in modeling the intricacies of contributions and benefits. This is a non-trivial challenge, given that the complexity of the Canada Pension Plan is second only to that of Canada's income tax system. Also relevant is a variety of assumptions – largely the same externally reviewed assumptions that the Chief Actuary uses (e.g. for inflation, earnings growth, convergence of men's and women's earnings, trends in retirement ages, mortality improvements, and disability rates). Specifically, for the DYNACAN results we present here, we use the assumptions of the 23rd statutory actuarial report as published in 2007 by the Office of the Superintendent of Financial Institutions (OSFI).

As well, the series of net benefits depend on the attribution principles used to allocate the benefits. The DYNACAN calculations assign the survivors' benefits and children's benefits to the individuals receiving them, rather than to the individuals whose contributions generated those entitlements. We attribute the relatively small CPP death benefits to the contributor, given their taxability as part of a deceased contributor's final tax return, and that they may be used to help to pay his/her funeral expenses. Similarly, we attribute retirement and disability benefits to the recipient beneficiaries. Where divorces and separations result in a splitting of pensionable earnings, affecting subsequent benefit entitlements, we assign the contributions to the contributors who made them, and the resulting benefits to the individuals receiving them. These several attributions are consistent with treatments in Canada's positive income tax system.

We calculate the internal rates of return in Microsoft Excel using its IRR function. Since this function takes as an argument an initial guess for the internal rate of return, we use the actuarial report's values for similar cohorts, or the previously derived internal rates of return for similar cohorts or sub-populations. Experimentation shows that the calculated internal rates of return are generally insensitive to these initial guesses.

2.4   DYNACAN vs. ACTUCAN real rates of return

As noted above, ACTUCAN is the actuarial valuation model developed and maintained by the Office of the Chief Actuary in Canada's Office of the Superintendent of Financial Institutions. ACTUCAN analyses provide the primary financial projections for the Canada Pension Plan, and for the periodic actuarial valuations mandated by the CPP's enabling legislation. DYNACAN, in contrast, exists primarily to provide plausible distributions of the ACTUCAN aggregate values, and to generate realistic point-in-time and longitudinal distributions of winners and losers resulting from prospective programme changes.

A standard feature of the periodic statutory actuarial reports is a presentation of the internal rates of return for selected cohorts. Table 1 displays, for those selected cohorts appearing in the most recent actuarial report, the ACTUCAN and DYNACAN real internal rates of return (i.e. rates that have been adjusted for the effects of inflation).

Table 1:   ACTUCAN and DYNACAN real CPP rates of return:
           selected birth-year cohorts

Birth-year	ACTUCAN (23rd)	DYNACAN
1940	6.2	6.1
1950	4.1	4.3
1960	3.0	3.3
1970	2.4	2.6
1980	2.2	2.3
1990	2.2	2.2
2000	2.2	2.1

The earlier birth-year cohorts have higher real internal rates of return because of the way that Canada phased in the CPP upon its creation in 1966. The primary reason for the trend is that members of the earlier cohorts could receive full benefits without contributing across the whole of their working lives; only years from 1966 onward counted for CPP contributions and calculations of average earnings. Earlier cohorts also benefited from lower contribution rates on their pensionable earnings. For later cohorts, the contribution rates (fractions of pensionable earnings) rose, from the 1966 rate of 3.6% of contributory earnings to the present 9.95% level. (That 9.95% combined employer/employee contribution level continues through to the end of the simulation period in 2130.) In addition, later cohorts had to contribute on earnings from age 18 onward, rather than only from 1966 onward. As well, the real value of earnings excluded from contributions declined, meaning that later cohorts contributed on a larger portion of their earnings.

Figure 1 presents these results graphically, including DYNACAN's results for all of the cohorts rather than just the set included in the actuarial reports. As in the tabular presentation, the DYNACAN results generally track the ACTUCAN results, despite the models' very different approaches to modeling CPP contributions and benefits. Both models exhibit the same general curve, with what seems to be an apparent asymptote for cohorts born after about 1980. For all of the cohorts, the DYNACAN rates lie within one third of a percentage point of the corresponding published ACTUCAN rates. The graph underscores the earlier finding that all birth-year cohorts beyond about 1980 should experience roughly the same real, before-tax, internal rate of return, slightly in excess of 2%.

Figure 1: Real before-tax CPP internal rates of return: ACTUCAN actuarial model and DYNACAN by 5-year cohort

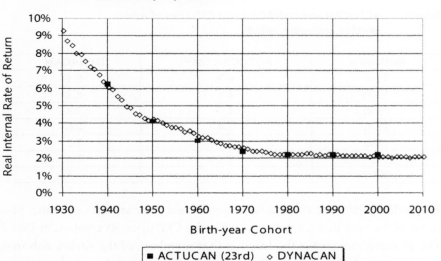

2.5 Rates of return by gender

Human Resources and Social Development Canada is the federal government department that administers the CPP. The Department's established policy on gender analysis requires managers and analysts to provide break-outs by gender as a matter of course. For example, the implementation section of the Gender Analysis Policy calls for --

- *"Collecting and considering data disaggregated by both sex and other demographic/diversity factors"*,
- *"Making data and analysis on gender issues widely available"*, and
- *"Factoring gender into all background analyses."*

Accordingly, it is appropriate here to break out these internal rates of return by gender, although the Chief Actuary does not provide a comparable analysis. Fortunately, the design of the DYNACAN model facilitates this decomposition. The DYNACAN output files identify the individual's gender for all contributions and benefits. This inclusion allows one to compile the requisite net flows (benefits less contributions) by birth year and calendar year, separately for men and women. The calculations of internal rates of return then parallel those for birth-year cohorts without gender breakouts. Indeed, this chapter calculated the DYNACAN overall rate of return values by summing together the gender-specific flows. Figure 2 displays the overall rates of return from Figure 1, supplemented by the various cohorts' gender-specific internal rates of return.

315

Not surprisingly, the rate of return patterns for men and women show the same downward tendency, reaching, for both, an asymptote for cohorts born after about 1980. The men's rates and women's rates naturally bracket the overall DYNACAN and ACTUCAN rates.

The women's real before-tax internal rates of return, by cohort, are consistently higher than the corresponding rates for men. We expect these higher women's rates because –

1. Women have a longer life expectancy; thus, for any given contribution history and retirement age, they tend to receive retirement benefits for more years than their male counterparts, raising their associated rate of return.

2. Women are, disproportionately, the beneficiaries of a CPP provision that allows contributors to drop, from the calculation of the average earnings that determine their pensions, years in which they were raising a child below the age of seven, provided that such a drop-out would improve their benefits.

3. Women disproportionately benefit from the mandatory divisions of earnings that occur upon marriage breakdown. With some exceptions, these divisions generally pool husbands' and wives' earnings for each year during the period of the union, and then assign one-half of that sum to each of the partners.

4. Women, with their longer average life spans, receive the bulk of survivors' benefits triggered by the death of a contributor spouse, an advantage (as regards the rates of return) that is compounded by the tendency for women to be younger than their spouses.

5. Women, with their lower labour force participation and lower average earnings, also benefit disproportionately from a number of CPP provisions designed to advantage persons with lower earnings. These include the general drop-out provisions for the calculation of average lifetime earnings, and the year's basic exemption that *excludes* certain earnings for purposes of contributions, but *includes* those same earnings for purposes of benefit calculations. As men's and women's earnings parameters continue to converge, this difference will diminish.

However, despite the higher rates for women, the before-tax real internal rates of return remain positive for both men and women, across all birth-year cohorts.

Figure 2: **Real before-tax CPP internal rates of return: Actuarial, DYNACAN and DYNACAN by birth-year cohort and gender**

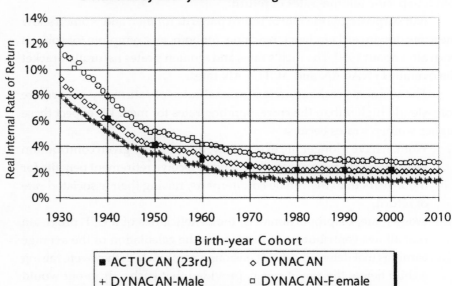

3   Sub-population rates of return

Just as one can look at the subset of a cohort that corresponds to a particular gender, one can also break cohorts out by other policy-relevant characteristics. That is, instead of just dividing a cohort out by gender, we can also divide a cohort by, say, whether individuals take up retirement benefits prior to reaching age 65, whether they have immigrated to Canada, or whether they have ever received any CPP disability benefits. Such analyses help give effect to the department's gender analysis policy as regards its provision for providing comparable analyses in respect of *"other demographic/ diversity factors"*.

In this chapter, we examine five groups of particular policy interest. They include – persons with low lifetime earnings, ever-married persons, immigrants, persons taking up retirement benefits prior to the "normal" retirement age of 65, and persons receiving a CPP Disability benefit. Other sub-populations might also be of interest, e.g. ever-divorced, or high-education, or those using the provisions to drop child-rearing years out of the calculation of average earnings, or the complements of the groups that we examine here. Still more focused sub-populations, such as "ever-married persons taking early retirement", might also be of interest, but such analyses may encounter sample size issues given that the department's gender analysis policy requires breakouts by gender when sample sizes permit.

The computational methods for the groups of special policy interest parallel those for gender-specific internal rates of return. We still break out the analyses by gender where sample size considerations permit. The analyses still reflect cohorts with common or similar birth-years, except that, out of concern for sample sizes, we combine the contribution and benefit flows for persons born in groups of five consecutive birth-years. The groupings extend from the set of birth-years 1930-1934, through the set 2005-2009. For the graphic presentations, we label each grouping with the central birth-year, e.g. 1932 for the grouping with birth-years in the range 1930-1934, and 2007 for the set 2005-2009. This level of aggregation is not strictly necessary for all of the sub-populations, but we apply it to all of them in the interests of consistency of presentation.

This chapter uses a common format across the five sections dealing with the five sub-populations. Each section begins with a brief discussion of the sub-population and its CPP policy significance, and of the relevant provisions in the Canada Pension Plan. It continues with a graphic showing the real before-tax rates of return, by five-year birth cohort grouping, separately for men and women, with the overall rates (as shown above) for all men and all women included for comparison purposes. A final portion of the discussion then briefly interprets those results in the context of CPP programme objectives. All of these analyses use a real, before-tax internal rates of return measure.

3.1 Low lifetime earnings

The Canada Pension Plan contains provisions that tend to advantage persons with low lifetime earnings. The major items include the following:

- CPP contributions are based on earnings less a level of excluded earnings, Year's Basic Exemption (YBE), while the calculated average earnings for an individual, largely proportional to retirement benefits, are based on earnings inclusive of that exemption. This means that lower earning individuals pay a lower average contribution rate on those earnings that determine their pensions.

- Persons with lower lifetime earnings tend to have greater year over year variability in participation and earnings levels. They thus tend to benefit more from the drop-outs (exclusions of certain years) used in the calculation of the average earnings that determine major components of CPP benefits.

- Disability rates are higher for persons with lower earnings, so that these persons are more likely to receive disability benefits, and to benefit from a drop-out of disability years in the calculation of the average earnings values used in benefit calculations. Further, disability pensions are relatively high, compared to retirement pensions, and persons receiving disability benefits do not pay contributions on any earnings accrued during their period of disability.

- Set against these provisions, persons with lower lifetime earnings also tend to die sooner, so that they do not, on average, receive retirement and survivor benefits for as many years. It is of considerable interest whether the plan provisions advantaging low-earning individuals outweigh their higher mortality as regards internal rates of return calculated on the net benefits received.

We identified low lifetime earnings individuals based on their lifetime totals of CPI-adjusted constant-dollar earnings, specifically, from age 18 through to age 64. For each combination of gender and birth-year cohort, we calculated an approximation for the median of the distribution of such lifetime earnings totals. For purposes of this analysis, we identified "low lifetime earnings individuals" as all those persons whose lifetime earnings fell below the approximate median for the gender and birth-year combination. With the low lifetime earnings individuals thus identified, we constructed time series of net constant dollar benefits by aggregating across all five of the consecutive birth-years in each of the 32 five-year, gender-specific, groupings. The number of individuals in the smallest such grouping exceeded 2,350. (Each such synthetic individual represents about 100 Canadians.) For three-quarters of the groupings, the number of individuals used for the internal rate of return calculation was greater than 5,000. Figure 3 displays, separately by gender, the real before-tax internal rates of return for low lifetime earnings individuals, as well as the comparison levels for all individuals.

Figure 3: **Real before-tax CPP internal rates of return: Low earners and all participants by 5-year cohort and gender**

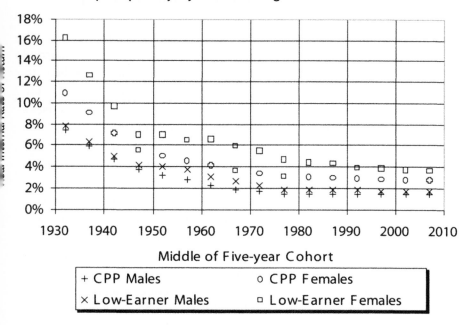

These before-tax rates of return show that the impacts of the Plan provisions favouring lower earnings individuals more than overcome their shorter than average lifespans. For each cohort grouping, and for both men and women, the internal rate of return for the lower earnings individuals non-trivially exceeds the corresponding rate for all CPP participants. The differentials are greater for women than for men, and tend to decline for later cohorts. From a policy perspective, the results are reassuring in that, by this measure of the Plan's value to its participants, lower earners are not collectively subsidizing those with higher earnings. In fact, the results suggest quite the reverse.

3.2 Ever-married

The Canada Pension Plan's contribution rules do not depend on marital status. However, its benefit calculations do contain provisions that tend to benefit married persons, both men and women. For example, there is a Child-Rearing Drop-Out (CRDO) provision that allows parents (who are, disproportionately, ever-married persons) to drop, from the calculation of the average earnings that determine their benefits, years spent raising a child under the age of seven, should such a drop-out be advantageous. As well, the Canada Pension Plan provides for the payment of a survivor's pension to most surviving spouses, or common-law partners, of deceased CPP contributors. The primary exception is for younger surviving spouses with no children. These survivors' benefits flow, inevitably, only to ever-married persons. In terms of aggregate CPP benefits paid, these survivors' benefits run a close third, by benefit type, to retirement benefits and disability benefits. This closeness occurs despite Plan provisions that give these spouses a smaller survivor's pension than was received, or would have been received, by the deceased spouse, and despite the Plan's "combined benefits" rules that reduce survivors' benefits when the sum of the survivor's own benefits and the survivors' benefits exceeds prescribed maxima. Because of differing mortality rates by gender; women's resulting longer expected lives; and the tendency of men to marry younger women, these survivors' pensions flow disproportionately to women. The relevant policy issue is whether and how much these several Plan provisions tend to advantage married Canadians, beyond their impacts as regards gender effects.

Because DYNACAN simulates marriage as one of its demographic events, we were able easily to identify individuals who had ever been married. Both the Canada Pension Plan, and DYNACAN, treat common-law unions as marriages. Those persons who had been "married" at any time during their lives were admitted to this sub-population; those who had not, were not. As with the low-earnings sub-population, we constructed time series of net constant dollar benefits by aggregating across all five of the consecutive birth-years in each of the 32 five-year, gender-specific, groupings. The number of individuals in the smallest such grouping exceeded 4,000. For more than three-quarters of the groupings, the number of individuals used for the internal rate of return calculation was greater than 7,000. Figure 4 displays, separately by gender, the real internal rates of return for ever-married individuals, as well as the comparison levels for all individuals.

Figure 4: **Real before-tax CPP internal rates of return: Ever-married and all participants by 5-year cohort and gender**

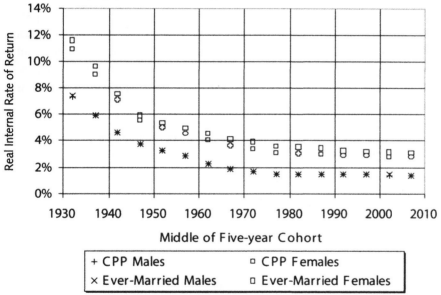

For women, the rates of return for the ever-married were, for all of the cohort groupings, slightly higher than for women as a whole. As anticipated, the differences declined across cohorts. This occurs because women in more recent cohorts have fewer children and earn progressively higher own-retirement pensions, that limit their ability to benefit from survivor pensions. For married men, who disproportionately die before their spouses, and who tend not to reduce their labour force participation to raise children, the rates of return are essentially equal to those of the broader male population for all of the cohort groupings. From a programme policy perspective, it is reassuring that the ever-married sub-population is not subsidizing the never-marrieds, and that any subsidy in the other direction is small, and restricted primarily to women.

3.3 Immigrants

Immigration is an extremely important component of Canadian demographics, having accounted for all or nearly all of recent Canadian population growth. The Canada Pension Plan itself is "immigration-blind". It contains no provisions specifically affecting immigrants as such. That is, immigrants and non-immigrants are subject to exactly the same rules for contributions, and for benefit calculations. An underlying principle is that immigrants will / should "proportionately" fund part of their retirements with entitlements built up abroad, before immigrating to Canada, and part through their participation in Canadian programmes such as the CPP after their arrival. Thus, one wants to examine immigrants' participation in the CPP to ensure that there is neutrality in their treatment. That is, one would not want to have the internal rates of return for immigrants be either significantly higher or appreciably lower than those for lifelong Canadians.

Figure 5: Real before-tax CPP internal rates of return: Immigrants and all participants by 5-year cohort and gender

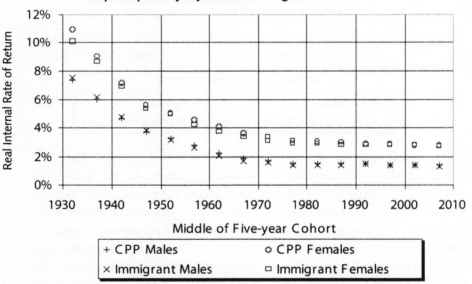

Because DYNACAN simulates immigration as one of its demographic events, we were able easily to identify individuals who had ever immigrated. We included in this sub-population those individuals who had immigrated to Canada, and excluded those who had not. As with the other sub-populations, we constructed gender-specific time series of net constant dollar benefits by aggregating across all five of the consecutive birth-years in each of the 32 five-year, gender-specific, groupings. Given the importance of immigration to Canadian demographics, there were no problems with sample sizes. The number of individuals in the smallest grouping exceeded 1,200. For more than half of the groupings, the number of individuals used for the internal rate of return calculation was greater than 5,000. Figure 5 displays, separately by gender, the real internal rates of return for immigrants, as well as the corresponding levels for all individuals.

The results are again clear. The before-tax internal rates of return for immigrants, male and female, lie very close to those of the rates for all CPP participants. Immigrants are neither subsidizing, nor being subsidized by, other Canadians to any appreciable extent. The results as displayed here show the immigrants with internal rates of return that are perhaps marginally smaller than those for all CPP participants. However, this result may be a slight understatement of their outcomes. The DYNACAN labour force module does not consider immigration status. However, labour force statistics indicate that immigrants tend to have, perhaps because of initial acculturation challenges, somewhat lower labour force participation rates and earnings than one might otherwise expect. As their residence in Canada increases, their labour force participation and earnings levels approach those of Canadian-born individuals with similar other characteristics. Thus, DYNACAN's histories for immigrants should probably share a bit more of the characteristics of lower-income Canadians. As seen above, this would likely result in slightly higher calculated internal rates of return. Overall, however, it appears likely that, as is desirable, the CPP is essentially neutral to immigrants in its impacts as measured by rates of return, just as it is neutral in its rules for CPP contributions and the computation of CPP benefits.

3.4 Early Retirees

The Canada Pension Plan permits contributors to begin drawing retirement benefits prior to the "normal" retirement age of 65. Approximately two-thirds of Canadians take advantage of this early-retirement provision. About half of these early retirees take up the benefits at the earliest permitted age of 60. Because early-retirement beneficiaries will, on average, receive their pensions over a longer period, the CPP applies an actuarial adjustment to maintain fairness. Retirement benefits for early retirees (those retiring before age 65) are calculated using the standard benefit formula, but are then reduced by 6% for each year that the claimant falls short of the normal retirement age of 65. Thus, an individual taking up the retirement benefit at age 60 would receive 70% of the benefit calculated using the standard formula. Such a reduction applies to the individual's benefits for the rest of his/her life. As well, once an individual is receiving a CPP retirement benefit, even if s/he returns to work, no further CPP contributions are payable.

Because DYNACAN simulates the retirement take-up decision as one of its demographic events, we were able easily to identify individuals who took early retirement. We included in this sub-population those individuals who had received any CPP retirement benefit prior to age 65, and excluded those who had not. As with the other sub-populations, we constructed gender-specific time series of net constant dollar benefits by aggregating across all five of the consecutive birth-years in each of the 32 five-year, gender-specific, groupings. Given the tendency of many Canadians to take early CPP retirement, there were no problems with sample sizes. The number of individuals in the smallest grouping exceeded 1,600. For more than two-thirds of the groupings, the number of individuals used for the internal rate of return calculation was greater than 4,000. Figure 6 displays, separately by gender, the real internal rates of return for early retirees, as well as the corresponding levels for all individuals.

Figure 6: **Real before-tax CPP internal rates of return: Early retirees and all participants by 5-year cohort and gender**

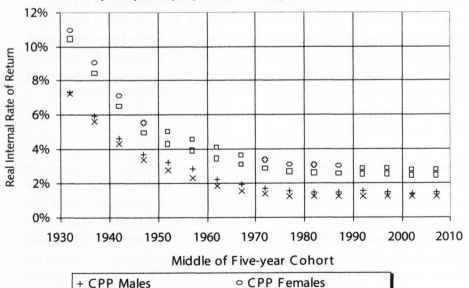

The results are clear. Early retirees, both men and women, for all of the cohorts examined, experience internal rates of return that fall slightly below the corresponding rates for all men or all women. The result is encouraging from a policy perspective. It would be counterproductive to be providing positive incentives for individuals to retire early. On the other hand, given that some early retirement is involuntary, it would be unreasonable for early retirees to be heavily subsidizing those retiring at age 65 or later. Finally, anticipating the results in the next section, we note that if disability beneficiaries (whom we generally deem to retire at age 65) were removed from the all-participants measures, then internal rates of return for the all-participants-less-disabled-participants would fall relative to the all-participants measures. That fall would lead to all-participants-less-disabled-participants measures that are closer to those of early retirees, reinforcing, for the non-disabled, the neutrality of the actuarial adjustment. The retirement benefit calculation neither significantly favours nor penalizes a decision to take up retirement benefits prior to the normal retirement age.

3.5 Disability beneficiaries

As part of its social insurance objectives, the CPP provides disability benefits to qualified contributors less than 65 who become disabled to the point that they cannot reasonably be expected to work. Disability emergences are strongly age-related; disabilities typically commence relatively late in participants' working careers. CPP disability benefits, although one does not expect them, by themselves, to raise recipients above established low-income cut-offs, are significant. Typically, they exceed the retirement pension a recipient with the same average earnings could expect at age 65. Moreover, if a disability beneficiary does have some earnings, those earnings are not subject to CPP contributions. However, if disability beneficiaries recover before age 65, they cease to receive disability benefits and become liable for contributions on subsequent earnings. At age 65, CPP disability benefits cease, being converted to a lower level of CPP retirement benefits, reflecting the availability of other seniors' benefits, e.g. those from Canada's Old Age Security and Guaranteed Income Supplement programmes. Unsurprisingly, CPP disability beneficiaries have significantly higher mortality probabilities, *ceteris paribus*, than the general population.

Because DYNACAN simulates disability and recovery among its demographic events, along with the individuals' work histories, we were again able easily to identify individuals eligible for disability benefits. We included in this sub-population those individuals who had received any CPP disability benefit, and excluded those who had not. As with the other sub-populations, we constructed gender-specific time series of net constant dollar benefits by aggregating across all five of the consecutive birth-years in each of the 32 five-year, gender-specific groupings. The number of individuals in the smallest grouping was only about 440, but over three-quarters of the groupings contained in excess of 1,200 individuals. Figure 7 displays, separately by gender, the real internal rates of return for persons receiving any CPP disability benefits, as well as the corresponding levels for all individuals.

Figure 7: Real before-tax CPP internal rates of return: Ever-disabled beneficiaries and all participants by 5-year cohort and gender

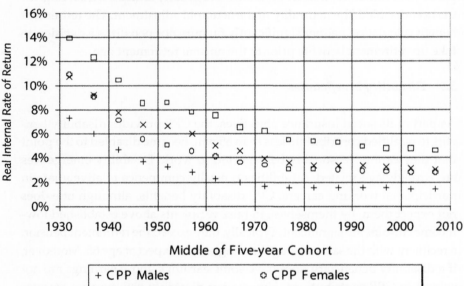

The internal rates of return for both men and women disability beneficiaries are substantially higher, 2% or more, than those for the general CPP population. The differences reflect the social insurance goals of the various CPP disability provisions. Those participants unfortunate enough to become disabled, as defined by the CPP's rather stringent standards, receive disability benefits during what would be their normal working lives. They also receive retirement benefits based on average incomes that exclude their periods of disability. In addition, they do not pay the employee portion of CPP contributions on any earnings received while they are disabled. Together, these provisions ensure that the internal rates of return for those receiving CPP disability benefits are substantially higher than those for the general CPP population. The higher rates occur despite the higher mortality rates among those disabled for CPP purposes.

4   After-tax rates of return

Internal rates of return based on the gross contributions paid and gross benefits received provide a reasonable first pass toward the examination of the CPP and the extent to which it is achieving its objectives. However, one will also want to assess internal rates of return on an after-tax basis rather than just the gross/pre-tax basis used in the first portion of this chapter. Canadian tax and benefit programmes typically take CPP contributions and benefits into account in calculating taxes and benefits payable. Thus, it makes sense to calculate internal rates of return that are based, not on *gross* contributions and benefits, but on the CPP's impacts on participants' *actual after-tax* purchasing power. Thus, for example, one would reduce the cost of CPP contributions to reflect the tax relief available in respect of the contributions. Similarly, one would reduce the value of CPP benefits received, to reflect the additional taxes payable on them, and the reductions in benefits that occur because CPP benefits form part of a benefit programme's income base. Fortunately, using microsimulation, we can ensure that the degree of such "scaling down" reflects individuals' particular circumstances rather than broad overall averages. After-tax internal rates of return then assess the value of the programme from the perspective of the CPP participants themselves, rather than that of the CPP programme. It addresses the balance of the purchasing power lost when participants contribute, versus the purchasing power gained when they receive benefits.

5   Approximating after-tax returns

Currently, DYNACAN does not explicitly model either taxes or income-tested benefits. Consequently, its adjustments for tax relief on contributions, the tax liability on benefit receipt, and the reductions in other benefits due to CPP receipt are only approximations. Morrison (2006) describes the "Gordian Knot" technology used for this approach. In broadest summary, one "borrows" appropriate marginal tax rates from a static microsimulation model. One assigns to DYNACAN individuals the marginal tax rates calculated for similar individuals in the static model, where the detailed tax/benefit calculations are possible. For example, if the similar individuals have a total marginal tax rate of 30% in terms of combined positive income taxes and reductions in income-tested benefits, then the after-tax gain from a CPP benefit would be 70% of the projected before-tax benefit. The index of comparability is, of course, restricted to variables available in both the static and dynamic models. Morrison (2008) provides additional detail on the calculations, material that is far too extensive to include in this chapter.

6   Preliminary after-tax results

328

The approximations inherent in the Gordian Knot technology mean that results derived using them must be regarded as preliminary. The approximations include not only the imperfect assignment of marginal tax rates, and their projection into the future, but also the assignment of tax relief for the portion of CPP contributions paid by employers. Current DYNACAN plans include the development of more sophisticated mechanisms for assigning marginal tax rates to DYNACAN's synthetic individuals. Longer-term plans include an explicit modeling of incomes, taxes, and benefits. Those developments should provide improved measures of CPP participants' changes in purchasing power resulting from CPP contributions and benefits. These improvements will translate into better measures of after-tax impacts and of real after-tax internal rates of return.

However, even with the current, imperfect measures of the purchasing power impacts of CPP contributions, we believe it is feasible to project reasonable preliminary measures for real after-tax rates of return for CPP participation. Figure 8 shows these real after-tax internal rates of return by gender and birth-year cohort. For comparison, we include the corresponding real before-tax internal rates of return seen earlier in Figure 2.

The results are straightforward. For cohorts born after about 1950, after-tax real internal rates of return fall below the corresponding before-tax rates for both men and women. For cohorts born after about 1980 the difference between before-tax and after-tax rates appears to stabilize at slightly over one-half of 1%, again for both men and women. The differences are consistent with changes in the positive tax system that provide less tax relief on CPP contributions than was formerly the case. However, the after-tax internal rates of return remain positive for all cohort and gender combinations. Given an apparent asymptote effect shown in Figure 8, for both men and women, they appear likely to remain that way.

Figure 8: **Real before/after-tax CPP internal rates of return: DYNACAN by birth-year cohort and gender**

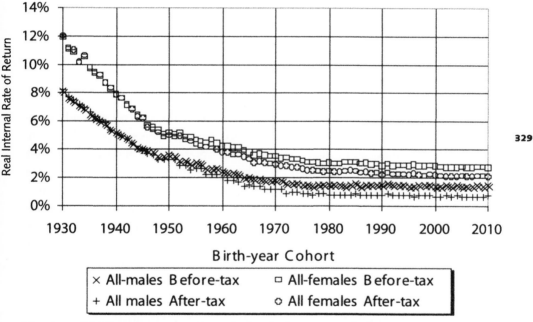

Morrison (2008) reports a number of other before-tax and after-tax internal rate of return results too extensive to include in this chapter. Highlights from those results include:

- **Before-tax sub-population internal rates of return for sub-populations not included in this chapter:** Results for both those (1) benefiting from the CPP's provision for preventing child-rearing from negatively impacting retirement pensions, and (2) affected by the income splitting provisions applicable to separated/divorced persons, show differential returns in the intended directions.
- **Analyses for sub-populations on a real after-tax basis:** For seven different sub-populations, including all of the sub-populations ad-

dressed in this chapter, the after-tax results generally show the desired differences, relative to results for the general population, with respect to policy objectives.

- **Relative levels of before-tax and after-tax real internal rates of return:** For all of the sub-populations, for both men and women, and for all of the cohorts after about 1950, the after-tax rates of return fall below their before-tax counterparts.
- **Sign of real after-tax internal rates of return:** However, for all of those sub-populations, and their complements, by gender, the real internal rates of return remain positive, with apparent asymptotes indicating that they are likely to remain positive for future cohorts.

7   Conclusions

How national retirement pension schemes treat different cohorts and different population sub-groups is a subject of enduring interest to policy-makers. One measure used in such analyses is the "internal rate of return" – the net benefit to individuals of their "pension" investment. Procedurally, the use of longitudinal dynamic microsimulation models to calculate internal rates of return is straightforward. The models' operation permits one to generate a longitudinal micro-level database of all of the participants' contribution and benefit "transactions" with the programme. Post-processing of that database then permits one to assemble the cohort-specific time series of net benefits (benefits less contributions) necessary for the rate of return calculations. Moreover, one can carry out the construction of these series by gender and for sub-populations of interest, and derive the internal rates of return specific to cohorts within those sub-populations.

Substantively, the calculation of internal rates of return can contribute to cross-model validation – e.g. DYNACAN's near-replication of before-tax, cohort-specific rates of return from another model, ACTUCAN, which is methodologically very different. The process of generating the rates of return can also contribute to other types of model validation. Intermediate results compiled in the generation of the return rates reported in this chapter enabled the identification and correction of a few small errors in DYNACAN's demographic modules. However, the substantive contributions of the exercise go further than these. This chapter shows how the development of internal rates of return for sub-populations can help assess the effectiveness of key programme provisions or provide insights into the programme's treatment of those sub-populations. Examples addressed in this chapter included the effectiveness of the disability insurance component of the CPP's social insurance objectives, and the largely neutral treatment of immigrants and early retirees relative to the broader population.

Those results remain, of course, subject to the usual constraints of sample size, and of dependencies on one's assumptions about the future (e.g. future wage and salary growth). However, even so, the approach permits assessments that would not be possible under a purely theoretical assessment of individual programme provisions. The internal rate of return approach automatically provides its results within the context of the broader programme, including the effects of all of the other CPP provisions, and permits the netting out of opposing tendencies – e.g. the programme provisions that advantage lower-earning participants in terms of their pension levels, versus the shorter life expectancies for such participants.

Inevitably, to the extent that they are useful to policy-makers, results such as these open the door to a variety of further analyses, and to a more formalized role in policy evaluation and development. A few examples, some of them already under development, will illustrate these possibilities, with the researcher being able to examine:

- Other sub-populations of policy interest, e.g. "ever a parent", or "ever a single-parent".
- Sub-sub-populations, e.g. low-earnings individuals who retire early.
- How a prospective policy change would affect cohorts' anticipated internal rates of return, thus including rate of return analyses as a standard part of policy development processes.

This chapter's second major contribution is an approximation for real, after-tax internal rates of return of the Canada Pension Plan. Although it is subject to a number of caveats and assumptions, the analysis provides a first look at internal rates of return calculated based on participants' effective gains and losses from participation in the Canada Pension Plan. That is, it attempts to assess participants' effective costs and benefits once one takes into account the reactions of the rest of the tax/transfer system. The resulting real after-tax rates of return are lower than the before-tax rates, but are still positive for all cohorts for both men and women, and for all of the examined sub-populations by gender.

References

Human Resources and Social Development Canada (2003) "Gender Analysis Policy", Human Resources Development Canada, Gender Analysis and Policy Directorate.

Ménard, J.-C. (Chief Actuary) (2007) "Actuarial Report (23rd) on the Canada Pension Plan as at 31 December 2006", Office of the Chief Actuary, Office of the Superintendent of Financial Institutions, Government of Canada, November.

Morrison, Richard J. (2000) 'DYNACAN', pp. 599-603 in: Gupta, A./Kapur, V. (eds.), *Microsimulation in Government Policy and Forecasting.* New York: North-Holland.

Morrison, Richard J. (2004) "DYNACAN Validation Note: CPP Internal Rates of Return", DYNACAN Working Paper, June.

Morrison, Richard J. (2006) "No, It's Knot: A Gordian Knot Approach for Projecting After-Tax Impacts in DYNACAN", DYNACAN Working Paper, September.

Morrison, Richard J. (2007) 'DYNACAN (Longitudinal Dynamic Microsimulation Model)", in: Gupta, A./Harding, A. (eds.), *Modelling Our Future: Population Ageing, Health and Aged Care.* International Symposia in Economic Theory and Econometrics Volume 16. Amsterdam: Elsevier B. V.

Morrison, Richard J. (2008) "Rates of Return for the Canada Pension Plan: Replication of Real Before-tax Rates of Return, and An Approximation for Real After-tax Rates", DYNACAN Working Paper, June.

Chapter 13

Simulating Employment Careers in the LifePaths Model: Validation across Multiple Time Scales

Geoff T. Rowe / Kevin D. Moore

1   Introduction

The LifePaths model is engaged in a project, the goal of which will be to produce credible simulations of public and private components of Canada's retirement income system. The use of LifePaths in this role has particular advantages: it provides a framework on which to integrate otherwise incomplete data; it has the flexibility to assess different income adequacy concepts; it permits projection of distributional outcomes; and it allows for a wide range of projection scenarios to assess sensitivity. LifePaths has previously been used to examine broad historical aspects of the intergenerational exchanges that are implicit in Canada's tax-transfer system (Wolfson et al., 1998; Wolfson and Rowe, 2007).

As indicated in Wolfson and Rowe (2007), Canada's public pension system can be described as having three tiers. The first tier is comprised of two cash transfers to the elderly (generally age 65+) based only on their current income, and financed out of general taxation. One is a taxable "demogrant" called the Old Age Security (OAS) pension. The other basic cash transfer is an income-tested benefit, the Guaranteed Income Supplement (GIS) programme, providing non-taxable monthly benefits to older Canadians. Together, these major programmes provide basic income guarantees for Canada's senior individuals and couples. As a result of a number of *ad hoc* increases over the years, their combined benefit levels have become such that very few of Canada's elderly have incomes below the "low income line".

The next tier is the Canada and Quebec Pension Plans (C/QPP), an earnings-related public pension plan that pays out a retirement pension essentially equal to 25% of average (updated) pre-retirement earnings (earnings capped at roughly the average industrial wage). The C/QPP plans also provide pre-and post-retirement survivor pensions, orphan and disability pensions, and a lump sum death benefit. These plans are financed by a payroll tax.

The third tier of Canada's public pension system is a set of tax incentives for private saving for retirement, either via individual accounts called Registered Retirement Savings Plans (RRSPs) or employer-sponsored plans (Registered Pension Plans or RPPs). The annual tax expenditure (foregone income tax revenue) in respect to these provisions may be considered comparable to the total annual cost of OAS/GIS or C/QPP. Thus, tax incentives are a significant component of the public system, and they are used disproportionately by those with above-average earnings.

The focus of the current project will be detailed simulation of future levels and distributions of retirement income and income replacement rates – together serving as indications of the future adequacy of Canada's retirees' incomes. This is a more complex task than was attempted previously, largely because of:

- the multi-level structure of Canada's retirement income system; and
- the particular challenge of modelling complete employment careers and earnings histories that can serve as a basis for credible simulations of accumulated pension entitlements and savings.

This chapter will provide an overview of the first steps being taken to validate LifePaths simulations of lifetime employment careers. This evaluation has two immediate aims:

1. to help clarify whether there are deficiencies in the simulation of career-long employment and/or earnings patterns; and, if so, to determine how these deficiencies might be remedied; and,
2. to document, as far as possible, the degree of realism that might be expected of simulations of the future by examining simulations of the past.

The chapter will be organized as follows: the second section will describe LifePaths' existing employment transitions module, the third section will evaluate the validity of LifePaths' simulations at annual and sub-annual time-scales and identify special concerns involved in assessing simulations of recurrent events (job starts and job separations) in the long-run (i.e. careers), the fourth section will present available results evaluating the accuracy of simulations at the time-scale of multiple decades, and the conclusion follows.

2 Employment transitions in LifePaths

2.1 *Modelled transitions*

LifePaths uses a three-category classification of employment status – employee (E), self-employed (SE), and not employed (NE). The model focuses on simulation of periods with or without earnings and, as such, we have not incorporated transitions involving unemployment. There are six transitions that can result in a change in employment status – as represented in Figure 1. LifePaths models all of these transitions. In addition, job changes that do not appear to involve an interruption of employment are also modelled by LifePaths (denoted here as E →E).[1]

Figure 1: Employment transitions in LifePaths

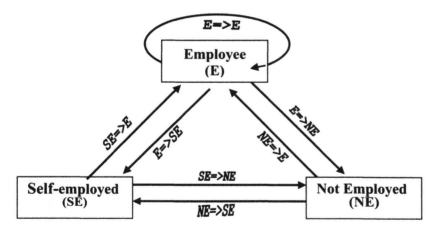

LifePaths relies heavily on data from the Labour Force Survey (LFS), a monthly, cross-sectional, representative sample survey of national and provincial labour market activity, in order to model these transitions in employment status.

---

1   The analysis of transitions has focused on changes involving the "main job". In principle, some E →E transitions could involve loss of a main job and retention of a pre-existing secondary job.

2.2 *The lifetime employment decision*

Since LifePaths simulates the lives of Canadians from birth to death, there will be an initial step at which it is determined whether or not the employment transition model will play any role in the simulation of a given life (Figure 2).

Thus, the first employment decision made in LifePaths is the decision to "ever work in a lifetime". This decision is critical to accurate simulation of women's historical employment patterns[2] and, in the present, it remains important for women at the lowest levels of educational attainment. Figure 3 displays observed and simulated proportions of women who chose never to work; for these purposes, women were grouped into education attainment categories and into single years of birth ranging from 1880 to 1960. Evidently, the proportion of women who will never be at risk of an employment transition is negligible in more recently born cohorts, except at the lowest levels of education. Corresponding proportions for men are lower than for women, but are still above 0.05 (5%) for recently born cohorts at the lowest levels of education.

336

Figure 2:   Sub-models of the LifePaths employment module

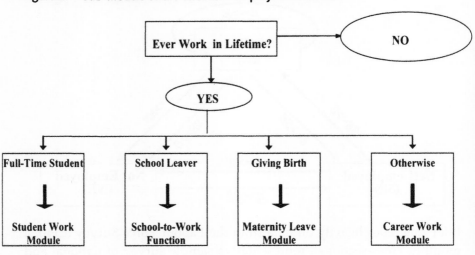

Figure 3: **Proportions of women who never worked for pay, by year of birth and by education (Primary Only, University [BA+], & Other), Labour Force Survey (LFS) data and LifePaths simulations**

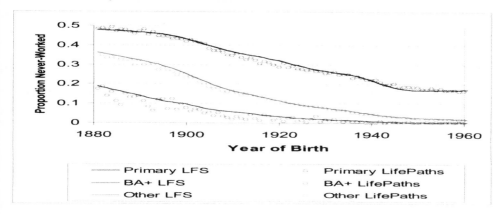

Patterns of employment activity differ systematically among demographic groups (women versus men, for example). And for a given person, employment behaviour changes when he or she enters a new phase of the life cycle; for example, the level and pattern of market work engaged in after leaving school will obviously be different from student work. Accordingly, different behavioural equations are employed for different demographic groups and/or different phases of life and LifePaths reflects these differences in separate employment transitions sub-models, as indicated in Figure 2. The remainder of this chapter will concentrate on LifePaths' "Career Work" model, since it forms the principal basis for simulation of career earnings streams and so, ultimately, of retirement income.

2.3 LifePaths' "Career Work" Model

An employment career might be said to consist of alternating spells of employment and non-employment that could begin just after the completion of education and likely terminates either with a decision to withdraw from the labour market or with death. In LifePaths, we have estimated a proportional hazards model to summarize the rates of occurrence of each type of transition – conditional on covariates. Details on all of the sub-models included in the LifePaths Employment Module may be found in Nguyen (2007).

As presented in Figure 2 above, the career employment equations determine the labour force transitions of a person during any period in which the person is 15 years old or older, not a full-time student, not a school leaver waiting for a first job, not on maternity leave, and not a permanent resident of a healthcare institution (only applicable to the elderly).

2.3.1 The hazard equations determining career employment

The career employment hazard equations determine the seven labour force transitions illustrated in Figure 1. These transitions were assumed to have cumulative conditional hazard functions [$H_t(X_t)$] of exponential form:

$$E(\ d\ |\ X,\ t\ ) = H_{t+1}(X_t) - H_t(X_t), \quad \text{where}$$
$$H_t(X_t) = \exp(b_1{}^*\ln(t) + b_2{}^*\ln(t)\ {}^*(t<12) + X_t\,B) \tag{1}$$

and where "d" is a binary variable which takes the value 1.0 if a main job was reported gained (transitions NE →E, NE →SE, SE →E, E →SE, and E →E) or reported lost (transitions E →NE, and E →NE) in the month since the previous interview, and which takes the value 0.0 otherwise (where t is the duration of working / not working measured in months, X is a vector of explanatory variables, b_1, b_2, and vector B are coefficients to be estimated).[3]

338

---

3   A technical note:

LifePaths is a continuous time implementation of the "latent waiting times" formulation of the classical competing risks model (Prentice et al., 1978): that is, random waiting times to all specified events (job separation, marriage, child birth, death, etc.) are generated and placed in an event queue; then, the event in the queue with the minimum waiting time becomes the next event to occur. At that point, the calendar is incremented by the amount specified, the event queue is refreshed and the simulation continues.

In order to use hazard equation estimates in LifePaths, a random waiting time for labour force transition events in LifePaths is generated as follows (given the simulation up to time T):

$h = dH/dT = \exp(b_1{}^*\ln(T) + b_2{}^*\ln(T)\ {}^*(T<12) + XB)\ {}^* d(b_1{}^*\ln(T) + b_2{}^*\ln(T)\ {}^*(T<12))/dT$
$= \exp(b_1{}^*\ln(T) + b_2{}^*\ln(T)\ {}^*(T<12) + XB)\ {}^* (b1 + b2{}^*(T<12)) / T$

Then, within each month – treating the hazard h as approximately constant – we make use of the constant-hazard survival function $S(t) = \exp(-h{}^*t)$ to obtain a random waiting time w: derived from h and with a uniform pseudo-random number U in place of S(t) (i.e., by solving $U = \exp(-h{}^*w)$ for w). Modgen is the extension of C++ in which LifePaths is written. Among other simulation tasks, Modgen ensures that a fresh random waiting time will be generated whenever an explanatory factor changes. In the case of employment transitions, a model that ensures a new random waiting time will be generated (at least) each month of the simulated lifetime (since duration in the employment state – measured in months – is one of the explanatory factors). Consequently, an employment transition cannot be simulated until a random waiting time of less than one month is generated.

Equation (1) was estimated for each of the seven labour force transitions displayed in Figure 1 and for males and females separately; thus there were a total of 14 equations. To estimate these equations, we used a longitudinal version of the LFS data covering the period from January 1976 to December 2004 in monthly steps. The LFS is a panel survey in which respondent households typically remain in the sample for six consecutive months. Thus, it is possible to reconstruct six-month fragments of longitudinal data from the monthly records of household members and estimate a range of interesting transitions models. These data are the best available single source for estimation purposes because of the rich survey content, large sample size (more than 37 million person-months of individual and family level data from about 6.5 million respondents), and a long historical coverage (nearly three decades). Further details on the construction, features, and validation of the longitudinal LFS file may be found in Rowe and Nguyen (2005).

The components of the vector of explanatory variables (X) are summarized in Table 2. The rationale for the inclusion of these variables is generally clear. Theoretically, there are other factors/variables that may also be important determinants of the labour force transitions. However the decision to include certain variables in the equations and not other variables depends not only on the hypothetical relationships and availability of the empirical data, but also on the existing makeup of LifePaths.

3 Validating simulated careers

3.1 *Validation at annual and sub-annual time scales: selected results*

As one of several validation measures of the model performance, we compared employment/population ratios (EPRs) for males and females by single year of age that were estimated from LFS data or, correspondingly, simulated in LifePaths.

Figure 4 shows the age profiles of these ratios for women in years 1976 and 2004, which are the first and the last year covered by the LFS data used for our estimation of the parameters. As seen from this figure, the age profile of women's employment changed substantially between 1976 and 2004. LifePaths captures the changes well, and the gaps between the simulated and the actual employment rates are small. (Corresponding comparisons for men and for each year between 1976 and 2004 showed that the simulated and actual EPRs were similarly close in each case.) It is worthy of note that this represents a relatively challenging test of the model; LifePaths simulates transitions between employment states in continuous time, but this validation test compares annual average stocks expressed as person-years employed per person-year lived at each age.

Table 1: Summary of variables included in seven career work hazard equations: 265 parameters were estimated for each of the 14 equations (7 transitions and 2 sexes)

Transition	Dependent Variable	Summary of Explanatory Variables
E →NE	$d_{E \to NE}$	1. Duration since entering the current status (months)
		2. Calendar years (binary variables)
E →E	$d_{E \to E}$	3. Age, in quadratic form with a spline at age 35 if age<65, linear if age> 66, and a separate binary for age 65
E →SE	$d_{E \to SE}$	4. Province of residence
		5. Spouse's labour force status
NE →E	$d_{NE \to E}$	6. Education level
		7. Presence of children (separate binary variables for children of age groups 0, 1-5, 6-15, and 16+)
NE →SE	$d_{NE \to SE}$	8. Year * Age Interactions (2) * (3)
		9. Year * Education Interactions (2) * (6)
SE →E	$d_{SE \to E}$	10. Year * Child Interactions (2) * (3)
		11. Year * Education * Child Age Interactions (2)*(6)*(7)
SE →NE	$d_{SE \to NE}$	12. Calendar month binary variables (seasonal impacts)

Figure 4: Average annual employment/population ratios for women by age in 1976 and 2004. LFS data and LifePaths simulations

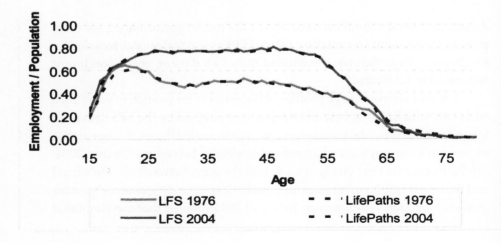

Figure 5 exhibits sub-annual aspects of employment in terms of weeks worked in the calendar year 2000 as reported in the 2001 Census and as simulated in LifePaths. These charts compare cumulative percentages of the male population reporting 0 weeks worked, at most 8 weeks worked, and so on, up to at most 48 weeks worked. Cumulative percentages facilitate visual comparison of observed and simulated patterns because each corresponding line on the respective charts is positioned entirely above the previous corresponding line.

Figure 5: Cumulative population percentage for selected weeks worked in year 2000. Males by age in 2001 with 0, 8, 16, 32, 40 & 48 weeks worked. 2001 Census data and LifePaths simulations

2001 Census Data: Males

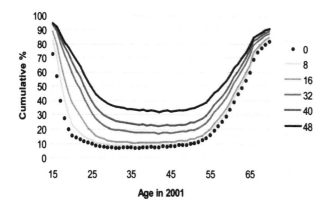

LifePaths Year 2000: Males

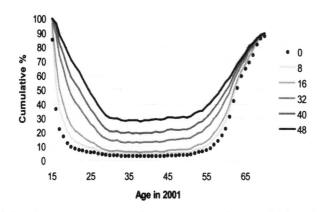

A limitation of the LFS data is that respondents remain in the survey for only six consecutive months. As such, it is impossible to unambiguously identify employment states or events that are part of an annual work pattern. The value of comparing census data with LifePaths simulations rests in the fact that we can hope to identify discrepancies apparent after aggregation over all seasons of the year. The greatest discrepancy between observed and simulated profiles appears to be the difference in the percentage at 0 weeks worked. It is tempting to associate this entirely with biases in the LifePaths model; the census data are comprised of annual recalls and reports of 0 or only a few weeks worked may be subject to considerable recall lapse. Evidently, agreement between the census data and LifePaths is relatively close enough and neither the census observations nor their synthetic counterparts can be assumed to be error-free.

3.2 Validation of careers: conceptual issues

The data on which the LifePaths employment transitions models were based are unusually rich, covers an unusually long historical period, and represents an unusually large sample; but, it does not identify characteristics of a career. As illustrated in Figure 6, respondents enter the LFS sample at random stages of their careers; at that point, we know their tenure in their current employment state and typically are able to track employment events over the following five months. But with available LFS data, we cannot distinguish, for example, between respondents who have previously had many different employers from those who have had few.

Figure 6:   **The LFS data cannot identify the stage of a career (e.g. cumulative employment spells)**

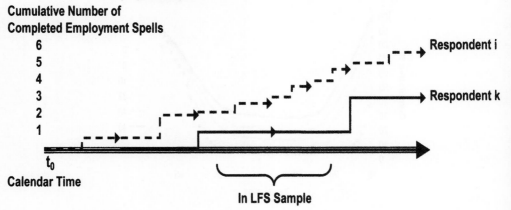

Until recently, we have not been in a position to even evaluate the magnitude of the problems arising because we had "employment spell" and not "career" data. This situation changed recently, when we began working with Statistics Canada's Longitudinal Worker File (LWF). The LWF is a 10% random sample of all Canadian workers, constructed by integrating data from four sources: the Record of Employment (ROE) files of Human Resources Development Canada (on worker separations), the T1 and T4 tax data files of Canada Customs and Revenue Agency, and the Longitudinal Employment Analysis Program of Business and Labour Market Analysis Division of Statistics Canada. The LWF provides longitudinal data on workers annual earnings, employment interruptions or separations, and on changes of employers over the period 1982 to 2004. However, as is frequently the case with administrative data, we are limited to stratifying the data mainly on basic demographic dimensions (e.g. age and sex), because critical dimensions like educational attainment are unavailable.

Another aspect of the problem is conceptual. Even given ideal career data, we would still not have a clear idea of how to best assess and correct for potential inadequacies in the LifePaths employment model. In effect, we do not have a definition of a "career" or a list of its essential properties. One consideration is that careers may differ from each other, because of underlying differences between individuals that remain relatively constant. In LifePaths' present form, successive simulated spells of employment will be correlated only to the extent induced by persistent states like education level or family composition; otherwise, simulated spells are conditionally independent.

From that perspective, an essential property of a career would involve long-run dependencies arising from so-called "shared frailties". These would be individual level random terms that could account for differences between individuals, but that induce inter-spell correlations because they are constant within individuals and can influence the chances of successive events. A model with this structure effectively partitions heterogeneity into that between individuals and that within spells (Clayton and Cuzick, 1985; Aalen and Husebye, 1991).

Shared frailties, as implemented in the LifePaths employment module, are in a form that has a special affinity with Weibull hazard models (Rowe and Lin, 1999). (Weibull models are characterized as having cumulative hazards that are a log-linear function of duration, as may be seen in equation [1]; LifePaths employment transition hazards are log-linear with a varying slope and may be termed piecewise Weibull.) Hougaard (1986a, 1986b, 1987) generalizes the Weibull to account for correlated spells using an unobserved random variable $\mathbf{Z}$ – a shared frailty. $\mathbf{Z}$ is intended to represent unmeasured personal and/or labour market characteristics that remain fixed over time. Hougaard exploits unique advantages of specifying $\mathbf{Z}$ as drawn from a Positive Stable distribution with parameter θ. If an individual's spell durations given $\mathbf{Z}$ are Weibull with scale parameter α and shape parameter β, then marginal spell durations are also Weibull:

$$E_Z(e^{-H(t)Z}) = e^{-H(t)^\theta} = e^{-\left(\frac{t}{\chi}\right)^{\theta\beta'}} \tag{2}$$

where the marginal shape parameter is β' and $\beta = \theta\,\beta'$.[4] Thus, Weibull models that have already been estimated can be transformed to a shared frailty model for specified values of θ. Hougaard demonstrates that θ can be estimated by $\sqrt{(1-r)}$, where $\mathbf{r}$ is the product moment correlation between log spell durations.[5] Thus far, use of shared frailties in LifePaths' applications has been limited to sensitivity studies, given the lack of data with which to measure inter-spell correlation.

A sceptic's characterization of the "Positive Stable-Weibull" shared frailty model might be that it was simply a technical fix. More generously, it might be observed that it merely corrects for a lack of correlation between the lengths of successive simulated employment spells in LifePaths. By construction, the characteristics of the marginal Weibull model should largely be preserved, so that the EPRs and other measures of population employment are minimally affected by changing the value of θ. Thus, in the absence of data on inter-spell correlation, we can not say whether this shared frailty model is actually solving an existing problem.

Another approach in the evaluation of the existing LifePaths model is to consider that a career should exhibit some form of adaptive behaviour. To some extent, the age terms in LifePaths will already reflect some degree of adaptation by displaying stereotypical career stages: entry, advancement, plateau, and withdrawal. With this in mind, we might hope to further identify specific omitted variable biases in the LifePaths "Career Work" equations that could be linked forms of adaptation. However, given the nature of the data available, examination of potential biases involving earnings levels may be the single most interesting avenue open to us.

---

4   The shared frailty model has the effect of shrinking all other hazard coefficients toward zero (Fine et al., 2003).

5   The relation between θ and r implies that only positive correlations can be accounted for in this model (i.e. $0 < \theta < 1$).

4   Validation at a multi-decade time scale: selected results

Our evaluation of careers simulated by LifePaths through the lens of LWF data is not yet complete. We have yet to understand all aspects of the LWF data as they might influence our interpretation of discrepancies between the LWF and LifePaths simulations. For instance, we have not been able to fully evaluate the comprehensiveness of the LWF's data coverage. In terms of longitudinal coverage issues, there are initial indications that a non-trivial number of the individual employment and earnings histories contained in the LWF are incomplete or fragmentary. This reflects a number of technical limitations associated with the LWF's construction, such as difficulties associated with reliably tracking and matching each individual's annual employment and earnings data every year for several decades through the use of personal identification numbers that were not designed or administered for this purpose, and consequently exhibit some instability over time. Unfortunately, in the LWF, it is generally not possible to authoritatively distinguish between lapses in longitudinal coverage and the real absence of employment and earnings.

There are other coverage issues. For example, employers are generally required to issue an ROE whenever an employee stops work either on a permanent or temporary basis: an ROE is required to establish eligibility for Employment Insurance (EI) benefits. However, for casual or part-time employees (who may not qualify EI benefits), ROEs are required only if they experience an earnings interruption of 30 days or more. Since, in theory, the LFS data will capture some of these interruptions, and we might expect to simulate more job losses than are reflected in the ROE data. In addition, prior to 1997, employers were not required to issue an ROE for employees working less than 15 hours per week. Additional work is required to reconcile what is known about the LFS concepts with verifiable aspects of the administrative data.

Figure 7 presents some encouraging initial findings. Recall that evaluating the validity of LifePaths' simulations of employment careers is an intermediate step towards evaluating the validity of LifePaths simulations of retirement income: the next step will be to consider the earnings streams that serve as the basis for retirement savings. Figure 7 provides an indication of the "bottom line"; these charts display the distribution of the sum of the stream of wages from 1983 to 2004 for men and women aged 30 in 1983 (i.e. 51 or still pre-retirement, in 2004). Given the age range involved, this represents the stream of earnings that is likely to be the major source of retirement savings. As may be seen, agreement between observed and simulated decile cut points is generally very good (in this case, since the observations are based on income tax data, no misalignment of concepts should be present). There are differences in the lowest two deciles that are substantial in percentage terms, but less so in absolute terms. However, among the decile groups at the median and above, discrepancies are in the order of 5% for men and for women. We cannot, as yet, make a judgement about how much of these errors may be attributed to errors arising in the course of simulation of the career rather than errors in the imputation of career wages given career employment. It seems likely that a significant portion of the discrepancies shown, particularly at lower levels of wages, reflect the lapses in longitudinal LWF coverage that we have identified and continue to evaluate.

Figure 7: **Deciles of total wages accumulated over the years 1983 to 2004 (constant 2004 \$). T4 (tax) data and LifePaths simulations for men and women aged 30 in 1983**

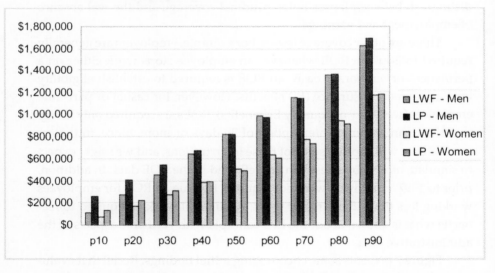

Another finding of this validation exercise is that LifePaths is currently generating far too many job separations. There are large discrepancies between the number of job separations simulated by LifePaths and those contained in the LWF. Further comparisons with the Labour Force Survey, the data source used to estimate the behavioural equations used by LifePaths, confirmed this, and suggest that this discrepancy is not a function of differences in concepts or population coverage.

This problem appears to be related to the application of the labour market transition equations to time scales not observed in the source data used to estimate them. As LifePaths is currently generating correct annualized employment to population rates by year, age and gender, it follows that the correct amount of time is being spent in employment in a given year, as demonstrated in Figures 4 and 5. The extra transitions away from employment, therefore, do not appear to be reducing the amount of time individuals are employed. This suggests that LifePaths is currently generating many spurious, "instantaneous" transitions from an employed state to a not-employed state, and then back to an employed state (E → NE →E). Further investigation confirmed that many such transitions appear to be generated. As these short spells have little impact on aggregate employment rates or wages, they were not noticed during the detailed validation of the LifePaths career work module done previously. While this is clearly a weakness of the model that will need to be addressed, it is largely inconsequential in terms of its impact on career employment and wages, and should therefore not be an impediment to the credible simulation and evaluation of issues relating to the Canadian retirement income system.

The possibility of correcting for "instantaneous" transitions has been explored from two distinct points-of-view: i) possibilities of over-/under-counting of events and ii) bias in the estimation of employment transition equations (particularly for hazards at durations of less than one month). The former might arise from the LFS data collection design. If E →NE transitions tended to take place toward the end of the month, then E →E transitions might be more likely to appear to be simple E →NE transitions, because the LFS interviews take place mid-month. As such, E →NE transitions should be over-counted and E →E transitions under-counted, which suggests that correction for the over-/under-count problem would only result in more "instantaneous" transitions. That in turn points to bias in employment transition hazards at durations of less than one month as the ultimate source of our problems. One remedy for this bias would be addition of an indicator variable representing durations of less than one month as a correction to the piecewise Weibull specification in Equation 1.[6] Yet another source for these biases relates to the neglect of the distinction between Permanent Layoff and Temporary Layoff in LifePaths. These represent different types of E →NE that can be expected to have different short-term dynamics (e.g. hazards

---

6   This correction amounts to a simple variation on the well-known "Zero-Inflated Count" models.

of less than one month). However, distinguishing between these two types of lay-off would require restructuring the Career Work module to account for an additional three types of employment transition. As this represents a relatively major change to LifePaths, these corrections will not be considered until the next time that employment transition equations are updated.

5   Conclusions

Developing modules for a microsimulation model requires an approach that differs from that best adopted when the main goal of analysis is to test specific hypotheses. A hazard model that is to be incorporated in a microsimulation model will perform poorly, if its right-hand-side variables cannot be accurately simulated. Yet, in some cases, elements of the simulation model must be incorporated for logical completeness, irregardless of whether there are data to shed light on the underlying behaviour (e.g. the LifePaths 'lifetime employment decision' may be one example). Thus, there are constraints on the design of microsimulation models that do not apply in the case of analysis, in isolation, of data collected from a single survey. The data required for estimation and validation of a given theoretical model may typically be available only on a piecemeal basis from a variety of sources. In many ways, the microsimulation model inevitably becomes a vehicle for data integration.

These issues are illustrated well in our attempts to validate LifePaths simulations of employment careers on sub-annual, annual, and multi-decade time intervals. This task is likely to always remain a work in progress. We continue to work to reconcile data concepts and to evaluate, try to resolve, or account for issues of data quality. In particular, we are looking to other sources of data to possibly allow us to better evaluate the apparent longitudinal coverage weaknesses of the LWF. Our experience with the LWF to date may be seen as a case-study of the tremendous technical difficulties associated with performing career-level validation, and of the limitations of administrative data.

Furthermore, additional work remains that will involve elaborating the properties of a "career" in ways that we can both observe in data and use for validation or enhancement of LifePaths. But, the investment of effort in validation can pay off with valuable suggestions for model improvements, as has been the case in the present exercise.

348

Nevertheless, despite flaws that have been identified in the model, preliminary results still suggest that LifePaths can provide highly credible simulations of career wages. There are clearly weaknesses in LifePaths' simulations of job separations that will eventually need to be addressed, but these are largely immaterial to the simulation of long-run career wages and time worked. Given this, we can be reasonably confident that LifePaths can credibly be used to simulate and evaluate issues relating to the Canadian retirement income system.

LifePaths' success is probably due more to the efforts that went into assembling pertinent data, than to the sophistication of its analytical techniques. In that sense, LifePaths' current success may be a testimony to the value of data integration.

References

Aalen, O.O./Husebye, E. (1991) 'Statistical analysis of repeated events forming renewal processes', *Stat. Med.* 10: 1227-1240.

Clayton, D./Cuzick, J. (1985) 'Multivariate Generalizations of the Proportional Hazards Model', *J.R.Statist.Soc.A* 148(2): 82-117.

Fine, J. P./Glidden, D. V./Lee, K. E., (2003) 'A simple estimator for a shared frailty regression model', *J.R.Statist.Soc.B* 65 (1): 317-329.

Hougaard, P. (1986a) 'Survival models for heterogeneous populations derived from stable distributions', *Biometrika* 73 (2): 387-396.

Hougaard, P. (1986b) 'A class of multivariate failure time distributions', *Biometrika* 73 (3): 671-678.

Hougaard, P. (1987) 'Modelling Multivariate Survival', *Scand J Statist.* 14: 291-304.

Nguyen, H. (2007) "Modeling Employment Status in LifePaths". Socio-Economic Modeling and Analysis Division Working Paper, Statistics Canada.

Prentice, R.L./Kalbfleisch, J.D./Peterson Jr., A.V./Flournoy, N./Farewell, V.T./Breslow, N.E. (1978) 'The Analysis of Failure Times in the Presence of Competing Risks', *Biometrics* 34: 541-554.

Rowe, G./Lin, X. (1999) "Modeling Labour Force Careers for the LifePaths Simulation Model". International Symposium on Combining Data from Different Sources, Statistics Canada, Ottawa.

Rowe, G./Nguyen, H. (2005) 'Longitudinal Analysis of Labour Force Survey Data', *Survey Methodology* Vol. 30: 105-114.

Statistics Canada – LifePaths: www.statcan.ca/english/spsd/LifePaths.htm.

Statistics Canada - Longitudinal Worker File [Business and Labour Market Analysis Division]: Catalogue no.: 75C0013.

Wolfson, M./Rowe, G./Gribble, S./Lin, X. (1998) 'Historical Generational Accounting with Heterogeneous Populations', in: Corak, M. (ed.), *Government Finances and Generational Equity*, Statistics Canada Cat. No. 68-513-XPB, Ottawa.

Wolfson, M./Rowe, G. (2007) 'Aging and Inter-Generational Fairness: A Canadian Analysis', in: Lambert, P. J. (ed.), *Research on Economic Inequality, Volume 15 – Equity*. Amsterdam: Elsevier.

Chapter 14

Employment Transitions and Earnings Dynamics in the SAGE Model

Asghar Zaidi / Maria Evandrou / Jane Falkingham /
Paul Johnson / Anne Scott

1 Introduction

The SAGE dynamic microsimulation model is an analytical tool with which to make projections and inform the development of social policy in Britain for the twenty-first century. As in other such models, the principal purpose is to study the implications of population ageing for pensions and issues regarding health and long-term care needs.[1] The model starts with a base population of individuals from a sample of the 1991 Census of Great Britain, and proceeds by updating each individual's status for every year in accordance with various life course transitions. The model specifies various demographic processes, education, employment, earnings, pension accumulation, health and disability and support networks.[2] This chapter describes the work undertaken in constructing the labour market module and highlights generic lessons that can be drawn from this work.[3]

---

1 Evandrou et al. (2001) provide the objectives and the work programme pursued in the ESRC-SAGE ("Simulating Social Policy for an Ageing Society") Research Group.

2 See O'Donoghue (2001) and Zaidi and Rake (2001) for a review of major dynamic microsimulation models; the latter also discusses pros and cons of alternative empirical choices to be made in building a dynamic microsimulation model. Harding (2007) provides a discussion on challenges and opportunities of dynamic microsimulation models.

3 The chapter draws upon a number of technical papers prepared while documenting the work undertaken by the SAGE team. In particular, the work reported here makes use of the information available in Zaidi (2004a, 2004b), Zaidi and Scott (2001), Scott and Zaidi (2004), and Scott (2004). Authors are grateful for the comments received from Paul Williamson and Marcia Keegan (NATSEM) on an earlier version of the chapter.

In modelling retirement incomes, it is necessary to generate for each individual a lifetime trajectory of labour market experience that is subsequently used to compute his/her accumulation of pension entitlements. The labour market module therefore simulates, for each year and for each individual, whether or not the individual will work, and how many weeks or months the individual will work in a single year. Subsequently, the module computes earnings generated from that work. The module also provides information about whether absences from the labour market are due to unemployment, inactivity due to studentship or inactivity of other kinds (principally, caring for children, caring for sick and disabled). Such distinctions between different forms of non-employment are critical inputs for the pension module: they determine whether and how individuals receive credits towards their pension entitlements.

Various factors are important in determining a credible simulation of a life course trajectory of employment and earnings. The requirements can be threefold:

1. Estimation of credible predictors of employment transitions and earnings dynamics from the existing datasets, including a plausible account of inter-cohort and intra-cohort differentials in lifetime labour force experiences;
2. Implementation of estimated employment and earnings equations on the base data, for simulation purposes, including undertaking all the imputations necessary in the base dataset to enable this implementation; and
3. The validation for logic and consistency of simulated results, and – if necessary – calibrations, so as to be able to reliably predict the impact of various policy scenarios for the future.

In line with these requirements, the main body of the chapter is organized into three sections. Section 2 describes the modelling of the labour force dynamics, covering both employment transitions and earnings dynamics. In Section 3, the implementation of the labour force event is discussed. Section 4 illustrates the methods adopted in testing the implementation of the labour force event – logic testing as well as statistical evaluation. Section 5 provides the conclusions.

2 Modelling labour force dynamics

In the SAGE model, individuals were subjected to employment dynamics from the year after they leave education, at an age between 16 and 22, until the year they retire, at 65.[4] The employment transitions took place on a quarterly basis, as this modelling choice facilitated accounting for sub-annual changes in employment. However, for computational efficiency, the employment transitions were all computed in a single event in the last quarter of the model year, after the annual demographic transitions had taken place.[5]

The labour force dynamics cover three aspects: in employment *status*; in the *level* (full-time/part-time), *type* (employee/self-employed), and *location* (sector, industry and occupation) of employment; and in earnings. Figures 1 and 2 display different processes and outcomes that are involved in these dynamics. They seek to illustrate all possible labour force transitions, and thus provide a framework within which to evaluate processes modelled in the SAGE model.

Figure 1 exhibits the employment status dynamics, starting with an entry into the labour market status and ending in retirement. Notably, it shows that the entry into the labour market may start with experiences of employment (full-time or part-time), unemployment or inactivity. The phenomenon of unemployment or inactivity right at the start of one's career is more frequently observed in recent times in Great Britain, and also serves as a strong predictor of labour market experience during the rest of the working life. From there onwards, individuals make transitions across other employment states or they maintain the same status as before. All transitions possible between the four alternative states of employment are shown at the bottom of Figure 1.

4　One of the guidelines adopted by the SAGE team is that no unnecessary effort will be expended on an accurate representation of characteristics that will have little or no effect on the simulated outcomes of interest. For this reason, we decided on a simple initial model in which education and working life are assumed discrete phases of the life course (and there is no return to education after entering the labour market). An implicit assumption is that the part-time work among full-time students does not count towards pension accumulation and such work has no impact on future employment experiences. Such generalizations helped us to simplify the work of implementation and also keep the model "smaller", easier to understand and faster to execute.

5　The impact of demographic changes on labour market transitions is relatively gradual (apart from the birth of a child), and it was considered unnecessary to tie employment transition probabilities to the demographic state at precisely the same time.

Figure 1:   Dynamics in the employment status

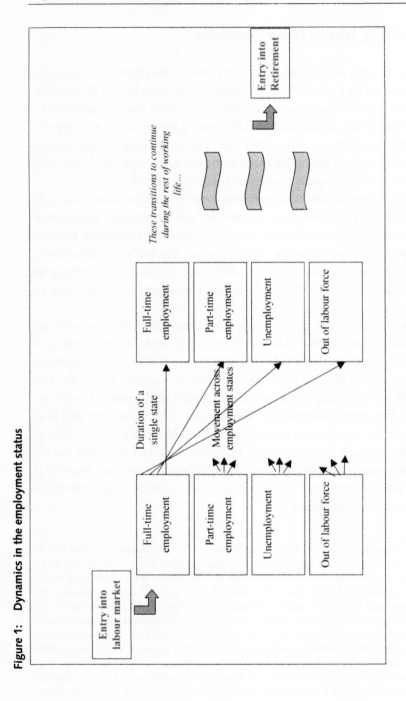

Notes: FT stands for full-time employment, PT for part-time employment, U for unemployment and N for inactivity status.

Figure 2:   Dynamics in the type and the location of employment

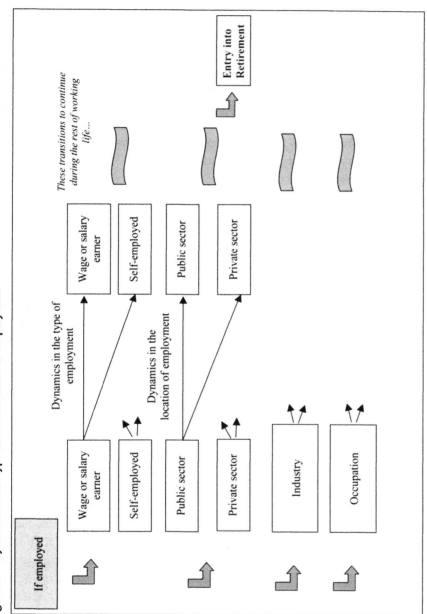

All employed persons were further categorized into subgroups on the basis of their level of employment (full-time or part-time), type of employment (employee or self-employed), sector of employment (private or public sector), industry (e.g. agriculture, manufacturing, or services) and occupation (e.g. manual or non-manual). The necessity and the significance of these attributes were determined by the differences in the empirical patterns of employment and earnings and differences in pension schemes across these categories. The arrows in Figure 2 point to the possible transitions that one can observe in the type and location attributes. The type and location attributes were taken as time-invariant attributes in the SAGE model.[6] All such attributes were determined at the time of completion of education (at age 22), and they include education level attained, industry, occupation and sector.

2.1 Predictors of employment dynamics

In order to distinguish between differential experiences of employment, we need to identify strong predictors for duration of and changes in employment, unemployment and inactivity. Since some predictors, such as gender, interact with many other predictors, it is crucial to identify the groups for which separate estimation should be carried out. For our purposes, the potential list of predictors and estimation groups had been constrained by the availability of variables in the base dataset.[7] However, we also imputed certain variables in the base data, using correlates between available and non-available variables in related sample surveys, which facilitated using a larger set of predictors for the simulation of employment dynamics.[8]

To estimate the pattern of transition between different employment states over time, two datasets that provide longitudinal information for the British population were available: the Quarterly Labour Force Survey (QLFS), and the British Household Panel Survey (BHPS). The QLFS had a much larger sample size, so we used this database to estimate employment dynamics. However, the panel element in the QLFS is restricted to five quarterly observations, and the earnings data are much less comprehensive

---

6   See Scott and Zaidi (2004) for reasons underlying this empirical choice as well as its implications.

7   See Zaidi and Scott (2001) for further discussion on issues relevant to the choice of the base dataset.

8   More details of imputation of missing variables are given in Scott and Zaidi (2004).

than in the BHPS. Therefore, we used the QLFS to derive parameters for employment transitions, whilst the BHPS was used for estimating earnings equations.

We used 27 waves of the QLFS, beginning with the December 1992 – February 1994 wave, and ending with the June 1999 – August 2000 wave. Each wave contains approximately 12,000 individuals who were followed over five quarters, providing four cases of transition/non-transition between employment states. In total, this dataset provided observations on over 1.2 million employment transitions. We grouped the data by year, where the years correspond to the quarter in which the respondent was first surveyed.[9] Our subsequent modelling work is based on the transitions that people observed between the 4th and 5th quarter, allowing us to take as much account of previous work history as possible by drawing upon the information on employment experience over the previous three quarters captured in the QLFS.

As a starting point, we initially considered three basic employment states – employed (E), unemployed (U) and inactive (N). Transitions between these states were to be modelled with a series of nested dichotomous choices, thus: E $\Rightarrow$ E or E $\Rightarrow$ non-E, and if non-E, then U or N (and likewise for transitions originating in U or N). However, our exploration of the QLFS data revealed that there was an additional transition of considerable importance for the British population – between full-time and part-time work. We therefore further subdivided those in employment into part-time and full-time employment. This was based on the variable FTPTWK: whether full- or part-time in the main job.[10] We therefore ended up working with four possible employment states – full-time work (FT), part-time work (PT), U and N. Instead of modelling this as a series of nested dichotomous choices, we chose to model it as a simultaneous polychotomous choice, using multinomial logit.

Models were estimated separately for four population groups:

---

9   Details of the data files used to construct the estimation database are provided in Zaidi (2004).

10   The variable FTPTWK was verified against reported total number of hours worked. In short, all those who work full-time have on average 40.5 hours of work per week, and all those who work part-time have on average 16 hours per week. Obviously, these averages hide some extreme values of working hours for both full-time and part-time workers.

1.   Males with non-advanced qualifications,[11]
2.   Males with advanced qualifications,
3.   Females with non-advanced qualifications, and
4.   Females with advanced qualifications.

The labour force state can take one of four values in a single quarter: 1. FT, 2. PT, 3. E, 4. N. Transitions between these states were determined by multinomial logistic regression models with four possible outcomes. Outcome 1, FT, was taken as the reference level, and in each model there were three equations giving the relative risk of outcomes 2, 3 and 4, in relation to outcome 1:

$$R_i = \exp\left(\beta_{i0} + \beta_{i1}X_1 + \beta_{i2}X_2 + \ldots + \beta_{ik}X_k\right) \quad (i = 2,3,4)$$

where X_j represent the values of predictor variables relating to characteristics of the individual and β_{ij} are coefficients provided in a parameter table. The relative risks R_2, R_3, R_4 were computed, depending on the individual's characteristics, and the relative probability thresholds were cumulated as:[12]

$$P_1 = 1; \quad P_2 = 1 + R_2; \quad P_3 = 1 + R_2 + R_3; \quad P_4 = 1 + R_2 + R_3 + R_4$$

A pseudo-random number r was generated in the range $(0, P_4)$ and compared in turn with $P_1, P_2,$ and P_3. The outcome was the first level i for which $r < P_i$.

Since the models were estimated for the four origin states for each of four population groups, defined by sex (2 levels) and possession of advanced qualifications (2 levels), there were 16 models and 48 equations. The explanatory terms in the regression equations were:

(Constant term)
Qualification (2 levels within advanced/non-advanced group)
Age (whole years)
Age squared

---

11   Education status was defined in a four-category variable: 1) "No qualifications", 2) "GCSE, etc.", 3) "A-level, etc.", and 4) "Higher qualifications". The first two categories define non-advanced levels of qualification, and the last two refer to advanced qualifications.

12   This method was considered more computationally efficient than the more conventional method where the thresholds are divided by P_4 and the random number is in the range $(0, 1)$.

Aged 16-22 (indicator)

Children: number and age of youngest (grouped interaction, 6 levels, for females only)

Partner employment status (3 levels: no partner, partner working, partner not working)

Health restricts work (indicator)

Status change in last year (indicator)

Duration of non-employment and age (3 levels for non-employed)

Employment sector (3 levels for employed)

Occupation (6 levels)

Industry (6 levels)

Most of the predictors were indicator (dummy) variables, while others were categorical variables and had coefficients for several levels represented by indicator variables. Age and age squared entered the equations as interval-level variables and had one multiplicative coefficient each.

Two variables of employment history had been of particular relevance. First, the variable *"duration of non-employment"*, calculated only for those who were currently non-employed, was measured in quarter years and was used only to distinguish those who have not had a job in the last eight years (i.e. threshold 32). Second, the variable *"status change in last year"* indicated a change between employment, unemployment or inactivity in the last year and is computed as a derived variable from the observed employment status in each of the last four quarters.

The results for the final specification of the regression equations estimated are reported in Tables 8 to 19 of Zaidi (2004a). As a way of an illustrative example, we include (in Annex A) results of the multinomial logit models for the origin state of **full-time work**, for both males and females and for those with advanced and non-advanced qualifications.

2.2   *Estimation of earnings equation*

The aim of the earnings equation has been to capture the cross-sectional heterogeneity amongst workers as well as determine how time-variant attributes affect earnings. A simple approach would have been to estimate the wage equation on the basis of a large cross-sectional dataset and use the resulting relationship for the prediction of wages in each model time period. However, this approach implies that individuals will be subject to the same cross-sectional variation in each time-period and the link with one's own wages of the immediate past will be lost.

This problem was resolved by working with both static and dynamic aspects of the random effect panel data model. Random-effect linear regression models, with first-order disturbance terms, for the log monthly earnings,[13] were estimated for all employees. To this, we added a separate single model for self-employed persons. The form of the equation is:

$$\log(y_{jt}) = \alpha + X_{jt}\beta + \mu_j + \varepsilon_{jt} \qquad (j = 1, ..., N; \; t = 1, ..., t_j) \qquad (1)$$

where u_j is the time-invariant individual effect, representing fixed unobserved attributes. The time variant error term, ε_{jt}, satisfies

$$\varepsilon_{jt} = \rho\varepsilon_{jt-1} + v_{jt} \qquad (2)$$

in which $|\rho| < 1$ and v_{jt} are independent and identically distributed with zero mean and standard deviation σ_v.

The dataset used for the estimation of earnings equations was derived from the 11 waves of the BHPS, covering the period 1990-2000. This survey was preferred for a number of reasons. *First*, the longitudinal nature of the BHPS data offered us the possibility to estimate a panel data model. *Second*, the quality of the wage variable was better than that recorded in other large-scale datasets (e.g. QLFS). *Third*, the survey provided detailed attributes of individual wages, including a possibility to work with both gross and net wages.

The estimation sample was restricted to those of working age and who had non-missing wage data. The sample was pooled across 11 waves of the BHPS; thus results were representative of the trends and patterns observed during the whole of the 1990s. The estimation groups for the wage equation were the same four population groups as used for employment transitions, defined by sex, and possession of advanced qualifications. In particular, the distinction across individuals with advanced and non-advanced qualification levels offered large explanatory power in wage progression.

A whole range of explanatory factors was tested to see their impact on wages. The potential set of explanatory variables and their different categorizations were chosen on the basis of their relevance but also their

---

13   Differences in the accounting period for earnings may affect accuracy in the model estimation, subsequently raising doubts on the credibility of simulation of earnings. See O'Donoghue et al. (2009) for a discussion.

availability in the base dataset and their inclusion in the estimation of employment transitions. Amongst the most notable are variables that report on the most recent employment experience. Other variables are age, age squared, educational attainment, occupation, industry, partnership status, employment status of the partner, whether health restricts work, and public/private sector distinction. Number of children living at home and age of youngest child (grouped interaction, 6 levels, for females only) have also been included. Full-time and part-time status, along with its interaction with other attributes, is also used. Part-time employment indicator was used in interaction with young age, private sector, employment history (for females) and professional/managerial occupation. Many of the predictors were common to the employment transition and wage equations. The regression results for the earnings equation are reported in Zaidi (2004b). As a way of an illustrative example, in Annex B, we report the coefficients of the final specification of the wage equation for male employees, with advanced and non-advanced qualifications.

It was useful to split the regression results (for the log wage) into three parts for implementation:

1. The time-invariant portion, which we term the base log wage. This includes the terms for: constant, qualification, occupation, industry, and the individual effect u_j of equation (1).

2. The time-variant error term. This auto-regressive term was initially drawn from a normal distribution with mean 0 and standard deviation σ_ε, and was updated each year using formula (2), where v_{jt} was drawn from a normal distribution with mean 0 and standard deviation σ_v, which was computed as $\sqrt{(1-\rho^2)}\,\sigma_\varepsilon$.

3. The time-variant deterministic portion, including terms for: age, age squared, health, children, partner's employment, employment history, part-time employment (including interactions).

The time-invariant portion and error term were assigned to each individual along with the other time-invariant characteristics upon entry to the labour market. Each subsequent year, and for each individual of working age, the error term was updated using stored parameters ρ (RHO) and σ_v (SIGMA_N).[14] Earnings were calculated after the labour market transitions for the year had been computed. NEMPHIST was also updated, reflecting the employment status in the fourth quarter of the current year, after the computation of employment transitions and earnings.

---

14 This method was considered more computationally efficient than the more conventional method where the thresholds are divided by P_4 and the random number is in the range (0, 1).

Table 1a: **Variables included in the population database for the labour market event**

ID	*Person identifier*
NSEX	*Sex* 1 "Male" 2 "Female"
NAGE	*Age in years*
NEDSTAT	*Educational status* 1 "No qualifications" 2 "GCSE, etc" 3 "A-level, etc" 4 "Higher qualification"
IDPART	*Partner's ID* 0 "n/a (not currently partnered)"
NCHILD	*Number of own/partner's children under 16*
NYCAGE	*Age of youngest child in family* -1 "unborn child (woman pregnant)" -9 "n/a (no children under 16)"
NHEALTH	*Health status* 0 "No health problem" 1 "Health restricts work"
NSECT	*Sector* 1 "Public employee" 2 "Private employee" 3 "Self-employed"
NINDUS	1 "Agriculture/ fishing/ Construction" 2 "Manufacturing/Energy & water" 3 "Catering/ transp/ communication" 4 "Finance" 5 "Public services" 6 "Other services"
NSOC	1 "Managers & administrators" 2 "Prof, assoc prof & tech" 3 "Clerical & secretarial" 4 "Craft/personal protec serv" 5 "Plant & machine operatives" 6 "Sales/ Other occupations"
NEMP1, NEMP2, NEMP3, NEMP4	*Employment status in each quarter* 1 "Employed full-time" 2 "Employed part-time" 3 "Unemployed" 4 "Inactive"
NDURLM	*Duration of labour market spell in quarters*
NEMPHIST	*Two-year labour market status history*
FWAGE_B	*Base log wage (time-invariant)*
FWAGE_E	*Wage error term (auto-regressive)*
MWAGE	*Annual earnings*

Notes: The table includes variables needed for computing derived variables, as well as direct predictors, in the labour market module. See Section 3.1 for a description of NDURLM and NEMPHIST. The health status variable was initially defined to be static and it was based on the presence of "limiting long-term illness" in the base dataset; subsequently, health transitions were also implemented during the whole of the working life.

Table 1b: Derived variables used in the labour market event

AGE2	Square of NAGE
NCHB	Number of children born
NEMP	Initial employment status for transition
EMPPT	Partner employment status 0 "No partner" 1 "Partner not employed" 2 "Partner employed"
CHNG	Status change in the last year
DAS	No job / sector lookup values
RHO, SIGMA_N	Coefficients for updating wage error term

3 Implementing the labour market event

The implementation part of the labour market module had been the most demanding part of the work undertaken in the SAGE model. Not only were the transition rules complex, with multiple states in the case of labour market status, and multiple estimation groups, but the dependence on variables included in other modules was complicated, and a large amount of information had to be imputed in the base data. This section describes briefly the salient aspects of this work.

For implementation purposes, some of the labour market variables were stored in the population database and could be referred to directly in the implementation rules; whilst others had to be computed as derived variables. Table 1a shows the names and coding of the variables in the population database, and Table 1b the derived variables.

3.1 *Employment history variables*

The variable NDURLM, mentioned in Table 1a, measured the length of the current employment spell, which was defined as the number of quarters during which the person has been either continuously employed or continuously non-employed. It was set to 1 whenever a transition results in a change between employment and non-employment, and incremented at each transition not resulting in a change. Other variables made use of the information recorded in NDURLM. For instance, the derived variable CHNG, "status change in last year", was set to 1 if NDURLM<4 and 0 if NDURLM>= 4 and the person was currently employed. If NDURLM>= 4 and NEMP4>2 (either unemployed or inactive), it is necessary to distinguish people who have switched between unemployment and inactivity in the last year. This was established by examining the variable *"employment status in each quarter"* (NEMP1 to NEMP4, each having values 3 or 4 in this case).

For earnings, we utilized the variable NEMPHIST, which indicates the previous two years' employment history categories, used in the equation for the time-varying portion of wages. Employment history was coded using the values 0=student (S), 1=employed (E), 3=unemployed (U), 4=inactive (N). The codes of NEMPHIST are shown below in Table 2.

The labels of NEMPHIST indicate the current status first, followed, in order, by the status in the previous two years. The current status is always E, "employed", when wages are being calculated. The history was based on the employment status in the last quarter of each of the previous two years. This choice was made in order to be consistent with the estimation data, which used employment status in the week before interview.

364

For the parameter estimation for females, the coding of the history variable was extended to cover the interaction with part-time working (by adding 100 to the value for women working PT). Thus, for males, the code values run from 0 (ESS) to 44 (ENN) and for females, from 0 to 144. In both cases, the reference category in the wage equation was 11 (EEE, FT).

Table 2: Coding of employment history variable

Codes	includes	labels†	FT code	PT code
0		ESS	0	100
1	3 4	EES EUS ENS	1	101
11		EEE	11	111
13		EEU	13	113
33	14 31	EEN EUE EUU) combined	33	133
34		EUN††) for all but	44	111/100
41		ENE) PT females	44	141
44	43	ENN ENU	44	144

Notes: † The labels indicate the current status first, followed, in order, by the status in the previous two years;   E = Employed; U = Unemployed; N = Inactive; S = Student.

†† EUN is combined for PT females with EEE or ESS according to level of education: non-advanced.

3.2   The labour market parameter tables and rules

There were 16 models of employment transitions, subdivided by sex, qualification group (2 levels) and origin state (4 levels). For each of these models
there were three equations, with up to 12 predictor variables. The coefficients associated with one or more predictors were grouped in panels in
the parameter table. The panels were named as:

> QUA (for qualification and age terms),
> CHA (for number of children and age),
> HPT (for health status and partner's employment),
> DAS (for employment duration, age and employment sector),
> SOC (for occupation) and
> IND (for industry).

Each panel contains three columns of beta coefficients (e.g. *BQUA2*, *BQUA3*,
BQUA4) for the three outcome levels: while outcome 1, full-time work,
was taken as the reference level, the beta coefficient gave parameters for
employment transitions to part-time work, unemployment and inactivity,
respectively. Panels also included one or more columns of lookup values for
the predictors. Some examples of the panels included in the employment
transitions parameter table are provided in Annex C.

Using the parameter table, *four* transitions of employment status were
performed: from the fourth quarter of the previous year to the first quarter
of the current year (NEMP4 to NEMP1) and then successively to the second,
third and fourth quarters of the current year. Each of the four employment
status variables (*"employment status in each quarter"*: NEMP1 to NEMP4) was
successively overwritten by the new value.

The parameter table for the simulation of wages was smaller than
that for employment transitions, since only the time-variant portion of the
log wage regression equation needed to be computed (nb. log base wage
was computed at the time of entry into the labour market), and there were
fewer equations. The table was arranged in sub-tables and panels, as for
the employment transition equations, but there were only five sub-tables:
four for employees, grouped by age and qualification group as above, and
one for self-employed persons. The panels included in the wage parameter
table are specified in Annex D, which also includes the full parameter table
for the time-variant component of the wage equation.

If a person had not worked at all during the year, there was no need to do any wage computation, and the wage was set to 0. Otherwise the time-variant portion of the log wage was computed separately for any periods of full-time and part-time work during the year, using the appropriate parameters. These terms were then combined with the base log wage and wage error term and exponentiated to obtain the quarterly full-time and part-time earnings. The annual earnings were assigned as a weighted sum, according to the time spent employed full-time and part-time during the year.

NEMPHIST was also updated, reflecting the employment status in the fourth quarter of the current year. These updates were performed after the computation of employment transitions and earnings. The assignment of labour market predictors on entry to the labour force took place in the *AgeOneYear* event and is described in Scott and Zaidi (2004). For the initial labour market status, NEMP4 was set to 3 "Unemployed" and NDURLM remains at its default value of 0. This was predicated on the supposition that new entrants were actively seeking work, and were not yet scarred by unemployment of a year or more. NEMPHIST also remained at 0, as this was the code for student history over the previous two years.

4   Testing and validation

A protocol for testing and validation of simulations of the labour force event was established, so as to see whether the model works as intended and to "validate" the simulated results.[15] This step was important as it contributed to enhancing the credibility of the model among its producers and users. For the labour market event, we performed *logic testing*, to check that the rules and parameter tables were correctly specified, and *statistical evaluation*, to check whether the model output was consistent with the data used to design the simulation.

4.1   Logic testing – employment transitions

Because of the large number of terms and predictor values, it was not practicable to check the rules for computation of the transition equations using log output for selected individuals. Instead, we used the predict command

---

15   Validation can be defined as the comparison of model's results with counterpart values that come from independent sources and are known to be "correct" and/or credible.

in Stata (Stata Corporation, 2001) which could output the values of the estimated outcome probabilities and the linear estimators, for any set of observations, immediately after estimating the logit model.

The first test undertaken compared the linear estimators and outcome probabilities estimated by Stata with probabilities computed by the simulation programme. It used a base dataset with 10,364 observations from the QLFS data. The test simulated the labour market event for one year only, using adapted transition rules, which performed only the first quarterly transition. The output data after one year was then analysed to see that the SAGE-derived variables and probabilities agreed with the ones generated by Stata's predict command. Errors were discovered in this way in the coding schemes of some of the variables. Further tests enabled checking of the allocation of outcome states and updating of duration, the re-computation of probabilities when states change, and the sequencing of the quarterly transitions, which were not covered by the first test.

Another test used a small base dataset containing 3 couples and 2 unpartnered individuals, running for two years. It executed the labour market event, which did all four quarterly transitions, with detailed log output. It also executed the *AgeOneYear* event, so that ages were incremented for the second year. The test was used to hand-check the derived variables, in particular partner employment status when the partner was older (including over 64) and the correct lookup in case of pregnancy. A further test, which was performed on output from a larger number of years, had been to check that there were no systematic differences in transition rates by quarter, depending on whether there had been changes earlier in the same year. This suggested that there were no differences in the rules between quarters. The output from the adjustment of employment status in the base data when there were no changes in the other population characteristics indicated that the labour market changes were smooth over each year.

4.2 Logic testing – earnings simulation

We used Stata's predict command to provide an alternative computation with which to test the earnings simulation. Since the earnings depended on employment in each quarter of the current year, we could not use a prediction from the base data, but used a sample of data from the first year simulation output and computed "out of sample" predicted log wages, using coefficient estimates saved in Stata for each estimation group. We added the error term from the base data to the predicted log wages, before the annual earnings were derived, and compared with the simulated earnings.

To check that the error terms were being updated correctly, the distribution of the error term after one year in each estimation group was checked to see that it was $N(0,\sigma_\varepsilon)$ and that the correlation with the base data error term was ρ. The updating of employment history was checked by tabulating new against old histories by current employment status. The initialization of the base wage and error term on entry to the labour market was checked by looking at their distributions for new entrants in the output for 1991 and 1992.

4.3   Statistical evaluation – employment transitions

For comparison with available time series, and with the estimation data (QLFS 1994-2000), we used a simulation from 1990 to 2000 and analysed all individuals of working age (16-59/64) at the time of the employment transition, including students, who were classified as inactive. The data included an average of 17,097 males and 15,960 females each year from 1990 to 2000.

We compared the simulated outcomes with the LFS time series for the UK produced by ONS, for 1991-2000, by sex (ONS, 2003). Table 3 shows the proportions of each sex who were employed, or active (employed or unemployed) at the beginning and end of the decade in the official figures and in the simulation. The proportions in the base data are also shown here for comparison purposes.

It can be seen that both employment and activity rates were much lower in the base sample than in the LFS for 1991. By the end of the decade, the employment rates for both men and women in the simulation were only marginally higher than those in the LFS, but the activity rates were around 1% higher for both sexes.

Table 3:   Employment states compared

	Male 16-64 (% employed)	Male 16-64 (% active)	Female 16-59 (% employed)	Female 16-59 (% active)
LFS Mar-May 1991	79.9	88.1	66.0	71.3
Base data (v. 1.6)	76.9	82.0	63.7	67.2
LFS Jun-Aug 2000	79.3	84.1	69.6	73.1
Simulation 2000 Q4	80.1	85.5	69.8	74.1

Note: Full-time students are included as inactive.

Further comparisons in the employment states over the 1990s with the LFS time series show that simulated rates converged with the LFS time series towards the end of the decade, but inactivity rates were too low.

4.4 Statistical evaluation – earnings results

Since earnings were dependent on the time spent in full-time and part-time employment during each year, we show results only for those who were employed full-time throughout the year in question. The analysis is of simulated data for the years 1991 to 1999. Tables 3 and 4 show statistics for the annual earnings (in 1991 prices, but 1993 earnings levels) for various subgroups of the population. The mean, standard deviation, median and 10th and 90th percentiles are shown.

Table 4 shows the distribution of earnings in each of the estimation groups, with self-employed disaggregated by sex. Self-employed earnings are more variable than those for employees. The relationship with sex and education status is as expected.

Table 4:   Earnings distribution by estimation group

Estimation group	mean	s.d.	p10	p50	p90	N
Male non-advanced	12664	6425	5945	11380	20983	43270
Male advanced	18501	9840	8321	16462	31077	55113
Female non-advanced	8153	4656	3498	7094	14070	31068
Female advanced	13314	8049	5355	11430	23495	23803
Male self-employed	17328	27229	2247	9237	38924	20147
Female self-employed	8043	12209	1027	4330	18091	2981

Notes: Educational attainmant is defined as: 1 "No qualifications" 2 "GCSE, etc" 3 "A-level, etc" 4 "Higher qualifications". The first two categories define non-advanced levels of qualification, and the last two refer to advanced qualifications.

The corresponding distributions for 1993 (the reference year) in the estimation data are given in Table 5. Note that the requirement to be employed full-time all year in the simulation is more restrictive than the requirement to be employed full-time in the week before interview in the BHPS. The number of female self-employed is also rather small to make a comparison. The distributions are roughly the same as in the simulation. Differences are to be expected because of compositional differences in the two datasets, Monte Carlo variation in the simulated data, and less-than-perfect model fit in the estimation data.

Table 5:   Earnings distribution in the estimation data for 1993

Estimation group	mean	s.d.	p10	p50	p90	N
Male non-advanced	13349	7999	6741	12029	21378	994
Male advanced	18180	9476	8378	16680	29069	773
Female non-advanced	9306	4405	4668	8807	14522	676
Female advanced	13937	6899	6282	12788	22818	439
Male self-employed	14293	13589	3148	10185	32407	384
Female self-employed	8663	8611	648	6481	18519	92

The distribution of earnings in the simulation by age group and sex is shown in Table 6. The full-time earnings of both sexes peak between the ages of 36 and 50, but the peak for women is less marked than that for men.

Table 6:   Earnings distribution by sex and age, for 1993

Age group	mean	s.d.	p10	p50	p90	N
Males						
16-22	8602	7632	3548	7256	14134	9060
23-35	14543	11653	5898	12242	24734	42993
36-50	19292	16295	7256	16401	32727	45936
51-64	15937	12625	5634	13378	27933	20541
All males	16171	13905	5681	13445	28454	118530
Females						
16-22	6582	3962	2636	5721	11434	7177
23-35	10352	6852	3992	8705	18552	22251
36-50	11550	8056	4193	9498	21422	21848
51-64	9771	7017	3559	8082	17981	6576
All females	10271	7242	3707	8453	18889	57852

5   Conclusions

The labour market module is a key element of every dynamic microsimulation model. Its requirements are manifold, including estimation of parameters of employment transitions and earnings dynamics from the existing datasets and undertaking all imputations necessary in the base dataset to enable the implementation of the labour market event. Then, there is the process of testing, evaluation and validation of simulated results to measure the credibility of the model. This chapter describes how this work had been undertaken for the SAGE dynamic microsimulation model of Great Britain.

The estimation data for employment transitions came from the Quarterly Labour Force Survey, covering the period between December 1992 and August 2000. This dataset had the advantage of large sample size, as it provided over 1.2 million observations on employment transitions, but it lacked information on employment history beyond a single year. However, the lack of a job in the last eight years, inferred from missing values, proved to be an important predictor of the probability of transition into employment.

For earnings, the estimation data were taken from the British Household Panel Survey, covering 11 waves during the period 1990-2000. Random effect linear regression models, with first-order autoregressive disturbance terms, produced cross-sectional earnings distributions for full-time workers that reasonably reflected the distributions in the donor data. The form of the equations allowed for a permanent individual component to be calculated once only, in the base dataset, and imputed by donation to new labour market entrants. This meant that the time-variant component, which had to be recalculated each year according to the individual's current circumstances, was relatively simple to compute.

Further validation of the long-term trajectories of employment and earnings produced by the model will be necessary. Unfortunately, there was little reliable independent data available with which to compare the simulated results. Period and cohort effects are also important and projection of future employment behaviour and earnings without disentangling these effects must inevitably entail some degree of doubt. We cannot assume that those entering the labour market in the 1990s will follow the same trajectories as the previous generation. In basing our estimations on 1990s data only (because of lack of availability of comprehensive data from earlier periods), we confound the cohort and period effects that shaped the experience of older people still in the labour market.

In analysing the results, account must also be taken of Monte Carlo and other sources of variation. Because of the high dependency of the outcomes on modelled changes in individual circumstances, model-runs with different random number seeds will produce varying outcomes at macro as well as individual level, and this variation should be assessed by making a number of different runs for each analysis. Analysis of other sources of variation, such as sampling and imputation variation in the base data and variation in parameter estimates, should be performed. It is possible that Monte Carlo variation in the execution of the transition rules will provide the biggest source of variation, especially as these differences are cumulative over time.

With these reservations in mind, the logic testing and statistical evaluation showed that the model produced a realistic distribution of employment and earnings, which was related to individual circumstances in a way that no static or macro model could achieve. It will also be possible to add alignment, or time-varying parameters, into the rules in future versions of the SAGE model, in order to explore the effects of different economic and policy scenarios in the future.

References

Evandrou, M./Falkingham, J./Johnson, P./Rake, K. (2001) *SAGE: Simulating Social Policy for an Ageing Society. A Research Agenda*. ESRC-SAGE Discussion Paper No. 1. London: London School of Economics.

Harding, A. (2007) Challenges and Opportunities of Dynamic Microsimulation Modelling, Plenary paper presented to the 1st General Conference of the International Microsimulation Association, Vienna, 21 August 2007.

O'Donoghue, C. (2001) 'Dynamic microsimulation: a survey', *Brazilian Electronic Journal of Economics* 4 (2): 45-61.

O'Donoghue, C./Leach, R./Hynes, S. (2009) 'Simulating Earnings in Dynamic Microsimulation Models', pp. 381-412 in Zaidi, A./Harding, A./Williamson, P. (eds.), *New Frontiers in Microsimulation Modelling*. Farnham (UK): Ashgate.

Office of National Statistics (ONS) (2003) *Historical Supplement to the Labour Market Statistics First Release*. London: National Statistics Virtual Bookshelf. http://www.statistics.gov.uk/OnlineProducts/LMS_FR_HS.asp (accessed November 2003).

Scott, A./Zaidi, A. (2004) *Education and Labour Market Predictors in the SAGE Dynamic Microsimulation Model*. ESRC-SAGE Technical Note No 9. London: London School of Economics.

Scott, A. (2004) *Implementation of Labour Market Transitions and Earnings in the SAGE Dynamic Microsimulation Model*. ESRC-SAGE Technical Note No 11. London: London School of Economics.

Stata Corporation (2001) *Stata Statistical Software Release 7.0*. College Station, Texas: Stata Corporation.

Zaidi, A./Rake, K. (2001) *Dynamic Microsimulation Models: A Review and Some Lessons for SAGE*. ESRC-SAGE Discussion Paper No. 2. London: London School of Economics.

Zaidi, A./Scott, A. (2001) *Base Dataset for the SAGE Model*. ESRC-SAGE Technical Note No. 2. London: London School of Economics.

Zaidi, A. (2004a) *Modelling Labour Market Dynamics in the SAGE Model*. ESRC-SAGE Technical Note No. 7. London: London School of Economics.

Zaidi, A. (2004b) *Estimation of Earnings in the SAGE Dynamic Microsimulation Model*. ESRC-SAGE Technical Note No. 10. London: London School of Economics.

Annex A: Regression results for employment transitions (from full-time work)

Table A.1: Relative risk ratio (derived from the multinomial logit models) of quarterly employment transitions of working age males, originating from full-time work status

Males	A-level or higher qualification						GCSE or lower qualification					Relative risk ratio
	Part-time		Unem-ployed		Inac-tive		Part-time		Unem-ployed		Inactive	
Age	0,771	***	0,976		0,682	***	0,778	***	0,985		0,741	***
Age squared	1,003	***	1,000		1,005	***	1,003	***	1,000		1,004	***
Couple	0,645	***	0,657	***	0,623	***	0,753		0,660	***	0,925	
Head of family unit	0,987		0,740	**	0,710		0,733		0,762	*	0,997	
Have child of age less than 2	1,155		0,753		0,457	*	1,541		0,944		0,788	
Lowest educational attainment	0,705	***	1,188	*	1,129		0,903		1,069		1,155	
Health restricts work	1,904	***	1,576	***	4,112	***	1,857	***	1,521	***	4,180	***
Employment history: employed for one year or more	0,203	***	0,118	***	0,128	***	0,250	***	0,132	***	0,184	***
Employment status: self-employed	2,881	***	0,786	**	0,591	***	2,357	***	0,784	*	0,690	**
Employment sector: private	1,169		1,493	**	0,922		1,122		1,160		0,906	
Managers and administrators	0,434	***	0,722	*	0,684	*	0,415	***	0,556	***	0,818	
Professionals and associated professionals	0,531	***	0,743	*	1,144		0,779		0,511	***	0,622	*
Clerical and secretarial occupations	0,681		1,291		1,224		0,354	***	0,672	**	1,162	
Craft related occup., personal and protective services	0,456	***	0,922		0,861		0,521	***	0,687	***	0,732	*
Plant and machine operatives	0,728		0,926		1,266		0,423	***	0,777	**	0,938	
Agriculture and fishing; construction	0,467	***	1,098		0,927		0,602	***	1,540	***	0,764	
Energy and water; manufacturing	0,483	***	0,972		1,000		0,407	***	1,098		1,137	
Banking and financial sector	0,584	***	0,777	*	0,743		0,976		1,409	**	1,322	
Public administation, education and health	1,350		0,799		0,827		1,178		1,152		1,078	
Other services	1,612	**	1,151		0,913		1,541	*	1,645	**	1,233	
1994/95	1,134		1,452	***	1,417	*	1,342		1,305	**	1,684	**
1995/96	1,436	*	1,362	**	1,314		1,124		1,312	*	1,426	
1996/97	1,555	**	1,104		1,290		1,246		1,269		1,592	**
1997/98	1,450	*	1,127		1,400	*	1,110		1,164		1,354	
1998/99	1,394		1,410	**	1,261		1,488	*	1,515	***	1,425	
1999/00	1,608	*	1,299		1,114		1,274		1,016		1,388	
Autumn	0,989		1,170		1,379	**	1,269		0,953		0,910	
Winter	1,046		0,949		0,715	**	0,986		1,196		0,916	
Spring	1,000		1,116		0,764	*	1,060		1,044		0,860	
Pseudo- R square	0,123						0,124					
Number of observations	69.431						46.053					

Notes: * significant at 10%; ** significant at 5%; *** significant at 1%

373

Table A.2: Relative risk ratio (derived from the multinomial logit models) of quarterly employment transitions of working age females, originating from full-time work status

Females	A-level or higher qualification						GCSE or lower qualification					Relative risk ratio
	Part-time		Unem-ployed		Inac-tive		Part-time		Unem-ployed		Inac-tive	
Age	0,876	***	0,908	**	0,710	***	0,905	***	0,919	**	0,780	***
Age squared	1,002	***	1,001	**	1,005	***	1,001	***	1,001	*	1,003	***
Couple	1,307	**	0,646	*	0,856		1,314	**	0,788		0,650	***
Have child of age less than 2	4,567	***	2,361	**	5,635	***	4,884	***	0,886		3,613	***
Have child of age 2-4	1,152		0,953		1,664		1,143		0,764		1,152	
Have child of age 5-9	1,060		1,361		1,217		1,040		0,856		0,828	
Have child of age 10-15	1,141		1,300		1,146		1,320	*	0,764		0,487	***
Number of children aged less than 16	1,268	**	0,972		0,969		1,275	**	1,340		1,748	***
Wife or partner of head	1,198		0,908		1,258		1,138		1,011		1,622	***
Lowest educational attainment	0,954		1,072		1,145		1,112		0,928		1,300	**
Health restricts work	1,570	***	1,358		3,575	***	1,507	**	1,115		3,800	***
Employment history: employed for one year or more	0,345	***	0,091	***	0,136	***	0,282	***	0,163	***	0,306	***
Employment status: self-employed	2,409	***	0,665		0,965		1,654	***	0,625		1,031	
Employment sector: private	1,082		1,705	**	1,044		1,008		1,019		1,367	*
Managers and administrators	0,429	***	1,055		0,773		0,399	***	0,613	*	0,902	
Professionals and associated professionals	0,547	***	0,707		0,899		0,578	***	0,740		0,858	
Clerical and secretarial occupations	0,561	***	0,886		0,940		0,538	***	0,645	**	0,820	
Craft related occup., personal and protective services	0,962		0,721		1,415		0,762	**	0,895		1,381	*
Plant and machine operatives	1,115		1,557		1,765		0,639	**	1,176		1,114	
Agriculture and fishing; construction	0,645		0,719		0,470		1,171		1,215		0,881	
Energy and water; manufacturing	0,598	***	0,865		0,848		0,572	***	0,866		1,157	
Banking and financial sector	0,836		0,798		0,476	***	0,843		0,890		0,945	
Public administation, education and health	0,789		1,042		0,743		1,137		0,662	*	1,045	
Other services	0,851		1,354		0,527	**	1,133		1,267		1,029	
1994/95	1,010		2,451	***	1,596	*	0,906		1,319		1,029	
1995/96	1,066		2,520	***	1,563	*	0,899		1,172		1,099	
1996/97	0,966		1,831	**	1,442		0,851		1,340		1,025	
1997/98	0,852		1,501		1,081		0,705	**	0,973		1,060	
1998/99	1,066		1,955	**	1,338		0,727	*	0,975		1,111	
1999/00	1,449	*	2,443	**	0,453	*	0,922		1,306		0,999	
Autumn	1,690	***	1,425	*	1,549	**	1,340	**	1,151		1,241	
Winter	1,078		0,837		0,818		1,161		0,723	*	1,009	
Spring	1,191		1,159		0,901		1,159		1,104		1,029	
Pseudo- R square	0,101						0,088					
Number of observations	28.522						29.340					

Notes: * significant at 10%; ** significant at 5%; *** significant at 1%

374

Annex B: Wage equation for male employees

Table B.1: Wage equation for male employees, further subdivided between those with advanced and non-advanced qualification

Males	Advanced qualification			Non-advanced qualification	
	Coefficient	Significance		Coefficient	Significance
Age	0,119	***		0,092	***
Age squared	-0,001	***		-0,001	***
Aged 16-22, working part-time	-0,415	***		-0,288	***
Health restricts work	-0,052	***		-0,040	**
No partner	-0,045	***		-0,051	***
Partner working	0,046	***		-0,010	
Employment history - ESS	-0,243	***		-0,640	***
Employment history - EES, EUS, ENS	-0,128	***		-0,289	***
Employment history - EEU	-0,108	***		-0,090	***
Employment history - EEN, EUE, EUU	-0,202	***		-0,171	***
Employment history - EUN, ENE, ENN, ENU	-0,327	***		-0,272	***
Employed part-time	-0,411	***		-0,689	***
Manager, part-time	0,077	*		0,230	***
Private sector, part-time	-0,157	***		0,127	**
Lowest educational category (within group)	-0,257	***		-0,107	***
Managers and administrators	0,196	***		0,171	***
Professionals and associated professionals	0,106	***		0,145	***
Clerical and secretarial occupations	0,031			0,032	*
Craft related occup., personal and protective services	0,047	**		0,062	***
Plant and machine operatives	0,065	***		0,081	***
Agriculture and fishing; construction	0,118	***		0,035	***
Energy and water; manufacturing	0,106	***		0,066	***
Banking and financial sector	0,103	***		0,107	***
Public administration, education and health	0,071	***		0,052	**
Other services	0,008			-0,053	**
Constant	4,801	***		4,973	***
rho_ar	0,414			0,350	
sigma_u	0,320			0,324	
sigma_e	0,261			0,280	
rho_fov	0,601			0,574	
R-sq within	0,416			0,378	
between	0,680			0,724	
overall	0,558			0,618	
Number of observations	8.867			9.551	

375

Notes: Model is the GLS estimator for random effects models, assuming the disturbance term is first-order autoregressive. Reference categories for the categorical variables: For occupation: Sales and other occupations; for industry: Catering, transport and construction; for partner: partner not working; for work history: EEE.

Annex C: The employment transitions parameter table – an example

The parameter table is arranged as 16 sub-tables corresponding to the 16 estimated models, indexed by sex (2 levels), qualification (2 levels) and origin state (4 levels). Each sub-table consists of six panels containing the groups of coefficients:

QUA	Qualification and age coefficients
CHA	Number and age of children
HPT	Health and partner's employment
DAS	Duration and age or sector
SOC	Occupation
IND	Industry

Categorical predictors were represented in the transition equations by a set of dummy variables taking the value 0 or 1 for each category. Since the categories are mutually exclusive, it was not necessary to compute $\beta_{ij}X_j$ for each of the dummies, but merely look up the β_{ij} for the relevant category and add this into the linear predictor expression. Thus, for a particular model, the three coefficients for each level of, e.g., NSOC are arranged as follows:

NSOC	BSOC2	BSOC3	BSOC4
1	-0.0519	-0.2371	0.0355
2	0.8051	-0.1384	-0.0693
3	-0.2335	-0.0687	0.1014
4	0.1350	-0.0328	-0.0053
5	0.9181	0.3084	0.1858
6	0	0	0

The NSOC column provides the lookup values. BSOC2 represents the log relative risk ratio of outcome 2 (part-time employment) compared to outcome 1 (full-time employment) associated with being in the relevant category of NSOC (relative to the reference category, 6), and so on. Note that the reference category had to be included explicitly in the panel, with zero coefficients. The fieldnames for the coefficients started with B, so as to indicate β, followed by SOC as an indicator of the predictor variable, and ending with a digit indicating the outcome level to which they refer.

Altogether, each panel has six rows of coefficients. Three panels have four columns: one lookup value and three coefficients (as shown in the SOC panel above). The other three panels, which contained interactions, had columns for two lookup values and three coefficients. The six panels therefore used 27 fields and 6 rows. The whole table has 3+27=30 fields and 16x6=96 rows.

Annex D: The wage parameter table – specification and initial values

There are five sub-tables in the wage parameter table and they are stacked vertically (as shown in Table D.1). The first four sub-tables are for employees, corresponding to the estimation groups male/female with advanced/non-advanced qualifications, indexed by NSEX (values 1, 2) and NEDSTAT (thresholds 2, 4). Self-employed people form a single separate estimation group and the parameters for this subgroup are included in the fifth sub-table. The sub-table for self-employed was differentiated by adding 2 to the NSEX value, and using threshold 4 for both NSEX and NEDSTAT.

Each sub-table has lookup values for the estimation subgroups, given by NSEX and NEDSTAT. They also have five panels, each having column(s) for lookup values (prefixed by N) as well as the value of the parameter (prefixed by B). The five panels are defined as follows:

AGE	(also used to store coefficients updating the error term),
CHILD	(number and age),
HPT	(health and partner's employment),
HISTORY	(including interaction with part-time work), and
SSP	(interactions of NSOC and NSECT with part-time work).

The full wage parameter table used in implementing the time-variant part of the wage equation is given in Table D.1. Below we illustrate the HISTORY panel in some more details.

The HISTORY panel was implemented as a full interaction with FT/PT. There were 8 rows corresponding to the groupings:

0	ESS
1 - 4	EES EUS ENS
11	EEE
13	EEU
14 - 33	EEN EUE EUU
34	EUN[16]
41	ENE
43 - 44	ENN ENU

Coefficients for full-time and part-time wages were stored in separate columns named BHISTF and BHISTP within the history panel. For males, where a full interaction was not estimated, the PT coefficients were obtained by adding the PT main effect to each of the FT coefficients. The categories used are listed in Table 2 above.

---

16   The coefficients for EUN ENE ENN ENU were equal for all but females employed part-time. For these, EUN was grouped with EEE or ESS according to the non-advanced or advanced qualifications the person has, and ENE (ENN ENU) form separate groups. For more details, see Zaidi (2004b).

Table D.1: Parameter table for time-variant component of the wage equation

NSEX	NEDSTAT	NAGE	BAGE	NYCAGE	NCHILD	BCHA	NHEALTH	NEMPPT	BHPT	NEMPHIST	BHISTF	BHISTP	NSOC	NSECT	BSSP
1	2	9	0.3502	1	0	0.0000	0	0	-0.0511	0	-0.6395	-1.3284	2	1	0.2300
1	2	10	0.2619	1	1	0.0000	0	1	0.0000	4	-0.2889	-0.9777	2	3	0.3570
1	2	11	0.0924	1	9	0.0000	0	2	-0.0100	11	0.0000	-0.6889	6	1	0.0000
1	2	12	-0.0011	4	9	0.0000	1	0	-0.0908	13	-0.0901	-0.7790	6	3	0.1270
1	2	22	-0.2879	9	9	0.0000	1	1	-0.0397	33	-0.1711	-0.8599	0	0	0.0000
1	2	64	0.0000	15	9	0.0000	1	2	-0.0497	34	-0.2715	-0.9604	0	0	0.0000
1	2	0	0.0000	0	0	0.0000	0	0	0.0000	41	-0.2715	-0.9604	0	0	0.0000
1	2	0	0.0000	0	0	0.0000	0	0	0.0000	44	-0.2715	-0.9604	0	0	0.0000
1	4	9	0.4141	1	0	0.0000	0	0	-0.0450	0	-0.2431	-0.6539	2	1	0.0774
1	4	10	0.2372	1	1	0.0000	0	1	0.0000	4	-0.1280	-0.5387	2	3	-0.0793
1	4	11	0.1192	1	9	0.0000	0	2	0.0457	11	0.0000	-0.4108	6	1	0.0000
1	4	12	-0.0014	4	9	0.0000	1	0	-0.0973	13	-0.1078	-0.5186	6	3	-0.1567
1	4	22	-0.4146	9	9	0.0000	1	1	-0.0522	33	-0.2018	-0.6125	0	0	0.0000
1	4	64	0.0000	15	9	0.0000	1	2	-0.0065	34	-0.3274	-0.7382	0	0	0.0000
1	4	0	0.0000	0	0	0.0000	0	0	0.0000	41	-0.3274	-0.7382	0	0	0.0000
1	4	0	0.0000	0	0	0.0000	0	0	0.0000	44	-0.3274	-0.7382	0	0	0.0000
2	2	9	0.4084	1	0	0.0000	0	0	0.0015	0	-0.5976	-1.3574	2	1	0.0575
2	2	10	0.3096	1	1	-0.0642	0	1	0.0000	4	-0.2691	-1.0729	2	3	0.0331
2	2	11	0.0613	1	9	-0.1816	0	2	-0.0616	11	0.0000	-0.5794	6	1	0.0000
2	2	12	-0.0007	4	9	-0.1679	1	0	-0.0308	13	-0.0522	-0.6166	6	3	-0.0244
2	2	22	-0.0315	9	9	-0.1581	1	1	-0.0323	33	-0.1466	-0.7929	0	0	0.0000
2	2	64	0.0000	15	9	-0.0788	1	2	-0.0939	34	-0.4341	-0.5794	0	0	0.0000
2	2	0	0.0000	0	0	0.0000	0	0	0.0000	41	-0.4341	-0.8530	0	0	0.0000
2	2	0	0.0000	0	0	0.0000	0	0	0.0000	44	-0.4341	-0.9703	0	0	0.0000
2	4	9	0.4374	1	0	0.0000	0	0	-0.0202	0	-0.1879	-0.6538	2	1	0.1958
2	4	10	0.2994	1	1	-0.1219	0	1	0.0000	4	-0.1148	-0.5862	2	3	0.1215
2	4	11	0.1100	1	9	-0.2905	0	2	-0.0108	11	0.0000	-0.5257	6	1	0.0000
2	4	12	-0.0014	4	9	-0.2116	1	0	-0.0418	13	-0.1292	-0.7532	6	3	-0.0743
2	4	22	-0.2296	9	9	-0.2280	1	1	-0.0216	33	-0.2152	-0.7961	0	0	0.0000
2	4	64	0.0000	15	9	-0.1555	1	2	-0.0325	34	-0.4021	-0.6538	0	0	0.0000
2	4	0	0.0000	0	0	0.0000	0	0	0.0000	41	-0.4021	-0.8557	0	0	0.0000
2	4	0	0.0000	0	0	0.0000	0	0	0.0000	44	-0.4021	-1.0288	0	0	0.0000
4	4	9	0.2950	1	0	0.0000	0	0	0.0000	0	0.0000	-0.5168	2	1	0.0000
4	4	10	0.8361	1	1	0.0000	0	1	0.0000	4	0.0000	-0.5168	2	3	0.0000
4	4	11	0.0759	1	9	0.0000	0	2	0.0000	11	0.0000	-0.5168	6	1	0.0000
4	4	12	-0.0009	4	9	0.0000	1	0	0.0000	13	0.0000	-0.5168	6	3	0.0000
4	4	64	0.0000	15	9	0.0000	1	2	0.0000	44	0.0000	-0.5168	0	0	0.0000

Chapter 15

Simulating Earnings in Dynamic Microsimulation Models

Cathal O'Donoghue / Ross H. Leach / Stephen Hynes

1 Introduction

Simulated earnings are one of the most important processes in dynamic microsimulation models used to analyse welfare, pensions and labour market policies. Aside from modelling earnings as the largest contribution to disposable income, this variable is used to generate pension contributions and entitlement, counter-factual or reservation wages and in determining eligibility for welfare benefits.

An earnings model must be able "…to capture the cross-sectional heterogeneity amongst the population of working people as well as demonstrating how time-variant attributes affect earnings (i.e. capture heterogeneity and state-dependence)" (Zaidi, 2004). The simulation must adequately reflect the relationship between earnings and their determinants such as schooling, labour market history and regional labour markets. It must also reflect the distribution of earnings observed in the population and the mobility of earnings over time. Thus the model needs to reflect three dimensions, observed heterogeneity reflected in the deterministic component of the model and unobserved cross-sectional and inter-temporal heterogeneity as part of the stochastic component of the model.

This chapter will look at how the results from econometric models of earnings are applied to dynamic microsimulation models, with an in-depth assessment of the effects of different accounting periods and pay-

This work was funded jointly by the Department of Work and Pensions, the Irish Department of Agriculture and Food's Research Stimulus Fund and the Irish National Development Plan.

ment mechanisms for earnings, which may lead to inaccuracies in model estimation through the different variance in earnings across groups that could have a significant impact on a microsimulation of earnings. Section 2 briefly summarizes human capital theory and its application to econometric models of earnings. Section 3 details the data and methodology, while Section 4 evaluates the performance of different earnings models using data for Ireland and the UK. Finally, Section 5 concludes.

2   Theoretical model

The earnings equations in this chapter draw upon Becker's Human Capital model,[1] which determines that logged earnings depend upon schooling, experience and other factors (Z) and unobserved variation (ε):

$$\ln Y = \beta_1 + \beta_2.Education + \beta_3.Experience + \beta_4 Z + \varepsilon$$

Where ability across individuals is the same, the rate of return to additional schooling can be identified from the education coefficient. The objective of earnings simulation models is to generate a distribution of earnings both cross-sectionally and inter-temporally, therefore a monte-carlo simulation method is used to generate error components. This method also has implications for the mean earnings in the population as the average non-stochastic earnings is lower than the stochasitic earnings due to the log normal nature of the distributiuon used in the models.

Variability of earnings can occur in two dimensions, cross-sectionally between persons and over time. In our model, this variability can depend both upon characteristics that we can observe in the deterministic part of the model and upon characteristics that we cannot observe in the stochastic part of the model.

Table 1 describes an overview of factors that have been used in dynamic microsimulation models to account for intra-personal correlation, the deterministic component of the model. The standard Mincer variables of schooling and experience (or age as a proxy) as well as sex are included in most models. Because of the different institutional characteristics such as

---

1   See a standard labour economics text, for example by Borjas (2003) for a full discussion of human capital theory.

Model	Country	Input Variables
DYNAMOD I and II	Australia	Experience, industry, occupation, labour market activity, family size, number of jobs, a proxy for nationality, and spouse earnings
HARDING	Australia	Age, education, invalidity status, number of hours worked, "ability and personal qualities"
Melbourne Cohort	Australia	Age, age^2 and age^3 (women)
DYNACAN	Canada	Weekly Wage (-1)*Education Status, Foreign, Non-English, Disabled, Age, Prov. Unemp. Rate, Weeks Worked (-1), Gender, Age, Employee (-1), Employee
LifePaths	Canada	Gender, educational attainment, duration since graduation
DESTINIE	France	Gender, Schooling, Experience, Experience^2
Sfb3	Germany	Age, education, time in labour force, sex, occupational status, marital status, labour force status and ability
LIAM1	Ireland	Occupational Group, Age, Age^2, Employee Last Year, Part-time, Married, Years in Education, Years in Work, Years in Unemployment, Years Ill, Years at Home, Years in Education^2, Years in Work^2, Years in Unemployment^2, Father's Education Level, Lone Parent, Number of Children, Spouse Unemployed, Spouse Not Participating, Civil Servant, Pension Member, Manager, Gender, Occupational Group, Education Level
DYNAMITE	Italy	Cohort, Education, Manager, Self-employed, Sector, Region, Gender, Headship, Part-time, Inverse mills ratio, Age
ANAC	Italy	Cohort, Education, Manager, Self-employed, Sector, Region, Gender, Headship, Part-time, Inverse mills ratio, Age
Italian Cohort Model	Italy	Sex, education, age, sector, activity, marital status
Japanese Cohort Model	Japan	Family Disposable income (head age <60): Age of the head of Family, Size of Employer, Occupation, Industry, Number of Income Earners in Household, Gender of Head, Main Source of Income. Family Disposable income (head age >= 60): Age of Head, Size of Employer, Home Owner, Head in FT work, Agricultural Sector, Occupation, Number of Earners, Gender
MIDAS	New Zealand	Decile: Age, gender, ethnicity, previous income decile
MOSART	Norway	Previous Wage, Education, gender, age, children, pension status
MICROHUS	Sweden	Wage$_{t-2}$, education, experience, gender
SESIM	Sweden	In-work: Age, age^2, education, number of children, place of residence, nationality, gender, cohabiting, participation$_{t-1}$. Age, age^2, education, number of children, place of residence, nationality, gender, household type, inverse Mill's ratio. Mill's Ratio: Age, age^2, education, number of children, place of residence, nationality, gender, household type, young child, regional unemployment rate
SVERIGE	Sweden	Relative wage rate last year, age, sex, education level, dummy if the person is in education, unemployment rate in that region
Swedish Cohort Model	Sweden	Gender, Age, Age^2
PENSIM	UK	Sex, Marital Status, age, years out of labour force, labour force status
Pensim2	UK	Education, potential experience, a proxy for hours, if the occupation contains a managerial or technical component, whether you work in the public sector, have a permanent job, an individual effect and transitory error component
SAGE	UK	Educational attainment, industry, occupation, health status, number and age of children
CORSIM	USA	Age, earnings$_{t-1}$, education, education*earnings, married$_{t-1}$, number of children, percent unemployment, youngest child's age, age, have child, marital status, race, sex, weeks worked$_t$, weeks worked$_{t-1}$
DYNASIM I & II	USA	Age, race, sex, education, South, disability, marital status, student
CBOLT	USA	
PRISM	USA	Age, sex, changed job this year, unemployed

Source: O'Donoghue (2001), Baekgaard (2002), Zaidi (2004).

wage bargaining, entry restrictions and set pay scales, different segments of the labour market may have different wage structures (see for example Nickell, 1982). Occupation, industry, contract status, sector and firm size for example may be important and are included in a number of models internationally.

Utilizing panel data, we may also be able to tell something about the unobserved individual heterogeneity. After identifying the impact of observed characteristics we may observe that an individual consistently earns higher (or lower) than the predicted wage from the econometric model. This persistent difference can be identified within a panel data econometric model, where the stochastic term (ε_{it}) can be divided into a time invariant individual effect (u_i) and a time variant effect (v_{it}): $\varepsilon_{it} = u_i + v_{it}$. The u term can be classified as a (relatively) permanent unobserved attribute such as ability, family background, work ethic etc.

While variation in the deterministic part of the model, described by Baekgaard (2002) as intra-personal correlation, will determine to some extent (up to about 50%) the variation in earnings, the stochastic term is an important factor. Baekgaard further describes influences of this stochastic term:

- Inter-personal correlation
- Inter-temporal correlation

2.1 Inter-personal correlation

Inter-temporal correlation relates to the fact that earnings of individuals within a family, particularly between partners, are observed to be correlated (see Galler, 1996). In other words in a system of two equations for two partners:

$$\ln Y_1 = \beta_{1,1} + \beta_{2,1}.Education_1 + \beta_{3,1}.Experience_1 + \beta_{4,1}Z_1 + \varepsilon_1$$

$$\ln Y_2 = \beta_{1,2} + \beta_{2,2}.Education_2 + \beta_{3,2}.Experience_2 + \beta_{4,2}Z_2 + \varepsilon_2$$

The stochastic terms are correlated:

$$\rho = Corr(\varepsilon_1, \varepsilon_2)$$

This can be due to the fact that people partner with similar people and that they have shared experiences. In this chapter, for simplification reasons and because the issue has been dealt with adequately in the microsimulation literature (Galler, 1996 and Baekgaard, 2002), we focus instead on inter-temporal correlation. This is the correlation between earnings of an individual over time.

Inter-temporal correlation

The combination of the deterministic and stochastic parts will determine the position of an individual in the earnings distribution, while changes in these components will determine inter-temporal variability. Utilising a single model allows for changes in earnings to be determined by changes in the explanatory variables. It does however make the assumption that the time variant stochastic component has the same distribution across the whole population. We shall see later that this may not be a valid assumption, as some groups such as workers in marginal employment may have higher stochastic variability than workers in more stable employment. Heteroscedasticity in this parameter may result in some groups having higher than expected inter-temporal simulated variation, with others lower than expected. We may therefore have to correct our models for this heteroscedasticity.

2.2   *Dependent variable: definition of earnings*

One of the issues that concern us in this chapter is the nature of the dependent variable. While we may be interested in lifetime income, in a dynamic microsimulation model where variables are simulated on an annual basis, the variable, annual earnings, is more important. We can define annual earnings as follows:

Annual Earnings = Hourly Earnings x Hours Worked per Week x Weeks Worked per Year plus Lump Sum Payments

Similarly weekly earnings can be defined as

Weekly Earnings = Hourly Earnings x Hours Worked per Week

There are thus a number of different definitions that can be and are used in the literature. While the hourly wage rate can be regarded as the return on human capital, both annual and weekly earnings can be considered as combining labour supply (in terms of hours worked) and the return on human capital. Depending upon the correlation between labour supply and the hourly wage rate, aggregating may have the impact of increasing or decreasing the variability of the dependent variable. Where we may see an effect is in the assumption relating to the distribution of the error term.[2] While hourly earnings typically follow a log-normal distribution, hours and weeks worked frequently exhibit non-normal, multi-modal distributions, which affect the performance of models that make the assumption of log-normality.

The choice of whether the dependent variable is net or gross of the tax-benefit system may also be important given the non-linear nature of the system, but we shall ignore this here as gross variables exist in the datasets considered in this chapter. Lazear (1986) distinguishes between salaried and piece-rate workers, where the earnings of salaried such as government officials depend entirely on their input to the firm at an agreed level in advance, while piece-rate workers such as salesmen are paid on individual or firm output. Other extra "lumpy" components included in annual earnings which may also alter the distribution of earnings include:

- Performance-related pay such as Commission pay, which depends upon performance; Piece rate, which depends directly upon quantity of goods or services produced and Bonuses and Profit Share that depend respectively indirectly and directly upon the performance of the company
- Working hours related pay such as overtime where the actual wage rate may vary with hours worked

Seiler (1984) conducted an empirical study of two "four-digit"[3] manufacturing industries and the outcome showed that workers who receive incentive pay potentially earn higher mean and more "dispersed" earnings than time-paid workers.

Based on the discussion above, it is apparent that bonuses, commissions, profit share and piece rates are theoretically comparable. They are all within the criteria of being dependent on either individual or firm output.

---

2   It should also be noted however that weekly and hourly earnings models are contingent on other parts of the simulation model in ways that annually earnings are not. Consequently, parts of the specifications of the weekly and hourly models may effectively have been suppressed.

3   "Four-digit" relates to the classification of an industry within a dataset – in this case the US Bureau of Labor Statistics set. Four digits provide a more precise definition than a common "two-digit" specification.

Therefore we will describe all these aspects of earnings together in one defi-nition referred to as "piece rates". We still consider salaried pay separately, as we do with hourly pay (including overtime).

Variation in skills and industries dictate the method of payment. High-skilled workers have greater bargaining power in the labour market, and can more easily demand a guaranteed level of income. Hence professional and managerial jobs are more likely to be salaried, which relates to the theory postulated by Seiler, whilst low-skilled jobs are characterized by hourly pay. In terms of salaries, as it is inefficient to constantly re-negotiate the level of pay, it is standard in labour market agreements to negotiate pay rises on a six-monthly or annual basis. Thus, it implies that the flexibility of these earnings, regardless of the business cycle, may not be that variable. Piece rates however are likely to be affected by the business cycle. Therefore they are likely to be more variable than salaried earnings.

Overtime may also affect earnings variability. Hourly-paid workers may receive overtime, while salaried workers usually do not. Bell and Hart (1999) for example show that plant/machine operatives are paid for virtu-ally every hour they work, whilst managerial/professional workers receive approximately 9/10ths of what they should be paid if they were paid for overtime hours at work. As overtime may also be affected by the business cycle, one may again see a differential degree of dispersion due to this variable.

Card (1995) looked at real wage cyclicality and found that the correla-tion between annual hours and unemployment rates, which is an indicator of movements in the business cycle, could result in an hours curve. The hourly wage is found to have the lowest elasticity with respect to the business cycle, followed by an annual hours measure. Annual earnings are shown to have the highest elasticity in respect to the business cycle backing up his assertion. Furthermore, analyses of different worker types and industrial sectors show that better educated workers have a lower elasticity than less educated workers, and similarly older workers are less prone to the busi-ness cycle than younger workers. The private sector is more sensitive to the business cycle.

Devereux (2001) identifies a further caveat. In economic booms some workers may take on extra employment. In this period they are likely to exhibit a rise in earnings – thus their pay is strongly pro-cyclical. When comparing to other groups who do not obtain extra employment in booms their pattern of earnings will be markedly different. Often professionals are bound by their contract to work for their employer only. Therefore, they are less likely than other groups to take on extra employment in periods of economic prosperity.

Focusing on workers who moved in and out of the workforce regularly, Bils (1985) found that wages were in fact very pro-cyclical for workers who move in and out of the workforce and less so for those who remain in stable employment. Another study by Solon et al. (1994) using the PSID found that using panel data to analyse real wage cyclicality has advantages over the pooled cross-section approaches employed. Using repeated cross-sections may skew the measured elasticity of real wages by a sizeable proportion.

3   Data and methodology

In this section we describe the datasets used in this analysis. In order to assess the robustness of the earnings models to different assumptions, we utilize two different national datasets for Ireland and the UK that have been used as part of two dynamic microsimulation model developments.

The Irish data are the *Living in Ireland Survey* (LII) collected 1994-2001, while the UK data are the British Household Panel Survey (BHPS) from 1991 to 2000. The accounting period for the dependent variable used in both datasets depends upon the typical pay period (week, fortnight or monthly normally). We can derive hourly earnings by dividing by the hours worked per week and derive annual earnings by multiplying by the number of weeks worked within the year. In both cases, we utilize gross earnings. The Irish data allow for *usual* annual earnings to be separated from *total* annual earnings that may include bonuses, commissions and overtime etc, while the UK data do not allow this. While self-employment incomes can be identified, the focus of this chapter is on employee income. Also our analysis, for reasons of brevity, is restricted to male earnings. Figure 1 details the age-earnings distribution for different education groups in Ireland and the UK, exhibiting the expected inverted u shape, with positive returns to education. The UK age-earnings distribution is flatter than the Irish distribution. In Figures 1 and 3 the scale is relative to the average for the population (average = 1).

Figure 1:   Earnings distribution

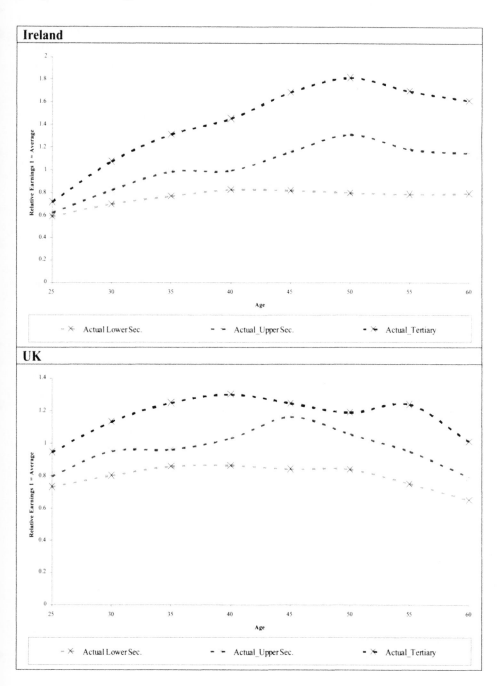

We utilize dummies for detailed educational attainment to represent the contribution of schooling to human capital. For historical reasons due to the variables that have been derived for the creation of earnings modules in the two national dynamic microsimulation models, we utilize slightly different definitions of experience, with the Irish data using a measure of lifetime years in and out of work, while the UK data simply use a proxy, potential experience which is a function of age and years in education.

Both models also contain variables that describe the nature of the job individual employees have:

- Occupation (based upon Standard Occupational Classifications – SOC)
- Industry (16 categories in Ireland and 9 categories in the UK)
- Permanent contract
- Public sector
- Membership of an occupational pension
- Part-time work

Region (NUTS II) and time dummies are also included in the models for each country.

Methodology

In the chapter thus far, we have identified a number of objectives for earnings modules in dynamic microsimulation models that simulated earnings should reflect

- The distribution of earnings relative to observed characteristics
- Changes in the cross-section earnings distribution over time
- Patterns of observed earnings mobility

We have also illustrated a range of issues that may affect these objectives

- The accounting period of earnings
- The definition of earnings in terms of the inclusion of lump-sum components
- The impact of mobility into and out of the labour market
- The impact of heteroscedasticity in terms of differential unobserved earnings variability of different population groups.

We estimate 8 different panel data econometric models to assess the impact of these characteristics detailed in Figure 2. A random effects panel data model is employed with an AR(0) specification of the stochastic time-variant error. While the models may not necessarily satisfy the Hausman test, as the individual effect may be correlated with the explanatory variables, we nevertheless continue to use random effects models instead of the fixed effects specification. This is because the population is not fixed in a dynamic microsimulation model and so the fixed effects model will not allow us to generate new individual effects. Similarly many of the labour market variables are largely time-invariant or at least vary very little and so the result is that much of the variability in the fixed effects model would be contained within the unobserved individual effect rather than in the explanatory variables and so is not appropriate for dynamic microsimulation.

Regression results for each of the 8 models are reported in Tables 2 and 3 in the Annex. Note that for models 5-8, we report two sets of estimates as in correcting for heteroscedasticity we group the population into two clusters containing characteristics that have respectively high and low variability. For space reasons, we do not report estimates for occupation, industry, region and wave dummies – these are however available from the authors on request. The results in general have expected signs with earnings rising with education and experience (with a falling rate of increase), negative in years out of work. Public sector, occupational pension membership and permanent contract are consistent with formal employment and all experience positive coefficients, while part-time work, more associated with marginal employment, has a negative coefficient. We also note that the R^2 is about 50% in Ireland and about 40% in the UK reflecting the better labour market histories used in the Irish data. The rho statistic varies between 0.5 to 0.8 meaning that between 50% and 80% of stochastic variability is accounted for by the time-invariant individual effect. As a result only about 10% to 25% of variability is unaccounted either by the deterministic component or the individual effect derived from the panel data.

While the objective of developing earnings modules in this chapter is to simulate earnings within dynamic microsimulation models, it may be difficult to evaluate the performance of the different modules simulated within one of these models. This is because we may not be able to differentiate between the impact of the earnings module and the interaction with other modules with the microsimulation model. For this reason, we simulate earnings, holding all other variables such as the labour market constant by simulating just earnings within the panel datasets on which the equations are estimated.

Figure 2: Models to be tested

1. Static, annual earnings (including lump sum) for all employees, not adjusting for heteroscedasticity
2. Static, annual earnings (including lump sum) for all employees (*who are in all 8 waves*), not adjusting for heteroscedasticity
3. Static, annual earnings (including lump sum) for all employees (*who are not new entrants to the labour market*), not adjusting for heteroscedasticity
4. Static, annual earnings (including lump sum) for all employees (who are not new entrants to the labour market), *adjusting for heteroscedasticity by estimating separate models for high and low variability*
5. Static, annual earnings (*not including lump sum*) for all employees (who are not new entrants to the labour market), adjusting for heteroscedasticity by estimating separate models for high and low variability
6. Static, *weekly earnings* (*including lump sum*) for all employees (who are not new entrants to the labour market), adjusting for heteroscedasticity by estimating separate models for high and low variability
7. Static, *hourly earnings* (including lump sum) for all employees (who are not new entrants to the labour market), adjusting for heteroscedasticity by estimating separate models for high and low variability
8. *Dynamic, annual earnings* (including lump sum) for all employees (who are not new entrants to the labour market), not adjusting for heteroscedasticity

4 Results I: simulating earnings and heteroscedasticity

The first model formulation to be tested is similar to the first models the authors estimated for the UK and Irish dynamic microsimulation models and as outlined in Table 1, the model is similar to those used across the literature, where a single static panel data earnings model is estimated without correction for heteroscedasticity. Figure 3 reports the age-education earnings relationship (as measured by the ratio of the average earnings for each group relative to the average for the population) for both actual and simulated earnings. The results are good for both countries for this model formulation. This is also the case for the other model formulations, so we do not report the intra-personal measures again.

Figure 3: Education and age-specific variation – Model 1

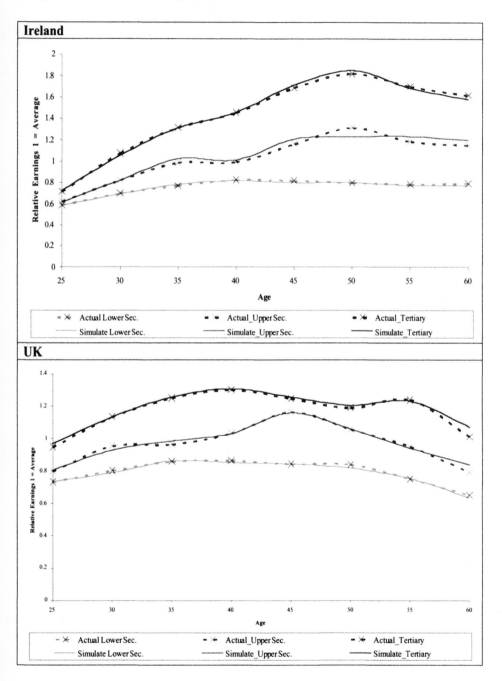

Figure 4:   Inter-temporal and cross-section distribution – Model 1

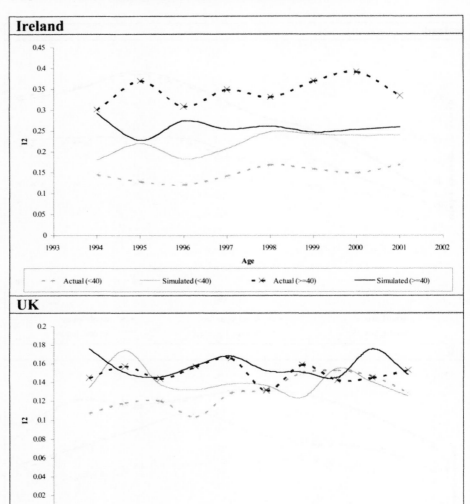

Inter-Temporal Variation – Corr(y_t, y_{t-1})		
	Ireland	**UK**
Actual	0.699	0.836
Simulated	0.894	0.864

In Figure 4, we consider how the model formulation performs in terms of its ability to recreate the changing cross-sectional earnings distribution over time and inter-temporal mobility. We measure cross-section variation using the half squared coefficient of variation (also referred to as the I_2 index of inequality),[4] while we use the correlation between current and lagged earnings as our measure of inter-temporal variability. Figure 4 highlights that, especially for the Irish case, the simulated cross-sectional earnings have quite a different distribution to the actual population. We compare actual and simulated variability for those aged over 40 and those aged 40 and under, finding that in Ireland there is a convergence to a mean variability across years that does not reflect the heteroscedasticity in age, while this is also the case in the UK, particularly for the early years of the simulation. The inter-temporal correlation is also poor in Ireland, where the observed correlation is about 75% of the observed correlation. As a result we are achieving less inertia, i.e. more mobility year on year in our simulations than observed in the actual data. The UK correlation of simulated earnings is about 95% of the observed correlation.

One potential reason for this poor performance is that model 1 is estimated across all employees. However new entrants may have more variability in their wages than the rest of the population. The time-variant stochastic error is designed to account for the unexplained inter-temporal variation that occurs in earnings for individuals such as pay rises that occur at a faster or slower pace than similar workers in the labour market. However, when we include long-term employees and new entrants, we are effectively combining two groups with different earnings distributions.

In model 2, we remove this as an issue by estimating a model and simulating only for the subgroup who remained in work for 8 or more years of the sample period, avoiding issues related to high volatility in earnings of marginal workers who enter and exit the labour market. In Tables 2 and 3 in the Annex, we notice a large fall in the standard deviation of the time variant stochastic term v for Ireland. There is much less of an issue in

---

4   I_2 is derived from the general formula for the Generalized Entropy Class of inequality measures and is given by half of the square of the

$$\text{Coefficient of Variation} = \frac{1}{\overline{y}}\left[\frac{1}{n}\sum_{i=1}^{n}(y_i - \overline{y})^2\right]^{1/2}$$

where the y's are the log of individual incomes and $\overline{y}$ is the arithmetic average in a population of n individuals. If everyone has the mean income, then the value is zero.

the British data. In Figure 5, we report our measures for this model. The performance for Ireland is substantially better. Although not perfect, the simulated cross-section variation tracks the actual cross-section better for under 40's. The correlation between simulated current and lagged earnings now is about 90% of the actual correlation in Ireland. Meanwhile in the UK, the cross-sectional performance is quite good, with a similar performance in terms of inter-temporal variability.

Using model 2 as the basis of simulating earnings, poses us some problems. While we can identify individuals who have worked at least 8 years in a row, as we need to simulate earnings for all individuals, we would be required to also estimate models for those who worked 7 years or less, resulting more of the same problem. One solution is to separately estimate an entry wage model for new entrants to the labour market and then to simulate earnings separately for those who are already in the labour market. In model 3, therefore we examine the performance of a model that falls between model 1, which contains all employees, and model 3, which contains only those who are in work for 8 years or more. Model 3 contains only those who have entered the labour market in the previous year. Figure 6 highlights that the performance of this model is slightly worse than model 2, but significantly better in the case of Ireland than model 1.

In Section 2, we highlighted a number of reasons in the literature why one might expect differential earnings distributions and mobility for different parts of the labour market. In Figure 7, we plot for a number of characteristics, the average variation in earnings by different characteristics. We regard low variability as groups who have a standard deviation less than 90% of the population standard deviation and high variability of the standard deviation of earnings for the group is more than 10% higher than the population standard deviation.

While no age group in the UK has a variability very different from the population, in Ireland the 50-55 and 65+ age groups have low variability, while the 25-30 year-old age group has high variability.

Figure 5:   Inter-temporal and cross-section distribution – Model 2

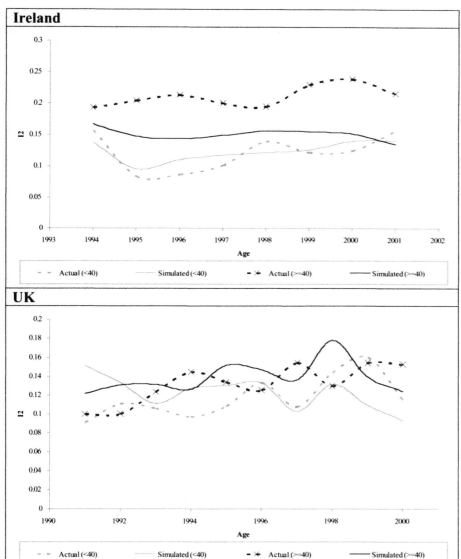

Inter-Temporal Variation – Corr(y_t, y_{t-1})		
	Ireland	**UK**
Simulated	0.821	0.828
Actual	0.910	0.877

Figure 6:   Inter-temporal and cross-section distribution – Model 3

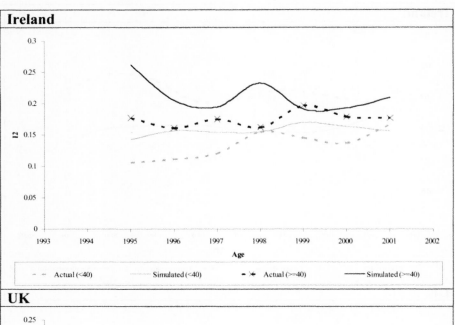

Inter-Temporal Variation – Corr(y_t, y_{t-1})		
	Ireland	**UK**
Actual	0.769	0.834
Simulated	0.894	0.864

Figure 7: **Heteroscedasticity – variation of earnings by explanatory variable**

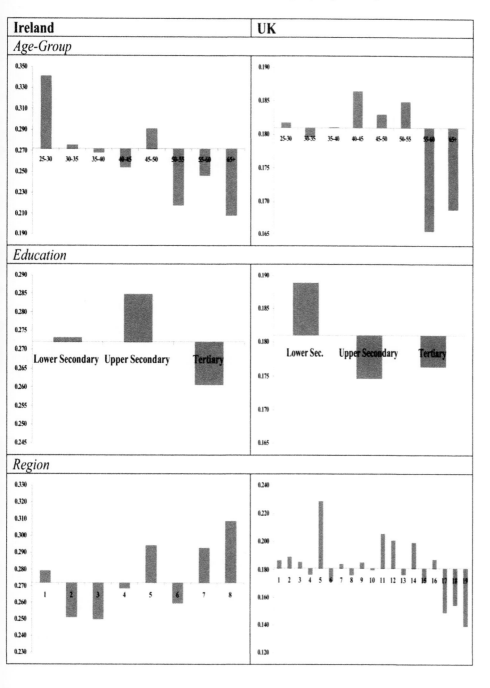

Figure 7 (continued)

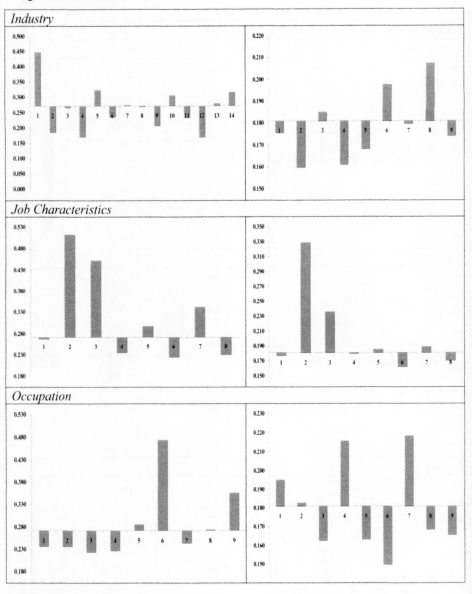

- For the regional categories in Ireland: 1. Border, 2. Dublin, 3. Mid-East, 4. Midlands, 5. Mid-West, 6. South-East, 7. South-West, 8. West. For the regional categories in the UK: 1. Inner London, 2. Outer London, 3. Rest of South East, 4. South West, 5. East Anglia, 6. East Midlands, 7. West Midlands, 8. Rest of West, 9. Greater Manchester, 10. Merseyside, 11. Rest of North, 12. South Yorkshire, 13. West Yorkshire, 14. Rest of Yorkshire.
- For the industry categories in Ireland: 1. Agriculture, 2. Mining and quarrying, 3. Manufacturing, 4. Electricity, gas and water supply, 5. Construction , 6. Wholesale, retail,

Amongst education groups, all groups in both countries have close to population standard deviations. This is noteworthy as education is often used to cluster employees to estimate separate earnings equations and error structures (see for example Harding, 1993 and Zaidi, 2004). Given the lack of significant differences between groups, a different type of clustering may be more effective.

In Ireland amongst the regions, only the Western region had a differential variability higher than the population, while in the UK, Wales, Scotland and Northern Ireland had a variability lower than the population with East Anglia, Rest of the North and South Yorkshire having a higher variability.

In the UK, employees in the energy and manufacturing sectors had lower wage variability, perhaps due to wage bargaining, while banking and insurance having a higher variability due in part to commissions and bonuses. Ireland has substantial variability across sectors in earnings with Mining and quarrying; Electricity, gas and water supply; Wholesale, retail, repair; Financial intermediation; Public administration and defence; Education having lower variability, while Agriculture; Construction; Real estate, renting& business activities; Other Services having higher variability.

Amongst other job characteristics, UK and Irish public servants have lower earnings variability, while in Ireland permanent workers and members of occupational schemes have lower variability, while part-time workers have higher variability in both countries. Amongst occupations, high-skilled white- and blue-collar workers have low variability in Ireland, but only associate professionals and skilled agricultural workers in the UK have lower variability. These results indicate that marginal workers will tend to have higher earnings variability than those working in more stable employment.

401

---

repair, 7. Hotels and restaurants, 8. Transport, storage and communication, 9. Financial intermediation, 10. Real estate, renting and business activities, 11. Public administration and defence, 12. Education , 13. Health and Social Work , 14. Other services. For the industry categories in the UK: 1 Agriculture, 2 Mining and quarrying, 3 Manufacturing, 4 Electricity, gas and water supply, 5 Construction , 6 Wholesale, retail, repair , 7 Hotels and restaurants, 8 Transports, storage and communication, 9 Financial intermediation.

- For the job characteristics categories in both Ireland and the UK: 1. Full-time, 2. Part-Time, 3. Not-Permanent, 4. Permanent, 5. Private Sector, 6. Public Sector, 7. Not Occupational Pension, 8. Occupational Pension.
- For the occupation categories in both Ireland and the UK: 1. Managers, senior officials, legislators, 2. Professionals, 3. Technicians and associated professionals, 4. Clerks , 5. Service, shop and sales workers, 6. Skilled agricultural/fishery workers, 7. Skilled craft/ trades workers , 8. Plant/machine operators/assemblers, 9. Elementary occupations.

Figure 8: Inter-temporal and cross-section distribution – Model 4

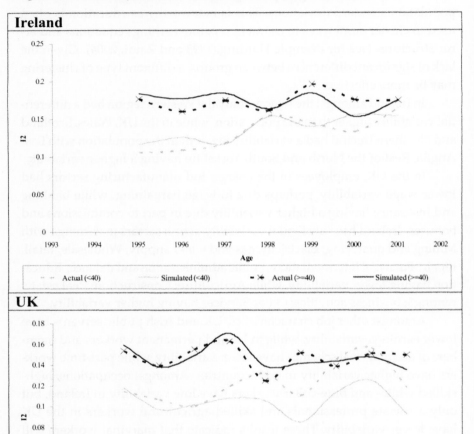

Inter-Temporal Variation – Corr(y_t, y_{t-1})		
	Ireland	**UK**
Actual	0.871	0.861
Simulated	0.899	0.864

In developing a new model, we need to be aware of the practical consideration of trying to minimize the number of earnings equations that are estimated. As individuals may move between job characteristics during their career, if these were all associated with different earnings equations, then we may find that their simulated earnings in a dynamic microsimulation model may jump around substantially. We therefore in model 4 opt for a compromise solution, classifying an individual as being in a "low variability" cluster if they are classified in one of the low income variability classes, with the remainder in another group. We then estimate two equations as outlined in model 4 in Tables 2 and 3. Figure 8 outlines the results for model 4, where we can observe an excellent outcome with the cross-sectional distributions simulated being very similar to the actual trend. Also the correlation between current and lagged variable is within 3.5% points in both countries. In all cases the inter-temporal correlations are high as expected due to the fact that inter-temporal variability in the explanatory variables is low and due to the high proportion of the error accounted for by the permanent component in both models.

403

5   Results II: dependent variable

The existence of bonuses, commissions and overtime payments may affect the distribution of earnings and the performance of an earnings model. Unfortunately, we cannot separately identify these variables for all waves in the BHPS, therefore in Figure 9, we report only the situation for Ireland. While the major improvement occurred when clustering the population into high and low variability groups, simulating earnings excluding lump-sum payments improves the model again, reducing the gap in correlations to 2%.

In Section 2, we highlighted that the choice of the accounting period such as hourly, weekly and annual earnings may influence the performance of an earnings model due in part to the fact that the labour supply may have a different distribution to that of hourly wages. In Figure 9, we consider a variant of model 4, this time simulating weekly earnings, which also by definition exclude lump-sum payments. Again, we see a further marginal improvement, with the gap in correlations down to within 0.75%. In moving to an hourly accounting period, the Irish model improves again to produce almost exactly the same results in actual and simulated. The UK model worsens slightly however.

Figure 9: Inter-temporal and cross-section distribution – Model 5

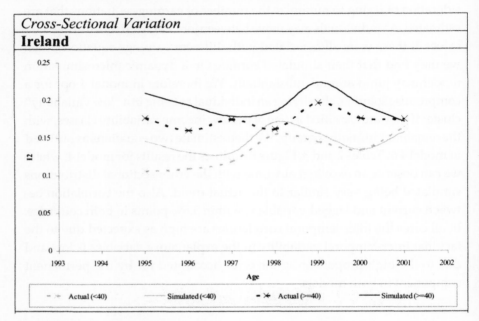

Inter-Temporal Variation – Corr(y_t, y_{t-1})	
	Ireland
Actual	0.889
Simulated	0.907

Figure 10: Inter-temporal and cross-section distribution – Model 6

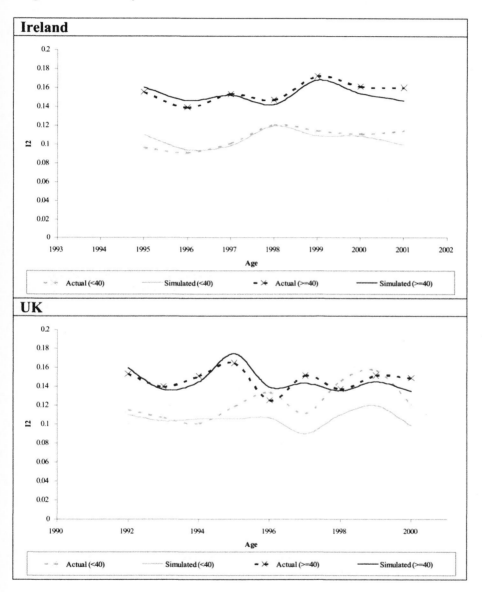

Inter-Temporal Variation – Corr(y_t, y_{t-1})		
	Ireland	**UK**
Actual	0.911	0.864
Simulated	0.9168	0.865

Figure 11: Inter-temporal and cross-section distribution – Model 7

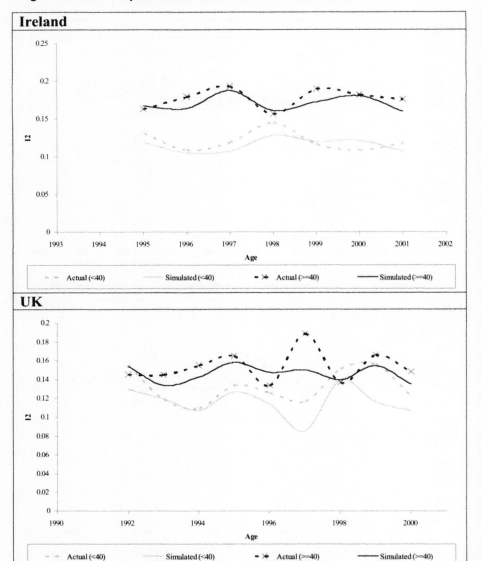

Inter-Temporal Variation – Corr(y_t, y_{t-1})		
	Ireland	**UK**
Actual	0.875	0.7425
Simulated	0.873	0.7279

6   Results III: dynamics

In this last section, we consider a variant where lagged earnings are included as an explanatory variable. We must realize however that including a lagged dependent variable will bias the estimates and so it would be preferable to use a different estimator such as a GMM estimator. However the simulation properties of equations based upon these estimators are not well-known in the microsimulation literature and so we do not for now utilize estimators of this kind, especially given the satisfactory outcome from the random effects models used thus far. The cross-sectional trends are slightly worse than in model 7. In Ireland the inter-temporal correlation is marginally better, but the UK correlation is substantially worse.

Even despite the worsening of the performance of the model, perhaps due to biases due to the lagged dependent variable, there are a number of reasons why one may be slow to utilize dynamic models in dynamic microsimulation models. Firstly the lagged variable will tend to dominate the impact of other explanatory variables. This may not be a problem if the distribution of the explanatory variables stays constant. However if one wished to change the pattern of explanatory variables as part of a scenario analysis, for example to simulate an alternative sectoral structure, one may not observe the expected response due to multicollinearity in explanatory variables. Therefore a dynamic model may not be sufficiently flexible for a dynamic microsimulation model. It may be preferable instead to utilize a more sophisticated error-component structure, e.g. AR(X); ARMA(X,Y), where one can capture some of the dynamic attributes of the data, but while maintaining the influence of explanatory variables in the simulation.

Figure 12: Inter-temporal and cross-section distribution – Model 8

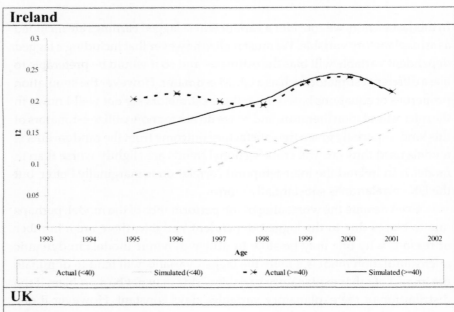

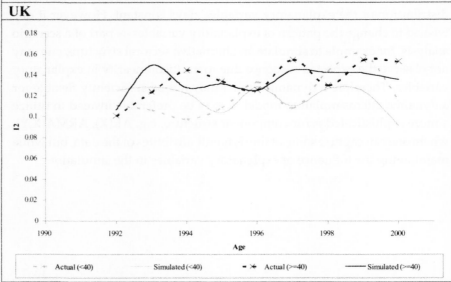

Inter-Temporal Variation – Corr(y_t, y_{t-1})		
	Ireland	**UK**
Actual	0.910	0.819
Simulated	0.910	0.877

7 Summary and conclusions

This chapter has looked at the methods applied in econometric models of earnings, how these methods are applied to dynamic microsimulation models, before investigating theoretical aspects of earnings. Methods applied to dynamic microsimulation models have followed the standard Mincer equation approach, but may fail to appropriately separate out differentials driven by economic conditions, where workers in receipt of some form of piece-rate observe greater variance in earnings over time. Understanding the dynamics of earnings is crucial for dynamic microsimulation models, such that the effects of policy modelling are appropriately understood.

We found that a number of choices that are not usually incorporated into dynamic microsimulation models have very important impacts upon the performance of earnings equations, namely

- Estimating earnings models on a subset of the population that did not enter the labour market in the previous year.
- Splitting the sample into a low earnings variability and another group to avoid problems associated with heteroscedasticity.
- Smaller improvements were found when using a narrower definition of income excluding lump-sum payments and using a shorter accounting period such as weekly earnings. Moving to hourly earnings had less of an impact. Difficulties and inflexibilities arose when trying to model a dynamic earnings model.

References

Baekgaard, H. (2002) 'Modelling the dynamics of the distribution of earned income', NAT-SEM.

Bell, D./Hart, R. (1999) 'Unpaid work', *Economica* 66: 271-290.

Bils, M. (1985) 'Real wages over the business cycle: evidence from panel data', *Journal of Political Economy* 93 (4): 666-689.

Borjas, G. (2003) *Labour Economics*, 3rd Edition, McGraw Hill.

Card, D. (1995) 'The wage curve: a review', *Journal of Economic Literature* 33: 785-799.

Devereux, P. (2001) 'The cyclicality of real wages within employer-employee matches', *Industrial and Labor Relations Review* 54 (4): 835-850.

Galler, H. (1996) 'Microsimulation of pension reform proposals: modelling the earnings of couples', in: Harding, A. (ed.), *Microsimulation and Public Policy*. Amsterdam: North Holland.

Harris, A./Sabelhaus, J. (2003) 'Projecting longitudinal earnings patterns for long-run policy analysis', Congressional Budget Office Technical Paper Series, 2003-2.

Harding, A. (1993) *Lifetime Income Distribution and Redistribution: Applications of a Microsimulation Model*. London: North-Holland.

Hart, R. (2004) *The Economics of Overtime Working*. Cambridge University Press.

Lazear, E. (1986) 'Salaries and piece rates', *Journal of Business* 59 (3): 405-431.

Mincer, J. (1974) *Schooling, Experience and Earnings*. New York: Columbia University Press.

O'Donoghue, C. (2001) 'Dynamic microsimulation: a survey', *Brazilian Electronic Journal of Economics* 4 (2): 45-61.

Seiler, Eric (1984) 'Piece rate vs. time rate: the effect of incentives on earnings', *The Review of Economics and Statistics* 66 (3): 363-376.

Solon, G./Barsky, R./Parker, J. (1994) 'Measuring the cyclicality of real wages: how important is composition bias?', *The Quarterly Journal of Economics* 109 (1): 3-25.

Zaidi, A. (2004), 'Estimation of earnings in the SAGE dynamic microsimulation model', SAGE Technical Note No. 10.

Annex – Regression Estimates for Ireland and the UK

Table 2:   Regression Estimates Ireland

Model	1	2	3	4	4	5	5	6	6	7	7	8
Cluster	1	2	3	0	1	0	1	0	1	0	1	1
Explanatory Variables												
Primary Cert. or equivalent	0.074 *	0.428	0.737	0.036 **	0.009 *	0.219	0.005 *	0.224	0.131 *	0.109	0.109 *	0.08
Some 2nd level, no exams	0.078 *	0.535	-0.136 **	0.082 *	0.052 *	0.165	0.047 *	0.135	0.14 *	0.002	0.075 *	-0.085
Group Cert. or equivalent	0.129	0.484	-0.093 **	0.12	0.107 *	0.107	0.106 *	0.111	0.215 *	-0.036	0.166 *	-0.124
Inter Cert. or equivalent	0.2	0.612	-0.107 **	0.178	0.14 *	0.232	0.135 *	0.235	0.234 *	0.112	0.189 *	-0.022
Junior Cert. or equivalent	0.189	0.589	-0.086 **	0.22	0.171 *	0.239	0.148 *	0.244	0.21 *	0.053	0.123 *	-0.034
Leaving Cert	0.29	0.724	-0.092 **	0.254	0.17 *	0.4	0.16 *	0.395	0.273 *	0.266	0.224 *	0.141
Post Leaving (PLC)	0.229	0.914	-0.086 **	0.214	0.196	0.23	0.183	0.203	0.293 *	0.085	0.273 *	0.044
Diploma	0.374	0.926	-0.018 **	0.334	0.293 *	0.481	0.278 *	0.48	0.394 *	0.368	0.331 *	0.238
Primary Degree	0.54	1.038	-0.037 **	0.508	0.402 *	0.714	0.385 *	0.711	0.521 *	0.599	0.455 *	0.513
Higher degree	0.669	1.178	0 ***	0.616	0.45 *	0.802	0.42 *	0.799	0.57 *	0.706	0.493 *	0.643
Years Worked	0.048 **	0.052 *	0 ***	0.042 **	0.04 ***	0.046 **	0.04 ***	0.045 **	0.039 **	0.041 **	0.036 **	0.044 **
Years Worked^2	-0.001 **	-0.001 **	0.007 **	-0.001 **	-0.001 **	-0.001 **	-0.001 **	-0.001 **	-0.001 **	-0.001 **	-0.001 **	-0.001 **
Years Not Worked	-0.048 **	-0.054 **	-0.001 **	-0.033 **	-0.035 **	-0.034 **	-0.034 **	-0.034 **	-0.03 **	-0.026 **	-0.014 **	-0.015 **
Years Not Worked^2	0 ***	0.003 ***	-0.007 ***	0 ***	0 ***	0 ***	0 ***	0 ***	0 ***	0 ***	0 ***	0 ***
Part-Time	-0.498 **	-0.299 **	0 ***	-0.395 **	-0.411 *	-0.24	-0.408 *	-0.236 **	-0.153 *	-0.074 *	0.46 **	0.427 *
Permanent Contract	0.275	-0.009 **	-0.24 **	0.268	0.313 **	0.154	0.312 **	0.146 **	0.126 **	0.088 **	0.07 **	0.102 *
Public Sector	0.03 **	0.045 **	0.06 *	0.062 **	0.059 **	0.071 **	0.066 **	0.079 **	0.021 **	0.039 **	0.073 **	0.076 **
Occ. Pension Membership	0.078 *	0.057 *	0.025 **	0.117	0.125 **	0.082 **	0.125 **	0.076 **	0.079 **	0.058 **	0.08 **	0.061 **
Constant	8.452 **	7.981 **	2.436 **	8.668 **	8.556 **	0 ***	0 ***	0 ***	0 ***	0 ***	0 ***	0.83 **
SD of u	0.376	0.255	0	0.356	0.358	0.364	0.353	0.355	0.302	0.3	0.3	0.314
SD of v	0.353	0.219	0.208	0.296	0.306	0.181	0.302	0.176	0.198	0.144	0.228	0.174
Rho	0.531	0.577	0.8	0.591	0.577	0.802	0.576	0.801	0.7	0.812	0.634	0.763
R^2	0.5	0.523	0.8	0.5	0.469	0.536	0.472	0.549	0.483	0.574	0.457	0.615
Sample Size	7926	2654	2320	5872	3946	1911	3942	1908	3942	1908	3938	1907

Table 3: Regression Estimates UK

Model	1	2	3	4		5		6		7		8
Cluster				0	1	0	1	0	1	0	1	1
Explanatory Variables												
GCSE	0.1 **	0.073 **	0.093 **	0.111 **	0.066 **			0.114 **	0.064 **	0.141 **	0.089 **	0.073 **
A Level	0.154 **	0.106 **	0.14 **	0.14 **	0.142 **			0.137 **	0.14 **	0.186 **	0.147 **	0.106 **
Degree	0.236 **	0.186 **	0.226 **	0.231 **	0.235 **			0.238 **	0.234 **	0.279 **	0.248 **	0.186 **
Higher Degree	0.408 **	0.352 **	0.435 **	0.436 **	0.454 **			0.431 **	0.454 **	0.447 **	0.431 **	0.352 **
Years Worked	0.036 **	0.035 **	0.035 **	0.031 **	0.036 **			0.032 **	0.036 **	0.032 **	0.033 **	0.035 **
Years Worked^2	-0.001 **	-0.001 **	-0.001 **	-0.001 **	-0.001 **			-0.001 **	-0.001 **	-0.001 **	-0.001 **	-0.001 **
Part-Time	-0.63 **	-0.488 **	-0.61 **	-0.651 **	-0.579 **			-0.636 **	-0.576 **	0.025	0.01	-0.488 **
Permanent Contract	0.1 **	0.044 **	0.061 **	0.084 **	0.089 **			0.092 **	0.09 **	0.141 **	0.068 **	0.044 **
Public Sector	-0.007	-0.004	-0.007	0 **	0.057 **			0 **	0.057 **	-0.16 **	0.109 **	-0.004
Occupational Pension Membership	0.067 **	0.049 **	0.058 **	0.069 **	0.031 **			0.064 **	0.03 **	0.087 **	0.035 **	0.049 **
Constant	8.857 **	9.002 **	0 **	0 **	9.236 *			5.359 **	0 **	1.565 **	0 **	9.002 **
SD of u	0.315	0.277	0.309	0.32	0.298			0.32	0.296	0.325	0.289	0.277
SD of v	0.203	0.199	0.193	0.203	0.156			0.2	0.156	0.218	0.162	0.199
Rho	0.706	0.659	0.719	0.711	0.785			0.718	0.782	0.689	0.76	0.659
R^2	0.405	0.378	0.398	0.387	0.424			0.385	0.425	0.374	0.417	0.378
Sample Size	13825	8581	10468	6261	4207			6206	4175	6618	4156	8581

Chapter 16

Continuous-time Microsimulation in Longitudinal Analysis

Frans Willekens

1   Introduction

In longitudinal analysis, individuals are followed in time and are observed either continuously or at points in time. The time to event, the sequence of events and the factors that influence timing and sequence constitute the object of study. Time is a continuous variable (exact time) or discrete variable (time interval). Longitudinal data are used to estimate parameters of event history or life history models. Individual life histories can be represented by sequences of states and sequences of events, that are transitions between states, and described by multistate transition models. The parameters of these models are transition intensities when time is represented by a continuous variable and transition probabilities when time is discrete (for details, see Willekens, 2001). Microsimulation contributes to longitudinal data analysis in a number of ways (Wolf, 1986, 2001). First, it generates individual event histories that are fully consistent with a set of transition intensities (probabilities). Second, it produces estimates of the full distribution of an outcome, in addition to the expected value that is produced analytically by most models. Third, it is helpful in examining the potential seriousness of defective data. Fourth, it may play a role in the imputation of missing

The research is part of the MicMac project, an international (European) project funded by the European Commission in the context of the Sixth Framework Programme. For details, see the MicMac website www.micmac-projections.org. I like to thank Dr. Jutta Gampe, Max Planck Institute for Demographic Research, Rostock, for extensive comments on an earlier draft. I also like to thank Douglas Wolf, a referee and the editors for their comments.

data. These contributions are enhanced when microsimulation is viewed as a form of sampling of a virtual population, an approach advocated by e.g. Wolf (2001) and adopted in this chapter.

Microsimulation in continuous time resolves three important problems of discrete-time microsimulation. The first is how to determine the sequence of events (transitions) rather than the state occupancies at successive points in time. The second is the precise measurement of the lengths of episodes between events. In discrete-time microsimulation the duration between events can be determined only approximately, whereas it can be determined precisely in continuous-time microsimulation. The third is how to handle multiple transitions during a same interval. In discrete-time microsimulation, multiple transitions during an interval are either omitted or assumptions about the ordering and the timing of the events are imposed exogenously. In continuous-time microsimulation, the theory of competing risks determines the timing and sequence. That allows a more accurate study of temporal sequence of events than in discrete time analyses. In addition the theory allows to model complex event sequences and interactions between events. The fact that microsimulation models in discrete time are not able to handle complex and interdependent event sequences is viewed as an important limitation (Zaidi and Rake, 2001: 19). The fourth problem that continuous-time microsimulation resolves is related to the third. It is the estimation of the number of events during an interval. In addition to resolving these problems, continuous-time microsimulation paves the way to an integrative framework that combines the *analysis* of life history data and the *synthesis* of life histories. That framework is rooted in probability theory and statistical theory and is extensively documented in the literature on survival analysis and event history analysis (see e.g. Blossfeld and Rohwer, 2002; Klein and Moeschberger, 2003; Andersen and Keiding, 2002; Putter et al., 2007; Meira-Machado et al., 2009). By adopting the established framework, microsimulation is embedded in event history analysis, which is an aim worth pursuing (see also Wolf, 1986 and Galler, 1997).

In event history models (also known as duration models, survival models and transition models) the variables of interest are the (waiting) time to event and sequences of events and states occupied. The time to event is a random variable. The distribution of the values of the random variable is described by the distribution function, the survival function, the probability density function and the hazard function. The *inverse distribution function* or *quantile function* is of prime importance in continuous-time microsimulation. The quantile function translates a probability into a real number, whereas the more commonly used distribution function and survival function translate a real number into a probability. The real number is the (waiting) time to event.

The chapter is organized as follows. Section 2 describes the method for generating waiting times to events from duration models. The approach is to use the inverse distribution function of the duration model. Once the function is specified, the generation of waiting times is straightforward. Section 3 presents numerical illustrations. Three illustrations are considered. The first is a simple one: a single event during a period of a given duration. The second illustration is a full multistate transition model with three states: healthy, disabled and dead. The multistate model is a continuous-time Markov model. That model, combined with a random generation of waiting times to transition, produces lifepaths for members of a virtual population. In this illustration the virtual population is homogeneous. The third illustration considers a heterogeneous population. Individuals are characterized by covariates. Some members of the virtual population participate in an intervention programme that includes prevention and treatment. The illustration expresses the nature and level of intervention in terms of the transition rates and assesses the impact of the prevention and treatment programmes on the probability of disability, the time at onset of disability and the numbers of years with disability. Section 4 concludes the chapter. Continuous-time microsimulation is implemented in a number of simulation models. They are listed in the Annex.

2   Inverse distribution or quantile function

The quantile function translates a probability into a real number. In the context of dynamic microsimulation it translates a probability of a transition into a (waiting) time to transition. This section presents the general method and applications to a few well-known transition models. Let U denote a random variable following a uniform distribution on the interval from 0 to 1: $U \sim U[0,1]$. Let T be a random variable measuring the time to an event or transition, where transition refers to a direct transition from an origin state to a destination state. The distribution of T is $F(t)$ with $F(t)$ the probability that T is less than or equal to t, i.e. the probability that the transition occurs in the interval from 0 to t. The survival function is $S(t) = 1 - F(t)$. At time t, i.e. during the interval from t to t+dt, the transition occurs at a rate

$$\mu(t) = -\frac{1}{S(t)}\frac{dS(t)}{dt}$$. The rate is the hazard rate or transition rate. Hence

$$S(t) = \exp\left[-\int_0^t \mu(\tau)\,d\tau\right] = \exp\left[-H(t)\right]$$

where H(t) is the cumulative hazard function.

The distribution function maps a real number (a particular value t of the random variable T) into a probability. The real number that is mapped into a probability is the *quantile* of the random variable (see Evans et al., 2000: 5). Hence, t is the quantile of T. With t is associated a probability, α say, and the distribution function gives the probability that T does not exceed t. The inverse distribution function or *quantile function* maps a probability (α) into a real number (t). In other words it maps a realization of U (denoted by α) into a realization of T (denoted by t). The inverse distribution function of T, denoted by $F^{-1}(t)$ and $G(\alpha)$, is the value of t (quantile) such that the probability that T takes on a value less than or equal to t, is α: $\Pr\{T \le G(\alpha)\} = \alpha = F(G(\alpha)) = F(t)$. $G(\alpha)$ gives the value t for which $F(t) = \alpha$. The quantile $G(\alpha)$ is the 100α percentile. The inverse survival function $Z(\alpha)$ is the quantile that is exceeded with probability α: $\Pr\{T > Z(\alpha)\} = \alpha = S(Z(\alpha))$. Inverse distribution functions are widely used in statistics, for instance to determine confidence intervals. Note that $Z(\alpha) = G(1-\alpha)$.

The inverse distribution function is used to generate random numbers from the distribution of a random variable. If G(T) is the inverse distribution function of T, then U = G(T) follows a uniform distribution on the interval from 0 to 1. In a Monte Carlo microsimulation a random draw from a distribution function involves two steps. First, a random value for the probability α is drawn from the uniform distribution U[0,1] (note that G(T) follows the distribution U[0,1]). Second, using the inverse distribution function $G(\alpha)$, the probability is mapped into a real number t, which indicates the timing of the transition. The first step is independent of the transition model used.

Common waiting time distributions include the exponential, the Weibull and the Gompertz distribution. If the waiting time to transition (T) follows an exponential distribution the transition occurs at a constant rate, i.e. the transition rate is constant. If the waiting time distribution is Gompertz, the transition rate changes exponentially with duration. If it is Weibull, the transition rate varies with duration following a power function of duration. The exponential distribution is used in most continuous-time dynamic microsimulation models, e.g. DYNAMOD, SOCSIM, LifePaths and PENSIM. In this section I consider the quantile function of three widely used transition rate models: the exponential model, the Gompertz model and the Cox model.

The exponential distribution is thoroughly documented by Balakrishnan and Basu (1996) and Evans et al. (2000). If T is exponentially distributed, the transition rate is constant. Let μ denote the constant transition rate. The survival function is $S(t) = \exp[-\mu t]$ and the distribution function is $F(t) = 1 - \exp[-\mu t]$. The inverse distribution function of T is

$$F^{-1}(t) = G(\alpha) = -\frac{\ln[1-\alpha]}{\mu}.$$

For a given transition rate (and the exponential model) it translates a transition probability into a waiting time to transition. With a draw α from a the uniform distribution U[0,1] is associated a time to event $t = G(\alpha)$.

In this section on theory, two distributions are considered that are not applied in this chapter: the Gompertz distribution and the Cox model. The Gompertz distribution of waiting times has two parameters, a scale parameter (μ) and a shape parameter (v). The transition rate changes exponentially; $r(t) = \mu \exp(v\,t)$ (with $\mu \geq 0$). If $v = 0$, the Gompertz distribution reduces to the exponential distribution. The survival function is

$$S(t) = \exp\left[\frac{\mu}{v}(1 - \exp(vt))\right]$$ and the distribution function is $1 - S(t)$.

The quantile function is

$$T = \frac{1}{v}\left[\ln\left(1 - \frac{v}{\mu}\ln(1-U)\right)\right]$$

where $U \sim U[0,1]$ is a random variable the values of which are uniformly distributed in the range from 0 to 1. A random draw from a Gompertz distribution is obtained in two steps, described above. First, a random number α is drawn from a uniform distribution over [0,1]. Second, the value of t is derived from the quantile function. Mueller et al. (1995: 558) generate a sample of waiting times from a Gompertz distribution.

The Cox proportional hazard model is given by $\mu(t|Z) = \mu_0(t)\exp[\beta'Z]$ where t is the time (duration), Z a vector of covariates, β the vector of regression coefficients and $\mu_0(t)$ the baseline hazard function, which is the hazard function for the group of individuals with characteristics equal to the reference categories of the elements of Z. For details on the Cox model, see any textbook on survival analysis or event history analysis. The survival function of the Cox proportional hazard model is $S(t|\mathbf{Z}) = \exp\left[-H_0(t)\exp(\beta'\mathbf{Z})\right]$ where $H_0(t)$ is the cumulative hazard function. The distribution function is $1 - S(t|\mathbf{Z})$. The quantile function of the Cox proportional hazard model is (Bender et al., 2005) $F^{-1}(t|\mathbf{Z}) = G(\alpha|\mathbf{Z}) = H_0^{-1}\left[-\ln(\alpha)\exp(-\beta'\mathbf{Z})\right]$. The quantile function determines the waiting time to a transition that is consistent with a probability of the transition when the probability depends on a constant transition rate and a set of time-independent covariates. The quantile function translates the transition rate (hazard rate) into a waiting time to transition. The translation involves the two steps listed above. The first step translates the transition rate into a realization of a random variable that follows a uniform distribution and the second step translates that realization into a realization of a waiting time distribution following a specific Cox model. For a discussion and application see Bender et al. (2005). A problem is that the Cox model is a semi-parametric model which leaves the baseline hazard unspecified. As a consequence, the cumulative hazard function H_0 is unknown and the inverse cannot be obtained. To obtain waiting times from the transition rates, the baseline hazard function must be specified. If the baseline hazard function is constant, the waiting times generated are exponentially distributed. Bender et al. refer to this model as the Cox-exponential model. They also discuss the Cox-Gompertz and the Cox-Weibull models. If the baseline hazard function is a Gompertz distribution, the transition rate varies exponentially with duration with a level that depends on the covariates.

In longitudinal microsimulation, the entire life course of an individual may be simulated before the simulation of the next individual starts. Waiting times are generated for several competing events and the next event and the time to that event are determined by the smallest waiting time. An alternative is to simulate a segment of life for all individuals before the simulation of the next segment starts. A segment can vary in length from a month to several years. An advantage of this approach is that at the beginning of each segment characteristics of other individuals and the context can be considered in determining transition rates. Segments may refer to windows of observation, periods during which for a given transition rate the duration dependence does not change (e.g. piecewise constant transition rates), and to time periods that are dictated by the application. For instance, demographic projections generally consider periods of one year. Consider duration intervals of length h years. If the waiting time t drawn at random from a waiting time distribution is less than h, the transition occurs during the observation window at time t. If t exceeds h, the transition does not occur. In case of a repeatable event, multiple transitions may occur during a period of h years. Many life events may occur more than once, i.e. job change, childbirth, marriage, and migration. Suppose an event is repeatable and its first occurrence is at t_1 ($t_1 <h$). The event occurs a second time during the interval if a second draw of a random variable from U[0,1] results in a value of t_2 that is less than or equal to $h - t_1$. In that case, the second event occurs at time t_1+t_2.

The assumption of fixed transition rates is for presentation only. Hazard rates are generally assumed to be piecewise constant, i.e. constant during intervals of a given length, usually one or five years. In that case, the exponential distribution is a step function with parameters that differ between intervals. For a particular interval, the random draws from the particular exponential distribution are kept only if the event time is in the interval.

If the event is a repeatable event, it may occur more than once during an interval of length h. Let t_1 denote the time at first occurrence. The probability that the event occurs a second time during the interval is the probability that it occurs during the interval from t_1 to h, which is of length $h - t_1$. That probability is

$$F(h-t_1) = 1 - \exp\left[-\int_{t_1}^{h} \mu(\tau)\, d\tau\right].$$

A random number α is drawn from the uniform distribution U[0,1] and the value of t_2 is determined that is consistent with that random number α. If $t_2 < h - t_1$, the event occurs a second time during the interval h, otherwise it does not. The sequence of events during the interval can be simulated in a similar way.

If t is less than the time till the end of the interval, the event occurs at t. Otherwise the event does not occur.

3   Illustration

Recall that a transition is an event that can be characterized by the time at occurrence, the origin state and the destination state. The origin state is denoted by i, the destination state by j and the waiting time to transition by the random variable T_{ij}. Let time be measured in years and fractions of a year. The rate of transition is μ_{ij}. Assume that the transitions occur in continuous time. Observations on times to transitions are manifestations of T_{ij} and the observed times to transitions are the basis for the statistical estimation of the transition rates. A discussion of the estimation is beyond the scope of this chapter. For methods, see e.g. Blossfeld and Rohwer (2002). The time to event T is generally analysed in terms of its distribution function F(t) and the associated survival function S(t), density function f(t), hazard function $\mu(t)$, quantile function $G(\alpha)$, and expected values of key indicators such as the expected waiting time to a transition E[T]. Note that the named distributions are equivalent and can be transformed one into another. The transition rates estimated from the data may be used to generate life histories that are consistent with the transition rates, using the quantile function. This is equivalent to sampling a virtual population with life histories governed by the empirical transition rates. Expected values serve as benchmarks to assess the results of the microsimulation. For large sample sizes the sample values should coincide with the expected values. This section consists of three subsections. Section 3.1 presents a transition with a single origin and a single destination. Multiple origins and multiple destinations are considered in Section 3.2. The aim is to determine the sequence and dates (times) of transition during the interval from 0 to h and to derive subsequently the length of episodes between transitions. The waiting time distributions are truncated at h. Conditional measures such as the expected waiting time to the event, provided the event occurs before h, are based on the truncated distribution. Section 3.3 introduces covariates and applies a transition model and continuous-time microsimulation to assess the effects of an intervention programme on the life histories of members of the virtual population.

3.1   Single origin and single destination

A simple model of T is the basic exponential transition rate model (see e.g. Blossfeld and Rohwer, 2002, Chapter 4). The exponential distribution has a single parameter that is independent of time or duration. For presentation, I assume a transition rate of $\mu = 0.2$.

The probability of a transition within a period of time is given by the distribution function. The probability of a transition within a year is F(1) = 1-exp(-0.2) = 0.18, i.e. 18%. The expected waiting time to a transition is E[T] = 1/0.2 = 5 years. It is

$$E[T] = \int_0^\infty \exp(-\mu\tau)d\tau = \int_0^\infty \exp(-0.2\tau)d\tau = \left| -\frac{1}{0.2}\exp(-0.2\tau)\right|_0^\infty = \frac{1}{0.2} = 5$$

The median waiting time to the transition, i.e. the time at which there is a 50% chance that the event occurred, is given by the inverse distribution function: $G(0.5) = -\dfrac{\ln[1-0.5]}{0.2} = \dfrac{\ln(2)}{0.2} = 3.5$ years. The probability of a transition reaches 25% at the upper quartile [G(0.25)] which is 1.44 years; the probability of a transition reaches 75% at the lower quartile [G(0.75)] which is 6.9 years. If the transition rate is 0.2, there is a 90% probability that the transition occurs before 11.5 years. Note that the probability that the transition occurs before the expected waiting time is 63.2%. The probability that no transition occurs between the start of the interval and τ ($0 \le \tau \le h$) is the survival function $S(\tau) = \exp[-0.2\,\tau]$.

The expected waiting time to transition during a period of h years is the total time expected to be spent in the origin state during h years. It is

$$E[T] = \int_0^h \exp(-\mu\tau)\,d\tau = \int_0^h \exp(-0.2\tau)\,d\tau = -\frac{h}{0.2}\Big|\exp(-0.2\tau)\Big|_0^h = -\frac{h}{0.2}\big[\exp(-0.2h)-1\big]$$

It is 0.91 if h = 1. The value is relatively high because the probability of experiencing the event during a year is relatively low and the waiting time is one year for persons who do not experience the event during the period of one year.

The expected time spent in the origin state during a period of h years is a weighted average of the expected sojourn time in the presence of a transition and the sojourn time in the absence of a transition: $E[T] = h*S(1) + E_e[T][1 - S(1)]$ where $E_e[T]$ is the expected waiting time to the transition provided the transition occurs during the interval. The sojourn time in the absence of the transition is h years. The expected sojourn time provided the transition occurs is

$E_e[T] = \dfrac{E[T] - hS(1)}{1 - S(1)}$ years. If h = 1, $E_e[T] = 0.48$. Under the exponential model, the transitions are concentrated in the first half of the year. If a transition occurs during a year, the probability that it occurs in the first half of the year is
$F(0.5)/F(1) = \big[1 - \exp(-\tfrac{1}{2}0.1)\big] / \big[1 - \exp(-0.1)\big] = 0.52$, which is 52%.

If the transition is repeatable, it may occur more than once during a period of h years. Suppose the rate is fixed at 0.2. The probability of *at least* two occurrences within a year is 1.75% and the probability of at least three occurrences is 0.11%. The probability of no occurrence during a period of one year is the survival function $\exp(-\mu) = \exp(-0.2) = 0.82$ or 82%. The probability of precisely one occurrence is 16.37% and the probability of exactly two occurrences is 1.64%. The probability of precisely n(t) occurrences during the period from 0 to t is given by the Poisson distribution:

$$\Pr\{N(t) = n(t)\} = \frac{(\mu t)^{n(t)} \exp[-\mu t]}{n(t)!}$$

where n(t)! is factorial n(t) which is the product $1 * 2 * 3 \dots * n(t)$.

The time intervals between occurrences are independent and exponentially distributed. Let D_n denote the duration between the n-1st and the n-th occurrence. The expected length of the interval between any two occurrences is $1/\mu$ (provided the length of "observation" is not constrained to a period of a given length). The time to the occurrence of rank n, T_n, is the sum of independent exponentially distributed variables D_n and is a gamma-distributed random variable. Hence the time to the n-th occurrence is the gamma distribution with parameters μ and n.

Consider a random sample of 1,000 subjects from the virtual population that experiences a single, non-repeatable transition at a constant rate of 0.2 per year. The (waiting) time to transition is drawn from an exponential distribution with parameters $\mu = 0.2$, using the method described above. Figure 1 shows the true survival and hazard distributions and the 'empirical' distributions based on the sample of the virtual population.

Figure 1: The exponential model ($\mu = 0.2$)

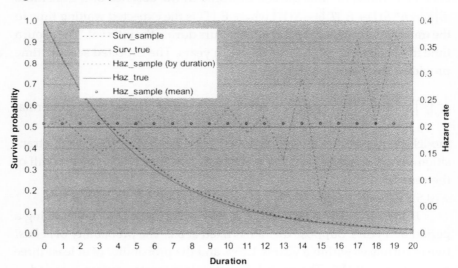

The "empirical" survival distribution (Surv_emp) based on simulated waiting time data is close to the true distribution as expected. For each duration the transition rate is calculated by dividing the number of transitions in the virtual population of 1,000 by the number of survivors in the mid-period. These duration-specific transition rates vary erratically around the true value of 0.2, especially at higher durations, which are drawn less frequently than lower durations. The mean transition rate is 0.204 (Haz_estim). It is estimated from the simulated waiting time data using the basic exponential transition rate model described by Blossfeld and Rohwer (2002, Chapter 4).

Suppose the transition is repeatable and we want to determine for each subject the number of occurrences during a period of one year (h=1). Each subject in the virtual sample is followed (observed) for a period of one year and transitions are recorded. For each transition that occurs, the time to transition and the rank of the transition are recorded. Statistical measures are calculated from the sample and the sample values are compared to expected values that are based on the theoretical distribution. Table 1 shows the results for three samples of size 1,000. The expected values are derived from the exponential distribution and the Poisson distribution, whatever distribution applies. In the first sample, 829 subjects do not experience a transition during the year and 171 experience at least one transition. Most of the subjects who experience at least one transition experience a single transition (152), 18 experience 2 transitions and 1 experiences 3 transitions. The total number of transitions experienced by the 1,000 subjects during that one year is 191 (152 + 18*2 + 1*3). In the second random sample, 203 subjects experience at least one transition. Of them, 189 experience a single transition, 12 experience 2 transitions and 2 have 3 occurrences during the year. The total number of transitions in that year is 219. The *expected* distribution of the subjects by number of transitions is given in the last column. The expected distribution of number of transitions is derived from the Poisson distribution. The number of transitions that the 1,000 subjects may expect to experience during the interval of one year, given the transition rate of 0.2, is 200 (=1,000 * 0.2).

The *expected* time to the first occurrence during the year, provided the transition occurs, is 0.48 years (see above). The expected times to subsequent occurrences are more difficult to obtain analytically. The sample mean of the waiting times to the transition follows directly from the microsimulation (sampling). In Table 1 the values are shown for three samples. Note that in Sample 3, the time to the third occurrence is less than the time to the second occurrence. The reason is that the two subjects that experience three occurrences during the year experience the first and the second occurrence earlier than the other subjects. Note also that the difference between the times at two consecutive occurrences does not yield the interval between transitions. To determine the interval, the times to transitions must be conditioned on a next transition. For instance, the time between the first and second transition should be calculated including only subjects that experience a second transition during the interval. These subjects may experience the first transition at different times (usually earlier) than subjects that do not experience a second transition. To illustrate the relation between the times to transitions and the number of transitions, consider Sample 1. The mean waiting time to the first transition is 0.50. The 18 subjects that experience two transitions during the year experience the first transition at 0.45 years, which is earlier than the overall average of 0.50 years. The 15 subjects with a single transition during the year experience the transition at 0.51 years, on average. The subject with three occurrences during the year experiences the occurrences at 0.51 years, 0.60 years and 0.96 years. The observation that subjects with more transitions during a given period experience the first transition earlier than other subjects is a general one.

Table 1: Number of occurrences and times to transition. Random samples of 1,000 transitions and expected values

Number of subjects by number of occurrences within a year	Random sample 1	Random sample 2	Random sample 3	Expected values
0	829	797	828	819
1	152	189	153	164
2	18	12	17	16
3	1	2	2	1
4	0	0	0	0
5	0	0	0	0
Total	1000	1000	1000	1000
Total number of occurrences within a year	191	219	193	200
Time to transition				
1	0.504	0.478	0.483	0.483
2	0.672	0.705	0.700	
3	0.960	0.740	0.596	
4	-	-	-	
5	-	-	-	

3.2 *Multiple origins and multiple destinations*

If an origin state may have several exits or if a transition may result in one of multiple destinations, each exit or destination may be viewed as competing to be the exit or destination. In other words, the exits or destinations represent competing risks. In the presence of multiple destinations, the destination must be determined in addition to the time to transition. The time to event (transition) is an exponential random variable. It follows an exponential distribution with parameter the total exit rate, which is the sum of destination-specific transition rates (see further). The number of persons selecting a particular destination in a set of possible destinations is a multinomial random variable (or binomial in case of 2 competing risks). The competing risk model is generally formulated in terms of latent times to transition (see e.g. Klein and Moeschberger, 2003: 50ff.).[1] Let T_j, $j = 1, 2,$ ..., J be a random variable denoting the unobservable time to occurrence of the transition to destination j, where J is the total number of destinations. T_j is a latent variable. In the theory of competing risks, observations on transitions consist of (1) the shortest time to transition, i.e. $t = \min (t_1, t_2, ..., t_J)$ and (2) the destination. The destination is represented by the random variable S. If a transition to state j has taken place at t_j, then t_j is a realization of T and the destination is j (S = j). The basic competing risk parameter is the hazard rate for risk j

$$\mu_j(t) = \lim_{\Delta t} \frac{P\left[t \le T < t + \Delta t, S = j | T \ge t\right]}{\Delta t}$$

which states that, in the presence of multiple destinations, the hazard rate is the product of the rate of transition in the small interval Δt and the probability that the destination is j, provided that the transition has not occurred before t. The total hazard rate is

$$\mu(t) = \sum_{j=1}^{J} \mu_j(t)$$

The destination-specific hazard rate at time t may be written as the product of the total hazard rate $\mu(t)$ and a probability $p_j(t)$ that the destination state after the transition is j, provided the transition occurs at time t:

$$\mu_j(t) = \mu(t) \, p_j(t)$$

In continuous-time microsimulation, two approaches may be distinguished to determine the time to transition and the destination. They are equivalent, however. The first, used in e.g. LifePaths, uses $\mu_{ij}(t)$, i.e. the

---

1   The approach is also used in the presentations of the LifePaths microsimulation model.

destination-specific hazard rates, and generates waiting times to transition for every possible destination j. The shortest waiting time is selected to determine the actual time to event and the destination. In case an interval of length h is considered, the transition occurs if t_j is in the interval. The second approach uses two random variables: $\mu(t)$ to determine the time to transition and $p_j(t)$ to determine the destination. The first random variable (time to event) is drawn from an exponential distribution to determine the timing of the transition. The destination is determined by a random draw from a uniform distribution U~U[0,1]. Let the draw be denoted by u. If u is less than $p_1(t)$, the transition is to the first destination, if $p_1(t) \le u < p_1(t) + p_2(t)$, the transition is to the second destination, if $p_1(t) + p_2(t) \le u < p_1(t) + p_2(t) + p_3(t)$, the transition is to the third destination, etc.

The competing risk model may easily be extended to a multistate model with hazard rates depending on state of origin and state of destination. The transition rate $\mu_{ij}(t)$ is the rate at which individuals, who occupy state i at time t, make a transition to state j. If the sample population is stratified by state occupied, the transition rates are conditioned on the state of origin, and the multistate model resembles the competing risk model. The transition rate by origin and destination $\mu_{ij}(t)$ may be written as the product of the rate of leaving state i $[\mu_{i+}(t)]$ and destination probability conditional on the state of origin $[p_{12}(t)]$ and conditional on leaving. For instance, the rate of a direct transition from state 1 to state 2 may be written as: $\mu_{12} = \mu_{1+} {}^* p_{12}$, where μ_{1+} is the exit rate from 1 and p_{12} is the probability that a subject leaving 1 transits to destination 2.

By way of example suppose the state space consists of three states: healthy (1), disabled (2) and dead (3). At the start of the process being simulated, all subjects are in state 1. The process is simulated for a period of 10 years. Suppose the transition rates are constant and equal to: $\mu_{12} = 0.12$, $\mu_{13} = 0.03$, $\mu_{21} = 0.06$ and $\mu_{23} = 0.06$. The rate of leaving state 1 (μ_{1+}) is 0.15 and the rate of leaving state 2 (μ_{2+}) is 0.12. The transition rates imply that 80% of the subjects leaving state 1 (healthy) move to state 2 (disability) and 20% move to state 3 (dead). Consider a sample of 1,000 subjects in state 1 at the start of the process. The *expected* state occupancies at different years are shown in Table 2. They are calculated by the following equation:

$$\mathbf{K}(t+1) = \mathbf{P}\,\mathbf{K}(t) = \exp[-\mathbf{M}]\,\mathbf{K}(t)$$

where $\mathbf{K}(t)$ is a vector of state occupancies indicating the number of subjects in each of the three states at time t. $\mathbf{P}$ is the matrix of transition probabilities. In this illustration, they are estimated from the transition rates using the linear approximation of the exponential model (for the derivation, see Willekens, 2006): $\exp[-\mathbf{M}] \approx [\mathbf{I} + \frac{1}{2}\mathbf{M}]^{-1}[\mathbf{I} - \frac{1}{2}\mathbf{M}]$

The transition rates are assembled in the transition matrix M:

$$\mathbf{M} = \begin{bmatrix} \mu_{11} & -\mu_{21} & -\mu_{31} \\ -\mu_{12} & \mu_{22} & -\mu_{32} \\ -\mu_{13} & -\mu_{23} & \mu_{33} \end{bmatrix} = \begin{bmatrix} 0.15 & -0.06 & 0 \\ -0.12 & 0.12 & 0 \\ -0.03 & -0.06 & 0 \end{bmatrix}$$

where $\mu_{ii} = \sum_{j=1}^{J} \mu_{ij}$. The matrix of transition probabilities for one-year intervals is

$$\mathbf{P} = \begin{bmatrix} p_{11} & p_{21} & p_{31} \\ p_{12} & p_{22} & p_{32} \\ p_{13} & p_{13} & p_{33} \end{bmatrix} = \begin{bmatrix} 0.863 & 0.053 & 0.000 \\ 0.105 & 0.890 & 0.000 \\ 0.031 & 0.057 & 1.000 \end{bmatrix}$$

The expected state occupancies at the beginning of each year from 0 to 10 are given in Table 2.

Table 2: State occupancies, expected values

Year	Healthy	Disabled	Dead
0	1000	0	0
1	863	105	31
2	751	185	64
3	658	244	98
4	581	286	133
5	517	316	167
6	463	336	201
7	417	348	235
8	379	353	268
9	346	354	300
10	317	352	331

To determine the *sample* values of the state occupancies at different durations, consider again a sample of 1,000 subjects in state 1 at the beginning of the process. Assume that the subjects do not differ with respect to the transitions between healthy, disabled and dead. All healthy people experience the same incidence rate of disability and the same death rate. Disabled persons experience the same recovery rate and death rate. We construct the lifepath of the 1,000 subjects during a 10-year period. Continuous-time microsimulation is used to determine, for each subject, the time to transition to disability, recovery, or death. Two random variables are generated. The first is the time to transition drawn from an exponential distribution that is characteristic for the state of origin. Healthy subjects leave the state of being healthy at a time that is determined by $\mu_{1+} = 0.15$. For each subject, the exit time is drawn from an exponential distribution with parameter $\mu_{1+} = 0.15$. The destination state is determined by drawing a random number from a uniform distribution. If the number is between 0 and 0.8, the healthy subject who discontinues to be healthy becomes disabled. If the number is between 0.8 and 1.0, the subject dies. The recovery and death of subjects with disability are determined in a similar way. The time to transition or exit time is drawn from an exponential distribution with parameter $\mu_{2+} = 0.12$ and the direction is determined by drawing a random variable from a uniform distribution. Recovery occurs when the random variable is between 0 and 0.6. If the value of the variable exceeds 0.6, the subject dies. Table 3 shows the state occupancies every year of the period from 0 to 10. The sample observations are close to the expected values. Note that all virtual subjects are followed for a period of 10 years. Censoring is at year 10.

Table 3:   State occupancies, sample values

Year	Healthy	Disabled	Dead
0	0	0	0
1	863	112	25
2	758	185	57
3	649	261	90
4	551	313	136
5	481	347	172
6	439	355	206
7	393	368	239
8	358	373	269
9	333	369	298
10	306	370	324

Of the 1,000 healthy subjects at the start of the process, 676 become disabled for at least some period and 172 die while healthy (including those who never became disabled and the 156 who recovered from disability before death). 153 die in disability. At the end of the observation at year 10, 306 are healthy, 370 disabled and 324 dead.

The sampling from the virtual population through microsimulation gives information on the population that cannot or cannot easily be obtained otherwise. The 1,000 subjects experience 1,157 transitions (Table 4). Most are from healthy to disability. 676 transitions initiate an episode of disability. Of the 676 episodes of disability, 156 end in recovery, 153 in dead and 367 are truncated when year 10 is reached. The table also shows the health status at death: 172 are healthy and 153 disabled.

Table 4:   Transitions, sample

ORIGIN	DESTINATION			
	Healthy	**Disabled**	**Dead**	**Total**
Healthy	0	676	172	848
Disabled	156	0	153	309
Dead	0	0	0	0
Total	156	676	325	1157

The healthy subjects that become disabled during the observation window of 10 years, become disabled after 3.9 years, on average. Disabled subjects that recover, recover at 5.9 years, on average. Although disabled subjects have a mortality that is twice that of healthy subjects, they die later than healthy subjects: 5.8 years versus 4.2 years. The difference is due to the relatively late onset of disability, the low recovery rate and the high death rate for healthy subjects that is independent of time since onset of the process. As a consequence, many healthy subjects die before the mean age at onset of disability.

A major advantage of continuous-time microsimulation is the possibility of multiple transitions within a year. The number of multiple transitions is relatively rare: 9.9% of the subjects experience two transitions and 0.4% three transitions.

The total number of years spent alive during the observation period is 8.3 years. An average subject spends 5.4 years healthy and 2.9 years disabled.

During the 10-year period, the 1,000 subjects follow 10 different lifepaths. The lifepath is the sequence of states. If H denotes healthy, D disabled and + dead, then a lifepath may be represented by a character variable. The most common path is HD (healthy – disabled). A total of 325 subjects follow that path. 217 subjects remain healthy throughout the 10-year period; they do not experience any transition. The lifepath is H. Of the 172 subjects who die while healthy, 161 die before experiencing a disability, 11 after recovery from a first period of disability and 3 after recovery from a second period of disability (Table 5). The table also shows the mean ages at transition, followed by the character denoting the transition. Note that subjects with multiple transitions generally experience the transition earlier than subjects with a single transition.

Table 5: Lifepaths during 10-year period, sample of 1,000 subjects

Pathway	Number	Name	Mean age at transition				
1	325	HD	4.24D				
2	217	H					
3	161	H+	4.03+				
4	150	HD+	2.68D	5.67+			
5	84	HDH	3.32D	6.79H			
6	40	HDHD	2.36D	4.88H	7.25D		
7	11	HDH+	1.96D	4.15H	5.77+		
8	7	HDHDH	1.49D	2.85H	5.74D	7.67H	
9	3	HDHD+	1.64D	3.86H	4.97D	6.78+	
10	2	HDHDHD	3.38D	3.92H	6.50D	8.04H	8.17D

3.3 Covariates and interventions

Hazard rates generally depend on personal attributes or covariates. Time-invariant covariates include sex and place of birth. Time-varying covariates include level of education, marital status, employment status, place of residence and health status. The time-path of time-varying covariates is a continuous-time process. It may be approximated by a discrete-time process when piecewise constant hazard rates are used and the covariates are allowed to change at the beginning of time intervals only. In that case, the values of the covariates are updated at the beginning of each interval and the hazard rate is obtained depending on the new values of the covariates. When covariates are allowed to change at any time during the interval, i.e. in continuous time, the interval is split in two or more subintervals and the hazard rates are derived for each subinterval. In other words, the hazard rates are updated whenever covariate values change. That procedure of interval splitting is similar to episode-splitting in event-history modeling (Blossfeld and Rohwer, 2002: 140ff.). The technique involves the splitting of episodes at every point in time where one of the time-varying covariates changes its value. Each of the original episodes is replaced by a contiguous set of subepisodes (splits) with appropriate values of the covariates. Interval splitting is implemented in LifePaths.

By way of example, consider the disability model and consider an intervention programme that reduces the incidence of disability and increases the rate of recovery once disability has struck. Subjects enrol in the programme at different ages and they remain enrolled till the end of the study period, which is 10 years. If a healthy subject enrols in the programme, the incidence rate of disability drops by 50%. Hence the rate after enrolment is 0.5 times the rate before enrolment. Subjects that are disabled and enrolled in the programme have a higher rate or recovery. The rate is assumed to be three times the rate for subjects not enrolled. Since subjects may enrol at any age, being enrolled is a time-varying covariate. The transition rates after enrolment may be written as

$$_k m_{12}^e(x) = m_{12}(x)\exp\left[(\ln 0.5)*{}_k X(x)\right]$$
$$_k m_{21}^e(x) = m_{21}(x)\exp\left[(\ln 3.0)*{}_k X(x)\right]$$

Where x denotes age, $_k m_{ij}^e(x)$ the rate at which subject k changes from state i to state j at age x, and $_k X(x)$ is the time-varying covariate that is equal to one if subject k is enrolled at age x and is 0 otherwise.

To determine who enrolled in the programme and at what age, i.e. to determine the values of $_k X(x)$, a random sample is drawn from the virtual population. It is assumed that, at the population level, 10% of the subjects not yet enrolled at the beginning of a year enrol in the programme. The enrolment rate is independent of the health status, but of course depends on the enrolment status. If the treatment programme is conditional on participation in the prevention programme, only healthy subject may enrol and the enrolment rate is dependent on the health status. Since the enrolment rate is independent of the health status, the expected proportion of subjects enrolled after a period of 10 years is 61.4% (=100*[1-1/(1+0.10)^{10}]). In the sample, 712 subjects enrolled, i.e. 71%. Table 6 shows the number of new yearly enrolments in the sample of the virtual population.

In the presence of the intervention programme, less subjects in the *sample* of the virtual population enter disability (613 versus 676) and more recover from disability (231 versus 156). More subjects die healthy (180 versus 172) because more subjects are healthy and are healthy longer. In the sample population, more subjects may expect to be healthy after 10 years (437 versus 306) and less are disabled (239 versus 370). Because of the intervention, subjects spend more years healthy (6.3 years versus 5.4 years) and less in disability (2.2 years versus 2.9 years). The expected number of years spent alive during the observation period decreases a little (8.4 years versus 8.3).

If the entire population enrols in the intervention programme at the start of the observation period, the effect is more significant. In that case the number of healthy years is 7.2 and the number of years in disability is 1.3. The total number of years lived during the observation period is 8.5.

Table 6:   Number of new enrolments by year

Year	Enrolment
0	124
1	84
2	80
3	83
4	62
5	58
6	51
7	64
8	34
9	42
10	30
TOTAL	712

4   Conclusion and discussion

Continuous-time microsimulation has some advantages over microsimulation in discrete time. The main advantage is that the dates of events and the sequences of events can be determined accurately using the theory of competing risks and continuous-time multistate transition models. Whereas in discrete-time microsimulation sampling from a uniform distribution determines the event occurrences, in continuous-time microsimulation the sampling is from a waiting time distribution. The main tool for continuous-time microsimulation is the inverse distribution function or quantile function. For a given transition model, the function translates the probability of a transition during an interval into a waiting time. Different transition models have different quantile functions. The method based on the quantile function is a general method that applies to all waiting time models and other models as well. The chapter illustrates the method using the exponential model. Other transition models for which quantile functions can be defined, may be applied in continuous-time microsimulation.

The ultimate aim of microsimulation is to produce a virtual population that closely resembles a real population and to use the virtual population to study characteristics of the real population and to perform experiments *in silico* that are not possible in real populations (*in vivo*). The major weakness of microsimulation is the dependence on the model. If the model is a weak representation of a population, then the results of microsimulation lack validity. In microsimulation, a good model is a necessary condition but it is not sufficient. The sample size also matters. The virtual population must be sufficiently large to closely resemble the real population. With today's computer technology, that weakness can easily be overcome.

With the advent of the R programming environment, continuous-time microsimulation is becoming more easy to implement. The standard R library generates quantile functions for a wide variety of probability distributions, including the exponential and the Weibull distributions but not the Gompertz and the Cox model. Some packages in the R library are particularly useful. For instance, the msm (multistate Markov model) package contributed by Jackson (2009) includes a function to estimate a continuous-time Markov model from empirical data and another function (sim.msm.r) that uses the model to simulate individual event sequences. Packages recently developed by Putter et al. (2007) and Meira-Machado et al. (2009) also estimate multistate transition models that may be used to simulate life histories. These developments substantially reduce the programming costs of continuous-time microsimulation. Computing time is not substantially larger than in discrete-time microsimulation. The reason is that the application of the quantile function does not involve any iteration. These developments are expected to enhance the use of continuous-time microsimulation in the study of life histories.

References

Andersen, P.K./Keiding, N. (2002) 'Multi-state models for event history analysis', *Statistical Methods in Medical Research* 11: 91-115.

Antcliff, S. (1993) 'An Introduction to DYNAMOD: A Dynamic Microsimulation Model', DYNAMOD Technical Paper no. 1, National Centre for Social and Economic Modelling, University of Canberra.

Balakrishnan, K./Basu, A.P. (1996) *The exponential distribution. Theory, methods and applications.* New York: Gordon and Breach Publishers.

Bender, R./Augustin, T./Blettner, M. (2005) 'Generating survival times to simulate Cox proportional hazard models', *Statistics in Medicine* 24: 1713-1723.

Blossfeld, , H.-P./Rohwer, G. (2002) *Techniques of event history modeling. New approaches to causal analysis.* Second edition. Mahwah, New Jersey: Lawrence Erlbaum Associates.

Evans, M./Hastings, N./Peacock, B. (2000) *Statistical distributions.* Third edition. New York: Wiley.

Galler, H.P. (1997) 'Discrete-time and continuous-time approaches to dynamic microsimulation reconsidered'. Technical Paper no. 13, National Centre for Social and Economic Modelling (NATSEM), Faculty of Management, University of Canberra.

Gribble, S. (1997) 'LifePaths: A longitudinal microsimulation model using a synthetic approach'. Paper presented in the conference "Microsimulation in Government Policy and Forecasting: International Conference on Combinatorics, Information Theory and Statistics" Maine Portland, Maine, USA, July 18-20, 1997

Hammel, E.A. (1990) *SOCSIM II,* Working Paper no. 29, Graduate Group in Demography, University of California, Berkeley.

Hammel, E.A./Hutchinson, D./Wachter, K./Lundy, R./Deuel, R. (1976) 'The SOCSIM Demographic-Sociological Microsimulation Program Operating Manual'. Institute of International Studies Research Monograph No. 27, University of California, Berkeley, California.

Holmer, M./Janney, A./Cohen, B. (2006) 'PENSIM overview'. Policy Simulation Group, U.S. Department of Labor, Washington, D.C.

Jackson, C. (2009) The msms package. Version 0.8.2. Reference manual. Available at the Comprehensive R Archive Network, http://cran.r-project.org/

Kelly, S. (2003) 'Forecasting wealth in an ageing Australia. An approach using dynamic microsimulation'. Paper presented at the 7th Nordic Seminar on Microsimulation Models, Helsinki, June 2003.

Klein, J.P./Moeschberger, M.L. (2003) *Survival analysis. Techniques for censored and truncated data.* Second edition. New York: Springer Verlag.

Klevmarken N.A./Olovsson, P. (1996) 'Direct and behavioral effects of income tax changes - simulations with the Swedish model MICROHUS', in: Harding, A. (ed.) *Microsimulation and Public Policy.* Amsterdam: North-Holland-Elsevier.

Meira-Machado, L./Uña-Álvarez, J. de/Cadarso-Suárez, C./Andersen, P.K. (2009) 'Multi-state models for the analysis of time-to-event data', *Statistical Methods in Medical Research* 18 (2): 195-222.

Mueller, L.D./Nusbaum, T.J./Rose, M.R. (1995) 'The Gompertz equation as a predictive tool in demography', *Experimental Gerontology* 30 (6): 553-569.

Putter, H./Fiocco, M./Geskus, R.B. (2007) 'Tutorial in biostatistics: competing risks and multi-state models', *Statistics in Medicine* 26: 2389-2430.

Rowe, G./Nguyen, H. (2004) 'Longitudinal analysis of labour force survey data', *Survey Methodology (Statistics Canada)* 30 (1): 105-114.

Spielauer, M. (2006) 'The "life-course" model, a competing risk cohort microsimulation model: source code and basic concepts of the generic microsimulation programming language ModGen'. Working Paper WP 2006-046, Max Planck Institute for Demographic Research, Rostock. Available at http://www.demogr.mpg.de/papers/working/wp-2006-046.pdf

Statistics Canada (2001) 'The LifePaths Microsimulation Model: An Overview'. http://statcan.ca/english/spsd/LifePathsOverview_E.pdf

Wachter, K.W./Blackwell, D./Hammel, E.A. (1998) 'Testing the validity of kinship microsimulation: an update'. Manuscript, www.demog.berkeley.edu/~wachter/

Willekens, F.J. (2001) 'Theoretical and technical orientations toward longitudinal research in the social sciences', *Canadian Journal of Population* 28 (2): 189-217

Willekens, F.J. (2006) 'The multistate model for biographic projections'. Manuscript.

Wolf, D.A. (1986) 'Simulation methods for analyzing continuous-time event history models', *Sociological Methodology* 16: 283-308.

Wolf, D.A. (2001) 'The role of microsimulation in longitudinal data analysis', *Canadian Studies in Population* 28: 165-179.

Zaidi, A./Rake, K. (2001) 'Dynamic microsimulation models: a review and some lessons for SAGE'. SAGE Discussion Paper no. 2 [SAGEDP/02]. ESRC SAGE Research Group, The London School of Economics, London. www.lse.ac.uk/depts/sage

Annex: Continuous-time microsimulation models

Few continuous-time microsimulation models exist. They include the SOC-SIM model developed by Hammel et al. at Berkeley (Hammel et al., 1976; Hammel, 1990),[1,2] the demographic PopSim part of the DYNAMOD model developed at NATSEM (Antcliff, 1993), MICROHUS of Uppsala University (Klevmarken and Olovsson, 1996), LifePaths of Statistics Canada (Gribble, 1997; Statistics Canada, 2001) and PENSIM of the US Department of Labor (Holmer et al., 2006). PENSIM uses the same algorithm as LifePaths (Holmer et al., 2006: 3). The algorithm consists of drawing a sample of waiting times to event and comparing waiting times, generated by hazard models, to determine the timing and sequence of events. For a description of several of these models, including LifePaths, see Zaidi and Rake (2001). Zaidi and Rake assert that "The LifePaths's choice of the continuous time is definitely desirable from a theoretical point of view, although the use of continuous time puts heavy demand on the underlying data and computer resources." (Zaidi and Rake, 2001: 16). The methodology of microsimulation in continuous time was discussed as early as 1986 by Wolf (1986). Researchers at Statistics Canada developed a general-purpose environment for programming microsimulation models, called Model Generator (ModGen). The ModGen language is a superset of the C++ programming language. This environment provides a common code-base for modellers which they can use to generate microsimulation models that are variants of LifePaths. Statistics Canada uses this environment to generate several special-purpose models such as the Population Health Model (POHEM) that uses the demographic module of LifePaths but replaces the mortality equations with a highly detailed model of morbidity and mortality. Spielauer (2006) provides a step-by-step documentation of a continuous-time microsimulation model programmed in ModGen and applied to study fertility change using survey data. Dynamic microsimulation models are transition rate (hazard) models; they use information on members of different birth cohorts to generate life histories of individuals. For a nice illustration, see Rowe and Nguyen (2004), as well as Spielauer (2006).

---

1   For an extensive bibliography, see www.demog.berkeley.edu/~wachter/socrefs.html
2   In SOCSIM, time is measured in integral months (Wachter et al., 1998: 10). The same approach is used in DYNAMOD (Kelly, 2003: 4).

Chapter 17

Welfare Effects of Alternative Financing of Social Security – Calculations for Belgium

Bart Capéau / André Decoster /
Kris De Swerdt / Kristian Orsini

1 Introduction

In Belgium, as in many other European countries, proposals are launched to reduce social security contributions and switch to indirect taxes as an alternative base to finance the social security system. The protagonists of these reforms guesstimate that labour market distortions will in this way be diminished, and, as a result, that unemployment rates would decline.

One strand in the literature uses macro and/or computable general equilibrium (CGE) models to assess the impact of either general or selective reductions of social security contributions (see among others Bassilière et al., 2005, Cockx et al., 2005 and Stockman, 2002 for Belgium, and Buscher et al., 2001, Böhringer et al., 2005 and Steiner, 2003 for Germany). The conclusions evidently depend on the specific measures that are scrutinized. But in general the broad result seems to emerge of a warning against overly optimistic expectations to lower persistently high unemployment rates by decreasing social security contributions. Certainly a general (i.e. non targeted) reduction of social security contributions has only a modest impact on aggregate employment. Moreover, in the long term, a compensation by means of indirect taxes might lead to neutrality at the level of labour

This is a revised version of a paper prepared for and presented at a conference organized by the Belgian FOD Sociale Zekerheid on 13 February 2006. A preliminary version has been presented at the 8th Nordic Conference on Microsimulation, 8 June 2006 in Oslo. Financial support from the Belgian FOD Sociale Zekerheid is gratefully acknowledged.

costs (and hence labour demand) due to compensating wage demands (see Steiner, 2003 and OECD, 1994).

The second, complementary, approach is framed within the incidence analysis of public finance and focuses on the distributional impact of this kind of reforms. This focus is mostly absent in the above-mentioned macro-models. Microsimulation models are the prime candidates here to serve as tools of analysis. Indeed, tax-benefit models in principle allow to calculate for a representative sample of households or individuals the impact benefit of the lowered social security contributions and the incidence of the tax instrument used to finance the operation. In practice however, this possibility is more limited than suggested. First of all, few microsimulation models cover the whole range of tax and benefit instruments that make up the chain from gross income (let alone labour cost) up to a disposable income concept. Some models are tailored to study the impact of personal income taxes, others focus more on social transfers and benefits, and still others only model the indirect tax system. One of the reasons is that there are few representative micro datasets that both contain reliable income information and at the same time detailed expenditure information to calculate indirect tax liabilities. A problem that we will also face in this chapter. Secondly, the integration of behavioural reactions – a core element in a CGE-model – is much more complex in the rich world of thousands of heterogeneous agents of a microsimulation model than in the stylized CGE-world. The rapid progress in micro-econometric estimation and simulation techniques of the last decades has therefore only recently found its way in the development of "behavioural microsimulation". Actually, this recent development seems to have reinforced the compartmentalization of the microsimulation field, by focussing more on subgroups of the population for which behaviour can be suitably modelled.

Both these factors make it far from straightforward to extend the general CGE-analysis of this kind of reform with distributional considerations. This chapter tries to fill this gap. In doing so, we are in line with the contribution by Bach et al. (2006). These authors analyse the increase of the standard VAT-rate from 16 to 19%, introduced by the new German coalition government in 2005, and became effective as of 1 January 2007. They produce both an "impact" analysis of the distributional consequences, and a second round effect, taking up behavioural response both on the expenditure side as on the supply side of the labour market. They do not dispose of one integrated microsimulation model, nor of a dataset covering both incomes and detailed expenditures, but cleverly link existing models and datasets.

We, too, do not aim at extending existing models or techniques. We rather combine two separately existing microsimulation models (and data-sets) to investigate the distributional effects of a shift in the financing source of social security away from taxing labour towards indirect taxes. We describe the distributional effects for the whole population, and we obtain results that are very similar to those in Bach et al. (2006). The reform is regressive in terms of disposable income and the currently living generation of pensioners is most liable to pay for the reform. They do not enjoy the reduced labour income tax, but they face nevertheless higher consumption prices. Yet, our approach differs from the mentioned paper in two respects.

First, our behavioural model of labour supply is more limited in scope since we are only able to model labour supply for couples. This limits the possibility to describe distributional effects for the whole population if we want to take into account behavioural reactions on the labour market. Secondly, more than Bach et al. (2006), we emphasize the role played by the welfare measure to assess the distributional impact of this kind of reforms. Traditionally, and certainly in policy-oriented analyses, one limits oneself to describe distributional patterns in terms of disposable income changes, at most corrected by means of a consumer price index. Yet theoretically sound welfare measures are available in the literature and have recently been extended and adapted for use in discrete choice models and microsimulation contexts (see, amongst others, Creedy and Kalb, 2005a, Dagsvik and Karlström, 2005 and Preston and Walker, 1999). In this chapter we want to investigate the sensitivity of the distributional picture of gainers and losers of a reform to the chosen welfare metric. A fortiori, when not only the allocation of the expenditure budget over the different consumption goods alters, but also the full income of the household is reallocated between consumption and leisure, it is important to capture the (supposedly negative) welfare impact of increased labour supply and labour market participation entailed by this kind of reform. The latter aspect has been pointed at in other recent contributions in the field like Aaberge et al. (2000) and Aaberge et al. (1995). To investigate this sensitivity we deliberately disconnect the normative tool used for assessing the change in the distribution of welfare, from the positive tool used to predict behavioural reactions both in commodity demands and labour supply. Our results confirm that even the choice of a specific cardinalisation affects the results. Therefore the particular choice needs to be motivated.

Using existing microsimulation models, we also share their limitations. Firstly, we do not appropriately deal with labour market imperfections and involuntary unemployment. Nor do we take into account partial or general equilibrium effects on the labour demand side. Also the impact of the reform on savings (future consumption) and durable consumption goods is not taken up in the present welfare analysis.

The structure of the chapter is as follows. The next section describes the reform we analyse and simulate. It also briefly reviews the datasets and microsimulation models that we will use. We explain how we have matched expenditure data in the underlying income dataset of the tax-benefit model, and how demand reactions and labour supply have been modelled. In section 3 we prepare the ground for the sensitivity analysis by describing the different possibilities to measure welfare effects of price changes. Section 4 presents the results of the reform without taking into account the labour supply reaction. We focus here on the sensitivity of the picture of gainers and losers to the chosen welfare concept. In section 5 we then introduce flexible labour supply for a *sub*sample of the population and redo the sensitivity analysis of the distributional picture to the chosen welfare concept. Section 6 concludes.

2 The simulated reform and the adopted microsimulation approach

2.1 *The reform and the assumption of an unchanged gross wage*

Most of the reforms analysed by means of macro or CGE-models concern reductions in social security contributions paid by the employer. Here, however, we have modelled a reduction of social security contributions paid by the employee. Indeed, we do not dispose of a model that covers the demand side of the labour market and the dependence of the labour cost on these contributions. We lower social security contributions paid by the employees by a substantial amount of 25%.

Moreover, we have assumed that the reduction of the social security contributions is fully shifted forward into an increase of the net wage. This presupposes a perfectly flexible labour demand. In that case, the reduction of the contribution is fully reflected into a corresponding increase in the net wage of the employee, and hence in disposable income. This assumption reflects the partial character of the analysis when we introduce labour supply reactions in the analysis.

Table 1:   Commodity breakdown, shares in disposable income, and indirect tax
            rates for the NIS budget survey 2001

Commodity aggregate	observed share in disposable income (NIS-budget survey 2001)	imputed share on (PSBH-survey 2001)	baseline indirect tax rate in % of producer price	consumer price baseline	consumer price reform	price change in %
Food	11.3	11.3	6.2	1.0620	1.0721	0.95
Drinks – Non Alcoholic	0.9	0.9	7.7	1.0772	1.0874	0.94
Drinks – Alcoholic	1.3	1.3	40.9	1.4090	1.4556	3.31
Tobacco	0.8	0.8	207.5	3.0746	3.3516	9.01
Clothing, footwear	4.7	4.7	20.8	1.2085	1.2482	3.28
Rent, Utilities, Heating	23.7	23.5	5.0	1.0502	1.0590	0.84
Private transport	6.3	6.5	47.4	1.4738	1.5155	2.83
Public transport	0.4	0.5	5.3	1.0525	1.0613	0.83
Hygienic, Health	5.8	5.9	7.7	1.0775	1.0919	1.34
Leisure commodities	12.8	12.7	10.7	1.1067	1.1267	1.81
Other commodities	11.2	11.3	7.2	1.0722	1.0860	1.28
Durables	10.3	10.2	20.9	1.2094	1.2493	3.30
Savings	10.5	10.5	0.0	1.0000	1.0000	0.00
Income	100.0	100.0	10.9	1.1086	1.1281	1.76

With fixed labour supply, and eventually even with an increase in employment, the foregone revenues from the social security contributions have
to be compensated. We have chosen to increase both the standard and the
reduced VAT-rate. We have crudely estimated how much we had to increase
both rates to obtain revenue neutrality in the case where labour supply was
fixed. It turned out that we had to increase the standard VAT-rate from 21%
to 25%, and the reduced rate from 6% to 7%.

  The resulting price change for the commodities on which our indirect
tax model is built, together with the budget shares and pre-reform indirect
tax rates are shown in Table 1. The first column shows the share in disposable

income for 13 expenditure categories and for savings as we observe them in the *budget survey*. In the next section we briefly discuss how we imputed budget shares in the *income survey*. These imputed shares are displayed in the second column. The third column shows the indirect tax rate for the aggregates in percent of the producer price for the baseline Belgian indirect tax system of 2005 and the rightmost columns give the resulting consumer prices expressed in terms of fixed producer prices normalized at unity. The implemented VAT change also induces substantial relative price changes. Since tobacco products not only bear VAT and excise duties, but also an ad valorem excise which is expressed as a percentage of the consumer price (hence also taxing VAT and excise duties), the consumer price for tobacco products goes up with 9%. For commodities subjected to the standard VAT-rate of 21%, the price increase amounts to around 3.3% (from 1.21 to 1.25), whereas the price of commodities taxed at the reduced rate goes up from 1.06 to 1.07, or 0.94%.

2.2 Data and models

Since the switch from social security contributions to indirect taxes affects both disposable income and expenditure patterns (through the change in consumer prices), we ideally would want to dispose of a database that contains gross incomes, labour supply and a detailed breakdown of expenditures for a representative sample of households, and one integrated microsimulation model which traces out the path from gross income to welfare generated by consumption and leisure. We do however not dispose of either of these. The representative household surveys with reliable income information (such as the PSBH, the Panel Study of Belgian Households) do not contain a detailed breakdown of expenditures, and the survey of the Belgian National Statistical Institute (NIS), containing details on expenditures, is judged to be less reliable and is certainly less detailed for income data. As far as the microsimulation models are concerned, several Belgian tax-benefit models (MISIM, MODÉTÉ) are available, and there is at least one indirect tax model (ASTER). But we lack one integrated microsimulation model, covering both direct taxes and benefits *and* indirect taxes.

We therefore first created one integrated database containing both incomes and expenditures. Next, different existing microsimulation models were linked. The database was created by imputing expenditures on a representative survey with income data (the PSBH-survey of 2001). For 13 aggregated expenditure categories and for savings (see the first column of Table 1) we estimated nonparametric Engel curves of the income share in the 2001 budget survey of the NIS. The technique and estimation results are described in Decoster and De Swerdt (2008).We then used the nonparametric regressions to impute shares for the same classification on the income survey. The imputed shares at population level are reported in the second column of Table 1: they fit the observed shares from the budget survey well.

To calculate the impact of lowering social security contributions on households' disposable income, the microsimulation model MODÉTÉ was used. MODÉTÉ is a Belgian standard static tax-benefit model developed by DULBÉA-ETE in the framework of the EU-project EUROMOD. It runs on the PSBH-survey of 2001 and it allows to simulate income assistance, child benefits, taxes and social security contributions. Pensions and unemployment benefits are not simulated as the PSBH does not collect all necessary information on past employment records. For more details, see Joyeux (1999). For our simulations with flexible labour supply the standard MODÉTÉ has been extended with a labour supply model for the subsample of couples, along the lines described in Orsini (2006).

To calculate the impact of changes in indirect taxes on the consumer prices for the commodity aggregates, we used the microsimulation model ASTER. The indirect tax system is the one of 2005 but we expressed all nominal amounts in Euros of 2001, the year of the budget survey.[1] The fourth column of Table 1 shows the resulting tax rate for the aggregates in % of the producer price.

In the Annex we explain how the behavioural models that we have put together mainly from other sources, allow to calculate the determinants of different evaluation measures, to be defined in the next section. Other models could equally well provide this material. We treat therefore all measures developed in the sequel *conditionally upon the results from a (set of) behavioural model(s)*.

3 Four concepts of welfare measurement

3.1 *Disposable income*

A common and popular approach to calculate the effects of tax reforms is to calculate the monetary benefits or losses in disposable income of different categories within the population. Disposable income is composed of

---

1   The excises are nominal amounts of 2005. They have been deflated to 2001 Euros by deflating them with a factor 0.9249, the ratio of the CPI in 2001 to the one of 2005.

gross labour income, which equals gross hourly wages, say w, times labour supply, denoted by L, *plus* non-earned income, say M, *minus* net taxes $T = \theta \left(wL, M, \zeta \right)$. *Net* taxes contain all income taxes *minus* any net of tax transfers of the government (such as net pensions or net unemployment benefits). These depend on gross labour income wL, non-earned income M and a number of other characteristics such as household composition, house ownership, composition and sources of non-earned income etc. The latter information is recollected in a variable ζ denoting the tax-benefit type of the household. It contains all the necessary information to calculate the income taxes recollected from and the benefits accruing to that household. Amongst other things, ζ contains the status on the labour market of different members of the household, because this may influence the amount of tax reductions or exemptions, as well as the tax liabilities.[2]

Hence, *disposable income*, say y, equals:

$$y = wL + M - \theta \left(wL, M, \zeta \right).$$

(1)

Consider now a reform of the tax-benefit system. We denote the tax-benefit system pre-reform by θ^0 and the post-reform situation by θ^1. If we *assume that labour supply L does not change due to the reform*, the *gain in disposable income*, say dy, equals:

$$dy \equiv y^1 - y^0 = \theta^0 \left(wL, M, \zeta \right) - \theta^1 \left(wL, M, \zeta \right),$$

(2)

where the superscripts 0 and 1 refer to baseline and reform respectively. Equation (2) shows that the impact effect on disposable income equals minus the change in tax liabilities. This allows to express the impact monetary cost of the reform to the government as the summation of the changes in disposable incomes across all households.

The reform of the tax-benefit system might affect different households and household members differently. Let us therefore introduce h as an indicator for households, and let the members of a household be indicated by j_h. Then gross labour income within a household, I_h, is written as $I_h = \sum_{j_h} w_{j_h} L_{j_h}$, where w_{j_h} and L_{j_h} are respectively the gross wage and the labour supply of household member j_h. Indicating the total net amount

---

2   In some European countries household income is taxed jointly, while in other countries the marginal tax rate is applied on spouses' incomes separately. In the latter case there are rules to divide common income, e.g. imputed rents from house ownership or interests on common savings accounts, to household members. In some cases there may be tax rules to split income from a single earner in the household across members without earned income.

of taxes – this is taxes *minus* benefits – for household h in situation s by $T_h^s = \theta^s (I_h, M_h, \zeta_h)$, we calculate the monetary cost of the reform to the government as:

$$\sum_h (T_h^0 - T_h^1) = \sum_h dy_h. \tag{3}$$

3.2   Real income

Purchasing power, and hence welfare, of nominal disposable income depends on the price level of consumer goods. Consumed quantities of goods by household h are denoted by $\mathbf{x}_h = (x_{h1}, ..., x_{hi}, ..., x_{hn})$ and the corresponding consumer prices, identical for all households, by $\mathbf{q} = (q_1, ..., q_i, ..., q_n)$. We assume that producer prices and gross wages are fixed.[3] Therefore, it is possible to normalize the producer prices of all consumer goods to one, and measure the associated quantities in monetary terms (in the application this will be in year 2001 Euros). The consumer prices are then equal to $q_i = 1 + t_i$ where t_i is the indirect tax rate on good i. The budget equation for household h reads as:

$$y_h = I_h + M_h - \theta (I_h, M_h, \zeta_h) = \mathbf{q}'\mathbf{x}_h. \tag{4}$$

The basic aggregation identity:

$$Q_h X_h \equiv \mathbf{q}'\mathbf{x}_h, \tag{5}$$

defines an implicit quantity level index X_h, associated with a chosen price level index Q_h. So, the nominal disposable income y_h, can be converted into a *real income* concept, X_h, measuring the quantity of consumer goods a household can buy with its budget, given the price level Q_h:

$$X_h \equiv \frac{y_h}{Q_h}. \tag{6}$$

Both the price index Q_h and the quantity index X_h are household-specific through the quantities $\mathbf{x}_h$ in (5). A joint reform of the tax-benefit system

---

3   This could be rationalized by a simplified Leontief model of the supply side of the economy which is linear in the – among each other – perfectly substitutable different types of labour supply, whose gross wages w_{j_h}, increased by the amount of employer taxes on labour demand, reflect the constant marginal productivities of different labour types.

(changing disposable income y_h) and indirect taxes (changing consumer prices) will affect these quantities by means of the classical demand function:

$$\mathbf{x}_h = f(\mathbf{q}, y_h). \tag{7}$$

We used the Stone price index as a specification for the household-specific price index Q_h:

$$\ln Q_h = \sum_i \omega_{ih} \ln q_i, \tag{8}$$

where

$$\omega_{ih} = \frac{q_i f(\mathbf{q}, y_h)}{y_h} \tag{9}$$

denotes the budget share of commodity i for household h.

Indexing again the pre-reform situation by a superscript 0, and the post-reform situation by a superscript 1, the *change in real income* for household h, $\mathrm{d}X_h$, obtained by deflating nominal disposable income by means of the price index, equals:

$$\mathrm{d}X_h \equiv \frac{y_h^1}{Q_h^1} - \frac{y_h^0}{Q_h^0}. \tag{10}$$

Obviously the ranking of winners and losers of a reform, induced by the gain concept in (10), might differ from the ranking induced by the change in welfare measured by change in disposable income in (2), and this for several reasons. Note first that even for a reform that only changes disposable income and keeps consumer prices constant, *i.e.* $\mathbf{q}_0 = \mathbf{q}_1$, the measure in (10) will differ from the one in (2) for two reasons. First of all, since households have a different allocation of the budget, they are affected differently by given price levels: the Stone price index differs across households because household budget shares differ across households. This cannot alter the sign of the evaluation by means of (10) as compared to the change in disposable income in (2), but it can alter the ranking of households in a distribution of winners and losers. Secondly, since the change in households' disposable income leads to changes in budget shares, the price index changes in the post-reform situation, even with constant consumer prices. This effect can even change the sign of the evaluation. Finally, if the reform also affects consumer prices, both, ranking and sign of the measure in (10) can differ from that of (2).

3.3 Consumption based welfare

The purpose of deflating nominal income y_h by means of a price index, is to approximate purchasing power, and hence quantities consumed. Yet, deflating by an *ad hoc* index, such as the Stone price index, is not always firmly grounded in theory. More theoretically sound is to start from an expenditure function, derived from the previously specified demand functions, $f(\mathbf{q}, y_h)$, and defined as:

$$y_h = e(\mathbf{q}, U),\qquad(11)$$

where U is the welfare level obtained from consumption $\mathbf{x}_h$, evaluated by means of the function $u(f(\mathbf{q}, y_h))$. This expenditure function can be used as a money metric welfare function for a household with disposable income y_h^0 and facing prices $\mathbf{q}^0$ as follows (see King, 1983):

$$mmu_h(\mathbf{q}^r, \mathbf{q}^0, y_h^0) = e\left(\mathbf{q}^r, u\left(f\left(\mathbf{q}^0, y_h^0\right)\right)\right),\qquad(12)$$

where $\mathbf{q}^r$ is a set of reference prices to convert welfare in the situation $(\mathbf{q}^0, y_h^0)$ into monetary units. We will use as reference prices the baseline prices $\mathbf{q}^0$. We can now construct a *consumption based welfare gain*, denoted by CWG, of the impact of a reform converting the baseline prices and disposable income $(\mathbf{q}^0, y_h^0)$ into the post-reform situation $(\mathbf{q}^1, y_h^1)$ for household h as follows:

$$CWG_h(\mathbf{q}^0, \mathbf{q}^1, y_h^0, y_h^1) \equiv e\left(\mathbf{q}^0, u\left(f\left(\mathbf{q}^1, y_h^1\right)\right)\right) - e\left(\mathbf{q}^0, u\left(f\left(\mathbf{q}^0, y_h^0\right)\right)\right) \qquad 13$$

The first term in the right hand side of the equation embodies the counterfactual situation of reaching the post-reform utility level at the pre-reform prices. It can be expressed by means of the compensated demand functions for consumption goods, denoted here as $\tilde{x}(\mathbf{q}, U)$:

$$e\left(\mathbf{q}^0, U_h^1\right) = \mathbf{q}^{0\prime}\tilde{x}\left(\mathbf{q}^0, U_h^1\right),\qquad(14)$$

where we denote the utility level in the post-reform situation by $U_h^1 \equiv u\left(f\left(\mathbf{q}^1, y_h^1\right)\right)$. In the application in this chapter, we simulated these compensated demands by calculating a real income effect on observed prereform demands, based on the nonparametric Engel curves.

Using (14), the consumption based welfare gain CWG_h in (13) can be rewritten as:

$$
\begin{aligned}
CWG_h\left(\mathbf{q}^0,\mathbf{q}^1,y_h^0,y_h^1\right) &= \mathbf{q}^{0'}\tilde{x}\left(\mathbf{q}^0,U_h^1\right)-y_h^0 \\
&= y_h^1-y_h^0-\left[y_h^1-\mathbf{q}^{0'}\tilde{x}\left(\mathbf{q}^0,U_h^1\right)\right] \\
&= dy_h-\left[\mathbf{q}^{1'}\tilde{x}\left(\mathbf{q}^1,U_h^1\right)-\mathbf{q}^{0'}\tilde{x}\left(\mathbf{q}^0,U_h^1\right)\right] \\
&= dy_h-\left[(\mathbf{q}^1-\mathbf{q}^0)'\tilde{x}\left(\mathbf{q}^0,U_h^1\right)+\mathbf{q}^{1'}\left(\tilde{x}\left(\mathbf{q}^1,U_h^1\right)-\tilde{x}\left(\mathbf{q}^0,U_h^1\right)\right)\right] \\
&= dy_h-\left[d1q_h+d2q_h\right],
\end{aligned}
\tag{15}
$$

where $d1q_h$ denotes the first term in the square brackets of the penultimate line in (15), and $d2q_h$ the second one.

Equation (15) shows how we have to correct the change in nominal disposable incomes (dy_h) to take into account the effect of the price change of consumption commodities. The first term, denoted by $d1q_h$, is an aggregate measure of price change. The weights in this measure are equal to the compensated demands evaluated at pre-reform prices but at an income that can assure the post-reform utility level U_h^1. Note that, contrary to the change in real income in (10), the consumption based welfare gain in (15) coincides with the change in disposable income when the reform does not alter the prices of consumption goods, i.e. when $\mathbf{q}^0 = \mathbf{q}^1$. The second term, $d2q_h$, vanishes when relative prices do not change. It can therefore be interpreted as the contribution to the welfare change due to a relative price change.

Summarizing, we have three different welfare measures with fixed labour supply:

1. the change in disposable income in (2);
2. the change in real income in (10), and
3. the theoretically more sound consumption based welfare gain in (15).

3.4 How much weight do we attach to leisure?

The expenditure function can also be defined for utility functions that value leisure, $l \equiv T - L$, i.e. total time endowment, T, minus labour supply, L; at a certain price, say π_l (see e.g. Creedy and Kalb, 2005a):[4]

$$
\mu \equiv e\left(q,\pi_l,U\right) = q'x-\pi_l L.
\tag{16}
$$

---

4   The expenditure function could also be defined in terms of full income $\mu + \pi_l T$, instead of in terms of virtual income μ. See Blundell et al. (1994: 22-27).

The welfare level U is in this case obtained from both, consumption *and* leisure: $U = u(\mathbf{x}, T - L)$. In this equation, consumption $\mathbf{x}$ and labour supply L should be replaced by observed values, or predictions according to a behavioural model. In the Annex we describe how we collected parts of existing behavioural models to allow for a two-step procedure, in which the allocation of disposable income to consumer goods is separable from the leisure-consumption choice, but, in general, the demand functions and the labour supply functions can be described as $f(\mathbf{q}, w_n, \mu)$ and $g(\mathbf{q}, w_n, \mu)$. In this equation, w_n is the *opportunity cost of leisure*, i.e. the net wage that can be obtained by supplying an additional unit of labour.

The price at which leisure should be valued in the expenditure function (16), which is a money metric utility function, is a normative choice. We choose to use the opportunity cost of leisure, w_n.

We calculated this opportunity cost on the basis of the individual gross wages w from the PSBH, if these were available or could be imputed. For households with individuals active in the labour market and for the unemployed, we determined the effective marginal tax rate, say θ', by simulating in MODÉTÉ an increase in labour supply of one hour and looking at the change in disposable income. This allows us to calculate for each individual a net wage rate w_n as:

$$w_n = \left(1 - \theta'\right)w. \tag{17}$$

We then chose the largest net wage among household members, as the net wage w_n. For the individuals that are unavailable for the labour market (in practice the retired) we imputed, quite ad hoc, the quantile value of the 25th percentile in the distribution of net wages obtained in the previous step.

The welfare gain corresponding to the expenditure function in (16) is equal to:

$$WG(\mathbf{q}^0, \mathbf{q}^1, w_n^0, w_n^1, \mu^0, \mu^1) = e\left(\mathbf{q}^0, w_n^0, U^1\right) - e\left(\mathbf{q}^0, w_n^0, U^0\right). \tag{18}$$

There is no a priori reason why the macro-economic objectives of the proposed reform (to activate unemployed) would coincide with the preferences of the individuals. Therefore we want to dispose of an evaluation tool that allows to be more or less generous towards the policy-makers' objective. The macro-economic employment objective could possibly be justified by an objective function that attaches less weight to leisure than the affected individuals.

To investigate the sensitivity of the welfare evaluation with regard to the weight attached to leisure in the welfare function, we have therefore chosen to separate the *positive* aspects in the analysis from the *normative* ones. For the positive part, we used a combination of existing empirical models to predict as secure as possible the behavioural reactions in terms of consumption (income and price effects) and labour supply. But once we have estimated consumption and leisure in both baseline and reform situation, these quantities can be plugged into another evaluation tool. As an example, we have used the CES-utility function, defined as:

$$u(\mathbf{x}, l) = \left[\delta_l^{1-\rho} l^\rho + \sum_{i=1}^{n} \delta_i^{1-\rho} (x_i)^\rho \right]^{\frac{1}{\rho}}, \tag{19}$$

where the δ_i's and δ_l are the share parameters of consumption goods and leisure, satisfying $\sum_{i=1}^{n} \delta_i + \delta_l = 1$; $\rho = 1 - \frac{1}{\sigma}$ and σ is the (Allen-Hicks) substitution elasticity. The share parameter δ_l is a measure for the weight attached to leisure in the evaluation and will be crucial in the sensitivity analysis.

For this CES-utility function, the expenditure function is obtained as:

$$e(\mathbf{q}, w_n, U) = \left(\phi(\mathbf{q}, w_n) \right)^{-\left(\frac{1-\rho}{\rho} \right)} U, \tag{20}$$

where $\phi(\mathbf{q}, w_n) \equiv \sum_i \delta_i q_i^{(1-\sigma)} + \delta_l w_n^{(1-\sigma)}$ is used as an abbreviated notation for a weighted average of prices $\mathbf{q}$ and w_n. Using the baseline prices as reference prices, the expression for the welfare gain in (18) then becomes:

$$WG_{\text{CES}} = [\phi(\mathbf{q}^0, w_n^0)]^{\frac{1}{1-\sigma}} \cdot (U^1 - U^0), \tag{21}$$

where the welfare levels U^0 and U^1 are obtained from:

$$U^s = \left[\delta_l^{1-\rho} \left(T - g \left(\mathbf{q}^s, w_n^s, \mu^s \right) \right)^\rho + \sum_{i=1}^{n} \delta_i^{1-\rho} \left(f_i \left(\mathbf{q}^s, w_n^s, \mu^s \right) \right)^\rho \right]^{\frac{1}{\rho}} \tag{22}$$

for $s = 0, 1$.

To be sure, the labour supply function $g(.)$ and the demand functions $f_i(.)$ are *not the ones* derived from the CES-framework. Functions g and f are modelled separately in a way which best predicts real world behavioural responses to policy changes (with the random utility model for labour supply, and QUAIDS for commodity demands). Next, we plug these new consumption and labour supplies into the normative evaluation tool (21) and (22) which does not have to fit the behavioural model. The additional parameter δ_l allows us to investigate whether the welfare evaluation of changing labour supply is sensitive to the weight attached to leisure in the evaluation function. But this separation of normative evaluation and behavioural modelling also allows to use (21) and (22) under different behavioural assumptions, such as e.g. fixed labour supply.

For the application we calibrated the CES-utility function in (19). Since our objective is to evaluate differences in assessment of macro-economic objectives and subjective welfare assessments of leisure, we wanted to reflect as close as possible the consumer's commodity preferences. Therefore the share parameters for the consumption commodities (the δ_i parameters) have been calibrated on the elasticities generated by the QUAID system referred to in the Annex. The calibrated values are displayed in Table 11 in the Annex. Next, we perform a sensitivity analysis on the share parameter of leisure by first fixing δ_l and then rescaling the share parameters of the consumption commodities proportionately such that all share parameters together sum to unity. The committed expenditures have been put equal to 0. Parameter ρ is related to the substitution elasticity σ by $\sigma = \dfrac{1}{1-\rho}$. The calibrated value of the substitution elasticity equals 0.696.

4 Results with fixed labour supply

4.1 Revenues

Table 2 shows the revenue effects of lowering social security contributions paid by the employee by 25% and increasing the standard VAT rate from 21 to 25% and the reduced rate from 6 to 7% under the assumption of fixed labour supply. All figures are in million Euros of 2001.

Even without labour supply effects, the assumption of a full shifting of the lower social security contributions into an increase of the net wage, leads to a substantial earning back effect through increased income taxes. The gross cost of 3292 million € is partially compensated by an increase in income taxes of 1473 million €. The remaining revenue loss is nearly covered by the mentioned increase in the indirect tax rates.[5] We are left with a cost of 155 million Euro.

---

5   The small difference between the aggregate change in disposable incomes (1813 million €) and the sum of changes in social security contributions and personal income taxes (1819 million €) is due to minor changes in means tested benefits.

In terms of the policy-relevant parameter of shares in government revenue for the three big categories of revenues: social security contributions, personal income tax and indirect tax, the reform reduces the share of social security contributions from 46.2% to 42.8%. Personal income taxes and indirect taxes go up from 41.6% and 12.1% to respectively 43.3% and 13.9%.

Table 2: **Effects on revenues in million Euros of 2001 of the reform with fixed labour supply**

	baseline	reform	change	
			mio €	%
gross income	122277	122277	0	0.0
disposable income	113617	115430	1813	1.6
social security contributions employee	14956	11664	-3292	-22.0
social security contributions employer	27915	27915	0	0.0
personal income taxes	38542	40015	1473	3.8
indirect taxes	11207	12865	1658	14.8

4.2 Standard analysis: changes in disposable income, in real income and in consumption

Table 3 summarizes the results for the reform under the assumption of fixed labour supply. All figures have been equivalized by means of the square root of household size. The deciles have been constructed on the basis of equivalized disposable income (excluding savings and durables) in the baseline, and contain 10% of the population of individuals.[6] Conditionally upon the predicted consumption behaviour post-reform, it turns out that most income classes are substantially affected by the policy. Only the change in real income in the 5th and 6th disposable income decile does not seem to be much affected by the reform (the change is not significantly different from zero). Note however that the averages can cover substantial individual differences in divergent directions.

---

6   Also the averages of the variables in the table have been weighted by the product of the number of individuals in the household and the household-specific weighting factor for the PSBH-survey.

Table 3: Changes in disposable income, real income and consumption based welfare gain (fixed labour supply)

	yearly equivalized disposable income (excluding savings and durable expenditures)			real income	price change			CWG	
	baseline	change	change	change	in €				
	in €	dy_h	in %	dX_h	$-d1q_h$	$-d2q_h$	in €	in %	
All	18605	240 (3.03)	1.29	11 (1.84)	-227 (1.47)	-29 (0.27)	-16 (1.97)	-0.19	
by decile of equivalized disposable income in baseline									
1	6814	54 (6.08)	0.79	-47 (5.33)	-107 (0.89)	-9 (0.27)	-61 (5.92)	-0.83	
2	10295	95 (4.36)	0.92	-47 (3.66)	-147 (0.77)	-15 (0.27)	-66 (4.01)	-0.64	
3	12520	140 (5.65)	1.12	-30 (4.73)	-173 (0.78)	-21 (0.34)	-54 (5.25)	-0.45	
4	14393	171 (5.94)	1.19	-21 (5.00)	-194 (0.79)	-25 (0.38)	-47 (5.63)	-0.36	
5	16198	216 (6.21)	1.33	3 (5.33)	-213 (0.79)	-27 (0.35)	-23 (5.99)	-0.15	
6	18189	235 (6.59)	1.29	4 (5.77)	-231 (0.70)	-30 (0.41)	-25 (6.50)	-0.15	
7	20285	296 (6.00)	1.46	40 (5.23)	-252 (0.94)	-32 (0.41)	13 (5.94)	0.09	
8	23018	342 (5.38)	1.49	61 (4.56)	-274 (1.10)	-36 (0.38)	32 (5.18)	0.19	
9	27277	393 (6.13)	1.44	74 (5.23)	-310 (1.54)	-40 (0.50)	43 (5.85)	0.23	
10	37118	459 (8.39)	1.24	77 (6.74)	-373 (3.21)	-53 (1.58)	34 (7.40)	0.14	
by age class of the household head									
< 18	5564	-108	-1.94	-255	-183	-4	-296	-2.47	
≥ 18	17437	277 (10.38)	1.59	31 (5.76)	-242 (5.93)	-24 (0.76)	11 (6.22)	-0.02	
≥ 30	18122	259 (4.70)	1.43	32 (2.71)	-223 (2.53)	-29 (0.41)	7 (2.92)	0.00	
≥ 40	20730	292 (5.09)	1.41	44 (3.19)	-242 (2.57)	-31 (0.49)	18 (3.46)	0.07	
≥ 50	21425	275 (7.72)	1.28	16 (4.65)	-257 (3.62)	-34 (0.74)	-16 (4.90)	-0.22	
≥ 65	12780	50 (2.17)	0.39	-108 (2.61)	-169 (2.45)	-24 (0.69)	-143 (3.34)	-1.13	
≥ 75	11565	43 (2.40)	0.37	-92 (2.72)	-144 (2.60)	-14 (0.52)	-114 (3.33)	-1.01	
by activity status									
non active	11353	54 (2.51)	0.48	-90 (2.47)	-154 (1.48)	-18 (0.35)	-118 (2.89)	-1.03	
active	21190	306 (3.01)	1.44	48 (1.79)	-253 (1.65)	-33 (0.31)	21 (1.94)	0.10	
*standard errors in parentheses									

453

The results in Table 3 are intuitive and broadly correspond to the findings of Bach et al. (2006) for Germany, but are nevertheless revealing. On average, the reform increases equivalized disposable income by 240 € (or 1.29%), but on average the associated price increase erodes this gain nearly completely when measured by means of the Stone price index deflator, and even turns the reform into a small loss as measured by means of the consumption based welfare gain measure.

However, the results are very unevenly distributed across income classes or other socioeconomic groupings. For the non-actives, disposable income is constant.[7] The reform entails an increasing pattern of the gain in disposable income across income classes, both in absolute and in relative terms, and in a relatively limited gain in disposable income for the older age classes.[8] The non-actives are of course hit by the price increase. This leads to an average loss of consumption possibilities of 118 € (or 1.03%) measured by means of the CWG. According to the same measure, only the upper four deciles succeed in compensating the price increase by a big enough increase in disposable income. For all other deciles there is a net loss. The decomposition by age class reveals how the reform triggers an intergenerational redistributive effect. The two oldest age classes lose more than 1%. For the age classes between 30 and 50, there is a welfare gain.

The assessment of the reform seems to be quite robust with regard to the choice of welfare measure. Of course, looking at the change in disposable income only is misleading. But correcting nominal income changes by means of a deflator like the Stone price index, or instead working with the consumption based welfare gain derived from the money metric utility framework does not make much difference as far as the distributional pattern is concerned. Note that the second component of the price change ($d2q_h$) is unimportant compared to the first factor ($d1q_h$) in equation (15). It is the general rise in the price level, not the change in relative prices, which causes the welfare losses.

In Table 4, we present a picture of the gainers and losers according to the different welfare measures considered thus far. This methodology was advocated by King (1983). It gives *an* answer to the frequently raised policy question: "Who gains? Who loses?".

---

7 To be consistent with the goods included in the CWG-measure, the figures for disposable income in Table 3 already subtract savings and expenditures on durable goods from disposable income. Therefore, disposable income of non-actives is no longer constant. Disposable income including savings and durable goods is constant for almost all non-actives.

8 There might be persons working, and thus paying social contributions, in households with a retired household head.

Table 4: Disposable income, labour supply and age for different orderings of gainers and losers (fixed labour supply)

ordering based on variable in row below	Quintile group of winners and losers				
	Q1	Q2	Q3	Q4	Q5
	equivalized disposable income (excluding savings and durable expenditures)				
abs change equiv disp income	12287	14958	16394	20757	30126
% change equiv disp income	12292	20785	19276	21069	24225
abs change equiv non durable exp	10621	14476	16930	21221	29794
% change equiv non durable exp	11762	16161	20515	21159	23448
abs change deflated non durable exp	15270	13300	18099	20197	26182
% change deflated non durable exp	12317	16221	20370	21475	22663
abs change consumption based welfare	15862	13670	18449	20117	24940
% change consumption based welfare	12614	16051	20632	21601	22146
	average weekly labour supply				
abs change equiv disp income	8.6	21.3	27.0	31.2	31.0
% change equiv disp income	8.6	22.9	26.9	30.5	31.3
abs change equiv non durable exp	5.5	16.1	27.3	31.7	30.4
% change equiv non durable exp	7.5	16.7	26.2	31.1	30.9
abs change deflated non durable exp	11.7	15.0	25.9	31.5	30.6
% change deflated non durable exp	8.9	17.3	26.5	31.5	30.1
abs change consumption based welfare	12.4	15.3	26.0	31.0	30.5
% change consumption based welfare	8.9	17.6	26.6	31.3	30.1
	age				
abs change equiv disp income	63.4	40.9	40.4	41.6	43.6
% change equiv disp income	63.4	43.6	40.5	43.1	40.9
abs change equiv non durable exp	65.0	54.8	40.6	40.8	44.2
% change equiv non durable exp	65.2	55.1	41.2	42.6	41.0
abs change deflated non durable exp	63.4	57.0	40.6	41.2	43.3
% change deflated non durable exp	62.1	58.8	41.5	42.3	41.8
abs change consumption based welfare	62.7	57.3	42.9	41.5	42.8
% change consumption based welfare	61.4	59.3	41.9	42.2	42.0

The table consists of three parts, each corresponding to a different household characteristic: equivalized disposable income, weekly labour supply (as a step to the analysis with flexible labour supply), and age of the household head. The different columns in the table correspond to five quintiles in the distribution of gains and losses. The column with heading Q1 shows the characteristics of the subgroup containing the 20% largest losers. The column with heading Q5 shows the characteristics of the 20% biggest winners of the reform. The different rows in each part of the table correspond to the choice of a different gain or loss concept. The first row, for instance, is obtained by ordering the population on the basis of the absolute change in equivalized disposable income (*including* savings and durable expenditures). Other rows order on changes in other variables, such as non-durable expenditures (taking savings and durables out of disposable income), on non-durable expenditures deflated by the Stone price index, or on the consumption based welfare gain. We also add the orderings based on the percentage changes, next to the absolute ones.

Looking at the first part of the table reveals whether the winners and losers of the reform can be differentiated according to their equivalized income, and whether the answer on this question is sensitive to the chosen welfare concept. The answer on the first question is affirmative. Focussing on a distribution of gainers and losers based on the absolute change in *global* equivalized disposable income (first row), disposable income (excluding savings and durable expenditures) increases with the position in the distribution from loss to gain. That means: the losers (e.g. group Q1) are the poorer households, the gainers are the richer ones. The pattern flattens out a bit when using the percentage change in disposable income instead of the absolute change. But also in this case, the reform turns out to be a regressive one. Leaving out savings and durable expenditures from the ordering concept by switching to changes in non-durable expenditures exacerbates this regressive pattern. For the ordering based on the absolute change, the ratio of the income of the 20% biggest winners to that of the 20% biggest losers is now three to one. The introduction of the price correction reduces the regressivity of the picture, although the remaining regressivity is substantial. The robustness with regard to the choice of correcting by means of the Stone price deflator or making use of the money metric utility of consumption based welfare is confirmed here.

The bottom two parts of the table repeat this picture of gainers and losers for two other characteristics. The middle part of the table shows average weekly labour supply for the groups of losers and winners. More or less independently of the chosen ordering concept, the losers group(s) mainly consist(s) of non-actives, while the households with actives are in the winners groups. This is in line with the third part of Table 4, where age of the household head in the group of the biggest losers is substantially above the one in the other groups.

4.3 Taking leisure into account

From the analysis sketched up to now, one might conclude that the choice of a specific evaluation measure, once corrected in one way or another for the effect of price changes does not matter much. In Table 5 this issue is elaborated more profoundly. It compares the picture of losers and winners according to consumption based welfare gain with the consumption based measure derived from the CES-utility function. The first row in each panel of Table 5 displays the characteristics of losers and winners when the ordering is based on the CWG-measure of equation (15). The next three rows show the CES-welfare gain of equation (21) for different values of the share parameter of leisure (δ_l). As mentioned before, we calibrated the share parameters, the δ_i's, for the different commodity aggregates such that they best fit the observed expenditure patterns. When attaching no weight to leisure ($\delta_l = 0$) both evaluation tools are exclusively consumption based. The picture of different categories of losers and winners is more affected by switching between those two evaluation tools than by using the change in real income as an alternative to the CWG-measure (see Table 4). Nevertheless, the qualitative results seem to be maintained. The non and less active are more concentrated among the (biggest) losers. The older generation is most liable to pay the bill.

From the macro-economic objective of the reform (activating unemployed) this result seems to be comforting. However, this objective does not have to coincide with the individual agent's objectives. To assess the welfare effect of the reform in case more weight is attached to leisure, we provide a similar losers/gainers picture for a higher share parameter of leisure (δ_l). It is striking that the importance attached to leisure does play a role, *even if labour supply is fixed*.

The results in Table 5 are surprising. If we increase the weight of leisure from 0 to 0.5 and then to 0.9, non-durable expenditures of the biggest losers decrease, while that of the middle groups in terms of loss increase. In this sense, the regressive pattern of the reform is exacerbated: poorer households seem to join the losers group. The group of biggest losers also becomes more predominantly populated by non-active people. The age of the biggest losers increases when $\delta_l = .5$ and then decreases for $\delta_l = .9$ but remains high. Also, the average weekly labour supply per capita of the biggest losers *decreases*. Increasing the share of leisure in the welfare evaluation tool, seems to shift not only more inactives into the group of the biggest gainers but also into the group of biggest losers.

This result is not due to the factor which transforms the utility difference into a money metric (the factor $\left[\phi(\mathbf{q}^0, w_n^0)\right]^{\frac{1}{1-\sigma}}$ in equation [21]). This factor is monotonously increasing in prices. Therefore gains and losses of people with higher net wage w_n are inflated relatively more than those of people with smaller wages. Due to the progressive tax system low income earners and unemployed tend to have a relatively high net wage, which might explain the unexpected result.[9] A similar analysis as in Table 5 for a welfare measure that is not expressed in monetary units, available from the authors upon request, largely provides the same puzzling results. Therefore, our choice of monetary valuation of leisure explained in Section 3.4, does not seem to affect the results too much.

Table 5: Disposable income, activity and age for different orderings of gain and loss (fixed labour supply)

ordering based on variable in row below	Quintile group of winners and losers				
	Q1	Q2	Q3	Q4	Q5
	equivalized disposable income (excluding savings and durable expenditures)				
change in consumption based welfare	15861	13670	18449	20117	24940
change in welfare, share leisure = 0.0	14949	14062	18647	20236	25170
change in welfare, share leisure = 0.5	12409	16453	20274	20232	23694
change in welfare, share leisure = 0.9	11624	17099	21070	20000	23257
	% of households that are non active				
change in consumption based welfare	80.3	66.1	12.6	1.1	1.9
change in welfare, share leisure = 0.0	86.6	57.1	6.8	1.9	1.5
change in welfare, share leisure = 0.5	95.2	49.8	3.5	0.2	5.1
change in welfare, share leisure = 0.9	95.5	52.4	1.0	1.8	6.1
	average weekly labour supply				
change in consumption based welfare	12.4	15.3	26.0	31.0	30.5
change in welfare, share leisure = 0.0	10.7	15.6	26.1	30.1	31.4
change in welfare, share leisure = 0.5	3.1	20.9	32.5	33.0	23.6
change in welfare, share leisure = 0.9	2.3	21.9	34.6	33.6	20.9
	age				
change in consumption based welfare	62.7	57.3	42.9	41.5	42.8
change in welfare, share leisure = 0.0	66.2	52.8	42.2	41.6	41.2
change in welfare, share leisure = 0.5	67.0	53.1	41.4	39.7	43.7
change in welfare, share leisure = 0.9	65.7	55.5	40.5	39.4	45.2

---

9   For the retired households we imputed the first quartile value of the distribution of the household net wage and therefore have a relatively low net wage by definition.

More seriously, it turns out that rank reversals in the classification of gainers and losers when increasing the weight of leisure in the utility function, occur for households with a different consumption level, but with the same amount of leisure. Hence, our results cannot be explained solely by the employment/leisure characteristics of the respondents. Differences in consumption behaviour remain to play a dominant role, even when attaching more weight to leisure.

So, despite some of the signals highlighted at the beginning of this subsection, the choice of welfare measure for evaluating a policy can play a crucial role, certainly for a more detailed analysis. We therefore argue for the need to justify the chosen welfare measure more carefully than is usually done, or to make the analysis independent from its particular choice. By lack of a more firm motivation for one of the measures provided, we pursue in the next section an example of the latter track.

4.4 Employment as a macro-economic objective

While the ranking of gainers and losers is affected by the weight of leisure in the evaluation function, even when labour supply is fixed, the fact that one is gaining or losing is not. In this subsection we therefore focus on this dichotomous picture of gainers and losers. We already notified that non-actives are among the losers. More surprising, and less prominent in the policy debate, is the fact that a non-negligible part of the actives is also affected negatively by the proposed reform (see Table 6). This might raise the question in how far the proposed reform does indeed stimulate employment.

Table 6:   Activity status of winners and losers (Frequency table)

	% non-actives	% actives	total
losers			
row percent	75.02	24.98	100.00
column percent	96.36	22.06	-
cell percent	39.26	13.07	52.33
winners			
row percent	03.11	96.89	100.00
column percent	03.64	77.94	-
cell percent	01.48	46.19	47.63
all			
row percent	-	-	-
column percent	100.00	100.00	-
cell percent	40.74	59.26	100.00

Before turning to this question, we first want to investigate whether there are some salient characteristics which differentiate losing actives from gaining actives. In Table 7 we give mean equivalized disposable income (including and excluding savings and durables) and labour supply per capita of losing and gaining active persons. As it turns out, none of these characteristics seems to clearly discriminate those categories. This raises the question, whether these results are due to the assumption of fixed labour supply, or whether the identified losers could improve their welfare as compared to the pre-reform situation by changing their labour supply. As a first step into this direction, we turn in the next section towards a quantitative analysis of the labour-incentive effects of the reform.

Table 7: Characteristics of active losers and winners

	equivalized disposable income (including savings and durables)
losers	20857
winners	21528
	equivalized disposable income (excluding savings and durables)
losers	15693
winners	16341
	weekly labour supply per capita
losers	28
winners	31

5 Introducing flexible labour supply

To estimate changes in labour supply following the reform of lowering social security distributions and increasing indirect taxes, we use the model of Orsini (2006 and 2008). The model is the by now standard one in which a multinomial logit is estimated for a set of discrete choice possibilities as far as labour supply is concerned (see Van Soest, 1995 for the basic reference, and Creedy and Duncan, 2002 and Creedy and Kalb, 2005b for overviews).

With our data, the model could only be estimated for a subset of households, viz. the couples. Evidently, we only considered the couples with adults at working age. The results discussed in this section therefore only cover this modelled subpopulation. The basic decision variable in such a model is the number of hours to work from a discrete set of available possibilities, e.g. full-time, half-time or unemployed. Each choice generates an income, available for consumption. Each pair of consumption and leisure, (C_{hj}, l_{hj}), that a household h can choose from a discrete set indexed by j, generates a random utility level:

$$V_{hj} = U\left(C_{hj}, l_{hj}\right) + \varepsilon_{hj},\tag{23}$$

where ε_{hj} is random disturbance term, reflecting preference heterogeneity. In the logit model, it is assumed that this variable has an Extreme Value Type I distribution, and is independent across choice options j. It is assumed that an agent chooses the alternative j that yields the highest utility.

In order to perform simulation exercises, we followed the Van Soest (1995) methodology of drawing repeatedly for each individual a set of random utility terms from the Extreme Value Type I distribution, such that the pre-reform choice, say $j*$, is the best option, i.e.

$$U\left(C_{hj*}, l_{hj*}\right) + \varepsilon_{hj*} \geq U\left(C_{hj}, l_{hj}\right) + \varepsilon_{hj} \quad \forall j .\tag{24}$$

For each such a draw the best choice in the post-reform situation is then determined by plugging the new disposable income resulting from the available labour supply options into the utility function. As a preliminary assessment, we then determined the post-reform labour choice as the average best option across all draws.[10] Because of this approach, most changes stem from the participation decision, while reactions at the intensive margin remain small. From the moment it is optimal for an agent to enter the labour market in only one particular draw, this individual (or household) is considered to be an entrant, although the average number of hours supplied might be small, since zero for all other draws.

Table 8 summarizes the labour supply effects by decile of equivalized disposable income (of the subpopulation only). We have summarized the transitions by categorising the population into households where at least one individual is active in the baseline, and the non-active households.

---

10 Duncan and MacCrae (1999: 34-35) mention that "The methods by which discrete models of labour market status are applied to discrete microsimulation are to a degree under-developed", certainly as far as the distributional analysis is concerned. Most papers who use behavioural microsimulation only report aggregate results for subgroups of the population. Dagsvik and Karlström (2005) derived the random expenditure function in the context of discrete choice, and for distributional analysis, several possibilities are discussed and compared experimentally in Creedy et al. (2004).

Table 8:   **Change in labour supply by decile of disposable income**

Decile	Total	non active in baseline		active in baseline with labour supply		
		stay non active	entry	un-changed	increased	decreased
1	112	10	62	20	19	1
2	99	2	3	53	38	3
3	104	1	0	72	30	1
4	109	0	0	89	16	4
5	107	0	0	84	20	3
6	105	1	0	85	18	1
7	117	0	0	101	12	4
8	124	0	0	108	14	2
9	119	0	0	99	16	4
10	113	0	0	94	10	9
Total	1109	14	65	805	193	32
L^0	27.573	0.000	0.000	32.194	20.711	29.623
L^1	27.670	0.000	1.018	32.194	20.950	29.304

Table 8 confirms that the participation effect is more important than the reaction at the intensive margin, but, as mentioned, this might be due to our choice of evaluation methodology. In line with many other studies, the participation effect is mainly relevant for the bottom of the income distribution. Note however from the bottom two lines of the table, where weekly household labour supply in the baseline and reform situations are displayed, that in terms of expected labour supply, the transition from non-participation to participation leads to a limited labour supply increase of a bit more than one hour a week.

Table 9 then repeats the analysis of the previous section by investigating the sensitivity of the distribution of winners and losers to the weight we attach to leisure in our normative evaluation tool. The table displays where we find the entrants of the labour market (upper panel), and the households who increase their labour supply (bottom panel) in the distribution of losers and gainers. The quintiles again contain 20% of the individuals for this sub-population and are constructed for different gain/loss concepts in the rows. The results are intuitive. Only looking at consumption, those households who are "activated" or increase their labour supply are overrepresented in the winners-part of the distribution. At the intensive margin (bottom part of the table) the effect of attaching more weight to leisure clearly moves households who increase their labour supply to the losers groups (quintiles 1 and 2). For the extensive margin the result is less clear and non-monotonic. Only when the weight attached to leisure is high enough, we do get a clear effect. This of course probably has to do with the small change in labour supply from 0 in the baseline to (on average) an expected value of slightly more than one hour after the reform.

Table 9: **Welfare effects of the reform for different orderings of gains and losses (flexible labour supply)**

ordering based on variable in row below	Quintile group of winners and losers					
	Q1	Q2	Q3	Q4	Q5	All
	% entrants in the labour market					
change consumption based welfare	5.7	2.5	1.0	1.8	17.9	6.0
change welfare, share= 0.0	8.2	1.1	2.0	0.3	17.4	6.0
change welfare, share= 0.5	7.7	1.6	0.8	0.7	20.4	6.0
change welfare, share= 0.9	27.1	0.0	0.0	0.0	1.7	6.0
	% actives who increase their labour supply					
change consumption based welfare	15.6	11.6	15.9	14.9	34.4	18.9
change welfare, share= 0.0	14.9	17.2	15.4	18.1	27.5	18.9
change welfare, share= 0.5	40.1	17.5	8.1	13.1	19.4	18.9
change welfare, share= 0.9	72.4	21.9	0.4	0.0	0.0	18.9

Table 10: **Winners and losers and labour supply incentives**

		percentage losers/winners		
δ_l	category	entrants	labour supply increase	labour supply decrease
0.00	losers	10.77	02.59	21.21
	winners	89.23	97.41	78.79
0.50	losers	23.08	17.62	00.00
	winners	76.92	82.38	100.0
0.90	losers	93.85	99.48	00.00
	winners	06.15	00.52	100.0

Finally, we confront the results of the welfare analysis with the macro-economic employment objective. From Table 10 one can notice that, even from the policy-maker's most favourable point of view to attach no weight to leisure, 11% of those who are activated by the policy, and 2.6% of those who are increasing labour supply lose by the measure. Naturally, these numbers increase when attaching more weight to leisure. Activating unemployed can impose a welfare cost on some agents, as well in terms of consumption (because of the rise in prices) and, naturally, also in terms of leisure.

6   Conclusion

In this chapter we analysed the distributional impact of lowering social security contributions and compensating the revenue loss by an increase in indirect taxes. For the empirical application, a link between two existing Belgian microsimulation models, MODÉTÉ for the tax-benefit system, and ASTER for the indirect tax part, was established. This was mainly accomplished by imputing detailed expenditures in the income data survey by means of nonparametric Engel curves. The behavioural models to predict changes in expenditure behaviour (QUAID for the ASTER model) and in labour supply (a discrete choice model) remained unconnected.

This empirical construction also deprived us from one – actually illusory – integrated measure of welfare change. We disconnected however the positive analysis from the normative evaluation. By using a flexible form like the CES-utility function to describe household welfare obtained from consumption and leisure, we investigated the sensitivity of the distributional analysis with respect to the chosen welfare measure, more specifically for the weight attached to leisure in the utility function.

The analysis with fixed labour supply is in line with recent results in other empirical papers like Bach et al. (2006) and confirms the prior expectation that there are considerable distributional effects of this shift in financing base. The currently living generation of pensioners are most liable to pay the bill. They do not profit from the reduced tax on labour income, but do pay higher consumption prices. In terms of equivalized disposable income, the reform is regressive. This picture is not really sensitive to the choice of measuring the welfare gain or loss by means of real income, defined as disposable income deflated with a Stone price index, or by using a money metric defined on consumption only. It is however sensitive to the decision to neglect or integrate leisure in the welfare concept used to assess the effect of the reform. Even with labour supply fixed, taking up leisure in the welfare function may seriously affect the picture of gainers and losers of a reform. We therefore concentrated on aspects of the evaluation which are independent of the choice of welfare function. About one quarter of the households with persons that are working lose by the measure. Despite the fact that these results might be the result of non-active losing members belonging to such households, this figure raises some doubts about the incentive effects of such a general reform.

The analysis with flexible labour supply, though limited to a subpopulation of couples only, seems to confirm this conjecture. The positive analysis is in line with the results found in many other papers that the labour supply effect is mainly found at the extensive margin of labour market participation. For the welfare analysis, the picture of gainers and losers evidently is affected by the weight attached to the lost leisure for individuals who enter the labour market or increase their labour supply. Yet, even when attaching no weight to leisure, about one tenth of the persons activated by the measure bears a welfare loss from the reform. To reconcile macro-economic objectives with welfare objectives, other or more fine-tuned measures seem to be in place.

465

References

Aaberge, R./Colombino, U./Strøm, S. (2000) 'Labour Supply Responses and Welfare Effects from Replacing Current Tax Rules by a Flat Tax: Empirical Evidence from Italy, Norway and Sweden', *Journal of Population Economics* 13 (4): 595-621.

Aaberge, R./Dagsvik, J.K./Strøm, S. (1995) 'Labour Supply Responses and Welfare Effects of Tax Reforms', *Scandinavian Journal of Economics* 97 (4): 635-659.

Bach, S./Haan, P./Hoffmeister, O./Steiner, V. (2006) 'Increasing the value-added tax to refinance a reduction of social security contributions? A behavioral microsimulation analysis for Germany', Working Paper DIW, Berlin.

Bassilière, D./Bossier, F./Bracke, I./Lebrun, I./Masure, L./Stockman, P. (2005) 'Sociale zekerheidsbijdrageverminderingen en alternatieve financiering van de sociale zekerheid: simulaties van beleidsvarianten', Planning Paper Federaal Planbureau, Brussel.

Blundell, R./Duncan, J. K./McCrae, J./Meghir, C. (2000) 'The Labour Market Impact of the Working Families Tax Credit', *Fiscal Studies* 21 (1): 75-104.

Blundell, R./Preston, I./Walker, I. (1994) 'An Introduction to Applied Welfare Analysis', pp. 1-50 in: Blundell, R./Preston, I./Walker, I. (eds.), *The Measurement of Household Welfare*. Cambridge University Press.

Böhringer, C./Boeters, S./Feil, M. (2005) 'Taxation and Unemployment: An Applied General Equilibrium Approach', *Economic Modelling* 22 (1): 81-108.

Buscher, H.S./Buslei, H./Goggelmann, K./Koschel, H./Schmidt, T.F.N./Steiner V./Winker P. (2001) 'Empirical Macro Models under Test. A comparative simulation study of the employment effects of a revenue neutral cut in social security contributions', *Economic Modelling* 18 (3): 455-474.

Cockx, B./Sneessens, H./Van der Linden, B. (2005) *Evaluations micro et macroéconomiques des allégements de la (para)fiscalité en Belgique*. Gent: Academia Press, Série Problèmes Actuels concernant la Cohésion Sociale.

Creedy, J./Duncan, A. (2002) 'Behavioural microsimulation with labour supply responses', *Journal of Economic Surveys* 16 (1): 1-39.

Creedy, J./Kalb, G. (2005a) 'Measuring welfare changes in labour supply model', *The Manchester School* 73 (6): 664-685.

Creedy, J./Kalb, G. (2005b) 'Discrete hours labour supply modelling: specification, estimation and simulation', *Journal of Economic Surveys* 19 (5): 697-734.

Creedy, J./Kalb, G./Scutella, R. (2004) 'Evaluating the Income Redistribution Effects of Tax Reforms in Discrete Hours Models', pp. 201-228 in: Amiel, Y./Bishop, J. (eds.), *Research on Economic Inequality, Vol. 12 Studies in Economic Well-being: Essays in the honor of John P. Formby*. Amsterdam: JAI-Elsevier Press.

Dagsvik, J. (1994) 'Discrete and Continuous Choice, Max-Stable Processes, and Independence from Irrelevant Attributes', *Econometrica* 72: 1179-1205.

Dagsvik, J./Karlström, A. (2005) 'Compensating variation and Hicksian choice probabilities in random utility models that are nonlinear in income', *Review of Economic Studies* 72 (1): 57-76.

Decoster, A./De Swerdt, K. (2008), 'Enriching income data with expenditure information: a semi-parametric imputation technique', CES Working Paper DPS 08.11, Centre for Economic Studies, KULeuven.

Duncan, A./MacCrae, J. (1999) 'Household Labour supply, childcare costs and in-work benefits: modelling the impact of the working families tax credit in the UK', Working Paper University of York, Department of Economics and Related Studies and Institute for Fiscal Studies.

Joyeux, C. (1999), 'Modété: un modèle de microsimulation pour la Belgique', *Cahiers Economiques de Bruxelles* 158 (2): 203-227.

King, M. (1983) 'Welfare analysis of tax reforms using household data', *Journal of Public Economics* 22 (1): 183-214.

OECD (1994) *The OECD Jobs Study: Evidence and Explanations*. Paris: OECD.

Orsini, K. (2006) 'Is Belgium Making Work Pay?', CES Working Paper DPS 05.06, Centre for Economic Studies, KULLeuven.

Orsini, K. (2008) Making Work Pay: Insights from Microsimulation and Random Utility Models, Proefschrift in de reeks van de Faculteit Economie en Bedrijfswetenschappen no. 275, KULeuven.

Preston, I./Walker, I. (1999) 'Welfare measurement in labour supply models with nonlinear budget constraints', *Journal of Population Economics* 12 (3): 343-361.

Steiner, V. (2003) 'Employment and wage effects of social security financing – An empirical analysis of the West German experience and some policy simulations', pp. 319-344 in: Addison, J./Welfens, P.J.J. (eds.) *Labour markets and Social Security,.Issues and policy options in the U.S. and Europe*. Berlin: Springer, 2nd ed.

Stockman, P. (2002) 'General and selective reductions in employer social-security contributions in the 2002 vintage of HERMES – A revision of WP 8-01', Working Paper Federaal Planbureau, Brussels.

Van Soest, A. (1995) 'Structural Models of Family Labor Supply: A Discrete Choice Approach', *Journal of Human Resources* 30 (1): 63-88.

Annex

In order to assess welfare post-reform we need to make predictions about changes in consumption and labour supply, when the latter is not considered to be fixed. We mainly used existing methods and models to arrive at that purpose, because we wanted to stress that different evaluations might be possible for one and the same behavioural reaction. We briefly summarize the sequence of models used, and refer the reader to the appropriate references for further details.

Recall that the reform we evaluated consists of a reduction of social security contributions paid by the employees by 25%. To finance the net reduction in revenues VAT-rates were increased. We took into account the effect of a higher net wage on taxable income and hence on income tax revenue and, when labour supply is flexible, also the reduced amount of unemployment benefits. Increasing the normal VAT-rate from 21% to 25%, and the reduced rate from 6% to 7% turned out to be (almost) revenue-neutral.

This reform causes a change in disposable income, a change in the general price level and the relative prices of consumption goods, and a difference in net wages.

The decision about the allocation of disposable income to the consumption goods is assumed to be weakly separable from the labour supply decision (and associated disposable income).

The effect of the change in disposable income and in the general price level on the allocation of total expenditures over the different commodities, is simulated by means of the same nonparametric Engel curve approach which was used to impute pre-reform budget shares on the PSBH income survey. The underlying methodology is explained in Decoster and De Swerdt (2008). We applied this technique on the new disposable incomes, deflated by a general Stone price index reflecting the living cost of a general change in consumption prices and defined as:

$$\ln Q_h = \sum_i \omega_{ih} \ln q_i, \tag{25}$$

where ω_{ih} refers to household h's budget share for commodity i and q_i to the consumer price for commodity i. Note that to estimate this real income effect, we use the income shares of the baseline in (25) to deflate disposable income before and after the reform. The implied median real income elasticities, resulting from this method, are reported in column 2 of Table 11 below.

Relative price changes are quantified on the basis of the price coefficient matrix of the QUAID-system underlying ASTER 3.0:

$$\omega_i^h = \alpha_i^h + \beta_i^h \log\left(\frac{y^h}{a^h(\mathbf{q})}\right) + \lambda_i^h \log\left(\frac{y^h}{a^h(\mathbf{q})}\right)^2 + \sum_j \gamma_{ij} \log q_i, \tag{26}$$

where y^h refers to total expenditures for household h.[11] The price index $a^h(\mathbf{q})$ was approximated by the Stone price index. The price coefficients (γ_{ij}'s) have been estimated on the National Accounts data, and hence do not take into account the preference heterogeneity, which does appear in the income coefficients β_i^h and λ_i^h. To implement the effect of the changes in relative prices, we only used the matrix of price coefficients $[\gamma_{ij}]$, since the effect of the change in real income has already been taken up by the nonparametric Engel curve. The demand system in (26) was not estimated for durables nor savings. We therefore put the corresponding γ_{ij}'s equal to 0 for the last two commodities. The median of the household-specific price elasticities are reported in column 3 of Table 11.

Table 11:   Commodity breakdown, income and price elasticities, and share parameters of the ces utility function

Commodity aggregate	real income elasticity (median)	relative price elasticity (median)	CES share parameter	
			δ_i	%
Food	0.48	-1.25	0.0340	11.6
Drinks-Non Alcoholic	0.42	-1.70	0.0027	0.9
Drinks-Alcoholic	0.99	-0.10	0.0054	1.8
Tobacco	-0.15	-1.07	0.0013	0.4
Clothing, footwear	1.03	-1.07	0.0222	7.6
Rent and Utilities	0.43	-1.32	0.0918	31.3
Private transport	1.08	-0.79	0.0221	7.5
Public transport	0.37	-8.73	0.0027	0.9
Hygienics, Health	0.74	-0.30	0.0214	7.3
Leisure commodities	0.99	-0.72	0.0552	18.8
Other commodities	0.75	-1.09	0.0346	11.8
Durables	1.08	-0.97	0.0000	0.0
Savings	1.97		0.0000	0.0

---

11   We omitted the second price index of a QUAID-system appearing in the denominator of the λ_i coefficient.

Finally, the labour supply decision is modelled along the lines developed by Dagsvik (1994). Such models explicitly recognize the institutional constraints on labour supply which result in a limited set of working time alternatives (inactivity, some part-time categories, full-time and over-time). Most importantly, however, the computational burden of estimating labour supply functions boils down to ML estimation of a conditional logit function.

The ML estimation allows to identify the preference parameters, conditional on the imposed functional form of the utility function. The approach is fully structural as it separates preferences from constraints, and it thus allows to simulate the effects of all possible changes in the budget constraints.

Discrete choice models of labour supply are based on the assumption that a household can choose among a finite number $J+1$ of working hours (J positive hours and non-participation); each choice $j = 0,...,J$ corresponds to a given level of disposable income C_{hj} (we suppose here that choice j=0 corresponds to non-participation) and each discrete bundle of leisure and income provides a different level of utility. The approach has become standard practice as it provides a straightforward way to account for taxes and benefits, hence nonlinear and nonconvex budget sets, and the joint labour supply of spouses. In effect, choices $j = 0,...,J$ in a couple correspond simply to all the combinations of the spouses' discrete hours. We assume that females may choose between working 0, 20, 40 or 50 hours, while men may work 0, 40 or 50 hours.[12]

The database contained almost no cases of males in couples working part-time. Labour supply was not modelled for singles, given the limited size of the sample. At the same time, we excluded couples where one or both partners are either self-employed or retired. In the first case, in fact, we do not dispose of information on working time, while in the second case the labour supply is fixed at zero.

---

12   Hours worked were censored at 80 hours per week and discretized into a new variable D_L according to the following rules for males and females:

$$D_L = 00, \forall L \in [0,10]$$
$$D_L = 40, \forall L \in [11,44] \quad \text{for males and}$$
$$D_L = 50, \forall L \in [45,80],$$

$$D_L = 00, \forall L \in [0,10]$$
$$D_L = 20, \forall L \in [11,34]$$
$$D_L = 40, \forall L \in [35,44] \quad \text{for females}$$
$$D_L = 50, \forall L \in [45,80].$$

Household's utility V_{ij} derived by household i from making choice j, corresponds to the sum of the deterministic part of the utility U_{hj}, which is assumed to depend on a function of spouses' leisure $l_{f_{hj}}$, $l_{m_{hj}}$, disposable income C_{hj} (equivalent to aggregate household consumption in a static framework) and household characteristics Z_h, and of a random term ε_{hj}:

$$V_{hj} = U(l_{f_{hj}}, l_{m_{hj}}, C_{hj}, Z_h) + \varepsilon_{hj}. \tag{27}$$

When the error term ε_{hj} is assumed to be identically and independently distributed across alternatives and households according to an Extreme Value Type I distribution, the probability that alternative k is chosen by household i is given by:

$$P_{hk} = \Pr(V_{hk} \geq V_{hj}, \forall j = 0, ..., J) = \frac{\exp U(l_{f_{hk}}, l_{f_{hk}}, C_{hk}, Z_h)}{\sum_{j=0}^{J} \exp U(l_{f_{hj}}, l_{m_{hj}}, C_{hj}, Z_h)}. \tag{28}$$

The likelihood for a sample of observed choices can be derived from that expression and maximized to estimate the parameters of function U. When actual working hours are used, the econometrician assumes that individuals choose freely their working hours and face no demand-side constraints.

We assumed a quadratic specification of the utility function as in Blundell et al. (2000). Hence, the utility function of a couple's household has the following form:

$$U_{hj} = \alpha_c C_{hj} + \alpha_{cc} C_{hj}^2 + \alpha_{lf} l_{f_{hj}} + \alpha_{llf} l_{f_{lj}}^2 + \alpha_{lm} l_{m_{hj}} + \alpha_{llm} l_{m_{hj}}^2 \tag{29}$$

$$+ \alpha_{clf} C_{hj} l_{f_{hj}} + \alpha_{clm} C_{ij} l_{m_{hj}} + \alpha_{lmlf} l_{f_{hj}} \cdot l_{m_{hj}}.$$

We assume that preferences vary across households through taste-shifters (age, number of small children) on income and leisure coefficients, and we follow Van Soest (1995) and introduce a dummy variable for part-time work, β_{pt}. Dummy variables also capture different aspects not explicitly treated in the model: search costs, rationing effect and dynamic maximization.

For more details on the model and on estimation results, see Orsini (2006 and 2008).

Chapter 18

Shooting at Moving Targets: Short- versus Long-Term Effects of Anti-Poverty Policies

Rembert R. G. De Blander / Ides Nicaise

1 Introduction

It is a well-established fact that the mobility into and out of poverty is rather high. Bane and Elwood (1986), for instance, report that "60% of those persons just beginning a spell of poverty will exit within two years". Some of the consequences of this observation are that the fraction of persistent poor is smaller and the fraction of people that were ever poor is larger than the instantaneous fraction of poor. Apart from obvious implications for policy, similar observations, combined with increased data availability, have led to a remarkable output focusing on the dynamics of social exclusion and poverty.

Among the recent research on poverty dynamics we find relatively simple models for poverty entry and exit with varying degrees of attention for different complications. Cappellari and Jenkins (2002), for instance, use a first-order Markov chain model and control for endogeneity of the initial conditions and for attrition. Breen and Moisio (2004) use a latent mover-stayer model with correction for measurement error in the poverty status. A more sophisticated approach models the duration before exit out of and re-entry into poverty (Callens, 2004, for 10 EU countries; Canto, 2002 for Spain; Devicienti, 2001, for the UK; Finnie and Sweetman, 2003, for Canada; Stevens, 1999, for a US sample, taking into account unobserved heterogeneity). Income mobility has also been modelled in a similar fashion (Cappellari, 2001; DiPrete and McManus, 2000; Jenkins, 2000; Cantó, 2000; Böheim

This research was funded by the Belgian Science Policy Office under the Social Cohesion programme (grant #SO/01/060).

et al., 1999; Stewart and Swaffield, 1999). A different but related research question considers persistence in welfare benefit uptake (Gustafsson et al., 2002). See also Alcock (2004) for a general discussion and Noble et al. (1998) for an overview.

In this chapter we present a joint Markov model for employment and poverty, conditional on educational attainment. This model is estimated in several stages. The three observed schooling levels are modelled using an ordered logit model. We consider the states employment and unemployment and estimate them with a state-dependent logit model. With respect to poverty we discern three states: insufficient protection (IP), minimum income (MI) and non-poverty (NP), which are state-dependently estimated using a multinomial logit model. To correct for the endogeneity of schooling and employment we include the generalized residuals (Cox and Snell, 1968; Gouriéroux et al., 1987) of the previous stages in each regression. This amounts to Heckman's (1976, 1978) control function approach adapted for ordered and multinomial choice equations (Dubin and McFadden, 1984). To correct for the initial selection effect, we also include control functions generated from static labour and poverty equations for the initial period. As a consequence of the joint modelling of poverty and social assistance benefit uptake, the poverty line we consider is the official threshold for obtaining income support. Finally, we resort to ex-post microsimulation (Merz, 1991) of three basic strategies against poverty: increasing the coverage of the minimum income, activation of the unemployed poor and raising the educational level of vulnerable groups. Using the estimated Markov model, we simulate the impact of these anti-poverty policies for the representatives of the respective target groups present in our sample over the period they were observed, i.e. a time horizon of five years. In the next section, we present our econometric model. Section 3 deals with the data and estimation results. In Section 4 the simulation results are presented. Finally, Section 5 concludes.

2   Empirical model

We assume that schooling is determined by the latent propensity for education

$$s_i^* = \alpha' x_i + u_i,$$

(1)

and we observe

$$
\begin{aligned}
s_i &= 1 \quad \text{if} \quad s_i^* \le \mu_1 \\
&= 2 \quad \text{if} \quad \mu_1 < s_i^* \le \mu_2 \\
&= 3 \quad \text{if} \quad \mu_2 < s_i^*
\end{aligned}
$$

Assuming that u_i are IID according to a logistic distribution, the probabilities to observe $s_i = 1,2,3$ are given by

$$
\begin{aligned}
\Pr[s_i = 1] &= \Lambda(\mu_1 - \alpha' x_i) \\
\Pr[s_i = 2] &= \Lambda(\mu_2 - \alpha' x_i) - \Lambda(\mu_1 - \alpha' x_i) \\
\Pr[s_i = 3] &= 1 - \Lambda(\mu_2 - \alpha' x_i)
\end{aligned}
\tag{2}
$$

with $\Lambda(y) = e^y / (1 + e^y)$.

In the first period, individual i is at work, when her employability

$$
w_{i1}^* = \beta_i' y_{i1} + \beta_2 d_{s_i=2} + \beta_3 d_{s_i=3} + v_{i1}
\tag{3}
$$

473

is higher than some threshold (0). In that case we observe $w_i = 1$, otherwise $w_i = 0$. We allow the errors u_i and v_t to be correlated, but assume a linear dependency between both error terms

$$
v_{i1} = \beta_4 u_i + \eta_{i1}.
\tag{4}
$$

Taking the expectation of (3) with respect to x_{it}' y_{it} and s_{it}, results in

$$
\mathrm{E}\left[w_{i1}^* | y_{i1}, s_i, x_i\right] = \beta_1' y_{i1} + \beta_2 d_{s_i=2} + \beta_3 d_{s_i=3} + \beta_4 \tilde{u}_i.
$$

When the instruments for s_i are valid, it holds that:
$\tilde{u}_i \equiv \mathrm{E}\left[u_i | x_i, y_{i1}, s_i\right] = \mathrm{E}\left[u_i | x_i, s_i\right]$. This last expression is also termed the generalized residual (Cox and Snell, 1968; Gouriéroux et al., 1987) of the schooling model (1-2). Its inclusion in equation (3) removes the bias due to the correlation between u_t and v_t. This can also be considered an extension of Heckman's (1976, 1978) control function approach to an ordered logistic choice equation, for which the expressions are given in De Blander and Nicaise (2005). From the second period on, the individual's employability is assumed to depend on the previous observed state $w_{i;t-1}$ as

$$
w_{it}^* = \beta_{1;w_{i;t-1}}' y_{it} + \beta_{2;w_{i;t-1}} d_{s_i=2} + \beta_{3;w_{i;t-1}} d_{s_i=3} + v_{it}.
\tag{5}
$$

This rather complicated notation means that the effect of a variable varies[1] depending on the state in $t-1$. Under the linearity assumption

$$v_{it;w_{i;t-1}} = \beta_{4;w_{i;t-1}} u_i + \beta_{5;w_{i;t-1}} v_{i1} + \eta_{it}, \tag{6}$$

the expectation of (5) can be written as

$$E\left[w_{it}^* \middle| y_{it}, w_{i;t-1}, s_i, x_i, w_{i1}, y_{i1}\right] = \beta_{1;w_{i;t-1}}' y_{it} + \beta_{2;w_{i;t-1}} d_{s_i=2} + \beta_{3;w_{i;t-1}} d_{s_i=3}$$
$$+ \beta_{4;w_{i;t-1}} \tilde{u}_i + \beta_{5;w_{i;t-1}} \tilde{v}_{i1},$$

where $\tilde{v}_{i1} = E\left[v_{i1} \middle| y_{i1}, s_i, w_{i1}\right]$. Linearity asumption (6) states that we allow the employability error v_{it} to be correlated with both its initial states' error and with the schooling error.

The same reasoning can again be applied for the poverty equations, with the modification that the endogeneity of the initial poverty state will be controlled for by two control functions. For the first period, the propensity for individual i of being in state k (i.e. IP or MI) is given by

$$p_{i1;k}^* = \gamma_{1;k}' z_{i1} + \gamma_{2;k} d_{s_i=2} + \gamma_{3;k} d_{s_i=3}$$
$$+ \gamma_{4;k}' w_{i1} + \gamma_{5;k} u_i + \gamma_{6;k} v_{i1} + \varepsilon_{i1;k}, \tag{7}$$

while for the other periods, it both depends on the previous state and we need to control for the initial conditions

$$E\left[p_{it;k;p_{i;t-1}}^* \middle| z_{it}, p_{i;t-1}, w_{it}, y_{it}, s_i, x_i, z_{i1}, p_{i1}\right] = \gamma_{1;k;p_{i;t-1}}' z_{it} + \gamma_{2;k;p_{i;t-1}} d_{s_i=2}$$
$$+ \gamma_{3;k;p_{i;t-1}} d_{s_i=3} + \gamma_{4;k;p_{i;t-1}}' w_{it} \tag{8}$$
$$+ \gamma_{5;k;p_{i;t-1}} \tilde{u}_i + \gamma_{6;k;p_{i;t-1}} \tilde{v}_{it}$$
$$+ \gamma_{7;k;p_{i;t-1}} \tilde{\varepsilon}_{i1;1} + \gamma_{8;k;p_{i;t-1}} \tilde{\varepsilon}_{i1;2}$$

where $\tilde{\varepsilon}_{i1;1}$ and $\tilde{\varepsilon}_{i1;2}$ are again given in De Blander and Nicaise (2005).

Two further remarks are in order. First, we do not fully exploit the panel structure of our data, nor the fact that several members of the same household may be included in the sample. However, White (1982) guarantees that, when the parameters are consistently estimated, their variance is given by

$$E\left[\frac{\partial^2 LL}{\partial\theta \cdot \partial\theta'}\right]^{-1} E\left[\frac{\partial LL}{\partial\theta} \cdot \frac{\partial LL}{\partial\theta'}\right] E\left[\frac{\partial^2 LL}{\partial\theta \cdot \partial\theta'}\right]^{-1},$$

a quantity which can easily be estimated. We apply this method since the use of a fixed effect estimator would not allow identification of the effect of schooling, and random effects merely allow some efficiency gains. Second, the fact that the control function needs to be estimated in a previous stage, is taken care of by the δ-method. For more details, see De Blander and Nicaise (2005).

1   In other words, when a variable is included in the model, its interaction with a dummy that indicates the previous state is included as well.

3   Estimation

3.1   Data

We consider three educational levels: primary or lower secondary education, upper secondary education and higher education; two labour market states: part- or full-time working (W) and non-working (U); and three poverty states:

- Insufficient protection (IP): family income lies below the legally guaranteed minimum income. For some reason, people in this state forego income support.[2] Note that some individuals in this state may draw an income from work or (other) social benefits. However this does not lift them above the official poverty line.
- Social assistance or minimum income (MI): the municipal social service pays the difference between earned income and the guaranteed minimum income.
- Non-poverty (NP): family income lies above the minimum income, irrespective whether it consists of wages or social security benefits.

From the above distinction it is clear that our definition of the poverty threshold is identical to the Belgian government's cut-off point for receiving social assistance. In the literature this poverty line is considered to result in an underestimation of the number of poor people. We nevertheless maintain it for the following reasons. First this threshold distinguishes a qualitatively different part of the population, those entitled to income support. Second, a higher poverty line would blur the difference between the IP and the MI states, making a model accounting for both poverty and social assistance dynamics much more difficult.

The dataset we use is a subset of the Panel Study of Belgian Households (Mortelmans et al., 2004), from which we retained all individuals out of school but not yet (early) retired, since pensioners, children and students are excluded from certain states. Our sample thus consists of 5,380 individuals, with monthly observations[3] on income and labour market status during the period 1993-1997 , totalling to 238,490 data points.

We present descriptive statistics for our sample in the Annex.

---

2   For a model of non-uptake see Riphahn (2001).
3   We reconstructed monthly income data by combining the yearly income and monthly activity variables from the panel. For a detailed account of the methodology, see Nicaise et al. (2004).

3.2 Results

3.2.1 Schooling

The first equation estimates the probability for an individual to have achieved a certain level of education, using an ordered logit model. The results of this estimation procedure are given in Table 1, from which the following conclusions can be drawn. Women, Catholics and younger birth cohorts generally have achieved higher educational levels. Parental social status also has the expected positive effect on the educational performance of their offspring. The influence of nationality at birth is statistically negligible after controlling for the other determinants. Likelihood-ratio tests for each group of dummies describing the same underlying continuous variable, are given in Table 2. Mother's employment is statistically insignificant at 1%, but significant at 5%, while the other determinants are all significant at 1%.

Table 1:   Determinants of educational attainment

Variable	b	s.e.	p
Gender (1=female)	0.0924	0.0542	0.088
Catholic	0.1848	0.0743	0.013
Born in Belgium	0.0445	0.0943	0.637
Born 40s	0.6921	0.1073	0.000
Born 50s	0.8175	0.1009	0.000
Born 60s	1.1071	0.1034	0.000
Born 70s	0.8418	0.1238	0.000
Father unemployed	-0.0811	0.3049	0.790
Father blue-collar worker	-0.5581	0.0892	0.000
Father white-collar worker	0.4188	0.1094	0.000
Father self-employed	0.0410	0.1124	0.715
Father executive	0.4668	0.1193	0.000
Mother unemployed	-0.1891	0.0929	0.042
Mother blue-collar worker	-0.3895	0.1325	0.003
Mother white-collar worker	-0.2036	0.1337	0.128
Mother self-employed	-0.3321	0.1292	0.010
Mother executive	-0.3941	0.2631	0.134
Father no education	-0.1508	0.1473	0.306
χ^2_{25}	0.2329	0.1111	0.036

Table 2: Likelihood ratio tests for each group of socio-economic background dummies in Table 1

	χ^2_{df}	df	p
Cohort	123.4462	4	0.000
Employment father	139.5040	5	0.000
Employment mother	12.1002	5	0.033
Education father	136.5826	4	0.000
Education mother	120.5392	4	0.000

3.2.2 Employment

The work status dummy-variable was estimated dynamically[4] from the second period onward, depending on the work status in the previous period, using a logit model. This dynamic model will subsequently be used to simulate the effects of activation and education policies on the poverty transitions. A priori we presume that those policies will have persistent effects both on labour market and poverty dynamics. In Table 3 we see that most regressors behave as expected. Education boosts both the probability to get and to stay at work, with the effect of higher education on access to work being almost twice as high as its effect on non-exit. Younger people have a higher probability of access to work, but also of job loss. In other words, youth unemployment is more volatile, while non-employment at later ages is more persistent. Unemployment in the countryside is also more persistent.

Women and single parents with more children and persons living in large families or in bad health, all have a lower probability of getting or staying at work. The lower probability of being at work experienced by non-Belgian EU citizens stems mainly from their slightly lower probability of keeping their job. The lower rate of employment of non-Europeans, on the other hand, is mainly caused by a lower probability of access to work.

Finally, the control function derived from the education equation has no significant effect on labour market transitions, but the correction terms with respect to initial employment status are significant. The latter effect points to the presence of an individual-specific error component. Indeed, the control functions for the initial conditions can be considered as a measurement (with error) of the individual-specific error component. There is thus a strong selection effect in the labour market dynamics. On top of this selection

---

4   The static probability of working in the initial period is not reported here (see De Blander and Nicaise [2005] for details and discussion).

effect, there is persistence in the probability of being at work: a likelihood-ratio test strongly rejects the null hypothesis of equality of the coefficients in both job entry and exit probabilities, i.e. the null of a static model.

Table 3:   Determinants of employment

previous state	unemployed			employed		
Variable	b	se	p	b	se	p
Upper sec. educ.	0.5066	0.0992	0.000	0.4583	0.0987	0.000
Higher education	1.3334	0.1573	0.000	0.7014	0.1500	0.000
Age < 25 y.	3.7765	0.2085	0.000	-0.3954	0.1461	0.007
Age 25-34 y.	3.8249	0.2005	0.000	1.0907	0.1403	0.000
Age 35-44 y.	3.4096	0.2012	0.000	1.6700	0.1405	0.000
Age 45-54 y.	2.2956	0.2076	0.000	1.4916	0.1431	0.000
Gender (1=female)	-0.7343	0.0681	0.000	-0.9813	0.0573	0.000
Cohabiting	0.2052	0.0749	0.006	0.4328	0.0621	0.000
Household size	-0.0373	0.0348	0.285	-0.1398	0.0281	0.000
# children < 12 y.	-0.2113	0.0462	0.000	0.0095	0.0393	0.809
# children 12-16 y.	-0.2814	0.0885	0.001	-0.1530	0.0754	0.042
Poor health	-0.2415	0.0367	0.000	-0.3118	0.0382	0.000
EU citizen	-0.2684	0.1416	0.058	-0.3493	0.1345	0.009
non-EU citizen	-1.1684	0.2156	0.000	-0.4311	0.1867	0.021
Urban residence	0.1481	0.0636	0.020	-0.1611	0.0564	0.004
Brussels region	-0.2369	0.1114	0.033	-0.0880	0.0901	0.329
Walloon region	-0.2178	0.0625	0.000	-0.2538	0.0568	0.000
Ec. growth	-0.0590	0.0363	0.104	0.0258	0.0353	0.465
Unempl. rate	0.1548	0.1591	0.330	-0.1737	0.1390	0.211
CF schooling	-0.0232	0.0398	0.561	-0.0305	0.0394	0.439
CF initial cond.	0.3870	0.0484	0.000	0.4910	0.0613	0.000
Constant	-7.0087	1.4495	0.000	6.0135	1.2635	0.000
# observations	69442			152933		
χ^2_{21}	2225.46		0.000	2928.97		0.000

3.2.3 Poverty

In this section we discuss the probability of finding oneself in one of the three poverty states, conditional on the state in the previous period.[5] The poverty state is given by a trinomial nominal variable, with reference category NP. In Tables 4-6, columns 2 and 6 list the parameter estimates.[6] Columns 4 and 8, on the other hand, give the effect a variable has on the probability of

---

5   Again we refer to De Blander and Nicaise (2005) for the static estimation for the initial period.
6   As usual, standard errors are reported between brackets. The probabilities of obtaining a larger estimate under the null of a parameter equal to zero are given in the columns to the right.

obtaining the concerned outcome. For continuous variables, we report the marginal effect $\partial \Pr[p = k]/\partial x$, while for binary independents we give the effect of a switch from zero to one for the complete observed sample, i.e. $\Pr[p = k|x = 1] - \Pr[p = k|x = 0]$.

A first striking conclusion with respect to entry into poverty, in Table 4, is the insignificant influence of employment status on the probability to enter MI. However, being at work significantly diminishes the probability of becoming insufficiently protected. Also, the self-employed are more likely to enter IP, but less likely to enter MI.

Both probabilities are inversely proportional to educational level. Being younger than 35 increases the probability of IP. Younger people are especially vulnerable to becoming poor, a finding which calls for special attention for this target group. Women, singles and smaller families or families with children have a higher probability of becoming poor. Single-parent households with older children are in addition more likely to enter MI. City dwellers and people in bad health have a higher likelihood of obtaining social assistance, as do people living in the Brussels area or Wallonia. In addition, people living in Brussels are less likely to be insufficiently protected. Note also that a rising unemployment rate increases the probability of falling below the threshold for social assistance eligibility, without resulting in a higher probability of uptake.

The control functions for the unobserved characteristics of schooling and initial working conditions are not significant. However, the initial poverty conditions and the work transitions' unobserved heterogeneity are significant. People who find (or keep) a job against the (observed) odds, are also more likely to stay out of poverty, while their probability of being in MI is unchanged. Likewise, people who inadvertently kept out of IP (and who thus have a negative associated control function), are more likely to stay out of poverty as well, without a similar effect on MI. Managing to keep out of MI against the (observed) odds increases one's likelihood to stay above the threshold altogether.

Table 5 reports the influence of determinants on the probability of leaving the IP state. A job, a degree of higher education and higher economic growth significantly diminish the likelihood of a prolonged stay in IP, while having no effect on a transition to MI. The IP state tends to be relatively more persistent for the self-employed and people living in Brussels. Upper secondary education, gender, cohabitation, health, nationality and degree of urbanization have no effect on transitions out of IP. Household size improves the chances of exit from poverty, but children decrease this probability.

Table 4: Probability of becoming poor (transitions from NP)

From NP to	IP				MI			
Variable	b (s.e.)	p	Effect on $\Pr[IP]$	p	b (s.e.)	p	Effect on $\Pr[MI]$	p
Working	-1.1015 (0.1796)	0.00	-1.55E-3 (3.10E-4)	0.00	-0.3233 (0.3368)	0.34	-5.64E-5 (6.00E-5)	0.36
Upper sec. educ.	-0.2749 (0.1815)	0.13	-2.82E-4 (1.60E-4)	0.09	-1.4547 (0.4490)	0.00	-1.96E-4 (6.00E-5)	0.00
Higher education	-0.6826 (0.3094)	0.03	-6.85E-4 (2.40E-4)	0.01	-2.6427 (0.7155)	0.00	-3.99E-4 (1.20E-4)	0.00
Self-employed	1.4407 (0.1676)	0.00	3.06E-3 (5.90E-4)	0.00	-1.4834 (1.0328)	0.15	-1.44E-4 (5.00E-5)	0.01
Age < 25 y.	0.9936 (0.2503)	0.00	1.67E-3 (6.10E-4)	0.01	1.7335 (0.6017)	0.00	6.50E-4 (4.60E-4)	0.16
Age 25-34 y.	0.7677 (0.2239)	0.00	1.01E-3 (3.50E-4)	0.00	0.9862 (0.5460)	0.07	2.09E-4 (1.60E-4)	0.18
Age 35-44 y.	0.2994 (0.2156)	0.17	3.44E-4 (2.60E-4)	0.19	0.8589 (0.5077)	0.09	1.71E-4 (1.30E-4)	0.19
Age 45-54 y.	0.3053 (0.2008)	0.13	3.61E-4 (2.60E-4)	0.16	1.1961 (0.4683)	0.01	2.93E-4 (1.80E-4)	0.10
Gender (1=female)	0.1951 (0.1118)	0.08	2.11E-4 (1.20E-4)	0.08	0.3111 (0.2314)	0.18	5.12E-5 (4.00E-5)	0.18
Cohabiting	-0.5229 (0.1172)	0.00	-6.49E-4 (1.70E-4)	0.00	-0.8804 (0.2578)	0.00	-1.85E-4 (7.00E-5)	0.01
Household size	-0.4502 (0.0759)	0.00	-4.86E-4 (8.00E-5)	0.00	-0.1549 (0.1131)	0.17	-2.53E-5 (2.00E-5)	0.18
# children < 12 y.	0.2260 (0.0924)	0.01	2.44E-4 (1.00E-4)	0.01	0.2131 (0.1431)	0.14	3.49E-5 (2.00E-5)	0.13
# children 12-16 y.	0.5921 (0.1487)	0.00	6.39E-4 (1.60E-4)	0.00	0.5276 (0.2393)	0.03	8.64E-5 (4.00E-5)	0.04
Poor health	0.0751 (0.0626)	0.23	8.11E-5 (7.00E-5)	0.23	0.2953 (0.1095)	0.01	4.84E-5 (2.00E-5)	0.02
EU citizen	0.1414 (0.2298)	0.54	1.63E-4 (2.80E-4)	0.56	0.3154 (0.3937)	0.42	5.99E-5 (9.00E-5)	0.48
non-EU citizen	0.2084 (0.2712)	0.44	2.49E-4 (3.50E-4)	0.47	0.5502 (0.4136)	0.18	1.18E-4 (1.20E-4)	0.31
City	-0.1556 (0.1044)	0.14	-1.63E-4 (1.00E-4)	0.12	0.6734 (0.2233)	0.00	1.30E-4 (5.00E-5)	0.02
Brussels region	-0.6159 (0.1858)	0.00	-5.35E-4 (1.30E-4)	0.00	0.8051 (0.3176)	0.01	1.84E-4 (1.00E-4)	0.06
Walloon region	0.0072 (0.1055)	0.95	7.70E-6 (1.10E-4)	0.95	0.5811 (0.2535)	0.02	1.00E-4 (5.00E-5)	0.04
Ec. growth	0.0326 (0.0433)	0.45	3.52E-5 (5.00E-5)	0.45	0.1496 (0.0945)	0.11	2.45E-5 (2.00E-5)	0.11
Unempl. rate	0.4513 (0.1760)	0.01	4.87E-4 (1.90E-4)	0.01	0.4836 (0.3708)	0.19	7.92E-5 (6.00E-5)	0.20
CF schooling	0.0986 (0.0813)	0.23	1.06E-4 (7.00E-5)	0.12	0.1791 (0.1865)	0.34	2.93E-5 (3.00E-5)	0.30
CF init. cond. work	-0.0869 (0.0556)	0.12	-9.38E-5 (5.00E-5)	0.09	-0.0616 (0.1100)	0.58	-1.01E-5 (2.00E-5)	0.57
CF work	-0.4955 (0.0419)	0.00	-5.35E-4 (5.00E-5)	0.00	-0.2617 (0.1816)	0.15	-4.28E-5 (3.00E-5)	0.14
CF init. cond. IP	0.3944 (0.0441)	0.00	4.26E-4 (4.00E-5)	0.00	0.0441 (0.1150)	0.70	7.15E-6 (2.00E-5)	0.70
CF init. cond. MI	0.2182 (0.0760)	0.00	2.36E-4 (6.00E-5)	0.00	0.5059 (0.1490)	0.00	8.29E-5 (2.00E-5)	0.00
Constant	-9.1036 (1.6233)	0.00			-13.0496 (3.4675)	0.00		
# observations	216076							
χ^2_{50}	1273.18	0.00						

Table 5: Probability of staying poor (transitions from IP)

From IP to	IP				MI			
Variable	b (s.e.)	p	Effect on Pr$[IP]$	p	b (s.e.)	p	Effect on Pr$[MI]$	p
Working	-0.7817 (0.1705)	0.00	-6.87E-2 (1.68E-2)	0.00	-1.8124 (0.7628)	0.02	-6.14E-4 (5.10E-4)	0.23
Upper sec. educ.	-0.2540 (0.2319)	0.27	-2.15E-2 (1.55E-2)	0.17	-0.2045 (0.7349)	0.78	1.54E-5 (4.10E-4)	0.97
Higher education	-0.9230 (0.4014)	0.02	-9.16E-2 (3.32E-2)	0.01	-1.5419 (1.3996)	0.27	-3.66E-4 (6.50E-4)	0.58
Self-employed	1.5282 (0.1749)	0.00	9.44E-2 (8.74E-3)	0.00	0.3162 (1.3140)	0.81	-5.11E-4 (4.90E-4)	0.29
Gender (1=female)	0.0948 (0.1111)	0.39	7.52E-3 (8.96E-3)	0.40	0.6137 (0.5714)	0.28	3.08E-4 (2.80E-4)	0.28
Cohabiting	-0.2114 (0.1271)	0.10	-1.63E-2 (1.01E-2)	0.11	-1.5415 (0.6967)	0.03	-9.43E-4 (8.10E-4)	0.24
Household size	-0.1092 (0.0540)	0.04	-8.06E-3 (4.38E-3)	0.07	-1.7022 (0.5763)	0.00	-9.57E-4 (4.80E-4)	0.05
# children < 12 y.	0.0682 (0.0819)	0.41	4.51E-3 (6.71E-3)	0.50	2.0163 (0.8038)	0.01	1.17E-3 (6.20E-4)	0.06
# children 12-16 y.	0.5725 (0.1804)	0.00	4.57E-2 (1.45E-2)	0.00	2.5879 (0.5473)	0.00	1.23E-3 (6.80E-4)	0.07
Poor health	0.0083 (0.0659)	0.90	4.51E-4 (5.35E-3)	0.93	0.4244 (0.2511)	0.09	2.49E-4 (1.90E-4)	0.18
non-EU citizen	0.2135 (0.2507)	0.39	1.67E-2 (1.73E-2)	0.34	-1.2078 (1.4321)	0.40	-5.00E-4 (3.80E-4)	0.19
City	-0.2031 (0.1230)	0.10	-1.77E-2 (1.06E-2)	0.10	0.3718 (0.5684)	0.51	3.88E-4 (4.90E-4)	0.43
Brussels region	0.3268 (0.1998)	0.10	2.46E-2 (1.31E-2)	0.06	-0.7844 (0.9231)	0.40	-4.54E-4 (3.60E-4)	0.21
Walloon region	0.1488 (0.1187)	0.21	1.24E-2 (9.34E-3)	0.19	-0.1937 (0.4833)	0.69	-1.98E-4 (3.20E-4)	0.53
Ec. growth	-0.1463 (0.0531)	0.01	-1.18E-2 (4.30E-3)	0.01	-0.3802 (0.4616)	0.41	-1.48E-4 (2.70E-4)	0.58
Unempl. rate	0.0187 (0.2060)	0.93	8.44E-4 (1.68E-2)	0.96	1.2859 (1.8486)	0.49	7.57E-4 (1.09E-3)	0.49
CF schooling	0.2062 (0.1114)	0.06	1.71E-2 (6.22E-3)	0.01	-0.2044 (0.2718)	0.45	-2.34E-4 (1.70E-4)	0.17
CF init. cond work	-0.0192 (0.0471)	0.68	-1.59E-3 (3.79E-3)	0.68	0.0171 (0.1971)	0.93	2.07E-5 (1.20E-4)	0.86
CF work	-0.4631 (0.0906)	0.00	-3.81E-2 (6.98E-3)	0.00	-0.0258 (0.2096)	0.90	2.36E-4 (1.60E-4)	0.15
CF init. cond. IP	0.0550 (0.0329)	0.09	4.50E-3 (2.64E-3)	0.09	0.0404 (0.1525)	0.79	-5.78E-6 (9.00E-5)	0.95
CF init. cond. MI	0.0753 (0.0685)	0.27	6.20E-3 (5.47E-3)	0.26	-0.0146 (0.2209)	0.95	-4.96E-5 (1.40E-4)	0.72
Constant	2.6787 (1.9033)	0.16			-12.3578 (17.0562)	0.47		
# observations	4596							
χ^2_{42}	712.59	0.00						

The initial conditions of both work and IP do not seem to influence the exit probability from IP. People with a high unobserved component in their education or in their probability of falling below the eligibility threshold also tend to stay longer in IP, while people with a high unobserved component in their transitions into work have a higher exit probability from poverty. We finally remark that our sample contains only 24 transitions from IP to MI, which corresponds to a transition probability of 0.53%.

In Table 6 we describe the transition probabilities from the MI state into IP or MI. As before, the number of transitions from MI to IP is very low and corresponds to a transition probability of only 0.71%. An obvious conclusion is that the mode of poverty in which people are situated is very persistent.

Having a job, living together and a high unemployment rate all promote exits from social assistance, the latter perhaps because it induces tighter controls of eligibility. Household size and the number of adolescent children, on the other hand, increase MI persistence. The control functions for education and the initial IP conditions are not significant. On the other hand, unobserveds causing initial employment tend to reduce a transition from MI to IP. Inadvertently finding a job decreases the likelihood of a prolonged stay in MI. An unexpected initial MI state keeps increasing the odds of staying in MI later on.

Table 6: Probability of staying poor (transitions from MI)

From MI to	IP				MI			
Variable	b (s.e.)	p	Effect on $\Pr[IP]$	p	b (s.e.)	p	Effect on $\Pr[MI]$	p
Working	1.0342 (1.3064)	0.43	6.92E-3 (8.94E-3)	0.44	-0.8780 (0.3679)	0.02	-4.52E-2 (2.24E-2)	0.04
Upper sec. educ.	0.3080 (1.6194)	0.85	1.56E-3 (4.90E-3)	0.75	-0.4266 (0.4362)	0.33	-1.72E-2 (1.78E-2)	0.33
Higher education	-2.0154 (2.2135)	0.36	-9.97E-4 (.)	.	-1.3658 (0.7674)	0.08	-7.75E-2 (6.67E-2)	0.25
Gender (1=female)	-0.1556 (0.8118)	0.85	3.86E-4 (1.24E-3)	0.76	-0.3913 (0.2771)	0.16	-1.28E-2 (8.35E-3)	0.13
Cohabiting	-0.9151 (1.5123)	0.55	6.08E-5 (2.69E-3)	0.98	-0.9942 (0.2515)	0.00	-4.29E-2 (1.30E-2)	0.00
Household size	-1.0780 (0.9879)	0.28	-2.45E-3 (1.56E-3)	0.12	0.3051 (0.1607)	0.06	1.25E-2 (5.47E-3)	0.02
# children < 12 y.	0.7464 (1.0758)	0.49	1.72E-3 (1.44E-3)	0.23	-0.2281 (0.2198)	0.30	-9.26E-3 (7.38E-3)	0.21
# children 12-16 y.	1.4485 (1.0238)	0.16	1.37E-3 (1.86E-3)	0.46	0.7064 (0.3480)	0.04	2.22E-2 (1.12E-2)	0.05
Poor health	0.1887 (0.4186)	0.65	1.95E-5 (7.00E-4)	0.98	0.1842 (0.1425)	0.20	6.12E-3 (4.71E-3)	0.20
non-EU citizen	0.5938 (2.1755)	0.79	-2.19E-4 (3.33E-3)	0.95	0.7429 (0.5487)	0.18	1.95E-2 (1.14E-2)	0.09
City	0.4543 (0.8566)	0.60	1.38E-3 (1.63E-3)	0.40	-0.2625 (0.2929)	0.37	-1.03E-2 (1.05E-2)	0.32
Brussels region	-0.2361 (1.7224)	0.89	-6.63E-4 (2.47E-3)	0.79	0.1962 (0.4855)	0.69	6.79E-3 (1.44E-2)	0.64
Walloon region	-0.9390 (0.9126)	0.30	-2.26E-3 (2.93E-3)	0.44	0.1111 (0.3030)	0.71	5.94E-3 (1.05E-2)	0.57
Ec. growth	0.2841 (0.3467)	0.41	2.60E-4 (5.80E-4)	0.65	0.1432 (0.1226)	0.24	4.52E-3 (4.02E-3)	0.26
Unempl. rate	-1.7234 (1.2064)	0.15	-1.49E-4 (2.29E-3)	0.51	-0.9188 (0.4832)	0.06	-2.92E-2 (1.55E-2)	0.06
CF schooling	0.1015 (0.5449)	0.85	-4.35E-6 (9.20E-4)	1.00	0.1076 (0.1887)	0.57	3.59E-3 (6.30E-3)	0.57
CF init. cond. work	-0.7033 (0.4855)	0.15	-1.09E-3 (5.50E-4)	0.05	-0.0946 (0.1243)	0.45	-2.10E-3 (4.02E-3)	0.60
CF work	-0.8030 (0.2151)	0.00	-4.40E-4 (3.90E-4)	0.26	-0.5761 (0.1133)	0.00	-1.88E-2 (3.71E-3)	0.00
CF init. cond. IP	0.7683 (0.4549)	0.09	7.11E-4 (1.04E-3)	0.49	0.3826 (0.2206)	0.08	1.21E-2 (7.22E-3)	0.10
CF init. cond. MI	-0.3439 (0.3288)	0.30	-9.52E-4 (7.00E-4)	0.17	0.1966 (0.0847)	0.02	7.47E-3 (2.37E-3)	0.00
Constant	15.0182 (11.1717)	0.18			10.4613 (4.4097)	0.02		
# observations	1703							
χ^2_{40}	558.63	0.00						

483

4 Microsimulation of policies

Every anti-poverty policy presumably has a different impact on the transition probabilities between the three poverty states. In this section, we will examine the effects of three broad categories of policies, by means of ex-post microsimulation of some typical examples of measures:

1. optimization of the coverage of social assistance: every household which becomes poor will get social assistance,
2. activation: a temporary job is offered to all jobless poor individuals,
3. education: low-skilled individuals are encouraged to obtain a diploma of upper secondary education.

Each of these strategies can be seen as representing one of three competing views on the welfare state: the traditional welfare state, the active welfare state or the knowledge-based society.

In our simulations we assume that the effects of each strategy apply as from January 1993, the beginning of our observation period. We will indeed apply ex-post microsimulation (Merz (1991): each policy will be applied to each member of their respective target groups present in our database. This procedure allows us to compare the different policies without having to generate hypothetical macro-economic time series or representative sample individuals.

The target groups consist of people to whom the conditions of the specific policy apply in January 1993. We will simulate the policies for these groups only and we do not consider "late joiners" into the respective programmes. For each individual, we know the starting poverty and employment states, or we can predict them using the static estimations for the initial period. We also know, for each individual, the labour market and poverty transition probabilities,[7] which allow us to construct a time-path of probabilities for both employment and poverty states. Comparing time-paths with and without policy intervention gives an indication of the impact of this policy over time.

4.1 Full coverage of the guaranteed minimum income

Under this scenario, everybody in IP in January 1993 receives social assistance. We assume that reception of income support entails behavioural

---

7   When a policy affects the labour market transitions, the poverty transition probabilities are obtained by predicting them with and without employment and then mixing them with the employment probabilities.

changes: conditional on observed characteristics, our target group will adopt the transition patterns of the MI group. The target group in our sample consists of 170 people in the IP state in January 1993.

Figure 1: Full coverage of the guaranteed minimum income: predicted effects on the time path of (non-)poverty

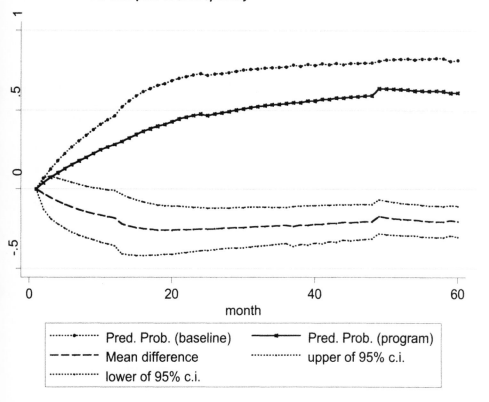

In Figure 1 three curves are plotted: the baseline probability curve depicts the time-path of non-poverty (for the target group of the measure) without any policy intervention; the curve labelled "predicted probability under the programme" describes the simulated time-path after application of the programme. For example, we notice that spontaneous exit out of poverty amounts to three-quarters after approximately two years. The third curve, at the bottom of the graph, represents the difference between the probabilities before and after intervention, with a 95% confidence interval band. As can be seen, the net anti-poverty impact of the "full coverage" strategy on the target group is significantly *negative*: approximately 20% more people (from the group) get stuck into income support, even after five years.

Table 7:   Steady state characteristics of the full coverage scenario

	Total Sample	Target Group		
		no programme	100% coverage	difference
$\hat{\Pr}[\text{NP}]$	96.85 (6.71)	79.34 (10.40)	63.44 (12.62)	-15.90 (15.19)
$\hat{\Pr}[\text{IP}]$	2.22 (6.68)	15.75 (9.85)	0.0	-15.75 (9.85)
$\hat{\Pr}[\text{MI}]$	0.93 (0.42)	4.91 (2.30)	36.56 (12.62)	31.65 (11.46)
$\hat{E}[t_{NP}]$	1116.53 (120.28)	116.91 (20.25)	116.91 (5.12)	0.00 (19.37)
$\hat{E}[t_{IP}]$	7.43 (0.92)	13.31 (1.94)	0.0	-13.31 (1.94)
$\hat{E}[t_{MI}]$	8.42 (2.12)	37.35 (27.02)	77.81 (65.61)	40.47 (48.24)

A successful policy should achieve the following objectives:

1. reduce the severity of poverty (i.e. close the gap between actual income and the minimum income threshold),
2. lift as many individuals as possible out of poverty by raising the exit rate,
3. prevent new entries into poverty by reducing the entry hazard.

The full coverage scenario achieves only the first of these three objectives: it closes the income gap but at the same time decelerates the exit rate and thus decreases the probability of non-poverty after five years significantly[8] to about 60%. In other words, this approach is purely curative: it alleviates extreme poverty, but raises the dependency on income support. The potentially positive effects of services related to social assistance on the exit rate are clearly offset by a "poverty trap" effect.

The impact of increased coverage can also be illustrated in a different way. Knowledge of the transition probabilities allows us to compute some steady-state parameters for each individual, which, averaged over the target group, are given in Table 7. For comparison, these numbers are also given for the total sample. The probability of being poor for the population out of school and not yet retired amounts to 3.15%, two thirds of which do not apply for social assistance. The mean duration of a spell in poverty is about 8 months for both the IP and MI states. Looking at the target group, the picture changes drastically. In the long run and without extra policy meas-

486

<hr>

8   Using a 5% significance level.

ures, about 21% of the target group live on or below the poverty threshold, with a mean spell of 13 months in IP and slightly more than 3 years in MI. A policy of 100% coverage by social assistance would *raise* the probability of poverty to 36.6% and the expected duration to almost 6.5 years.

These findings do sound somewhat paradoxical: strengthening the safety net raises the poverty risk. Of course this conclusion follows directly from the yardstick with which we chose to measure the effects of a policy. In no way do we advocate the abolishment of social assistance, which at least reduces the severity of poverty. On the other hand, this exercise also shows the potentially adverse effects on the poverty *dynamics* of an increase in social assistance coverage.

4.2 Activation

In this scenario, the unemployed poor get a job for a period of one year. A first expected, direct effect is that this job will increase the exit probability from, and lower the (re-)entry hazard into poverty. A second, indirect effect is that persistence in employment will sustain this effect after the end of the programme.

Table 8:   Steady state characteristics of the activation scenario

	no programme	activation	difference
$\hat{Pr}[NP]$	74.56 (9.23)	75.76 (11.69)	1.20 (5.33)
$\hat{Pr}[IP]$	12.82 (8.48)	12.17 (0.44)	-0.65 (5.14)
$\hat{Pr}[MI]$	12.62 (3.33)	12.07 (2.28)	-0.55 (1.48)
$\hat{E}[t_{NP}]$	126.12 (20.18)	141.47 (36.46)	15.35 (19.06)
$\hat{E}[t_{IP}]$	10.58 (1.93)	10.14 (1.56)	-0.44 (0.68)
$\hat{E}[t_{MI}]$	47.90 (25.06)	45.11 (17.90)	-2.79 (8.19)

The target group in our sample consists of 160 individuals in January 1993, who are offered and supposed to accept a job at that moment. Without any programme, about 30% of the poor unemployed manage to be at work after years. A first direct effect of the activation policy is that the estimated probability of being at work rises by about 5.5% four years after the programme is finished. Of the participants, however, more than 60% become unemployed again. From month 11 up to month 33, the activation programme has a significant[9] positive effect on the probability of non-poverty. In reality, the poverty alleviation effects of this policy will strongly depend on the quality and the suitability of the job offered, parameters unaccounted for in this simulation. By setting the "at work"-dummy equal to one, we implicitly assume that the programme provides jobs of the same quality as those that are otherwise performed voluntarily by persons with comparable characteristics (except for the duration which is kept fixed here).

Figure 2: Activation scenario: anti-poverty effects

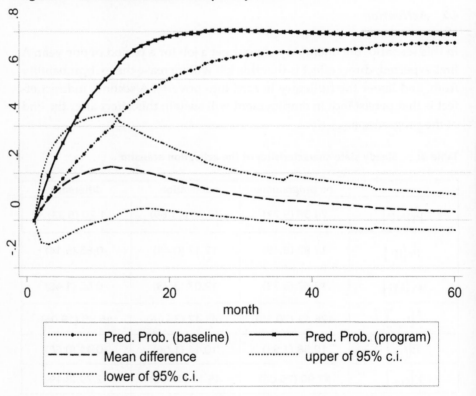

The activation policy (see Figure 2) now seems to affect mainly the *timing* of poverty exits. The direct effects are (a) a substantial increase of the exit and (b) a decrease of the entry probability. After 12 months the programme

---

9   Using a 5% significance level.

reaches its maximum impact: it lifts an extra 23% of the participants above the poverty line, compared to the trend without intervention. Later on, this result diminishes as the policy reaches its ceiling while the baseline poverty odds keep diminishing. The net residual effect of this programme is about 3.70% four years after its termination. The modest long-term residual effect of this policy can also be noticed from Table 8: the steady-state probability of being non-poor increases by about 1.2%. The mean spell out of poverty, however, increases from 10.5 to 12 years. Eventually, the difference in steady states decays to zero.

We like to stress that our focus on poverty probabilities does not imply that we consider non-poverty a good regardless of other considerations. We consider this work as a first stage on which then later cost-benefit or welfare assessments can be based, taking into account for instance the trade-off between income and leisure.

4.3 Education

The most recent welfare state paradigm stresses education and knowledge as determining factors of social integration. We translate this into a scenario where the lowest-skilled are encouraged to obtain a degree of upper secondary education, which is simply operationalized by forecasting the poverty outcomes under the assumption that the target group has obtained the upper secondary degree. In the "youth variant", the target group consists of all low-skilled below the age of 25, in the "learn-fare" variety it is made up of the poor low-skilled younger than 50 years.

Table 9: Steady state characteristics of the education scenario, target group <25y

	no programme	education	difference
$\hat{\Pr}[\text{NP}]$	91.80 (13.51)	96.83 (9.71)	5.03 (13.57)
$\hat{\Pr}[\text{IP}]$	3.33 (12.99)	2.04 (0.07)	-1.28 (13.13)
$\hat{\Pr}[\text{MI}]$	4.87 (1.46)	1.13 (1.11)	-3.75 (1.39)
$\hat{E}[t_{NP}]$	342.40 (122.14)	734.34 (54.94)	391.95 (114.30)
$\hat{E}[t_{IP}]$	6.98 (1.12)	5.19 (0.60)	-1.79 (1.13)
$\hat{E}[t_{MI}]$	18.20 (6.07)	10.59 (5.07)	-7.61 (4.63)

Figure 3: Education scenario, target group<25 y: anti-poverty effects

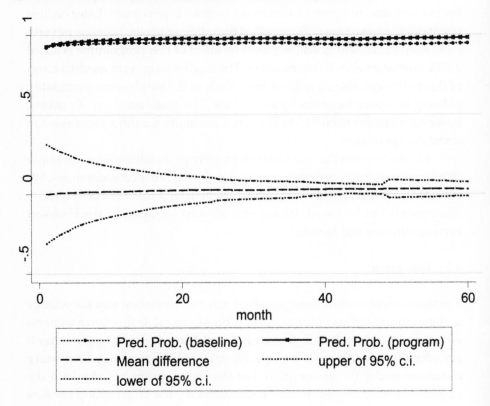

The first target group in our sample consists of 192 individuals who, in January 1993, are younger than 25 and have no degree of upper secondary education. Of these 179 (93.23%) are not poor, 4 (2.08%) are insufficiently protected and 9 (4.69%) receive social assistance. The small number of low-skilled school-leavers living below the poverty line can be explained by the fact that most of them still live with their parents. Some form of protection seems to spring from their social capital. However, since we consider a period of five years, our model should implicitly account for the period in which these youngsters leave their parental household to live on their own. Nevertheless, a degree of upper secondary education seems to offer some extra and lasting protection against poverty of slightly over 5%.

Figure 4: Education scenario, target group poor <50y: anti-poverty effects

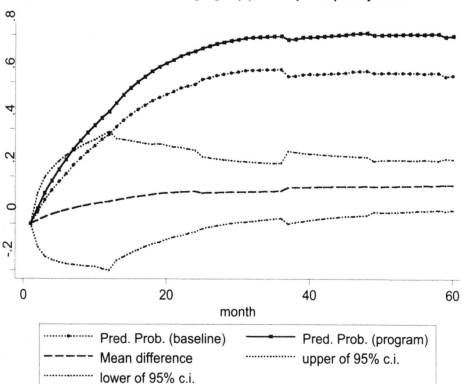

Table 10: Steady state characteristics of the education scenario,
target group poor <50y

	no programme	education	difference
$\hat{\text{Pr}}[\text{NP}]$	63.90 (16.62)	80.89 (9.26)	16.99 (13.91)
$\hat{\text{Pr}}[\text{IP}]$	14.41 (12.83)	10.80 (0.21)	-3.60 (10.83)
$\hat{\text{Pr}}[\text{MI}]$	21.70 (7.45)	8.31 (4.42)	-13.39 (6.04)
$\hat{\text{E}}[t_{NP}]$	67.78 (26.60)	123.51 (12.59)	55.73 (21.38)
$\hat{\text{E}}[t_{IP}]$	12.85 (2.45)	9.96 (1.47)	-2.88 (2.32)
$\hat{\text{E}}[t_{MI}]$	64.77 (31.38)	38.00 (36.99)	-26.77 (19.47)

In the second variant (learnfare), the target group consists of 67 low-skilled poor respondents below the age of 50. Figure 4 again shows the lasting effects of increased education. From month 29 on, these positive effects are statistically significant.[10] The probability of being above the poverty line increases by 17%. This relatively large impact is also reflected in a 40% decrease of the mean spell duration in social assistance.

4.4 Policy implications

Despite the methodological and data problems discussed in Sections 2 and 3, the following conclusions seem to emerge from our analysis.

- Raising the *coverage of social assistance*, while alleviating the harshest effects of poverty, also tends to increase the number of poor through the poverty trap effect. Admittedly, the findings relate to the period 1993-1997 in Belgium, in the context of a sluggish economy and rather "passive" income compensation policies. In the meantime, work incentives have been built into the social assistance regulations and benefits have been linked with activation. Nevertheless, the simulation warns against the possible perverse effects of mere income compensation.
- Getting people into *work* for a limited period (one year) affects mainly the timing of the poverty exits, but has less effect on the steady state parameters. Exits from poverty accelerate in the short run. However, the longer-term impact of activation is very modest unless high-quality jobs are offered (e.g. combinations of work and training).
- The *education* scenario appears to yield the most substantial and durable effects, especially when focused on those living in poverty (learnfare variant).

In order to make the estimated effects of the three strategies comparable, we have to take into account the size differences of the initial target groups. To do so we reweighed the reported results. In Table 11 the poverty impact of policies is reported as a percentage of the overall group of poor people (IP and MI) in the initial period (226 individuals). Raising the coverage of social assistance will increase the steady state fraction of poor people by up to 11.96%. This result is the net effect of the decreased share of under-protected people (11.85%) and the increased share of people receiving social assistance (23.81%). The net steady-state impact for the activation policy, during the fourth year after the programme amounts to 0.85%, but theoretically, it further decays to zero in the future. The relatively small figures for

---

10   Using a 5% significance level.

the "youth variant" of the education policy reflect the fact that only 13% of the target group was poor as well. The fraction of originally poor people helped by the programme is thus accordingly small.

Table 11: Net steady-state impact of policies as a fraction of the total number of poor in the initial period

	NP	IP	MI
100% coverage	-11.96%	-11.85%	+23.81%
Activation	+0.85%	-0.46%	-0.39%
Education of the young	+0.29%	-0.07%	-0.22%
Education of the poor	+5.04%	-1.07%	-4.03%

Upon comparing the strategies with each other, increasing the coverage of MI has (by definition) the highest impact on extreme poverty (IP), while improving education of the low-skilled has the highest overall impact (IP and MI), strikingly more than activation of the unemployed. And yet, all in all, none of the simulated strategies appear to provide the panacea against poverty. More perversely, the major part of the gain in non-poverty[11] originates from a reduction in the fraction of people receiving the minimum income, while the sub-population of really poor seems less affected.

The rather modest impact of our simulations is of course partly due to the criterion we use to compare the different policies (fraction of the initially poor who remain poor in the long run), which is of course affected by a sizable deadweight effect. The negative connotation of the latter term seems rather unfair, since the fact that so many initially poor finally escape poverty reflects both the effectiveness of other existing poverty-alleviating measures and the adaptability of human nature to difficult conditions.

5   Conclusion

In this study we model employment and poverty states as a discrete first-order Markov process, taking into account endogeneity of schooling. Using this model, we then evaluate the impact of different policies on the poverty dynamics by ex-post microsimulation. The policies we assess are exemplars of currently prevailing social policy paradigms: the traditional welfare state, the active welfare state and the knowledge-based society.

---

11   Except for the 100% coverage scenario.

When the *duration of poverty spells* or the *probability of being poor* is taken as the criterion for evaluation, our research indicates that (a) increased coverage of the guaranteed minimum income has adverse effects, (b) activation has large short-term and small long-term positive effects, and (c) learnfare has lasting positive effects.

At the same time, our dynamic approach proved to be much more realistic in predicting the impact of policies. Given the high degree of mobility into and out of poverty, the net effects of anti-poverty measures appear to be much smaller than a static model would predict. Moreover, depending on the type of policy adopted, long-term effects may be much greater or smaller than short-term effects.

References

Alcock, P. (2004) 'The Influence of Dynamic Perspectives on Poverty Analysis and Anti-Poverty Policy in the UK', *Journal of Social Policy* 33 (3): 395-416.

Bane, M.J./Ellwood, D.T. (1986) 'Slipping Into and Out of Poverty: The Dynamics of Spells', *Journal of Human Resources* 21 (1): 1-21.

Böheim, R./Ermisch, J.F./Jenkins, S.P. (1999) 'The Dynamics of Lone Mother's Incomes: Public and Private Income Sources Compared', ISERWorking Paper 1999-05, University of Essex, UK.

Breen, R./Moisio, P. (2004) 'Poverty Dynamics Corrected for Measurement Error', *Journal of Economic Inequality* 2 (3): 171-191.

Callens, M. (2004) 'Essays on Multilevel Logistic Regression', Unpublished PhD Thesis, K.U.Leuven.

Cantó, O. (2000) 'Income Mobility in Spain: How Much Is There?', *Review of Income and Wealth* 46 (1): 85-102.

Cantó, O. (2002) 'Climbing Out of Poverty, Falling Back In: Low Income Stability in Spain', *Applied Economics*, 34 (15): 1903-1916.

Cappellari, L. (2001) 'Earnings Mobility among Italian Low Paid Workers', ISER Working Paper, 2001-13, University of Essex.

Cappellari, L./Jenkins, S.P. (2002) 'Who Stays Poor? Who Becomes Poor? Evidence from the British Household Panel Survey', *Economic Journal* 112 (478): C60-C67.

Cox, D.R./Snell, E.J. (1968) 'A General Definition of Residuals', *Journal of the Royal Statistical, Society B* 30 (2): 248-275.

De Blander, R./Nicaise, I. (2005) 'Maatschappelijke keuzen, structurele armoede en sociale kost', HIVA Rapport 975, HIVA, K.U.Leuven.

Devicienti, F. (2001) 'Poverty Persistence in Britain: A Multivariate Analysis using the BHPS, 1991-1997', ISERWorking Paper 2001-02, University of Essex.

DiPrete, T.A./McManus, P.A. (2000) 'Family Change, Employment Transitions, and the Welfare State: Household Income Dynamics in the United States and Germany', *American Sociological Review* 65 (3): 343-370.

Dubin, J.A./McFadden, D.L. (1984) 'An Econometric Analysis of Residential Electric Appliance Holdings and Consumption', *Econometrica* 52 (2): 345-362.

Finnie, R. / Sweetman, A. (2003) 'Poverty Dynamics: Empirical Evidence for Canada', *Canadian Journal of Economics-Revue canadienne économique* 36 (2): 291-325.

Gouriéroux, C. / Monfort, A. / Renault, E. / Trognon, A. (1987) 'Generalized Residuals', *Journal of Econometrics* 34 (1-2): 5-32.

Gustafsson, B. / Muller, R. / Negri, N. / Voges, W. (2002) 'Paths Through (and Out of) Social Assistance', in Saraceno, C. (ed.), *Social Assistance Dynamics in Europe. National and Local Poverty Regimes.* Bristol: The Policy Press.

Heckman, J.J. (1976) 'The Common Structure of Statistical Models of Truncation, Sample Selection and Limited Dependent Variables and a Simple Estimator for Such Models', *Annals of Economic and Social Measurement* 5 (4): 475-492.

Heckman, J.J. (1979) 'Sample Selection Bias as a Specification Error', *Econometrica* 47 (1): 153-161.

Jenkins, S.P. (2000) 'Modelling Household Income Dynamics', *Journal of Population Economics* 13 (4): 529-567.

Merz, J. (1991) 'Microsimulation – a Survey of Principles, Developments and Applications', *International Journal of Forecasting* 7: 77-104.

Mortelmans, D. / Casman, M.T. / Doutrelepont, R. (2004) *Elf jaar uit het leven in België. Socio-economische analyses op het Gezinsdemografisch Panel PSBH.* Ghent, Belgium: Academia Press.

Nicaise, I. / Groenez, S. / Adelman, L. / Roberts, S. / Middleton, S. (2004) *Gaps, Traps and Springboards in European Minimum Income Systems.* Leuven: HIVA / Loughborough: CRSP.

Noble, M. / Cheung, S.Y. / Smith, G. (1998) 'Origins and Destinations – Social Security Claimant Dynamics', *Journal of Social Policy* 27 (3): 351-369.

Riphahn, R.T. (2001) 'Rational Poverty or Poor Rationality? The Take-Up of Social Assistance Benefits', *Review of Income and Wealth* 47 (3): 379-398.

Stevens, A.H. (1999) 'Climbing Out of Poverty, Falling Back In – Measuring the Persistence of Poverty Over Multiple Spells', *Journal of Human Resources* 34 (3): 557-588.

Stewart, M.B. / Swaffield, J.K. (1999) 'Low Pay Dynamics and Transition Probabilities', *Economica* 66: 23-42.

White, H. (1982) 'Maximum Likelihood Estimation of Misspecified Models', *Econometrica* (1): 1-25.

Annex: Descriptive statistics

Table 12: Descriptive statistics for the variables used in the schooling estimation

Variable	Baseline value	#	Other values	#	%
Education	≤ Lower sec.	1850	Higher sec.	1676	31.15
			Higher Educ.	1854	34.46
Gender	Male	2736	Female	2644	49.15
Religion	Other	878	Catholic	4502	83.68
Place of birth	Other	525	Belgium	4855	90.24
Birth decade	30s	663	40s	987	18.35
			50s	1358	25.24
			60s	1389	25.82
			70s	983	18.27
Father's profession	Miscellaneous	1662	No	24	0.45
			Labourer	1545	28.72
			Employee	752	13.98
			Self-employed	783	14.55
			Professional	614	11.41
Mother's profession	Miscellaneous	1560	No	2358	43.83
			Labourer	364	6.77
			Employee	420	7.81
			Self-employed	605	11.25
			Professional	73	1.36
Father's education	Miscellaneous	953	No	905	16.82
			≤ Lower sec.	1930	35.87
			Higher sec.	741	13.77
			Higher Educ.	851	15.82
Mother's education	Miscellaneous	932	No	1034	19.22
			≤ Lower sec.	2208	41.04
			Higher sec.	680	12.64
			Higher Educ.	526	9.78

Table 13: **Descriptive statistics for the variables used in the employment and poverty estimations**

Variable	Baseline value	#	Other values	#	%
Poverty status	NP	231478	IP	5056	2.12
			MI	1956	0.82
Employed	No	76301	Yes	162189	68.01
Education	Lower sec.	79959	Higher sec.	73442	30.79
			Higher ed.	85089	35.68
Self-employed	No	217420	Yes	21070	8.83
Age	55 ≤ age	25816	age < 25	25994	10.9
			25 ≤ age < 35	66068	27.7
			35 ≤ age < 45	70812	29.69
			55 ≤ age < 65	49800	20.88
Gender	Male	119924	Female	118566	49.72
Living together	No	65315	Yes	173175	72.61
Nationality	Belgian	221145	EU	9997	4.19
			Non EU	7348	3.08
City	No	169623	Yes	68867	28.88
Region	Flanders	104877	Brussels	28873	12.11
			Wallonia	104740	43.92
Variable	Mean	StdDev	Min	Max	
HH size	3.2679	1.3235	1	10	
# children age < 12	0.7433	1.0255	0	7	
# children 12 < age ≤ 16	0.1403	0.3912	0	3	
health	1.9705	0.7783	1	5	
Macro growth %	1.6386	1.828	-1.52	3.41	
Unemployment %	9.3515	0.4466	8.6	9.8	

Part IV:
Macro-Micro Linkages and
Environmental Polices

Chapter 19

A Dynamic Analysis of Permanently Extending the 2001 and 2003 Tax Cuts: An Application of Linked Macroeconomic and Microsimulation Models

Tracy L. Foertsch / Ralph A. Rector

1 Introduction

In the United States, the President's budget for fiscal year 2007 included a number of proposals to extend expiring tax provisions. The most significant involved extending the lower marginal rates on ordinary income enacted under the 2001 Economic Growth and Tax Relief Reconciliation Act (EGTRRA) and the preferential rates on individual net capital gains realizations and dividend income enacted under the 2003 Jobs and Growth Tax Relief Reconciliation Act (JGTRRA). The President's budget also proposed raising the alternative minimum tax (AMT) exemption amount and continuing the AMT's unrestricted use of some nonrefundable personal tax credits. Without such an AMT fix, extending EGTRRA and JGTRRA would spur significant growth in the number of taxpayers subject to the AMT.

In this chapter we use a microsimulation model of the federal individual income tax and the Global Insight (GI) short-term U.S. Macroeconomic Model[1] combined with calibration techniques to analyse the economic and budget effects of permanently extending some of EGTRRA's and JGTRRA's expiring provisions. The extension plan analysed is similar to that considered

---

[1] The Global Insight model is used by private-sector and government economists to estimate how important changes in the economy and public policy are likely to affect major economic indicators. It contains several variables that can be used to simulate changes in tax policy. The methodologies, assumptions, and conclusions presented here are entirely the work of the authors. They have not been endorsed by, and do not necessarily reflect the views of, the owners of the Global Insight model.

by the U.S. Treasury Department's Office of Tax Analysis (OTA) in a 2006 dynamic analysis of the President's tax relief proposals (U.S. Department of Treasury, 2006b). The plan permanently extends:

- JGTRRA's preferential tax rates on capital gains and dividends,
- EGTRRA's lower marginal tax rates on ordinary income,[2] and
- EGTRRA's provisions raising after-tax income.

The economic and budget effects of this extension plan are measured against the Congressional Budget Office (CBO) January 2006 baseline projections (CBO, 2006). CBO's baseline projections embody the rules and conventions governing a current-services federal budget (Williams, 2005). Thus, they project gross domestic product (GDP), prices, individual and corporate incomes, and net federal saving, among other economic and budget variables, over the 10-year budget period assuming the continuation of current levels of federal spending.

They also assume current-law tax policy. Throughout this chapter, "current law" refers to current law as defined by CBO in January 2006. CBO's January 2006 baseline projections assume that the preferential tax rates on individual capital gains and dividend income enacted under JGTRRA expire at the end of calendar year 2008 and that the lower marginal rates on ordinary income enacted under EGTRRA expire at the end of calendar year 2010. As a result of its current-law assumptions, CBO projects a sharp increase in current-law federal income tax revenues and some slowdown in economic activity after 2010.

When compared to CBO's baseline, our results indicate that permanently extending EGTRRA and JGTRRA produces modest economic gains. Between 2011 and 2016, real (inflation-adjusted) GDP is on average over 0.5% higher and an average of over 700,000 new jobs are created. Individual incomes and the federal personal income tax base also expand, helping to reduce the cost of the extension plan to the Treasury.

The remainder of this chapter is organized as follows. The next section describes the extension plan. The third section discusses our procedures for calibrating to CBO's baseline projections and for simulating the economic and budget effects of a change in tax policy. The fourth section reviews the conventional revenue and marginal rate effects of the extension plan as estimated using the microsimulation model. The fifth and sixth sections then consider the macroeconomic and dynamic revenue effects as estimated using both the Global Insight model and the microsimulation model.

---

2   See Joint Committee on Taxation (2001) for additional information on EGTRRA's expiring provisions.

2   The extension plan

The extension plan permanently extends a select set of provisions enacted under the 2001 and 2003 tax laws. It includes three broad components.

2.1   *Permanent extension of JGTRRA's preferential tax rates on capital gains and dividend income*

Under current law, capital gains tax rates for individuals will revert to 10% or 20% and individual dividend income will be taxed at ordinary income tax rates beginning in 2009. Under the extension plan, the maximum capital gains tax rate will be permanently lowered to 15%.[3] In addition, qualified dividend income (generally from domestic corporations and qualified foreign corporations) will be taxed at the same rates as capital gains.

2.2   *Permanent extension of EGTRRA's lower marginal tax rates on ordinary income*

With no change in current law, ordinary tax rates are set to revert to their pre-EGTRRA levels in 2011. Pre-EGTRRA law includes five regular marginal tax rates – 15%, 28%, 31%, 36%, and 39.6%. Table 1 shows our projections of the tax rate structure for single filers and married couples filing a joint return assuming no extension of EGTRRA's marginal rate provisions.

Under the extension plan, EGTRRA's 10% tax bracket is made permanent for a portion of income that would otherwise be taxed at the 15% rate. The 10% taxable income bracket is projected to end at $8,500 for singles and $17,000 for married couples in 2011. The end point for the 15% bracket remains roughly the same for singles but increases for married couples. The widths of the remaining four brackets change very little.[4] However, the associated regular marginal tax rates are reduced to 25%, 28%, 33%, and 35%, respectively.

---

3   Under the extension plan, the capital gains tax rate is reduced to 0% for realizations that would otherwise be taxed at the regular marginal income tax rate of 10%.

4   In Table 1, inflation adjustment accounts for small differences between projections of the pre-EGTRRA tax brackets and the extension plan tax brackets. In law, the base amount for the widths of the 25%, 28%, 33%, and 35% brackets do not change.

Table 1: Projected 2011 ordinary income tax schedules for the pre-EGTRRA baseline and the extension plan

Single Filers				Married Couples Filing a Joint Return			
Pre-EGTRRA		Extension Plan		Pre-EGTRRA		Extension Plan	
Tax Rate	Taxable Income	Tax Rate	Taxable Income	Tax Rate	Taxable Income	Tax Rate	Taxable Income
15%	$1-34,500	10% 15%	$1-8,500 $8,501-34,550	15%	$1-57,650	10% 15%	$1-17,000 $17,001-69,100
28%	$34,501-83,600	25%	$34,551-83,600	28%	$57,651-139,300	25%	$69,101-139,350
31%	$83,601-174,400	28%	$83,601-174,450	31%	$139,301-212,300	28%	$139,351-212,350
36%	$174,401-379,100	33%	$174,451-379,250	36%	$212,301-379,100	33%	$212,351-379,250
39.6%	Over $379,100	35%	Over $379,250	39.6%	Over $379,100	35%	Over $379,250

Notes: EGTRRA = Economic Growth and Tax Relief Reconciliation Act. Taxable income bracket amounts are based on tax provisions and projected inflation under each plan.

2.3 Permanent extension of provisions of EGTRRA increasing after-tax income

504

The provisions primarily raising after-tax income include the $1,000 child tax credit, marriage penalty relief, and the phase-out of itemized deductions and personal exemptions.

Child Tax Credit. Under current law, the child tax credit will fall to $500 in 2011 for each qualifying child under the age of 17. It will generally not be refundable except for families with three or more qualifying children. Under the extension plan, the child tax credit is $1,000 per child, and the credit is partially refundable.

Marriage Penalty Relief. Under current law, the basic standard deduction and the regular 15% tax bracket revert to their pre-EGTRRA levels in 2011. Thus, the standard deduction for married couples filing a joint return will be about 1.67 times the standard deduction for an individual filing a single return. Similarly, the top of the 15% tax bracket for married couples filing a joint return will be about 1.67 times the top of the 15% bracket for a single filer. EGTRRA raises the standard deduction and the top of the 15% bracket for married couples filing a joint return to 2 times those amounts applying for a single filer (see Table 1). The extension plan makes this increase in the standard deduction and the 15% bracket permanent.

Phase-out of Itemized Deductions and Personal Exemptions. Under current law, the phase-out of itemized deductions and personal exemptions will be reinstated. We project that most taxpayers with adjusted gross income (AGI) exceeding $169,550 in 2011 will have to reduce their itemized deductions. Single filers with AGI greater than $169,550 and married couples filing a joint return and having an AGI exceeding $254,300 will also have to reduce their personal exemptions. Under the extension plan, itemized deductions and personal exemptions do not phase out.

3 Model calibration and tax policy simulations

We calibrate two models to CBO's baseline economic and budgetary projections. The first model is the Global Insight short-term U.S. Macroeconomic Model. The second is a microsimulation model of individual income tax returns. We calibrate both models to CBO's January 2006 baseline economic and budgetary projections.[5]

A CBO-like baseline forecast is constructed using the Global Insight model and the details that CBO publishes about its baseline economic and budgetary projections. We use the resulting CBO-like forecast to infer the implications of CBO's current-law assumptions for key macroeconomic variables like personal consumption, investment, employment, and the components of national income and product accounts (NIPA) personal income. In combination with Statistics of Income (SOI) data, the microsimulation model uses the CBO-like baseline revenue forecast and estimated relationships between NIPA personal income and non-NIPA taxable income to project individual income tax data that are consistent with CBO's published baseline projections.

3.1 Calibrating the macroeconomic model

We first calibrate the Global Insight model to CBO's published economic projections and NIPA federal revenue and spending projections.[6]

Calibrating the Global Insight model to CBO's current-law baseline involves iteratively adjusting a control forecast.[7] This is a multi-step process. In each step, we set variables in the GI model to replicate CBO's published

---

5 See Foertsch and Rector (2006) for details of the baseline calibration procedure.
6 Global Insight provided a detailed outline of a methodology for calibrating the GI model to CBO's baseline projections. We used that outline to create a series of AREMOS programmes, making adjustments and additions to GI's basic methodology where appropriate. AREMOS is Global Insight's proprietary modeling language.
7 GI's February 2006 U.S. Macroeconomic Forecast is used as the control.

baseline projections. We then solve the GI model so that those variables that have not been targeted adjust. In essence, we are using econometrically estimated relationships and accounting identities within the GI model to create a forecast that is consistent with what we know about CBO's baseline economic and budgetary projections.

Calibration of the Global Insight model to CBO's baseline projections proceeds in seven steps.

Step 1. We set key forecast assumptions and economic variables. Key forecast assumptions include the price of oil, the value of the trade-weighted U.S. dollar exchange rate, and the federal social insurance tax rate. Key economic variables include the unemployment rate, the 3-month Treasury bill rate, the 10-year Treasury note rate, and price levels.

Setting price levels early in the calibration procedure is critical because many exogenous federal spending (outlays) variables in the Global Insight model are in real terms. Thus, a price level variable is needed to convert CBO's nominal baseline budgetary projections for those variables into con-

sistent real targets.

Step 2. We set federal spending net of federal interest payments. Federal spending broadly includes consumption spending, transfer payments, and other spending items in the federal government's budget. CBO publishes its projections for most – but not all – of the Global Insight model's NIPA federal spending variables. In those instances where CBO does not provide NIPA baseline projections, we derive needed targets using either the GI control forecast or CBO's published projections of budget (unified) federal outlays.

Step 3. We adjust the components of GDP so that they are consistent with not only CBO's projections of real GDP and real federal spending but also CBO's current-law assumptions.

A target for real personal consumption obtained using information from only the control forecast is likely to be too high. This is because the control forecast assumes a partial extension of EGTRRA's and JGTRRA's expiring provisions. Thus, the control forecast projects a far more gradual increase than does CBO in NIPA personal income tax revenues as a share of GDP. It also projects higher levels of NIPA personal disposable income as a share of GDP – particularly after 2010.

We derive a target for real personal consumption using statements from CBO (2006) about CBO's expectations for annual rates of growth in personal consumption. We also apply some judgement about the likely impact on personal saving of not extending EGTRRA's and JGTRRA's expiring provisions.

Step 4. We derive a target for potential (full-employment) GDP that is consistent with CBO's projections of the rate of growth in potential GDP and the rate of growth in the potential labour force (CBO, 2006:44). CBO does not regularly publish estimates of the level of either variable. Thus, we adjust the projected levels of both variables in the control forecast to be consistent with CBO's published growth rate projections.

Step 5. We adjust the components of NIPA taxable personal income. CBO's NIPA taxable personal income includes wage and salary income, personal interest income, personal dividend income, personal rental income, and proprietors' income. CBO typically publishes projections of only NIPA taxable personal income and wage and salary income. We use information from the control forecast to derive targets for the remaining components of NIPA taxable personal income. When possible, we also adjust our targets to reflect CBO's current-law assumptions.

Step 6. We adjust the CBO-like forecast to target CBO's baseline projections of NIPA federal tax receipts. NIPA federal tax receipts include taxes from the rest of the world, taxes on production and imports, and taxes on personal and corporate incomes. CBO publishes projections of all four.

Setting federal taxes on personal and corporate incomes in the CBO-like forecast requires that we separately target both average effective federal income tax rates and the GI model's federal personal and corporate income tax bases. In the GI model, the federal personal income tax base is a function of both NIPA taxable personal income and individual capital gains.

The GI model includes an approximation of the federal corporate income tax base. It defines the federal corporate income tax base as before-tax corporate (book) profits minus rest-of-world corporate profits and the profits of the Federal Reserve. We indirectly target CBO's published projections of corporate profits by iteratively adjusting the statistical discrepancy in the CBO-like forecast.[8]

Step 7. We set the stock of publicly held federal debt to be consistent with CBO's published projections of unified federal surpluses. In addition, we fine-tune average effective federal tax rates on personal and corporate

---

8   The Global Insight model defines corporate (book) profits as Gross National Product (GNP) net of consumption of fixed capital, taxes on production and imports, transfer payments by business, interest payments by business, net surpluses of government enterprises, employer-paid payroll taxes, wage and salary income, other labour income, proprietors' income, personal rental income, and the statistical discrepancy. In the NIPA, the statistical discrepancy is the difference between GDP and Gross Domestic Income (GDI).

incomes and for federal contributions to social insurance so that the final CBO-like forecast is consistent with CBO's published projections of federal tax receipts.

3.2 Calibrating the microsimulation model

We next calibrate the microsimulation model of individual income tax returns to CBO's baseline projections. The final CBO-like forecast provides income, price level, and some budgetary variables used in this calibration.

The microsimulation model consists of four primary components – the core base-year data, a federal income tax and payroll tax calculator, an optimizing routine that ages (extrapolates) the core base-year data, and routines that read data and parameter input files and generate output from the model.[9] The first three components are described in greater detail below.

The first component consists of base-year

- Tax return data from the Internal Revenue Service/Statistics of Income (SOI) Division Public Use File[10] and
- Household survey data from the U.S. Census Bureau's March Current Population Survey (CPS)/Annual Income and Demographic File.[11]

The two files are statistically matched to produce the core base-year data used in the microsimulation model.[12] The SOI and CPS matched file is hierarchically structured. It contains family and person level records populated with data from the CPS and tax return records populated with data from the SOI.

The second component reads the matched file and replicates the process of calculating individual income and payroll taxes in the base year and future

---

9   The fourth primary component of the microsimulation model consists of routines that are used to read data and parameter input files and to generate output from the model. Output from the model is stored in an Excel workbook. It includes both model results and the tax and economic parameter values used during the simulation.

10 See Weber (2004) for information on Public Use Tax File. SOI has issued public use files for almost every year since 1960.

11 The CPS is a monthly survey of about 50,000 households conducted by the U.S. Bureau of the Census for the Bureau of Labor Statistics (BLS). The CPS provides estimates of employment, earnings, hours of work, and other labour force characteristics by a variety of demographic characteristics, including age, gender, and race. Supplemental questions to the CPS provide additional information on education, health, and employee benefits. For a general overview of the design and methodology of the CPS, see U.S. Census Bureau and Bureau of Labor Statistics (2002). For additional information on the Annual Demographic Survey (March CPS Supplement), see U.S. Census Bureau (2005).

12 Data from other sources are also used in the microsimulation model. Those other sources include the Survey of Consumer Finance (SCF) and the Consumer Expenditure Survey (CE).

years. It can also be used to simulate the process of calculating individual taxes under different tax plans by changing year-specific input parameters. Those input parameters include regular income tax rates, alternative minimum tax rates, preferential rates on long-term net capital gains realizations, and preferential rates on qualified dividend income.

The third component adjusts the matched file to reflect projected changes in demographic and economic variables. Income amounts are first adjusted to account for changes in general price levels. A linear programme algorithm is then used to compute the minimum sample weight adjustments needed for the model to reflect projected changes both at the aggregate level and by income class. The process of aging the core base-year data involves four major steps.[13]

Step 1. We use the CBO-like forecast to update all nominal income values on individual tax returns. We also update all targets for demographic variables.

Step 2. We sequentially target four broad measures of individual income by percentile class. Total income is divided into wages and salaries, business income, non-capital gains investment income, and income from other sources. It encompasses both gross income reported on individual tax returns (gross tax return income) and non-taxable income.[14]

Step 3. We target more detailed measures of the components of gross tax return income. Most of the targets are for components of NIPA personal income, with some important exceptions. Those exceptions include small business corporation (S-Corporation) net income, taxable pension and annuity income, net capital gains, and gains from the sale of other assets.[15]

The final CBO-like baseline forecast provides a number of NIPA measures of personal and business income. These include wage and salary income, investment income, proprietors' income, other business income, transfer payments to persons, and corporate profits.

We use NIPA data to estimate the amount of income reported on tax returns.[16] We also use NIPA data to estimate other NIPA-based compo-

---

13   See Foertsch and Rector (2006) for additional information.

14   Gross tax return income here is a broad income measure that approximates the Internal Revenue Code's definition of gross income reported on Form 1040.

15   We obtain projections of capital gains realizations from Table 4-4 in CBO (2006: 92). We develop independent estimates for the remaining non-NIPA sources of personal income.

16   In estimating detailed personal income targets, we rely upon unpublished tables from the Bureau of Economic Analysis (BEA) comparing the components of NIPA personal income and Internal Revenue Service (IRS) federal adjusted gross income. We also rely upon annual Survey of Current Business articles describing the major categories used to reconcile the differences between personal income and federal AGI (Ledbetter, 2004).

nents of gross tax return income. Those components include proprietors' (farm and non-farm) gains and net losses,[17] income from rents and royalties, income from trusts and estates, and the pass-through net income from S-Corporations that is included in NIPA corporate profits. Social Security income is introduced as a separate target because a portion of Social Security benefits are included in taxable income.

Differences between NIPA measures of personal income and measures of gross tax return income can be substantial. This is because NIPA personal income and gross tax return income are defined differently and are constructed using data from different sources. The Bureau of Economic Analysis (BEA) produces annual tables that compare the two measures of income. Those tables identify and provide estimates of the adjustments needed to reconcile the definitional and reporting differences. Those reconciliation adjustments are used to calculate an "adjusted" personal income that approximates AGI. The discrepancy between "adjusted" personal income and AGI is called the "AGI gap". We forecast a combination of data about personal income, reconciliation adjustments, and the AGI gap to develop separate estimates for the NIPA-based components of gross tax return income.

The sum of our forecasts of the components of NIPA-based income and non-NIPA-based income approximates the taxable income base that CBO uses to project federal receipts from the individual income tax. CBO does not provide its projections for most of the components of gross tax return income. As a result, there can be differences between income amounts we use and those projected by CBO.

Step 4. Finally, we compare CBO's projections of individual income tax collections with estimates of tax liability calculated by the microsimulation model. Tax payments are divided into withholding, estimated payments, and final payments. The payments are aggregated to estimate fiscal year revenue collections. An additional adjustment is made to reflect payments for fees, penalties, and other collections.

We modify our targets for the distribution of gross tax return income by size of income by marital filing status when there are material differences in the revenue projections. For incomes up to the 95th percentile, the initial targets for income distribution are based on estimates derived from an analysis of the Panel Survey of Income Dynamics (PSID). Distribution

---

17   NIPA does not separately report the sum of gains and losses for proprietorships or other businesses. Losses are instead added to gains to derive an aggregate net amount for proprietorship income. We use IRS data to estimate the historical relationship between the aggregate amount of proprietors' income and the amount of net gains and losses.

targets for higher income taxpayers are based on historical tax return data. Adjustments may be needed because a large proportion of the total federal income tax is paid by a relatively small proportion of taxpayers at the top end of the income distribution. Slight changes in assumptions about the number of tax returns in the top classes can produce significant changes in total revenue projections.

3.3 Simulating the economic and budget effects of a change in tax policy

Calibrating a macroeconomic model of the U.S. economy and a microsimulation model of the federal individual income tax to a common baseline yields a consistent starting point for dynamic policy analysis. We apply an additional calibration procedure to ensure that final dynamic revenue estimates from the macroeconomic model are broadly consistent with revenue estimates from the microsimulation model.

Our tax policy simulations proceed in three steps.

First, we use the microsimulation model to estimate the revenue effects of the proposed change in tax policy under baseline economic assumptions. The proposed tax policy can involve a change in current-law federal income tax rates, a change in the federal individual income tax base, or both. The microsimulation model is used to estimate the change in federal income tax revenues. It also produces estimates of marginal tax rates on three types of income – ordinary income, long-term capital gains realizations, and dividend income – under the proposed tax policy and current law.

Second, we use the Global Insight model to estimate the dynamic revenue effects of the same policy change. Estimated changes in federal tax revenues and marginal tax rates from the microsimulation model are used as inputs into a simulation with the GI model. The macroeconomic simulation produces an alternative to the CBO-like baseline forecast. That alternative (non-baseline) forecast includes the dynamic effects of the proposed policy on a large number of economic variables, including GDP, prices, interest rates, and employment.

Third, we update the microsimulation model to reflect the dynamic effects of the proposed tax policy on individual and business incomes. This is done using procedures similar to those developed for baseline calibration. Thus, NIPA components of personal and business income along with price level variables and some NIPA budget variables from the alternative forecast are used to estimate target values for non-taxable income and gross

tax return income on individual income tax returns. We use those targets
to update individual and business incomes in the microsimulation model
so that they are consistent with the GI model's alternative forecast for the
components of NIPA personal income.

We continue to iterate between the microsimulation model and the Global Insight model. Revenue estimates and marginal rates from the updated
microsimulation model are used as inputs into a new simulation with the
GI model. The alternative forecast that results provides a new set of income
targets for the microsimulation model. Revenue estimates from the GI model
and the microsimulation model are compared after each iteration. We consider a tax-policy simulation complete when differences between changes
in federal tax revenues from the GI model and the microsimulation model
are small or can be accounted for by definitional and other differences in
the federal income tax bases used in the two models.

**Figure 1:   Differences between individual income tax receipts after calibration
of the Microsimulation and Global Insight models, calendar years
2009-16**

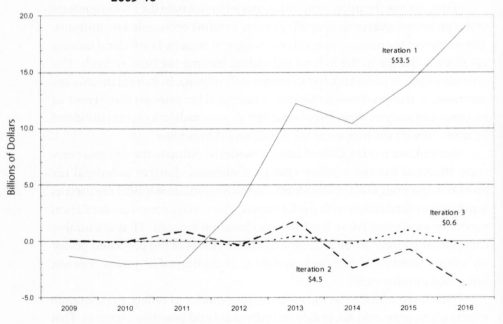

Note: Amounts shown are differences between Global Insight and microsimulation model estimates of the
change in federal individual income tax revenues over 10 years. Changes in revenues are given as
differences from the Congressional Budget Office's January 2006 baseline budgetary projections.

We followed this iterative procedure in estimating the economic and budget effects of the extension plan. Revenue estimates from the two models converged quickly (see Figure 1). In the first iteration, the total change in personal income tax revenues implied by the Global Insight model exceeded the total change in estimated individual income tax revenues implied by the microsimulation model by almost $54 billion over 10 years. By the third iteration, well under $1 billion separated the estimated total changes in income tax revenues from the two models.

4 Revenue estimates and the marginal rate effects of the extension plan

Table 2 shows two sets of revenue estimates.[18] Revenue estimates from the *baseline* forecast start from CBO's January 2006 baseline income projections and give the revenue effects of the extension plan under conventional assumptions. This means that the revenue estimates assume that changes in tax policy do not affect baseline projections of GDP, prices, incomes, or net federal saving, among other economic and budget variables.

4.1 Revenue estimates from the income-adjusted forecast

Revenue estimates from the *income-adjusted* forecast include the macroeconomic ("dynamic") effects of the extension plan on CBO's baseline projections. They do so because the income-adjusted forecast updates the federal individual income tax base in the baseline forecast to reflect the economic and budget effects of the extension plan. For the same change in tax policy, revenue estimates from the income-adjusted forecast can differ substantially from those from the baseline forecast.

Revenue estimates starting from CBO's baseline income projections put federal income tax revenues $1,048.8 billion below CBO's baseline revenue projections over the 10-year budget period (see "Estimate from the Baseline Forecast" in Table 2).[19] In comparison, in February 2006, the Treasury Department (2006a: 143-146) estimated that extending EGTRRA's lower tax rates on ordinary income, JGTRRA's preferential tax rates on

---

18 In Table 2, estimated changes in federal individual income tax revenues include net refundable credits.

19 Baseline revenue projections are the sum of CBO's current-law projections of federal estate, business, and individual income tax revenues.

capital gains and dividend income, and EGTRRA's $1,000 child tax credit and marriage penalty relief would change federal tax revenues by about –$1,022.4 billion (including outlays for changes in net refundable credits). The income-adjusted forecast implies a smaller reduction in federal income tax revenues (see "Estimate from the Income-Adjusted Forecast" in Table 2). It puts federal income taxes $866.9 billion below CBO's baseline federal revenue projections over 10 years.

The estimated change in federal income tax revenues would be significantly higher – nearly twice as large in the income-adjusted forecast – if not for the change in revenues from the AMT. The extension plan includes no additional increases in the AMT exemption amount or indexing of the AMT brackets to inflation. Without these, an ever larger number of middle-income to upper-income taxpayers will become subject to the AMT. For example, the U.S. Treasury Department (2006c) estimates that with permanent extension of EGTRRA and JGTRRA and no additional AMT relief, the number of individual AMT taxpayers will jump from 5.5 million in 2006 to almost 26 million in 2007 and over 56 million in 2016.

Many more taxpayers would be subject to the AMT because the tax cuts under the extension plan effectively put the regular income tax liability below the minimum tax liability. The increased difference between the minimum tax liability and the regular income tax liability has been characterized as a "claw back".[20] The estimated change in federal income tax revenues is less than it otherwise would be because the AMT takes back tax reductions from the extension plan.

Table 2: Change in federal individual income tax revenues from current law under the extension plan, billions of dollars

	2007-16 (Fiscal Year Totals)	
	Change in Federal Income Tax Revenues[a]	Change in Alternative Minimum Tax
Estimate from the Baseline Forecast	-1048.8	767.3
As a Share of Federal Tax Revenues (%)[b]	-5.4	4.0
Estimate from the Income-Adjusted Forecast	-866.9	797.3
As a Share of Federal Tax Revenues (%)	-4.5	4.1

---

20   As defined here, "claw back" is the result of a phase-out of the AMT exemption amount for taxpayers with high levels of AMT income. See Esenwein (2005) for additional details.

Notes: a) Estimated changes in federal individual income taxes include net refundable credits. In the baseline forecast, refundable credits increase by roughly $56.9 billion over 10 years. In the income-adjusted forecast, they increase by around $54.3 billion. The U.S. Treasury Department (2006a: 143-146) puts the total change in refundable credits from permanently extending the child tax credit and marriage penalty relief at $59.2 billion.

b) Federal tax revenues equal the sum of the Congressional Budget Office's January 2006 baseline projections of federal estate, business, and personal income tax revenues.

Table 3:   Effects of the extension plan on average marginal individual income tax rates

	2011-16 (Calendar Year Average)
	Average Percent Change from Current Law[a]
Capital Gains	-24.1
Dividend Income	-52.8
Ordinary Income[b]	-7.8

Notes: a) The average percent change from current law is calculated using marginal tax rates from the income-adjusted forecast.

b) Ordinary income includes all income that does not qualify as a capital gain.

4.2   *The extension plan's marginal rate effects*

The extension plan dramatically lowers marginal tax rates on capital gains, dividend income, and ordinary income (see Table 3). For example, between 2011 and 2016, current-law marginal tax rates on capital gains and dividend income fall by an average of around 24% and 53%, respectively. The drop in the marginal tax rate on ordinary income is not as steep. However, between 2011 and 2016, marginal tax rates on ordinary income are on average almost 8 percentage points below baseline levels.

5   Macroeconomic effects of the extension plan

The extension plan has a positive economic impact (see Table 4). Between 2011 and 2016, total employment expands by an average of over 700,000 jobs annually, and the unemployment rate drops an average of 0.1 percentage point. That drop in the unemployment rate occurs despite the increase in the rate of labour force participation spurred by lower marginal tax rates on labour income.[21] Over the same period, real disposable income rises by nearly $200 billion, and personal saving climbs sufficiently to push the personal saving rate 0.8 percentage point above baseline levels.

---

21   The labour force participation rate is calculated by dividing the projected civilian labour force by the population aged 16 years and older. The increase in the labour force participation rate is forecast to average almost 0.2 percentage point in 2016.

Permanently extending JGTRRA's preferential rates on capital gains and dividend income permanently reduces the cost of capital to business. Real non-residential fixed investment responds positively, climbing an average of nearly $9 billion annually between 2011 and 2016. The economy's stock of productive capital is bolstered as a result, and real potential GDP expands in every quarter between 2009 and 2016. Reflecting that increase in the economy's productive potential, real GDP exceeds CBO's baseline projections by $60.2 billion by 2016.

Two factors mitigate the economic benefits of the extension plan. First, in the simulations, rising output and falling rates of unemployment prompt the Federal Reserve to increase the federal funds rate despite little change in the rate of consumer price index (CPI) inflation.[22] Yields on Treasury notes and bills and on corporate and other debt rise as a result, increasing the cost of capital to business. Second, increases in the AMT nearly halve the tax reduction under the extension plan (see Table 2), limiting gains in personal disposable income, consumption, and saving. They also boost the average effective marginal tax rate on ordinary income, which might offset incentives for supplying more labour.[23]

5.1 Incentive effects of the extension plan

The macroeconomic effects simulated here stem primarily from reducing the disincentives to work, save, and invest created by the expiration of those provisions of EGTRRA and JGTRRA lowering marginal tax rates on capital gains, dividend income, and ordinary income. Permanently extending the $1,000 child tax credit, marriage penalty relief, and repeal of the phase-out of itemized deductions and personal exemptions also has some effect on economic activity. However, they tend to do so by increasing refundable credits and after-tax incomes.[24]

In general, tax relief measures that reduce marginal tax rates on capital and labour income will produce bigger gains in GDP than do measures that only tinker with the size of after-tax income. This is because cuts in marginal tax rates both increase the after-tax wage rate and lower the cost

---

22   We use an econometrically-estimated reaction function in the GI model that adjusts the effective interest rate on federal funds in response to changes in the unemployment rate and the rate of inflation in the CPI.

23   The AMT is nearly a flat tax with two brackets, 26% and 28% (Esenwein, 2005). See Brauer (2004) and Joint Committee on Taxation (2005) for discussion of the impact of the AMT on average marginal tax rates and labour supply.

24   Refundable credits are modeled as a change in federal transfer payments to persons and, thus, as a change in federal outlays.

of capital. They therefore tend to encourage individuals to work more and businesses to invest. Increases in labour supply, saving, and the domestic capital stock follow.

New or bigger personal deductions and tax credits typically do not have the same incentive effects. They do little to spur employment and new business investment. And they boost after-tax incomes, not after-tax wage rates. Thus, individuals can increase or even maintain the same level of after-tax income by working the same or fewer hours.

Table 4: **Macroeconomic effects of the extension plan relative to the CBO's January 2006 baseline projections, fiscal years 2011-16**

	2011	2012	2013	2014	2015	2016	(Average) 2011-16
Real GDP[a]	67.8	97.2	85.5	78.8	70.2	60.2	76.6
Total Employment[b]	568	880	870	750	647	539	709
Unemployment Rate[c]	-0.1	-0.2	-0.2	-0.2	-0.1	-0.1	-0.1
Real Disposable Personal Income[a]	148	203	204	209	211	208	197
Real Personal Consumption[a]	73	115	122	125	125	123	114
Personal Saving Rate[d]	0.7	0.8	0.8	0.8	0.8	0.7	0.8
Real Gross Private Domestic Investment[a]	22.0	30.4	12.5	6.2	2.8	1.7	12.6
Real Non-Residential Investment[a]	12.8	21.4	11.6	4.1	1.5	2.0	8.9
Full-Employment Capital Stock[a]	18.7	39.0	47.6	46.7	44.8	44.0	40.1
CPI Inflation[e]	0.0	0.0	0.0	0.1	0.1	0.1	0.1
Treasury Bill, 3 Month[f]	0.1	0.3	0.2	0.2	0.2	0.1	0.2
Treasury Bond, 10 Year[f]	0.1	0.3	0.2	0.2	0.2	0.2	0.2

Notes: GDP = gross domestic product; CPI = consumer price index; CBO = Congressional Budget Office. The economic effects of the extension plan are measured relative to the CBO's January 2006 baseline economic and budgetary projections.

a) Difference in billions of inflation adjusted dollars (indexed to 2000 price levels).

b) Difference in thousands of jobs.

c) Difference in the percent of the civilian labour force.

d) Difference in the percent of disposable personal income.

e) Difference in the percent change from a year ago.

f) Difference in an annualized percent.

5.2 Response of labour to permanently extending EGTRRA's lower marginal tax rates on ordinary income

Permanently extending EGTRRA's reduction in the top four individual tax rates lowers overall effective marginal tax rates on labour income. Several of the Global Insight model's labour supply variables are adjusted to reflect the likely effects of lower marginal rates on labour force participation and average weekly hours worked. Those variables include the full-employment civilian labour force, the civilian labour force aged 16 to 64 years, the civilian labour force aged 65 years and over, and the average work week under full employment in the non-farm, business sector.

All adjustments to the model's labour supply variables are small. For those aged 65 years and older, we assume a total wage elasticity between 0 and 0.3.[25] That total wage elasticity breaks down into a participation elasticity falling between 0.1 and 0.2 and an average-hours elasticity not exceeding 0.1. For those aged between 16 and 64 years, a participation elasticity not exceeding 0.15 is assumed. In this simulation, average hours worked for those in this age group are assumed to be unresponsive to changes in both payroll and personal income tax rates. For the full-employment labour force and hours worked, a weighted average of the above elasticities is used to determine labour's responsiveness to changes in tax rates. The weights applied equal each of the above age cohort's share of the total civilian labour force.

Average weekly hours worked (full-employment and actual) over all age groups generally rise, but only negligibly, between 2011 and 2016. The civilian labour force increases an average of about 0.4% between 2011 and 2016. For those aged between 16 and 64 years, labour supply rises by roughly the same amount. In comparison, OTA in its dynamic analysis of a similar extension plan simulates an increase in total labour supply averaging between 0.5% and 0.7% between 2011 and 2016 (U.S. Department of the Treasury, 2006b:20).

5.3 The response of investment to permanently extending JGTRRA's preferential rates on capital gains and dividend income

Permanently extending JGTRRA's preferential rates on capital gains and dividend income is simulated in the Global Insight model as a reduction

---

25 A CBO memorandum puts the total wage elasticity for the population as a whole between 0 and 0.3 (Russek, 1996). The total wage elasticity breaks down into a participation elasticity that falls between 0.1 and 0.2 and an average hours elasticity that does not exceed 0.1. All labour supply elasticities are further multiplied by 0.25 to obtain a quarterly pattern. All implied reductions in labour force participation and average hours worked are phased in over two years.

in the firm's cost of capital. We introduce that reduction into the GI model through an increase in the value of the Standard & Poor's (S&P) 500 index of common stocks, which lowers the dividend yield on the S&P 500 and thus the firm's cost of equity.

Predictions of any change in stock prices should perhaps be viewed with some scepticism. However, current taxes on corporate income, dividends, and capital gains likely play some role in reducing the value of the corporation to the shareholder and thus depress stock prices (Golob, 1995). Lowering taxes on capital gains and dividend income should therefore have some positive effect on stock returns.

The "new" and "old" views of the economic effects of dividends are taken into account when calculating the increase in the S&P 500 in the GI model.[26] Under the "new" view, the S&P 500 rises permanently. Under the "old" view, that same increase in the S&P 500 is phased out over the 10-year budget period. An average of the two views gives the change in the S&P 500 that is assumed to follow the permanent extension of JGTRRA's preferential rates on capital gains and dividend income.

Changes in the S&P 500 under both the old and new views are derived using an equation that links changes in the cost of equity with changes in marginal tax rates on capital gains and (S&P 500) dividends. A static estimate of the change in the cost of equity is obtained using a separate equation for the after-tax rental price of capital.[27] That equation expresses the after-tax price of – or return to – equity as a weighted average of the after-tax return to dividends and the after-tax return to capital gains. An explicit expression for the after-tax return to equity is obtained by equating that weighted average with the after-tax return to corporate debt.

We use data from various sources to obtain initial estimates of the change in the cost of equity likely under the extension plan. The microsimulation model is used to generate estimates of marginal tax rates on individual capital gains and dividend income under current law and permanent extension of JGTRRA's lower rates on capital gains and dividends. We use those marginal tax rates on capital gains and dividend income to calculate the change in the after-tax return on equity. We set the before-tax return on corporate debt and the dollar value of S&P 500 dividends using baseline data from the final CBO-like baseline forecast. Finally, we use S&P

---

26 Page (2003) provides a more detailed description of the treatment in macroeconomic models of the old and new views of the economic effects of dividends.
27 This analysis is based on a static comparison of the cost of equity under the extension plan and current law. The static analysis assumes that the extension plan has no effect on baseline levels of the economic and financial-market aggregates used to calculate the change in the value of the cost of capital and the S&P 500.

500 data to determine the share of firm investment financed with debt and the share of corporate income allocated to dividends.[28]

The implied static changes in the value of the S&P 500 have a noticeable effect in the simulations. Permanently reducing the tax rate on dividend income gives a static increase in the S&P 500 averaging roughly 1% under the old and new views combined between 2009 and 2016. Permanently lowering the tax rate on capital gains gives a static increase in the value of the S&P 500 averaging about 2.3% between 2009 and 2016.[29]

Those static changes in the value of the S&P 500 are adjusted if necessary so that the simulated change in the S&P 500 is in line with other estimates of the impact of capital gains and dividends tax cuts on the value of U.S. equities. In a frequently cited study by the American Council for Capital Formation, the Standard & Poor's chief economist, David Wyss, attributes about 7.5% of the increase in the S&P 500 between 1997 and 1999 to the 1997 Taxpayer Relief Act's (TRA 97) lower taxes on capital gains (Thorning, 1999).[30] In a back-of-the-envelope calculation, Poterba (2004) estimated that JGTRRA's 2003 dividend tax cuts could increase aggregate U.S. equity values by about 6%.[31]

We use smaller estimates of the static effects on the value of the S&P 500 of permanently lowering dividend taxes. This is in part because there is some dispute in the literature regarding the magnitude of the impact of dividends tax cuts on equity values. For example, Auerbach and Hassett (2005) find that a change in dividend taxes – particularly a permanent change – can have a significant effect on equity markets. However, a Federal Reserve Board working paper using a similar methodology finds little evidence that cuts in capital taxation have boosted U.S. equity prices (Amromin et al., 2005).

---

28   We use 10-year averages (1992–2002) for all publicly traded companies included in the Standard & Poor's Compustat database. We assume that 46% of all dividends paid out by corporations are subject to personal income taxes (Gale, 2002).

29   An empirical literature links stock market reactions to capital gains tax policy. Shackelford (1999) provides a survey of empirical work on the impact of the 1997 Taxpayer Relief Act and the 1998 Internal Revenue Service Restructuring and Reform Act on equity values.

30   Alternatively, Shackelford et al. (2006) examine the effects of personal capital gains taxation on asset prices in the period surrounding the announcement of TRA 97's capital gains tax cuts. Their analysis incorporates both the demand-side capitalization effects and the supply-side lock-in effects of a change in the capital gains tax rate. Shackelford et al. (2006) find evidence of initial price declines (a capitalization effect), followed by price increases after the official announcement of TRA 97's cuts in the tax rate on capital gains (a lock-in effect). Their results seem to suggest that the two effects approximately offset one another.

31   Poterba (2004) obtains this 6% estimate by using an S&P 500 price-earnings ratio to capitalize CBO projections of the annual flow of forgone dividend taxes.

6   Dynamic revenue effects of the extension plan

The extension plan puts federal tax revenues $696.4 billion below CBO's baseline projections ("Total Receipts with Income-Adjusted Projections" in Figure 2). We estimate that the revenue loss to the Treasury would be much higher, $991.9 billion ("Individual Income Tax with Baseline Projections" in Figure 2), if not for the dynamic effects of the extensions on incomes and federal tax collections.[32] Over 10 years, the dynamic revenue feedbacks equal the difference between -$696.4 billion and -$991.9 billion. In 2009 and 2010, dynamic revenue feedbacks do not exceed about $9 billion. But they more than treble in size in each of the final 6 years, reaching $56 billion in 2016.

Such revenue feedbacks can be divided into three components: revenue feedbacks from the microsimulation model, revenue feedbacks from other federal taxes not calculated using the microsimulation model, and an adjustment attributable to differences in the individual income tax bases used in the Global Insight model and the microsimulation model.

Revenue feedbacks from the microsimulation model total around $179.4 billion over 10 years ("Individual Income Tax Feedback" in Figure 2). They are obtained by subtracting the revenue effects from the income-adjusted and baseline forecasts (see Table 2).[33] Revenue effects from the two forecasts differ because the income-adjusted forecast updates incomes in the baseline forecast to reflect the extension plan's dynamic effects on incomes. The income-adjusted forecast implies a decline in federal individual income tax revenues totaling $812.5 billion over 10 years ("Individual Income Tax with Income-Adjusted Projections" in Figure 2).[34] That $812.5 billion revenue loss is calculated by comparing estimated federal individual income tax revenues from the income-adjusted forecast with the baseline projections of federal tax revenues underlying the baseline forecast.

Revenue feedbacks from other federal taxes not calculated using the microsimulation model include corporate income taxes, payroll taxes, and taxes on production and imports. They are estimated using the Global Insight model. They exceed $116 billion over 10 years (the sum of "Corporate Income Tax Feedback" and "Feedback from Other Taxes" in Figure 2). Combining

---

32   In Figure 2, estimated changes in federal individual income tax revenues exclude net refundable credits.

33   Thus, this $179.4 billion is the difference between revenue effects from the income-adjusted forecast (-$812.5 billion) and the baseline forecast (-$991.9 billion).

34   Table 2 shows an estimated change in federal individual income tax revenues (from the income-adjusted forecast) of $866.9 billion. Subtracting a $54.3 billion increase in net refundable credits from this $866.9 billion gives the $812.5 billion revenue loss reported in Section 6 and included in Figure 2.

revenue feedbacks from the microsimulation model with revenue feedbacks from other federal taxes gives dynamic revenue feedbacks of $295.5 billion over 10 years.

That $295.5 billion in dynamic revenue feedbacks implicitly includes a small adjustment for differences in the federal income tax bases used in the Global Insight model and the microsimulation model. This adjustment sums to under $1 billion over 10 years. It is necessary because of measurement and definitional differences between the baseline levels of personal income in the Global Insight model and individual income in the microsimulation model.

Figure 2: Dynamic revenue feedbacks from the extension plan, billions of dollars, fiscal years 2007-16

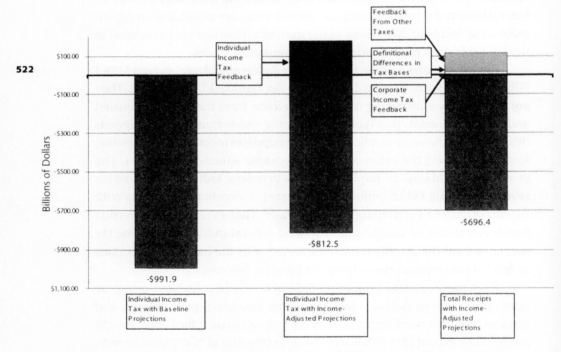

Notes: The microsimulation model is used to estimate the change in federal individual income tax revenues. "Individual Income Tax Revenues with Baseline Projections" equal the estimated change in total receipts when the macroeconomic effects are not included. Estimates of federal individual income tax revenues exclude net refundable credits. Federal taxes not calculated using the microsimulation model include corporate income taxes, payroll taxes, and taxes on production and imports.

7 Concluding remarks

We calibrate a macroeconomic model of the U.S. economy and a micro-simulation model of the federal individual income tax to CBO's January 2006 baseline economic and budgetary projections. We then do a separate calibration of the two models to simulate the economic and budget effects of permanently extending some of EGTRRA's and JGTRRA's expiring provisions. In our simulations, the extension plan boosts economic activity. However, the AMT's expanding reach offsets some of the economic gains.

We plan to extend our calibration and simulation procedures in several directions. Most notably, we plan to increase the number and quality of the links between the microsimulation and macroeconomic models. For example, the microsimulation model could be used to estimate the labour supply response to a change in average effective marginal tax rates. That estimated labour supply response could then be used as an input into simulations with the macroeconomic model.

References

Amromin, G./Harrison, P./Liang, N. et al. (2005) 'How did the 2003 dividend tax cut affect stock prices and corporate payout policy', Working Paper No. 57, Finance and Economics Discussion Series, Divisions of Research and Statistics and Monetary Affairs, Federal Reserve Board. (http://www.federalreserve.gov/pubs/feds/2005/200557/200557pap.pdf) [accessed 30 October 2008]

Auerbach, A. J./Hassett, K. A. (2005) 'The 2003 dividend tax cuts and the value of the firm: an event study', Working Paper No. 11449, National Bureau of Economic Research. (http://www.nber.org/papers/W11449) [accessed 30 October 2008]

Brauer, D. (2004) 'CBO's projections of the labor force', Congressional Budget Office Paper. (http://www.cbo.gov/ftpdocs/58xx/doc5803/09-15-LaborForce.pdf) [accessed 30 October 2008]

Congressional Budget Office (2006) 'The budget and economic outlook: fiscal years 2007 to 2016'. (http://www.cbo.gov/ftpdocs/70xx/doc7027/01-26-BudgetOutlook.pdf) [accessed 30 October 2008]

Esenwein, G. (2005) 'The alternative minimum tax (AMT): income entry points and "take back" effects', Congressional Research Service Report for Congress. Order code RS21817.

Foertsch, T. L./Rector, R. A. (2006) 'Calibrating macroeconomic and microsimulation models to CBO's baseline Projections', Publication 1500, The IRS Research Bulletin: Recent Research on Tax Administration and Compliance. (http://www.irs.gov/pub/irs-soi/06foertsch.pdf) [accessed 30 October 2008]

Gale, W. G. (2002) 'About half of dividend payments do not face double taxation', *Tax Notes* 839.

Golob, J. E. (1995) 'How would tax reform affect financial markets?', Federal Reserve Bank of Kansas City Economic Review. (http://www.kc.frb.org/PUBLICAT/ECONREV/PDF/4q95golb.pdf) [accessed 30 October 2008]

Joint Committee on Taxation (2005) 'Present law and background relating to the individual alternative minimum tax', JCX-37-05. (http://www.house.gov/jct/x-37-05.pdf#search=%22jct%20capital%20gains%20phase%20out%20range%22) [accessed 30 October 2008]

Joint Committee on Taxation (2001) 'Summary of provisions contained in the conference agreement for H.R. 1836, the Economic Growth and Tax Relief Reconciliation Act of 2001', JCX-50-01. (http://www.house.gov/jct/x-50-01.pdf) [accessed 30 October 2008]

Ledbetter, M. A. (2004) 'Comparison of BEA estimates of personal income and IRS estimates of adjusted gross income, new estimates for 2001, Revised Estimates for 1959-2000', Survey of Current Business. (http://www.bea.gov/bea/ARTICLES/2004/04April/0404PI&AG.pdf) [accessed 30 October 2008]

Page, B. (2003) 'How CBO analyzed the macroeconomic effects of the president's budget', A Congressional Budget Office Paper. (http://www.cbo.gov/ftpdocs/44xx/doc4454/07-28-PresidentsBudget.pdf) [accessed 30 October 2008]

Poterba, J. (2004) 'Taxation and corporate payout policy', Working Paper 10321, National Bureau of Economic Research. (http://www.nber.org/papers/w10321) [accessed 30 October 2008]

Russek, F. S. (1996) 'Labor supply and taxes', Congressional Budget Office Memorandum. (http://www.cbo.gov/ftpdocs/33xx/doc3372/labormkts.pdf) [accessed 30 October 2008]

Shackelford, D. A./Dai, Z./Maydew, E. et al. (2006) 'Capital gains taxes and asset prices: capitalization or lock-in?' Working Paper 12342, National Bureau of Economic Research. (http://www.nber.org/papers/w12342) [accessed 30 October 2008]

Shackelford, D. A. (1999) 'Stock market reactions to capital gains tax changes: empirical evidence from the 1997 and 1998 tax acts', Working Paper, Fall 1999.

Thorning, M. (1999) 'Capital gains taxation and US economic growth', Testimony before the Standing Committee on Banking, Trade and Commerce of the Senate of Canada. (http://www.accf.org/publications.php?pubID=104) [accessed 30 October 2008]

U.S. Census Bureau (2005) 'Current Population Survey, 2005 Annual Social and Economic (ASEC) Supplement', March. (http://www.census.gov/apsd/techdoc/cps/cpsmar05.pdf) [accessed 30 October 2008]

U.S. Census Bureau and Bureau of Labor Statistics (2002) 'Current Population Survey: Design and Methodology', Technical Paper 63RV (TP63RV), March. (http://www.census.gov/prod/2002pubs/tp63rv.pdf) [accessed 30 October 2008]

U.S. Department of the Treasury (2006a) 'General explanations of the administration's fiscal year 2007 revenue proposals'. (http://www.ustreas.gov/offices/tax-policy/library/bluebk06.pdf) [accessed 30 October 2008]

U.S. Department of the Treasury, Office of Tax Analysis (2006b) 'A dynamic analysis of permanent extension of the president's tax relief'. (http://www.treasury.gov/press/releases/reports/treasurydynamicanalysisreporjjuly252006.pdf) [accessed 30 October 2008]

U.S. Department of the Treasury, Office Tax Policy (2006c) 'Tax relief kit – the toll of two taxes: the regular income tax and the AMT'. (http://www.ustreas.gov/offices/tax-policy/library/tax_relief_kit.pdf) [accessed 30 October 2008]

Weber, M. (2004) 'General Description Booklet for the 2001 Public Use Tax File', Individual Statistics Branch, Statistics of Income Division, Internal Revenue Service, October. (http://www.nber.org/~taxsim/gdb/gdb01.pdf) [accessed 30 October 2008]

Williams, C. (2005) 'What is a current-law economic baseline?' Congressional Budget Office Economic and Budget Issue Brief. (http://www.cbo.gov/ftpdocs/64xx/doc6403/EconomicBaseline.pdf) [accessed 30 October 2008]

Chapter 20

Linking Microsimulation and Macro-Economic Models to Estimate the Economic Impact of Chronic Disease Prevention

Laurie J. Brown / Anthony Harris / Mark Picton /
Linc Thurecht / Mandy Yap / Ann Harding /
Peter Dixon / Jeff Richardson

527

1 Introduction

This chapter, using type 2 diabetes in Australia as a case-study, has two aims. First, it examines the development of a methodology that links microsimulation and macro-economic modelling for testing robust scenarios to support the making of broad policy decisions about public health investment and human capital agendas aimed at improving workforce participation and productivity. Second, it illustrates this methodology by investigating the possible effects of a hypothetical diabetes prevention program on health and economic outcomes. While microsimulation models (MSM) are well suited to modelling individual units within a particular system (e.g. how people or families interact with the income support system), the strength of macro-economic models is their capacity to model change within the entire economy. Conversely, the weakness of micro-models is that they operate within a closed system without considering the broader economic environment in which the micro-units are acting. Also micro-models typically only model first-round effects where the response of agents to the change imposed

This work was supported by the Australian National Health and Medical Research Council Health Service Research Grant (Grant ID 334114) "Modelling the Economics of the Australian Health Care System for Policy Analysis".

on the system is not captured. Whilst this is true of static MSM, dynamic MSM with behavioural components do have the potential to provide a more complete resolution of the system to a new post-shock equilibrium. An alternative class of economic models is computerized general equilibrium (CGE) models that provide an economy-wide perspective of a given shock after the economy has fully equilibrated. However, a weakness of macro-models is that they provide no insight into how aggregate changes in the economy and the new equilibrium solution affect individuals. The opportunity offered by linking models operating in these separate domains is the complementary nature of their respective strengths and weaknesses.

Chronic disease is reaching epidemic proportions in developed nations around the world. Diabetes has been a National Health Priority Area in Australia since 1996 with nearly one million adult Australians having type 2 diabetes and a further 16.4% of Australians aged 25 years or above having "pre-diabetes" (Dunstan et al., 2002). The number of Australian adults with diabetes has more than doubled since 1981 (Dunstan et al., 2002; AIHW, 2002) and numbers are expected to continue to grow as the population ages and becomes more overweight and less physically active. Diabetes is associated with major disability, reduced quality of life and shortened lifespan. Diabetes as either the underlying or associated cause of death accounts for over 5% of all deaths in Australians aged 25 years and over (AIHW, 2005).

Type 2 diabetes, however, is largely preventable. The natural history of type 2 diabetes includes a pre-diabetic state of impaired glucose metabolism (impaired glucose tolerance [IGT] and impaired fasting glucose [IFG]) estimated to be between 5 and 12 years in duration (Sherwin et al., 2004; Vinicor et al., 2003). This presents an opportunity to intervene to prevent or delay the onset of diabetes. Key risk factors for the development of type 2 diabetes include: age, genetic factors, physiological factors such as weight, pre-diabetes, or gestational diabetes, behavioural factors of physical inactivity and poor nutrition, and socio-environmental influences.

Strong, consistent evidence from large, well-designed clinical trials has definitively shown that maintenance of modest weight loss through diet and physical activity reduces the incidence of type 2 diabetes in high-risk persons by about 40-60% over three to four years (Centers for Disease Control and Primary Prevention Working Group, 2004). Three recent major international randomized clinical trials have demonstrated the prevention of type 2 diabetes in individuals with IGT through intensive lifestyle modification: the Finnish Diabetes Prevention Study (Tuomilehto et al., 2001); the

US Diabetes Prevention Program (Diabetes Prevention Program Research Group, 2002; Eddy et al., 2005); and the Da Qing IGT and Diabetes Study (Pan et al., 1997).

To date, public health initiatives in Australia aimed at combating diabetes have typically been limited to opportunistic screening programs for diabetes (Shaw and Chisholm, 2003; Colagiuri et al., 2004). However, diabetes prevention and management has been firmly established as a key action item on Australia's national policy agenda with the Commonwealth, State and Territory Government leaders identifying diabetes as one of four priority areas where work will be undertaken on specific reform proposals as the first part of their human capital reform agenda. This agenda aims to improve workforce participation and productivity, in particular to:

- Reduce the proportion of the working age population not participating and/or under-participating in paid employment due to illness, injury or disability;
- Reduce the incidence of preventable chronic disease and serious injury amongst the working age population;
- Reduce the prevalence of key risk factors that contribute to chronic disease; and
- Increase the effectiveness of the health system in achieving health outcomes.

The research reported in this chapter is set within this policy context and is organized as follows. A brief overview of linking micro- and macro-economic models is provided in the following section. Section 3 then describes the modelling and economic methods that have been used to investigate the economic costs and benefits of a diabetes prevention program. The results of the modelling are presented in Section 4 followed by some concluding remarks.

2   Linking micro- and macro-models

The number of researchers developing micro-/macro-economic models is still very small worldwide and while approaches and techniques are still in their "infancy", advances in econometric and computational methods are leading to a growing interest in this type of modelling (Davies, 2004). Anderson (1990) suggests that there are three reasons to link micro- and macro-models: the outputs from a macro-model can be used as an input to a micro-model and to align the predictions of the micro-model; to enable general equilibrium feedbacks and interactions among variables in the micro-model; and to provide a micro-economic basis for aggregate behaviour. These benefits largely reflect a macro-centric view of modelling. However, in the context of the health system, there are a number of advantages stemming from the linking of micro- and macro-models to examine health-related policy issues, including:

- Improved integration of the health sector within the overall economy by providing a more detailed description of the use of health services by individual agents;
- Better integration of the various sectors within the health system;
- The capturing of externalities from the provision and use of health services (e.g. improvements in labour productivity);
- Bringing a longer-term focus to the effects of government interventions in the health sector;
- The highlighting of constraints within the economy that may impinge on the health sector (e.g. shortfalls in the health workforce); and
- Better assessment of the effect of a macro-shock on the use of health services by individual families.

The first attempt to describe a process for linking models that operate at differing levels of aggregation was by Orcutt (1967) who envisaged multiple models being linked through, "adaptors and key variables used as interme-diaries" (p. 120). The approach involved models that describe part of the economy being linked as modules that together would describe the overall system. The most succinct summary of alternative approaches to linking micro- and macro-models is provided by Bækgaard (1995) who identifies the following methods:

1. Top-down approach in which the micro-model is adjusted to match an exogenous macro-aggregate;
2. Bottom-up approach in which a change generated in the micro-model is used to adjust the macro-model;
3. Recursive linkage approach in which there is a two-way lagged inter-action between models; and
4. Iterative approach in which the two models are solved simultaneously within each period.

A fifth approach, proposed by Toder et al. (2000), involves the micro- and macro-models being solved separately over the full simulation period, with the models then calibrated and resolved until convergence is achieved. A further alternative is to build a model that inherently includes both a micro-

and macro-dimension. Davies (2004) refers to such models as the *integrated* approach, in contrast to a *layered* approach in which different types of models are brought together. The MOSES model (Eliasson, 1996) and DYNASIM (Orcutt et al., 1976) are examples of integrated models.

While a fully integrated model is compelling in principle, it is perhaps telling that most models in the literature take a recursive-linkage approach, suggesting that including both dimensions within the one model may give rise to its own difficulties. An interesting discussion of the problems and limitations encountered with early modelling work on MOSES, including the trade-off between macro-economic and micro-economic stability, is provided by Eliasson (1986).

A focus on labour supply – workforce participation or productivity reforms – appears to be a common feature of linked models developed to date. For example, Arntz et al. (2006) analyse welfare reform proposals designed to encourage labour force participation in Germany at the lower end of the wage distribution. Data on changes in the labour supply in response to a policy shock are recursively passed between the macro CGE and a micro labour supply model until the two models converge. Fredriksen et al. (2007) combine a detailed dynamic microsimulation model of government pension expenditures and a large CGE model to estimate the extent to which reforms of the Norwegian public pension system improve fiscal sustainability and stimulate employment. The models were linked through the iterative exchange of data relating to the changes in labour supply and government pension expenditures. Aaberge et al. (2007) present an integrated micro-macro-model of the Norwegian economy in which the two models are iteratively resolved with changes in the labour supply determined within the micro-model used by the CGE to determine changes in wage rates, cash transfers and capital income.

Within Australia, there have been only limited attempts to link micro- and macro-models. Perhaps the earliest Australian example is provided by Meagher and Agrawal (1986) in which output from a CGE model was used to re-weight the 1981-82 National Income and Housing Survey (IHS). At the macro-level, a shock was imposed on the economy relating to taxation reform with the distributional consequences then assessed at the micro-level. Linkage of the two models was achieved by the top-down passing of changes to key variables that were used to re-weight the IHS and to revise average factor incomes. This approach was updated by Dixon et al. (1996), who foreshadowed an iterative linking of a CGE model to either a static or dynamic MSM. In related work, Polette and Robinson (1997) used the top-down approach to link an aggregated version of the MONASH CGE to the microsimulation model of the Australian income support system.

There are only limited examples of the application of a linked micro- and macro-model within the health field. One example is a model of long-term care in the United Kingdom and the health care costs associated with the elderly (Hancock et al., 2005). In this work projections of long-term care expenditure and the distributional impact of state-financed care were investigated through the linking of a macro-projections model with a microsimulation model that permits the analysis of the distributional consequences of different funding options.

3 Micro-macro-modelling of diabetes prevention

In order to investigate the economy-wide impacts of a hypothetical diabetes prevention program, we have linked a micro-model of diabetes prevalence, through a labour supply model using a bottom-up approach, to a CGE model (Brown et al., 2006). The three models involved in this research are: 1) the "Diabetes Model (v06.1)" which is a population projection based diabetes prevention and econometric outcomes model; 2) a conventional household labour supply model; and 3) "MONASH", a CGE model of the Australian economy. The Diabetes Model first quantifies the reduction in cases of type 2 diabetes by sex and age in each three-year period of the simulation expected to result from the diabetes prevention program. The reduction in cases by age and gender is then used as an input into the econometric model, in order to predict the additional number of persons in employment in each period. The macro-economic effect of the shock involving both government expenditure on the prevention program and the resulting increase in the labour supply is then quantified in MONASH.

3.1 Specification of the Diabetes Prevention Scenario

The hypothetical diabetes prevention program that was modelled aims to reduce the progression of individuals at high risk of type 2 diabetes through early detection by screening and early lifestyle intervention. The scenario was based on the intensive lifestyle intervention trialled in the Finnish Diabetes Prevention Study (Tuomilehto et al., 2001). The intervention activities (e.g. one-to-one counselling or group sessions covering nutrition, physical activity, weight management etc.) and the attributable effects (e.g. changes in waist circumference, blood pressure, lipids, smoking and exercise) mirror those in the Finnish program. The Finnish trial essentially involved a resource-intensive recruitment and screening component and an individualized approach to lifestyle intervention supported with group-based activities. The intervention was most intensive during the first year, followed by a two-year maintenance program (Lindstrom et al., 2003).

Overall, about 925,000 individuals were expected to participate in the intervention program.The scenario in this modelling exercise targeted all Australians aged 55-74 years plus those aged 45-54 years with one or more risk factors for diabetes (approximately 5.9 million persons in 2005). It was assumed that about half of the target population would participate in an initial screening program with 50% of these individuals going on to have further testing. All those likely to be diagnosed as having pre-diabetes are assumed to participate in the prevention program (about a third of those having the follow-up testing). In addition, an equivalent number of individuals were assumed to participate in the program because their risk factor profile puts them at risk of the disorder.

It was assumed that the prevention strategy runs over a three-year period and that only one prevention program occupies each three years, i.e. a program commences at the beginning of a three-year simulation cycle and finishes at the end of the period. The prevention strategy was modelled against a base case, the parameter values of which reflected current growth in the prevalence of risk factors. The simulation period was 21 years from 2005 to 2026, and it was assumed that the program would be funded by the Australian Commonwealth Government.

3.2   Diabetes Model

The Diabetes Model is a complex cell-based population projection model that generates a time-series of cross-sectional prevalence based "snap shots" of the adult Australian population over the simulation period. The model comprises 3,456 cells representing the combination of eight key diabetes risk factors: sex (2 groups); age (6 groups); income (4 categories); waist circumference (2 categories); blood pressure (2 categories); abnormal cholesterol (2 categories); physical activity (3 categories); and smoking history (3 categories). The cell-based structure of the model is underpinned by AusDiab, unit record data from the Australian Diabetes, Obesity and Lifestyle Study (Dunstan et al. 2002). The prevalence of both pre-diabetes and diabetes are determined for each cell based on its specific set of risk factors, with the model's population base updated every three years to reflect both population ageing (ABS 2006) and changes in the prevalence of the modifiable risk factors.

Modelling a prevention strategy involves changing the number of people that have a particular set of risk factors and "moving" them into another cell reflecting their new set of characteristics following participation in the prevention program. This is based on parameter values that reflect the likely impact of the program on the prevalence of different risk factors. Specific prevention programs target only a proportion of the population, e.g. those at high risk of diabetes, and only a proportion of these individuals may participate in a lifestyle intervention program. The model first identifies which unit records fall into at-risk groups. A random number generator is then used to select records to represent those participating in the program. The model then makes changes in line with the expected outcomes of the program to the biometric and other risk factor characteristics of the selected records. Cell weights are then recalculated based on the new distribution of values in the unit record dataset. A record may be selected in more than one cycle with the cumulative impact of the interventions being carried forward across the simulation.

Having derived the expected number of people in each cell at the end of each cycle, the number of persons expected to have pre-diabetes or diabetes is then calculated by assigning to each cell the probability of having either condition determined from two logistic regression models derived from AusDiab. Multiplying the probability of pre-diabetes or diabetes by the cell population produces the number of persons expected to have each condition. The model then generates various epidemiological results, disability-adjusted life years and economic results in terms of the cost effectiveness, cost utility and cost benefit of the program. The costs and benefits associated with a particular prevention strategy can be assessed against a chosen comparator which is typically set as the 'base case'. The base case simulates current trends in diabetes prevalence, risk factors, current screening and detection practices, i.e. the status quo.

3.3 Household Labour Supply Model

The underlying theoretical model used to examine labour market outcomes is one of a conventional household labour supply. The individual is assumed to make a trade-off between labour and leisure subject to a constraint of full income. The decision to enter the labour force is the first part in a two-part decision on hours supplied. The final outcome of hours worked will depend on both labour supply and the demand for that individual's labour. Since health affects productivity, modelling the relationship between employment and its determinants in a single equation will include elements of both supply and demand. For the results presented in this chapter, the relationship between employment and health (diabetes) is estimated in an econometric model and no distinction is made between employment and labour force participation, or account taken of the impact of health on hours worked. In that sense, the approach is similar to that taken by Mullahy and Sindelair (1996) and the analysis can be interpreted as an analysis of labour market outcomes rather than a labour supply decision. While the focus is on employment rather than hours, the decision to work part- or full-time for those in work is also investigated.

All positive labour outcomes, L, are called "employment" and they will depend on:

$$L = L(h, X, \theta) \tag{1}$$

where h is the health status of the individual, X are exogenous observable household characteristics that affect productivity, and θ are unobserved household characteristics that affect labour outcomes.

In this kind of structural model, much attention has been paid in the literature to the issue of measuring the true underlying health of individuals. The most common measure of health status used is overall self-reported health. However, while at any point in time there may be a correlation between self-reported health status and employment, this may well be due to bias in measurement as individuals who report no employment misrepresent their health status for, among other reasons, self-esteem. It might seem obvious therefore that a more objective measure of health should be used. The problem, however, is to find adequate proxies for the health conditions that affect activity. If we restrict the issue to one disease such as diabetes we assume that other illnesses either do not affect the activity decision or are uncorrelated with diabetes. Moreover, if we only use a clinical measure such as the presence of active disease, we lose information on the true relationship between health and behaviour that might be intrinsic to the self-reported subjective measure.

Consequently, in this study we have chosen to use a measure of health status, confirmed by physical measurement as important for the problem at hand – diagnosis of diabetes. In the main analysis, this is the only illness variable included in the statistical model of employment. In a second analysis, a more general measure of health status is also included. We recognize the potential endogeneity of this general measure in terms of a causal link between employment and reported health status and this is investigated using an instrumental variable (IV) technique that removes the endogenous part of the general measure of health.

The statistical analysis is based on the 1999-2000 AusDiab stratified random sample of households whose members completed a questionnaire and had a physical examination (n=11,247). All of the analyses were weighted to reflect the over-25-years-of-age Australian population.

3.3.1 Modelling Individual Health Status

The true individual underlying health status h in (1) is unobserved. Since we are interested specifically in the role of diabetes in labour activity, h could be proxied by a variable measuring a diagnosis of diabetes. In the main analysis, we do precisely this. A potential problem with this approach is that other important health factors may have been excluded that are correlated with diabetes and this may lead to error in variables bias. One potential approach is to include other measured illness variables from the survey. However, the AusDiab survey is limited in its measurement of other conditions and largely confined to physical conditions that may be related to diabetes. This approach therefore was not pursued. As an alternative, a measure of health status (SF-36) is included directly in the estimation of (1). As Cai and Kalb (2006) argue it seems reasonable to regard many aspects of the SF-36 measure as objective measures of health status (physical limitations for example) and as such a good proxy for short-term and long-term aspects of health status in addition to diabetes. However, even such a measure may be subject to some form of the endogeneity described above.

An alternative approach is to regard the SF-36 measure as a more general imperfect proxy for perceived health status. Following the general ideas in Disney et al. (2003) (albeit in a static framework), we assume that true health is a linear combination of exogenous individual characteristics x and objective measures of health z. The latent counterpart to h is h* measured with error e and we can write:

$h^* = h + e$

$h^* = x\beta + z\gamma + (v + e)$

$h^* = x\beta + z\gamma + u$ (2)

(2) is estimated using OLS, with h^* the SF36 summary measures of physical and mental health. The predicted values are then used as an instrument in a second-stage discrete choice model of labour activity:

$L^* = a + h^*\beta1 + x\beta2 + z\gamma + e$ (3)

$L = 1$ if $L^* > 0$ and 0 otherwise

(3) is estimated using logistic regression. The odds ratio of employment if diagnosed with diabetes compared to those not diagnosed is calculated as [(P.employ / P.not employ) | diabetes] / [(P.employ / P.not employ) | no diabetes]. The marginal effect is the predicted change in employment if diagnosed with diabetes compared to no diabetes calculated at the mean of all covariates $(P(E=1 | D=1)–P(E=1 | D=0))$. Labour supply variables include years of age, education, marital status, and number of children. The estimates are made for men aged 35-64 and women aged 25-59 years. In addition, separate estimates are provided for each 10-year age band for men and women.

    In summary, the main approach taken was to estimate (3) using a physical measure of diabetes (with and without the summary measures of the SF-36 as additional health status measures). The second approach was to instrument general health status by physical measures of exercise and weight from a first-stage linear regression and to test for exogeneity. In the second approach the procedure used is IVPROBIT in STATA 9.1.

3.4 MONASH CGE Model

MONASH is a recursive dynamic computable general equilibrium model (Dixon and Rimmer 2002). It generates a picture of the economy as it would develop in the absence of unknown policy or other shocks. Using macro-economic forecasts developed in consultation with other economic modellers and detail on technical and taste change at the commodity and industry level, the MONASH model depicts an economy changing over time.

    Within the forecast, there is detail about the accumulation of capital due to investment and depreciation as well as government and private debt owed both within Australia and to foreigners. The combination of these factors generates forecasts for 107 industries over time. Industry prospects depend on economy-wide conditions and commodity- and industry-specific technical change.

In the context of policies affecting diabetes – and through it, workforce participation – this dynamic base case forecast is important, since the size and structure of the economy is liable to change a great deal over the period of the policy's operation.

Policy results for MONASH are generated as percentage deviations from the base case. A policy that has an adverse impact on an industry that is forecast to be growing in the base case will show up as a negative deviation from the base case. The industry will still be growing, but more slowly than it would have done in the absence of the policy change. A policy that causes an industry to expand will show up as a positive deviation from the base case, which means that the industry would be growing even faster than in the forecast. This is important because it allows us to focus only on the policy-induced changes rather than attributing all growth over the period of the policy's impact to the policy.

3.4.1 Policy closure

The policy simulation employed here is a standard policy or deviation closure modified in two ways:

1. The employment gains due to diabetes prevention are imposed exogenously on the model; and
2. Income taxes are allowed to vary in order to keep the Australian Federal Government deficit a constant proportion of GDP. This is done to ensure that the increased government expenditure required by the prevention program is explicitly paid for by taxpayers. Allowing the additional expenditure to displace existing expenditure or "funding" it by running down the budget surplus would overstate the benefits of the policy.[1]

---

1   This simulation does not examine the specifics of financing the policy and does not account for behavioural responses to tax changes. A policy such as this could be financed by raising taxes when the expenditure occurs and lowering them when the savings associated with prevention occur, by debt or by reallocating money from other parts of the government budget. The closure adopted here is non-committal about financing specifics and merely ensures that the policy is paid for and that the effects of changes in fiscal position are not allowed to influence the results.

3.4.2 Specification of shocks

The shocks imposed during the policy simulation to health costs and employment were the net costs of the diabetes prevention program (Table 3) and the estimated gains in employed persons (not including SF-36) (Table 8). The three-year shocks generated from the Diabetes and household labour supply models were annualized, then percentage shocks were calculated against the MONASH base case. The shocks to MONASH variables emp_hours and f5dom ("Health") are given in Table 1 where emp_hours is the aggregate level of employment in hours and f5dom ("Health") is a shift term for government domestic demand for health. The growth in the number of diabetes cases

Table 1:   Policy shocks in the MONASH CGE model

	Annual % Change	
Shock	emp_hours	f5dom
2006	0.0069	2.3764
2007	0.0080	0.0000
2008	0.0093	0.0000
2009	0.0100	-0.0107
2010	0.0120	-0.0316
2011	0.0143	-0.0309
2012	0.0175	-0.0676
2013	0.0189	-0.0802
2014	0.0192	-0.0783
2015	0.0196	-0.1147
2016	0.0193	-0.0832
2017	0.0196	-0.0812
2018	0.0203	-0.0959
2019	0.0206	-0.1197
2020	0.0215	-0.1168
2021	0.0218	-0.1307
2022	0.0221	-0.1020
2023	0.0231	-0.0996
2024	0.0249	-0.2004
2025	0.0253	-0.1217
2026	0.0265	-0.1187
Cumulative	**0.3813**	**0.6700**

Note: emp_hours is the aggregate level of employment in hours and f5dom is a shift term for government domestic demand for health.

prevented is sufficiently strong to outweigh the effect of the growth in the workforce in the base case, meaning that the shock to emp_hours increases over the policy simulation. The shocks to government demand for health indicate that the prevention program involves a sharp initial increase in spending. Spending is sustained at around this level until 2015 and then decreases back towards the base case. At the start of the program, there is a 2.38% increase in spending on health. By 2026, the total shock to government spending on health is 0.67% above the base case. We assumed that the additional workers from the labour supply model supplied hours in the same way as existing workers. Integrating the interactions between health, labour force characteristics, effective labour supply and employment outcomes in a more comprehensive fashion is a matter identified for future work.

4 Results

540

In this section results of the diabetes prevention program, the employment effect this generates and the flow-on impact on the macro-economy are presented. In the previous section, even after allowing for savings to the health system, it was shown that there was a net cost from implementing the prevention program (Table 3). In this section it will be seen that the macro-economic gain associated with the increased labour supply, and its flow-on effects through the economy, exceed these first-round net costs. However, while the annual increase in real GDP peaks at 0.33% relative to the base case, a positive impact on real GDP does not occur until eight years into the simulation.

4.1 Prevention of type 2 diabetes

If current trends in population ageing and modifiable risk factors for type 2 diabetes continue over the next 21 years in Australia, then the number of Australians aged 25 years and over who will have type 2 diabetes will increase by over 70% from around 1 million to 1.8 million persons (Table 2). However, under the prevention scenario, the number of adults expected to have type 2 diabetes in 2026 is 30% lower (550,000 cases) than if current trends in diabetes risk factors continue. As the prevention program only targets individuals at high risk, the majority of prevented cases occur among those of working age.

Table 2: Growth in number of adult Australians with type 2 diabetes

	June 2005		June 2026					
			Base Case		Prevention Scenario		Cases Prevented	
								% Base Case
	(No. '000)	%	(No. '000)	%	(No. '000)	%	Base Scenario	Base Case
Males								
25-34	4.547	0.32	6.009	0.37	6.009	0.37	0	0.0
35-44	39.403	2.63	52.409	3.10	52.409	3.10	0	0.0
45-54	98.331	7.07	128.798	8.14	59.878	3.78	68.92	53.5
55-65	151.524	13.74	224.858	14.92	106.451	7.06	118.407	52.7
65-74	138.879	20.29	276.605	21.37	113.350	8.76	163.255	59.0
75+	145.992	28.39	326.805	29.14	326.805	29.14	0	0.0
All Males	578.677	8.72	1,015.485	11.50	664. 902	7.53	350.583	34.5
Females								
25-34	3.270	0.23	4.334	0.28	4.334	0.28	0	0.0
35-44	29.767	1.96	39.257	2.40	39.257	2.40	0	0.0
45-54	78.119	5.55	101.134	6.40	56.741	3.59	44.393	43.9
55-65	114.561	10.52	175.867	11.38	100.955	6.53	74.912	42.6
65-74	109.144	15.20	218.117	15.94	127.180	9.29	90.937	41.7
75+	147.046	19.56	282.167	20.52	282.167	20.52	0	0.0
All Females	481.907	6.97	820.876	9.05	610.635	6.73	210.241	25.6
Persons								
25-34	7.817	0.27	10.343	0.32	10.343	0.32	0	0.0
35-44	69.171	2.29	91.666	2.75	91.666	2.75	0	0.0
45-54	176.450	6.30	229.933	7.27	116.619	3.69	113.314	49.3
55-65	266.086	12.14	400.725	13.13	207.407	6.80	193.318	48.2
65-74	248.023	17.69	494.722	18.58	240.530	9.03	254.192	51.4
75+	293.038	23.15	608.972	24.39	608.972	24.39	0	0.0
All Persons	1,060.584	7.83	1,836.362	10.26	1,275.537	7.13	560.825	30.5

Type 2 diabetes is associated with significant health care costs. Table 3 shows the estimate of these costs and the savings that are expected to occur as an outcome of the prevention program. The diabetes literature indicates that the costs for a diabetic patient are approximately 1.7 times the cost for a person with normal glycaemia (Oliva et al., 2004; Nichols and Brown, 2005; Clarke et al., 2006). In the Diabetes Model, we assumed the following cost ratios where 1.00 is the average annual per capita direct health care cost for the "non-diabetic" population: 1.70 for individuals with diagnosed type 2 diabetes; 1.50 for undiagnosed; and 1.30 for pre-diabetes. For the prevention scenario, cases newly detected through the screening activities of the program were assigned a cost half-way between undiagnosed and diagnosed (1.60). These individuals would have additional costs associated with the initiation of diabetes treatment but because their duration of the disorder would be considerably less than the mean duration of diabetes in the diagnosed group, they are less likely to incur the same costs of care. The results are in 2005 constant dollar values and are the additional direct health care costs attributable to diabetes (i.e. costs normally incurred by the 'non-diabetic' population were subtracted from the costs incurred by each diabetic group).

542

As Table 3 indicates, the prevention program leads to an increase in direct health care costs in the first three years compared with the base case because the program increases the detection of type 2 diabetes with flow-on effects to treatment costs. The reduction in the number of people with type 2 diabetes then offsets increases in treatment costs for newly detected cases. The total cost of the prevention program is over $A2 billion per triennium (average cost per participant of around $A2,200). By 2023-26, the estimated savings in direct health care costs contribute to over 90% of the program costs.

Table 3: Direct health care costs and cost savings ($A million, 2005 constant dollars)

	2005-08	2008-11	2011-14	2014-17	2017-20	2020-23	2023-26
Base Case							
Diagnosed	3,675.2	4,012.0	4,366.1	4,746.1	5,131.6	5,506.7	5,884.4
Undiagnosed	2,625.2	2,865.7	3,118.6	3,390.1	3,665.4	3,933.4	4,203.1
Total	6,300.4	6,877.8	7,484.7	8,136.2	8,797.0	9,440.1	10,087.5
Prevention Scenario							
Diagnosed - established	3,591.5	3,783.9	3,888.2	3,934.8	3,949.6	3,902.9	3,761.5
- newly detected	1,525.8	1,638.1	1,741.8	1,844.4	1,938.2	2,000.8	2,045.6
Undiagnosed	1,341.5	1,409.2	1,462.5	1,506.2	1,538.0	1,582.3	1,653.7
Total	6,458.8	6,831.2	7,092.6	7,285.5	7,425.7	7,486.0	7,460.8
Savings (Base Scenario)	-158.4	46.5	392.1	850.8	1,371.3	1,954.1	2,626.7
Cost of Prevention Program	2,050.3	2,212.1	2,363.5	2,501.2	2,649.4	2,762.5	2,823.9
Net Cost of Program	2,208.7	2,165.6	1,971.4	1,650.4	1,278.2	808.4	197.2

4.2   Diabetes and employment

Table 4 shows the proportion of the Australian population with and without diabetes who are in employment by age group and gender based on the 1999-2000 AusDiab survey data. For men under 65 years, the population-weighted proportion of those in the sample conditional on diabetes is considerably lower than those without diabetes, although only in the age group 45-54 do the 95% CI suggest a statistically significant difference. In the case of women, only the 45-54 year age group suggests a statistically significant lower rate of employment for those with diabetes.

Table 4:   Probability of employment by diabetes status

Age group	Proportion without diabetes in employment	95% CI	Proportion with diabetes in employment	95% CI
Males				
35-44	0.900	[0.847,0.952]	0.845	[0.688,1.002]
45-54	0.885	[0.839,0.931]	0.756	[0.632,0.880]
55-64	0.623	[0.569,0.677]	0.388	[0.187,0.589]
65-74	0.166	[0.119,0.213]	0.076	[0.020,0.131]
Females				
35-44	0.725	[0.690,0.761]	0.541	[0.330,0.753]
45-54	0.735	[0.693,0.778]	0.588	[0.437,0.740]
55-64	0.388	[0.340,0.437]	0.235	[0.110,0.359]
65-74	0.052	[0.027,0.077]	0.033	[-0.009,0.076]

Note: The employment probabilities presented in this table control for sex, age, educational attainment, marital status and the presence of children. Additionally, the number of men and women with diabetes not in employment is too low in the age group 25-34 years for a reliable estimate of proportions.

The common variables used in all of the regressions and the results of the logistic regression of employment on diabetes status and human capital variables are shown in Tables 5 and 6. For men the mean of the marginal effects of diabetes on employment for those aged 25-64 years is -0.063 (95% CI -0.553, 0.426). For women aged 25-59 years, the mean of the marginal effects is -0.101 (95% CI -0.242, 0.041) (Table 6).

Table 5: Employment odds ratio for diabetes

	Males aged 25-64 years	Females aged 25-59 years	Males aged 25-64 years	Females aged 25-59 years
	Employment odds ratio (1)	Employment odds ratio (2)	Employment odds ratio (3)	Employment odds ratio (4)
Diagnosed diabetes	0.525**	0.554*	0.713	0.618
	[0.339,0.813]	[0.344,0.894]	[0.467,1.087]	[0.379,1.008]
High school education	1.979***	1.500	1.727*	1.420
	[1.378,2.842]	[0.939,2.399]	[1.147,2.602]	[0.856,2.358]
Higher education	2.481***	2.325***	2.100***	2.211***
	[1.849,3.328]	[1.644,3.287]	[1.582,2.787]	[1.585,3.083]
Age	8.750*	11.475***	21.738***	12.365***
	[1.286,59.539]	[3.365,39.131]	[4.431,106.645]	[3.920,39.000]
Age squared	0.733**	0.751***	0.659***	0.748***
	[0.590,0.911]	[0.650,0.867]	[0.553,0.786]	[0.655,0.853]
Married	2.722***	1.092	2.692***	1.004
	[1.924,3.853]	[0.861,1.386]	[1.574,4.606]	[0.795,1.267]
Children	0.895	0.566**	0.827	0.556**
	[0.569,1.407]	[0.395,0.810]	[0.539,1.268]	[0.391,0.791]
Standardized Physical Health Summary			1.083*** [1.060,1.106]	1.030*** [1.015,1.045]
Standardized Mental Health Summary			1.045*** [1.027,1.064]	1.016*** [1.010,1.022]
Constant	0.081	0.013**	0.000***	0.001***
	[0.002,3.358]	[0.001,0.183]	[0.000,0.001]	[0.000,0.014]

Note: * p<0.05, ** p<0.01, *** p<0.001 95% confidence intervals in parentheses

Table 6: Marginal effect of diabetes on employment

	Females aged 25-59 years (1)	Males aged 25-64 years (2)	Females aged 25-59 years (3)	Males aged 25-64 years (4)
	Employment average of marginal effects	Employment average of marginal effects	Employment average of marginal effects	Employment average of marginal effects
Diagnosed diabetes	-0.131*	-0.091*	-0.103	-0.037
	[-0.242,-0.019]	[-0.162,-0.020]	[-0.214,0.008]	[-0.086,0.012]
High school education	0.079	0.076***	0.068	0.051**
	[-0.008,0.167]	[0.039,0.112]	[-0.027,0.163]	[0.017,0.086]
Higher education	0.169***	0.110***	0.156***	0.074***
	[0.101,0.236]	[0.077,0.143]	[0.092,0.220]	[0.047,0.102]
Age	0.500***	0.266*	0.505***	0.311***
	[0.247,0.753]	[0.057,0.475]	[0.270,0.740]	[0.163,0.459]
Age squared	-0.059***	-0.038**	-0.058***	-0.042***
	[-0.088,-0.029]	[-0.061,-0.015]	[-0.085,-0.031]	[-0.058,-0.026]
Married	0.018	0.140***	0.001	0.113**
	[-0.031,0.068]	[0.073,0.207]	[-0.046,0.048]	[0.038,0.188]
Children	-0.115**	-0.014	-0.116**	-0.019
	[-0.187,-0.044]	[-0.069,0.041]	[-0.186,-0.047]	[-0.063,0.024]
Standardized Physical Health Summary			0.006*** [0.003,0.009]	0.008*** [0.006,0.010]
Standardized Mental Health Summary			0.003*** [0.002,0.004]	0.004*** [0.003,0.006]
Observations	3827	3761	3827	3761

Notes: Marginal effects are P(E=1|diabetes=1) - P(E=1|diabetes=0). 95% confidence intervals in parentheses.
* $p<0.05$, ** $p<0.01$, *** $p<0.001$. Adjusted for survey stratification.

Table 7 gives the marginal effects from a logistic regression with the same variables as Table 4 but with a separate regression for each age and gender group. There is a consistent trend towards a lower employment rate among those with diabetes for men and women in each age group above the age of 35 years. In only two age groups, however, is there a statistically significant effect of diabetes on employment at $p<0.05$.

545

Table 7:   Employment average marginal effect of diabetes by age group
            and gender

Age group	Marginal effect	95% CI	Marginal effect including SF-36 physical for male and physical and mental for females	95% CI
Male				
35-44	-0.037	[-0.199,0.126]	0.015	[-0.079,0.110]
45-54	-0.110*	[-0.206,-0.013]	-0.046	[-0.110,0.017]
55-64	-0.137	[-0.280,0.006]	-0.101	[-0.240,0.037]
65-74	-0.068*	[-0.127,-0.010]	-0.060	[-0.120,0.001]
Female				
35-44	-0.183	[-0.394,0.028]	-0.173	[-0.404,0.058]
45-54	-0.111	[-0.264,0.043]	-0.074	[-0.234,0.086]
55-64	-0.089	[-0.201,0.023]	-0.065	[-0.191,0.062]
65-74	-0.014	[-0.053,0.026]	-0.006	[-0.057,0.044]

Note: Marginal effects are P(E=1|diabetes=1) - P(E=1|diabetes=0).

Including the physical and mental health summary scores of the SF-36 in the employment equation had a substantial impact on the estimated marginal effect of diabetes. For women the reduction in the marginal effect is 0.028 but for men the marginal effect is reduced from 0.091 to 0.037. The mental health summary score had a high correlation with diabetes status (0.72) for men. It may be that multi-collinearity does not allow us to separate out the effects of diabetes from the general measure of health status. For women the correlation was lower for mental health (0.04) but higher for physical health (0.25). Given this, it may be more reasonable to predict the effect of diabetes on employment as somewhere in the range given in Table 7.

The IV model with an instrument for the SF-36 physical summary score improved the p-value and increased the marginal effect of diabetes on employment for men aged 35-64 years to -0.08. For women aged 25-59 years, instrumenting the SF-36 mental summary score increased the marginal effect on employment to -0.126. However, in the case of women, a Wald test failed to reject the exogeneity of the SF-36 measure and the instrument was not estimated precisely in the employment equation (p>0.376).

For those in work, it may be that diabetes makes it more difficult to work full-time or in higher-paid employment. We found some evidence that for men aged 25-64 years who were employed, diabetes reduced weekly household before tax income by around $A145 (95% CI -316, 27).

However, there is considerable uncertainty about the size of this effect and no statistically significant difference was found either for this group or for any of the 10-year age groups for women or men. For women in employment diabetes increased the probability of part-time compared to full-time work by 0.03 (95% CI -0.182, 0.114).

The severity of symptoms associated with diabetes is likely to influence the capacity to work and the decision to seek employment. The AusDiab survey contains information on the complications of diabetes. We re-estimated the employment equations including as explanatory variables the neuropathy disability score and the experience of leg or foot pain. Neither was statistically significant in explaining the probability of employment either for the population as a whole or for those with diabetes.

Finally, we use the marginal effects given in Table 7, applied to the expected number of cases of type 2 diabetes prevented through the secondary prevention program (Table 2), to estimate the likely increase in employment that might occur as a consequence of the lifestyle modification of individuals at high risk of diabetes. Note that these predictions are imprecise as the confidence intervals on the marginal effects in Table 7 are wide. We use these rather than the marginal effects in Table 6 in order to present estimates at a more disaggregate level. Applying the aggregate effects from Table 6 will predict similar if less precise employment effects overall. As Table 8 shows, by 2026 labour supply is estimated to increase by somewhere between 25,000 and 35,000 employed males and 8,700 and 13,000 employed females. As the next section shows, this has economy-wide implications.

4.3 Diabetes shocks to the economy

Perhaps the most striking economic results in this simulation are macro-economic. Real GDP rises, but by less than the increase in employment (Figure 1). The initial fall in GDP occurs because both consumption and investment are lower in the short term. Consumption falls because of the extra taxes required to finance the policy. Consumers spend out of after-tax income. Investment falls because cheaper labour at a given level of income reduces the rental price of capital.

Over time, however, real GDP, consumption and investment all grow relative to the base case. The positive impact of the increase in the labour supply gradually outweighs the negative influence of higher taxation. In addition, the degree to which taxation is higher than the base case falls, since the additional expenditure required to finance the program diminishes as a proportion of the base case.

Over the long term, investment adjusts to provide capital for the additional workers in the economy. In the MONASH model, capital is available to a small country like Australia at a fixed expected rate of return. The long-term response to an increase in workforce participation is an expansion of capital as well as labour.

Table 8: Estimated gains in employed persons, 2005-2026

	June 2008	June 2011	June 2014	June 2017	June 2020	June 2023	June 2026
Marginal effect							
Male							
45-54	511	1,220	2,334	3,443	4,665	6,349	7,581
55-64	686	2,201	4,114	6,671	9,468	11,625	16,222
65-74	540	1,090	2,970	4,499	6,089	8,640	11,101
Total	1,737	4,510	9,418	14,614	20,222	26,614	34,904
Female							
45-54	338	812	1,587	2,142	3,019	3,944	4,928
55-64	440	1,110	1,754	2,911	4,062	5,545	6,667
65-74	68	199	348	561	867	991	1,273
Total	846	2,121	3,689	5,614	7,948	10,480	12,868
Marginal effect including SF-36							
Male							
45-54	214	510	976	1,440	1,951	2,655	3,170
55-64	506	1,622	3,033	4,918	6,980	8,570	11,959
65-74	476	962	2,621	3,970	5,373	7,623	9,795
Total	1,196	3,094	6,629	10,328	14,304	18,849	24,925
Female							
45-54	225	541	1,058	1,428	2,013	2,629	3,285
55-64	321	811	1,281	2,126	2,967	4,050	4,869
65-74	29	85	149	240	371	425	546
Total	576	1,437	2,488	3,794	5,351	7,104	8,700

Figure 1:   Change in real GDP and employment, 2006-2026

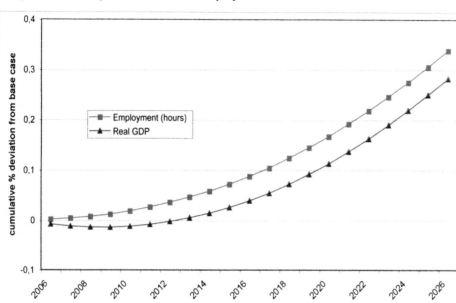

The economy is about 0.33% larger than the base case by 2026 (Figure 2). This sounds like a small number, but it is around $A6.4 billion above the 2026 base case. The economy by then is substantially larger than now, so it may be helpful to consider that 0.33% of 2006 GDP is more than $A2 billion.

Figure 2:   Change in real GDP, consumption and investment, 2006-2026

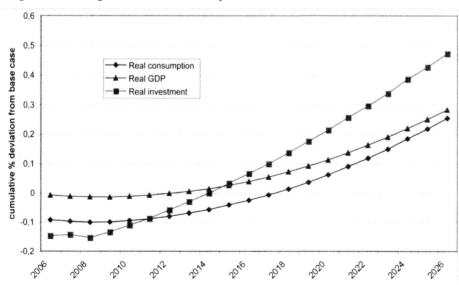

As the economy grows, demand for imports grows. In MONASH, it is assumed that Australia faces fixed prices for imports (in a given year) but downward-sloping demands for exports. An expansion of both exports and imports – due to the expansion of the whole economy in this simulation – has the effect of driving down the terms of trade relative to the base case (Figure 3) as exporters face lower prices as they sell more. In the early years of the simulation, when the economy is a little smaller overall, the opposite can be seen: depressed trade volumes and associated improvement in the terms of trade (Figure 3).

Figure 3:   Change in exports, imports and terms of trade, 2006-2026

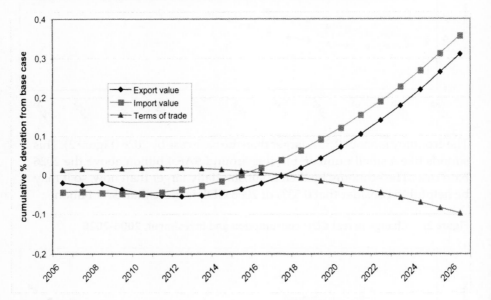

5   Discussion and conclusions

It is clear that diabetes prevention programs of the kind modelled in this simulation exercise do have the capacity to significantly reduce the health and economic costs of type 2 diabetes projected to occur in the next two decades. The hypothetical prevention program modelled may seem costly at over $A2 billion per triennium. This in part reflects the large population at risk of type 2 diabetes in Australia and the relatively high participation rate modelled. The challenge from a public health perspective is whether such a prevention program can be implemented in Australia on a sustainable basis and whether the attributable effects in reducing the health and economic burden of diabetes can be achieved.

To date, research linking diabetes and workforce participation has mainly occurred at the micro-level with a similar finding of a negative relationship between diabetes and employment outcomes (Ng et al., 2001; Vijan et al., 2004; Tunceli et al., 2005). The effect of diabetes on employment for those of working age in Australia is particularly evident in men aged between 55 and 64 years. In women, the largest decrease in employment appears to be for those aged 35-44 years.

There is evidence that perceived ill health, as measured by the summary SF-36 scores, has an independent effect on the probability of employment. Table 5 suggests that a one standard deviation reduction in both summary measures of health status (10 points) would reduce the probability of employment by 0.09 for women aged 35-59 years and 0.12 for men aged 35-64 years. The marginal effect on employment of having diabetes, for those one standard deviation below the Australian population average for both the SF-36 summary measures of physical and mental health, is -0.07 for men [95% CI -0.161 0.0190] and -0.12 for women [-0.237 -0.002]. Thus, for those who have diabetes and have significant symptoms of ill health there is an even lower likelihood of being in employment than implied in Table 6.

We found little evidence in the AusDiab survey of a reduction in household income for those in employment and only weak evidence of a reduction in hours of work associated with diabetes. However, the survey was not detailed on the hours of work for individuals, spousal income or work patterns, and we were not able to infer anything about the productivity effects of diabetes in the population. At the elementary level, a healthy population is critical to workforce participation and productivity. Focusing on the health outcomes needed to enhance participation and productivity and thus the future living standards of Australians are the objectives of the human capital stream of the reform agreed by the Australian Commonwealth and all State and Territory Governments.

A key contribution of this research has been the linking of micro-level health and employment outcomes to economy-wide effects which has not been undertaken before in Australia, nor to our knowledge elsewhere. The results demonstrate that preventive health care interventions have value beyond their effects on direct health care expenditures and beyond their effects on health – the prevention program would not be deemed to be cost-effective if savings in direct health care costs was the only outcome measure used. However, the flow-on effects from increased workforce participation and earnings can have quite large effects on the broader economy and evaluation of policies needs to account for these economy-wide implications. This is particularly so at present when there is considerable concern about workforce participation in the context of an ageing population. Furthermore, the economic impact of diabetes is likely to worsen substantially as the prevalence of diabetes increases, given the trend of diabetes among young adults.

Increased workforce participation leads to real GDP being higher than it would have been in the absence of the policy. Normally, there might be a question about whether this was a real gain to society, since it involves people undertaking more work. In this case, however, there are strong reasons to suppose that those undertaking the additional work are more than adequately compensated for their time, and to the extent that both real GDP and real consumption rise in the MONASH simulation, the policy is worthwhile despite the fact that it causes net health costs and taxes to rise. There is also a strong argument for focusing not only on short-term but long-term commitments as the results suggest that the expansion of capital and labour as a result of increased workforce participation will lead to real GDP being higher in the long run.

Type 2 diabetes is used as the example in this chapter. We argue that the modelling methodology illustrated forms a template for a broader and more comprehensive economic evaluation of public health strategies for the prevention of chronic disease in Australia and internationally. While both micro- and macro-approaches are able to provide powerful insights over the domain that is individually being modelled, there are inherent questions that cannot be answered by these models when used in isolation. Linking models that capture dynamics at both the micro- and macro-level offers the potential for deeper insights to be gained on how a given policy shock will affect both individuals and economic aggregates.

It is notable that the majority of research in the field has focussed on linkages effected through population and labour market variables. Indeed, the diabetes example described above achieved a linkage through just such a mechanism. While novel insights were provided on the macro-economic effect of reducing the prevalence of diabetes over the 21-year period the prevention program was modelled, no feedbacks between the micro- and macro-level were captured. Future attention in this particular work could perhaps be directed towards enriching the flow of information between the levels of modelling and achieving greater feedbacks between the models. To the extent that these paths of integration can be enhanced, a more complete understanding of the true effect of a hypothesized shock to the economy and individuals' health status will be revealed.

References

Arntz, M./Boeters, S./Gürtzgen, N./Schubert, S. (2006) 'Analysing welfare reform in a micro-simulation-AGE model: The value of disaggregation', Conference paper presented at the 8th Nordic Seminar on Microsimulation Models, Oslo, Norway, June 8-9, 2006.

Aaberge, R./Colombino, U./Holmøy, E./Strøm, B./Wennemo, T. (2007) 'Population ageing and fiscal sustainability: Integrating detailed labour supply models with CGE models', pp. 259-290 in: Harding, A./Gupta, A. (eds.), *Modelling Our Future: Social Security and Taxation* (Volume I). Amsterdam: Elsevier.

Anderson, J. M. (1990) 'Micro-macro linkages in economic models', in: Lewis, G.H./Michel, R.C. (eds.), *Microsimulation Techniques for Tax and Transfer Analysis*. Urban Institute Press.

Australian Bureau of Statistics (2006) *Population projections, Australia, 2004 to 2101*, Catalogue Number 32220. Canberra: Australian Bureau of Statistics.

Australian Institute of Health and Welfare (2002) *Diabetes: Australian Facts 2002*, AIHW Cat No CVD 20 (Diabetes Series No 3). Canberra: AIHW.

Australian Institute of Health and Welfare (2005) 'Diabetes related deaths in Australia 2001-2003', *AIHW Bulletin 32*. Canberra: AIHW.

Bækgaard, H. (1995) 'Integrating micro and macro models: mutual benefits', International Congress on Modelling and Simulation Proceedings Volume 4 (Economics and Transportation). Australia: University of Newcastle.

Brown, L./Harris, A./Picton, M./Thurecht, L./Yap, M. (2006) 'Estimating the health and economic impacts of the prevention of type 2 diabetes in Australia – Linking micro and macro-economic models', 28th Australian Conference of Health Economists, Perth, 28-29 September.

Cai, L./Kalb, G. (2006) 'Health status and labour force participation: Evidence from Australia', *Health Economics* 15 (3): 241-261.

Centers for Disease Control and Prevention Primary Prevention Working Group (2004) 'Primary prevention of type 2 diabetes mellitus by lifestyle intervention: Implications for health policy', *Annals of Internal Medicine* 140 (11): 951-957.

Clarke, P./Kelman, C./Colagiuri, S. (2006) 'Factors in influencing the cost of hospital care for people with diabetes in Australia', *Journal of Diabetes and its Complications* 20 (6): 349-355.

Colagiuri, S./Hussain, Z./Zimmet, P./Cameron, A./Shaw, J. (2004) 'Screening for Type 2 diabetes and impaired glucose tolerance: The Australian experience', *Diabetes Care* 27 (2): 367-371.

Davies, J. (2004) 'Microsimulation, CGE and macro modelling for transition and developing economics', paper prepared for United Nations University/World Institute for Development Economics Research (UNU/WIDER), Helsinki.

Diabetes Prevention Program Research Group (2002) 'Reduction in the incidence of type 2 diabetes with lifestyle intervention or metformin', *The New England Journal of Medicine* 346 (2): 393-403.

Disney, R. / Emmerson, C. / Wakefield, M. (2003) 'Ill health and retirement in Britain: A panel data-based analysis', Institute of Fiscal Studies Working Paper 03-02.

Dixon, P. / Malakellis, M. / Meagher, T. (1996) 'A microsimulation / applied general equilibrium approach to analysing income distribution in Australia: Plans and preliminary illustration', Industry Commission Conference on Equity, Efficiency and Welfare, Melbourne, Australia.

Dixon, P.B. / Rimmer, M.T. (2002) *Dynamic general equilibrium modelling for forecasting and policy*. Amsterdam: North Holland.

Dunstan, D. / Zimmet, P. / Welborn, T. / de Courten, M. (2002) 'The rising prevalence of diabetes and impaired glucose tolerance: The Australian Diabetes, Obesity and Lifestyle study', *Diabetes Care* 25 (5): 829-34.

Eddy, A. / Schlessinger, L. / Kahn, R. (2005) 'Clinical outcomes and cost-effectiveness of strategies for Managing People at High Risk for Diabetes', *Annals of Internal Medicine* 143 (4): 251-263.

Eliasson, G. (1986) 'The Swedish Micro-to-Macro Model: Idea, design and application', in: Orcutt, G. H. / Merz, J. / Quinke, H. (eds.), *Microanalytic Simulation Models to Support Social and Financial Policy*. Netherlands: Elsevier Science Publishers.

Eliasson, G. (1996) 'Endogenous economic growth through selection', in: Harding, A. (ed.), *Microsimulation and Public Policy*. North-Holland.

Fredriksen, D. / Heide, K.M. / Holmoy, E. / Solli, I.F. (2007) 'Macroeconomic effects of proposed pension reforms in Norway', pp. 107-142 in: Harding, A. / Gupta, A. (eds.), *Modelling Our Future: Social Security and Taxation* (Volume I). Amsterdam: Elsevier.

Hancock, R. / Comas-Herrera, A. / Pickard, L. / Wittenberg, R. (2005) 'Who will pay for long-term care in the UK? Projections linking macro- and micro-simulation models', *Fiscal Studies* 24 (4): 387-426.

Lindstrom, J. / Louheranta, A. / Mannelin, M. / Salminen, V. / Eriksson, J. / Uusitupa, M. / Tuomilehto, J. (2003) 'The Finnish Diabetes Prevention Study (DPS)', *Diabetes Care* 26 (12): 3230-3236.

Meagher, G.A. / Agrawal, N. 1986 'Taxation reform and income distribution in Australia', *Australian Economic Review* 19 (3): 33-56.

Mullahy, J. / Sindelair, J. (1996) 'Employment, unemployment and problem drinking', *Journal of Health Economics* 15 (4): 409-434.

Ng, Y.C. / Jacobs, P. / Johnson, J. (2001) 'Productivity losses associated with Diabetes in the US', *Diabetes Care* 24 (2): 257-261.

Nichols, G. / Brown, J. (2005) 'Higher medical care costs accompany impaired fasting glucose', *Diabetes Care* 28 (9): 2223-2229.

Oliva, J. / Lobo, F. / Molina, B. / Monereo, S. (2004) 'Direct Health Care Costs of Diabetic Patients in Spain', *Diabetes Care* 27 (11): 2616-2621.

Orcutt, G. H. (1967) 'Microeconomic Analysis for Prediction of National Accounts', in: Wold, H. / Orcutt, G. H. / Robinson, E. A. / Suits, D. / de Wolff, P. (eds.), *Forecasting on a Scientific Basis – Proceedings of an International Summer Institute*. Portugal: Curia.

Orcutt, G. / Caldwell, S. / Wertheimer II, R. / Franklin, S. / Hendricks, G. / Peabody, G. / Smith, J. / Zedlewski, S. (1976) *Policy exploration through microanalytic simulation*. Washington DC: The Urban Institute.

Pan, X.R. / Li, G.W. / Hu, Y.H. / Wang, J.X. / Yang, W.Y. / An, Z.X. / Hu, Z.X. / Lin, J. / Xiao, J.Z. / Cao, H.B. / Liu, P.A. / Jiang, X.G. / Jiang, Y.Y. / Wang, J.P. / Zheng, H. / Zhang, H. / Bennett, P. / Howard, B. (1997) 'Effects of diet and exercise in preventing NIDDM in people with impaired glucose tolerance. The Da Qing IGT and Diabetes Study', *Diabetes Care* 20 (4): 537-544.

Polette, J./Robinson, M. (1997) 'Modelling the impact of microeconomic policy on Australian families', Discussion Paper 20, National Centre for Social and Economic Modelling, University of Canberra.

Shaw, J./Chisholm, D. (2003) 'Epidemiology and prevention of type 2 diabetes and the metabolic syndrome', *Medical Journal of Australia* 179 (7): 379-383.

Sherwin, R.S./Anderson, R.M./Buse, J.B./Chin, M.H./Eddy, D./Fradkin, J./Ganiats, T.G./ Ginsberg, H.N./Kahn, R./Nwankwo, R./Rewers, M./Schlessinger, L./Stern, M./ Vinicor, F./Zinman, B.; American Diabetes Association; National Institute of Diabetes and Digestive and Kidney Diseases (2004) 'Prevention or delay of type 2 diabetes', *Diabetes Care*, 27 (Supplement 1): 47-54.

Toder, E./Favreault, M./O'Hare, J./Rogers, D./Sammartino, F./Smith, K./Smetters, K./Rust, J. (2000) 'Long term model development for social security policy analysis', Final Report to the Social Security Administration, USA, The Urban Institute.

Tunceli, K./Bradley, C./Nerenz, D./Williams, L./Pladevall, M./Lafata, J. (2005) 'The impact of diabetes on employment and work productivity', *Diabetes Care* 28 (11): 2662-2667.

Tuomilehto, J./Lindström, J./Eriksson, J.G./Valle, T.T./Hämäläninen, H./Ilanne-Parikka, P./Keinänen-Kiukaanniemi, S./Laasko, M./Louheranta, A./Rastas, M./Salminen, V./ Uustipa, M. (2001) 'Prevention of Type 2 diabetes mellitus by changes in lifestyle among subjects with impaired glucose tolerance', *The New England Journal of Medicine* 344 (18): 1343-50.

Vijan, S./Hayward, R./Langa, K. (2004) 'The impact of diabetes on workforce participation: Results from a national household sample', *Health Services Research* 39 (6): 1653-1669.

Vinicor, F./Bowman, B./Engelgau, M. (2003) 'Diabetes: Prevention needed', *The Lancet* 361 (9357): 544.

Chapter 21

Microsimulation Meets General Equilibrium – A New Tool for Applied Policy Analysis

Markus Clauss / Stefanie Schubert

1 Introduction

Bourguignon and Spadaro (2006) provide an excellent discussion on the use of microsimulation models as a tool for analysing policy reforms and their impact on redistribution and poverty. Their paper also points out the limits of this tool and hints at future research directions in this field. One of the directions mentioned was that of combining microsimulation and CGE models.

In our chapter, we briefly describe the general methods of microsimulation and general equilibrium modelling. We provide a detailed presentation of the microsimulation model STSM and the computable general equilibrium model PACE-L, as well as the linkage of both models. The combination and full integration of microsimulation and computable general equilibrium (CGE) models has led into a new era of computational modelling (Davies, 2004). At the cutting edge of economic research, the Centre for European Economic Research (ZEW, Mannheim) uses a combined CGE-microsimulation model for Germany to analyse policy implications arising from different reform proposals.

Microsimulation models and computable CGE models are usually separately employed for the evaluation of policy reform proposals. The main advantage of microsimulation models lies in the micro-foundation created by using individual household data. This allows the calculation of partial equilibrium labour supply effects, from which we draw a detailed analysis of gainers and losers after a reform proposal. The main disadvantage of using a microsimulation model is that general equilibrium effects and feedback effects are neglected. This means that results are calculated under the assumption that, e.g. wages and interest rates do not change. In contrast, CGE models take these effects into account but are usually based on aggregated household types. The loss of information within the household sector makes a detailed analysis of the reform effects impossible. Therefore, the combination of microsimulation and CGE-models to combine the advantages of both types and to reduce the disadvantages of each model type is a further logical development.

All in all, the recent developments in microsimulation models for Germany are dominated by three research institutes[1]: the German Institute for Economic Research (DIW), the Institute for the Study of Labour (IZA) and the Centre for European Economic Research (ZEW).[2] While the DIW uses a microsimulation model, the IZA has established a combined CGE-microsimulation model, albeit with only one representative household in the CGE-model. The ZEW, as a stand-alone, uses a fully integrated CGE-microsimulation model with approximately 4,000 households.

The chapter is organized as follows: In Section 2 the microsimulation model is illustrated, which algebraically describes the household labour supply model used to consider behavioural response. We also describe the data used, as well as the most important German tax-transfer regulations. Section 3 refers to the general equilibrium modelling. A general overview is followed by the presentation of the general equilibrium model PACE-L. The linkage of the microsimulation model STSM to the general equilibrium model PACE-L is given in Section 4. Section 5 concludes and presents an outlook for further research.

2   Microsimulation

It was Guy Orcutt (1957) who brought microsimulation models into social sciences as a new type of modelling that is based on distributions, and therefore can be regarded as micro-based. Although this was a revolutionary contribu-

---

1   Besides these research institutes, microsimulation models are also applied and maintained at universities or at the Institute of Employment Research, a department of the Federal Employment Service.

2   See for example: Haan/Wrohlich (2007), Bargain et al. (2005), Haan (2006), Wrohlich/Steiner (2008), Wrohlich (2006), Bonin et al. (2003), Brenneisen/Peichl (2007 a,b), Peichl/Schaefer (2006), Arntz et al. (2008), Clauss/Schnabel (2008), Arntz/Boeters/Guertzgen (2006).

tion, the employment of microsimulation models in economic analysis actually developed three decades later. The explanation can be found in the access to individual-based data (e.g. the German Socio-Economic Panel / GSOEP started in 1984) and in growing computing power (Harding and Gupta, 2007: 7-8).[3]

Microsimulation models, in particular tax-benefit microsimulation models, use a detailed representation of a tax system to simulate policy reforms. Structurally, microsimulation models are based on micro-data with detailed information on socio-demographic variables (i.e. number of children in household, age, sex or education), incomes, taxes, benefits and working time of households and individuals. If the micro-data are a representative sample of the population, the simulated effects also serve as forecast for the possible impact of the proposed reforms.

There are two main branches of microsimulation models. On the one side, there are static models that do not consider the behavioural responses of the households / individuals after the policy changes have come into effect. These arithmetic models simulate only the so-called "morning-after effects" or "first-round effects". On the other side, there are models which also allow for behavioural reactions by integrating a household labour supply model. The estimated labour supply effects also establish a partial equilibrium, since the labour supply side of the household sector is also regarded. These so-called "second round effects" are transferred and assessed in the following distribution and poverty analysis.

A very promising development is EUROMOD (Sutherland, 2001, 2007) which is a popular European microsimulation model covering 15 EU Member States and is continuously expanding. For Germany in particular, Wagenhals (2004) gives an overview of the existing microsimulation models applied to the German economy, although it is not clear if all of them still exist. Peichl (2005) gives an overview on the existing branches of simulation models. In addition, he also outlines the developments in Germany.

2.1 The ZEW Tax and Benefit Microsimulation Model (STSM)

The ZEW tax and benefit microsimulation model (STSM) is a static microsimulation model for empirical analysis of the impact of taxes, social security contributions and transfers on the income and labour supply of private households in Germany. The data base is the GSOEP, which is a yearly based

---

3   See Lenhard (2004) for an illustration of creating a full computerized decision-making system (for the weather forecast).

panel study of 12,000 representative households of the German economy.[4] The present microsimulation model uses the variables of the 2005 wave which are complemented with retrospective information from 2006.

2.1.1 Household Labour Supply Model

The STSM integrates both a simulation model for the German tax and transfer system and an econometrically estimated labour supply model. We use a structural model of household labour supply to transfer the outcomes of the STSM in behavioural responses of the households. We assume that the individual faces different hour categories, which produce different utilities according to the preferences of the individual. The individual decides to choose the hour category with the highest utility. Married or cohabiting couples are regarded as one decision-maker, jointly maximizing their utility.[5]

We use a linear translog utility function as proposed by van Soest (1995). For each individual we assume a weekly time endowment (TE) of 80 hours. We identify leisure as $lm_i = TE - h_i$ and $lf_i = TE - h_i$ where lm indicates the weekly leisure of the male and lf the weekly leisure of the female of the respective household i.

$$U_k(x_k) = x_k' A x_k + \beta' x_k + \varepsilon_k \qquad (1)$$

The utility of category k U_k is as linear function in x_k, containing monthly disposable income and leisure of the household in natural logarithm $(\log y_i, \log lm_i, \log lfi)$. The unobserved part is defined by ε_k which is assumed to be iid. The symmetric 3x3 matrix A contains the coefficients of the interactions and quadratic terms of the included variables, and the vector β contains the coefficients of the linear terms.

There are also further covariates that enter the utility function which controls different preferences for leisure ("taste shifters") of households (i.e. age, education, number of children, regional dummy for Eastern Germany, nationality, dummy for part-time or full-time employment).

The probability of a decision-maker now choosing category k instead of category l is given by:

---

4   See Haisken De-New and Frick (2005).
5   An extension of the unitary household model would be to focus on intra-household sharing of incomes, which has been done with a collective household model in Beninger/ Laisney/Beblo (2007).

$$\mathrm{Pr}_k = \mathrm{Pr}(U_k > U_l) = \mathrm{Pr}\left(\left(x_k' A x_k + \beta' x_k\right) - \left(x_l' A x_l + \beta' x_l\right) > \varepsilon_l - \varepsilon_k\right) \forall l \quad (4)$$

The equation is solved by making a distributional assumption about the unobserved part of the utility function. In particular, it is assumed that the density for each unobserved part of the utility function follows a Gumbel or type I extreme value distribution.

$$f(\varepsilon_j) = \exp(-\varepsilon_j) \exp(-\exp(-\varepsilon_j)) \qquad (5)$$

As shown by McFadden (1974, 2001), the difference of the unobserved parts then follows a logit distribution. The probability of choosing category k can thus be written as

$$\mathrm{Pr}_k(U_k > U_l) = \mathrm{Pr}(X = k) = \frac{\exp\left(x_k' A x_k + \beta' x_k\right)}{\sum_m \exp\left(x_m' A x_m + \beta' x_m\right)}, \forall l \neq k \qquad (6)$$

The parameters of the conditional logit model are estimated by maximum likelihood, assuming the IIA-assumption holds (see Equation 6).

$$L = \prod_{i=1}^{n} \prod_{j=1}^{m} \mathrm{Pr}(H = j)^{d_{ij}} \qquad (7)$$

Here $\mathrm{Pr}(H = j)$ describes the choice probability of category j, and d_{ij} is defined as an indicator which takes the value $d_{ij} = 1$ if household i has chosen category j and 0 if this is not the case.

2.1.2 Data basis and selection of households

For the empirical implementation of the STSM, a dataset is needed that contains the necessary person and household characteristics, is representative of the German population, contains a sufficient number of cases and is up-to-date. The GSOEP basically fulfils these requirements. However, there are some restrictions – like the missing information about household assets, which are required to detect transfer entitlements, and the limited information on tax rebates. All in all, the GSOEP, with all its advantages and disadvantages, embodies the best compromise for the tax-transfer-simulation out of all the micro-datasets available today for Germany.

Income and transfers cannot be simulated for every household in the GSOEP. A selection of households is taken for various reasons. On the one hand, the simulation of hypothetical incomes for alternative employments requires information about the entitlement to unemployment benefit in the case of unemployment. This entitlement can be deduced from employment participation during the three previous years, the information about which is contained in the GSOEP. Since the income information has been collected retrospectively in the succeeding year, only those households who have participated in the survey in four consecutive years enter the simulation.

Missing values for workers' compensation, duration of employment, and earnings from rent and lease are being imputed if they can be deduced sufficiently from other information. In case where this is not possible, the households are eliminated from the simulation. Finally, those households are excluded for which the required information about the head of the household or the partner's marital situation is missing. For a simulation of the incomes depending on the amount of employment, only the householder's or the partner's amount of employment is varied. Certain information such as the potential entitlement to unemployment benefit are thus only needed for the head of the household and their partners – and households are accordingly only excluded if the information was missing for these persons.

From the group of the remaining households, those persons who live in one household together with the householder, but are neither relatives nor cohabitants, are excluded. A further selection of households results from the designated application of the STSM to simulate the employment behaviour of employees. In economic theory, the labour-supply decision is usually modelled as a trade-off between utility from consumption or leisure. This trade-off between temporary consumption and leisure cannot be assumed to be the same for all types of persons facing the labour-supply decision. This concerns, for example, retired persons, trainees, persons in military/civil service as well as students. The self-employed persons' labour-supply decision should be significantly different from the one made by employees. The analysis thus focuses on certain groups of employees and unemployed, for whom a similar consumption- and leisure-utility calculation can be assumed. We do not include the following groups of persons:

- persons younger than 20 or older than 65 years of age,
- recipients of pension, retirement transition or early-retirement payments,
- trainees (school, university, vocational training etc.),
- persons in maternity leave or military/civil service, and
- mainly self-employed persons.

Legal income tax regulations, which are only relevant for these types of persons, were not implemented. Thus, for these persons, simulations cannot be done. We differentiate householders and partners with variable and with invariable labour supply. Three types of households that are treated differently result in the following:

1. households with flexible householder and flexible partner (flexible households),
2. households with flexible householder or flexible partner (mixed households), and
3. households with inflexible householder and inflexible partner (inflexible households).

For single-households, the second type of household does not apply. Households in which neither the householder nor the partner display a variable labour supply (group three) are excluded from the labour supply simulation. Single-households are excluded from the simulation if the householder had no variable labour supply. Group one, in which both the householder and the partner have a flexible labour supply in couple-households, can thus be included in the simulation of labour-supply reactions. The second group, in which either the householder or the partner shows a flexible labour supply, represents a special case. For these mixed couple-households, a simulation of the labour-supply reactions is done, but they are technically treated as single-households. The detection of the net household income depending on the employment behaviour is done for the partner with flexible labour supply for different amounts of employment while, for the partner with inflexible labour supply, actual working time is considered.

For the simulation of income depending on the employment behaviour, only the first and second group (the flexible and mixed households) are relevant. For an analysis of the actual incomes without behavioural responses, the third group can also be included.

2.1.3 Regulations of the tax and benefit system

The ZEW microsimulation model calculates the disposable household income, as well as the taxes and benefits. The calculation of these outcomes is based on a very detailed representation of the German tax and transfer system, summarized very briefly below.

The net disposable household income detected in the STSM is derived from the components stated in Table 1. The first part of the table contains the household's income; the second part lists the wage-replacement benefits and transfers; and the third part applies the deductions.

Table 1: Components of the household net income

	Income components
1	Income from employment + Income from assets + Income from rent and lease + Income from self-employment, agriculture, forestry,
2	+ child benefit + raising benefit + housing benefit + unemployment benefit I and II + social assistance
3	- social security contributions - taxes
	disposable household net income

Incomes

The data contain the information on actual wages or salary received, which enables us to calculate the income from employment. For the simulation of different market states we estimate the hourly wage rate of each individual, which is then multiplied by the associated working time.[6] The pieces of information about the incomes from assets contained in the data are limited in several ways. Firstly, we only have information on the returns through interest and dividends and, secondly, the returns on interest and dividends are not differentiated by types of investment but are displayed as a total amount. Thus, it is assumed that the entire revenues can be considered as earnings from assets. The information about incomes from rent and lease

---

6   For individuals who are not in employment, we estimate a wage regression with selection correction as proposed by Heckman (1976).

is rather incomplete. We either can observe income from rent or lease of moveable assets or from the surrender of rights. In the data only income from rent and lease of real property are explicitly listed. The data also show missing values to a relevant extent for the information about interest and acquittance payments, as well as for operating expenses which are associated with income from rent and lease. To avoid elimination of these cases on the one hand – and trying not to skew the data on the other hand – we replaced the missing information. Income from agriculture and forestry, from business and from self-employment are not collected separately in the GSOEP. Special regulations for these types of income in the income tax law can thus not be considered. As mentioned earlier, the self-employed are excluded from the labour supply simulation. Income from self-employment is therefore only measured through the channel of supplementary income. Since it is not possible to disentangle whether supplementary income is from self-employment or from employment, it is assumed to be 100% from self-employment.

Benefits

We have information on the number, the relation to the householder and the age of persons in the household. As such we can identify and model child benefits by multiplying the number of children by the respective rate of 154 Euro (from the fourth child onwards the rate amounts to 179 Euro). We restrict the availability of child benefits to children under the age of 26 and we apply the deduction rule (if the child's income exceeds 7,680 Euro per annum). On the other side, there exist child tax allowances of 5,808 Euro for each child. We implement a yield test to decide whether the household benefits more from child benefits or from child allowances. The information on the number of children is also used to model the child-raising benefit. As there are two alternatives offered by the legislation, we assume that the standard rate is chosen. This rate amounts to 300 Euro per month. It is assumed that one person could always dedicate himself/herself to raising the child in the sense of the legislation if he or she is not employed for more than 19 hours per week or receiving unemployment benefit, assistance or child-raising benefit for a similar activity. In cases this precondition is met by persons with a child younger than 2 years, and if certain income thresholds are not exceeded, generally, an entitlement to child-raising benefit is fulfilled.

The amount of actual rent is collected in the SOEP. Generally, it is known whether and how many heating- and hot-water costs are included within the rent, so that a rent adjusted by these components can be calculated. If the information is missing – regardles of whether or not heating- and hot-water costs are contained in the rent – it is assumed that they are not contained. Thus, the actually paid rent according to the Housing Benefit Law may possibly be overestimated in some cases. The potential impact of this overestimation on the simulated housing benefit is, however, already limited by the ceiling amounts of rent eligible for benefit applying to the housing-benefit calculation. In the case that the information about the actually paid rent is missing entirely, the ceiling amounts eligible for benefit are imputed. The actual amount of housing benefit results from bulky tables, which consist of three dimensions. These are the household-size, the amount of rent or encumbrance to consider, and the monthly family income. These tables were not directly transferred into the simulation but were approximated by a function for each household-size.

In the GSOEP we can also refer to employment and unemployment spells. This information, and the questionnaire about receiving unemployment benefits, serve to identify the entitlement in Unemployment Benefit I (UB I). This benefit is income-related and the duration in UB I strongly depends on the prior employment record. It offers a replacement rate of 60% for persons without dependent children and 67% for others. In return, the Unemployment Benefit II (UB II) is basically a minimum income programme for all households in which at least one person is considered to be a labour force participant, but with means-testing. As such we simulate the entire UB II in our model without referring to actual transfer payments. The basic amount is 345 Euro. For each partner or adult child in the household, 80% of the basic amount is paid. For example, for a couple without children, the minimum income level (net of rent payments) is 621 Euro per month. There are supplementary payments for extraordinary situations (e.g. for single parents, for disabled persons, for special dietary requirements of sick persons etc.). For children, a lower monthly rate is paid. In general, the rent for "adequate housing" is also added. The Social Assistance comprises equivalent rates and is analogously simulated. The differences to UB II are first, that no labour force participant exists within the household and second, the different allowances for the means-testing.

Deductions
Social security contributions comprise pension, health and employment contributions up to the upper social security contribution limit. The GSOEP does not contain detailed information about which health insurance com-

pany the person has chosen. We circumvent this information deficit by applying average rates for Germany. However, we incorporate the specific social security contribution regulations which accrue to atypical employments like mini-jobs (up to 400 Euro gross monthly income) and midi-jobs (from 400 to 800 Euro gross monthly income). Moreover, taxes are deducted by applying the contemporary tax-scheme. As the German tax system is a progressive tax system, offering income splitting for married couples, we assume that married couples always choose joint income taxation.

3   General equilibrium

General equilibrium models allow analyses of exogenous shocks, taking into account the whole economy rather than parts of it. These models account for all factor markets as well as for markets for goods. Economic agents, such as households, firms or the government, are represented through income balance equations and demand and supply functions. The agents' decisions result from the respective optimization problem: households choose the utility-maximizing labour-leisure combination, while firms decide about the cost-minimizing factor input combination. On each market, supply and demand are balanced by an adjustment of relative prices using the so-called "market clearance conditions". However, it is possible to allow for markets which do not clear. This applies especially to the labour market, where unemployment plays an important role.[7]

Within a model that includes n markets, Walras Law states that only $n-1$ markets are independent from each other (see Mas-Colell et al., 1995). This implies that if all markets except one are in equilibrium, then the last market must also be in equilibrium. Although the model represents n markets, only $n-1$ prices can be determined. Fixing a numeraire, the Walrasian equilibrium can be characterized by $n-1$ equations $n-1$ variables which determine relative prices rather than absolute price levels.

3.1   Applying general equilibrium models

Computable (CGE) or applied general equilibrium (AGE) models combine the theoretical general equilibrium framework and statistical data to improve

---

7   See Böhringer et al. (2005) for a CGE-analysis including union wage-bargaining and the effects on employment and unemployment.

practical relevance. The use of these models allows for an operationaliza-
tion of complex research questions which cannot be solved analytically.
Furthermore, economic results can be quantified, thus pointing out which
effects dominate and which are of minor importance. Therefore, CGE models
represent an important tool for analysing and comparing potential reform
scenarios ex-ante.

Applied general equilibrium models were pioneered by Johansen
(1960), who established the CGE modelling tradition, which started in the
1970s (see, e.g. Ballard et al., 1985a; Shoven and Whalley, 1984). Currently,
general equilibrium models that are solved numerically are widely used by
research centres, e.g. the World Bank and the European Commission (see,
e.g. Böhringer and Löschel, 2005).

These models use data which typically come from national accounts.
The macro-economic data are used to build a social accounting matrix (SAM,
see, e.g. Pyatt and Round, 1985), which comprises all economic flows of an
economy for a certain period. It includes all economic agents of the general equilibrium model. According to economic theory, an agent's sum of
expenditure equals that of his/her revenues. Applying statistical data, this
condition is generally not met due to various reasons. Therefore, different
approaches were made to address this problem and to provide a consistent social accounting matrix (e.g. the Cross Entropy Method – Robinson et
al., 2001).

Given a consistent database, all required parameters of the model can
be calibrated (see Mansur, 1984, for an overview of calibration). Here, one
assumes that the status quo economy is in equilibrium, which is reflected
by the data. Solving the model equations for the parameters to be calibrated
and plugging in prices and amounts of the benchmark year yields the unknown parameters. The calibration procedure can be interpreted as a point
estimation of parameters (see Böhringer and Wiegard, 2003). Admittedly, it
would be preferable to estimate these parameters using econometric methods. But this would require a lot of observations for each parameter, which
are often not available.

3.2 *The PACE-L Model: the model framework*

PACE-L is a static general equilibrium model built to analyse policy reform
proposals. The model represents a small open economy. We apply the Armington assumption to seven representative firms producing 12 homogeneous

commodities and services, using capital, labour and intermediate inputs. The model distinguishes between low and high-skilled labour. Workers are mobile, but they can only change sectors during a period of unemployment. Matching of unemployed workers with vacant jobs occurs at random. Capital is also assumed to be mobile among sectors.

One of the model's distinctive features is the incorporation of decentralized wage-bargaining in both the labour markets for low-skilled and high-skilled individuals. In each labour market, an employers' organization and a labour union are engaged in wage negotiations, which are modelled as a "right-to-manage" Nash-bargaining. We assume that the bargaining parties have rational expectations about the labour demand outcome. Furthermore, the model includes a discrete choice labour supply module that allows for the distinction between labour supply at the intensive margin and labour at the extensive margin.

The detailed formulation of the model reads as follows: for the production sectors, we assume that each individual firm is small in relation to its respective sector. All firms in one sector interact through monopolistic competition, which means that they produce variants of the sectoral output good Y_S thus attracting different consumers. This is how a firm can exploit market power in the respective market segment. From this it follows that output prices p_{ys} consist of costs of primary inputs and intermediary inputs plus a fixed mark-up m_S. The budget constraint of the respective firm can be written as:

$$(1 - m_s)p_{y,s}Y_s = \sum_{ss} p_{a,ss}A_{ss,s} + r(1 + t_k)K_s + \sum_i w_{i,s}(1 + t_{l,i})L_{i,s}, \quad (8)$$

where

$A_{ss,s}$ = intermediary input from Armington good ss,
K_s = capital input,
$L_{i,s}$ = labour input of skill type i

Profits in sector s are given by

$$\pi_s = m_s p_{y,s}Y_s.$$

To derive optimal demand for intermediate and value-added inputs, we apply a nested constant-elasticity-of-substitution (CES) production structure.

The inputs consist of low-skilled labour and a composite of high-skilled labour and capital (HK-aggregate). This reflects the empirical evidence that low-skilled labour is a relatively good substitute for the HK-aggregate – whereas the substitution elasticity between capital and high-skilled labour is relatively low. The cost functions of the value-added aggregate $c_{va,s}$ and the HK-aggregate $c_{hk,s}$ for each sector s can be written as:

$$
c_{va,s} = \left[\beta_s^L \left(\frac{w_{L,s} \cdot (1 + t_{l,s,L})}{\overline{w}_{L,s} \cdot (1 + \overline{t}_{l,s,L})} \right)^{1-\sigma_s^L} + (1 - \beta_s^L) c_{hk,s}^{1-\sigma_s^L} \right]^{\frac{1}{1-\sigma_s^L}}
$$

$$
c_{hk,s} = \left[\beta_s^H \left(\frac{w_{H,s} \cdot (1 + t_{l,s,H})}{\overline{w}_{H,s} \cdot (1 + \overline{t}_{l,s,H})} \right)^{1-\sigma_s^H} + (1 - \beta_s^H) \left(\frac{r(1 + t_{k,s})}{\overline{r}(1 + \overline{t}_{k,s})} \right)^{1-\sigma_s^H} \right]^{\frac{1}{1-\sigma_s^H}} ,
$$

(9)

where

β_s^L = benchmark value share of L in *VA* aggregate,

β_s^H = benchmark value share of H in *HK* aggregate,

$w_{i,s}$ = wage of skill group i (gross of wage tax),

r = rental rate of capital,

σ_s^L = elasticity of substitution in *VA* nest,

σ_s^H = elasticity of substitution in *HK* nest,

$t_{l,i}$ = social security contributions of labour of type i

$t_{k,s}$ = capital input tax,

and the "bar" superscript denotes benchmark values. Cost minimization at each nest yields the following demand functions for the primary factors at the sectoral level:

$$K_s = Y_s \left(\frac{c_{va,s}}{c_{hk,s}} \right)^{\sigma_s^L} \left(c_{hk,s} \frac{\bar{r}(1+\bar{t}_k)}{r(1+t_k)} \right)^{\sigma_s^H},$$

$$L_{H,s} = Y_s \left(\frac{c_{va,s}}{c_{hk,s}} \right)^{\sigma_s^L} \left(c_{hk,s} \frac{\overline{w}_{H,s}(1+\bar{t}_{l,H})}{w_{H,s}(1+t_{l,H})} \right)^{\sigma_s^H}, \tag{10}$$

$$L_{L,s} = Y_s \left(c_{va,s} \frac{\overline{w}_{L,s}(1+\bar{t}_{l,L})}{w_{L,s}(1+t_{l,L})} \right)^{\sigma_s^L}.$$

We assume that in each sector, an employer's association and a trade union bargain over wages following the right-to-manage approach: parties bargain over wages and, subsequently, firms decide on labour demand, taking the bargained wages as given. The bargaining outcome results from the maximization of a Nash function. This Nash function includes both parties' objective functions and respective fallback options. The objective function of the employer is given by its profit π_s, while the fallback option implies zero profits. The Nash function Ω_s can be written as:

$$\ln \Omega_s = \ln \pi_s + \rho_{H,s} \ln \Gamma_{H,s} + \rho_{L,s} \ln \Gamma_{L,s}. \tag{11}$$

where $\rho_{r,s}$ denotes bargaining power of both skill types L, H relative to the firm's bargaining power. For each skill type, the union's objective function $\Gamma_{r,s}$ is employment $L_{r,s}$ times the value of a job $V_{r,s}$ minus the value of unemployment $V_{U,r}$:

$$\Gamma_{r,s} = L_{r,s} \left(V_{r,s} - V_{U,r} \right) \tag{12}$$

According to the literature on search unemployment (e.g. Pissarides 1990), the values of the labour market states are recursively determined as weighted averages of the incomes in the case of employment and unemployment. The weights are computed from the transition probabilities between the labour market states, which are employment and unemployment. This means the value of a job $V_{r,s,t}$ in period t is given by:

$$V_{r,s,t} = \frac{1}{1+r} \left[I_{r,s}(1 + npc_{r,s}) + (1 - \mu_{r,s}) V_{r,s,t+1} + \mu_{r,s} V_{U,r,t+1} \right]. \tag{13}$$

$\mu_{r,s}$ represents the sector-specific separation rate from employment to unemployment, $npc_{r,s}$ is a non-pecuniary pay component, and $I_{r,s}$ is the average disposable income of an employed worker. Using the steady-state assumption, we can replace the value of employment of the previous period by its value of the current period. We can use the difference between the value of employment and unemployment to simplify the Nash function by:

$$V_{r,s} - V_{U,r} = \left[\frac{I_{r,s}(1 + npc_{r,s}) - rV_{U,r}}{r + \mu_{r,s}} \right], \tag{14}$$

to yield an objective that only depends on the average disposable income $I_{r,s}$ of an employed worker. In contrast, the value of unemployment $V_{U,r}$ is assumed to be exogenously given. The wage resulting from the bargaining negotiations is, in turn, used to calculate the average income in case of employment.

Given the wages for low and high-skilled workers, which result from the bargaining negotiations, firms decide about their labour demand according to the labour demand equations displayed above. The difference between labour supply and demand endogenously determines unemployment. In equilibrium, job-seekers must be indifferent between any two of the sectors.

The household sector comprises three representative households – two worker households and one capitalist household. One representative worker household captures individual households with flexible labour supply. These individual households derive utility from leisure and consumption. To derive optimal labour supply, we use the same discrete choice model (van Soest, 1995) as the microsimulation model. Labour supply finally determines the disposable household income which is used for consumption. In contrast, the second representative worker household includes all households whose labour supply is assumed to be fixed. The third household is endowed with capital and property rights of the firms. Only the household mentioned last takes a consumption-savings decision. The representation of this decision follows the approach of Ballard et al. (1985b), where the household purchases an investment good representing a fixed-coefficient composite of all goods (Böhringer et al., 2005).

We assume identical consumption spending patterns for all three aggregate households. Aggregate consumption C, which is equal to the sum of the consumption of the three household types, is distributed among the different consumption goods C_z according to a CES function:

$$\frac{C_z}{\overline{C}_z} = \frac{C}{\overline{C}}\left(\frac{P_C}{\overline{P}_C}\frac{\overline{P}_{z,c}}{p_{z,c}}\right)^{\sigma_c},$$

(15)

$$\frac{P_C}{\overline{P}_C} = \left[\sum_z \theta_z^C \left(\frac{p_{c,z}(1+t_{c,z})}{\overline{p}_{c,z}(1+\overline{t}_{c,z})}\right)^{1-\sigma_c}\right]^{\frac{1}{1-\sigma_c}},$$

(16)

where

P_C = consumer price index,
θ_z^C = benchmark value share of consumption good z,
$p_{c,z}$ = producer price of consumption good z,
$t_{c,z}$ = consumption tax,
σ_c = elasticity of substitution in consumption,

A reform scenario is always modelled as a budget-neutral reform by fixing the government budget T in real terms according to the benchmark level. Government revenues consist of taxes on capital K_s, labour, consumption C_z of commodity z, output Y_s and profits π_s :

$$T = \sum_s t_{k,s}\, rK_s + T_{MS} + \sum_z t_{c,z}\, p_{c,z}C_z + \sum_s t_{y,s}\, p_{y,s}Y_s + \sum_s t_\pi \pi_s,$$

(17)

where $t_{k,s}$ is the capital tax rate, $t_{c,z}$ the consumption tax rate, $t_{y,s}$ the output tax rate, and t_π the profit tax rate. r, $w_{i,s}$, $p_{c,z}$ and $p_{y,s}$ denote the respective prices. The profit tax includes all other taxes paid by firms. T_{MS} is the balance of labour income taxes plus social security contributions minus transfer payments of the individual households.

3.2 The PACE-L Model: the application to the German economy

We apply the theoretical general equilibrium model to the German economy. Various sources of data are used to build a consistent database representing the equilibrium status quo, which is taken as the standard for our comparative analyses. Macro-economic data for the CGE-model is taken from national accounts. We use the 2002 input-output table (IOT) provided by the

Federal Statistical Office of Germany, which contains a consistent dataset of economic transactions for 71 sectors. From the IOT, we derive the value of capital services, total labour income and profits. The German Federal Bank's publication on annual accounts of West-German enterprises supplies another important figure for calculating profits, namely the profit per Euro of sales ratio net of taxes. The value of capital services is calculated as the difference between total capital earnings and profits. Mark-up rates result as the ratio of profits over sales. Furthermore, we apply data of the employment statistics register to divide total labour income into earnings of low-skilled and high-skilled individuals. An employee without a vocational or academic degree is considered as unskilled. We derive the tax rates applied at the aggregate level from the tax revenue statistics of the Federal Ministry of Finance (BMF, 2002).

Furthermore, some econometric estimates are taken from publications, such as substitution elasticities for the production sectors (Falk and Koebel, 1997). Complementary information on factor price elasticities are taken from Buslei and Steiner (1999). Armington elasticities required for the production of the Armington goods from imports and domestically produced goods are taken from Welsch (2001).

The data source of the household type covering individual households with flexible labour supply is the German Socio-Economic Panel (GSOEP). In contrast to other CGE models, which use aggregated household data from national accounts or use microdata to build highly aggregated household types, we directly use individual data without aggregation (see Arntz et al., 2008, for different aggregation levels of households). Moreover, the required data are derived using the fully sophisticated microsimulation model rather than simplified tax and transfer rules. The details of linking the two models are presented in the following section.

4   Linking the models

The microsimulation model of Section 2 and the CGE model of Section 3 are linked to combine the advantages of both models. Firstly, the microsimulation model based on individual household data is used to calculate all those parameters which are required to run the CGE model. This comprises the parameters given in Table 2:

Table 2:   Transfer microsimulation – CGE model: parameters

Parameter	Depending on
Estimated Parameters	
Parameters utility function	Household
Gross wage	Household, person
Calculated and Statistical Parameters	
Household weight	Household
Dummy skill type	Household, person, skill type, scenario
Taxes	Household, working hours, scenario
Transfers	Household, working hours, scenario
Marginal tax rate	Household, person, working hours, scenario
Gross income	Household, working hours, scenario
Disposable income	Household, working hours, scenario

Table 2 reveals that the microsimulation model does not only provide for calculated parameters but also econometric estimates. Furthermore, some parameters vary, e.g. concerning labour supply options, and have to be derived for all dimensions. Disposable income, for example, depends on labour supply options or labour supply option combinations for couples resulting in 5 (5 x 5=25) simulated values for single (couple) households.

The data are transferred to the CGE model that additionally uses macro-economic data for the national accounts and other sources. Within the CGE model, the labour supply module and the CGE module are kept separate and iterated until a global solution results. First of all, the labour supply module produces the labour supply reactions of our policy measures. Given the partial equilibrium nature of this analysis, wages and unemployment rates are held constant. The intermediate results of the first round equal those of the pure microsimulation model. The resulting labour supply is aggregated by skill type and transferred to the CGE module. Running the CGE module, we derive wage reactions and changes in the unemployment rate resulting from the change in labour supply. The changes in wages and income taxes required to balance the public budget are fed back to the labour supply module for the next iteration, where the next round's labour supply effects are computed. This continues until the two modules converge. Transferring data from the labour supply module to the CGE module requires the aggregation of individual labour supply per skill type, which is measured in efficiency units. We assume that the individual wages move in proportion to the average macro-economic wage of the respective skill group. When transferring data from the CGE module to the labour supply module, it is therefore firstly necessary to adjust individual wages and, secondly, to account for the change in the income tax rate, which is used to balance the government's budget in the CGE module.

Figure 1:   The Combined Microsimulation-CGE-Model

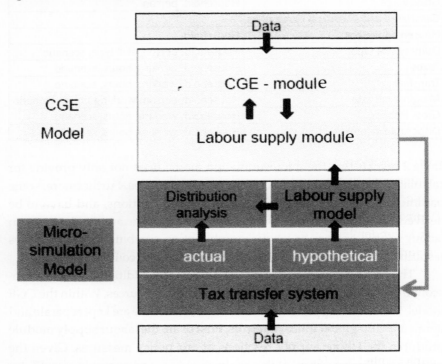

The CGE model yields the overall solution. Given equilibrium wages, tax rates and labour supply, this information can be transferred back to the microsimulation model. Using the microsimulation model has the advantage that the results can be analysed at a highly detailed level, since the model includes an advanced tool to investigate distributional and allocative effects.

As Figure 1 reveals, the labour supply model appears twice. At the current state of the art, technical problems resulting from the data transfer between the microsimulation and the CGE model exceed the addional effort, which is caused by formulating the labour supply model twice. However, a further development of such a combined model would be to re-establish the position of the labour supply model, and iterate between the microsimulation model and the CGE model.

5 Conclusion

In our chapter, we illustrate the development of the most up-to-date microsimulation CGE model in Germany, which defines the new state of the art in modelling policy analysis. The development of our combined microsimulation-CGE model at the Centre for European Economic Research (ZEW, Mannheim) has been initiated by the work of Arntz et al. (2008). The authors extend the already existing CGE model by integrating more than 3,000 individual households, which were linked to the microsimulation model. In their work, they compare the standard CGE model comprising 26 household types with the highly disaggregated version of their extended model. They show that the usage of a disaggregated model with individual households allows for a better distinction of the extensive and intensive labour supply effects compared to an aggregated model with a certain number of representative, or only one representative household. This becomes very important in evaluating the likely participation effects of a policy reform. Moreover, the authors find that the inclusion of general equilibrium effects can be fundamental in the valuation of the impact of policy reform proposals. In particular, allocative and distributive effects vary between the aggregated and disaggregated model versions, while the differences in macro-economic variables are of minor importance.

An application of this model to a policy reform is presented by Franz et al. (2007). The authors quantify economic effects of the so-called "Hartz IV" welfare reform. The key element of this reform, which has already been implemented in 2005, is to merge the two co-existing transfer systems. The authors aim to quantify the economic effects that can be traced back to this welfare reform. Since only few people are marginally affected, relatively small general equilibrium effects were calculated. The distribution analysis showed that a positive labour supply reaction of former transfer recipients only translates into slight employment gains.

The combined microsimulation-CGE model has also served the Council of Economic Experts (Sachverständigenrat, 2007) when evaluating the employment and labour supply effects of the introduction of a basic income proposal. This reform proposal includes dramatic changes for most households, while also influencing the wage setting and unemployment to a high degree. In both of these analyses, the distributional analysis gives valuable insights into the effects at the individual household level that cannot be analysed using an aggregated CGE model. At the same time, feedback effects covered by the general equilibrium approach influence wages, incomes and the overall effect, and should thus necessarily be taken into account.

Although Guy Orcutt (1967) suggested linking models that operate at different levels of aggregation, attempts to do so have remained limited. The combination of Computable General Equilibrium models (CGE) and microsimulation models heralds a new era of computational modelling. Future research in this field is set to face many black boxes and pitfalls. Nevertheless, the combination of microsimulation models and general equilibrium analyses proves very promising as it opens up new perspectives in economic analysis.

References

Arntz, M./Boeters, S./Gürtzgen, N./Schubert, S. (2008) 'Analysing Welfare Reform in a Microsimulation-AGE Model – The Value of Disaggregation', *Economic Modelling* 25: 422-439.

Arntz, M./Boeters, S./Gürtzgen, N. (2006) 'Alternative Approaches to Discrete Working Time Choice in an AGE Framework', *Economic Modelling* 23: 1008-1032.

Atkinson, A./Sutherland, H. (1988) *Tax Benefit Models*. ST/STICERD, LSE London.

Ballard C./Shoven, J.B./Whalley, J. (1985a) 'General Equilibrium Computations of the Marginal Welfare Costs of Taxes in the United States', *American Economic Review* 75 (1): 128-138.

Ballard, C.L./Fullerton, D./Shoven, J.B./Whalley, J. (1985b) *A General Equilibrium Model for Tax Policy Evaluation*. The University of Chicago Press; National Bureau of Economic Research.

Bargain, O./Caliendo, M./Haan, P./Orsini, K. (2006) 'Making Work Pay in a Rationed Labour Market', IZA Discussion-Paper, 2033.

Baroni, E./Richiardi, M. (2007) 'Orcutt's Vision, 50 years on', Working Paper no. 65. Torino: Labor, Center for Employment Studies.

Beninger, D./Laisney, F./Beblo, M. (2007) 'Welfare Analysis of Fiscal Reforms: Does the Representation of the Family Decision Process Matter? Evidence for Germany', *Journal of Population Economics* 20(4): 869-893.

Brenneisen, F./Peichl, A. (2007a) 'Welfare Effects of Tax Reforms', *Finanzwissenschaftliche Diskussionbeiträge* Nr. 07-05.

Brenneisen, F./Peichl, A. (2007b) 'Documentation Welfare Module FiFoSiM', *Finanzwissenschaftliche Diskussionsbeiträge* Nr. 07-04.

Blundell R.W/MaCurdy, T. (1999) 'Labour Supply: a Review of Alternative Approaches', in: Ashenfelter/Card (eds.), *Handbook of Labour Economics*, vol. 3a. North Holland.

BMF (2002) Kassenmäßige Steuereinnahmen nach Steuereinnahmen nach Steuerarten in den Kalenderjahren 2002-2005. www.bundesfinanzministerium.de.

Böhringer, C./Boeters, S./Feil, M. (2005) 'Taxation and Unemployment: An Applied General Equilibrium Approach for Germany', *Economic Modelling* 22 (1): 81-108.

Böhringer, C./Löschel, A. (2005) 'Climate Policy Beyond Kyoto: Quo Vadis? A Computable General Equilibrium Analysis based on Expert Judgements', *Kyklos* 58 (4): 467-493.

Böhringer, C. / Wiegard, W. (2003) 'Methoden der angewandten Wirtschaftsforschung: Eine Einführung in die nummerische Gleichgewichtsanalyse', ZEW Discussion Paper No. 03-02, Mannheim.

Bonin, H. / Kempe, W. / Schneider, H. (2003) 'Household labor supply of low-wage subsidies in Germany', *Schmollers Jahrbuch (Journal of Applied Social Science Studies)* 123(1): 199-208.

Bourguignon, F. / Spadaro, A. (2006) 'Microsimulation as a tool for evaluating redistribution policies', *Journal of Economic Inequality* 4 (1): 77-106.

Buslei, H. / Steiner, V. (1999) *Beschaeftigungseffekte von Lohnsubventionen im Niedriglohnbereich.* Baden-Baden: Nomos.

Citro, C. / Hanushek, E. (1991) *Improving Information for Social Policy Decision – The Uses of Microsimulation Modelling.* National Academic Press Washington DC.

Clauss, M. / Schnabel, R. (2007) 'Distributional and behavioural effects of the German Labour Market Reform', ZEW Discussion Paper No. 08-006, Mannheim.

Creedy, J. / Duncan, A. (2002) 'Behavioural Microsimulation with Labour Supply Responses', *Journal of Economic Surveys* 16: 1-38.

Davies, J. (2004) Microsimulation, CGE and Macro Modelling for Transition and Developing Economies, Mimeo, University of Western Ontario.

Falk, M. / Koebel, B. (1997) 'The Demand of Heterogeneous Labour in Germany', ZEW Discussion Paper 97-28, Mannheim.

Franz, W. / Gürtzgen, N. / Schubert, S. / Clauss, M. (2007) 'Reformen im Niedriglohnsektor – eine integrierte CGE-Mikrosimulationsstudie der Arbeitsangebots- und Beschäftigungseffekte', ZEW Discussion Paper No. 07-085, Mannheim.

Haan, P. / Wrohlich, K. (2007) 'Optimal Taxation: The Design of Child-related Cash and In-Kind Benefits', DIW Discussion Paper Nr. 737, Berlin

Haan, P. (2006) 'Much ado about nothing: Conditional logit vs. random coefficient models for estimating labour supply elasticities', *Applied Economics Letters* 13: 251-256.

Haisken De-New, J. / Frick, J. R. (2005) DTC-Desktop Compendium to the German Socio-Economic Panel (GSOEP).

Harding, A. (1996) *Microsimulation and Public Policy.* Amsterdam: North Holland.

Harding, A. / Gupta, A. (2007) 'Introduction and Overview', in: Harding, A. / Gupta, A. (eds.), *Modeling our Future: Population Ageing, Social Security and Taxation.* International Symposium in Economic Theory and Econometrics, Vol. 15. Amsterdam: Elsevier.

Heckman, J. J. (1976) 'The Common Structure of Statistical Models of Truncation, Sample Selection and Limited Dependent Variables and a Simple Estimator for Such Models', *Annals of Economic and Social Measurement* 5: 475-492.

Johansen, L. (1960) *A Multi-Sectoral Study of Economic Growth.* Amsterdam: North Holland.

Lenhard, T.H. (2004) 'The Idea of Full Computerized Decision Making According to the Weather Forecast', *Podium der Wirtschaft* 6: 47-58.

Mansur, A. / Whalley, J. (1984) 'Numerical Specification of Applied General Equilibrium Models: Estimation, Calibration, and Data', pp. 69-127 in: Scarf, H.E. / Shoven, J.B., *Applied General Equilibrium Analysis,* Cambridge.

Mas-Colell, A. / Whinston, M.D. / Green, J.R. (1995) *Microeconomic Theory.* New York: Oxford University Press.

McFadden, D. (2001) 'Economic Choices', *The American Economic Review* 91 (3): 351-378.

McFadden, D. (1974) 'Conditional Logit Analysis of Quantitative Choice Behavior', pp. 105-142 in: Zarembka, P (ed.), *Frontiers in Econometrics.* New York: Academic Press.

Merz J. (1991) 'Microsimulation – A Survey of Principles, Developments and Applications', *International Journal of Forecasting* 7: 77-104.

Orcutt, G. (1957) 'A new type of socio-economic system', *Review of Economics and Statistics* 58: 773-797 (reprinted with permission in *International Journal of Microsimulation* 1 (1): 3-9, Autumn, at http://www.microsimulation.org/IJM/V1_1/IJM_1_1_2.pdf).

Orcutt, G. (1967) 'Microeconomic Analysis for Prediction of National Accounts', in: Wold, H./Orcutt, G. H./Robinson, E. A./Suits, D./de Wolff, P. (eds.), *Forecasting on a Scientific Basis – Proceedings of an International Summer Institute*. Lisbon: Gulbenkian Foundation.

Peichl, A./Schaefer, T. (2005) 'Documentation FiFoSim: Integrated tax benefit microsimulation and CGE model', *Finanzwissenschaftliche Diskussionsbeiträge* Nr. 06-10.

Peichl, A. (2005) 'Die Evaluation von Steuerreformen durch Simulationsmodelle', *Finanzwissenschaftliche Diskussionsbeiträge* Nr. 05-01.

Pissarides, C.A. (1990) *Equilibrium Unemployment Theory*. Oxford: Basil Blackwell.

Pyatt, G./Round, J. (1985) *Social Accounting Matrices: A Basis for Planning*. The World Bank.

Robinson, S./Cattaneo, A./El Said, M. (2001) 'Updating and Estimating a Social Accounting Matrix Using Cross Entropy Methods', *Economic Systems Research* 13 (1): 47-64.

Sachverständigenrat zur Begutachtung der gesamtwirtschaftlichen Entwicklung (2007) *Das Erreichte nicht Verspielen, Jahresgutachten 2007/2008*. Wiesbaden. Sachverständigenrat.

Shoven, J.B./Whalley, J. (1984) 'Applied General Equilibrium Models of Taxation and International Trade: An Introduction and Survey', *Journal of Economic Literature* 23: 1007-1051.

Steiner, V./Wrohlich, K. (2008) 'Introducing Family Tax Splitting in Germany: How Would It Affect the Income Distribution, Work Incentives, and Household Welfare?', *Public Finance Analysis* 64 (1): 115-142.

Sutherland, H. (2001) 'EUROMOD: an integrated European Benefit-tax model, Final Report'. EUROMOD Working Paper EM9/01.

Sutherland, H. (2007) 'EUROMOD – The Tax-Benefit Microsimulation Model for the European Union', in: Harding, A./Gupta, A. (eds.), *Modeling our Future: Population Ageing, Social Security and Taxation*. International Symposium in Economic Theory and Econometrics, Vol. 15. Amsterdam: Elsevier.

Van Soest, A. (1995) 'A Structural Model of Family Labour Supply: a Discrete Choice Approach', *Journal of Human Resources* 30: 63-88.

Wagenhals, G. (2004) 'Tax-benefit microsimulation models for Germany: A Survey', *IAW-Report/Institut für Angewandte Wirtschaftsforschung* (Tübingen) 32 (1): 55-74.

Welsch, H. (2001) 'Armington Elasticities and Product Diversity in the European Community: A Comparative Assessment of Four Countries', Working Paper, University of Oldenburg.

Wrohlich, K. (2006), 'Labor Supply and Child Care Choices in a Rationed Child Care Market'. DIW Discussion Paper Nr. 570, Berlin.

Chapter 22

Higher Immigration – Empirical Analyses of Demographic and Economic Effects for Norway

Nils Martin Stølen / Inger Texmon / Vibeke O. Nielsen

1   Introduction

Like most other OECD countries Norway will face an ageing population in the next decades. The growth in supply of labour is slowing down, and the old-age dependency ratio is expected to become significantly higher. Although the approved reform of the Norwegian pension system is expected to reduce future growth in the pension burden, a substantial increase seems unavoidable. The ageing population may also cause an increased demand for labour in production of health and welfare services. In the period 2006-2008 there was a substantial general growth in demand for labour in Norway, and as a consequence immigration increased significantly. If the higher immigration persists, this will obviously have large impacts on the aggregate population, its composition and the size of the labour force. But higher immigration also means higher demand for labour, and the effect on public budgets is not obvious because after some years of residence immigrants will be entitled to public pensions and health and welfare services, especially in the long run when they get old.

The effects from higher immigration are analysed in the economic literature, and especially in the US these questions have been offered great attention.[1] Storesletten (2003) has analysed the effects from higher immigration based on data from Sweden. In Denmark the effects from higher immigration as a means to secure fiscal sustainability in financing the welfare state is one of the questions that is discussed by the Danish Welfare Commission (2004).

---

1   See among others Borjas (1994) and Lee and Miller (1997) for a survey.

A common finding in the analyses reported above is that the economic effects from immigration are rather small, especially when the analyses are based on reasonable and realistic assumptions about the number of immigrants. But the analyses also indicate that the results may be significantly affected by the age structure of the immigrants and the extent of integration in the host country's labour market. Labour market statistics from Norway show that the extent of integration depends on the reason for immigration, country of origin, gender, education, tightness in the labour market and the period of residence. While participation rates for immigrants from Nordic and EU-countries are high, they are commonly much lower for refugees and other immigrants from more distant and poor countries. The extent of integration naturally increases by duration of residence and level of education, while immigrants usually are more severely hurt than Norwegians by slack in the labour market.

As pointed out by Kemnitz (2003) and Storesletten (2003) the economic effects of immigration are naturally more positive if the immigrants are young. It is necessary, however, to take into consideration that even young immigrants become older in the long run. Thereby they accrue the right to pension entitlements. The need for health care and other welfare services also increases by age. The analyses by Storesletten indicate that the positive effect on government budgets from increased immigration is smaller in a country like Sweden compared to the US, as the level of publicly financed pensions and welfare services is higher.

Even though the existing analyses provide a lot of information about economic effects from immigration it is possible to increase knowledge about the empirical effects related to different assumptions by a combined use of Statistics Norway's demographic and economic models. A static approach is an obvious limitation in most of the earlier analyses from the US and Norway. These analyses usually concentrate on the contribution from the immigrated part of the population in a single year regarding the effects on employment, production, tax revenues and government expenditures. As pointed out by Storesletten (2003) calculations based on information from a single year will be of limited value compared with an analysis that takes into account the entire life course for the immigrants. His approach by estimating the present value for government incomes and expenditures from increased immigration is thus a step forward compared with the static analyses. This method also makes it possible to estimate the sensitivity of shifts in the most important assumptions regarding the composition and integration of immigrants.

However, in relation to the question of whether increased immigration may improve sustainability of public finances in the long run, there are some limitations to Storesletten's approach. As a consequence of an increasing share of elderly in most Western countries, the burden of financing the welfare state will increase. Storesletten takes this aspect into account by assuming a higher tax level than the present to obtain sustainability for public finances in Sweden. Assumptions about the tax level, the level of government expenditures and the rate of interest are important in determining the estimated partial effects from higher immigration. Storesletten takes this into account by assuming a higher tax level than the present to ensure the sustainability of public finances in Sweden. But this approach doesn't allow for the likelihood that tax levels will increase as time passes, in order to finance the higher expenditures of later years. These problems are recognized by Storesletten, and he is also aware of the possibility of general equilibrium effects on prices and wages as discussed by Borjas (1994).

A macro-economic model with overlapping generations (OLG), as used in the analyses by Beetsma et al. (2003) and by the Danish DREAM-model team in their analyses for the Danish Welfare Commission (2004), is probably one of the most appropriate approaches to analyse economic effects from higher immigration. A macro-economic analysis is thus the final target in the second part of this project. A weakness with the earlier general equilibrium analyses, also remarked by Storesletten (2003), is that they may be too simple including "relatively few elements of heterogeneity". To meet this criticism our analysis will be based on a combination of models for demographic projections, dynamic microsimulation of the development of the labour force and pension expenditures (the MOSART-model), partial models for projections of the demand for public services and a macro-economic computable general equilibrium model (MSG).

The results from the demographic projections are included in the economic models in a consistent way, and the results from the partial projections for labour supply, pension expenditures and demand for public services will be used as inputs in the general equilibrium model. All the details incorporated in these models mean that some of the most relevant effects of higher immigration may be better handled than with only an aggregated macro-economic OLG-model. The aim of this chapter is to present the most important direct effects from higher immigration, including size and composition of population, labour force and main public sector welfare services and pension expenditures. The inclusion of these direct effects in an overall macro-economic analysis remains work in progress.

Although the size of net immigration to Norway has shown a positive trend during the past decades, there have also been large fluctuations. These fluctuations are mainly caused by shifts in the Norwegian demand for labour, crises in different parts of the world important for the flow of refugees, immigration policy and the enlargement of the EU to include countries from Eastern Europe. It is very difficult to know exactly how large net immigration will be in the future. As the main aim of this chapter is to analyse demographic and economic effects, assumptions in accordance with the demographic projections from Statistics Norway are chosen. These assumptions and their effects on the total population and its composition are further discussed in Section 2.

It is also difficult to make good projections on the composition of future immigrants by country / region of origin and the reason why they go to Norway. In this chapter we have chosen to focus on analysing the effects from higher labour immigration and the accompanying flows of family members. By using different assumptions the analysis could have been extended to analyse the effects from e.g. a higher number of refugees. As presented in Sections 2 and 3 typical labour immigrants to Norway are young relative to the host population, and to a large extent integrated in the Norwegian labour market. There are different groups of labour immigrants. Those who are granted permission for residence and work for more than 6 months are included in the Norwegian Population register and in the demographic and economic models based on register information. Temporary workers (less than 6 months) in Norwegian firms are not registered as inhabitants. They are included as employed according to the National Accounts though, and ought to be included in a macro-economic analysis. Demand for services from foreign firms and the self-employed is not counted as employment, but as an import of services.

The effects from different assumptions about immigrants on labour supply and pension expenditures are discussed in Section 3, and the effects on demand for public services are presented in Section 4. The conclusions from this first part of the project are summarized in Section 5.

584

2   Demographic effects

The demographic projections presented in this chapter are made by Statistics Norway's transition matrix model for population projections named BE-FREG. The model takes account of fertility, mortality, internal and external migration in projecting the population by gender, age and municipality, one year at a time, using a cohort-component method. In the medium alternative of the projections from Statistics Norway (2008) the total fertility rate is assumed to be constant at 1.85. Life expectancy at birth is expected to increase between 7-8 years towards 2060, and somewhat more for men than for women.

Probably due to a strong demand for labour and low unemployment in Norway, net immigration increased from 18,000 persons in 2005 to about 45,000 persons in 2008. The increase in net immigration was especially high among persons from new EU countries in Eastern Europe. After a period of higher immigration return migration will also increase, reducing net migration for a given size of gross immigration. In the medium alternative of the demographic projections from May 2008, net immigration is assumed to decrease from 40,000 persons in that year to 20,000 towards 2040. A main objective of this chapter is to discuss the effects from alternative assumptions. In a low alternative net immigration is assumed to decrease to 10,000 persons per year towards 2040, and in a high alternative from above 47,000 persons in 2009 to about 32,000 in 2040. This corresponds to what may be considered as a realistic range of variation in the long run.

The age composition of immigrants may be quite important for determining the economic effects from immigration, and the large net migration to Norway in the last years is mainly made up of young persons compared to the Norwegian population as presented in Table 1 and Figure 1. Observations from the previous years 1998-2007 constitute the basis for the assumption of the age structure for immigrants in the demographic projections from 2008. Only a few of the immigrants are older than 67, and the share over 45 is also rather small. The propensities to emigrate are naturally much higher for earlier immigrants than for Norwegians, and also differ by age and gender. For immigrants over 55 there is a small net emigration. The impression of a young age structure is thus strengthened if we look at net immigration. The propensities for return migration are higher among persons who have immigrated to Norway for work, and are lower for families with children.

Table 1:   Age structure by gender for the entire population, gross immigrants and net immigrants to Norway. Observations from the period 1998 to 2007 (in percent)

	0-15	16-19	20-44	45-66	67+
Entire population					
Both	20.5	5.3	34.1	27.1	13.0
Men	10.5	2.7	17.4	13.7	5.4
Women	10.0	2.6	16.7	13.4	7.5
Gross immigration					
Both	20.7	5.8	62.3	9.8	1.3
Men	10.5	2.6	32.0	5.8	0.6
Women	10.2	3.2	30.3	4.1	0.7
Net immigration					
Both	24.4	8.3	64.2	3.4	-0.3
Men	12.2	3.9	33.7	2.0	-0.4
Women	12.2	4.4	30.5	1.4	0.0

Although the young age structure among immigrants should persist, in the long run it seems impossible to adjust immigration to keep the ratio between the number of persons in working age and the number of adults constant. As pointed out by, among others Lesthaeghe et al. (1988), a policy with this aim would demand an accelerating growth in the number and share of immigrants. According to Blanchet (1988) such a policy could also demand large fluctuations in the size of immigration between different periods. From a practical and a political point of view it would therefore be out of the question that higher immigration could be a sufficient means to solve the ageing problem in a particular country. However, in an analysis by Espenshade et al. (1982) it is pointed out that increased immigration may be an efficient tool to prevent a reduction in the number of inhabitants in a situation where total fertility is below the level of reproduction. An adjusted and constant level of immigration may under these circumstances contribute to keep the size and the composition of the population relatively constant, with the exception of a growing number of elderly caused by increasing life expectancy and far larger cohorts than earlier reaching retirement age. For Norway an earlier analysis by Texmon and Østby (1989) shows that an increase in net immigration may help to moderate the ageing of the population.

Alternative assumptions about the age structure for immigrants are presented in Figure 1. One alternative is composed of a higher share of young immigrants in the age group 15-35 counterbalanced by a lower share of children. In the other alternative the share of immigrants in the age group 15-35 is lower than in the medium one, offset by a higher share of children and a somewhat higher share of immigrants older than 35.

Figure 1: Alternative assumptions of age structure among immigrants compared with the entire population in 2008. Percent

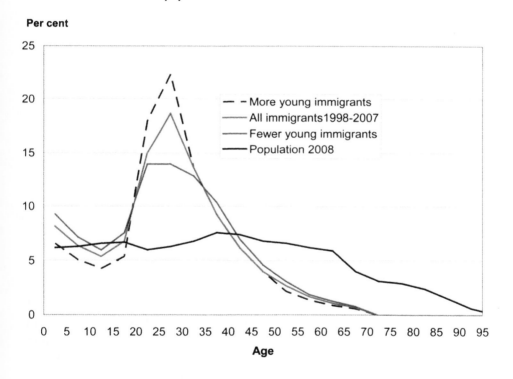

Per cent

By combining the different alternatives for the size of net immigration with the different alternatives for the age structure in the case of high immigration, the effect on the total population in Norway towards 2060 is presented in Figure 2. The effects on the number of inhabitants by age groups in 2050 compared to the situation in 2008 are shown in Table 2. From this perspective the assumption about net immigration is of substantial importance for the size of the population.

Figure 2:   Projections of total population under different assumptions about net immigration (in million inhabitants)

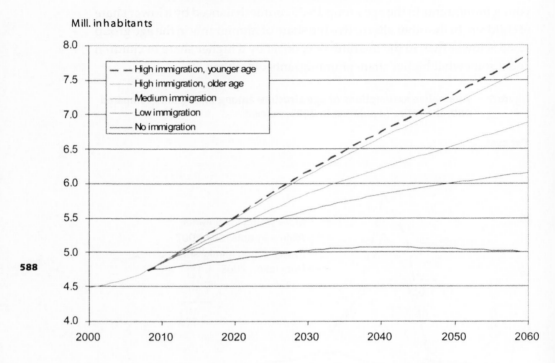

With an assumption of no net immigration the total number of inhabitants will start to decline after 2040, and the total population would only grow by about 300,000 persons from 2008 to 2050. In the alternative with low net immigration the size of the total population in 2050 will be about 1.3 million persons higher than in 2008. In the medium alternative, the total population may increase further by more than 540,000 persons towards 2050. With the assumptions from the high alternative in combination with the observed age structure from the period 1998-2007, the total population in 2050 will increase by about 2.4 million persons, or about 50% compared to 2008. The alternative assumptions about the age structure among immigrants from Figure 1 are only of minor importance for the total population. The number of inhabitants will be somewhat higher if a larger part of the immigrants is in the age group 15-35 because this will probably cause a higher number of births.

Table 2: **The number of inhabitants in different age groups in 2050 under different assumptions about net immigration; 1000 persons and relative numbers**

Age group	2008 Registered	2050 No net migration	2050 Low migration	2050 Medium migration	2050 High migration
		1000 persons			
0-15	971	857	1 053	1 174	1 322
16-19	252	226	270	299	334
20-44	1 616	1 442	1 780	1 988	2 243
45-66	1 285	1 301	1 570	1 720	1 907
67+	614	1 222	1 333	1 373	1 423
Total	4 737	5 048	6 006	6 553	7 229
		Relative numbers			
0-15	100	88	109	121	136
16-19	100	89	107	118	132
20-44	100	89	110	123	139
45-66	100	101	122	134	148
67+	100	199	217	224	232
Total	100	107	127	138	153

589

The assumptions about the size and age structure of net immigrants are also of importance for the age composition of the entire population. The number of persons 67 years and more is more modestly influenced than the younger age groups, even in 2050. In this year the number of persons 67 years and more will be more than twice the number of persons in this group in 2008 irrespective of the level of immigration. The size of the younger age groups is more affected by the assumptions about immigration because of the young age structure among immigrants, immigration of families with children and somewhat higher fertility among immigrated women than among Norwegians.

Without any net immigration at all, the number of persons in the youngest age groups (including the group 20-44) will be significantly lower in 2050 than today. In this case ageing causes the ratio between the population in working age 20-66 and the population 67 years and more to be reduced from 4.73 in 2008 to 2.26 in 2050. But from Figure 3 it is evident that the general ageing of the Norwegian population is the main reason for the fall in this maintenance ratio irrespective of the level of immigration. Net immigration has to increase far outside the range of what has been considered as realistic (and probably politically acceptable) to counteract this development. In the medium alternative the ratio in 2050 is estimated to be 2.71. The age structure of the immigrants is of some importance for the maintenance ratio. But even with the assumptions high, younger age, alternative, the ratio in 2050 will not be higher than 3.01.

Figure 3: Number of persons age 20-66 relative to number of persons 67+

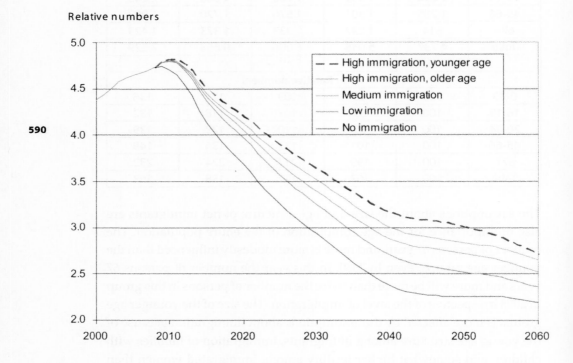

Relative numbers

3 Effects on labour supply and pension expenditures

The effects from immigration on labour supply and pension expenditures are analysed using Statistics Norway's dynamic microsimulation model MOSART (cf. Fredriksen, 1998). While projections of satisfactory quality for labour supply probably could have been made by transition matrix methods linked to the demographic projections, this is obviously not the case for projections of pension expenditures. The main reason is that tax and benefit rules are detailed and complicated, and different parts of the population face different parts of the rules. Therefore there are substantial problems of aggregation in calculating the total effects on government budgets of changes in taxes and benefits. To meet these problems, the use of microsimulation models advocated among others by Orcutt et al. (1986) has been more common in the last decades to support the government with analyses regarding the effects of changes in social and financial policies.

The basic idea in microsimulation modelling is to represent a socio-economic system by a sample of decision units, e.g. persons, and then model possible events that may happen to these units. Contrary to what is possible in a macro-economic approach, the detailed and complicated tax and benefit rules may be exactly reproduced. Aggregated numbers are obtained by multiplying the variable of interest for each unit with its sample weight and summing across the sample.

From a representative sample of the population in a base year the MOSART model simulates the further life course for each person in the population. The life course is simulated by possible transitions from one state to another by utilizing transition probabilities depending on each person's characteristics. The transition probabilities are estimated from observed transitions in a recent period. Events included in the simulation are migration, death, birth, marriage, divorce, educational activity, retirement and labour force participation. Public pension benefits are calculated from labour market earnings and other characteristics included in the simulation. Included in the model are old age pensions, disability pensions, survival pensions and early retirement pensions. The model is thus well placed to analyse the effects on pension expenditures of the number of immigrants and their characteristics.

The analyses in this chapter are based on a representative sample from 1993. The demographic development of this sample is calibrated to observed statistics up to 2007, and subsequently to the demographic projections discussed above. Labour market participation rates, and the propensities to study, enter into disability and retire, are calibrated to observed levels from 2006. The necessary information about distribution of incomes between individuals over the life cycle is based on observations from a longer period.

As the majority of immigrants are young, the assumption about the size of net immigration will be of considerable importance for the projected size of the labour force over subsequent decades. In addition to the number of immigrants and their age structure, the effect will also depend on the degree of integration of immigrants into the Norwegian labour market. Tables 3 to 5 report the most recent available employment rates for immigrants. In the fourth quarter of 2007, a period when the Norwegian labour market was very tight, the average participation rate for first generation immigrants was about 8 percentage points lower than the population average. In the years to come participation rates may be somewhat lower.

Table 3:   Employment rates among immigrants by region of origin and gender; 4th quarter 2007, percent of persons 15-74 years of age

	Total	Men	Women
Entire population	**71.6**	**74.8**	**68.4**
First generation immigrants, total	**63.3**	**69.2**	**57.3**
Nordic countries	74.5	76.8	72.2
Other countries in Western Europe	72.0	77.0	65.1
New EU countries in Eastern Europe	75.9	81.3	66.9
Other countries in Eastern Europe	61.9	65.0	59.4
North America and Oceania	64.2	70.0	58.6
Asia	56.3	63.1	50.0
Africa	49.0	55.5	40.9
South and Central America	65.3	71.4	60.5

Source: Statistics Norway.

Amongst immigrants, participation rates differ by country / region or origin, gender, age and years of residence. Average participation rates are higher for immigrants from the Nordic countries, other countries in Western Europe and new EU countries in Eastern Europe. The main reason for these high average participation rates is the young age structure of these immigrants, as pointed out in Section 2. Immigrants are underrepresented in the older age groups where participation rates generally are lower. Average participation rates for immigrants from other countries in Eastern Europe, North America and Oceania and South and Central America are also about 7-10 percentage points lower than for the entire population, while the participation rates for immigrants from Asia, and especially Africa, are rather low. Larger cultural differences, lower basic education and training and the fact that a larger part of the immigrants from these parts of the world are refugees, are possible explanatory factors for the low participation rates.

Participation rates for women are generally lower than for men, and except for immigrants from the Nordic countries and other countries in Eastern Europe, the differences between male and female participation rates are larger for first generation immigrants than for the entire population. Especially, the participation rates for female immigrants from Asia and Africa are quite low.

Table 4: Employed immigrants by region of origin and age; 4th quarter 2007 (in percent)

	15-24	25-39	40-54	55-74
Entire population	**60.0**	**83.4**	**84.3**	**52.7**
First generation immigrants, total	**51.2**	**69.0**	**70.0**	**44.6**
Nordic countries	68.0	83.8	84.2	53.6
Other countries in Western Europe	44.0	81.4	82.0	53.9
New EU countries in Eastern Europe	64.2	78.9	81.0	54.6
Other countries in Eastern Europe	53.5	70.3	68.7	33.1
North America and Oceania	33.4	71.0	73.5	51.2
Asia	48.6	61.9	60.9	29.9
Africa	40.3	52.8	53.1	30.3
South and Central America	54.3	68.2	72.3	47.4

Source: Statistics Norway.

The differences between employment rates for immigrants from different regions also show up when they are presented by age. Employment rates for immigrants from the Nordic countries, other countries in Western Europe and new EU countries in Eastern Europe are at about the same level as for the entire population in the age groups over 25, while they are especially low for immigrants from Asia and Africa. For the youngest age group 15-24 employment rates for immigrants from the Nordic countries and new EU countries in Eastern Europe are even higher than for the entire population as a great part of them immigrate to Norway to work.

Table 5:   Employed immigrants by region of origin and period of residence;
4th quarter 2007, percent of persons 15-74 years of age

	-4 years	4-6 years	7+ years
First generation immigrants, total	**61.2**	**64.0**	**64.3**
Nordic countries	78.2	80.9	72.6
Other countries in Western Europe	72.0	78.7	70.9
New EU countries in Eastern Europe	77.7	79.4	69.3
Other countries in Eastern Europe	50.0	66.1	64.5
North America and Oceania	56.0	67.8	67.8
Asia	42.4	58.4	60.1
Africa	40.9	50.5	52.6
South and Central America	53.4	68.9	68.7

Source: Statistics Norway.

For immigrants from most parts of the world employment rates increase by duration of residence up to 4-6 years. This observation is in accordance with the results from an analysis by Blom (1997). The lower average employment rates for immigrants from several regions after seven or more years of residence are probably due to composition effects because many of the immigrants from these countries go to Norway for work for a shorter or longer period and then return to their country of origin. Those who stay are often older, and their families may also have arrived for reunification. The figures are therefore influenced by lower employment rates among women and older persons of working age. The significant increase in employment rates by period of residence for immigrants from more distant parts of the world reflects the fact that it may take several years before these groups are integrated in the labour market, and even after more than seven years of residence, employment rates for immigrants from Asia, and especially Africa, are significantly lower than for immigrants from other regions.

In the present version of the MOSART model immigration is represented in a simplified way. Only net migration is included, and immigrants are not divided by region of origin. A more detailed treatment of immigration would have been beneficial, and this is especially the case for modelling of gross immigration and emigration. However, as it is very difficult to make good assumptions about the future composition of immigrants to Norway by country of origin, it is questionable how much such an extension of the model would improve model results. On the other hand, when the immigrated part of the population is growing, a more detailed treatment may be beneficial to pick up the effects from observed heterogeneity and alternative assumptions about the development in different characteristics.

Because of the difficulties in making good assumptions about the composition of immigrants and their participation in the Norwegian labour market several decades ahead, we have chosen to focus on the effects from higher labour immigration. This means that we assume that the main part of the extra immigrants in the case of high immigration arrives from the Nordic countries, other countries in Western Europe and new EU countries in Eastern Europe, and that these immigrants have high participation rates, as presented in Tables 3 to 5. A standard assumption in the MOSART model is to assign somewhat lower participation rates to immigrants than to Norwegians of equal age and gender. In the model this is done by linking participation rates to educational level. Due to weaknesses in the registration of the educational level of new immigrants in the Norwegian administrative systems, a large part of them are registered with educational status unknown. And persons with unknown education are assumed to have somewhat lower participation rates. This assumption may thus be interpreted as a low participation alternative for labour immigrants, while setting participation rates equal to those of Norwegians of equal age and gender represents a high participation alternative. For refugees and asylum seekers, especially for persons immigrating from Asia and Africa, reasonable participation rates are obviously lower than the standard MOSART assumptions.

Based on these assumptions about immigrant labour market participation, together with the assumptions about the size of net immigration flows discussed in Section 2, the projected effect on the labour force is presented in Figure 4. After some decades the alternative assumptions have substantial effects on the number of persons in the labour force. If net immigration ceased in 2008 the number of persons in the labour force would start to decrease from 2018. By 2050 the labour force would be about 140,000 persons lower than in 2008. This decline is caused by a fertility rate for Norwegian women below the level of reproduction. If, instead, the assumption of low net immigration holds, the Norwegian labour force may increase by more than 400,000 persons between 2008 and 2050; and in the medium immigration alternative, the labour force may increase by a further 300,000 persons. If we additionally assume that the participation rates for labour immigrants equal the participation rates for Norwegians of corresponding age and gender, a further 75,000 persons will be added to the labour force by 2050. Thus, the different assumptions about the size of net immigration are far more important than assumptions about participation rates.

Consequently, under the assumption of high net immigration and standard participation rates, the labour force in 2050 is estimated to increase by about 370,000 persons more than in the medium alternative, whilst high net immigration with high participation rates leads to a labour force about 480,000 persons larger. Compared to 2008, the labour force in this final alternative may increase by more than 1.2 million persons, or close to 50%, by 2050.

Figure 4: **Projections of the labour force under different assumptions about net immigration (1000 persons)**

1000 persons

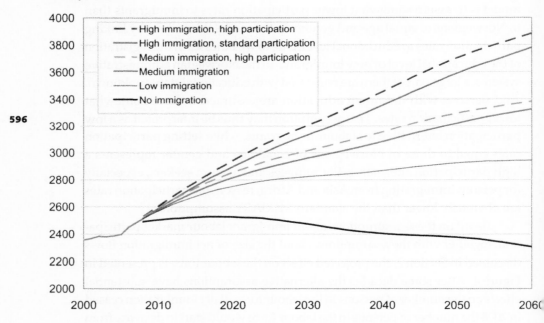

While higher immigration is an effective tool to secure increased supply of labour in the short run, it is not so obvious that this development may counteract lack of labour and improve government budgets in the long run. The MOSART model is well-suited to analyse the long-term effects for two central items of public expenditures: old age pensions and disability pensions. As shown in Table 6 the assumption about the size of net immigration will be of some importance for the number of old age pensioners and disability pensioners. The increasing number of pensioner immigrants will cause the total effect on government budgets to be lower than the partial positive effect from increased tax incomes, that grow approximately proportionally with labour supply.

Table 6: The number of old age pensioners and disability pensioners in 2050 under different assumptions about the size of net immigration (1000 persons)

	2005	2050			Percentage change from 2005		
		Low	Medium	High	Low	Medium	High
Old age pensioners	607	1347	1382	1435	122	128	136
Disability pensioners	307	374	414	460	22	35	50

Figure 5: Projections of the contribution rate for pensions in the National Insurance Scheme under different assumptions about size of immigration and participation rates among immigrants (in percent)

Per cent

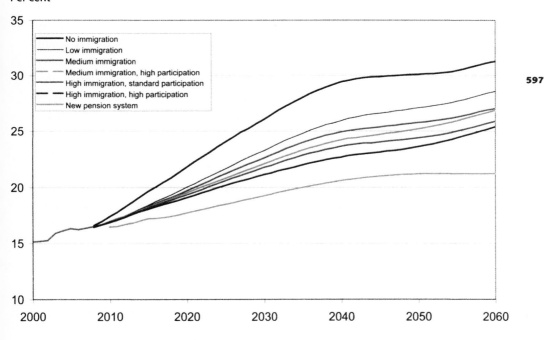

597

Figure 5 shows the effects from higher immigration on government budgets calculated by a contribution rate for the National Insurance Scheme including old age pensions, disability pensions and survivors' pensions that are financed through government budgets. The contribution rate is defined as the public expenditures for these pensions relative to total labour incomes, also taking into account that the tax level for pensioners is about half the level for persons in the labour force. As a consequence of the ageing population and increased building up of entitlements when the present pension system matures, maintaining the present system means a growing contribution rate from 16.5% in 2008 to more than 25.7% in 2050 based on the medium alternative for fertility, life expectancy and immigration. With the assumption of low net immigration the contribution rate in 2050 may be 1.4 percentage points higher, while it may be 2.2 percentage points lower in the case of high immigration and high participation rates.

The effects on the age structure from alternative assumptions about the size of immigration are rather small compared with effects from the ageing of the Norwegian population towards 2050. As discussed in connection with Table 2, the ageing of the Norwegian part of the population will cause a large fall in the maintenance ratio towards 2050 and, compared to this development, alternative assumptions about immigration will only have modest effects. Although higher immigration causes an increase in the labour force, the effects on the contribution rate will be somewhat counteracted as a result of higher pension expenditures when the immigrants get older, especially in the long run. This result is in accordance with earlier Norwegian analyses of the effects from the size of immigration on the contribution rate by Fredriksen (1998). It is also in accordance with the international literature referred to in Section 1.

Without any net immigration at all from 2008, the contribution rate would have reached 30% in 2050. Compared to this case the assumptions about net immigration in the medium alternative mean a significant reduction of the future pension burden. In Figure 5 we have also included a line showing the estimated effect on the contribution rate from the approved Norwegian pension reform that is going to be operative from 2011. The distance between this line and the medium immigration alternative in 2050 equals the distance between the medium alternative and the alternative with no immigration. But net immigration has to increase to, and stay constant at, almost 50,000 persons per year to give an effect corresponding to that of the pension reform. And in the future net immigration would have to increase further to maintain the contribution rate at the lower level resulting from the pension reform, due to the ageing of the Norwegian population continuing beyond 2050, and the long-run ageing of initially youthful immigrants.

The partial effect on the contribution rate of higher labour participation rates amongst immigrants is also significant, as is shown in Figure 5. In particular, higher labour force participation as an alternative to disability is an efficient means of reducing contribution rates. This effect causes the numerator in the expression for the contribution rate to decrease whilst the denominator increases. A higher incentive to stay at work is one of the main elements of the present economic policy in Norway.

4   Effects on demand for public services

Just like anyone else, immigrants will also demand public services. In the short run the demand for educational services as a part of the integration process may cause the age- and gender-specific user propensities to be larger than for corresponding Norwegians. Especially refugees and asylum seekers may cause extra public expenses in the first years after arriving to Norway, not only as a part of the integration process, but also because they need direct economic support and a place of residence. However, these direct public expenses are not taken into account in the present analyses of the effects from higher immigration. The immigrants are assumed to arrive in order to find work, and they are partly followed by their families. As some of the present immigrants to Norway are refugees and asylum seekers, a comparison of immigration projection alternatives may underestimate the total costs of the existing immigration as the direct costs are not taken into account.

The analyses of the extra demand for public services as a consequence of higher immigration are made by using a demographic projection model with fixed user propensities by age and gender. Of course it would have been advantageous to have information of age- and gender-specific user propensities for immigrants from different regions of origin. However, as net immigration to Norway has increased partly from zero since the beginning of the 1970s, there are still only a few elderly immigrants. Therefore the statistics for use of public services among immigrants by region of origin are not well-established.

The public services in the projection model are separated into individual and non-individual services. The individual services include kindergartens, day care facilities for school children, compulsory schooling, upper secondary school, higher education, homecare services, long-term care at institutions, hospitals and psychiatry. Demand for these services is projected by constant user propensities. For non-individual services like public administration, water supply and sewage treatment, transport and cultural services, their demand is assumed to increase in line with the total population.

Figure 6: Demand for labour in public services directed towards children and education under different assumptions about net immigration (1000 person-years)

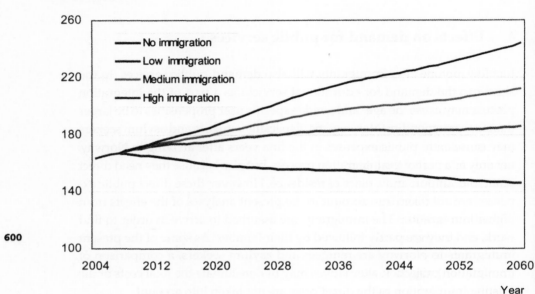

Figure 7: Demand for labour directed towards public health and long-term care under different assumptions about net immigration (1000 person-years)

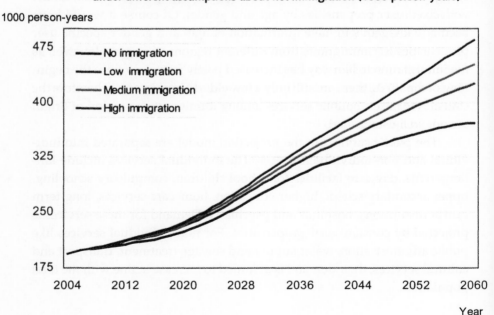

The total effects from higher immigration on demand for public services will be included in the macro-economic analyses in the ongoing second part of the project. As projected employment in public services is an exogenous input in the macro-economic model, this indicator is chosen for presentation here. Because a lot of employees in public services in Norway work part-time, "person-years" (or person-hours) is a more relevant indicator than the number of persons. In this chapter we only focus on the effects for the two most important aggregated sectors: public services directed towards children and education, and those directed towards health and long-term care. In 2007 the number of person-years in these sectors respectively constituted about 31 and 37% of total public employment. The projected development measured in 1000 persons-years is presented in Figures 6 and 7. The projected shares relative to total employment will emerge as part of the subsequent macro-economic analyses (not reported here).

In public services directed towards children and education, demand for labour is projected to decrease in the case of no immigration when standards of services are assumed to be constant. This is caused by lower birth rates than necessary to maintain the number of children (and also the entire population). Given low net immigration there will be a slight increase in demand for labour, mainly concentrated in the first 20 years. The demand for labour will increase further if we assume a medium level of immigration. In the case of high immigration, the number of person-years spent servicing children and education will have to increase by 40% from 2004 to 2050 in order to keep up with demand.

In public health and long-term care the ageing of the Norwegian population will cause a significant growth in demand for labour irrespective of the level of immigration. Increasing need for old age care is the main component. As only a minor part of the immigrants have reached the age where they need old age care, even by 2060, the main effect of higher immigration for services from health care and social services relates to increased demand for hospital services. The total demand for labour in health and long-term care will increase by 80% without immigration, and by 120% given high net immigration. If we look at health care only, the total demand for services is twice as high with high immigration as compared to the case with no immigration.

Although higher immigration causes increased demand for public services, especially in the long run when immigrants get older, the increased need for labour in these sectors only amounts to a small part of the growth in the labour force. In 2050 our models project that there will be 1.3 million more people employed in the high immigration, high participation scenario (mainly working age immigrants) compared to when there is no immigration at all. The difference in demand for individual public services is only 190,000 person-years between the two alternatives, indicating the relative unimportance of immigration compared to demographic ageing in terms of generating additional service demands.

If, instead, we look at development from 2008 to 2050, under the medium immigration alternative, the labour force is projected to increase by about 700,000 persons while the demand for labour in public services directed towards children, education, health and long-term care is estimated to increase by 340,000 person-years in the same period. Immigration may thus facilitate growth in public services without reduction of employment in other industries. However, it should be remembered that the effect on demand for public services is not exhausted in 2050, since after this date new immigrants will continue to reach the age when the need for health care is large.

5 Conclusions so far and plans for further analyses

The analyses so far show that immigration is quite important for the number of inhabitants and the size of the labour force. In a period of some decades different yearly assumptions about the number of net immigrants may accumulate to figures of substantial magnitude. There is also strong evidence that immigrants are young relative to the host population. A main question is to what degree and how fast they are integrated in the Norwegian labour market. Labour market participation rates depend on age, gender, country of origin, reason for immigration and period of residence, and participation rates seem to be rather high for typical labour market immigrants from the other Nordic countries, other countries in Western Europe and new EU countries in Eastern Europe. Higher immigration, as experienced in Norway in recent years, and especially labour market immigration, is of some importance for public finances, but a substantially higher and continuously increasing net immigration flow seems to be necessary to counteract the ageing of the Norwegian population and secure fiscal sustainability in the long run, even bearing in mind that immigrants grow old in the long run and themselves become entitled to pensions and public services.

To analyse long-term macro-economic effects for labour market and fiscal sustainability we plan to put the partial direct effects from higher immigration analysed in this chapter into Statistics Norway's dynamic computable general equilibrium model MSG. This reflects the strength of Statistics Norway's model portfolio. Results from demographic projections and the corresponding partial effects on labour supply, pension expenditures and demand for public services, estimated via microsimulation, may be used in a consistent way as inputs in an overall macro-economic analysis.

References

Beetsma, R./Bettendorf, L./Broer, P. (2003) 'The budgeting and economic consequences of ageing in the Netherlands', *Economic Modelling* 20: 987-1013.

Blom, S. (1997) 'Tracing the interaction of refugees in the labour market, a register approach', *Statistical Journal of the United Nations ECE* 14: 243-265.

Blanchet, D. (1988) 'Immigration et régulation de la structure par âge d'une population', *Population* 43 (2): 293-309.

Borjas, G.J. (1994) 'The Economics of Immigration', *Journal of Economic Literature* 32 (4): 1667-1717.

Danish Welfare Commission (2004) *Fremtidens velfærd kommer ikke af sig selv. (Future welfare does not arise by itself)*. Copenhagen, www.velfaerd.dk.

Espenshade, T.J./Bouvier, F.L./Arthur, W.B.(1982) 'Immigration and the stable population', *Demography* 1 (19): 125-133.

Fredriksen, D. (1998) *Projections of Population, Education, Labour Supply and Public Pension Benefits – Analyses with the Dynamic Microsimulation Model MOSART.* Social and Economic Studies 101, Statistics Norway.

Kemnitz, A. (2003) 'Immigration, Unemployment and Pensions', *Scandinavian Journal of Economics* 105 (1): 31-47.

Lee, R.D./Miller, T.W. (1997) 'The Future Fiscal Impact of Current Immigrants', in: Smith, J.P./Edmonton, B. (Eds.), *The New Americans*. Washington, DC: National Academy Press.

Lesthaeghe, R. et al. (1988) 'Are Immigrants Substitutes for Births'?, Working Papers, Free University of Brussels.

Orcutt, G.H./Merz, J./Quinke (eds.) (1986) *Micro Simulation Models to Support Social and Financial Policy*. New York: North Holland.

Statistics Norway (2008) *Population projections – National and regional figures, 2008-2060*, www.ssb.no/english/subjects/02/03/folkfram_en/

Storesletten, K. (2003) 'Fiscal Implications of Immigration – A Net Present Value Calculation', *Scandinavian Journal of Economics* 105 (3): 487-506.

Texmon, I./Østby, L. (1989) *Innvandringens betydning for befolkningsutviklingen i Norge (The Effects from Immigration on the development of the Norwegian population)*. Reports 89/4, Statistics Norway.

Chapter 23

Complying with the Kyoto Targets: An Assessment of the Effectiveness of Energy Taxes in Italy

Rossella Bardazzi / Filippo Oropallo / Maria Grazia Pazienza

As is well-known, European Union environmental policy is deeply focused on the issue of climate change. Fighting climate change requires a long-term perspective and international actions and the EU has played a major role in "regime building" in this context.

As regards policy tools, a great support for *market-based instruments* can be found in European policy (and in the Kyoto Protocol), as opposed to the traditional command and control approach,[1] and the European Carbon Trading Scheme represents a major success of recent European policy. However, no comparable achievement has been reached in the tax area and, despite several efforts to design an European Carbon Tax, a supranational environmental tax is still lacking. All European countries act autonomously in this field, with the partial exception of an energy tax directive[2] that sets minimum levels of taxation for some energy products in order to avoid harmful fiscal competition.

In the EU-27, total greenhouse gas emissions decreased by 8% from 1990 to 2005. The contribution of the manufacturing sector has been noticeable: the reduction was approximately 17% for EU-27 and 10% for EU-15 compared to base-year levels. As for CO_2 emissions, data show a very slight decrease for EU-27 (-3.5%) and an increase for EU-15, whereas a conspicuous decrease can be found for manufacturing in almost all countries (-17% for

---

1   According to the OECD (1997: 15), economic instruments can be defined as "those policy instruments which may influence environmental outcomes by changing the costs and benefits of alternative actions open to economic agents ... economic instruments create incentives that encourage people acting more-or-less in their own best interests, simultaneously, to treat the environment in a way that is in the best interests of society".

2   Directive 2003/96/EC.

EU-27). These emission trends show that the EU-15 is not on track to meet its Kyoto target with existing measures and will need to consider carbon sinks and the other flexible mechanisms. Despite this unsatisfactory performance, overall environmental policy in Europe cannot be considered unsuccessful, in particular with regard to energy consumption trends. Unfortunately, in the Italian case, total greenhouse gas emissions rose by 12.1% compared to the base-year level (13% for CO_2). This tendency shows that Italy currently has a considerable distance to its burden-sharing target, even if carbon sinks and other flexible mechanisms are taken into account. According to EEA (2007), Italy is the only European country that appears unable to meet the Kyoto target at the moment. At least some responsibility can be found in policy design and implementation: Italian environmental policy appears confused, wavering and highly influenced by the pressure of lobbies. Notwithstanding some results in decreasing CO_2 intensity, manufacturing CO_2 emissions are still increasing and without evidence of de-coupling, probably because of a general scarcity of environmentally-related investments.

606

After reviewing some important characteristics of environmental taxes and recent emission trends in Italy, we present summary results from a previous ex ante microsimulation analysis to briefly describe the short Italian experience of the Carbon tax reform. In the final sections of the chapter we extend this model to provide an ex post assessment of the efficacy of energy taxes in Italy with regard to the effect on CO_2 emissions and input mix of industrial sectors by estimating a fixed effect model on a panel of more than 5,000 firms.

1 General characteristics of environmental taxes: energy taxes vs. carbon taxes

As is widely known, the main argument in favour of market-based instruments over regulation is that, in theory, the cost to society of reducing environmental damage is minimized.[3] If a price signal is used to reach an environmental standard, pollution abatement will be undertaken at minimum cost. This is because for firms with a relatively high cost of abatement, it is cheaper to pay the charge than to reduce emissions. On the contrary, firms facing low abatement costs find it cheaper to abate rather than pay the charge. In other words, unlike the traditional command and control ap-

---

3   See for instance Tietenberg (2006).

proach to environmental policy, economic instruments allow the polluter to choose the level of output and pollution, but a cost is imposed for the pollution produced. If correctly set, the Pigouvian tax rate must be equal to the marginal damage and, as a consequence, if marginal damage varies across countries, tax rates should be set at different levels.

A general evaluation of environmental taxes[4] can be made with regard to different criteria. As an example of market-based instruments, environmental taxes are generally characterized by economic efficiency (in static and dynamic terms), good efficacy (or environmental effectiveness[5]), and relatively low monitoring and administrative costs. On the other hand, the effect on competitiveness has been a major concern of policy-makers in considering possible applications of taxes to energy and other goods and an eventual trade-off between environmental policy and growth policy has to be considered. Moreover, the possibility that environmentally-related taxes, mainly energy taxes, can have a regressive impact on household income distribution and, therefore, on the political acceptance of such a policy, has to be seriously taken into account.[6]

Within this context, a carbon tax is a specific environmental tax that is levied on the carbon content of fossil fuels, which is an efficient way of assigning costs to the carbon dioxide emissions they release when burned for energy.[7,8] Contrary to the case of local pollution, in the case of climate change the marginal damage can be quantified homogeneously across countries.[9] Summing up, an energy tax is imposed on fuels (both fossil fuels and carbon-free sources as nuclear power and renewables), while a carbon tax is restricted to carbon-based fuels only. This difference can explain why a carbon tax is believed to be more efficient in reducing emissions: an energy

---

4   Defined as "any compulsory, *unrequited* payment to general government levied on tax-bases deemed to be of particular environmental relevance. The relevant tax-bases include energy products, motor vehicles, waste, measured or estimated emissions, natural resources, etc." (see OECD, 2006: 26).

5   The extent of the efficacy depends, among other elements, on the amount of the tax and the availability of substitutes to allow for a change in behaviour. Another crucial element to take into account is the existence, and the range of, exemptions.

6   On this issue, see Pearson (1995) and OECD (2006).

7   Since there is a fixed proportion between carbon and carbon dioxide, it is possible to convert a carbon tax into a carbon dioxide tax. Therefore, the two terminologies are equivalent.

8   A carbon tax equalizes the marginal abatement cost across fuels, and in this way realizes the minimization of the total cost of abatement.

9   Considering several estimates, the social cost of carbon ranges between \$3 and \$95 per tonne of carbon dioxide (see IPPC [2007] or the Stern Review [Stern, 2006]).

tax works through the general cost-saving mechanism, while a carbon tax adds to the cost-saving channel the fuel-substitution channel.

The effectiveness of environmental taxes on industrial firms can be evaluated by using a variety of modelling approaches. First of all, an *ex ante simulation* can be employed in order to provide information on the short-term effect of taxes. This analysis can be based on past behaviour or be merely arithmetical, in the sense that the model simply considers the change in the budget constraint that agents face because of environmental tax, without taking into account any behavioural change. Notwithstanding this evident limitation, microsimulation-based ex ante analysis can calculate the maximum revenue effect of the change in the tax for several typologies of agents, with the objective of assessing the gainers and the losers after the reform.

On the other hand *ex post analysis* replicates the observed behaviour of the system in order to disentangle the different contributions to the observed pattern (i.e. the change of input intensity attributable to tax as opposed to the change attributable to price variation). As a result, the output of the ex post analysis can be employed – as a behavioural starting point – in future ex ante evaluation.

In this chapter we combine the two approaches by estimating the ex post behaviour of firms starting from an arithmetical microsimulation model. Among all criteria for ex post evaluation of environmentally-related taxes, as proposed by OECD (1997), we focus on the ability of tax in reducing CO_2 emissions; however, as pointed out by Agnolucci (2004: 8), it is very difficult to distinguish between the effect of taxes and their effectiveness: assessing the efficacy of tax implies "ascertaining the effects of tax in relation to the expected objectives and targets or to other instruments". As regards the Kyoto target of emissions abatement, for instance, countries implement multiple policies and there is no defined target for each policy.

1.1 Current use of energy and CO_2 taxes in Europe and in Italy

Almost all developed countries use environment-related taxes, and the majority of them have a long experience in this regard; these taxes raise revenues between 2.5% and 4% of GDP and constitute on average 8% of total revenues. In many respects, energy taxes are the most significant environment-related taxes because they generate large revenues (more than

90% of total environmental tax revenue comes from energy and vehicles).[10] Energy taxation in the EU is currently regulated by Directive 2003/96/EC (the directive came into force in 2004), setting minimum tax rates for a broad range of energy products. This Directive has widened the scope of the pre-existing EU energy taxation (by including electricity, natural gas and coal) and has increased the minimum rates for transport fuels that had been set by the previous Directive. As a result of these policies, on the whole, taxes on energy increased between 2000 and 2004, and this is particularly true for taxes on fuels.

With regards to Italy, revenue from environmental taxes exhibits a striking increase in nominal terms (80% between 1990 and 2005). However, the importance of environmental taxes in the Italian taxation system has decreased: the revenue from environmental taxes as a proportion of both total taxes and gross domestic product show a remarkable decline between 1990 and 2005. The same trend has been shown for energy taxes.

At EU level, environmental policy has been gaining increasing importance as a device for building integration and taking a leading role in global environmental planning. From this perspective, an environmental pan-European tax has several positive attributes, as it constitutes a market-based instrument and, at the same time, a potential revenue for the EU budget, to be designed directly by the Commission. Moreover, greater harmonization in carbon tax can be efficient as variation in damage costs across countries is of minor importance. A prominent role for environmental taxes was planned for the first time with the EU carbon/energy tax (known as the European carbon tax, COM[92] 226). However, without a general agreement, the proposal was firstly amended and eventually withdrawn by the Commission in 2001. In the meanwhile, because of the lack of an agreement, several European countries have unilaterally introduced supplementary CO_2 taxes, or reshaped their existing energy taxes (among them Sweden, Norway, Finland, Denmark, Italy and Germany).[11]

609

---

10   It is not possible to make a distinction between energy taxes and carbon taxes in official revenue figures. However, it is worthwhile to recall that an energy tax is paid on the quantity of energy consumed, whereas the tax design of a carbon tax should be based only on emissions or on the CO_2 content of fossil fuels.

11   An overview on European carbon tax experiences can be found in Bardazzi et al. (2004).

1.2 The Italian carbon tax

The Italian Carbon tax entered into force in 1998 (law 488/98) with the aim of reducing environmentally damaging outputs by reshaping the previous energy-related tax rates and including coal and other energy products with high emissions. Moreover, the Italian carbon tax reform was designed as a fiscally neutral reform: the increase in revenue was offset by a decrease in existing social contribution rates. In other words, the reform was based on the "double dividend" hypothesis, where the first dividend was the supposed emission cut and the second dividend an increase in full-time employment through a cut in the labour tax wedge.[12] Furthermore the fiscal neutrality approach has helped to alleviate competitiveness concerns and to increase the political acceptability of the reform. The tax rates originally foreseen in 1999 were supposed to gradually increase up to a target level in 2005, as shown in Table 1.

Table 1:   Italian Carbon Tax: main tax rates as provided by law

		1998 (*)	1999	2005
Coal	Euro/1000 kg	0	2,63	21,61
Coke	Euro/1000 kg	0	3,52	30,59
Diesel	Euro/1000 lt	386.03	403,21	467,84
Diesel (heating fuel)	Euro/1000 lt	386.03	403,21	467,84
Heavy oil – industrial use (high sulphur content)	Euro/1000 kg	46.48	63,75	128,73
Heavy oil – industrial use (low sulphur content)	Euro/1000 kg	23.24	31,39	62,04
LPG (fuel vehicle)	Euro/1000 kg	305.57	284,77	206,58
LPG (heating fuel)	Euro/1000 kg	185.52	189,94	206,58
Petrol - leaded	Euro/1000 lt	574.04	578,24	594,05
Petrol - unleaded	Euro/1000 lt	518.25	570,66	594,05
Methan (fuel vehicle)	Euro/1000mc	0	10,85	51,65
Methan (industrial use)	Euro/1000mc	0.01	12,50	20,66

Note: (*) Tax rates in force in the pre-reform system.
Source: Law 488/98.

An ex ante estimation of the impact of the full reform on a manufacturing firm's competitiveness has been performed with a microsimulation model by Bardazzi et al. (2004). The simulation shows that, despite the very high increase for some energy products (such as coal or heavy oil) with respect

---

12   Moreover a form of earmarking, through subsidies to environmentally-related investments, was designed.

to the pre-reform situation, the compensatory decrease in social contributions would have succeeded in offsetting the increase in energy input expenditure: as a consequence the reform shows an overall negligible effect on profitability (-0.6% for the Gross Operating Surplus), even if impacts appeared highly differentiated by sector due to the variability of energy expenditure as a component of intermediate costs and of the share of labour costs (Table 2).[13]

Table 2: Carbon tax effects on sectoral profitability: ex ante microsimulation analysis on 2000 dataset comparing 2000 and proposed 2005 tax rates

	Change, as a percentage of Gross Operating Surplus in 2000		
	Change in social contributions	Change in energy taxes	Gross Operating Surplus
13-14 Mining	-0.37	5.29	-4.91
15-16 Food	-0.42	0.93	-0.51
17 Textiles	-0.57	1.13	-0.56
18 Wearing apparel	-0.65	1.64	-0.99
19 Luggage, footwear	-0.55	0.37	0.18
20 Wood	-0.42	0.70	-0.28
21 Pulp, paper	-0.42	1.56	-1.14
22 Publishing	-0.52	0.18	0.33
24 Chemicals	-0.37	1.16	-0.79
25 Rubber, plastic products	-0.52	0.59	-0.07
26 Other non-metal. mineral products	-0.41	4.01	-3.60
27 Metallurgic products	-0.46	4.98	-4.52
28 Fabricated metal products	-0.51	0.55	-0.03
29 Machinery, equipment n.e.c.	-0.59	0.25	0.34
30 Office machinery, computers	-0.63	10.36	-9.73
31 Electrical machinery	-0.63	0.29	0.34
32 Communication equipment	-0.36	0.08	0.27
33 Medical, optical instruments	-0.48	0.13	0.35
34 Motor vehicles	-0.71	0.48	0.22
35 Other transport equipment	-0.57	0.25	0.31
36 Furniture and other manufact. products n.e.c.	-0.56	0.31	0.25
Total	-0.50	1.11	-0.60

Source: Bardazzi et al. (2004).

611

---

[13] The ex ante evaluation compared the effective tax rates in 2000 with the proposed, but never implemented, 2005 tax rates.

As regards results by firm size, very small firms (2-9 persons employed) show on average a higher level of losses from the reform. This is due to the fact that only 25% of the firms of this size have at least one regular employee and, as a consequence, only few firms can benefit from the cut in social contribution rates.[14]

In fact, due to rising international energy prices, the original tax design were not implemented in full, with the planned upwards tax rate revisions halted in 2000. Since then, only minor changes have occurred.

Summing up, Table 2 shows the results of a pure counter-factual simulation, as the full set of planned tax increases did not occur. But what can be said about efficacy of the actual changes in tax rates that took place between the end of the 1990s and 2004? And is there any role for environmental taxes in the process of Italian compliance with Kyoto targets?

2   The microsimulation model and the data

The DIECOFIS microsimulation model for Italian firms is the tool used here to evaluate the impact of energy taxes on industrial energy demand. DIECOFIS has been built and used in recent years within a project financed by the EU Commission in the FP5 framework.[15] Several public policy evaluations have been carried out with this tool to monitor (ex-ante/ex-post) the *effectiveness* of public programmes and to foresee the *effects* of public choices on firms within an impact analysis, ceteris paribus.[16] In particular this microsimulation model is designed to analyse the effects of taxes on enterprises and reproduces the fiscal burden on firms of several items such as social contributions, a regional tax on economic activity (IRAP), corporate taxes and energy excises. Its features make it a very original and path-breaking device for policy impact analysis and for studies on firms' behaviour in

---

14   More than 90% of all Italian firms belong to the class of 1-9 persons employed. According to Eurostat classification, Italy has the second-highest share of micro-enterprises in the European Union (Eurostat, 2008).

15   DIECOFIS (Development of a System of Indicators on Competitiveness and Fiscal Impact on Enterprise Performance) is a project financed by the Information Society Technologies Programme (IST-2000-31125) of the European Commission and coordinated by the Italian National Institute of Statistics (ISTAT, coordinator Paolo Roberti). The model is run at ISTAT where data are produced but the Institute bears no responsibility for analysis or interpretation of the data.

16   See, among others, Bardazzi, Parisi and Pazienza (2004).

the field of taxation. The coverage of Italian firms includes both small and large enterprises. In fact the DIECOFIS model is based upon a large and detailed database called EISIS (*Enterprise Integrated and Systematized Information System*) which is a micro-funded multi-source business data bank built at the Italian National Statistical Office.[17] The model covers all active enterprises except for those belonging to Agriculture, Forestry and Fishing, to the Financial Sector and to the Public Sector. For studies on energy issues a special (reduced) version of the model has been used in order to take advantage of the statistical information about the energy uses and expenses by firms collected in the Manufacturing Product Survey (*Prodcom*), which covers all manufacturing firms with more than 19 employees and a sample of small manufacturing enterprises with more than 2 and less than 19 employees. These micro-data are very interesting for our purposes as, among other information, they record consumption and expenditures for several energy products. A matching procedure has been built to link the micro-data in the main database with the *Prodcom* energy-related information: as an exact matching was not possible, a statistical matching procedure was implemented in order to reconstruct information at a micro level. Data in the two surveys are merged through a cell-based integration procedure where *Prodcom* is the donor survey and a subset of EISIS related to manufacturing firms with more than 2 workers is the receiving dataset.[18] This matched dataset is available for the years 2000 and 2004 and covers respectively about 18,000 and 20,000 units of the manufacturing sector with more than 2 workers. The distribution of firms in our data for the year 2004 is presented

---

17   The integrated and systematized information system on enterprises is the result of an integration process of different administrative sources. The first step of this process is the selection of the "spine" information that will be used as a basis for the integration process. In this case, the "spine" is constituted by the statistical register of Italian active enterprises (ASIA) which represents the best "hanger" for data integration purposes. On this hanger, information from the following sources has been added: Large Enterprise Accounts (SCI); Small and Medium Enterprise Survey with less than 100 workers (PMI); Manufacturing Product Survey (Prodcom); Foreign Trade Archive (COE); other surveys such as the Community Innovation Survey (CIS) and the ICT Survey. All of the above ISTAT surveys are based on common EUROSTAT standards and classifications.

18   The cell is an aggregation of units of the same activity sector (NACE 3 digits), employment class (3-19, 20-99, 100-249, >250), geographical area (NW, NE, C, SI). Through these common variables 1,350 cells are identified in the donor survey and matched with firms with the same characteristics in the receiving dataset. The integration procedure and the evaluation of the quality of its performance are presented in the DIECOFIS project deliverables at http://petra1.istat.it/diecofis.

in Table 3 where units are classified according to the NACE 2-digit classification and their size in terms of workers. Both of these characteristics are very important for interpreting our estimation results.[19]

Table 3: Firms' distribution by sector and size (2004)

Sector of economic activity	Employee classes (row percentages, weighted frequencies)			Weighted frequencies	Sample frequencies
	3-49	50-250	> 250		
13-14 Mining	97.1	2.8	0.0	2095	396
15-16 Food	97.0	2.6	0.4	29691	1984
17 Textiles	93.9	5.4	0.6	13225	1578
18 Wearing apparel	97.3	2.4	0.2	19957	933
19 Luggage, footwear	96.2	3.6	0.3	11243	808
20 Wood	98.2	1.7	0.1	13744	730
21 Pulp, paper	90.7	8.0	1.2	2894	493
22 Publishing	97.0	2.7	0.3	11431	714
24 Chemicals	83.1	13.3	3.6	3823	1215
25 Rubber, plastic products	91.5	7.8	0.8	8606	818
26 Other non-metal. mineral products	95.4	4.0	0.6	13812	1421
27 Metallurgic products	84.2	13.5	2.3	2679	856
28 Fabricated metal products	96.8	3.0	0.2	48267	1776
29 Machinery, equipment n.e.c.	91.3	7.6	1.1	21405	2137
30 Office machinery, computers	95.1	4.2	0.7	754	176
31 Electrical machinery	94.0	5.2	0.8	9137	1056
32 Communication equipment	91.3	6.6	2.1	2303	372
33 Medical, optical instruments	95.6	3.7	0.7	6028	612
34 Motor vehicles	74.1	19.0	6.9	1372	419
35 Other transport equipment	92.5	6.0	1.4	2534	450
36 Furniture and other products n.e.c.	96.2	3.5	0.2	19255	1182
Total	95.2	4.2	0.6	244259	20127

Source: DIECOFIS Model

---

19 NACE is the sector classification established by Eurostat, see Commission Regulation 29/2002.

Energy data in our dataset include information about expenditures (net of value added taxes) as well as consumption in physical units of several types of energy (electricity, coal, LPG, diesel, gasoline, metallurgic coke, petroleum coke, fuel oil, natural gas, and others). The firm's fiscal burden on energy is computed by applying the excise tax rates of a specific year for each economic activity to the firm's energy consumption by product. Energy prices by source (net of taxes) for each industrial company are endogenously determined. Several indicators are calculated regarding the energy intensity of each firm's industrial production: the weight of the CO_2 tax payments on the endogenous energy expenditure as well as the share of energy costs on intermediate production costs.

Some patterns of energy consumption for the manufacturing sectors may be identified from our micro-data. As shown in Table 4, at the NACE 2-digit level of classification, electricity is the predominant energy source in most sectors. Its share ranges from a minimum of one third of total energy used – sector 26, non-metallic mineral products – to a maximum of three quarters for sector 32 – manufacturing of communication equipment. The use of natural gas as second most-important energy source is also widespread among economic manufacturing activities, while the consumption of other products is more concentrated on specific sectors as production processes require. Finally, energy intensity (tons of oil equivalent over value added) is on average 0.145 but varies between manufacturing activities, reaching a peak value of 0.7 in the most energy-intensive sector (metallurgic products).

For certain energy sources (such as diesel, fuel oil, natural gas and electricity) a variability of prices before taxes can be identified that depends upon firm size. In Table 5, we can observe that smaller firms are penalized with higher prices whereas large enterprises can obtain favourable prices for large amounts on a special contract basis – as for natural gas and electricity – which allows for reductions up to 20% of the average price.

Table 4: Sectoral shares of energy consumption by product and energy intensity (2004)

	coal	die-sel	fuel oil	natural gas	elec-tricity	oth-ers	energy intensity
13-14 Mining	0.3	50.2	3.4	5.4	37.9	2.8	0.303
15-16 Food	0.3	6.4	4.3	37.6	50.1	1.4	0.248
17 Textiles	0.2	2.3	3.8	33.9	59.1	0.6	0.232
18 Wearing apparel	0.0	12.6	1.9	38.0	45.5	2.0	0.071
19 Luggage, footwear	0.0	6.7	3.7	28.3	59.8	1.4	0.058
20 Wood	0.0	7.3	1.7	26.5	63.8	0.7	0.101
21 Pulp, paper	0.0	1.1	1.5	63.3	33.7	0.4	0.190
22 Publishing	0.0	6.0	0.2	23.3	69.3	1.1	0.265
24 Chemicals	1.1	1.8	11.4	34.4	50.3	0.9	0.156
25 Rubber, plastic products	0.0	1.9	0.9	14.2	82.7	0.3	0.312
26 Other non-metal. mineral products	3.7	3.8	4.8	35.8	32.5	19.4	0.221
27 Metallurgic products	34.9	0.7	2.9	18.5	35.5	7.4	0.698
28 Fabricated metal products	0.0	5.9	0.7	27.8	63.3	2.3	0.100
29 Machinery, equipment n.e.c.	0.0	7.4	1.1	26.6	62.4	2.3	0.054
30 Office machinery, computers	0.0	3.1	0.0	14.8	78.5	3.6	0.021
31 Electrical machinery	0.0	5.3	0.4	21.1	70.0	3.3	0.041
32 Communication equipment	0.0	2.7	0.7	18.8	77.6	0.3	0.187
33 Medical, optical instruments	0.0	6.3	0.9	16.9	74.8	1.1	0.046
34 Motor vehicles	0.0	2.2	0.4	29.7	67.1	0.7	0.126
35 Other transport equipment	0.0	3.6	2.0	27.5	66.3	0.7	0.068
36 Furniture and other products n.e.c.	0.0	8.2	2.1	18.3	69.4	2.0	0.093
Total	9.0	3.9	3.5	29.5	48.3	5.7	0.145

Source: DIECOFIS Model.

Table 5: Energy prices by products for manufacturing firms, year 2004 (average=100)

	diesel	heavy oil	natural gas	electricity
under 50 workers	100.16	100.41	100.67	100.18
50 to 250	97.50	95.95	89.95	97.57
above 250	92.39	83.59	80.58	91.38

Source: DIECOFIS Model.

The remainder of this chapter builds upon the microsimulation analysis of carbon tax previously described in section 1.2. Although the planned series of reforms were not implemented in full, 1998 did see the introduction of carbon taxes in Italy for the first time. The aim, therefore, is to evaluate the environmental effects, in terms of emission reductions, that the introduction of carbon taxes in 1998 set in-train, and to investigate the impact that those changes in carbon taxation had on the demand for specific energy sources.

To this end a balanced panel of firms from the previously described dataset has been built. This panel includes manufacturing firms surveyed both in 2000 and 2004 for which we can analyse possible changes in energy consumption and CO_2 emissions. For each year around 5,600 firms have been selected, of which approximately 60% have at least 100 workers (Large Enterprises, LE); these firms cover about 40% of the total value added of manufacturing sectors. CO_2 emissions have been imputed for each firm using the NAMEA (National Accounting Matrix including Environmental Accounts) accounts on the basis of the types and amounts of energy use and their specific CO_2 emission factors.

3   Environmental effects of the Italian carbon tax

In this study we verify the environmental impact of the implementation – although limited as described in the first part of the chapter – of the carbon tax introduced in 1998. We also investigate the essential features of industrial companies' energy demand for some specific products, with a particular focus on the elasticity to the specific tax component of the energy cost. If energy taxes have affected firms' behaviour, both in choosing a less-pollutant bundle of production inputs and in implementing investments for emission abatement technologies, estimating the elasticities of energy input demands to the rate of carbon tax offers some quantitative insights into the potential impact of a future tax change on energy consumption and, consequently, on CO_2 emissions.[20]

Following the introduction of a carbon tax, tax rates increased in line with the planned path of annual uprating until the year 2000. Between 2000 and 2004, rising global oil prices led to a reduced range of carbon tax increases on diesel, LPG, natural gas fuel, fuel oil and electricity. This scaling back of carbon tax increases may help to explain the lack of success in reducing Italian CO_2 emissions that was outlined in the introduction to this chapter.

In the light of this policy change, the impact of carbon taxation on CO_2 emissions will clearly have been less than anticipated by our original ex ante

---

20   A similar issue has been investigated with regard to Scandinavia by Enevoldsen et al. (2007).

model. However, our panel data on changes in firm behaviour between 2000 and 2004 still allow us to model, ex post, the effect on CO_2 gas emissions of a range of factors: the change of the weight of the carbon tax rate relative to full energy price, the change in energy intensity (built on the ratio of energy consumption in tons of oil equivalents and value added), the variation of the share of expenditures for emission abatement and waste disposal on production costs, and the variation in total value added by enterprises.

The left-hand panel of Figure 1 shows the relationship between changes in CO_2 emissions and changes in carbon tax (measured as a proportion of the full energy price). As expected a negative link emerges, although individual firms clearly show significant variability around this broader trend. Moreover, as the right-hand panel of Figure 1 shows, the pattern of changes in CO_2 emissions varies significantly across the different industrial sub-sectors. For this reason indicators of specific manufacturing activities will also be included in our ex post model.

Figure 1: Changes in CO_2 emissions, 2000-2004

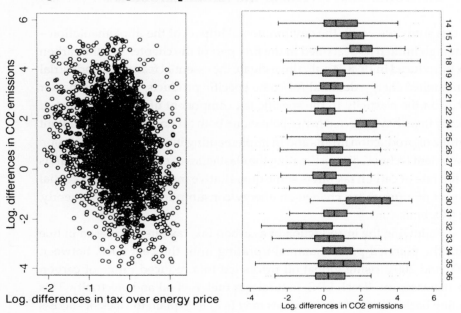

Model results are summarized in Table 6.[21] The explanatory variables show the expected signs: the emissions are reduced as the tax ratio on energy

---

21 The scatter distribution of dependent and independent variables presented some outliers (mostly due to misreporting), which were eliminated from our panel.

cost increases and as the energy intensity and the value-added reduces. Environmentally-related expenditures positively contribute to the reduction of CO_2 emissions.

Table 6: Results for CO_2 emission variations (linear regression with robust variance estimates)

Differences in CO_2 emissions (2004-2000) (log)	Coef.	Std. Err.	t	P>ltl	95% Confidence Interval	
Differences in tax over average energy price (2004-2000) (log)	-0.13	0.04	-3.7	0.0	-0.20	-0.06
Differences in energy intensity (2004-2000) (log)	0.93	0.02	51.6	0.0	0.89	0.96
Differences in environmental expenditures over total production cost (2004-2000) (log)	-0.05	0.01	-3.7	0.0	-0.08	-0.03
Differences in value added (2004-2000) (log)	1.22	0.04	28.3	0.0	1.14	1.31
13-14 Mining	0.12(*)	0.10	1.2	0.2	-0.07	0.31
15-16 Food	1.44	0.04	35.6	0.0	1.36	1.51
17 Textiles	1.88	0.06	32.1	0.0	1.77	2.00
18 Wearing apparel	1.95	0.24	8.3	0.0	1.49	2.42
19 Luggage, footwear	1.60	0.11	14.4	0.0	1.38	1.81
20 Wood	0.57	0.08	7.2	0.0	0.42	0.73
21 Pulp, paper	-0.23	0.09	-2.7	0.0	-0.40	-0.06
22 Publishing	-0.51	0.11	-4.7	0.0	-0.72	-0.29
24 Chemicals	2.54	0.05	53.5	0.0	2.45	2.64
25 Rubber, plastic products	0.47	0.06	7.8	0.0	0.35	0.59
26 Other non-metal. mineral products	0.38	0.06	5.9	0.0	0.25	0.51
28 Fabricated metal products	-0.26	0.05	-5.0	0.0	-0.37	-0.16
29 Machinery, equipment n.e.c.	0.66	0.05	14.2	0.0	0.57	0.76
30 Office machinery, computers	4.04	0.51	8.0	0.0	3.05	5.03
31 Electrical machinery	0.59	0.09	6.5	0.0	0.41	0.77
32 Communication equipment	-0.19(*)	0.24	-0.8	0.4	-0.67	0.29
33 Medical, optical instruments	0.47	0.15	3.2	0.0	0.18	0.75
34 Motor vehicles	0.39	0.08	5.0	0.0	0.24	0.55
35 Other transport equipment	0.28(*)	0.17	1.7	0.1	-0.05	0.61
36 Furniture and other products n.e.c.	-0.36	0.09	-4.1	0.0	-0.54	-0.19
R-squared	0.676					

(*) Not significant. Sector 27 (Metallurgic products) is omitted as reference sector.

Although all coefficients are statistically different from zero, the major role in explaining changes in emissions is played by the energy content and the cyclical trend of production, as the coefficient of the tax variable is much smaller (-0.13). However, this result does not contradict the conclusion generally drawn from ex-post evaluation studies that all CO_2 taxes have contributed to reduce emissions. The weakness of the observed impact may be mainly attributed to the limited variation both in gas emissions and in tax rates already pointed out.

The group of coefficients for the industrial sub-sectors is jointly significant (as shown by the F-test performed on the group of coefficients). Thus industry-specific characteristics are relevant to the impact of carbon taxes on CO_2 emissions.[22] Sectoral indicators show that only firms in the pulp and paper industry (sector 21), the printing and publishing industry (22), and communication equipment (32) perform relatively (and significantly, in statistical terms) worse than the metallurgic sector in reducing their gas emissions: these activities are among those covered by the EU emission trading scheme as deemed among the most energy-intensive industrial sectors and therefore a large effort in emission abatement will soon be required to fulfil the obligations of the European Directive.

4   The demand of some energy products: a fixed effect model

Panel data offer a large flexibility with respect to modelling latent heterogeneity not measurable across different enterprises. In the following we present the estimate of the firms' demand for diesel, natural gas, fuel oil and electricity. For the firms of our panel, these products represent 60% of total energy inputs in the year 2000, and the 75% in 2004 as the use of other inputs such as solid fossil fuels decreased. Among these, electricity and natural gas cover the highest share as expected. The demand of each energy product estimated here, takes the following form:

$$\log(energy\_input)_{it} = \alpha_i + \beta_i \log(VA)_{it} + \beta_2 \log(price)_{it} + \beta_3 \log(tax)_{it} + \beta_4 \log(p\_energy)_{it} +$$
$$+ \beta_5 \log(p\_electr) + \beta_6 (dum\_subsector) + \theta_t + u_i + \varepsilon_{it}$$

The input demand measured in physical terms (log),[23] is a function of value added, input price (net of taxes), an input-specific tax component, the price

---

22   All coefficients are computed with respect to sector 27, Metallurgic products, which has been dropped as the most energy-intensive industrial sub-sector.

23   The unit of measure is ton for diesel and fuel oil, thousand of cubic meters for natural gas and Kwh for electricity.

of all other energy inputs used by each firm (excluding the product in question and electricity), the electricity price, and sectoral characteristics. We intend to investigate the effect on energy demand of the price and fiscal components for each specific product and of the electricity price – which is a major energy input for most sectors, and of the residual bundle of energy carriers used by each firm. The parameter θ_t denotes time dummies that are included to capture the effect of variations in unobserved variables that affect all enterprises in the same way. The parameter β_1 represents the elasticity with respect to value added, while the elasticity of the demand to the price of each product is denoted by β_2, and finally the parameter β_3 indicates the percentage change of consumption due to the unit energy tax.

This model can be estimated by assuming a common intercept for all observations (pooled or cross-section regressions) or by taking into account the panel structure of the data and supposing the relevance of company-specific fixed effects, allowing the intercepts to be different for each firm to control for heterogeneity of the companies. The model with fixed effects can capture the unobserved variables at the firm level u_i – such as the adoption of energy-saving technology and the management attention devoted to the energy content of the production process – that influence each energy input demand. We have run both a pooled regression and a fixed effect model.[24] Results presented here are limited to the latter because the fixed effect model both theoretically and empirically performs better in capturing the latent heterogeneity in the firm panel. Moreover, we have decided to run the model for two different groups of companies to verify how firm size (in terms of number of workers) affects the demand parameters.[25] Estimation results of the complete set of equations for all products are presented in the Annex. Here we present the parameters of own-price elasticities and energy tax elasticities for each product demand (Table 7).

All own-price elasticities have the expected negative sign with the exception of electricity consumption where large enterprises have a positive (not significant) elasticity to price before tax, whereas the SMEs' estimate is -0.77. One interpretation of this result is that large manufacturing companies are, in general, large users receiving electricity at higher voltage and at a

---

24 We have also compared the fixed effect model with a random effect model on a simpler specification of the demand equation. The Hausman test for all equations was significantly greater than zero meaning that the difference in coefficients with respect to a random effect model is systematic.

25 The two groups include firms up to 100 workers (Small and Medium Enterprises, SME) and firms with more than 100 workers (Large Enterprises, LE).

lower price, so they are less reactive to price changes, as special conditions are provided in their contracts and prices are more stable.[26]

Table 7: Estimates of own-price and energy tax elasticities

Own-price elasticities		
	Small and medium enterprises	Large enterprises
diesel	-0.372	-0.472
natural gas	-1.683	-1.708
fuel oil	-0.567 (*)	-0.893
electricity	-0.768	0.182 (*)
Elasticities to Energy taxes		
	Small and medium enterprises	Large enterprises
diesel	-0.988 (*)	-3.046
natural gas	-3.233	-2.384
fuel oil	-0.502 (*)	-2.456
electricity	-0.433	-0.517

Note: (*) Not significant (below the 95% confidence level).

In general, for all other energy products considered here large firms do react slightly more to price changes and particularly natural gas demand is the most price-elastic with parameters above -1.5% for all companies.

Most important for the purpose of this study is the estimate of the effect of carbon tax changes on energy product demands (bottom panel of Table 7). For all estimated equations, this parameter has the expected (negative) sign and in most cases is statistically different from zero. For diesel and fuel oil, the estimated value is higher for large companies and is always bigger than price elasticity: energy product demand is more reactive to changes in tax rates than in net prices, perhaps because changes in taxes are perceived

---

26 Italian prices for industrial use of electrical energy, both gross and net of taxes, are among the highest in Europe. The explanation of higher electricity prices in Italy is to be found in the higher tax burden as well as, especially, in the low plant efficiency and in the mix of fuels with a high cost per thermal of unit supplied (ENEA, 2005).

to be more permanent than price changes[27] and therefore their impact on energy demand is higher. These large estimated values imply that there are opportunities to reduce energy consumption, and then gas emissions, at a low cost by appropriately changing carbon tax rates.

The demand of natural gas is particularly sensitive to tax changes, as its consumption has progressively increased in the Italian manufacturing sector substituting the use of solid fossil fuels. From our estimates, SMEs have larger values than LEs for the tax parameter: this result is robust also with respect to the introduction of dummy variables to capture industrial sub-sector-specific differences in technological constraints. Finally, companies of every size reduce their demand of electricity by about 0.5% for every percentage point of increase in carbon taxes per unit of energy. This is the lowest value of the tax elasticities in our set of equations, thus supporting the view that carbon/energy taxes have a lower effect on industrial electricity consumption because there is no adequate substitute for this energy carrier (Enevoldsen et al., 2007). This argument may also be supported by the estimates of parameter β_5 in our equations to investigate how the (gross) price of electricity affects each product demand: most of our estimates are positive but not statistically significant, with the exception of diesel demand where an increase of the electricity price leads to a large increase in consumption for both small and large companies.

As for the other variables included in our equations, whose results are presented in Tables 1-4 of the Annex, some remarks are worthwhile. All elasticities to value added for energy products considered here are positive and significant (except for fuel oil) and do not present large differences between the two groups of large and small/medium enterprises: the only exception is for diesel where the elasticity for LEs (+0.65) is almost twice that of SMEs (+0.42).[28]

---

27   Barker et al. (1995) suggest this interpretation to explain why taxes should give polluters a bigger incentive to reduce CO_2 emissions.

28   Results of the pooled regression for the same products (not reported here) show a larger value for value-added elasticity, very close to 1.0 for all energy consumptions (i.e. constant returns to scale). This result is consistent with estimates of a simpler model by Bjørner and Jensen (2002) and supports the idea that cross-section (pooled) estimates based on variation in the variables between companies may be better to capture long-term effects while the fixed effect model focuses on the behaviour of the (continuously existing) companies over time and these within-estimates should be interpreted as short-term elasticities. Agnolucci (2004) correctly identifies these short-term coefficients with values smaller than one as an indication of increasing returns to scale: the model indeed suggests that increasing the energy input in the production function by a certain factor t raises the output by a factor which is larger than t.

Our covariates also include the average price of energy products consumed by each firm other than the input of each equation and electricity as mentioned above. However, this variable is never significant, thus showing that our results on price and tax parameters are robust to price changes of other energy products.

Although our panel consists only of two years of observations, the time dummy has a significant effect both in diesel and in natural gas consumption: in 2004, economic activity in the manufacturing industry was basically stagnant compared with the year 2000 although, on a general level, the modest growth in levels of activity has not been accompanied by an improvement in the structural characteristics of the system in terms of energy required for each level of activity.[29] Finally, industrial sub-sector characteristics are relevant to explain some of the demand variability, as shown by the test on the group of coefficients reported at the bottom of each table in the Annex.

624

6 Final remarks

The Italian path towards compliance with the Kyoto targets so far appears very unsatisfactory compared to the other EU members. This result can partly be explained by the scarcity of (private and public) resources devoted to investment in energy-saving and energy-renewable technologies. On the other hand, the traditional environmental policy instrument, i.e. Pigouvian taxes, has not been managed in a coherent and consistent manner. In fact, a carbon tax reform has been introduced in 1998 by reshaping the previous energy-related tax rates and including coal and other energy products with high emissions. The tax rates originally foreseen in 1998 were supposed to gradually increase up to a target level in 2005, but in a framework of rising international energy prices, the original tax design has never been implemented and in fact only some minor tax rates revisions have been installed since the year 2000. On the basis of a microsimulation model for Italian firms, in this chapter we make an assessment of the effectiveness of the current

---

29 According to the 2005 Report on Energy and the Environment by ENEA (Italian National Agency for New Technologies, Energy and the Environment), the increase of energy consumption in an extended phase of stagnation of production depends mainly on the resilience of sectors with greater energy intensity and on the simultaneous cutback of sectors with a lower specific consumption, but that represent significant shares of overall industrial output.

environmental tax system on energy products (a mix between an energy tax and a carbon tax). This analysis has been performed on a microsimulation model of manufacturing firms between the years 2000 and 2004. A regression analysis on the effect of taxes on CO_2 emissions and an input demand analysis for some energy products show the efficacy of environmental taxes, even in a framework of rising energy prices.

References

Agnolucci, P. (2004) "Ex Post Evaluation of CO2 Taxes: A Survey", *Working Paper 52*, Tyndall Centre.

Bardazzi, R./Oropallo, F./Pazienza, M.G. (2004) 'Accise energetiche e competitività delle imprese: un'applicazione sull'esperimento della carbon tax' (Energy Taxes and Industrial Competitiveness: The Case of Italian Carbon Tax), *Economia delle fonti di energia e dell'ambiente* 3: 121-164

Barker, T./Ekins, P./Johnstone, N. (1995) *Global Warming and Energy Demand*. London: Routledge.

Bjørner, T.B./Jensen, H.H. (2002) 'Energy Taxes, Voluntary Agreements and Investment Subsidies: a Micropanel Analysis of the Effect on Danish Industrial Companies' Energy Demand', *Resource and Energy Economics* 24: 229-249.

EEA (2007) *Greenhouse Gas Emission Trends and Projections in Europe 2007*, EEA Report No 9/2007.

Enevoldsen, M.K./Ryelund, A.V./Andersen, M.S. (2007) 'Decoupling of Industrial Energy Consumption and CO_2-Emissions in Energy-intensive Industries in Scandinavia', *Energy Economics* 29: 665-692.

Eurostat (2008) 'Enterprises by Size Class Overview of SMEs in the EU', *Statistics in Focus* 31/2008.

IPCC (2007) Fourth Assesment Report, www.ipcc.org

OECD (1997) *Evaluating Economic Instruments for Environmental Policy*. Paris: OECD.

OECD (2006) *The Political Economy of Environmentally Related Taxes*. Paris: OECD.

Pearson, M. (1995) 'The Political Economy of Implementing Environmental Taxes', *International Tax and Public Finance* 2 (2): 357-373

Stern, N. (2006) 'Review on the Economics of Climate Change', H.M. Treasury, UK. http://www.sternreview.org.uk

Tietenberg, T. (2006) *Economia dell'Ambiente*. McGraw Hill.

Annex

Table A.1: Fixed effects model – demand of diesel

| | Small Enterprises | | Large enterprises | |
	Coef	Robust S.E.	Coef	Robust S.E.
Log_value added	0.415**	0.131	0.646***	0.154
Log_price_diesel	-0.372*	0.173	-0.472*	0.199
Log_tax_diesel	-0.989	0.796	-3.047**	1.080
Log_price_energy	-0.135	0.076	-0.053	0.085
Log_price_electr	1.868***	0.534	1.497*	0.620
time	-0.182	0.137	-0.676***	0.151
Sector 14	-0.086	0.888	(dropped)	
Sector 15	-0.350	0.986	1.068	1.833
Sector 17	-0.934	1.082	2.739	2.221
Sector 18	-0.981	1.110	3.682	2.236
Sector 19	-1.242	1.077	1.839	2.137
Sector 20	0.015	1.138	0.335	1.404
Sector 21	-0.312	1.038	-0.936	2.165
Sector 22	1.166	1.368	0.855	2.954
Sector 24	-1.168	0.961	1.240	1.831
Sector 25	-0.678	0.779	-0.830	1.437
Sector 26	-0.553	0.864	2.031	1.276
Sector 28	0.005	0.338	1.050	1.093
Sector 29	-0.234	0.688	0.879	1.168
Sector 30	0.004	1.312	(dropped)	
Sector 31	0.262	1.360	1.276	1.765
Sector 32	0.377	1.078	0.861	2.485
Sector 33	0.384	0.835	1.597	1.808
Sector 34	-0.485	1.450	0.730	1.673
Sector 35	-0.133	0.806	0.417	1.446
Sector 36	-0.604	0.745	0.458	1.290
_cons	10.505	5.427	17.502*	7.331
R-Square Overall	0.060		0.110	
R-Square Within	0.168		0.312	
corr(u_i, Xb)	-0.192		-0.504	
Observations	2923		4685	

* p<0.05, ** p<0.01, *** p<0.001

Test on Sectors:	SME	F(20,	1057) =	1.28	Prob > F =	0.1819
Test on Sectors:	LE	F(18,	1670) =	6.21	Prob > F =	0.0000

Note: R-square within is a measure of goodness-of-fit after the fixed effects have been controlled for.
Heteroscedasticity robust standard error of estimate are reported (S.E.).

Note: corr(u_i, Xb)is the correlation index between the fixed effect u_i and the model Xb

Table A.2: Fixed effects model – demand of natural gas

| | Small Enterprises | | Large enterprises | |
	Coef	Robust S.E.	Coef	Robust S.E.
Log_value added	0.543**	0.168	0.443**	0.138
Log_price_natgas	-1.684***	0.413	-1.708***	0.443
Log_tax_natgas	-3.234*	1.477	-2.384*	1.008
Log_price_energy	-0.112	0.084	0.011	0.069
Log_price_electr	0.345	0.452	0.294	0.383
time	-0.238**	0.077	-0.120	0.065
Sector 14	-1.159	2.784	(dropped)	
Sector 15	-0.990	1.246	0.143	1.127
Sector 17	-0.086	1.300	-0.924	1.485
Sector 18	0.378	1.298	0.129	1.668
Sector 19	-0.740	1.259	-0.919	1.339
Sector 20	-0.236	2.119	-1.177	1.493
Sector 21	1.406	1.394	-0.004	1.182
Sector 22	1.355	1.816	-0.002	1.265
Sector 24	-0.526	1.163	-0.745	1.099
Sector 25	-0.425	1.136	-1.132	1.127
Sector 26	-0.538	1.101	-0.924	1.743
Sector 28	-0.580	0.429	-0.254	0.823
Sector 29	-0.513	0.781	-1.050	0.860
Sector 30	0.173	1.536	(dropped)	
Sector 31	0.512	1.127	-1.379	0.963
Sector 32	1.723	1.306	-1.002	1.216
Sector 33	0.630	1.014	-1.390	1.117
Sector 34	0.267	0.812	-0.737	1.293
Sector 35	-1.269	0.906	0.465	1.447
Sector 36	0.186	1.472	-1.654	0.999
_cons	15.469**	5.500	15.598***	4.459
R-Square Overall	0.152		0.248	
R-Square Within	0.167		0.098	
corr(u_i, Xb)	-0.095		0.0916	
Observations	2915		4880	

* p<0.05, ** p<0.01, *** p<0.001

627

					Prob > F =	
Test on Sectors:	SME	F(20,	1066) =	7.31	Prob > F =	0.0000
Test on Sectors:	LE	F(18,	1762) =	2.78	Prob > F =	0.0001

Note: R-square within is a measure of goodness-of-fit after the fixed effects have been controlled for.
Heteroscedasticity robust standard error of estimate are reported (S.E.).

Note: corr(u_i, Xb)is the correlation index between the fixed effect u_i and the model Xb

Table A.3: Fixed effects model – demand of fuel oil

	Small Enterprises		Large enterprises	
	Coef	Robust S.E.	Coef	Robust S.E.
Log_value added	0.306	0.307	0.223	0.251
Log_price_fueloil	-0.567	0.361	-0.894**	0.303
Log_tax_fueloil	-0.502	1.463	-2.457**	0.813
Log_price_energy	-0.049	0.228	-0.363	0.280
Log_price_electr	-1.133	1.479	-0.754	0.741
time	-0.028	1.066	1.297*	0.620
Sector 14	6.884*	3.471	(dropped)	
Sector 15	-2.601***	0.401	(dropped)	
Sector 17	5.912***	0.865	(dropped)	
Sector 18	7.035***	0.703	2.575***	0.337
Sector 19	(dropped)		2.282***	0.395
Sector 20	-0.568	1.016	-1.672	1.891
Sector 21	7.296***	0.969	2.143	2.383
Sector 22	(dropped)		-1.906	2.383
Sector 24	3.809***	0.545	(dropped)	
Sector 25	2.728*	1.082	0.039	2.375
Sector 26	5.264***	0.526	0.786	2.381
Sector 28	2.646**	1.014	0.379	1.057
Sector 29	4.529**	1.432	0.280	1.055
Sector 30	(dropped)		(dropped)	
Sector 31	(dropped)		-1.969	1.889
Sector 32	(dropped)		(dropped)	
Sector 33	2.043	1.085	(dropped)	
Sector 34	(dropped)		-1.408	1.937
Sector 35	4.138**	1.486	2.224	2.395
Sector 36	-4.008	2.191	1.663	1.821
_cons	-2.165	7.703	13.719*	6.280
R-Square Overall	0.017		0.105	
R-Square Within	0.141		0.198	
corr(u_i, Xb)	-0.8223		-0.2672	
Observations	1772		2967	

* p<0.05, ** p<0.01, *** p<0.001

Test on Sectors:	SME	F(10,	508) =	177.68	Prob > F =	0.0000
Test on Sectors:	LE	F(13,	880) =	469.63	Prob > F =	0.0000

Note: R-square within is a measure of goodness-of-fit after the fixed effects have been controlled for.
Heteroscedasticity robust standard error of estimate are reported (S.E.).

Note: corr(u_i, Xb)is the correlation index between the fixed effect u_i and the model Xb

Table A.4: Fixed effects model – demand of electricity

	Small Enterprises		Large enterprises	
	Coef	Robust S.E.	Coef	Robust S.E.
Log_value added	0.403***	0.100	0.365***	0.108
Log_price_electr	-0.768*	0.363	0.182	0.293
Log_tax_electr	-0.433***	0.069	-0.517***	0.042
Log_price_energy	-0.046	0.069	0.007	0.072
time	0.053	0.046	-0.036	0.050
Sector 14	0.190	1.363	(dropped)	
Sector 15	-0.441	1.141	-0.185	0.741
Sector 17	-0.603	1.267	-0.347	1.039
Sector 18	-0.866	1.239	-0.386	1.170
Sector 19	-1.107	1.185	-0.658	0.972
Sector 20	0.291	1.335	-1.066	0.833
Sector 21	-0.186	1.281	-0.163	0.962
Sector 22	1.273	1.529	0.185	1.353
Sector 24	-0.111	1.110	-0.337	0.735
Sector 25	0.162	1.019	-0.348	0.738
Sector 26	-0.612	1.167	-0.259	1.648
Sector 28	-0.105	0.493	-0.345	0.518
Sector 29	-0.337	0.679	-0.603	0.559
Sector 30	0.567	1.289	(dropped)	
Sector 31	0.252	0.966	-0.553	0.674
Sector 32	1.641	1.244	-0.054	1.267
Sector 33	0.365	1.008	-0.463	0.724
Sector 34	0.275	0.941	-0.686	1.043
Sector 35	-0.422	0.681	0.215	0.718
Sector 36	0.374	1.333	-1.500*	0.663
_cons	3.804	2.067	6.975***	2.088
R-Square Overall	0.355		0.555	
R-Square Within	0.198		0.347	
corr(u_i, Xb)	0.1358		0.2405	
Observations	3064		4895	

* p<0.05, ** p<0.01, *** p<0.001

Test on Sectors:	SME	F(20, 1152) =	0.84	Prob > F =	0.6680
Test on Sectors:	LE	F(18, 1777) =	1.12	Prob > F =	0.3213

Note: R-square within is a measure of goodness-of-fit after the fixed effects have been controlled for.
Heteroscedasticity robust standard error of estimate are reported (S.E.).

Note: corr(u_i, Xb)is the correlation index between the fixed effect u_i and the model Xb

List of Contributors

Ben Anderson, Technology and Social Change Research Centre, University of Essex, now at: Department of Sociology, University of Essex, UK

Rossella Bardazzi, Dipartimento di Studi sullo Stato, Università di Firenze, Italy

Muriel Barlet, Department of General Economic Studies, National Institute of Statistics and Economic Studies (INSEE), Paris, France

Elisa Baroni, Institute for Futures Studies, Stockholm, Sweden

Mark Birkin, School of Geography, University of Leeds, UK

Didier Blanchet, Department of General Economic Studies, National Institute of Statistics and Economic Studies (INSEE), Paris, France

Laurie J. Brown, Professor, National Centre for Social and Economic Modelling, University of Canberra, Australia

Bart Capéau, K.U.Leuven, Belgium

Graham P. Clarke, School of Geography, University of Leeds, UK

Markus Clauss, ZEW Centre for European Economic Research, Mannheim, Germany

Paola de Agostini, Technology and Social Change Research Centre, University of Essex, now at: Department of Sociology, University of Essex, UK

Rembert R.G. De Blander, Unité d'économie rurale and Center for Economic Studies, Université catholique de Louvain, Belgium

André Decoster, K.U.Leuven, Center for Economic Studies, Leuven, Belgium

Kris De Swerdt, K.U.Leuven, Center for Economic Studies, Leuven, Belgium

Peter B. Dixon, Sir John Monash Distinguished Professor, Centre of Policy Studies, Monash University, Australia

Matias Eklöf, Institute for Futures Studies, Stockholm, Sweden

Maria Evandrou, Professor of Gerontology, Director Centre for Research on Ageing, School of Social Sciences, University of Southampton, UK

Jane Falkingham, Professor, Associate Dean (Research), Faculty of Law, Arts and Social Sciences, University of Southampton, UK

Francesco Figari, Institute for Social & Economic Research (ISER), University of Essex (UK), DI.S.E.FIN., University of Genoa, Italy

Tracy L. Foertsch, Office of Tax Analysis, The US Department of the Treasury, Washington D.C., USA

Daniel Hallberg, Institute for Futures Studies, Stockholm, and Department of Economics, Uppsala University, Sweden

Ann Harding, Professor, National Centre for Social and Economic Modelling, University of Canberra, Australia

Anthony Harris, Professor, Centre for Health Economics, Monash University, Australia

Stephen Hynes, Head, Rural Economy Research Centre, Galway, Ireland

Paul Johnson, Vice-Chancellor and President, La Trobe University, Victoria, Australia

632

Guyonne Kalb, Melbourne Institute of Applied Economic and Social Research, University of Melbourne, Australia

Jose-Maria Labeaga, Institute for Fiscal Studies, Madrid, Spain

Selma Laidoudi, Technology and Social Change Research Centre, University of Essex, now at: Markit Trade Processing, UK

Ross H. Leach, Department for Work and Pensions, London, UK, now at ILO, Geneva

Thomas Le Barbanchon, Department of General Economic Studies, National Institute of Statistics and Economic Studies (INSEE), Paris, France

Sylvie Le Minez, Department of General Economic Studies, National Institute of Statistics and Economic Studies (INSEE), Paris, France

Thomas Lindh, Institute for Futures Studies, Stockholm, and Department of Economics, Växjö University, Sweden

Justine McNamara, National Centre for Social and Economic Modelling (NATSEM), University of Canberra, Australia

Kevin D. Moore, Modelling Division, Statistics Canada, Ottawa, Canada

Richard J. Morrison, the DYNACAN Team, Human Resources and Social Development Canada

Thomas Morrison, National Centre for Social and Economic Modelling (NATSEM), University of Canberra, Australia

Ides Nicaise, Higher Institute for Labour Studies and Department of Education Sciences, Catholic University of Leuven, Belgium

Vibeke O. Nielsen, Unit for Public Economics, Research Department, Statistics Norway

Cathal O'Donoghue, Head, Rural Economy Research Centre, Galway, Ireland

Xisco Oliver, Universitat de les Illes Balears, Palma de Mallorca, Spain

Filippo Oropallo, ISTAT / Italian National Statistical Office, Rome, Italy

Kristian Orsini, Center for Economic Studies, K.U.Leuven, Belgium

Maria Grazia Pazienza, Dipartimento di Studi sullo Stato, Università di Firenze, Italy

Mark Picton, Research Fellow, Centre of Policy Studies, Monash University, Australia

Ralph A. Rector, Office of Tax Analysis, The US Department of the Treasury, Washington D.C., USA

Phil Rees, School of Geography, University of Leeds, UK

Jeff Richardson, Professor, Centre for Health Economics, Monash University, Australia

Piet Rietveld, Department of Spatial Economics, VU University, Amsterdam, the Netherlands

Geoff T. Rowe, Modelling Division, Statistics Canada, Ottawa, Canada

Stefanie Schubert, WHU – Otto Beisheim School of Management, Vallendar, Germany

Anne Scott, Retired, formerly at the SAGE ESRC Research Group, Department of Social Policy, London School of Economics, UK

Amedeo Spadaro, Paris School of Economics and Universitat de les Illes Balears, Palma de Mallorca, Spain

Nils Martin Stølen, Unit for Public Economics, Research Department, Statistics Norway

Robert Tanton, National Centre for Social and Economic Modelling (NATSEM), University of Canberra, Australia

Inger Texmon, Division for Social and Demographic Research, Research Department, Statistics Norway

Thor O. Thoresen, Research Department, Statistics Norway

Linc Thurecht, Senior Research Fellow, National Centre for Social and Economic Modelling, University of Canberra, Australia

Eveline S. van Leeuwen, Department of Spatial Economics, VU University, Amsterdam, the Netherlands

Antonia Weston, Technology and Social Change Research Centre, University of Essex, now at: GeoData Institute, University of Southampton, UK

Frans Willekens, Netherlands Interdisciplinary Demographic Institute, Netherlands Royal Academy of Sciences (NIDI-KNAW), The Hague, and Professor of Population Studies, University of Groningen, the Netherlands

Paul Williamson, Department of Geography at the University of Liverpool, UK

Michael Wolfson, Assistant Chief Statistician, Analysis and Development, Statistics Canada

Belinda Wu, School of Geography, University of Leeds, UK

Mandy Yap, Research Fellow, National Centre for Social and Economic Modelling, University of Canberra, Australia

Asghar Zaidi, Director Research at the European Centre for Social Welfare Policy and Research in Vienna, Austria

Jovan Žamac, Department of Economics, Uppsala University, and Institute for Futures Studies, Stockholm, Sweden

Ping Zong, Technology and Social Change Research Centre, University of Essex, now at: Office for National Statistics, UK

Asghar Zaidi is Director Research at the European Centre for Social Welfare Policy and Research in Vienna. Until recently, he has been a Senior Economist at the Social Policy Division, OECD, Paris, where he worked on issues related to pension policy in OECD countries. In the past, he worked as Economic Advisor at the Department for Work and Pensions of the United Kingdom, and as a researcher at the Social Policy Department of the London School of Economics and University of Oxford. His work interests include economics of ageing (particularly pension reforms and their impact on retirement incomes), implications of living costs of disability on poverty and resource measurement, and dynamic microsimulation modelling (in particular those used for pension trends and their underlying factors). He has been the Vice-President of the International Microsimulation Association since 2007. He is currently a research affiliate at the German Economic Research Institute (DIW Berlin), the Centre for the Analysis of Social Exclusion, London School of Economics, and the Centre for Research on Ageing, Southampton University.

Ann Harding has recently been re-elected President of the International Microsimulation Association and has published four books on microsimulation with Elsevier (1993, 1996, 2*2007). After working on major policy reviews in several Federal Government departments, Ann was appointed Professor of Applied Economics and Social Policy and Director of the National Centre for Social and Economic Modelling (NATSEM) at the University of Canberra in January 1993. She is an internationally recognized expert in the fields of microsimulation modelling, income distribution, and tax/transfer policy. Ann has played a key role for the past 14 years in constructing sophisticated data and models that can be used to assist policy-makers in assessing the revenue and distributional consequences of possible policy options. In 1996 Ann was elected a Fellow of the Academy of Social Sciences and in 2003 was elected President of the International Microsimulation Association. Ann holds a PhD from the London School of Economics and a Bachelor of Economics with First Class Honours from Sydney University.

Paul Williamson is a Senior Lecturer in the Department of Geography at the University of Liverpool in the UK. He was awarded his PhD from the University of Leeds for his work on a microsimulation model of health care for the elderly. Dr Williamson is the editor of the International Journal of Microsimulation and is particularly interested in spatial microsimulation models and in small area analyses.

For Product Safety Concerns and Information please contact our EU
representative GPSR@taylorandfrancis.com Taylor & Francis Verlag GmbH,
Kaufingerstraße 24, 80331 München, Germany

Printed and bound by CPI Group (UK) Ltd, Croydon, CR0 4YY
11/04/2025
01843977-0010